Windows® Administration at the Command Line

Windows® Administration at the Command Line

for Windows Vista™, Windows® 2003, Windows® XP, and Windows® 2000

John Paul Mueller

Wiley Publishing, Inc.

Acquisitions and Development Editor: Thomas Cirtin
Technical Editor: Russ Mullen
Production Editor: Felicia Robinson
Copy Editor: Cheryl Hauser
Production Manager: Tim Tate
Vice President and Executive Group Publisher: Richard Swadley
Vice President and Executive Publisher: Joseph B. Wikert
Vice President and Publisher: Neil Edde
Book Designers: Maureen Forys, Happenstance Type-O-Rama, Judy Fung
Compositor: Craig Woods, Happenstance Type-O-Rama
Proofreader: Rachael Gunn
Indexer: Nancy Guenther
Anniversary Logo Design: Richard Pacifico
Cover Designer: Ryan Sneed

Published simultaneously in Canada

ISBN: 978-0-470-04616-6

For general information on our other products and services or to obtain technical support, please contact our Customer Care Department within the U.S. at (800) 762-2974, outside the U.S. at (317) 572-3993 or fax (317) 572-4002.

Wiley also publishes its books in a variety of electronic formats. Some content that appears in print may not be available in electronic books.

Library of Congress Cataloging-in-Publication Data

Mueller, John, 1958-

Windows administration at the command line for Windows 2003, Windows Vista, Windows XP, and Windows 2000 / John P Mueller.

p. cm.

ISBN 978-0-470-04616-6 (paper/website)

1. Microsoft Windows (Computer file) 2. Operating systems (Computers) I. Title.

QA76.76.O63M8423 2007

005.4'46--dc22

2007006195

10 9 8 7 6 5 4 3 2 1

This book is dedicated to my long-suffering wife, Rebecca, who has always supported me in my writing—I couldn't ask for a better friend.

Acknowledgments

Thanks to my wife, Rebecca, for working with me to get this book completed. I really don't know what I would have done without her help in researching and compiling some of the information that appears in this book. She also did a fine job of proofreading my rough draft and page proofing the result. Rebecca also helps a great deal with the glossary and keeps the house running while I'm buried in work.

Russ Mullen deserves thanks for his technical edit of this book. He greatly added to the accuracy and depth of the material you see here. Russ is always providing me with great URLs for new products and ideas. However, it's the testing Russ does that helps most. He's the sanity check for my work. Russ also has different computer equipment from mine, so he's able to point out flaws that I might not otherwise notice.

A number of people read all or part of this book to help me refine the approach, test the coding examples, and generally provide input that all readers wish they could have. These unpaid volunteers helped in ways too numerous to mention here. I especially appreciate the efforts of Eva Beattie, who read the entire book and selflessly devoted herself to this project.

Matt Wagner, my agent, deserves credit for helping me get the contract in the first place and taking care of all the details that most authors don't really consider. I always appreciate his assistance. It's good to know that someone wants to help.

Finally, I would like to thank Tom Cirtin, Felicia Robinson, Cheryl Hauser, and the rest of the editorial and production staff at Sybex for their assistance in bringing this book to print. It's always nice to work with such a great group of professionals and I very much appreciate the friendship we've built over the last seven books.

Acknowledgments

About the Author

John Mueller is a freelance author and technical editor. He has writing in his blood, having produced 73 books and over 300 articles to date. The topics range from networking to artificial intelligence and from database management to heads down programming. Some of his current books include a Windows power optimization book, a book on .NET security, and books on Amazon Web Services, Google Web Services, and eBay Web Services. His technical editing skills have helped over 52 authors refine the content of their manuscripts. John has provided technical editing services to both *Data Based Advisor* and *Coast Compute* magazines. He's also contributed articles to magazines like DevSource, InformIT, SQL Server Professional, Visual C++ Developer, Hard Core Visual Basic, asp.netPRO, Software Test and Performance, and Visual Basic Developer. Be sure to read John's blog at `http://www.amazon.com/gp/blog/id/AQOA2QP4X1YWP`.

When John isn't working at the computer, you can find him in his workshop. He's an avid woodworker and candle maker. On any given afternoon, you can find him working at a lathe or putting the finishing touches on a bookcase. He also likes making glycerin soap and candles, which comes in handy for gift baskets. You can reach John on the Internet at JMueller@mwt.net. John is also setting up a Web site at `http://www.mwt.net/~jmueller/`. Feel free to look and make suggestions on how he can improve it. One of his current projects is creating book FAQ sheets that should help you find the book information you need much faster.

Contents at a Glance

Contents

Introduction

When was the last time you visited the command line? A few administrators live there, but many others have forgotten about it over the years. When Microsoft originally introduced Windows, the assumption was that you no longer needed the command line and many people left it behind completely. After all, why bother with the command line when you can access everything you need from the graphical environment? The problem is that the Windows graphical user interface (GUI) doesn't actually provide access to everything on your system. In addition, all of that mousing around wastes considerable time and effort. You can't easily replicate your actions either; many people have tried, and failed, to produce a macro recorder for the graphical portion of Windows. Every time that you want to perform a task, you start it from scratch, which means that you have plenty of opportunities for making mistakes. *Windows Administration at the Command Line* reveals the command line to you. Using the information in this book, you not only discover the vast array of commands that are at your disposal but you also see how to automate those commands so that you can save significant time and effort while performing administrative tasks.

Just in case you thought that the command line would go away in Vista in favor of Windows PowerShell, you should look at all of the command line changes in this edition of the book. In fact, you'll find the special icon shown at the beginning of this paragraph throughout the book to show just how many changes Microsoft has made to the command line in Vista. If you want a summary of the changes, check out Appendix B. The command line is alive and well in Vista. Not only is Microsoft supporting it, but you'll find a wealth of updates as well. Make sure to read about Windows PowerShell in Chapters 18 and 19 though—future versions of Windows will very likely move toward this new environment for administrators. No matter which command line interface you choose, *Windows Administration at the Command Line* provides the resources you need to work effectively and efficiently.

Overcoming GUI Problems

As an example of the flawed behavior of the GUI, just try locating the word *Microsoft* in the executables on your hard drive. You'll find that the task is impossible because Windows doesn't search executables and just barely searches data files. Many people have complained about the flawed performance of the search mechanism in Windows. Many people end up getting third party utilities to help them search for the data that Windows should help them find, utilities with dubious reputations for compromising security. *Windows Administration at the Command Line* shows you a better way, one that relies on a free utility supplied with Windows that will never divulge your personal information to anyone else. Check out the FindStr utility in Chapter 4 and you'll discover the high-speed search mechanism used by people in the know. The FindStr utility is but one of hundreds of commands and utilities discussed in this book. Just think about what you can do with all of those free resources! Not only will you accomplish your work faster and with fewer errors, but by reading this book, you can save your company a significant investment in third party products that might not do the job anyway.

No other book has the level of detail provided by *Windows Administration at the Command Line*. I scoured the Internet looking for all of the details about every Windows command and utility I could find. In some cases, the information you see in this book appears nowhere else. Much of the extra information in this book is the result of 20 years of hard won experience at the command line starting with DOS and moving through the current version of Windows. This book gives you the benefit of the experience of many network administrators as told on their Web sites and through correspondence in email.

This book offers something for everyone. Everyone needs to locate files on their hard drive. If you think the GUI is going to help you, think again. After a few frustrating searches, you'll wish for a better tool and you already have it in the form of the `Dir` command. Unlike the Windows GUI, the `Dir` command actually locates the files you request on the hard drive. The interesting thing is that the `Dir` command is very easy to use. Anyone can employ this command with very little training.

In fact, I included Chapter 1 of this book for those who have little or no experience with the command line. Chapter 1 helps you discover techniques for using the command line effectively and configuring it to meet your specific needs. Even if you're a complete command line novice, you can use this book to get started by reading Chapter 1 first and becoming familiar with the command line.

Goals for Writing This Book

My initial goal for writing this book was to overcome the frustration of using the command line. I constantly had to look up commands on the Internet because I couldn't find a single resource that answered all of my command line questions. After performing some research online, I found that many other developers, administrators, and even average users were just as frustrated as I was. Consequently, writing a book about the command line seemed like an ideal way to help everyone. This book is the result. Never again will you spend hours looking for the right answer to a command line question; you'll find them here.

Of course, documenting the command or utility usually isn't enough. It's important to know all of the caveats of using the command or utility and answer questions such as how much damage it could cause to a system. In many cases, you also need additional common information, such as a cultural identifier. Consequently, as I wrote the book, I tried to provide as many tidbits of additional information as I could. These tidbits turn the documentation entries from functional into truly useful.

You'll also find a wealth of Real World Scenarios in this book. Each of the Real World Scenarios tells you about the commands or utilities in general from a real world perspective. All of the stories in these sections are real. Some of them did happen to me; many others didn't. I did change the names of those involved to protect the innocent. The point of all these Real World Scenarios is to provide you something that simple documentation can't: a perspective of why you should care about a command or utility and how you can use it safely.

Along with all of the other documentation, I wanted to share a few of my favorite techniques for working at the command line. You'll find scripts that I have used for many years in this book to perform work at the command line. The batch files and scripts have seen real world use and you can use them too. Copy the scripts or batch files out of the book and use them as is, or modify them to meet your specific needs.

Who Should Read This Book?

Anyone can read this book. In fact, the first five chapters of the book are useful for anyone who uses Windows regardless of experience level. The amazing array of commands that Windows hides at the command prompt will give you the tools you require to get more work done with a lot less effort. Gone are the frustrations of using graphical tools that simply don't work most of the time.

I did anticipate a certain level of knowledge for even the novice command line user. You should have a good idea of how to work with Windows. For example, you might want to think twice about using the commands in this book if you don't know how to perform a search of the hard drive using Windows. In addition, you should be familiar with the mouse and relatively well acquainted with the keyboard. This book doesn't teach Windows basics—it goes right to the command line and helps you to start working there immediately. However, some command line information might not make as much sense if you don't already have at least some Windows experience.

Starting with Chapter 6 and moving on to Chapter 17, this book is targeted toward the needs of developers and administrators. The average user will never require the commands listed in Chapter 6. In fact, developers and administrators will use them only on occasion. These powerful commands help you perform tasks that you generally can't perform using the GUI. In fact, you'll even find a section that describes a technique for accessing Microsoft's secret functions within the Windows DLLs. See the "Accessing Functions within DLLs" section of Chapter 6 for details.

Developers and administrators also need to automate tasks in today's hectic IT environment. Chapters 7 through 11 help you get the most out of Windows automation features, which are actually quite formidable once you know how to use them. Should Windows fail to provide some functionality, Chapters 12 through 14 provide tips and hints on third party applications you might want to use. Chapters 15 through 17 provide an all-important view of the .NET Framework. Did you know that you can compile JScript using the .NET Framework? Most people don't know about this feature because Microsoft hasn't advertised it. Without spending a single penny, you can create your own JScript executable that can take full advantage of the .NET Framework. Check out this technique in the "Understanding the JSC Compiler Supplied with .NET" section of Chapter 14.

Chapters 18 and 19 provide a preview of what Vista looks like at the command line. All I can say after working with Vista and Windows PowerShell for a while is wow (you can download Windows PowerShell for other versions of Windows as well and I tell you how to do it)! What you'll see in these chapters is going to amaze you. Vista and Windows PowerShell represent a significant and long anticipated departure from the command line of the past. Yes, you can still use all of the older techniques in this operating system, but the new features are going to amaze you with their ability to get work done quickly, efficiently, and with fewer potential security issues. You get all this and better documentation besides. Windows PowerShell is a fully extensible command line shell, very much in the same vein as UNIX shells, only a lot more powerful.

Conventions Used in This Book

It always helps to know what the special text means in a book. The following table provides a list of standard usage conventions. These conventions make it easier for you to understand what a particular text element means.

TABLE I.1: Standard Usage Conventions

CONVENTION	EXPLANATION
`Inline Code`	Some code will appear in the text of the book to help explain application functionality. The code appears in a special font that makes it easy to see. This monospaced font also makes the code easier to read.
`Inline Variable`	As with source code, variable source code information that appears inline will also appear in a special font that makes it stand out from the rest of the text. When you see monospaced text in an italic typeface, you can be sure it's a variable of some type. Replace this variable with a specific value. The text will always provide examples of specific values that you might use.
`User Input`	Sometimes I'll ask you to type something. For example, you might need to type a particular value into the field of a dialog box. This special font helps you see what you need to type.
`Filename`	A variable name is a value that you need to replace with something else. For example, you might need to provide the name of your server as part of a command line argument. Because I don't know the name of your server, I'll provide a variable name instead. The variable name you'll see usually provides a clue as to what kind of information you need to supply. In this case, you'll need to provide a filename. Although the book doesn't provide examples of every variable that you might encounter, it does provide enough so that you know how to use them with a particular command.
[***`Filename`***]	When you see square brackets around a value, switch, or command, it means that this is an optional component. You don't have to include it as part of the command line or dialog field unless you want the additional functionality that the value, switch, or command provides.
File ➤ Open	Menus and the selections on them appear with a special menu arrow symbol. "File ➤ Open" means "Access the File menu and choose Open."
italic	You'll normally see words in italic if they have special meaning or if this is the first use of the term and the text provides a definition for it. Always pay special attention to words in italic because they're unique in some way. When you see a term that you don't understand, make sure you check the glossary for the meaning of the term as well. The glossary also includes definitions for every nonstandard acronym in the book.
`Monospace`	Some words appear in a monospace font because they're easier to see or require emphasis of some type. For example, all filenames in the book appear in a monospace font to make them easier to read.
`URLs`	URLs will normally appear in a monospace font so that you can see them with greater ease. The URLs in this book provide sources of additional information designed to make your development experience better. URLs often provide sources of interesting information as well.

Part 1

Standard Windows Utilities

In This Section:

Chapter 1

Using the Command Line Effectively

- Understanding Why the Command Line Is So Important
- Considering the Methods Available for Working at the Command Line
- Viewing the Commands by Purpose
- Updating Your Current Utilities at the Microsoft Download Center
- Configuring the Command Window
- Understanding Internal Commands
- Defining the Vista Command Line Differences

At one time, everyone worked at the command line. In fact, when you started the computer, you saw a command prompt and you never really left it the entire time you worked with the computer. I'm dating myself, of course, because no one's worked exclusively at the command line for many years. The days of DOS are gone and the command line is seemingly gone with it—or is it? The command line still exists and you can use it to make your life easier. In addition, working at the command line can help you automate tasks and work considerably faster. A good understanding of the command line can even help you work with fewer errors because most command line applications work or they aren't based on the input you provide. Of course, this begs the question of why people aren't using the command line if it's so great. This chapter answers that question; it helps you understand why the command line has fallen out of favor and why you should consider making it part of your life again.

Working at the command line doesn't mean that you have to perform tasks manually or memorize arcane syntax. It's true that you had to do that in the past to an extent, but even in the past, people created batch files so all they needed to remember was the batch file name and not the difficult series of command line switches for executing a command. Windows makes working at the command line a lot easier. You can even automate tasks so that you never actually go to the command line; you can tell Windows to perform all of that work for you. Consequently, working at the command line could mean putting a batch file together and then telling Windows to execute it for you. Working at the command line need not be time consuming or difficult.

Something to consider about the command line is that it contains a lot more than you might think. Many savvy administrators and power users know that Windows provides a number of command line utilities. However, few people realize just how many utilities there are. Would you believe that this book discusses 280 command line utilities of various types for all Windows users and a significant number more for Vista users? In fact, after performing the research for this book, I concluded that many of the most interesting Windows features aren't in the graphical user interface (GUI); they're at the command line. By the time you finish this book, you'll have gained an understanding of just how capable Windows is at the command line.

Understanding Why the Command Line Is So Important

You might have been there the day that Microsoft released Windows. The original reason for this product was twofold. First, it let users run more than one application at a time—something that required a kludge at the DOS prompt. Second, it provided a friendly interface that made using a computer easier. No longer did you have to remember command names; all of them appeared on screen so you could simply select the command you wanted to execute. The first version of Windows went over like a lead balloon, and the second version wasn't far behind, but by the third version, Microsoft had something workable—something people could use to perform their tasks without worrying about the command prompt.

Over the years Windows has delivered on its promise to make applications easier to use—at least the applications that you must sit in front of to use. For example, I wouldn't consider going back to a character mode word processor and I doubt very much that I'd want to write complex applications at the command line. Unfortunately, computing activities aren't limited to those tasks that you perform in real time in front of the display. Almost everyone has a task they must perform in the background or at least when they aren't present. The most common task that you should perform is backing up your data. Not only is there no need for you to be present when the backup occurs, but using your computer can be detrimental to getting a good backup because you should have all of the files closed. These noninteractive tasks always benefit from the command line because ease of use isn't an issue. When you perform a backup, you want it to be fast, accurate, and repeatable.

Okay, so you can count the number of tasks you need to automate on one hand? However, working at the command line can do a lot more for you than simply automate tasks that should take place in the background. Have you ever searched for text within a file using the Windows GUI and found that Windows Explorer can't locate text that you know appears within a certain folder? (Even with the advanced indexing features of Vista, you still can't find certain files because Vista doesn't index them and may not even provide direct access to them through the GUI.) Many people have found Windows Explorer lacking. Even when Windows Explorer can find the text, it isn't always accurate, and it's seldom fast. Interestingly enough, the command line offers utilities that can make searching for specific files quite fast and always accurate. For example, the FindStr utility discussed in Chapter 4 can help you locate text in any kind of file. You can even look inside binary files such as executables for particular strings. Everyone needs to search for data, and using the command line is usually faster than working with a GUI simply because the GUI gets in the way and slows things down.

Security has become a major issue with every cracker on the Internet seeking entry to your machine. However, have you ever wondered what's really running on your machine? You can't tell from the GUI. The best view you can get in most versions of Windows is Processes tab of the Task Manager that you can access by right-clicking the Taskbar and choosing Task Manager from the context menu. Vista adds a new Services tab that tells you about the services running on your system, but the addition only provides a little more help. Figure 1.1 shows the output from the Vista version of this application.

Unfortunately, Figure 1.1 shows only part of the story at best. For one thing, all of those SvcHost entries hide services that are running on your system (which is why that Services tab in Vista is so handy), which could be anything from the driver for your display adapter to a Windows service that is leaving you wide open to attack. However, you can't tell what's running on your system from Figure 1.1. Figure 1.2 shows the output of the TaskList command line utility. Suddenly you know about all of those SvcHost entries. As you can see, a single entry can host more than a few services. In addition, you now have access to a special number, the Process Identifier (PID). The PID lets you learn more about the application. In short, if you really want to know what your system is doing, you have to use the command line to do it. Don't worry too much about the TaskList utility right now; you'll find a discussion of its full capabilities in Chapter 5.

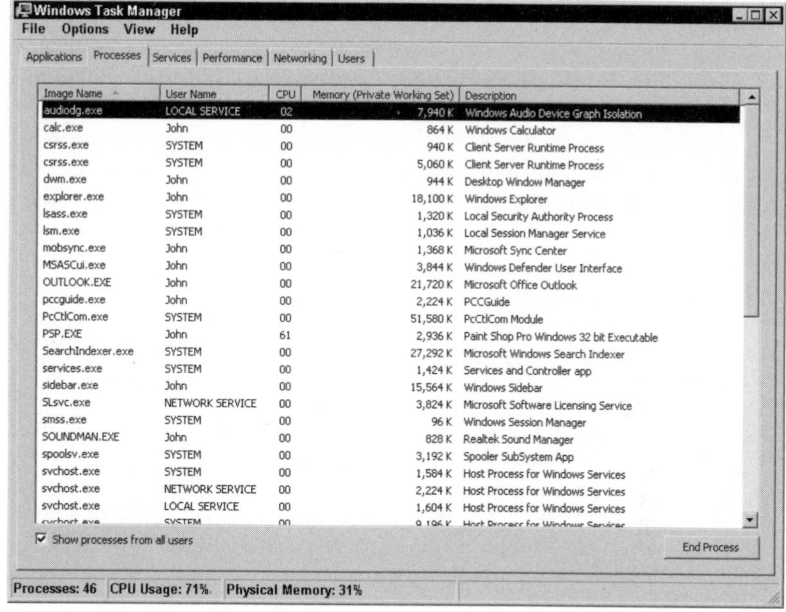

FIGURE 1.1
Task Manager only provides a partial view of the applications running on your system.

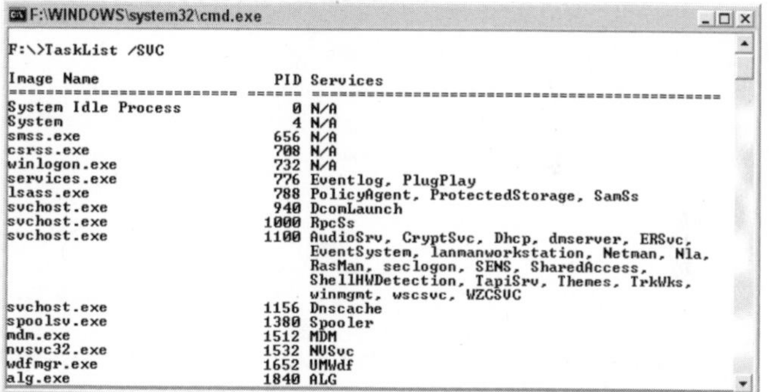

FIGURE 1.2
TaskList provides a complete picture of the applications running on your system.

The command line makes a wealth of powerful tools available. For example, you can discover the exact address for a Web site you visit frequently, so you can avoid making assumptions about emails that enter your inbox with an address, rather than human readable Web site name. On days when access to the Web sites you visit seems especially slow, you can use command line utilities to detect whether your local ISP is the problem or the problem is somewhere else that your Internet Service Provider (ISP) can't control before you call to complain. You can also use command line tools to locate local resources or those on a network. In fact, command line utilities can help you learn more about your system than you might think is possible.

The command line is important because it frees you from the constraints of the GUI that was supposed to make your life easier. Sure, you don't want to use the command line for everything, but it's good to know about the command line when you want to perform tasks quickly or you need low-level information about your system. The command line does require that you learn something about your machine, but this short section should have already demonstrated that you need the additional information the command line provides to keep your system safe and functioning fully.

The Command Line Made Easy

Some people are of the opinion that the command line works one way. You type in a command and hope that you got all of the information right and received the correct result, which you then have to interpret. This entire activity sounds quite difficult, somewhat boring, and error prone to say the least. You have to wonder why someone would put themselves through all that pain. However, the command line isn't anything like the scenario just mentioned. Actually, if you know a few simple rules, using the command line doesn't have to be hard at all. The following sections describe some of the methods you can use to work at the command line.

Using Utilities Directly

Generally, you'll being using the command line by working with the utilities directly. After all, it's a little hard to create a batch file or script if you don't know how the command works. However, using a command doesn't have to be hard. All you need to remember are two simple characters, /?. That command line switch says, "Help me!" The command usually will help by presenting you with some options for using it.

To open a command line, select the Start ➤ Programs ➤ Accessories ➤ Command Prompt command. You'll see a command prompt. Whenever you open a command prompt using this method, it opens in your home directory on the hard drive. Type **TaskList /?** and press Enter. Figure 1.3 shows what you'll see. (I've scrolled back to the top so you can see the major entries.)

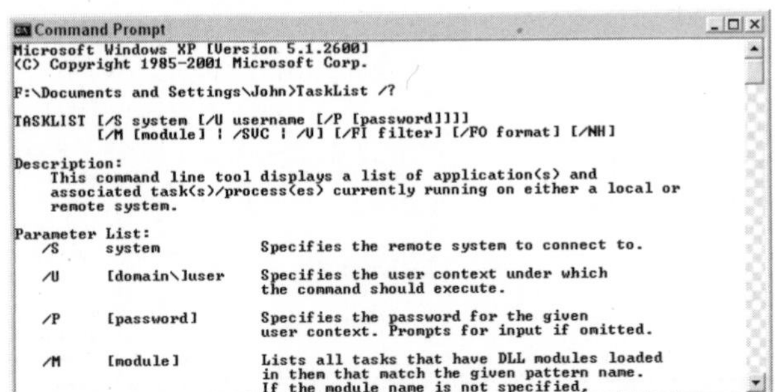
Command Prompt
Microsoft Windows XP [Version 5.1.2600]
(C) Copyright 1985-2001 Microsoft Corp.
F:\Documents and Settings\John>TaskList /?
TASKLIST [/S system [/U username [/P [password]]]]
[/M [module] | /SVC | /V] [/FI filter] [/FO format] [/NH]
Description:
This command line tool displays a list of application(s) and
associated task(s)/process(es) currently running on either a local or
remote system.
Parameter List:
/S system Specifies the remote system to connect to.
/U [domain\]user Specifies the user context under which
the command should execute.
/P [password] Specifies the password for the given
user context. Prompts for input if omitted.
/M [module] Lists all tasks that have DLL modules loaded
in them that match the given pattern name.
If the module name is not specified,

FIGURE 1.3
Make things simple; ask the command for usage instructions.

The first piece of information is the usage instructions for the command. A set of square brackets ([]) tells you about an optional input. In this case, everything is optional; you can use TaskList by itself.

A slash (/) tells you about a command line switch. Sometimes command line switches appear with a dash (-) instead. In either case, a command line switch configures the command to perform a task in a specific way. For example, TaskList doesn't normally display services, but you can tell it to display services by adding the /SVC command line switch.

Some command line switches depend on other command line switches. You'll see the command line switches nested within multiple layers of square brackets in this situation. For example, if you want to supply a password for logging into a remote system to view the tasks running on it, you must also supply the `/System` and `/Username` command line switches.

In other cases, command line switches are mutually exclusive. The command line will separate these switches with the pipe (|) symbol. The `TaskList` command won't allow you to use the /M command line switch with the /SVC switch; you must select one or the other.

After the usage information, you'll normally see a description section for newer commands. The description tells you what task the command performs and why you would want to use it. Sometimes this information is quite complete, as it is with the `TaskList` command, and in other cases, you'll still be scratching your head after you read the description. Older commands don't provide a description at all; you just have to know what task they perform, which is why many people don't use them.

A description of the individual parameters (or arguments and inputs) comes next. These entries tell you how to use the individual command line switches. You'll also discover other kinds of information you must provide. For example, the `Dir` (directory) command information shown in Figure 1.4 tells you that you can provide a drive letter, followed by a colon, followed by a directory path, and ending with a filename specification. None of these entries is a command line switch, but they're all important parameters.

The final section is a list of examples. Only a few commands provide this kind of information, but it's always helpful when they do. The examples come in many forms. The `TaskList` command provides a list of filters first, so you can see how to get the output you want. It provides actual usage examples next so you can see what to type at the command line. The point is that most people could use a command at the command prompt if they simply knew the simple /? command line switch. Go ahead and try it out now with the `TaskList` and `Dir` commands. You'll want to keep the /? command line switch in mind as you read about other commands in this book. Try it out with every one of them and you'll find that most commands provide some information, usually enough to jog your memory when you need to use it.

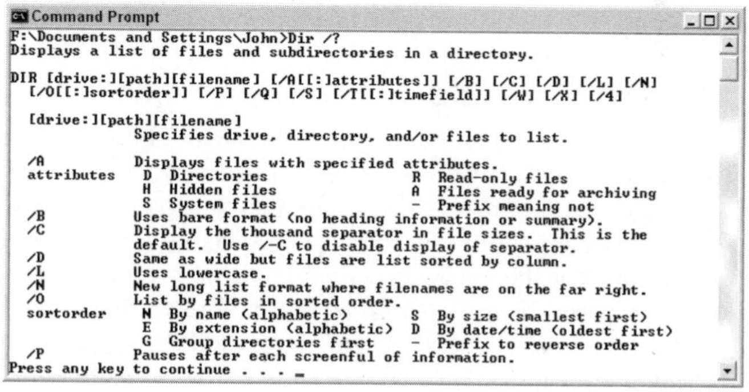

FIGURE 1.4 Sometimes you provide text input as well as command line switches.

```
Command Prompt
F:\Documents and Settings\John>Dir /?
Displays a list of files and subdirectories in a directory.

DIR [drive:][path][filename] [/A[[:]attributes]] [/B] [/C] [/D] [/L] [/N]
  [/O[[:]sortorder]] [/P] [/Q] [/S] [/T[[:]timefield]] [/W] [/X] [/4]

  [drive:][path][filename]
              Specifies drive, directory, and/or files to list.

  /A          Displays files with specified attributes.
  attributes   D  Directories                R  Read-only files
               H  Hidden files               A  Files ready for archiving
               S  System files               -  Prefix meaning not
  /B          Uses bare format (no heading information or summary).
  /C          Display the thousand separator in file sizes.  This is the
              default.  Use /-C to disable display of separator.
  /D          Same as wide but files are list sorted by column.
  /L          Uses lowercase.
  /N          New long list format where filenames are on the far right.
  /O          List by files in sorted order.
  sortorder    N  By name (alphabetic)       S  By size (smallest first)
               E  By extension (alphabetic)  D  By date/time (oldest first)
               G  Group directories first    -  Prefix to reverse order
  /P          Pauses after each screenful of information.
Press any key to continue . . .
```

Real World Scenario

STORING COMMANDS IN BATCH FILES

I've worked at the command line for years, so you might assume that I have all of these commands memorized by now. However, like many people, I find that memorizing all of the commands, their parameters, and their command line switches is just too much work. However, discovering the required parameters one time isn't too much work. That's where batch files come to my aid. I use batch files to remember specific command sequences for me.

When you need to store one or more commands so you don't have to remember them every time you want to use them, a batch file can do the job. In fact, you can create batch files that have a limited amount of intelligence so they don't perform the same task in the same way every time. Batch files are the first method that many people use to automate the command line. I have batch files that I wrote over 18 years ago when I started with computers and I'm still using them today. In short, a good batch file can last a very long time. The thing to remember about batch files is that they're very easy to write, only have a little intelligence (so there isn't any heavy coding), and don't require anything special to execute. You'll discover how to work with batch files in Chapter 7.

Writing Scripts

Scripts are the next step up in complexity. A script uses a simple programming language to accomplish tasks. You can't create complex applications using a script. For example, you wouldn't want to write a word processor using a script. However, scripting languages provide more intelligence than a batch file can. In addition, you can access some of the functionality that Windows provides. Consequently, rather than rely on utilities for every action, you can ask Windows for some help in automating your tasks.

A script requires a special environment to run. Windows provides this environment in the form of a script interpreter. The interpreter reads every line of code you write in your script and performs the task it requests. Writing scripts is a little harder than writing batch files, but not nearly as difficult as writing an application with a full-fledged programming language. Consequently, scripts are exactly what many people need to automate tasks when they don't want to learn a full-fledged programming language, yet find batch files less robust than they'd like. You'll discover how to work with scripts in Chapter 8.

Most of the tasks you perform using scripts have standard requirements and needs to execute successfully. Active Directory, the Windows enterprise database, requires some special handling to work correctly. Chapter 9 discusses the scripting requirements for this special environment and helps you create scripts that make working with Active Directory a lot easier.

Scheduling Tasks

No matter how you work with the command line, whether you use individual commands, batch files, or scripts, you can schedule a task to run at a specific time. For example, if you want to defragment your hard drive every night, you can schedule the `Defrag` command described in Chapter 6 to run automatically. Of course, you'd better be certain that everything is set up correctly before you assume the computer can perform the task on its own. Many people begin using the Task Scheduler to run tasks that they could forget during normal work hours and then progress to after-hours tasks. You'll find a discussion of the Task Scheduler in Chapter 10 and after-hours task scheduling in Chapter 11.

Relying on Third Party Utilities

The fact that Microsoft doesn't spend much time advertising the command line should tell you something. The tools that Microsoft provides for working at the command line are basic, simple, and not always the best tools at your disposal. Third party tools for working at the command prompt have been around for a long time. Most of these products are mature, fully tested, and quite capable of making your command line experience everything it should be. Part 3 of this book, Chapters 12, 13, and 14, provides you with a wealth of third party utility resources.

Viewing the Commands by Purpose

The commands on your system have a particular purpose in most cases. The name doesn't always reveal the purpose. Depending on the documentation provided with the utility, you might still have a hard time figuring it out. However, they all do have a particular purpose. For example, the `Dir` command helps you locate files and directories (folders) on your machine and the `TaskList` command helps you discover which applications are running. The `Dir` command performs a data-specific task, while the `TaskList` command is a monitoring application. The following sections describe the classifications of commands that you'll find at the command prompt.

Data Specific

Many of the commands that Windows provides are data specific. You use them to perform infrastructure tasks such as creating and removing directories. Other commands help you create, delete, and edit files. You'll find that the `Sort` command lets you sort the contents of a file. Some of the commands display data on screen, while others send the file content to the printer. A few of the commands perform management tasks. For example, you can perform a bulk copy of your files using the `XCopy` command. All of these commands appear in Chapter 2.

The data-specific commands are important for a number of reasons. For example, you can write a batch file that lets you set up the entire directory structure for a new user. A new user setup can require seconds instead of hours. In addition, you can be certain that every user will have precisely the same setup every time, which means that you'll spend less time supporting a network and more time getting other work done.

Using the data-specific commands can save you considerable time in other ways. Most companies archive files either when a project finishes or during standard intervals in the process of working with a client. Batch files can make it significantly easier to create the archive, but you need to know the commands required to create the data infrastructure and move the files first.

System Status

Computer systems today are very complex. The combination of software and hardware that makes the computing environment as useful as it is can also hide problems and eventually damage the very data they were used to create. Knowing the status of your system is important. However, discovering the status information can be hard without the use of the command line. Something as simple as knowing what equipment you have installed can make a big difference when it comes time to manage the system. Chapter 3 tells you all about the system status commands.

Real World Scenario

USING STATUS INFORMATION TO YOUR ADVANTAGE

Failures of any kind on a computer can prove frustrating. The question of where to start looking for the problem can be the first and last question that many people ask. It's too easy to see the computer as a box that has a problem and assume there isn't any place to look. I've talked more than a few people through computer problems by simply telling them about the status indicators that the computer provides. In many cases, Microsoft provides these commands as a means for their support staff to locate a problem for you at some outrageous hourly rate, but there isn't any reason you can't use the tools too.

For example, one command problem that people encounter is a failed audio system. You can check the event log and then view the information about the sound system using the Control Panel applets. In addition, you can use a utility such as DXDiag to perform audio checks on your system. You might even use performance monitoring to look for hidden audio problems. Of course, you have to remember to do all of these things. However, as the book progresses, you'll find that you can also access all of this information from the command prompt. A batch file might be all you need to perform a carefully executed diagnostic check using the same steps every time. The results are consistent input about your audio system and no missed checks, which means that you have a good chance of locating an error without paying anyone.

Of course, you don't want to spend all of your time managing the system and obtaining the status information. You can also use the command line to set up performance monitors, alerts, and logs. Of course, you can use the Performance console in the Administrative Tools folder of the Control Panel to perform the required setups, but that means performing the task manually. If you have more than one computer to manage, it's a lot easier to set up a script or batch file to perform the required setups once and then automate the task on every machine you manage.

TIP If you think that utilities such as DXDiag (DirectX Diagnostics) require use of a GUI to perform any useful work, be prepared for a surprise in Chapter 3. Many of these utilities sport a command line interface that you can use to manage computers from your desk, rather than running from place to place looking for information. A GUI is great when you're sitting at the machine because it does make things easier, but the command line interface makes things faster and more convenient when working from a remote location.

File and Resource Management

Files and other resources are always a source of concern for a computer system. The resources you have at your disposal determine the kind and amount of work you can perform with the computer system. Data isn't simply a collection of information that you use to create a report, it's a resource that you have to manage. The utilities in Chapter 4 all provide some type of resource management. The chapter begins by looking at file commands, such as those you can use to detect strings within a file, but it also includes other resources. For example, this chapter shows how to manage the power configuration settings on a system from the command prompt. You'll also find commands for a number of services including the Remote Access Server (RAS).

Security and System Monitoring

Monitoring on a computer can take several forms. There's the kind of monitoring that you perform to ensure the computer is operating at peak efficiency that appears in Chapter 3. However, if you only check the performance of your computer, you'll almost certainly notice that it decreases with time. The reason is simple: overall computer health is a combination of performance, reliability, and security. Often, you increase one part of the triangle at the expense of the other two. For example, increasing the performance of the computer by overclocking the hardware will almost certainly result in reduced reliability and could impair security as well.

Chapter 5 focuses on the kind of monitoring that improves security from a number of perspectives. The security monitoring in this chapter doesn't necessarily keep intruders out, but it focuses on the kind of monitoring that dissuades outside intrusion and improves system health. For example, by maintaining strict control over the network, you not only improve overall system security but you also improve the performance and reliability of the computer as well.

Developer and Low-level Tasks

Microsoft has always tried to provide support for the developer community by including helpful utilities for them as part of Windows. For example, after you install a program, the developer can use the ShutDown utility to restart your system and ensure that the changes to system DLLs load. However, developers aren't the only ones to use this utility. I include a quick shutdown feature for my system using a simple shortcut as explained in the "Shutting the System Down with the ShutDown Utility" section of Chapter 6. Using this simple shortcut shortens a relatively long shutdown process into one that takes seconds (sometimes less). Of course, you have to know when to use and when to avoid a quick shutdown.

Most of these low-level utilities work with the system in ways that could be dangerous in the wrong hands. Consequently, you'll want to view this chapter only if you have the skills required to work with system resources safely. For example, the DiskPart utility could wipe out your hard drive, so it's important that you not use it unless you understand disk partitioning.

Active Directory

Some tools are specifically for managing enterprise systems. All of the Active Directory utilities described in Chapter 9 fall into this category. In fact, because of the nature of these utilities, the chapter describes them in the light of usage with scripts immediately, rather than assuming you'll use the utilities in a stand-alone mode. If your company uses Active Directory, this chapter can save you significant time and frustration, while making your setup considerably more reliable.

Services

Windows services are a special breed of applications. In fact, many people ignore them completely. However, services are simply a kind of application, one that executes in the background unobserved, often waiting for a special system event to occur. If you haven't really paid attention to services before, you can view them using the Services console located in the Administrative Tools folder of the Control Panel. Figure 1.5 shows a typical view of services.

Unfortunately, failure to manage services can cause all kinds of problems. For example, every service uses system resources, so keeping a service that you don't need running can slow system performance. Some services, such as Messenger (not associated with Windows Messenger), can actually open security holes in your system. By using command line utilities combined with batch files, you can start and stop services as you need them. For example, I start the development-oriented services on my system only when I plan to develop code; the rest of the time, I keep them disabled so they don't use resources or open security holes. Starting and stopping is a matter of double-clicking a simple batch file, which makes it incredibly easy to maintain a secure and efficient environment.

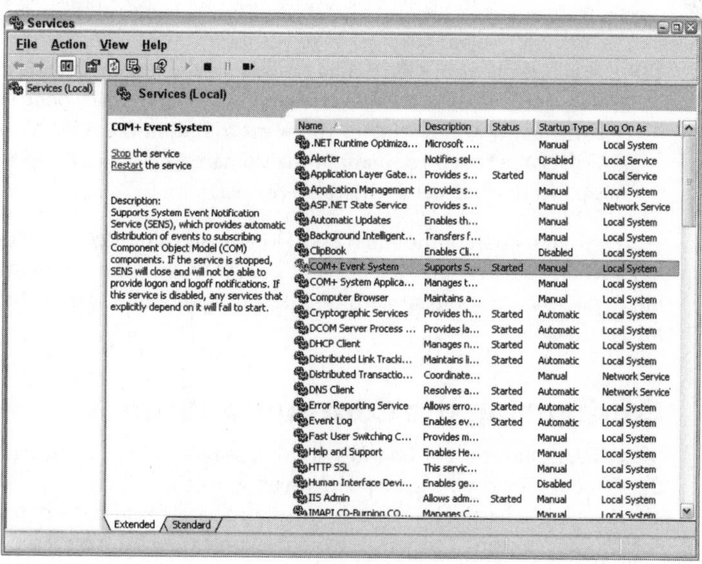

FIGURE 1.5
Managing services is an important reason to use command line utilities.

WARNING The names and order of services can vary by Windows version. For example, Figure 1.5 shows the Windows XP names of the services. In most cases, these names are unchanged from Windows 2000 and remain the same in Windows 2003. Vista makes the largest changes to service names and even old favorites have new names. Because you need the actual names of services to use some command line utilities, you'll want to verify that any older batch files that manipulate services still work when you move them to a new version of Windows.

Task Scheduling

It's not always convenient to run commands while you're using the computer for work. In other cases, you want to ensure the command runs even if you get busy in meetings. You can resolve both needs by using the Task Scheduler. Chapter 10 tells you how to use the Task Scheduler to improve the efficiency of your system, while Chapter 11 provides a special focus on after-hours scripting using the Task Scheduler. In both chapters, you'll discover new techniques for using command line utilities to control the Task Scheduler so it performs as you expect.

Updating Your Current Utilities at the Microsoft Download Center

You might already know about the Microsoft Download Center at `http://www.microsoft.com/downloads/search.aspx`. If you don't, you should visit it before you go any further in the book. This Web site provides access to updates for all of Microsoft's products, including those that the Windows Update and Office Web sites don't automatically update for you.

The Microsoft Download Center usually displays the current favorite or target applications at the top. If you visit the Web site often, you'll want to check out this list immediately to obtain the current versions of applications you already have installed on your system.

Immediately below the list of favorites (you usually have to scroll down), you'll see a search form where you can search for applications by keyword and technology. In many cases, the most efficient search is to look for applications by technology because Microsoft sometimes uses arcane terminology for the updates.

TIP If you really have a hard time finding an application you need at the Microsoft Download Center, go to Google Advanced Search at `http://www.google.com/advanced_search`. Type the name of the product you want to find in the With All of the Words field. Type the `www.microsoft.com` domain in the Domain field. Click Google Search and you should find the application you need with relative ease.

The final section of the Microsoft Download Center contains download categories. Use these links when you have an idea of what you need, but don't know the name. As an example, you might have heard about something interesting on a newsgroup, but might not know precisely what Microsoft calls it.

Configuring the Command Window

Many users start the command window, see the typical command prompt, and just assume that they'll never see anything else. However, you can easily configure the command window to appear as you want, at least within limits. You can access these features by clicking the box in the upper left corner and choosing Properties from the context menu. You'll see a properties dialog box with four tabs. Each of these tabs is described in the sections that follow.

Setting the Window Options

The Options tab shown in Figure 1.6 defines how the command window reacts when you open it. The Cursor Size option controls the size of the cursor, with small being the default. The Large option provides a block cursor that is very easy to see. The Display Options determine whether you see the command window full screen or as a window. Using the full screen mode when you have a number of tasks to perform is easier on the eyes.

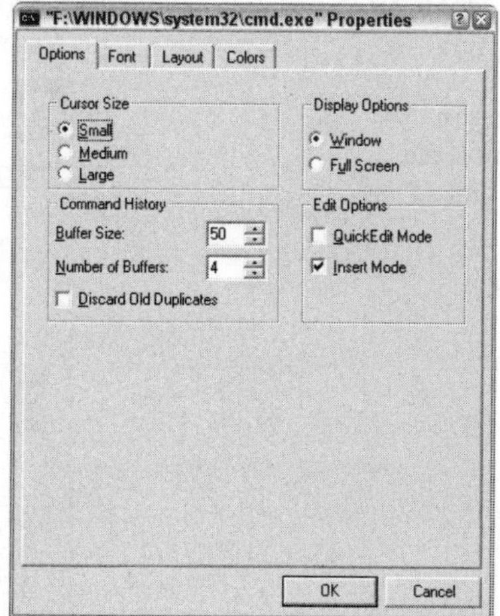

FIGURE 1.6
The Options tab helps you control the appearance and behavior of the command window.

NOTE Vista doesn't let you run the command window in full screen mode by changing the Display Options setting. This particular option is missing when you view the dialog box shown in Figure 1.6. However, you can set the option by changing the command line prompt shortcut options. If you want to use full screen mode all of the time, right-click the Command Prompt entry in the Start ➢ Programs ➢ Accessories menu and choose Properties. Select the Options tab of the Command Prompt Properties dialog box and select Full Screen in the Display Options group.

The Command History is especially important. The Buffer Size option determines the number of commands the buffer will store. Every command requires memory, so increasing this number increases the amount of memory the command prompt requires. Increase this number when you plan to perform a number of complex commands. A smaller number will save memory for larger command line applications. The Number of Buffers Option controls the number of individual histories. You need one history for each process (application environment) you create. Generally, the four shown work fine.

The Edit Options determine how you interact with the command window. Check the QuickEdit Mode when you want to use the mouse to work with the entries directly. The only problem with using this feature is that it can interfere with some commands such as Edit that have a mouse interface of their own. The Insert Mode option lets you paste text into the command window without replacing the text currently there. For example, you might copy some information from a Windows application and paste it as an argument for a command.

Changing the Font

The Font tab shown in Figure 1.7 controls the font used to display text. The font size automatically changes when you resize the window, but you can also control the font size directly using this tab. The raster fonts give the typical command line font appearance that works well for most quick tasks. The Lucida Console font works better in a windowed environment. It's easier on the eyes because it's smoother, but you might find that some applications won't work well with it if they create "text graphics" using some of the extended ASCII characters. The extended ASCII characters include corners and lines that a developer can use to draw boxes and add visual detail.

FIGURE 1.7
Use the Font tab to control the size of the text in the command window.

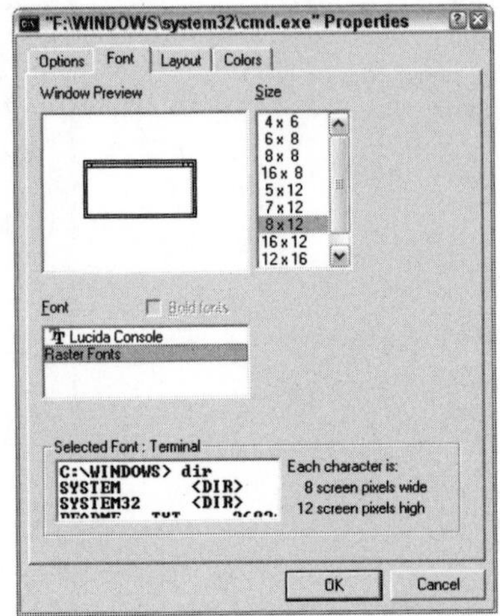

Choosing a Window Layout

The Layout tab shown in Figure 1.8 has the potential to affect your use of the command window greatly when working in windowed mode. The Screen Buffer Size controls the width and height of the screen buffer, the total area used to display information. When the Window Size setting is smaller than the Screen Buffer Size, Windows provides scroll bars so you can move the window around within the buffer area and view all it contains. Some commands require a great deal of space for display purposes. Adjusting the Screen Buffer Size and Window Size can help you view all of the information these commands provide.

The Window Position determines where Windows places the command window when you first open it. Some people prefer a specific position on the screen so they always know where a new command window will appear. However, it's generally safe to check Let System Position Window to allow Windows to place the command window on screen. Each command window will appear at a different, randomly chosen, position on screen.

Defining the Text Colors

Microsoft assumes that you want a black background with light gray letters for the command window. Although DOS used this setting all those years ago, many people today want a choice. The Color tab lets you choose different foreground, background, and pop-up colors for the command window (even though Figure 1.9 doesn't show the colors, it does present the dialog box layout). You can modify the window to use any of the 16 standard color combinations for any of the text options. Use the Select Color Values options to create custom colors.

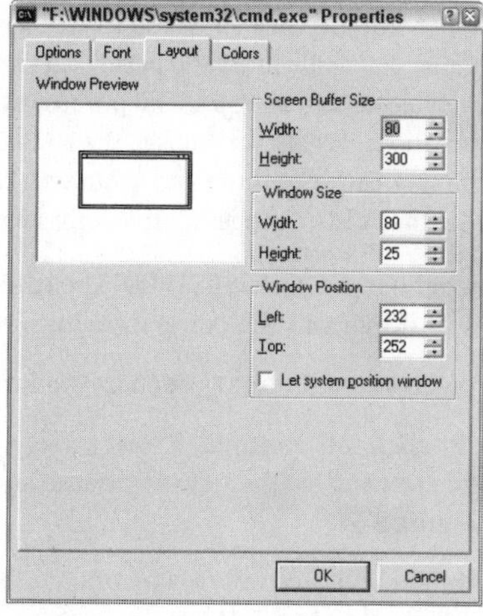

FIGURE 1.8
Change the size and positioning of the command window using the Layout tab.

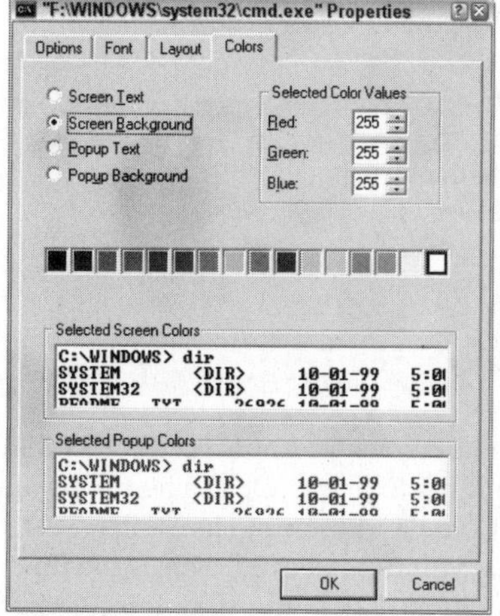

FIGURE 1.9
Modify the text colors for an optimal display using the Colors tab.

Placing a Command Prompt at Your Fingertips

It's possible to change the Windows Explorer registry settings so that you can get a command prompt wherever you need one. For example, say you're viewing the System32 folder and see a utility that you've never seen there before. You can use this registry change to right-click the folder and choose Command Prompt Here from the context menu to see a command prompt in that folder, rather than your home folder, as normal. Use the following steps to make this change manually.

1. Select the Start ➢ Run command. Type `RegEdit` in the Open field and click OK. You'll see the Registry Editor.

NOTE When working with Vista, you'll often see a User Account Control (UAC) dialog box appear that asks whether you really intend to perform a particular action. Although this dialog box can become quite annoying, it does serve a useful purpose in alerting you to actions from viruses and other nefarious applications. Whenever you see the UAC dialog box and know that you've started a particular action, simply click Continue and Vista will continue the action (assuming you have the proper rights). See the "Vista Changes for the Command Line" section of the chapter for more details.

2. Open the `HKEY_CLASSES_ROOT\Folder\shell` folder. Right-click this folder and choose New ➢ Key from the context menu. The Registry Editor will create a new type for you.
3. Type **Command_Prompt_Here** as the key name and press Enter.
4. Right-click the `Command_Prompt_Here` key and choose New ➢ Key from the context menu. Type **command** for the new key name and press Enter. You now have two new keys, as shown in Figure 1.10.
5. Right-click the command key and choose New ➢ String Value from the context menu. Type **cmd.exe /k \"cd %1\"** as the new string value. Exercise extreme care with this step. Press Enter. The new value should look like the one shown in Figure 1.10.
6. Close the Registry Editor.

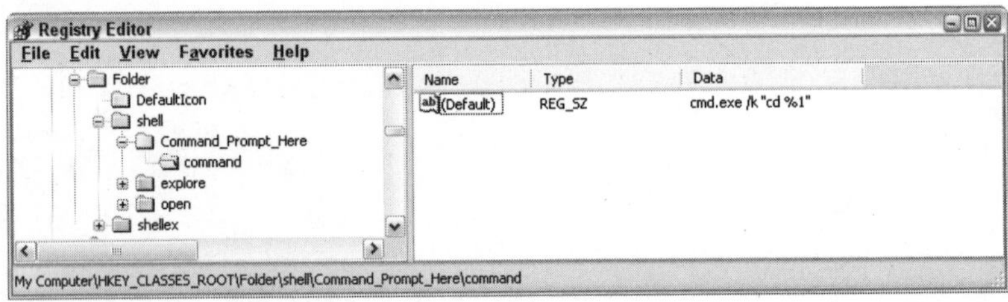

FIGURE 1.10 Create new registry keys to hold the Command Prompt Here context menu option.

Congratulations, you now have a tool that you can use to create a command prompt directly from Windows Explorer. Open a new copy of Windows Explorer, right-click a folder, and you'll see the new Command Prompt Here entry. Select this option to create a new command prompt in the folder that you right-clicked. This is the first use of the command line in this book. You can learn more about `CMD.EXE` in the "Using the CMD Switches" section of Chapter 7.

You don't have to go through this set of steps every time you want to add this feature to a copy of Windows. The following registry script will perform the same task. To use this approach, open a copy of Notepad and type the script shown here precisely, as shown.

```
Windows Registry Editor Version 5.00

[HKEY_CLASSES_ROOT\Folder\shell\Command_Prompt_Here]
@="Command Prompt Here"

[HKEY_CLASSES_ROOT\Folder\shell\Command_Prompt_Here\command]
@="cmd.exe /k \"cd %1\""
```

When you finish, select the File ➢ Save command. Type **CommandPromptHere.REG** in the File Name field. Choose All Files in the Save as Type field. Click Save. You now have a new registry script for adding the Command Prompt Here feature. All you need to do is double-click this file in Windows Explorer to make the addition.

Understanding Internal Commands

This chapter has used the term *command* for everything you execute at the command line. In reality, you need to view the command line as having multiple command types. Some commands, such as `TaskList.EXE`, appear as separate files. This book will use the term *utility* for these kinds of commands from now on. A utility always resides in a separate file and you can look it up using the `Dir` command.

Some commands don't exist in separate files; they reside in the host program that you use to interact with the computer. The host program for the command prompt is `CMD.EXE`. If you want to try it out, use the Start ➤ Run command to display the Run dialog box. Type **CMD** in the Open field and click OK. You'll see a command prompt. `CMD.EXE` doesn't end after it opens the command prompt; it remains in the background to receive and react to your keystrokes.

The `CMD.EXE` file also has a number of internal commands. These special keystrokes tell `CMD.EXE` to perform a task for you. For example, the `Dir` command is an internal `CMD.EXE` command. You won't find `Dir` listed as an executable anywhere on your hard drive. This book lists all internal commands as commands. Consequently, you'll see the TaskList utility and the `Dir` command discussed later in the book.

Other utilities create a host environment and you'll discover the commands in those host environments as you read the book. For example, the TelNet utility discussed in Chapter 4 provides a host environment where you'll type commands. These commands don't exist outside TelNet, just as the `Dir` command doesn't exist outside of `CMD.EXE`.

Vista Changes for the Command Line

Microsoft is well known for maintaining backward compatibility whenever possible despite a strong desire to add new features to an operating system or application that serve to complicate administrative tasks. However, you're going to find that Vista represents a change in tactic. Everyone has complained for so long about the security problems in Windows that Microsoft has finally decided to do something about the issue (proving yet again that you should be careful about what you wish for). Working at the command line is considerably harder in Vista than in any previous version of Windows, partly because of the new security features and partly because of significant changes to some command line features. The following sections provide an overview of these various changes and help you understand them better.

Understanding User Account Control (UAC) Changes

The UAC features of Windows serve to increase security by reducing the chance that an application can perform any act on the user's behalf, without the user's knowledge. Vista assumes that every user is a standard user, even administrators. If you have an administrator account, you must elevate your privileges from standard user to administrator to perform many tasks. In most cases, this means clicking Continue when you see the UAC dialog box asking whether you really mean to perform a particular task. Let's just say that the feature is incredibly annoying for anyone who spends their day working at the command line, but it does serve a useful purpose. Used correctly, UAC ensures that no one can perform an action on your behalf without your knowledge. Given that administrators have considerable power, this feature is especially useful to administrators who might become targets of nefarious individuals. After all, you don't want to suffer the embarrassment of being the source of a virus, adware, or spyware on the very network that you're supposed to protect.

However, UAC goes far further than simply asking whether you want to perform a particular task. In some cases, it can actually prevent you from performing tasks despite having an administrator account. For example, you're going to find that Vista severely hampers your access to the Windows and System32 folders even with an administrator account. Vista meets any attempt to change anything in the folders with disapproval that is seemingly impossible to overcome. The same holds true for the root directory of the boot drive. Network drives are nearly impossible to access as well. In fact, except for your personal data folders, Vista is locked down so tight that many administrative tasks are all but impossible to perform, even with an administrator account. The "Overcoming UAC Problems," "Giving Yourself Permission," and "Setting Vista Zones on Network Drives" sections of the chapter provide you with details on how you can overcome some of these issues. The bottom line is that Vista is all about security. Microsoft has thrown backward compatibility out the window in order to achieve some level of additional security.

Overcoming UAC Problems

The main source of woe for most administrators in Vista is the UAC. Before you can do anything, you'll need to override the UAC, at least for a while. It's actually better if you can override UAC to gain the privileges you need and then return Vista to its default state. Fortunately, you'll find all of the UAC controls in one place. Open the Local Security Policy applet found in the Administrative Tools folder of the Control Panel. Select the Security Settings\Local Policies\Security Options folder as shown in Figure 1.11. The figure shows the default settings should you ever need to restore them.

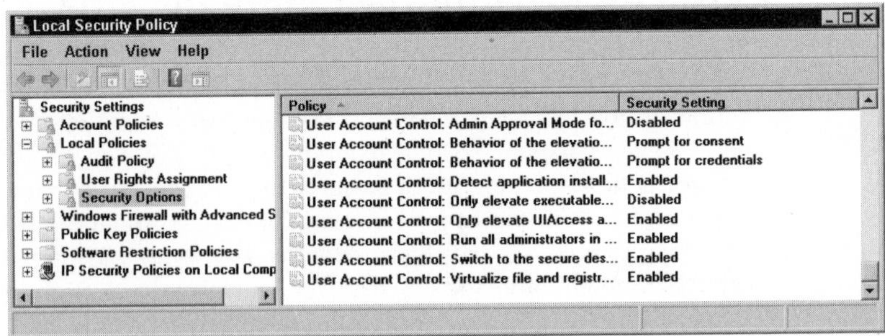

FIGURE 1.11 The User Account Control policies affect your ability to work with the system as an administrator.

The best way to get your system configured is to turn off everything, reboot the system, and make the changes you need (see the "Giving Yourself Permission" and "Setting Vista Zones on Network Drives" sections for details). After you set the required permissions, return Vista to its previous state so you can obtain the security features that Vista provides. Remember that changing the settings isn't enough since a change to policy won't affect your security token until after you reboot. Always make the required changes and then reboot to add those changes to your security token.

Giving Yourself Permission

Vista handles security differently from previous versions of Windows. First, you don't have permission to use anything other than your personal folder until you specifically request that permission. If UAC is still in force, Vista will reject any request to change security in the root folder of the boot drive (the one that has the Windows folder) even if you have an administrator account. Consequently, you must disable UAC to give yourself permission to access the drive.

Second, you'll quickly discover what it means to be a standard user. Whenever you open Windows Explorer, it opens with standard user credentials, which means you can't change anything even if you have administrator privileges and disable UAC. Instead of starting Windows Explorer normally, you'll need to right-click Start ➢ Programs ➢ Accessories ➢ Windows Explorer and choose Run as Administrator from the context menu. This action gives you a version of Windows Explorer with administrator privileges. Now, you can right-click the root directory and choose Properties from the context menu. Select the Security tab and add your account to the list as shown in Figure 1.12. Adding a group won't grant you the privileges you think it will—you must add your personal user account to the list.

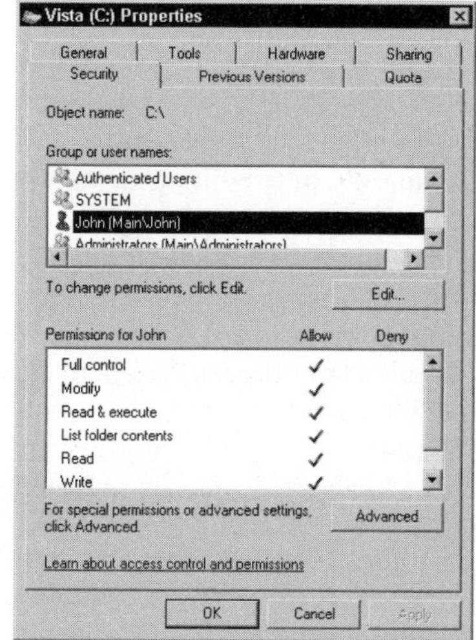

FIGURE 1.12
Grant yourself permission to make changes to your own hard drive.

Third, you'll be amazed to find that rights don't flow as they once did. Microsoft has specifically blocked the flow of rights from the root directory to the Windows and System32 folders. Consequently, you must also add your account to these folders if you want to access them as shown in Figure 1.12. Rights do flow from the root folder to other folders on the boot drive.

Setting Vista Zones on Network Drives

Vista treats every network drive as an Internet drive. Choose View ➢ Status Bar in Windows Explorer and you'll notice that the status bar shows that all network drives are now in the Internet zone, which severely limits what you can do with them. The purpose of this change is to make it harder for viruses, adware, and spyware to spread from machine to machine. However, it also makes it nigh on to impossible for an administrator to perform any task remotely. Unless you want to spend your days running from machine to machine, you need to change the zone of those network drives.

Admittedly, you'll only want to change the zone for drives that you actually work with regularly. You may even want to elevate their privileges when working with a special account. It depends on how much you value this particular Vista feature. The following steps help you set the zone for your network drives.

1. Choose a network drive. Double-click the zone icon in the Windows Explorer status bar. You'll see the Internet Security Properties dialog box.

2. Choose the Trusted Sites zone and click Sites. You'll see the Trusted Sites dialog box.
3. Type the URL for the network machine, such as `file://winserver` when the machine's name is winserver. Click Add. The new location appears in the trusted zone list.
4. Click Close to close the Trusted Sites dialog box and OK to close the Internet Security Properties dialog box. Your network drive is now accessible as it was in previous versions of Windows.

Understanding Vista Doesn't Support Old Commands

Vista changes some of the command line commands that have existed since the days of DOS. For example, you're going to notice a change in the `Choice` command (described in the "Using the Choice Command" section of Chapter 7). Many of the changes are obviously for security reasons, but changes to commands such as `Choice` simply end up breaking batch files for no apparent reason. Microsoft hasn't offered any reason for many of these changes, but you'll find them all listed as the book progresses.

Some commands are missing entirely. Microsoft chose not to support some commands that are obviously long in the tooth and it isn't hard to understand why. Some commands have simply become dangerous to use because they work completely different from other commands and because very few people use them. However, some command changes occur because of the way Vista operates. For example, Microsoft has replaced the BootCfg utility with the BCDEdit utility because Vista uses an entirely different method to store the boot configuration. You'll also see these changes listed throughout the book.

The bottom line for anyone using Vista is that you need to test every batch file to determine whether Vista changes have modified their behavior. Even simple batch files are prone to break in the new environment. Look for the changes in the chapters of this book whenever you have a question about some new Vista behavior.

TIP Don't always assume that a Vista command or utility change has affected your batch file. In some cases, batch files will cease to work because you don't have the required permissions. Always try to start the batch file by right-clicking it and choosing Run as Administrator before you assume that the command or utility won't work. Remember that security is everything in Vista.

Getting Started with Command Line Tasks

If you're anything like me, you're a little overwhelmed by now at what the command line can do for you. I've always used the command line. In fact, I've had some batch files hanging around since the days of DOS—yes, really, that long. However, until you take time to look at what the command line has to offer, you don't know what's there. Microsoft certainly doesn't make the command line the centerpiece of its advertising. In fact, the command line is one of the least understood and explored parts of Windows. Consequently, this book is your doorway to a new world. Not only will you perform tasks faster, with less effort, and more precisely, but you'll have a distinct edge over those around you as well. While they fiddle with an excessively time-consuming GUI, you're speeding along at the command line and making yourself look quite good in the process.

Of course, before you can begin working at the command line, it pays to make sure that your system is ready. Before you go any further, make sure you get on Windows Update and download all of the latest patches for your system. Check your Office installation and all of those third party utilities as well. Go to the Microsoft Download Center and look around for the downloads you've missed. An updated system normally yields the best set of fully updated utilities that will perform best and with the fewest possible errors. Make sure you get your command line prompt set up and add the required registry entries to put a command prompt at your fingertips as well. If you're using Vista, make sure you follow the procedures in the "Vista Changes for the Command Line" section of the chapter to set up your system for command line use in Vista. If you don't perform this setup, you'll find that most of the commands and utilities in this book won't work at all.

Chapter 2 begins showing you the command line utilities. It focuses on commands that affect data in some way. You'll discover how to work with files and directories. It also shows some of the command line editors at your disposal. You don't have to use these editors, but they can help you create batch files and perform other tasks that make your command line experience better. Chapter 2 also provides your first look at the registry and some of the productivity utilities that you'll script later in the book. For example, it describes how to use the backup utility at the command line.

Chapter 2

Completing Data-Specific Tasks

- Creating and Modifying Data Files and Directories
- Displaying Data Files
- Determining File and Directory Status
- Performing Backups with the NTBackup or WBAdmin Utilities
- Working with ODBC Data Sources
- Managing the Windows Registry

Many of the tasks you perform at the command line relate to data in some way. You might want to create new files, archive existing files, create new directories, set up the home location for a new user, or perform any number of other tasks. The point is that you need to manage your data in some way.

NOTE You might not have run across the term *directory* in the past. Windows currently uses the term *folder* to describe what amounts to a directory. In fact, it actually uses an icon that looks like a folder. In the past, DOS and other command line users relied on the term *directory* to describe a container for holding files. Many of the commands and utilities described in this book still use the term *directory*. You can interchange directory and folder freely; they mean the same thing.

Data management doesn't just include working with files and directories. Creating a backup of your system regularly provides insurance against a multitude of disasters, including virus attacks. Even though this chapter doesn't provide you with a backup strategy, it does show you how to use NTBackup (WBAdmin for Vista) from the command line, which will allow you to automate the backup process. Backup automation is a great way to ensure you create a backup regularly, even if you're prone to forgetting when you have to perform the task manually.

Creating data connections is also a requirement, especially for older applications. This chapter shows how to manage Open Database Connectivity (ODBC) Data Source Names (DSNs). Applications rely on DSNs to create connections to the server. Many people are unaware that you can work with ODBC from the command line and create every connection using the ODBC Data Source Administrator located in the Administrative Tools folder of the Control Panel.

A final type of Windows data is the database that holds all your Windows and application settings called the registry. The registry is simply another form of data in some respects. Backing up this database can save you significant rework if your system fails for some reason. The backup will contain all of the essential settings for your system so that you can recover quickly. Of course, you can perform other registry tasks from the command line too.

Creating and Modifying Data Files and Directories

Files hold the actual content that a computer uses to perform tasks. Files generally come in two forms: application and data. An application file holds some form of executable content. In most cases, the executable content is in the form of machine code instructions: essentially special codes that the processor can understand without any interpretation. However, executable content can come in the form of tokens or even text that another application interprets and passes along to the processor.

Data files contain information. The information can appear in many forms and might include binary data. For example, graphics files are pure binary data that an application must interpret and present as an image for you. Likewise, some data files contain pure ASCII text, which is a series of numeric codes that the system interprets as text for you. Some data files, such as Word documents, are a mixture of text and binary data. However, the bottom line is that all data files contain some type of information, rather than executable content.

Directories act as storage containers for both files and other directories. The graphic image of folders in Windows Explorer shows you the arrangement of files and directories on a Windows system. The hard drive doesn't actually see the data in this way, but the vast majority of command line utilities do. Special utilities let you see the data as it actually appears on the hard drive, but this book doesn't discuss utilities such as Debug to that degree. Now that you have some idea of how all of these components work together, the following sections tell you about the commands and utilities you can use to maintain the data files and directories on your system.

Opening Remote Directories with the Append Utility

The Append utility lets you open multiple directories as if they exist in the current directory. In short, this utility lets you consolidate several directories into a single directory on the hard drive. The other directories don't actually appear in the current directory; the Append utility only makes them appear that they do. This utility uses the following syntax:

```
APPEND [[drive:]path[;...]] [/X[:ON | :OFF]] [/PATH:ON | /PATH:OFF] [/E]
```

The following list describes each of the command line arguments.

drive: Specifies the drive you want to use to append directories. The drive is always a letter. If you want to use a drive on another machine, you must first map the drive using Windows and then use the mapped drive letter for access.

path Contains one or more paths on the drive that you specify. Separate multiple paths using a semicolon (;). If you want to append paths from multiple drives, you must execute the Append utility multiple times, once for each drive.

/X:ON or X:OFF Defines whether you can use the appended path to perform file searches and application execution or just to open files. The default setting is X:OFF, which only allows you to use the appended path to open files.

/PATH:ON or /PATH:OFF Determines whether the appended path is included with commands that rely on a path. For example, if you have C:\Temp included within the path statement and use /PATH:ON with the Append utility, any requests to C:\Temp automatically include the appended path as well. However, if you select /PATH:OFF, the appended paths aren't included as part of the path. The default setting is /PATH:ON.

/E Stores all of the appended directories in an environment variable named APPEND. You can only use this command line switch the first time you execute Append within a particular command line window. However, other command line windows aren't affected by this command line switch; the APPEND environment variable only exists within the command line window in which you executed the Append utility and only for the time the command line window is open.

Executing Append with just a semicolon clears all of the appended paths for a particular directory. Running Append by itself will list the appended paths for a particular directory.

NOTE Windows XP and above ignores the results of the Append utility. Microsoft supplies the Append command in these versions of Windows for DOS batch file compatibility. When the appended directory feature is important, store the appended directories in the APPEND environment variable using the /E command line switch and then use the environment variable to search for files in other directories. As an alternative, you can employ data redirection (see the "Employing Data Redirection" section of this chapter for details). The Subst utility can also help by assigning long paths to a drive letter. You can also employ some direct substitutes for the Append utility, such as the shared folder redirection technique discussed at `http://windowsxp.mvps.org/sharedfolders.htm` (the TweakUI utility provided by Microsoft at `http://www.microsoft.com/windowsxp/downloads/powertoys/default.mspx` makes this process easier by providing a graphical interface). Consider modifying the path as described in the "Setting and Viewing Application Paths with the *Path* Command" section to make executables accessible.

Copying Files with the *Copy* Command

The Copy command lets you create a copy of a file that exists in one directory into another directory. You can create copies on other drives, even drives that you map using Windows. In addition, this command works with nonfile devices such as the printer or keyboard. Generally, users rely on the functionality provided by Windows Explorer to move and copy files. However, the extensive list of command line switches provided by the Copy command makes it extremely flexible for use in batch commands. In addition, using some switches, such as the ASCII file transfer option for text files, can improve overall Windows copy performance. This utility uses the following syntax:

```
COPY [/D] [/V] [/N] [/Y | /-Y] [/Z] [/L] [/A | /B ] source [/A | /B]
     [+ source [/A | /B] [+ ...]] [destination [/A | /B]]
```

The following list describes each of the command line arguments.

source Defines the source of the data that you want to copy. The source is usually a file, but you can use devices as a source of data. See the "Understanding Command Line Devices" sidebar for details. You can use wildcard characters to specify the filenames. See the "Working with Wildcard Characters" sidebar for details.

destination Defines the output location for the data that you want to copy. The destination is usually a file, but you can use devices as a destination for data. See the "Understanding Command Line Devices" sidebar for details.

/A Copies the file as ASCII text. Using this technique improves Copy command performance. However, using this command line switch with a binary file will result in data loss.

/B Copies the file in binary mode. Many files fall into the binary category, even though you might think they are standard text files. For example, a Word DOC file is a binary file because it contains control and other characters that won't transfer well using the /A command line switch.

/D Decrypts the destination file. This special Windows command line switch decrypts files that are encrypted using Windows encryption features. If you don't use this command line switch, the destination remains encrypted.

/L Copies a symbolic link to the target instead of the actual file pointed to by the symbolic link when the source is a symbolic link. This command line switch is only available in Vista.

/N Creates a destination file with an 8-character filename and a 3-character file extension. Use this command line switch when you must create destination files for older systems that rely on the DOS 8.3 naming convention. Avoid using this command line switch on files with long filenames unless you really do want to create a compatible file.

/V Verifies the destination file is the same as the source file. Writing files with verification improves reliability at the cost of performance. Windows writes the destination and then performs a file comparison when using this command line switch.

/Y and /-Y Suppresses or enforces the prompt for overwriting destination files with the same name as the destination file provided as input to the Copy command. Use the /Y command line switch in batch files where you know the batch file will overwrite an existing destination file. The /-Y command line switch is the default, so you never need to use it.

/Z Copies files to network destinations in a restartable mode. If the network connection fails, the Copy command gives you the option of restarting the copy from the current file position. This command line switch makes it possible to copy large files using less reliable network connections.

One of the more important features of the Copy command is the ability to combine two files. For example, you might download a large file as two file fragments from an Internet site to reduce the problems associated with downloading a single large file. Combine the two file fragments to create a complete file by typing a plus sign (+) between source files like this:

```
COPY FilePart1 + FilePart2 CompleteFile
```

When the Copy command completes, CompleteFile will contain the sum of the two file fragments.

When using the Copy command with the console, you must add an end of file marker to the input by pressing Ctrl+Z. The end of file marker will appear as ^Z on screen, which signifies it as control character 26. Pressing Enter after ^Z copies the file to the destination you indicate. The end of file marker doesn't appear when you send the resulting file to the console as output. Likewise, if you want a printer to output the partial page of data you sent to it, output a Ctrl+L character to it. You can see a complete list of standard control characters at http://www.cs.tut.fi/~jkorpela/chars/c0.html.

Understanding Command Line Devices

You can access a number of devices from the command line. Some devices accept input, others output, and some accept both. These devices always reference a physical device of some type. In some cases, the device isn't attached to your machine, but it's accessible from your machine, such as a network printer. Many commands and utilities let you use a device in place of a drive letter as an argument. For example, the Copy command lets you use input from a device to create a file. You can also use a file as output to a device. Here's the standard list of command line devices.

CON The system console, which is the combination of keyboard and monitor used to access the computer system. Input comes from the keyboard and output goes to the monitor.

PRN The default printer. You must configure network printers to provide a port to support a command line device. The port appears on the Ports tab of the network printer's Properties dialog box. Even if your printer can provide bidirectional communication, the PRN device is only capable of output.

LPT1 through LPT4 The printer attached to the first through fourth printer (parallel) ports. The device need not physically attach to the parallel port; Windows can redirect the output to the physical device for you. You must configure network printers to provide a port to provide a command line device. The port appears on the Ports tab of the network printer's Properties dialog box. Even if your printer can provide bidirectional communication, the LPT devices are only capable of output.

AUX The auxiliary device; the one serviced by the first serial port (COM1). It's usually better to reference COM1 directly for readability in batch files. The AUX device is a holdover from the early days of DOS.

COM1 through COM4 The communication device attached to the first through fourth serial ports. Although standard outputs for this port include modems, you can connect printers as well. The serial port can act as both an input and an output device. You can configure network printers to use a COM port instead of an LPT port using the Ports tab of the network printer's Properties dialog box.

NUL The output doesn't go anywhere. The NUL(L) device is also known as the bit bucket.

**CLOCK$** This device is supposed to access the real-time clock. In reality, the device normally doesn't work in modern systems and Windows makes no effort to provide required redirection. You should avoid using the CLOCK$ device.

Removing Files with the *Del* and *Erase* Commands

The `Del` and `Erase` commands are functionally equivalent. The two commands started with different versions of DOS, but they perform the same task now: erasing files that you no longer need from the hard drive. Unlike the deletion that Windows performs, the files don't end up in the Recycle Bin; the deletion is permanent. These commands use the following syntax:

```
DEL [/P] [/F] [/S] [/Q] [/A[[:]attributes]] names
ERASE [/P] [/F] [/S] [/Q] [/A[[:]attributes]] names
```

The following list describes each of the command line arguments.

`names` Defines the file or directory names to remove from the hard drive. You can use wildcard characters to specify the filenames. See the "Working with Wildcard Characters" sidebar for details. Deleting a directory also deletes all of the files that the directory contains. Consequently, these commands can be exceptionally destructive.

`/A` Deletes files or directories based on their attributes. See the "Changing File and Directory Attributes with the Attrib Utility" section of Chapter 4 for details on working with attributes at the command prompt.

NOTE Vista adds the `L` attribute for reparse points and the `I` attribute for nonindexed files. The `I` attribute is a little tricky because you see it when the file isn't indexed versus when it has the required feature such as when you use the other attributes. These new attributes help you work with new file system features.

`/F` Forces the deletion of files marked with the read-only attribute. Normally, the commands prompt the user to delete such files.

`/P` Prompts the user to delete every file. This command line switch provides a safety factor, but also increase the time required to delete files.

/Q Deletes files based on a wildcard specification without prompting the user first. Normally, the utilities will prompt the user before deleting all of the files in a directory.

/S Deletes the specified files from all subdirectories. This command comes in handy when you want to remove all of the files with a given name on a hard drive. Windows often creates multiple copies of files; locating them all can be difficult.

WORKING WITH WILDCARD CHARACTERS

You might wonder how you can make your use of commands and utilities even more efficient. Most of these utilities will let you work with multiple files at once, but you need to know the secret of specifying multiple files. Wildcard characters let you specify a group of files or directories without naming each file or directory individually. There are two standard wildcard characters: * and ?. The asterisk (*) specifies any number of characters, while the question mark (?) specifies a single character. You can use the two wildcard characters in combination to create complex file specifications to locate just about any file.

Most people are familiar with the * character. Typing `Dir S*.TXT` at the command line locates every text file in the current directory that begins with an S. However, you can use the * in any location. For example, typing `Dir *S*.TXT` at the command line would locate any text file that contains an S in any part of its name. Likewise, typing `Dir *S.TXT` would locate any text file that contains an S at the end of its name. You can also use the * for the file extension. Typing `Dir S.*` locates any file with S as a filename, but with any file extension.

The ? is far more selective than the * and many people fail to recognize its value. For example, typing `Dir S??.TXT` at the command line will locate any text file with three characters in its filename that begins with the letter S. Consequently, this command will locate `SUB.TXT` and `SUN.TXT`, but not `SUBST.TXT` or `RUN.TXT` (notice that even though `RUN.TXT` contains three letters, it doesn't begin with an S). Like the *, you can use the ? wildcard character anywhere in the filename. For example, you can type `Dir *.EX?` to locate both compressed and uncompressed executable files in the current directory. Without the selectiveness of the ? wildcard, you might end up with files that you didn't really want to find.

Removing a Directory Tree with the *DelTree* Command

VISTA

The `DelTree` command is a super delete; it removes all of the subdirectories and files in a particular directory, and then removes the specified directory as well. The command is quite fast and permanent. Yes, you can recover a directory removed with `DelTree` using a special file recovery program, but you should use this particular command with caution. Vista doesn't support the `DelTree` command. This command uses the following syntax:

```
DELTREE [/Y] [drive:]path [[drive:]path[...]]
```

The following list describes each of the command line arguments.

drive Specifies the drive where the directory is located.

path Specifies the absolute or relative path of the directory to remove.

/Y Forces the deletion of the specified path without asking the user first. You can use this option within a batch file to speed processing when you know that you want to delete the directory without user intervention.

NOTE Unlike many commands that add, remove, or modify directories, you can specify multiple paths using the `DelTree` command. This feature makes the command especially powerful and means that you can enter a single command to perform a significant amount of file and directory deletion.

Modifying Files with the Edlin Utility

Edlin is a relic from a previous time. It actually predates the PC when it comes to the user interface because it edits files line by line. Someone who worked with a mainframe in the 1960s would probably feel right at home using Edlin, but most modern users won't. The important things to remember about Edlin are

- You can find it in every Microsoft operating system and some non-Microsoft operating systems as well.
- It uses the same interface everywhere you find it.
- The executable is extremely small and portable at 12 KB.
- It always works.

Figure 2.1 shows an example of how Edlin appears with a file loaded.

FIGURE 2.1
Edlin is an ancient editor that works in any environment.

```
F:\WINDOWS\system32\cmd.exe - Edlin Temp.TXT
F:\>Edlin Temp.TXT
End of input file
*list
        1:*Hello
        2: This is Edlin!
        3: It's a line editor with an ancient interface.
        4: The best part about Edlin is that it works anywhere.
        1:*^Z
        3: It's a line editor with an ancient interface.
*?
Edit line                    line#
Append                       [#lines]A
Copy                         [startline],[endline],toline[,times]C
Delete                       [startline][,endline]D
End (save file)              E
Insert                       [line]I
List                         [startline][,endline]L
Move                         [startline],[endline],tolineM
Page                         [startline][,endline]P
Quit (throw away changes)    Q
Replace                      [startline][,endline][?]R[oldtext][CTRL+Znewtext]
Search                       [startline][,endline][?]Stext
Transfer                     [toline]T[drive:][path]filename
Write                        [#lines]W
*_
```

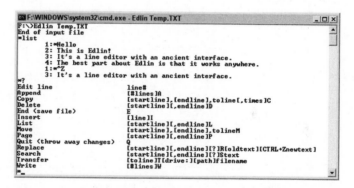

Figure 2.1 actually shows a number of Edlin features. The first line shows how to start Edlin by providing the name of the file you want to edit. Edlin can load any file, even binary files, if you provide the `/B` command line argument.

When you start Edlin, it doesn't display anything (yes, it's that primitive). You must type the `List` command and press Enter to show the content of the file, which you then edit one line at a time. Press Ctrl+Z to stop editing the text.

Typing a ? and pressing Enter displays the list of Edlin commands that comes next in Figure 2.1. Here's the one feature that I like about Edlin: it has a very capable search feature that doesn't assume anything about the file.

Finally, you type **`Quit`** and press Enter to end the editing session. Even though this editor works everywhere, you'll want to find a substitute such as the Edit utility described in the "Modifying Data Files with the Edit Utility" section of Chapter 7.

Repairing System Databases with the ESEnTUtl Utility

Windows has a number of associated databases. Of course, there's the main database, the registry, which contains all of the system, user, and application settings. The "Managing the Windows Registry" section of this chapter discusses this very important database. However, Windows also contains a number of other databases that you don't normally hear about. These databases reside in System Database (SDB) files. Some of these databases record application setup. You'll find that they normally have a `Setup.SDB` filename. Other databases record service pack status and have names such as `AppHelp.SDB`, `AppH_SP.SDB`, `DrvMain.SDB`, `MSIMain.SDB`, and `SysMain.SDB`. Still other databases keep track of security or other system settings that don't appear in the registry such as `SecEdit.SDB`. In short, Windows hides a lot of information in places other than the registry. You can access all of these other databases using the Extensible Storage Engine Technology Utility (ESEnTUtl).

Not every SDB file on your hard drive is a database. To confuse matters, Microsoft also uses the SDB extension for some text-based files. For example, the `Setup.SDB` file for Visual Studio is a text-based file. You can read it using Notepad as shown in Figure 2.2. The text entries in this file can tell you a lot about the application, but the information isn't in a form that ESEnTUtl can manage. A true SDB file contains binary data.

FIGURE 2.2
Verify that an SDB file is actually a database before you use ESEnTUtl to manage it.

```
setup.sdb - Notepad
File Edit Format View Help

[Dialog Page Order]
COMPage,[vs70pgui.dll]-[BB81D810-3F9B-11D3-A50C-00C04F5E0BA5] : Start Page
COMPage,[vs70pgui.dll]-[9FE307C0-3646-11d3-A508-00C04F5E0BA5] : Options Page
COMProgPage,[vs70pgui.dll]-[BB81D811-3F9B-11D3-A50C-00C04F5E0BA5] : Install Page
COMPage,[vs70pgui.dll]-[1920CC5D-5BE5-45d4-9C1C-3513D334C71C] : Install Page

[Version]
Signature="$CHICAGO$"
Provider="Visual Studio .NET Enterprise Architect 2003 - English"

[GUID to Friendly Name Mapping]
04D3D264-4A22-11d2-ACC7-00C04F8EEBA1,GFN_ Setup.exe
98A7F199-EEC2-11d2-ACDB-00C04F8EEBA1,GFN_ CommandLine
FFA0ABAC-4A7F-11d2-B8F9-00C04F797FB8,GFN_ WizardUI
DECDD26F-5491-11d2-BEE7-00C04F797FB8,GFN_ Default Scenario Factory
DECDD272-5491-11d2-BEE7-00C04F797FB8,GFN_ Custom Scenario
DECDD273-5491-11d2-BEE7-00C04F797FB8,GFN_ Typical Scenario
48121B76-8BDE-11d2-AF04-00C04F797FB8,GFN_ Minimal Scenario
DECDD274-5491-11d2-BEE7-00C04F797FB8,GFN_ Complete Scenario
9DE4FE99-5700-11d2-ACC7-00C04F8EEBA1,GFN_ SetupDB
9DE4FE9A-5700-11d2-ACC7-00C04F8EEBA1,GFN_ SetupLog
20D9416D-742D-11d2-AF03-00C04F797FB8,GFN_ Change Folder
2B0A7483-8D57-11d2-941D-00C04FA35008,GFN_ Default Dependency UI
9D194CF1-7A6A-11d2-940E-00C04FA35008,GFN_ Dependency Manager
A4F9DC85-1881-11d3-8896-00C04F72D91B,GFN_ Cartman Agg Component
E0A7B954-1881-11d3-8896-00C04F72D91B,GFN_ Cartman Contain Component
24A501BA-90A1-11d2-AF05-00C04F797FB8,GFN_ CD Info Manager
1B7EA23A-93CB-11d2-AF07-00C04F797FB8,GFN_ Template Manager
5F2C847D-96A6-11d2-AF0A-00C04F797FB8,GFN_ Disk Info Manager
01D92EBE-A8E3-11d2-BCEE-00C04F797FB8,GFN_ Account Manager
6AF63660-A8EA-11d2-BCEE-00C04F797FB8,GFN_ Setup Validation
053A4C40-121B-11d3-A823-00C04FB1799F,GFN_ PageFile Requirements
05B2109B-13B7-11d3-A823-00C04FB1799F,GFN_ Processor Requirements
8269DCC4-1457-11d3-A823-00C04FB1799F,GFN_ Platform Requirements
F06AFA52-145A-11d3-A823-00C04FB1799F,GFN_ RAM Requirements
A5F918AB-5E66-11d2-ACCA-00C04F8EEBA1,GFN_ Core Password
5DFE21F0-BBA9-11d2-BCF8-00C04F797FB8,GFN_ Core AutoLogon
496A525F-E168-11d2-ACD9-00C04F8EEBA1,GFN_ Core AutoLogon Previously Enabled
A5F918AC-5E66-11d2-ACCA-00C04F8EEBA1,GFN_ Core User Name
A5F918AD-5E66-11d2-ACCA-00C04F8EEBA1,GFN_ Core Organization
A5F918AE-5E66-11d2-ACCA-00C04F8EEBA1,GFN_ Core PID 20
```

WARNING The ESEnTUtl utility is extremely powerful. Used incorrectly on the wrong file, it can wipe out security settings or make your system unbootable. Consequently, make sure you understand this utility completely before you use it. Always make a copy of any database before you modify it. Verify as many changes as possible against the Microsoft Knowledge Base before you make them.

The ESEnTUtl utility doesn't provide you with much help. In fact, you'll hardly find this utility mentioned at all in the Windows help file or many of the other Microsoft resources. One place you'll find it mentioned is the Microsoft Knowledge Base. Many Windows problems require you to use ESEnTUtl as a means of repair. The following list contains just a few examples from the Microsoft Knowledge Base (use the `http://www.google.com/search?hl=en&lr=&q=ESEnTUtl+site%3Asupport.microsoft.com&btnG=Search` Google search URL to obtain a complete list):

HOW TO: Use Ntdsutil to Manage Active Directory Files from the Command Line in Windows 2000 `http://support.microsoft.com/default.aspx?scid=kb;en-us;315131`

You receive an "Access is denied" error message when you install the Bluetooth stack and detect a Bluetooth device in Microsoft Windows XP Service Pack 2 `http://support.microsoft.com/?kbid=892891`

You cannot add a Windows component in Windows XP `http://support.microsoft.com/?id=884018`

Event ID 2108 and Event ID 1084 occur during inbound replication of Active Directory in Windows 2000 Server and in Windows Server 2003 `http://support.microsoft.com/default.aspx?scid=kb;en-us;837932`

The ESEnTUtl operates in several modes. Each mode performs a different task with the SDB file. Here's the syntax for each mode.

```
Defragmentation
     ESENTUTL /d <database name> [options]
Recovery
     ESENTUTL /r [options]
Integrity
     ESENTUTL /g <database name> [options]
Repair
     ESENTUTL /p <database name> [options]
Checksum
     ESENTUTL /k <database name> [options]
File Dump
     ESENTUTL /m[mode-modifier] <filename>
Copy
     ESENTUTL /y <source file> [options]
```

The options vary by mode. However, some options are common to all or most modes. Here's a list of the common options.

/8 Defines the database page size as 8 KB. Normally, ESEnTUtl detects the page size automatically. Use this option only when told to do so as part of a Microsoft Knowledge Base article or when you experience problems reading a database.

/o Suppress the Microsoft logo. You can use this option to create output for reports or as input to another database.

/s<Streaming *Filename*> Sets the filename for streaming data output. The default setting is `NONE`. Use this switch when you want to send data to a destination using streaming data techniques, rather than a simple dump. This switch applies to the defragmentation, integrity, repair, and file dump modes.

/t<Database *Filename*> Sets the temporary database filename. The default setting is `TEMPDFRG*.EDB`. Normally, you won't need to change the database filename because ESEnTUtl already supports multiple temporary databases. This switch applies to the defragmentation, integrity, and repair modes.

NOTE Some of the modes use the same option switch for different purposes. Consequently, don't assume that the `/f` switch for the defragmentation mode performs the same task as the `/f` switch for the integrity mode.

Defragmentation removes excess space from the database and can improve system performance by reorganizing the database. The database becomes defragmented after long use because the system adds and removes entries without placing them in the optimal position (much as a hard drive becomes defragmented through use). The defragmentation-specific options include:

/f<*file*> Sets the filename for streaming data defragmentation. The default setting is `TEMPDFRG*.STM`. Normally, you won't need to change this setting.

/i Prevents ESEnTUtl from defragmenting the streaming file.

/p Preserves the temporary database. Generally, ESEnTUtl deletes the temporary database once all of the changes are incorporated into the main database.

/b<Database *Filename*> Creates a backup copy of the database prior to defragmentation using the specified filename. It's always a good idea to use this option so that you have another copy of the database should the defragmentation fail.

Recovery helps you overcome database errors. ESEnTUtl rebuilds the database using log entries. This is a typical feature of transactional databases where the database manager logs every action. The recovery-specific options include:

/l<*path*> Defines the location of the log files used to recover the data. The default setting is the current directory. Normally, you don't need to change this setting because the log files usually appear in the same directory as the database.

/s<*path*> Defines the location of any system files, such as the checkpoint file, required to perform the recover. The default location is the current directory. Normally, you don't need to change this setting because the system files usually appear in the same directory as the database.

/i Ignores any mismatched or missing database attachments. However, by ignoring these missing elements, you risk database damage. Use this option only when the database is already damaged and the recovery is a last ditch effort at reconstruction.

/d[*path*] Defines the location of database files. The default setting is the current directory. The default setting when you specify this option without a path is the directory originally logged in the log files, which may be different from the current directory.

Integrity checking verifies that the database is in an operational state and doesn't contain any structural errors. You can perform an integrity check when you suspect the database may contain errors, but don't want to perform any changes until you know that it does. The integrity-specific options include:

/f<*name*> Defines the prefix to use for name of report files. The default setting uses the name of the database, followed by `.integ.raw`.

Repair mode actually changes the database. The most common repair simply removes the damaged entries. This action can result in various kinds of data loss that affect system operation. For example, you could lose some of the security settings for your system. Always make a backup of the database before you repair it. The repair-specific option includes:

/f<*name*> Defines the prefix to use for the name of report files. The default setting uses the name of the database, followed by `.integ.raw`.

Checksum mode verifies that the file doesn't contain any bit level errors. The checksum acts as a means of verifying the data itself is error free. Compare this check with an integrity check and you'll notice that the two provide complementary error checks. You should perform both checks on a database when you suspect that it contains errors. The checksum mode only supports the `/8` and `/o` options.

File dump mode lets you view the content of the database in a nondestructive manner. It's the same as performing a query on any database. However, given the nature of these databases, the processing of querying content is slightly different. Instead of asking for the address of a customer or the number of widgets sold during the month of June, these queries obtain specifics about the database itself. The file dump-specific options include.

/t<*Table Name*> Performs a database dump for a specified table only. Use a metadata dump to obtain a list of the tables within the database.

/v Provide verbose output for the specified command. Even though ESEnTUtl always accepts this option, some file dump mode modifiers can't provide additional information. For example, performing a file dump of the database header won't yield any additional results because the initial command always provides complete information.

In addition to options, the file dump mode supports a modifier that determines the kind of data it provides as output. You combine this modifier with the `/m` command line switch. For example, to dump the database header, you use the `/mh` command line switch. The following list describes the file dump modes:

H This is the default modifier. It obtains the database header information. The header contains a wealth of information about the database, such as the database type and an indication of whether it uses a streaming file. In addition, you can discover the last backup date and other essential maintenance information about the database. You can see a header dump by typing **ESENTUTL /mh SecEdit.SDB** in the `\WINDOWS\security\Database` folder and pressing Enter.

NOTE This book uses the `\Windows` folder because that's the most common setup for modern machines. However, your Windows folder might appear as `\WinNT` or something else depending on how you installed Windows. The universal method of accessing the Windows directory is to use `\%WINDIR%` for the `\Windows` directory and `\%SYSTEM%` for the `\Windows\System32` directory. Because some utilities won't allow the use of environment variables, the book will use `\Windows` and `\Windows\System` as a consistent means of identifying these directories.

k A checkpoint file uses the CHK file extension. This file contains a checkpoint in the database transactions. The system writes each transaction to memory and log files first, and then commits them to the database. The reason for this system is twofold. First, writing the information to memory and a log file makes it possible to record transaction steps without changing the database, making it easier to commit and rollback transactions as needed. Second, using this approach makes it possible to write information to the database in the most efficient manner possible, which enhances overall system performance. The checkpoint is a reference to the transaction stream; it indicates that all of the transactions prior to the checkpoint appear in the database. Those after the checkpoint could appear in the database, but more likely appear in memory or in a log file. You can see a checkpoint by typing **ESENTUTL /mk EDB.CHK** in the `\WINDOWS\system32\CatRoot2` folder and pressing Enter.

l A log file uses the LOG file extension and normally appears in the same folder as a CHK or SDB file. However, sometimes Windows places the log files in an associated folder, as is the case with the security logs. The log files contain a record of current transactions—either completed or in process. You can use the `/r` command line switch with a log file to roll back or reprocess transactions on the database. You can see a log file by typing **ESENTUTL /ml EDB.LOG** in the `\WINDOWS\system32\CatRoot2` folder and pressing Enter.

`m` Metadata tells you about the content of a database. When you execute this command, you'll see a listing of the tables and indexes associated with the database, along with some statistical information about each entry. You can use this command to obtain a list of tables to use with other ESEnTUtl command line switches. You can see an example of metadata by typing **ESENTUTL /mm SecEdit.SDB** in the `\WINDOWS\security\Database` folder and pressing Enter.

`s` This modifier tells you how much space each of the tables and indexes within the database are using. You can use this command to determine whether you need to defragment the database using the `/d` command line switch. The best way to determine how much space the database should use is to defragment the database and use this command to take a snapshot of the defragmented size. When the database exceeds some threshold (normally 150 percent of the defragmented size), defragment the database and take another snapshot. You can see the size of the security database by typing **ESENTUTL /ms SecEdit.SDB** in the `\WINDOWS\security\Database` folder and pressing Enter.

Copying lets you create another copy of a log file, streaming file, or database in a secondary location. The default utility settings copy the data from a source location to the current location, but you can change that behavior by using the `/d` command line switch as follows.

/d<Destination *Filename*> Copies the file to the specified destination, rather than using the current directory and the same name as the source file.

Decompressing Files with the Expand Utility

The Expand utility lets you open the contents of a cabinet (CAB) file or compressed file and extract the contents. Generally, you'll use it to extract a missing file from a CD or other media, most notably Windows files. The advantage of using this utility is that you can use it with batch or script files to automate repair actions. An administrator can save time and effort using this approach for common repairs or repairs must be made to a group of machines.

USING MODERN COMPRESSION TECHNIQUES

Computing constantly changes, but some command line utilities don't keep up. Either they work fine as is, or Microsoft simply decides to let a third party do the job. At one time, CAB files were the only form of compression widely available to Windows users. Today, third party utilities, such as WinZip (a shareware utility you can download and try before you buy), have largely replaced the need for this particular utility when working with CAB files. However, you must still use Expand when working with compressed files—those that have an underscore as part of their file extension. For example, you'd always use Expand to expand a file named `MyApp.EX_` to `MyApp.EXE`. To make things easier for administrators, WinZip has a command line add-in (`http://www.winzip.com/wzcline.htm`) that you can use much like the Expand utility for a much broader range of compressed file types. Even so, you'll still find that you need the Expand utility, in some cases, such as when you use the recovery console, simply because it's the only tool available.

You can use the Expand utility in one of several ways. The information you provide depends on the way in which you want to use the utility. This utility uses the following syntax:

```
EXPAND [-r] Source Destination
EXPAND -r Source [Destination]
EXPAND -D Source.cab [-F:Files]
EXPAND Source.cab -F:Files Destination
```

Essentially, you must always provide at least two kinds of information or make an assumption about the output of the utility. For example, if you supply the source filename and use the `-r` command line switch, Expand will make an assumption about the output filename based on the source filename. The following list describes each of the command line arguments.

`Source` The name of the compressed file. The Expand utility works with single compressed files (those with an underscore in the file extension) and CAB files. It doesn't work with newer MSI, ZIP, or other compressed files.

`Destination` The name of the uncompressed file when working with a single file. The destination folder for the uncompressed files when working with a CAB file.

`-r` Renames the destination filenames based on the source filename. For example, when you supply `MyApp.EX_` as the source filename, Expand automatically uses `MyApp.EXE` as the output filename. This option works by using the full name of the file that's embedded as part of the compressed file. (The XVI32 utility explored in the "Using XVI32 to View Files in Depth" section of Chapter 12 tells you how to view inside of a file.)

`-D` Displays the list of files in the source file. When used with a single compressed file, you'll see only a single filename as output. CAB files normally contain multiple files.

`-F:`*`Files`* Decompresses one or more selected files within a CAB file. You can specify multiple files by supplying wildcard characters. (See the "Working with Wildcard Characters" sidebar for details.) Don't use multiple copies of the `-F` command line switch to specific multiple discrete files. When you want to expand single files from a CAB file, you must use the Expand utility once for each file.

The Expand utility is extremely useful because it doesn't require a running copy of Windows to work. For example, you can use this utility from the Recovery Console where other third party utilities will fail to work. Microsoft has created a Knowledge Base article to discuss the various scenarios for using the Expand utility at `http://support.microsoft.com/default.aspx?scid=kb;en-us;888017`.

Creating Directories with the *MD* and *MkDir* Commands

The `MD` and `MkDir` commands are equivalent. Both of these commands create a new directory from the command line. Windows automatically recognizes the new directory, and you can see it within Windows Explorer and use it from applications. One of the more interesting ways to use this command is within a batch file to create a directory structure for some task or to set up a new user. This utility uses the following syntax:

```
MKDIR [drive:]path
MD [drive:]path
```

The following list describes each of the command line arguments.

drive The drive to use when creating the new directory. The default is to use the current drive.

path The absolute or relative path to use when creating the new directory. The default is to create the new directory as a subdirectory of the current directory. However, you can specify an absolute or relative path as needed. See the "Understanding Absolute and Relative Paths" sidebar for additional details. These commands create all of the directories required to provide the full path in the specification, so you might create multiple directories when specifying a long path.

Understanding Absolute and Relative Paths

Some people get confused by the term *path* at the command line. The path is simply the list of directories from the root (topmost) directory to the current directory. The current directory is the one that you're working in at any given time.

The command line specifies the root directory with a simple backslash (\). When you go down a level, you add the directory name to the list. For example, if you move to the MyDir directory, then the path becomes `\MyDir\`. You can expand this list to any level of detail required to describe the current directory. For example, when you move to the SubDir directory from the MyDir directory, then the path becomes `\MyDir\SubDir\`.

Many commands and utilities require path information. Most of them can use either an absolute or relative path. An absolute path always expresses the full path from the root directory to the current directory. For example, when you're in the SubDir directory, the absolute path is `\MyDir\SubDir`. The relative path describes the hierarchy in reference to the current directory. Consequently, the relative path for SubDir is SubDir. Notice that you don't begin a relative path with a backslash.

When working with directories using commands, you often need to specify a destination using either an absolute or a relative path. For example, if you want to create a new subdirectory in the SubDir directory, you could type **`MD NewDir`**. This form of the command uses a relative path. The same command using an absolute path would appear as `MD \MyDir\SubDir\NewDir`. You might think the absolute path form wastes time, but it's always more accurate than using a relative path and eliminates the possibility of creating a directory where you didn't expect it.

The command window also provides support for two special relative paths. The first is the current directory, which is specified as a single period (`.`). The second is the parent directory (the one directly above the current directory in the directory hierarchy), which is specified as a double period (`..`). Many commands and utilities, such as the CD, benefit from this current directory and parent directory shortcut terminology.

Moving Files and Renaming Files and Directories with the *Move* Command

The `Move` command is functionally equivalent to copying a file or directory and then erasing it in the current directory. This command uses the following syntax:

```
Move one or more files:
MOVE [/Y | /-Y] [drive:][path]filename1[,...] destination
Rename a directory:
MOVE [/Y | /-Y] [drive:][path]dirname1 dirname2
```

The following list describes each of the command line arguments.

drive Specifies the drive to use for the file or directory. The default is to use the current drive.

path Specifies the absolute or relative path to use for the file or directory. The default is to use the current directory. However, you can specify an absolute or relative path as needed. See the "Understanding Absolute and Relative Paths" sidebar for additional details.

filename1 Defines one or more filenames to move. Separate multiple filenames using a comma.

destination Defines the output location for the data that you want to copy. The destination can include a drive letter and path (absolute or relative). When working with a single file, you can also rename the file by specifying a different filename.

dirname1 Defines the source directory when moving a directory from one location to another. Moving a directory always moves any subdirectories and files that the directory contains. Generally, you can move directories to another location on the same drive, but you can't move directories to another drive. The Microsoft recommendation is to use Move only to rename directories.

dirname2 Defines the destination directory when moving a directory from one location to another.

/Y and /-Y Suppresses or enforces the prompt for overwriting destination files with the same name as the destination file provided as input to the Move command. Use the /Y command line switch in batch files where you know the batch file will overwrite an existing destination file. The /-Y command line switch is the default, so you never need to use it.

Setting and Viewing Application Paths with the *Path* Command

The Path command controls a very important environment variable. The path is the environment variable that lets you access executables even if they aren't in the current directory when at the command prompt. For example, a typical path includes the \Windows\System32 directory on your machine so you have access to the majority of Windows utilities. Without the path, you'd need to supply the path for every command you want to execute. Imagine typing \Windows\System32\TaskList every time you want to discover which tasks are running on your system.

The problem is that Microsoft can't anticipate every application path needed for your system. For example, when you install SQL Server on a machine, you need another path to access the SQL Server executables with ease. Fortunately, many application vendors ease the use of paths by adding them for you to the Windows permanent path. This registry setting contains the paths to the applications you commonly use. You can view the permanent path by right-clicking My Computer and choosing Properties from the context menu. Select the Advanced tab. Click Environment Variables and you'll see the Environment Variables dialog box shown in Figure 2.3. The path appears in the System Variables list (it appears highlighted in the figure).

You'll normally use the Environment Variables dialog box or a direct registry edit to modify the permanent path. However, sometimes you need to add a path for just the current session. The Path command helps you make short-term path changes that affect a specific command window. This command uses the following syntax:

```
PATH [[drive:]path[;...][;%PATH%]
PATH ;
```

FIGURE 2.3
The permanent path appears as part of the environment variables for your system.

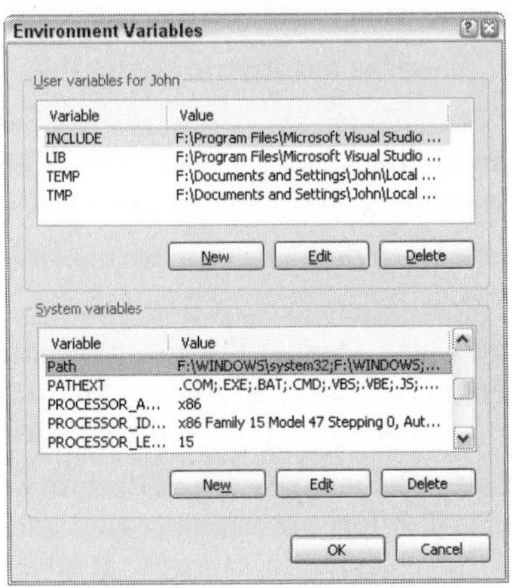

The following list describes each of the command line arguments.

drive Specifies the drive to use for the path entry. The default is to use the current drive, current being relative to where you are at any given moment. Always define a drive when changing the path to avoid unwanted drive reference problems.

path Specifies the absolute path to use for the entry. You can't use a relative path with the Path command. Separate multiple path entries with a semicolon (;).

%PATH% Obtains the current path environment variable value. In fact, you can access any other environment variable by enclosing it within percent signs (%). The "Managing Environment Variables with the Set Command" section of Chapter 3 provides details on working with environment variables. Any environment variable that contains path information can appear as part of the Path command. The most common environment variable used for this purpose is %WINDIR%, which contains the location of the current Windows directory.

Typing **Path** at the command line and pressing Enter always shows you the current path. If you haven't changed the path in any way, the Path command will show you the permanent path for your system. When you need to add a temporary path, always type the new path information followed by the %PATH% environment variable so that you don't lose the current path information. Finally, if you really do want to clear the path, Type **Path** followed by a semicolon and press Enter. This syntax clears the Path environment variable for the current command window only; using it won't affect your system as a whole.

Storing and Retrieving Directories with the *PushD* and *PopD* Commands

Windows maintains a directory stack that you can use to store locations that you visit. You use this stack to store directory information and then retrieve it as needed. The PushD and PopD commands provide access to the directory stack and help you move around your hard drive more efficiently.

TIP Think about a stack as you would a stack of pancakes. Fry a pancake and you can add it to the top of the stack. Get hungry and you can remove a pancake from the top of the stack to eat it. The first (bottom) pancake on the stack is always the last pancake off. When the pancakes are all gone, the stack is empty.

If you move around your hard drive a lot, using the PushD and PopD commands can save you considerable typing time. However, most people use these commands to simplify batch files. No matter which way you use them, the directory stack is a handy way for tracking your movement. These commands use the following syntax:

```
PUSHD [path | ..]
POPD
```

The following list describes each of the command line arguments.

path Specifies the absolute or relative path to change to from the current location. See the "Understanding Absolute and Relative Paths" sidebar for additional details.

The PushD and PopD commands can also use Command Extensions to change to a network drive. When you use PushD in this manner, Windows automatically maps a drive to the network path for you. The PopD command treats the networked drive as it would any other mapped drive for your system. You can learn more about Command Extensions in the "Understanding Command Extensions" section of Chapter 7. Notice that you can also specify the next directory as the parent directory by using the `..` syntax with the PushD command.

Recovering Lost Files with the Recover Utility

The Recover utility provides a last ditch method of recovering files from a bad hard drive. Depending on the hard drive failure, you might be able to recover some files, but not others. For example, when the hard drive experiences a head crash, the files located within the damaged portions of the hard drive will become unreadable because the media that contained the files is gone. However, files that aren't in the damaged section are unaffected; you can recover them in many cases. The Recover utility lets you move these undamaged files from the damaged drive to an undamaged drive. You'd normally use this utility after you had tried to recover the drive information using the ChkDsk command. This utility uses the following syntax:

```
RECOVER [drive:][path]filename
```

The following list describes each of the command line arguments.

drive Specifies the drive to use as a source for file information.

path Specifies the absolute path to use as a source for file information.

filename Specifies the name of the file you want to recover. You must specify the name of a file and cannot use wildcards with this command. The utility performs a low-level search for the information on the hard drive. Consequently, this command can require a long time to run. When you want to search for multiple files, it's usually more efficient to create a batch file containing all of the filenames and let the computer work while you do something else.

WARNING The Recover utility won't work with deleted files. In addition, it doesn't work if the File Allocation Table (FAT) is damaged in such a way that the utility can't discover the beginning file entry. Since most file systems provide a minimum of two FATs, it's unlikely that you'll lose the FAT.

Removing a Directory with the *RD* and *RmDir* Commands

The RD and RmDir commands perform the same task; they remove an empty directory from your hard drive. If you attempt to remove a directory that contains any files, the command displays an error message. Removing old directories cleans up the hard drive and makes it easier to find existing data. In addition, each directory consumes a minuscule amount of space on the hard drive that removing the directory frees. These commands use the following syntax:

```
RMDIR [/S] [/Q] [drive:]path
RD [/S] [/Q] [drive:]path
```

The following list describes each of the command line arguments.

drive Specifies the drive where the directory is located.

path Specifies the absolute or relative path of the directory to remove.

/S Removes all of the subdirectories and files in the specified directory along with the directory itself. This feature removes the safety feature that tells you when a directory contains files, but does make these commands easier to use within a batch file. This command line switch makes the `RD` and `RmDir` commands equivalent to the `DelTree` command.

/Q Forces removal of the directory tree without asking the user first. You can use this option within a batch file to ensure the batch continues to run without user intervention.

Renaming a File or Directory with the *Ren* and *Rename* Commands

The `Ren` and `Rename` commands both let you rename files and directories (the Microsoft documentation only mentions files, but the commands do work with directories). Using these commands is definitely faster than renaming them manually using Windows Explorer when you have a lot of files to change. These commands use the following syntax:

```
RENAME [drive:][path]filename1 filename2
REN [drive:][path]filename1 filename2
```

The following list describes each of the command line arguments.

drive Specifies the drive to use for the file or directory. The default is to use the current drive.

path Specifies the absolute or relative path to use for the file or directory. The default is to use the current directory. However, you can specify an absolute or relative path as needed. See the "Understanding Absolute and Relative Paths" sidebar for additional details.

filename1 Defines the file or directory that you want to rename. You can use wildcard characters with this command. For example, if you want to rename all TXT files to have a TEXT extension, you'd type **REN *.TXT *.TEXT** and press Enter.

NOTE Unlike Windows Explorer, the Ren and Rename commands won't constantly ask you about file extension changes. Although this means you'll spend less time clicking the Yes button, it also means that you could accidentally rename files that you didn't want to rename.

filename2 Defines the new file or directory name. If you use a wildcard character for `filename1`, then you generally have to use a wildcard character to this argument as well. When in doubt, always test the renaming strategy using sample files.

Replacing Existing Files with the Replace Utility

The Replace utility replaces a file in a destination folder with a file from a source folder. You can use it to copy files in a source folder to a destination without worrying and all of the usual warnings that Windows provides. The utility can also place unique files from the source folder into a destination folder. This utility uses the following syntax:

```
REPLACE [drive1:][path1]filename [drive2:][path2] [/A] [/P] [/R] [/W]
REPLACE [drive1:][path1]filename [drive2:][path2] [/P] [/R] [/S] [/W] [/U]
```

Notice that the two command lines use distinctly different command line switch sets. For example, you can't use the /A and the /S command line switches together. The following list describes each of the command line arguments.

drive1/drive2 Specifies the drive for the source and destination. The default is the current drive.

path1/path2 Specifies the absolute or relative path to use for the source and destination. The source must be different from the destination. The default is the current directory.

filename Defines the file or directory that you want to replace. You can use wildcard characters with this command. See the "Working with Wildcard Characters" sidebar for details.

/A Adds any new files to the destination directory. Normally, the Replace utility will only replace files. You cannot use this command line switch with the /S or /U switches.

/P Prompts the user for confirmation prior to replacing a file or adding a new file.

/R Replaces read-only files, as well as unprotected files. By default, the Replace utility only replaces standard read/write files.

/S Replaces all of the files in subdirectories of the destination directory. The Replace utility replaces all occurrences of the file. If a destination directory and a subdirectory both contain an instance of a file, the Replace utility replaces both instances of that file. You can't use this command line switch with the /A switch.

/W Waits for the user to insert a floppy disk or other removable media before beginning the replacement. Generally, you'd use this option as part of a batch file where the replacement requires more than one disk.

/U Replaces files that are older than the source files. When the destination files are the same age or newer than the source files, the Replace utility doesn't replace them. This command line switch is a safety feature that ensures you don't overwrite newer updates with older files.

Sorting File Content with the Sort Utility

The Sort utility is an amazing utility in that it can sort any text file. You can use this utility to perform analysis of output from other commands. For example, you could use it to perform a custom sort of a directory listing. The sort mechanism considers locale, so you can sort data based on a specific language. In addition, the Sort utility works on extremely large files, so you don't have to worry about getting halfway through a sort and having the sort fail. (Large sorts can take a while because the Sort utility writes any data that won't fit in memory to disk.) This utility uses the following syntax:

```
SORT [/R] [/+n] [/M kilobytes] [/L locale] [/REC recordbytes]
     [[drive1:][path1]filename1] [/T [drive2:][path2]] [/O
     [drive3:][path3]filename3]
```

The following list describes each of the command line arguments.

`/+n` Specifies the comparison character. The default is to use the first character of each line as a starting point. By using another character as a starting point, you can change the sort order of the data. For example, the `Dir` command won't let you sort a directory listing by time without first sorting it by date. If you're interested in sorting the listing by time, you could set the sort to use the time, `/+13`, as the starting point for the sort. This particular sort is handy because some vendors, including Microsoft, have used the time as a method of indicating the version number of their DLLs. Consequently, sorting by the time can provide a very fast indication of version number as long as you know what the time indicator means (vendors often provide this information in their knowledge bases).

NOTE There's no space between the /+ command line switch and the starting position of the sort. However, there's a space between the other command line switches and their arguments. Make sure you add or remove space as appropriate or the Sort utility will fail with an invalid command line switch error message.

`/L[OCALE] Local` Overrides the default system local, which is always the locale you selected for your Windows setup. Unfortunately, the only active override for Windows XP and newer systems is the C locale. The C locale provides a fast collating sort using binary differentiation, rather than language-specific sorting. Although this sort is quite fast, it might not always produce the results you need if your language uses diacritical marks. The sort is always case sensitive.

`/M[EMORY] Size` Defines the amount of memory in KB to use. Sort requires a minimum of 160 KB to perform its task. It's important to remember that the command window doesn't provide the same amount of memory as your machine contains. Generally, all modern machines will have 640 KB of main memory available in the command window, with some memory used by command window components and some required by Sort itself. You can check the amount of available memory using the Mem utility (see the "Determining Memory Status with the Mem Utility" section of Chapter 3 for details). The only time you need to set the memory size is if Sort fails due to memory constraints. Sort will use 90 percent of available memory to maximize performance as a default.

`/REC[ORD_MAXIMUM] Characters` Defines the maximum number of characters in a record. The default size is 4,096 characters. However, you can specify up to 65,535 characters in a record. Larger record sizes use more memory for each record. Consequently, keeping the record size as small as possible will improve Sort efficiency.

`/R[EVERSE]` Reverses the sort order. Instead of sorting A to Z, the output will appear in Z to A order. Likewise, Sort will also reverse number order.

`drive1` Specifies the drive for the sort input. The default is the current drive when you specify a filename.

`path1` Specifies the absolute or relative path to use for the sort input. The default is the current directory when you specify a filename.

`filename1` Defines the name of the file that you want to sort. If you don't provide a filename, Sort will use the standard input device, which is usually the keyboard for Windows, as the input. You can change the standard input by using redirection (see the "Employing Data Redirection" section of this chapter for details), but providing a filename normally provides faster results.

/T[EMPORARY] [drive2:][path2] Determines the directory used to hold the temporary files for the sort. Normally, you don't need to use this command line switch because it's easier to use the system temporary directory (the default) for storage. However, you might want to use this option if the current drive is low on storage space or you want to use a faster drive to hold the temporary data to promote faster sorting.

/O[UTPUT] [drive3:][path3]filename3 Specifies the location of the output. You must provide a filename as a minimum when using this command line switch. The drive3 and path3 arguments let you place the file on a different drive and directory. If you don't specify this command line switch, the Sort utility sends the output to the standard output, which is the console.

Associating a Folder to a Drive with the Subst Utility

The Subst utility is one that just about anyone can use. It makes a directory look like a new drive to a user. In fact, this effect shows itself in Windows Explorer, so the Subst utility has a lasting impact on your system. This utility uses the following syntax:

```
SUBST [drive1: [drive2:]path]
SUBST drive1: /D
```

The following list describes each of the command line arguments.

drive1 Specifies the drive to substitute for the directory specification you provide. The default is the current drive.

drive2 Specifies the drive that contains the directory for substitution. The default is the current drive.

path1 Specifies the absolute or relative path to substitute. The default is the current directory.

/D Terminates the directory substitution. You can also terminate the substitution using Windows Explorer.

USING THE SUBST UTILITY EFFECTIVELY

The Subst utility performs a task that you can't perform within the Windows GUI. It makes directories easily accessible to users. Instead of digging through the directory hierarchy, the user can access the directory using a drive letter. In addition, you can use the Subst utility to equalize all systems on a network, even if the various machines have different drive configurations. For example, you could set all machines to use Drive X as the word processing directory. The Subst utility can also make network reconfigurations invisible to the user. If you set Drive X as the word processing drive, it doesn't matter where the actual directory appears on the network and you can move it around at will. Here's an example of the Subst utility used to redirect the G:\Windows directory to the L drive.

```
Subst L: G:\WINWORD
```

The substitute drive letter always appears first; the directory appears second. Type **Subst** by itself to display a list of substituted directories. You can obtain additional ideas and detailed information about this technique by reviewing the TechRepublic article at http://techrepublic.com.com/5100-10877_11-5975262.html?tag=nl.e064.

Displaying a Directory Structure with the Tree Utility

If you've ever tried to get a complete picture of the directory structure of your hard drive using Windows Explorer, you know the task is tough. Windows Explorer focuses on helping you perform tasks, so it tends to focus your attention on a specific set of directories on the hard drive. In fact, the default settings actually hide many directories from view. The Tree utility hides nothing. It's easy to become quite overwhelmed by the amount of information it provides. This utility uses the following syntax:

```
TREE [drive:][path] [/F] [/A]
```

The following list describes each of the command line arguments.

`drive` Specifies the drive to examine. The default is the current drive.

`path` Specifies the absolute or relative path to examine. The default is the current directory.

`/F` Displays the filenames in each directory as well as the directory names.

`/A` Displays the output using standard ASCII characters, rather than extended ASCII characters that have a graphical appearance.

One of the best reasons to use the Tree utility is to explore your drive looking for places to clean out old information. Figure 2.4 shows typical output from this utility. This utility can also help you locate hidden directories and even provide a certain level of virus detection because most virus writers are counting on you to use Windows utilities to explore the hard drive. The fact that you can run this utility from the recovery console means that you can even use it to explore the drive for rootkits—a particularly nasty form of virus that actually hides itself from view when Windows is operating.

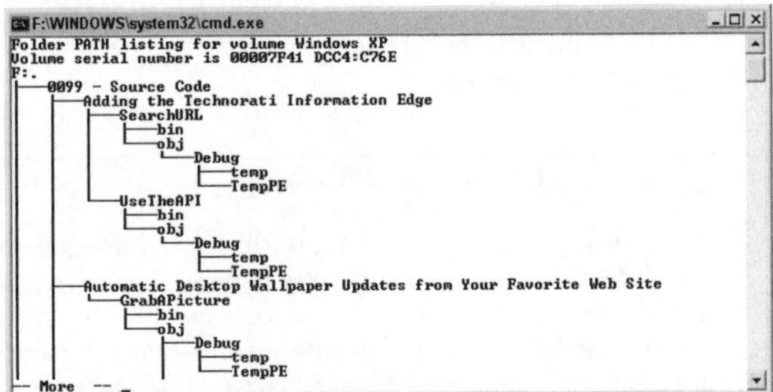

FIGURE 2.4
The Tree utility provides a detailed display of the directories on your hard drive.

WARNING Rootkits are particularly dangerous viruses because you don't even know you have one. They hide by using the operating system to trick you into not seeing the folders that store the executables. The rootkit writer doesn't want you to know the rootkit is in place, so don't expect a rootkit to do anything odd or strange. In fact, unlike common viruses, rootkits often go out of their way not to use your system to propagate because that action would expose them. Because of the level of integration a rootkit requires with the operating system, even removing a rootkit is going to cause problems because now your system is compromised at a low level. This book doesn't provide you with enough information to rid your system of a rootkit, but the Tree utility can help you detect one when used correctly. Obviously, third party utilities specifically designed for the task will locate a rootkit faster. If you suspect your system has a rootkit installed, you'll want to spend time viewing online resources such as the Rootkit Web site at `http://www.rootkit.com/`. You can learn more about rootkits at `http://en.wikipedia.org/wiki/Rootkit`.

Validating File Operations with the *Verify* Command

The `Verify` command is very simple. It's an on or off setting that you use to tell the command processor how to interact with your files. Setting verify on forces the command processor to check every file that it writes for errors before proceeding with the next file. However, using verify exacts a significant performance penalty, so the default setting is to have it off. The verify setting is a remnant from the early days of the PC when hard drives were less reliable than they are now. This command uses the following syntax:

```
VERIFY [ON | OFF]
```

Executing `Verify` by itself will display the current verify setting status. Generally, you'll keep the verify setting off unless you're copying files that require absolute verification. For example, you might want to use this setting when creating a disk for a presentation at work where errors aren't tolerated.

Performing Bulk File Transfers with the XCopy Utility

The XCopy utility is one of the few that even Microsoft mentions regularly because it's so handy to have. You use the XCopy utility to perform bulk file transfers from anywhere on a local network to anywhere else on a local network. In addition to copying single files, XCopy can copy entire directory structures. It also has a wealth of command line switches so you have precise control over the copying process. This utility uses the following syntax:

```
XCOPY source [destination] [/A | /M] [/D[:date]] [/P] [/S [/E]] [/V]
      [/W] [/C] [/I] [/Q] [/F] [/L] [/G] [/H] [/R] [/T] [/U] [/K] [/N]
      [/O] [/X] [/Y] [/-Y] [/Z] [/B] [/EXCLUDE:file1[+file2][+file3]...]
```

The following list describes each of the command line arguments.

TIP **Vista administrators should consider moving to the RoboCopy utility to perform some tasks. You can find a description of the new RoboCopy utility in the "Performing Robust File Transfers with the RoboCopy Utility" section of the chapter.**

`source` Specifies which files to copy. You can use wildcard characters to define the file specification. See the "Working with Wildcard Characters" sidebar for details. The file specification can also include a drive and absolute or relative path.

`destination` Specifies the destination for the files. When working with a single file, you can also specify a new filename for the file.

`/A` Copies only the files with the archive attribute set. Copying the files doesn't change the attribute status, so you need to use the Attrib utility (described in the "Changing File and Directory Attributes with the Attrib Utility" section of Chapter 4) to change the archive bit. Some people use this particular feature to create a simple, but effective, backup utility. They send any changed files to a hard drive on another machine, and then clear the archive attribute. As an alternative, if you know the copying methodology works without flaw, you can use the `/M` command line switch.

`/M` Copies only the files with the archive attribute set. However, unlike the `/A` command line switch, this command line switch does reset the archive bit.

`/D[:Month-Day-Year]` Copies files changed on or after the specified date. When you leave out the date, then XCopy only copies the file when the date of an existing file in the destination is older than the source file. If the dates are the same or newer, then XCopy doesn't copy the file.

/EXCLUDE:Definition1[+Definition2][+ Definition3]... Excludes files or directories based on the strings you provide. For example, specifying `.TXT` as a string will exclude all text files from the copy. On the other hand, specifying a string such as `\MyDir` will exclude the entire `\MyDir` subdirectory from the copy. You can make strings ambiguous to describe a number of conditions. For example, including the string `My` would include files or directories with the word *My* in them as any part of the name, including the extension. You can create multiple excludes by separating each exclude string with a plus sign (+).

/P Prompts the user before creating each destination file.

/S Copies all files in the current directory, plus all subdirectories and their files except empty subdirectories. You can't use this command line switch to create an empty directory structure for a user or application; use the `/E` command line switch instead.

/E Copies all files in the current directory, plus all subdirectories and their files including empty subdirectories.

/V Verifies each new file as the system writes it. This command line switch overrides the system verify setting.

/W Waits for the user to insert a floppy disk or other removable media before beginning the copy process. Generally, you'd use this option as part of a batch file where the copying process requires more than one disk.

/C Forces XCopy to continue copying files even when an error occurs. Normally, XCopy stops when it encounters the first copy error.

/I Forces XCopy to assume the destination is a directory when the destination doesn't exist and you're copying more than one file. Otherwise, XCopy displays a message asking the user whether the destination is a file or a directory. This will cause a batch file to halt to wait for user participation.

/Q Copies the files without displaying the filenames. You can use this option in a batch file where you don't necessarily want the user bothered or aware of everything that's happening in the background.

/F Displays full source and destination filenames while copying, including both the drive and the path. Normally, XCopy displays only the filenames. This feature often comes in handy when diagnosing problems with complex batch files because it shows precisely where XCopy copies each file.

/L Displays a list of files that XCopy would copy, without actually copying them. This is a diagnostic mode where you can log the files and verify the command line syntax produces the desired result.

/G Copies encrypted files to a destination that doesn't support encryption. This is a Windows-specific command line switch. The resulting destination files are unencrypted when you complete the copy, so using this command line switch can result in a security hole in your system.

/H Copies any files marked hidden or system. Normally, XCopy only copies the files without these attributes since hidden and system files are normally associated with operating system requirements (they aren't data files).

/R Forces XCopy to overwrite read-only files. Normally, XCopy won't overwrite read-only files to preserve their content.

/T Creates the directory structure, but doesn't copy any of the files. You can use this feature to create an empty directory structure for a new user or application without compromising data that might appear in an existing pattern directory structure. This command line switch won't include empty directories and subdirectories in the source. To include the complete directory structure in the destination, combine the /T and /E command line switches.

/U Copies only the source files that already exist in the destination. You could use this feature to perform updates on another system without compromising any unique files in the source system.

/K Copies all of the file and directory attributes. XCopy normally resets some of the attributes, such as read-only.

/N Creates a destination file with an 8-character filename and a 3-character file extension. Use this command line switch when you must create destination files for older systems that rely on the DOS 8.3 naming convention. Avoid using this command line switch on files with long filenames unless you really do want to create a compatible file.

/O Copies the file ownership and Access Control List (ACL) information. The ACL provides security for the file. If you don't use this command line switch, the destination system will use the default security settings for that system, which might not provide sufficient security for sensitive data.

/X Copies the file audit settings in addition to the file ownership and ACL information. File auditing monitors each file as Windows opens, closes, or modifies it. Using file auditing helps you track user and system activities, but does cause a performance hit.

/Y and /-Y Suppresses or enforces the prompt for overwriting destination files with the same name as the destination file provided as input to the XCopy command. Use the /Y command line switch in batch files where you know the batch file will overwrite an existing destination file. The /-Y command line switch is the default, so you never need to use it.

/Z Copies networked files in restartable mode. If the copy process stops for any reason, XCopy will attempt to restart the file copy.

/B Copies a symbolic link to the target instead of the actual file pointed to by the symbolic link when the source is a symbolic link. This command line switch is only available in Vista.

Performing Robust File Transfers with the RoboCopy Utility

The RoboCopy utility is new to Vista. Those of you who have it might remember RoboCopy as a feature of the Windows Resource Kit in the past. Unfortunately, the version of RoboCopy in Vista won't work with earlier versions of Windows. It does, however, include a number of new additions from the version found in the resource kit.

TIP You can find the Windows Resource Kit version of the RoboCopy utility at `http://www.microsoft.com/downloads/details.aspx?FamilyID=9d467a69-57ff-4ae7-96ee-b18c4790cffd`. This version does work with all versions of Windows. In addition, if you like RoboCopy but don't like using the command line, you can find a GUI wrapper for it at `http://www.gotdotnet.com/codegallery/codegallery.aspx?id=d162e46a-006e-4438-8cd6-c9b0cdb51862`. The GUI wrapper doesn't support the Vista additions to RoboCopy yet.

RoboCopy is a sort of super XCopy utility, in that you can copy a large number of files from one location to another. However, RoboCopy also provides a considerable number of file selection options and even job options, so that you can submit a copy requirement as a job. The source and destination can include Universal Naming Convention (UNC) paths, in addition to the standard paths. Unlike XCopy, you don't have to resort to odd logging methods because RoboCopy has them built in so you can see precisely what happened during the copying process. In addition, RoboCopy is forgiving in that it provides retry options to ensure a copy process has the best possible chance to succeed. This utility uses the following command line syntax:

```
ROBOCOPY Source Destination [File [File]...] [Copy Options] [File Selection
Options] [Logging Options] [Retry Options] [Job Options]
```

WARNING **The command line switches for RoboCopy aren't the same as the command line switches for XCopy. Consequently, you can't perform a simple search and replace in your batch or script files to use RoboCopy; you must completely rewrite the command.**

The copying options define how RoboCopy performs copying tasks. For example, you might want to include all of the folders in the copied location, even those that are empty, so you'd use the /E command line switch. The following list describes each of the `copy` command line arguments.

/S Copies all files in the current directory, plus all subdirectories and their files except empty subdirectories. You can't use this command line switch to create an empty directory structure for a user or application; use the /E command line switch instead.

/E Copies all files in the current directory, plus all subdirectories and their files including empty subdirectories.

/LEV:n Copies only the top-level subdirectories specified by *n*. For example, if n is 3, then RoboCopy only copies three subdirectories down. If there's a fourth level subdirectory, it won't appear in the copy.

/Z Copies the files using restartable mode. Using restartable mode means that you can restart the operation should an external force interrupt it. Normally, RoboCopy restarts an operation from the beginning with the retry options, but this command line switch restarts the copy with the failed file.

/B Copies files using backup semantics. When using this mode, you must have the backup right. Using backup semantics helps you overcome some obstacles where you might ordinarily receive an access denied error, such as copying a file for which you have only the write privilege. The resulting copy has all of the same Access Control List (ACL) entries as the original, so this feature doesn't cause a breach in security.

/ZB Attempts to perform the copy using restartable mode first (see the /Z command line switch) and then uses backup mode if restartable mode fails.

NOTE **Using the /Z, /B, or /ZB command line switches can slow RoboCopy performance because the utility must perform additional file tracking as it makes a copy. However, the performance loss is more than overcome when working with unreliable network connections because you gain additional flexibility in handling troublesome files.**

/EFSRAW Copies all of the encrypted files in the Encrypting File System (EFS) Read-After-Write (RAW) mode.

/COPY:<Copy Flags> Defines which elements to copy from the source files to the destination files. For example, you might want to copy all of the owner information, but don't really care about the auditing information. The following list defines the copy flags.

D Data

A Attributes

T Time stamps

S Security (NTFS) ACLs

O Owner info

U Auditing info

/DCOPY:T Copies the directory time stamps. RoboCopy normally uses the current time for the time stamps.

/SEC Copies the files with all of the security information intact. This command line switch has the same effect as the /COPY:DATS command line switch.

/COPYALL Copies all of the file information with the files. This option makes a nearly mirror copy of the data from the source to the destination. Using this option is equivalent to using the /COPY:DATSOU command line switch.

/NOCOPY Performs a copy without copying any of the file data. This feature is useful with the /PURGE command line switch. You can also use it when checking for potential copy errors since the process is extremely fast when you don't copy the file data.

/SECFIX Repairs the security information for a set of destination files. This option lets you update the security information without copying the file data, making the repair very fast. You can learn more about this feature in the Knowledge Base article at http://support.microsoft.com/kb/323275.

/TIMFIX Repairs the time stamps for a set of destination files. This option lets you update the time stamps without copying the file data, making the change quite fast. This feature works very much like the /SECFIX command line switch, except it affects the time stamps, rather than security.

/PURGE Deletes the files in the destination directory that no longer exist in the source folder. Consequently, the files in the destination directory match the files in the source directory after you use this command line switch.

WARNING Use the /PURGE command line switch with extreme care. Even a small error in the command line arguments can delete a significant number of destination data. Whenever you use the /PURGE command line switch, the RoboCopy utility removes any files that exist as part of the Extra file class. See the sidebar entitled, "An Overview of RoboCopy File Classes" for additional details.

/MIR Creates a mirror image of the source directory in the destination directory. Using this command line switch is equivalent to combining the /E and /PURGE command line switches.

/MOV Moves only the files in the source directory to the destination directory. RoboCopy deletes the files in the source directory after copying them to the destination directory.

/MOVE Moves both files and subdirectories from the source directory to the destination directory. RoboCopy deletes the files and subdirectories in the source directory after copying them to the destination directory.

/A+:[RASHCNET] Adds the requested attributes to the copied files. RoboCopy actually provides access to more attributes than the Attrib utility. The following list describes each of the attributes.

- R: Read-only
- A: Archive
- S: System
- H: Hidden
- C: Compress
- N: Nonindexed
- E: Encrypted
- T: Temporary
- O: Offline (/XA and /IA command line switches only)

TIP NTFS actually supports a number of attributes that you can't readily access. You can find them discussed at http://www.febooti.com/products/filetweak/online-help/.

/A-:[RASHCNET] Removes the requested attributes from the copied files. The meanings of the attributes are the same as the /A+ command line switch.

/CREATE Creates a directory tree and zero-length files. You can use this feature when you need to copy the infrastructure from one location to another without copying the data.

/FAT Removes the long filenames from the destination files. All the files appear using the 8.3 File Allocation Table (FAT) file system format.

/256 Turns off the long path support that RoboCopy provides. If RoboCopy detects a long path, it raises an error. The only time you'd need to use this feature is if the destination doesn't support long paths. For example, if you wanted to copy to an older system with DOS (or even some camera or flash drives), you would probably want to use this command line switch.

/MON:n Monitors the source directory and performs a copy when more than *n* changes occur. Unlike XCopy, you can use RoboCopy to keep source and destination files synchronized automatically.

/MOT:m Monitors the source directory and performs a copy after *m* minutes if RoboCopy detects a change. You can use this option to keep the number of copies under control for a high activity directory. RoboCopy uses a set amount of system resources, rather than using resources based on activity as the /MON:n command line switch does.

/RH:hhmm-hhmm Defines the hours when RoboCopy can run. You can use this feature to ensure that copies only occur during nonpeak hours or after work. Use a 24-hour clock when defining the time range. For example, 1 P.M. is actually 1300.

/PF Determines the RoboCopy run hours on a per file basis instead of checking at the beginning of each pass. This option does incur a performance penalty because RoboCopy must check to determine whether a copy is allowed for each file, but it does mean that the copying process will conform better to the hours set by the /RH command line switch.

/IPG:n Determines the Inter-Package Gap (IPG) value in milliseconds (ms). A higher IPG frees bandwidth for other uses on slower network paths. A lower IPG helps RoboCopy perform better and accomplish tasks faster.

RoboCopy also provides a complex set of file selection options. These options determine which files actually appear in the destination directory. RoboCopy supports the following file selection option.

/A Includes files with the archive attribute set. The operating system sets the archive attribute whenever anything changes a file. This option doesn't reset the archive attribute, which makes it useful when you want to create a backup of archived files later.

/M Includes files with the archive attribute set. This option resets the archive attribute, so this is the command line switch to use when you use RoboCopy for backup purposes.

/IA:[RASHCNETO] Includes only the files that have the requested attributes set. See the /A+ command line switch for details.

/XA:[RASHCNETO] Excludes all of the files that have the requested attributes set. See the /A+ command line switch for details.

/XF <File> [<File>]... Excludes any files that match the specified names or paths. The specifications can include wildcard characters.

/XD <Directory> [<Directory>]... Excludes any directories that match the specified names or paths. The specifications can include wildcard characters.

/XC Excludes Changed files. See the "An Overview of RoboCopy File Classes" sidebar for details on this file class.

/XN Excludes Newer files. See the "An Overview of RoboCopy File Classes" sidebar for details on this file class.

/XO Excludes Older files. See the "An Overview of RoboCopy File Classes" sidebar for details on this file class.

/XX Excludes eXtra files and directories. See the "An Overview of RoboCopy File Classes" sidebar for details on this file class.

/XL Excludes Lonely files and directories. See the "An Overview of RoboCopy File Classes" sidebar for details on this file class.

/IS Includes Same files. See the "An Overview of RoboCopy File Classes" sidebar for details on this file class.

/IT Includes Tweaked files. See the "An Overview of RoboCopy File Classes" sidebar for details on this file class.

/MAX:n Defines the maximum file size to include in bytes. Excludes any file larger than *n* bytes.

/MIN:n Defines the minimum file size to include in bytes. Excludes any file smaller than *n* bytes.

/MAXAGE:n Defines the maximum file age to include. Excludes any file older than *n* days old. You can also specify a date.

/MINAGE:n Defines the minimum file age to include. Excludes any file newer than *n* days old. You can also specify a date.

/MAXLAD:n Defines the maximum last access date to include. Excludes any file unused in *n* days. You can also specify a date.

/MINLAD:n Defines the minimum last access date to include. Excludes any file used in *n* days. You can also specify a date.

/XJ Excludes junction points for both directories and files (normally included with the results).

/FFT Assumes FAT File Times (FFT), which have a 2-second granularity.

/DST Compensates for one-hour daylight standard time (DST) time differences.

/XJD Excludes junction points for directories.

/XJF Excludes junction points for files.

Many command line utilities try an operation once and then fail if it doesn't succeed. RoboCopy continues to retry the task until you press Ctrl+C, in most cases, to stop the process manually (even RoboCopy gives up after 1 million retries). You can also tell RoboCopy how to react to failure conditions. The following list describes the retry options.

/R:n Modifies the number of retries on failed copies to *n*. The default setting is 1 million retries.

/W:n Defines the wait time between retries. The default setting is 30 seconds.

/REG Saves the `/R:n` and `/W:n` command line switches in the registry as default settings.

/TBD Tells RoboCopy to wait for sharenames To Be Defined (TBD). This command line switch addresses retry error 67.

Given everything that RoboCopy can do, you might not want to wait for it to accomplish a task. Consequently, RoboCopy provides logging options that you can use to output data to a permanent location. The following list describes the logging options.

/L Provides a list of files only. RoboCopy doesn't copy, time-stamp, or delete any files.

/X Produces a report of all eXtra files, not just those selected.

/V Produces verbose output, which includes skipped files.

/TS Includes source file time stamps in the output.

/FP Includes the full pathname of files in the output.

/BYTES Prints the sizes of files in bytes.

/NS Doesn't log file sizes.

/NC Doesn't log file classes.

/NFL Doesn't log filenames.

/NDL Doesn't log directory names.

/NP Doesn't display a progress indicator showing the percent copied.

/ETA Shows the estimated time of arrival of copied files. This option is helpful when copying large files over slow networks.

/LOG:file Outputs status to the log file and overwrites any existing log.

/LOG+:file Outputs status to the log file and appends the information to any existing log.

/UNILOG:file Outputs status to the Unicode log file and overwrites any existing log.

/UNILOG+:file Outputs status to the Unicode log file and appends the information to any existing log.

/TEE Outputs status to the console window, as well as the log file.

/NJH Doesn't include a job header with the output.

/NJS Doesn't include a job summary with the output.

/UNICODE Outputs status using Unicode rather than ASCII characters.

You may want to use RoboCopy to perform complex tasks over the weekend or during a downtime. If you're using RoboCopy as one means of backup for your system, you might want to perform the task at night. In all of these situations, you'll want to create a RoboCopy job to perform the task. The following list describes the job options.

/JOB:jobname Uses parameters from the named job file to perform a task. A job file is simply a list of RoboCopy and other commands that define what you want RoboCopy to do—a kind of script. The text file can contain any number of RoboCopy commands. You can also use the `Set` command to create local variables to hold values that you want RoboCopy to use (see the "Managing Environment Variables with the *Set* Command" section of Chapter 3 for details).

/SAVE:jobname Saves the current command line arguments to the named job file. This is one of the easiest ways to create a job file for use with the `/JOB` command line switch.

/QUIT Quits after processing command line so that you can view any arguments. This is a way to test jobs without actually performing the tasks that the jobs request.

/NOSD Specifies that you haven't defined a source directory in the job file. RoboCopy uses the current directory.

/NODD Specifies that you haven't defined a destination directory in the job file. RoboCopy uses the current directory.

/IF Includes external files as part of the current job. This feature lets you concatenate multiple jobs together and perform them as a unit.

An Overview of RoboCopy File Classes

RoboCopy classifies files in several ways to make handling specific file conditions easier. The following list provides an overview of the RoboCopy file classes:

Lonely A lonely file exists in the source directory, but not in the destination directory. If you perform an update copy using RoboCopy, the utility copies the file to the destination.

Tweaked Tweaked files exist in both the source and destination directories. The file size and time stamp are the same. However, the attributes (those set with the Attrib utility) differ. You can fix this problem by specifically copying the attributes from the source to the destination. A standard copy won't affect the attributes when the file falls into this class.

Same The source and destination files are the same in all respects.

Changed The file exists in both the source and destination directories. The time stamp for both files is also the same. However, the file size differs. RoboCopy doesn't consider the status of the attributes when placing a file into this class.

Newer The file exists in both the source and destination directories. The time stamp of the file in the destination directory is newer than the one in the source directory. RoboCopy doesn't consider the status of the file size or attributes when placing a file into this class.

Older The file exists in both the source and destination directories. The time stamp of the file in the source directory is newer than the one in the destination directory. RoboCopy doesn't consider the status of the file size or attributes when placing a file into this class.

eXtra An extra file exists in the destination directory, but not in the source directory. You can use the /PURGE command line switch to remove extra files. However, use the /PURGE command line switch with extreme care because a typo can cause RoboCopy to delete the entire destination directory.

Mismatched The entry exists as a file in the source directory and as a folder in the destination directory. RoboCopy reports this problem in the output log, but doesn't attempt to fix it.

Displaying Data Files

Creating data file output is a necessity even at the command line. The output methods provided at the command line won't provide highly formatted reports, but they will provide you with the data you need in a usable format. The following sections describe techniques you can use to output data from the command line.

Working with Line Printers

Unless you're working with an older mainframe or Unix setup, you probably won't ever run into a line printer. Line printer technology is outdated and not used all that often today. Today's modern equivalent isn't even a line printer; it's more likely a high-speed printer configured to provide the equivalent services. Of course, this might cause you to ask why there's a line printer topic in this chapter. It turns out that setting up a line printer is one of the ways you can share your printer (network or local) with a Linux machine. In fact, this technology is so embedded that some vendors like Hewlett-Packard provide print servers to provide Line Printer Daemon (LPD) services (see `http://h20000.www2.hp.com/bizsupport/TechSupport/Document.jsp?objectID=bpj02836` for details).

Windows provides a special LPD service to provide line printer support. The LPD service is an older TCP/IP service that you install with the Print Services for Unix (found in the Other Network File and Print Services folder in the Windows Components Wizard dialog box). However, installing the server isn't enough. You'll need to configure the LPD service to provide a number of queues that users can use for printing. You can find an excellent procedure for performing the LPD configuration at `http://www.le.ac.uk/cc/dsss/docs/print-lpr.shtml`.

TIP If you're serious about providing Linux print services through an LPD server, you might want to use one of the better utilities on the market. A good starting product is the SDI LPD server found at `http://www.sdisw.com/LPD/default.htm`. This server provides a nice graphical interface that makes it easy to manage your print queues. In addition, because this product is shareware, you can try it before you buy it.

Once you have a printer configured to use LPD, you might wonder how to access it. The LPQ utility lets you see the status of the printer. The LPR utility lets you send output to the printer. Interestingly enough, these same utilities appear on both Macintosh and Linux systems, which is why these systems can access the LPD server on your Windows machine without problem. Both of these utilities work at the command line as described in the following sections.

Troubleshooting the Line Printer Daemon with the LPQ Utility

The Line Printer Queue (LPQ) utility provides status information that you can use to troubleshoot a LPD server. You can use this utility to display the status of each document in the queue. Vista doesn't support the LPQ utility. Use the LPD Print Service instead. This utility uses the following syntax:

```
LPQ  -Sserver -Pprinter [-l]
```

The following list describes each of the command line arguments.

`-Sserver` Defines the name or IP address of the server hosting the LDP service. You use the standard network name of the machine when working with Windows. Notice that there isn't any space between the `-S` command line switch and the server name. In addition, the command line switches for this utility are case sensitive; typing `-s` or `/s` isn't the same as typing `-S`.

`-Pprinter` Specifies the name of the LDP printer queue. This isn't the name of the printer, but the name of the printer entry you create as part of setting up an LPD server. The name you see in the Printers and Faxes folder is the same as the name of the LPD server queue for that printer.

`-l` Displays the server information in verbose mode. This setting doesn't make much of a difference on Windows systems; you see the same information. However, you might see more information when accessing other platforms such as Linux. Note that this command line switch is a lowercase L.

Using the LPQ utility is relatively easy. For example, my machine's name is Main and I configured a LaserJet printer connection on it using the techniques described earlier in this section. Typing **`LPQ -SMain -PLJ5`** at the command prompt provides the display shown in Figure 2.5.

TIP There's nothing odd or strange about using an LPD server on Windows. Any printer you configure this way still provides the same management window as any other printer you connect to your machine or access from the network. You can use this GUI display to manage the print jobs in the queue. These features include all of the standard Windows features such as changing job priority, pausing a job, or canceling all jobs. The only difference is the server used to service the print queue.

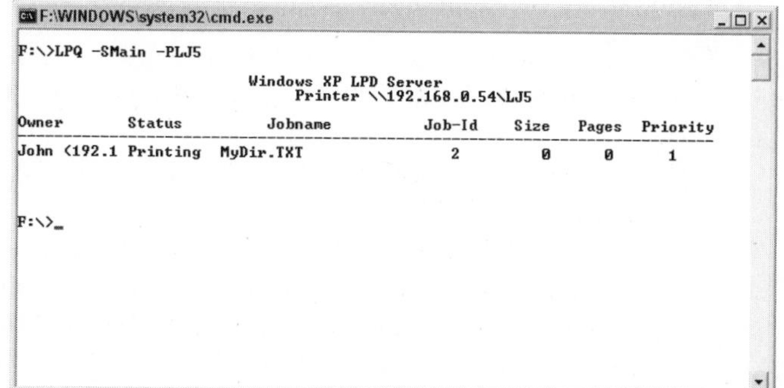

Figure 2.5
The LPQ utility tells you about the status of a selected printer queue on your machine.

SENDING A PRINT JOB TO A PRINTER WITH THE LPR UTILITY

VISTA

The Line Printer Request (LPR) utility sends a print job to the printer. When working at the command line, you'll normally send text files, but the LPR utility can also accommodate binary files and PostScript. Vista doesn't support the LPR utility. Use the LPR Port Monitor instead. This utility uses the following syntax:

```
LPR -S server -P printer [-C class] [-J job] [-o option] [-x] [-d] filename
```

The following list describes each of the command line arguments.

-S *server* Defines the name or IP address of the server hosting the LDP service. You use the standard network name of the machine when working with Windows. Notice that there isn't any space between the -S command line switch and the server name. In addition, the command line switches for this utility are case sensitive; typing -s or /s isn't the same as typing -S.

-P *printer* Specifies the name of the LDP printer queue. This isn't the name of the printer, but the name of the printer entry you create as part of setting up an LPD server. The name you see in the Printers and Faxes folder is the same as the name of the LPD server queue for that printer.

-C *class* Defines the job classification to use for the burst page. You must define print jobs for the server to use this feature.

-J *job* Defines the job name to print on the burst page. You must define print jobs for the server to use this feature.

-o *option* Determines the type of the file. The default setting is a text file. The only standardized option value is a 1, which indicates a binary or PostScript file. The presence of this option doesn't mean that the printer can handle the file you send or that Windows won't strip control characters. Make sure you read the Microsoft Knowledge Base articles on this topic, such as the one found at http://support.microsoft.com/kb/124735/EN-US/, before you create binary print jobs.

-x Enforces compatibility with SunOS4.1.x and prior when working with a remote printer.

-d Places this data file at the front of the print queue. The default is to place the data file at the end of the queue.

Generally, you won't need to use all of the LPR options. For example, you can print a text file on a Windows machine simply by specifying the server name, the print queue, and the name of the file as shown here:

```
LPR -SMain -PLJ5 MyDir.TXT
```

NOTE Once you establish an LPD server on your system, you can use the associated printer as you would any other printer from Windows applications. Consequently, the LPR utility is like any other command line utility for printing—it lets you create basic output from the command line. However, LPD servers and their associated printers require special setup to pass control characters and other non-ASCII data. Make sure you understand and configure your LPD server setup before you use it for general application output.

Printing Data Files with the Print Utility

The Print utility represents the fastest and easiest way to send data to a printer for output. However, you don't have many choices when you use this technique. The only change you can make is to define the print device to use for output. Otherwise, the Print utility relies on all of the defaults that you assign to the printer. This utility uses the following syntax:

```
PRINT [/D:device] [[drive:][path]filename[...]]
```

The following list describes each of the command line arguments.

/D:*device* Specifies the device to use for output. The default setting uses the printer attached to LPT1.

drive Specifies the drive that holds the file for printing. The default is the current drive.

path Specifies the relative or absolute path of the file you want to print. The default is the current directory.

filename Specifies one or more files to send to the printer for output.

Outputting Data Files with the *Type* Command

The Type command is a simple method of displaying the content of a file on screen. You use this utility with text files; it won't display control codes in a readable form and stops displaying text when it sees an end of file character (ASCII 26). This utility uses the following syntax:

```
TYPE [drive:][path]filename
```

The following list describes each of the command line arguments.

drive Specifies the drive that holds the file for display. The default is the current drive.

path Specifies the relative or absolute path of the file you want to display. The default is the current directory.

filename Specifies the file you want to display on screen.

Many people combine the Type command with other commands and utilities to achieve special effects. In addition, you can use redirection to augment the functionality of the Type command. By using the correct redirection, you can use the Type command to send raw text to the printer reliably. The following sections describe data redirection and the use of the most common Type command partner utility, the More utility.

Employing Data Redirection

Data redirection is the process of sending data from one command or utility to another command or utility. You can also redirect command or utility output to a device (see the "Understanding Command Line Devices" sidebar in this chapter for details on standard devices) or a file. Redirection provides the means for sending output to a location other than the standard output device (the console), obtaining input from a device other than standard input (the keyboard), and using something other than the standard error device (usually the console) to report problems. The command line supports three forms of redirection: input, output, and pipe. Each requires use of specialized symbols.

One of the most common forms of redirection is the pipe and it uses the pipe symbol (|) that appears over the backslash on most keyboards. In fact, the pipe is much older than the PC and appears in the earliest Unix operating systems (see the history at `http://www.linfo.org/pipes.html` for details). The pipe accomplishes what its name implies; it acts as a pipe between small applications. You connect the applications using the pipe and data flows between the applications using the pipe. For example, you can temporarily connect the Dir command to the Sort command to create a customized directory output using a command like this:

```
Dir /A-D | Sort /+13
```

The resulting command obtains a listing of the current directory, without the directory entries and sorts them by the time column. Figure 2.6 shows the results of this command.

Redirection always works with a file or other streaming device. You never use redirection with another command. The two types of redirection are input and output, with output being the most commonly used. To output the results of a command such as `Dir` or `Sort` to a file, you use a greater than sign (>) or output redirection pointer. Windows clears the file if it exists and places the command output in it. However, you might want to place the results of several commands into a file. In this case, you use two greater than signs (>>). A double output redirection pointer always appends the output of a command to the existing file. Here's an example of sending the output of the `Dir` command to a file:

```
Dir *.TXT > MyFile.TXT
```

FIGURE 2.6
Combining commands and utilities makes the command prompt extremely flexible.

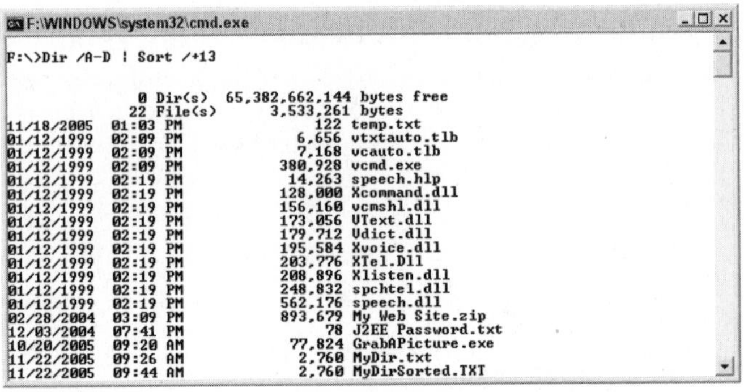

```
F:\WINDOWS\system32\cmd.exe

F:\>Dir /A-D | Sort /+13

               0 Dir(s)  65,382,662,144 bytes free
              22 File(s)      3,533,261 bytes
11/18/2005  01:03 PM               122 temp.txt
01/12/1999  02:09 PM             6,656 vtxtauto.tlb
01/12/1999  02:09 PM             7,168 vcauto.tlb
01/12/1999  02:09 PM           380,928 vcmd.exe
01/12/1999  02:19 PM            14,263 speech.hlp
01/12/1999  02:19 PM           128,000 Xcommand.dll
01/12/1999  02:19 PM           156,160 vcmshl.dll
01/12/1999  02:19 PM           173,056 VText.dll
01/12/1999  02:19 PM           179,712 Vdict.dll
01/12/1999  02:19 PM           195,584 Xvoice.dll
01/12/1999  02:19 PM           203,776 XTel.Dll
01/12/1999  02:19 PM           208,896 Xlisten.dll
01/12/1999  02:19 PM           248,832 spchtel.dll
01/12/1999  02:19 PM           562,176 speech.dll
02/28/2004  03:09 PM           893,679 My Web Site.zip
12/03/2004  07:41 PM                78 J2EE Password.txt
10/20/2005  09:20 AM            77,824 GrabAPicture.exe
11/22/2005  09:26 AM             2,760 MyDir.txt
11/22/2005  09:44 AM             2,760 MyDirSorted.TXT
```

In this case, you'd end up with a file called `MyFile.TXT` that contains a list of all of the text files in the current directory.

Input relies on the less than symbol (<) or input redirection pointer. You can always use a file as input to a command that's expecting text or record data. In some cases, you can use file input to generate commands as well. The point is that a file or other streaming device acts as input. Although it's extremely uncommon, you also have access to a double input redirection pointer (<<). This symbol appends input to previous input for a command.

The combination of an output redirection pointer and an input redirection pointer can be the same as a pipe. Here's an example of the two forms of redirection used together:

```
Dir /A-D > MyFile.TXT
Sort /+13 < MyFile.TXT
```

In this case, the output of the `Dir` command appears in `MyFile.TXT`. The second command uses `MyFile.TXT` as input to the `Sort` command. The result is the same as the pipe example shown in Figure 2.6.

Although you can only include one redirection symbol on a command line, you can use as many pipes as needed to accomplish a task. This means that you can create a series of pipes to connect any number of commands and create some interesting command sequences. For example, you can combine the `Dir`, `Sort`, and `More` commands as shown here to provide output where you see one display at a time (see the "Using the More Utility" section for details on the More utility).

```
Dir /A-D | Sort /+13 | More
```

Using the More Utility

The More utility is one of the few utilities that you never use by itself. You always use this utility with some other utility or command. The More utility pauses the display so that you can see output that normally requires multiple screens to display. For example, you can combine the More utility with the `Dir` command to display the list of files in a directory one screen at a time. One of the most common uses of the More utility is to provide a means of paging output from the `Type` command. You can also use redirection to input files to the More utility; the implied partner in this case is the `Type` command. This utility uses the following syntax:

```
MORE [/E [/C] [/P] [/S] [/Tn] [+n]] < [drive:][path]filename
command-name | MORE [/E [/C] [/P] [/S] [/Tn] [+n]]
MORE /E [/C] [/P] [/S] [/Tn] [+n] [files]
```

The following list describes each of the command line arguments.

drive Specifies the drive that holds the file for display. The default is the current drive.

path Specifies the relative or absolute path of the file you want to display. The default is the current directory.

filename Specifies the file you want to display on screen.

/E Enables the More utility extended feature set. You'll find a discussion of these features later in this section.

/C Clears the display prior to displaying a page. Normally, the More utility provides a continuous display, so you can scroll back and forth through the screen buffer.

/P Expands form feed characters as displayable information, rather than reacting to them as an actual form feed.

/S Removes excess blank lines from the display. The More utility squeezes multiple blank lines into a single blank line.

/Tn Changes the number of spaces for each tab. The default setting is 8 spaces.

NOTE You can specify the command line switches in the `MORE` environment variable. For more information on using environment variables, see the "Managing Environment Variables with the *Set* Command" section of Chapter 3.

+n Displays the first file starting at line *n*. This feature lets you continue displaying a file from a known position after stopping a display during a previous session.

files Specifies a list of files to display. The More utility sends the files to the `Type` command in the order specified. It separates each file with a blank. You must provide the list of files as the last argument.

The More utility includes an extended mode that you enable using the `/E` command line switch. The extended mode provides additional functionality to make it easier to work with output files. For example, you can display a few additional lines to see part of a continuation of data in a file. The following list describes the extended mode commands, which you can type at the `More` prompt.

P *n* Displays the next *n* lines of the file. Type the `P` command. You'll see a `Lines` prompt. Type the number of lines to display and press Enter.

S *n* Skips the next *n* lines of the file (doesn't display them). Type the `S` command. You'll see a `Lines` prompt. Type the number of lines to display and press Enter.

F Displays the next file in the list. If there's no next file, the More utility ends. This action doesn't necessarily end the previous application in the pipe. Press Ctrl+C to end the previous command (such as `Type`) as necessary.

Q Quits the More utility without displaying any additional data. This action doesn't necessarily end the previous application in the pipe. Press Ctrl+C to end the previous command (such as `Type`) as necessary.

= Shows the number of the current line of text. For example, if the More utility is currently displaying the 49th line in the file, you'll see `Line: 49` as part of the `More` prompt.

? Shows the list of extended commands.

<space> Displays the next page of the file.

<enter> Displays the next line of text in the file.

The More utility provides a simple prompt at the bottom of the command window for entering display commands. You can only move forward in a file, not backward. Whenever you enter a command, the `More` prompt extends to request any additional information. Figure 2.7 shows the `More` prompt after typing the `P` command. Notice that the prompt contains the `Lines:` entry, which lets you input the number of lines to display.

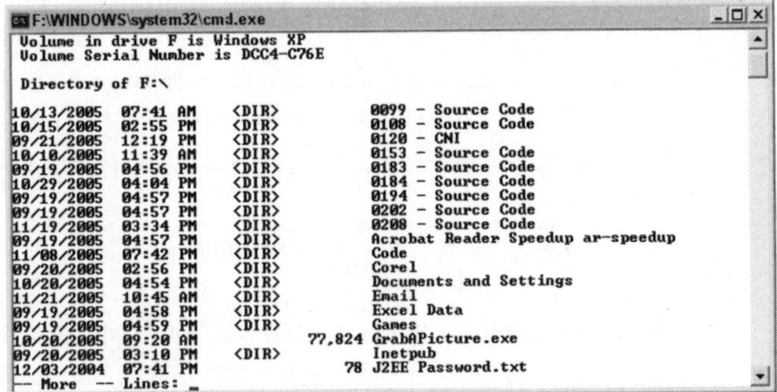

FIGURE 2.7
Using the More utility in extended mode makes it easy to manipulate the on-screen display.

Performing a Formatted Printout with Notepad

Many people associate Notepad with a utility that you use in the Windows GUI, and that's where you use it most often. However, Notepad and many other applications have a hidden side. Unfortunately, you won't discover this hidden side by typing the command name followed by a `/?`. Notepad and other Windows applications won't provide you with any help for using them at the command line, yet this command line functionality still exists.

To locate such functionality, you must rely on the registry editor, RegEdit. To start this utility, type **`RegEdit`** at the command line and press Enter. At this point you need to look at the `HKEY_CLASSES_ROOT` hive. Locate the extension of the file that you want to work with. The example uses the `.txt` entry shown in Figure 2.8. The `(Default)` entry shown in the right pane contains the essential information; the file association. (For more information about file associations see the "Working with File Associations and Types" section of the chapter.)

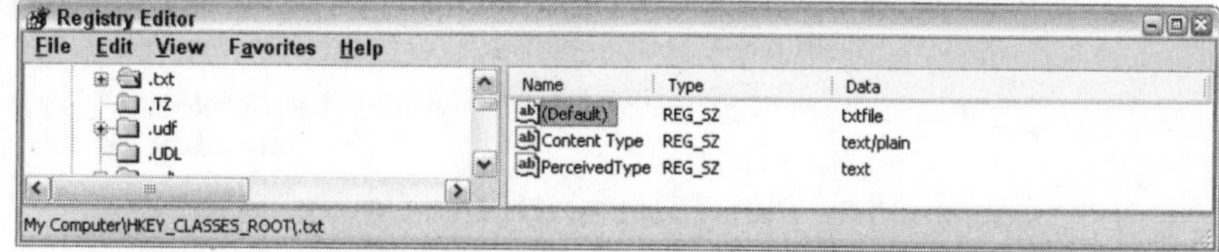

FIGURE 2.8 Locate the extension of the file you want to print from the command line.

Now that you know the file association, locate its entry in the registry. Figure 2.9 shows the entries for the txtfile association. The entry you want is the command for the print command shown highlighted in the figure. Notice that this command calls on Notepad with an undocumented `/p` command line switch to perform the printing. The `%1` after the command line switch is the name of the file. Consequently, if you want to print a text file at the command line using Notepad, you simply type **`Notepad /p`** ***`filename`*** and press Enter.

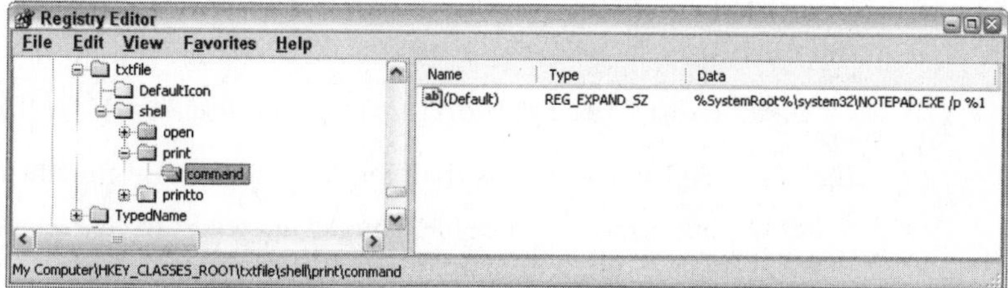

FIGURE 2.9 The file association provides clues as to how to use graphical utilities at the command line.

Determining File and Directory Status

Knowing where you are in the directory system is essential because you must execute commands in the correct directory to obtain the correct result. In addition, you need to know how to move from directory to directory and establish the status of a file when compared to another file. Understanding how Windows interacts with files is also important. All of these tasks rely on special status commands at the command line. The following sections describe each of these commands and utilities in detail.

Determining the Current Directory and Changing Directories with the *CD* and *ChDir* Commands

The `CD` and `ChDir` commands perform the same two tasks. First, you can use these commands to establish your current location at the command line. Second, you can use these commands to move to another directory. You can display the current directory by typing `CD` or `ChDir` without any arguments and pressing Enter. These commands use the following syntax:

```
CHDIR [/D] [drive:][path]
CHDIR [..]
CD [/D] [drive:][path]
CD [..]
```

The following list describes each of the command line arguments.

`drive` Specifies the new drive. The default is the current drive.

path Specifies the relative or absolute path of the new directory. The default is the current directory. You can use a double period (`..`) to specify the parent directory of the current directory.

/D Changes the current drive as well as the directory.

Comparing Two Files with the Comp Utility

Sometimes it's helpful to compare two files to determine what has changed or to verify that the files are precisely the same. A common use of this technique is to compare two text files. The files could contain anything from data to application settings. Another way to use this technique is to verify that no one has tampered with executable files. Viruses and other forms of intrusion often modify executable files. Just looking at the file isn't enough in many cases to verify the damage. However, keeping a known good copy of the file on an unmodifiable source, such as a CD, and using this simple comparison utility is often enough to detect the problem. It also provides you with a way of expunging the intruder from your executables by copying the known good executable from the CD (of course, you still have to consider registry entries and other ways intruders often use to rebuild themselves). This utility uses the following syntax:

```
COMP [data1] [data2] [/D] [/A] [/L] [/N=number] [/C] [/OFF[LINE]]
```

The following list describes each of the command line arguments.

data1 Specifies the source file. You can use wildcard characters to define multiple comparisons. For example, `*.DLL` will compare every dynamic link library in the source directory against a DLL with the same name in the destination directory.

data2 Specifies the destination file. You can use wildcard characters to define multiple comparisons. However, the source and destination specifications must compare. If the source contains just one file, then the destination will also contain one file as well.

/D Displays the differences in decimal format (as numeric values for each character, whether there's an ASCII equivalent or not). This is the optimal setting when comparing binary or executable files.

/A Displays the differences as ASCII characters. This is the optimal setting when comparing text files of any type (including INI or other settings files and standard data files in XML or other format).

/L Displays the line numbers for differences. The Comp utility compares the two files line by line, where the carriage return (ASCII character 13), linefeed (ASCII character 10), or both designate the end of a line.

/N=*number* Performs a comparison of the specified number of lines in each file beginning with the first line.

/C Performs a case-insensitive comparison of the two files. Normally, Comp will consider an uppercase letter different from a lowercase letter.

/OFF[LINE] Forces the Comp utility to compare files even when the files have the offline attribute set.

Performing Advanced File Comparison with the FC Utility

The FC utility is a slightly advanced form of the Comp utility described in the previous section. You can use it for the same types of activities, but perform a more flexible comparison of the two files.

For example, this utility has a comparison mode specifically designed for binary files. This utility uses the following syntax (the first is for ASCII files; the second is for binary files):

```
FC [/A] [/C] [/L] [/LBn] [/N] [/OFF[LINE]] [/T] [/U] [/W] [/nnnn]
   [drive1:][path1]filename1 [drive2:][path2]filename2
FC /B [drive1:][path1]filename1 [drive2:][path2]filename2
```

The following list describes each of the command line arguments.

/A Displays only the first and last lines for each set of differences. Normally, the FC utility (like the Comp utility) displays every line for a set of differences, making the output difficult to read when the files have a lot of differences.

/B Performs a binary comparison of the two files. This means that the FC utility won't interpret control characters such as linefeed, carriage return, and end of file character (ASCII character 26) as it would when performing an ASCII comparison.

/C Performs a case-insensitive comparison of the two files. Normally, FC will consider an uppercase letter different from a lowercase letter.

/L Performs an ASCII text comparison of the two files. This setting means that control characters become important in the comparison, as do the actual character meanings.

/LB*n* Defines the maximum acceptable mismatches between the two files. When FC reaches *n*, it stops performing the comparison.

/N Displays the line numbers for differences. The FC utility compares the two files line by line, where the carriage return (ASCII character 13), linefeed (ASCII character 10), or both designate the end of a line.

/OFF[LINE] Forces the FC utility to compare files even when the files have the offline attribute set.

/T Forces the FC utility to retain tabs within the output. Normally, it displays tabs using the default number of spaces (usually 8) between characters.

/U Performs a Unicode comparison of the two files. Unicode character sets include additional characters to meet the needs of languages other than English. In addition, Unicode character sets often include characters designed to express both scientific and mathematical output.

/W Compresses tabs and spaces for the purposes of comparison. You'd use this feature when comparing two data files where the content is important, but the manner of presentation isn't. Using this technique would let you compare the actual content of a raw data file against its formatted counterpart.

/nnnn Specifies the number of consecutive lines that must match after a mismatch to continue the comparison. If the source and destination files don't compare more often than this number allows, then FC discontinues the comparison.

[drive1:][path1]filename1 Specifies the source file. You can use wildcard characters to define multiple comparisons. For example, `*.DLL` will compare every dynamic link library in the source directory against a DLL with the same name in the destination directory.

[drive2:][path2]filename2 Specifies the destination file. You can use wildcard characters to define multiple comparisons. However, the source and destination specifications must compare. If the source contains just one file, then the destination will also contain one file as well.

Working with File Associations and Types

Strictly speaking, you don't need to know anything about file associations or file types to work with files from the command prompt. However, Windows does need to know this information when working with files in the GUI. Whenever a user double-clicks a file, Windows looks up the file association based on the file extension, locates the file type information, and then executes an application to load the file based on what it finds. Consequently, knowing something about the file associations and types on your system is important, but it isn't something that you'll use from the command prompt.

Windows provides two commands for working with file associations and types. You use the `Assoc` command to determine and set the file associations. The file association will connect a specific file type with an extension. The `FType` command defines the file type information. For example, you can specify what happens when a particular file type receives a request to open a file. The file types all rely on verbs, action words, to define specific tasks. The most common of these verbs are open and print, but depending on the file type, you might find many others.

The `Assoc` and the `FType` commands work together to show the relationships between file extensions and file types, and to allow you to modify these relationships. For example, an administrator could create a batch file to set up a user machine to use specific applications to handle certain kinds of files. The following sections describe these two commands.

Determining and Creating File Associations with the *Assoc* Command

The `Assoc` command can display or change the association between a file extension and a file type. For example, when you type **`Assoc .TXT`** and press Enter, the `Assoc` command responds with `.TXT=txtfile` on a Windows system using the default setup. This command uses the following syntax:

```
ASSOC [.ext[=[fileType]]]
```

The following list describes each of the command line arguments.

`.ext` Specifies the file extension that you want to assign or display. The file extension must begin with a period or the utility will fail. For example, you must type **`.TXT`** instead of TXT alone.

`fileType` Specifies the file type to assign to the file extension. The file type must exist within the registry (create it if necessary using the `FType` command). Always place an equals sign between the file extension and type. For example, to associate the .TXT extension with the txtfile type, you'd type **`Assoc .TXT=txtfile`** and press Enter at the command line.

Determining and Creating File Types with the *FType* Command

The `FType` command can display the open verb action or set the action for this verb for any file type on your system. You can also use it to create new file types as needed to express a specific file requirement. The `FType` command only works with the open verb, not any of the other verbs (such as print) that the file type might contain. Even so, this command is invaluable in setting up a system quickly.

A file type always includes the file type name and the associated action. For example, if you type **`FType txtfile`** at the command prompt and press Enter, the `FType` command responds with `txtfile=%SystemRoot%\system32\NOTEPAD.EXE %1` on a system using the default setup. In this case, txtfile is the file type. The action appears after the equals sign. The `%SystemRoot%` environment variable points to the Windows directory on your machine. The System32 directory contains many of the executable files including both EXEs and DLLs. The application that Windows will start to load is a text file in Notepad. The `%1` after Notepad is a placeholder for the file. You can include as many placeholders as required by the application. The action can also include any command line switches that the application requires to handle the file type. This command uses the following syntax:

```
FTYPE [fileType[=[openCommandString]]]
```

The following list describes each of the command line arguments.

fileType Specifies the name of the file type to display or change. Many common file types use the file extension followed by the word file as a name. For example, Windows normally associates a file with a .TXT extension with the txtfile file type.

openCommandString Defines the action to take when a user double-clicks a file or otherwise requests that Windows open it. The action must include the application location and application name (including file extension). You may optionally include command line arguments, placeholders, and other application input as needed.

Taking Ownership of Files with the TakeOwn Utility

VISTA

Vista provides a new method of taking ownership of a file using the TakeOwn utility. Given the importance that User Account Control (UAC) places on ownership for security reasons, using this utility could help you around some of the problems that UAC can create in user access. (See the "Understanding User Account Control (UAC) Changes" section of Chapter 1 for details on how UAC affects your use of the command line.) In some cases, you might find that you have to take ownership of a file to manipulate it effectively. The TakeOwn utility uses the following syntax.

```
TAKEOWN [/S system [/U [domain\]username [/P [password]]]] /F filename [/A] [/R
[/D prompt]]
```

The following list describes each of the command line arguments.

/S system Specifies the remote system that you want to check. In most cases, you'll also need to supply the /U and the /P command line switches when using this switch.

/U [domain\]user Specifies the username on the remote system. This name may not match the username on the local system. You'll need to supply a domain name when working with a domain controller.

/P [password] Specifies the password for the given user. You can provide the command line switch without specifying the password on the command line in cleartext. The system prompts you for the password. Using this feature can help you maintain the security of passwords used on your system.

/F filename Specifies the object that you want to own. The object can be a file or directory. You can include a sharename when required. TakeOwn also lets you use wildcard characters to define the file or directory specification.

/A Gives the Administrators group ownership of the object, instead of the current user (or the user whose credentials you supplied).

/R Performs a recursive search for files meeting the file specification. TakeOwn searches the current directory first, and then all subdirectories.

/D prompt Provides a default answer when the current user doesn't have the list folder permission for a particular directory. The acceptable answers are Y to take ownership of the directory or N to skip the directory.

Performing Backups with the NTBackup Utility

VISTA

Windows has included the NTBackup utility virtually unchanged for many versions. However, you won't find it included with Vista. You use the WBAdmin utility described in the "Performing Backups with the WBAdmin Utility" section of the chapter in place of NTBackup when working with Vista. This utility lets you create a backup of your system data using a file, tape drive, formatting floppy, or even a prepared CD (for those of you who want to use CD, check out sources such as Windows IT Pro at `http://www.windowsitpro.com/Article/ArticleID/24412/24412.html`).

NOTE This section concentrates on using NTBackup from the command line. It doesn't make any recommendations as to how to back up your system. You won't find any instructions on setting up NTBackup or a demonstration of how to use it with your media of choice. Refer to a Windows user book, such as my book, *Teach Yourself Microsoft Windows XP in 21 Days* (Sams, 2002), for information of this type.

NTBackup comes with a number of limitations. For example, you can't easily use NTBackup to back data up to a writable DVD or a blank CD. Always rely on a third party utility for these needs. This utility uses the following syntax:

```
ntbackup backup [systemstate] "@bks file name" /J {"job name"} [/P
     {"pool name"}] [/G {"guid name"}] [/T { "tape name"}] [/N {"media
     name"}] [/F {"file name"}] [/D {"set description"}] [/DS {"server
     name"}] [/IS {"server name"}] [/A] [/V:{yes|no}] [/R:{yes|no}]
     [/L:{f|s|n}] [/M {backup type}] [/RS:{yes|no}] [/HC:{on|off}]
     [/SNAP:{on|off}]
```

The following list describes each of the command line arguments.

backup Sets NTBackup to perform a backup action (as contrasted to a restore action). The utility currently provides support only for the backup action. You cannot restore a backup from the command line.

systemstate Specifies that NTBackup should create a backup of the system state for the host machine. The system state includes the registry, boot files, the COM class registration database, and other data that you might not select normally. You can only backup system state information for the local machine using NTBackup; you cannot back up system state information for a remote machine. One way around this problem is to perform local backups on the other machine to a file and then perform a backup of that file. In fact, this requirement is one reason that you would want to perform backups from the command line, rather than using the graphical interface. The Microsoft Knowledge Base article at `http://support.microsoft.com/default.aspx?scid=kb;en-us;315412` provides additional information about performing remote system state backups. Saving the system state limits the backup to either the Normal or Copy backup type.

@filename Determines the name of the Backup Selection (BKS) file that NTBackup uses for the backup operation. The BKS file contains a list of drives and directories that you want to include in the backup. It also contains directories, file extensions, and individual files that you don't want included in the backup. You can use the graphical interface to create this file. However, you could also automate file creation using a number of command line utilities. The BKS file is plain text, so you can view it using Notepad. The entries appear on individual lines and consist of either standard drive and directory or UNC drive and directory specifications. You exclude a drive or directory by entering its location followed by the `/Exclude` command line switch. You can find any BKS files created by the GUI in the `\Documents and Settings\<User Name>\Local Settings\Application Data\Microsoft\Windows NT\NTBackup\data` folder of the host machine.

`/J "job name"` Specifies the job name to enter into the log file. The job name must appear within double quotes after the command line prompt. You use the job name to describe the files and folders you are backing up with the current job. The job name also includes the date and time you backed up the files and the type of media used for the backup (such as tape or file).

`/P "pool name"` Specifies the media pool to use for the backup. The main (default) media pool is backup. However, you can choose any subpool that appears in the Backup Destination field on the Backup tab of the graphical interface. Common subpools include 4mm DDS and File. You can't use the `/A`, `/G`, `/F`, or `/T` command line switches when you use this command line switch.

`/G "GUID name"` Specifies that you want NTBackup to use a Globally Unique Identifier (GUID) in place of a tape name to identify the backup tape. Do not use this switch in conjunction with `/P`.

`/T "tape name"` Specifies that you want NTBackup to assign a particular tape name to the tape as a form of identification. Do not use this switch in conjunction with `/P`.

`/N "media name"` Defines the name of a new tape (instead of overwriting an existing tape). You can't use this switch with the `/A` command line switch.

`/F "file name"` Defines the disk, path, and filename for a disk-based backup. The backup appears in a file, rather than on removable media such as a table. You can't use the `/P`, `/G`, or `/T` switches with this command line switch.

`/D "set description"` Specifies a label for a backup set that could consist of multiple tapes. The backup set identifies the backup as a whole, rather than an individual piece of media.

`/DS "server name"` Performs a backup of the Directory Service file for the specified Microsoft Exchange Server.

`/IS "server name"` Performs a backup of the Information Store file for the specified Microsoft Exchange Server.

`/A` Appends the current backup to an existing backup on media with space to store the backup information. You must combine this switch with either the `/G` or `/T` command line switches. Do not use this switch in conjunction with `/P`.

`/V:{yes|no}` Verifies the data after completing the backup when using the `/V:yes` command line switch. Even though verification requires additional time and system resources, the verification also acts as a safety feature. If you don't verify the backup, you don't know whether the backup actually worked. The tape or other media could appear blank when you need to use it to restore the system. Notice that there's a colon (`:`) between the command line switch and the option selection you choose.

NOTE The `/V`, `/R`, `/L`, `/M`, `/RS`, and `/HC` command line switches default to whatever settings you use in the graphical interface. For example, if you turn on hardware compression in the graphical interface, then using the `/HC:on` command line switch doesn't do anything. However, using the `/HC:off` command line switch will turn off hardware compression. Adding the command line switches won't hurt anything, but you don't have to add them when you know how the graphical interface is set up.

/R:{yes|no} Restricts access to the backup to the owner or members of the Administrators group. This security setting can help keep tape data safe.

/L:{f|s|n} Specifies the type of log file that NTBackup maintains: (f)ull, (s)ummary, or (n)one. It's never a good idea to create a backup without a log file because you won't have a permanent record of any errors. Use the summary option only when disk space is an issue.

/M {normal | copy | differential | incremental | daily} Specifies the backup type. The normal backup creates a backup of all of the requested files and resets the archive bit. A copy backup creates a backup of all of the requested files, but doesn't reset the archive bit. A differential backup creates a backup of only the files that have changed since the last normal or incremental backup and doesn't reset the archive bit. An incremental backup creates a backup of only the files that changed since the last normal or incremental backup; it does reset the archive bit. A daily backup creates a backup of the files that have changed during the current day; it doesn't reset the archive bit. The archive bit is a special file bit that shows the file has changed. Backup programs use this bit to mark the file as backed up depending on the kind of backup you choose. Notice that this particular command line switch lacks a colon between the command line switch and the option selection you choose.

/RS:{yes|no} Performs a backup of the migrated data files located in Remote Storage. You don't need to use this command line switch to back up the local Removable Storage database that contains Remote Storage placeholder files. When you back up the `%SystemRoot%` folder, NTBackup automatically backs up the Removable Storage database as well.

/HC:{on|off} Sets the tape drive to use hardware compression when available. Generally, hardware compression not only adds storage capacity, it also improves performance.

/SNAP:{on|off} Specifies that this backup is a volume shadow copy when set to on. A volume shadow copy is a backup that precisely mimics the original volume. You can use this type of backup to perform a complete system setup.

Performing Backups with the WBAdmin Utility

VISTA

The WBAdmin utility is new to Vista. Even though it provides you with considerably more functionality than NTBackup, you'll find that it's actually easier to use in many cases. Part of the ease of use comes from the modes that WBAdmin supports. You use a particular mode by typing WBAdmin followed by the mode keywords, such as Start Backup. However, you'll also find that WBAdmin provides considerably fewer options than NTBackup. For example, you must back up an entire volume or mount point. The following list describes each of the modes.

Start Backup Starts the backup process. You'll need to provide backup information as command line arguments.

Stop Job Ends the current backup or recovery.

Get Versions Displays a list of backups that you can use for recovery purposes.

Get Items Displays a list of items found in a particular backup.

Get Status Obtains the status of the current backup or recovery.

Three of the options are quite simple to use. Simply type the mode name and WBAdmin performs the required task without any additional input. For example, when you use the Stop Job mode,

WBAdmin stops the current backup or recovery without asking for any additional information. Since you can run only one job at a time, the process is quite simple.

The Get Versions and Get Status modes also provide simple output. When working with Get Versions, you see a list of backups you have performed. The information provided by this mode acts as input to the Get Items mode where you have to supply a specific version. The Get Status mode simply shows the progress of the current backup or recovery.

The last two modes do require additional input from you. The following sections describe these two remaining modes.

Start Backup

The Start Backup mode lets you perform a backup of the system. This mode uses the following syntax:

```
WBADMIN START BACKUP -backupTarget:{TargetVolume | TargetNetworkShare}
-include:VolumesToInclude [-noVerify] [-quiet]
```

The following list describes each of the command line arguments.

-backupTarget:{TargetVolume | TargetNetworkShare} Defines the location of the backup. You must provide a drive letter or a UNC path to a shared location on a network drive.

-include:VolumesToInclude Defines the volumes or mount points that you want to back up. You can't define individual elements such as directories.

-noVerify Performs the backup without a verify. Although this option is considerably faster, it's also quite risky because you don't know whether the backup is any good.

-quiet Creates the backup without displaying the usual messages.

When you start a backup, the system retrieves any required volume information and then displays several messages unless you choose the `-quiet` option. After the backup starts, you'll see several status messages. The status messages continue until the backup is complete.

Get Items

After you create a backup using the Start Backup mode, you can use the Get Versions mode to obtain a list of backups for your system. The version identifier is usually a date and time (GMT, not local). With the version identifier in hand, you can list the items in a backup. This mode uses the following syntax:

```
Usage: WBADMIN GET ITEMS -version:VersionIdentifier
[-backupTarget:{VolumeName | NetworkSharePath}]
[-machine:BackupMachineName]
```

The following list describes each of the command line arguments.

-version:VersionIdentifier Defines the version identifier for the backup that you want to list. Use the Get Versions mode to obtain a list of versions.

-backupTarget:{VolumeName | NetworkSharePath} Defines the backup target you want to use for listing purposes. This option is helpful when you use multiple backup targets.

-machine:BackupMachineName Defines the machine you want to list. This option is helpful when you back up multiple machines in a single version.

Working with ODBC Data Sources

Many people see Open Database Connectivity (ODBC) as old hat—technology that has gone the way of the dinosaur. However, this technology is still alive and well for many applications because it's so universal. You'll find that there are many more ODBC database drivers than any other type for Windows systems. Consequently, even though this technology is outdated, many developers still use it because ODBC is very reliable, available on just about any Windows system, and well understood. The following sections describe two ODBC command line topics.

NOTE This discussion shows how to configure ODBC sources at the command line. It doesn't demonstrate how to create database applications based on those sources, nor does it tell you how to create a data source for a specific vendor product. Refer to a programming manual for your language of choice to discover how to work with ODBC data sources in an application. Your database product manual should contain information about how to configure the database for use with ODBC.

Configuring the ODBC Environment with the ODBCConf Utility

The ODBCConf utility helps you configure ODBC at the command line, rather than using the ODBC Data Source Administrator utility available in the Administrative Tools folder of the Control Panel—listed as the Data Sources (ODBC) console. You can use this utility to configure new data sources, check data source status, and perform other tasks on a remote machine from the command line. This utility uses the following syntax:

```
ODBCConf [/S] [/C] [/R] [/F Filename] [/E] [/L{n | v | d} Filename] [/A {Action}]
```

The following list describes each of the command line arguments.

/S Prevents ODBCConf from displaying any error messages. Normally, it's a better idea to redirect the error message output to an error log when working with a remote system so that you can determine whether the actions succeeded.

/C Forces ODBCConf to continue executing actions even if an action fails. This command line switch works well in situations where you need to perform multiple independent actions.

/R Performs the requested actions after a system reboot.

/F *Filename* Performs actions based on an input file. The response file contains a list of actions and all of the required input information. This option is often the best solution when you plan to perform a configuration on multiple machines or multiple times on the same machine.

/E Erase the response file when the action completes. Use this command line switch with the /F switch.

/L{n | v | d} *Filename* Sets the ODBCConf utility to output a log. You must provide a logging mode of (n)ormal, (v)erbose, or (d)ebug, along with a filename for the log. For example, `/Lv MyLog.LOG` would output a log in verbose mode to the `MyLog.LOG` file. The normal mode outputs the least information, while the debug mode outputs the most information. Using debug mode consumes considerable disk space and slows execution of any actions. You must use this command line switch to see any changes that ODBCConf makes since the utility doesn't display successful actions.

/A *{Action}* Defines one or more actions to perform. The action must appear within curly brackets ({ }).

The ODBCConf utility requires some type of action input to perform any task. You can provide a list of actions directly on the command line or you can use a response file. When working at the command line, you can include multiple `/A` command line switch entries. The ODBCConf utility executes these switches in order, so you must create the command line to reflect the required order. For example, you can't register a new Microsoft Data Access Components (MDAC) version until after you register its accompanying server. The following list describes each of the documented actions for the ODBCConf utility (some people have reported undocumented actions that I wasn't able to confirm).

REGMDACVERSION Version Registers a new version of the MDAC as specified by the Version argument. Normally, Microsoft performs this task for you as part of installing the new MDAC on your machine.

SETFILEDSNDIR Changes the File DSN directory to the specified value. The default setting is the `\Program Files\Common Files\ODBC\Data Sources` directory.

TIP Whenever you work with directory names that contain spaces, always enclose the directory name in double quotes. For example, to change the File DSN directory, you might type **`ODBCConf /lv ODBCConf.log /a {SETFILEDSNDIR "F:\Program Files\Common Files\ODBC\Data Sources"}`**. Notice that the directory name is enclosed in double quotes so that the command line utility treats it as a single entity.

INSTALLDRVRMGR Installs a new driver manager.

INSTALLDRIVER Configuration Path Installs a new ODBC driver. The configuration argument is the configuration name, which you modify using the CONFIGDRIVER action. You must obtain this information from the database vendor. In fact, some vendors, such as Oracle, do provide files with all of the required information provided. The path is the location of the new driver.

INSTALLTRANSLATOR Configuration Path Installs a new code page translator. The configuration argument is a name that you use to reference the code page translator configuration. Modify the configuration using the CONFIGDRIVER action. You must obtain the configuration data from the database vendor. The path is the location of the new driver.

CONFIGDRIVER Name Parameters Configures a driver for use. The name argument is the name of the driver configuration supplied as part of an INSTALLDRIVER or INSTALLTRANSLATOR action. The parameters argument contains name value pairs that define the configuration for the driver. The name is followed by an equals sign, which is followed by the argument. You can use this action to configure an existing driver on the user's machine as long as you know the driver configuration name.

CONFIGDSN Name DSN | Attributes Creates a new user DSN entry that's accessible only by the current user. The name is the name of the driver supplied during installation. The DSN is the name of the DSN as it will appear in the ODBC Data Source Administrator utility. The attributes describe the information required to make the database connection. For example, a SQL Server DSN might include these arguments: `"SQL Server" "DSN=Northwind|Server=(Local)|Description=SQL Server|Database=Northwind||"`. In this case, the DSN uses the SQL Server configuration. The action creates a DSN named Northwind that uses the (Local) instance of SQL Server and the Northwind database.

CONFIGSYSDSN Name DSN | Attributes Creates a new system DSN entry that's accessible by everyone on a particular machine. In all other ways, this action works like the CONFIGDSN action.

REGSVR Path Registers a new MDAC server on the machine. The path argument specifies the location of the server DLL. You normally combine this action with the REGMDACVERSION action to register a new MDAC server.

Creating an ODBC Data Source at the Command Line

More than a few people have experienced problems using the ODBCConf utility because it often requires use of complex command line syntax. However, there's an easier way of adding an ODBC data source to remote machine. Simply add the data source using a file DSN. These DSN files normally appear in the `\Program Files\Common Files\ODBC\Data Sources` folder of the remote system. Adding a DSN file automatically adds the DSN to the remote machine. (The application must take the file DSN into account or adding the DSN using this technique might not work.)

Although every database uses a different configuration strategy, the file DSN is always a text file with a DSN extension. It's essentially a form of INI (initialization or configuration) file. Here's an example file DSN for an Access database.

```
[ODBC]
DRIVER=Microsoft Access Driver (*.mdb)
UID=admin
UserCommitSync=Yes
Threads=3
SafeTransactions=0
PageTimeout=5
MaxScanRows=8
MaxBufferSize=2048
FIL=MS Access
DriverId=25
DefaultDir=G:\Access
DBQ=G:\Access\db1.mdb
```

Notice that this DSN includes such information as the database driver and the user identifier. It also includes the location of the Access database and other information to control access to it. You can easily create such a file using the ODBC Data Source Administrator utility, make any required changes to the text file for the remote system, and then copy it to the remote system's file DSN directory.

Managing the Windows Registry

You can perform an amazing number of tasks on the registry from the command line, which is very useful because a registry repair from the recovery console can make an unbootable system bootable. The following sections explore several registry utilities that you can use at the command line. The most powerful of these utilities is RegEdit, which lets you add, delete, copy, save, restore, export, or import all or part of the registry.

WARNING This chapter doesn't provide detailed information about the inner workings of the registry. Make sure you have a good backup of any system before you make changes to the registry. Exercise caution in making registry changes even when you have a good backup. Never make a change to the registry unless you fully understand what the change will do.

Modifying the Registry with the RegEdit Utility

The RegEdit utility is an extremely powerful utility, yet it's one of the most undocumented utilities available on your machine. The Microsoft recommended command line switches for the RegEdit utility appear in the Knowledge Base article at `http://support.microsoft.com/kb/q82821/`. The Knowledge Base article limits you to the /V and /S command line switches. The RegEdit utility itself doesn't display any helpful information when you try the /? command line switch. The Windows help file just barely discusses using the utility in GUI mode. In short, not only is this utility extremely powerful but you won't get much help from Microsoft in using it. This utility uses the following syntax:

```
RegEdit [Filename] [-v] [-s] [-e RegFilename Key] [-l:Path] [-r:Path]
     [-c RegFilename] [-d Key]
```

The following list describes each of the command line arguments.

`Filename` Specifies the name of a file that contains registry information. A registry file normally has a REG file extension. You can use a batch file to restore previously saved registry entries. For example, you might use this technique to set up a new system with user settings that you saved earlier.

`-v` Opens RegEdit in advanced (verbose) mode. If you're familiar with the standard registry appearance, you'll suddenly notice some registry keys that RegEdit didn't display before. Use this option with care; all of the registry settings are editable if you have the proper permissions and the new settings tend to have dramatic system results.

`-s` Suppresses any informational messages. You can use this feature to make a batch file installation work in the background.

-e RegFilename Key Exports the requested key to the specified registry file. You can use this command line switch within a batch file to save user settings prior to a system change. For example, typing **`Regedit -e Test.REG "HKEY_CURRENT_USER\Software\Nico Mak Computing"`** and pressing Enter at the command prompt will save the WinZip application settings to a file named `Test.REG`. Notice that you must enclose keys with spaces in the name in double quotes to ensure the RegEdit utility will interpret them correctly.

`-l:`*`Path`* Specifies the path for the `System.DAT` file to edit in the registry. The system database contains systemwide settings such as the `HKEY_LOCAL_MACHINE` hive. You can use this option to edit a registry on another machine as long as that machine allows remote editing. Use this option with the `-c` command line switch to create a new user based on an existing setup.

`-r:`*`Path`* Specifies the path for the `User.DAT` file to edit in the registry. The user database appears in the individual user directories and contains the `HKEY_CURRENT_USER` hive. You can use this option to edit a registry on another machine as long as that machine allows remote editing. Use this option with the `-c` command line switch to create a new user based on an existing setup.

`-c` ***`RegFilename`*** Creates a new registry based on the content of the registry entries in `RegFilename`. This command line switch is destructive. It completely destroys the `System.DAT` and `User.DAT` files for the affected user and reconstructs them using the contents of the supplied registry file. With this in mind, you must use this command line switch with a registry file containing a full registry backup. Otherwise, you'll leave the system in an unbootable state.

`-d` ***`Key`*** Deletes the specified key. This switch appears to work fine on Windows 9*x* systems, but doesn't work with Windows NT and above. The command line switch deletes the requested key from the registry.

It's unfortunate that the -d command line switch doesn't work on newer systems. One way around this problem for Windows XP and above users is to create a negative key registry file and then register it as normal. To create such a file, open Notepad or any other text editor. Enter the following code into the file.

```
REGEDIT4
[-HKEY_CLASSES_ROOT\Test]
```

The negative key entry will delete a key named Test from the HKEY_CLASSES_ROOT hive. Try creating the HKEY_CLASSES_ROOT\Test key and then running this file. You'll find that RegEdit removes the key without any problem.

Scripting Registry Entries with the RegIni Utility

The RegIni utility lets you perform registry manipulations that involve security or other configurations. You can also use it to perform a list of registry modifications as a script, rather than individually using RegEdit. The most common use of this utility is to modify the security settings for the registry as explained by the Knowledge Base article at http://support.microsoft.com/?kbid=245031. The Knowledge Base article at http://support.microsoft.com/?kbid=237607 has additional information on using this utility for security purposes. You can find a more complete discussion of how to use RegIni, including creating scripts using a number of techniques, on the Windows IT Library site at http://www.windowsitlibrary.com/Content/237/2.html. This utility uses the following syntax:

```
RegIni [-m \\computername] scriptname
```

The following list describes each of the command line arguments.

scriptname Specifies the name of the file containing the registry script.

-m *computername* Specifies the name of the computer on which to perform the modifications. The default is the local computer.

Adding and Removing Servers with the RegSvr32 Utility

Your machine has a wealth of Component Object Model (COM) servers installed on it. These servers perform a broad array of tasks too numerous to mention here. In all cases, these servers make a lot of registry entries; even a simple server makes a lot of entries and you won't want to add or delete them manually. Fortunately, the RegSvr32 utility makes it easy to add and remove COM server entries. This utility uses the following syntax:

```
RegSvr32 [/u] [/s] [/i[:Arguments] /n] Filename
```

The following list describes each of the command line arguments.

Filename The name of the file that contains the COM server. In most cases, the file will have a DLL extension, but it could have a number of other extensions including EXE and OCX.

/u Unregisters a server.

/s Suppresses any informational messages. Using this option lets you create an installation batch file.

/i[:Arguments] Calls a special function within the COM server named DllInstall. You may optionally pass command line arguments. The server vendor will provide you with a list of command line arguments that you can pass the COM server.

/n Suppresses the call to the standard DllRegisterServer function within the COM server. This special function normally registers the server for you, making all of the required registry entries. You can only use this command line switch with the `/i` switch.

Getting Started with Command Line Tasks

This chapter has demonstrated the many commands and utilities that Windows provides for working with data of all types. Data is the lifeblood of any computer system and it's likely the lifeblood of your business as well. Without proper data management techniques, intruders can easily compromise your data and you'll have a very hard time getting it back. Even though you can maintain your data using GUI tools, the detailed view of command line utilities in this chapter should show you that Windows has a lot more to offer than you might have thought.

The most important task you can perform with your newfound command line knowledge is to create a backup of your system. Start by creating a backup of your registry. Once you have the registry backup on your hard drive, create backups of all of your essential data. Of course, you don't necessarily need to back up every application on your hard drive, but make sure that every bit of data does appear as part of your backup list.

Chapter 3 moves on to system status information. Knowing what your system is doing at any given time is important. Crackers have a very difficult time infiltrating systems where everyone is aware of what is going on. Even when they do manage to overcome your defenses, they can't stay very long if you're aware of their every activity. It's not a perfect solution, but exercising awareness is one of the best ways of keeping other people out of your system. In addition, by exercising awareness, you can also detect drops in performance and reliability as equipment ages. In fact, perceptive users can often detect an impending hardware failure long before it actually occurs.

Chapter 3

Discovering the System Status

- Getting System Status Information
- Recording System Status Information
- Working with Performance Information

Without the proper tools, it's easy to become confused about the status of your system. The hard drive light goes on even though you haven't touched the machine for the last minute or so and you may wonder what's happening. What you don't know about the system status can be harmful. Knowing the system status can alert you to all kinds of problems that can remain otherwise hidden. For example, by knowing the system status, you can detect a failing hard drive or power supply long before the device actually fails. This information gives you time to plan for a replacement, rather than react to a failure. System information can also alert you to viruses and covert user activity. Being aware of your computer surroundings is always a good idea.

This chapter won't try to persuade you that Windows has everything needed to maintain perfect control over system status information. In fact, even Microsoft admits that there's a strong need for third party utilities for managing Windows. However, Windows provides a lot more in the way of system status information than you might think. Obtaining this information isn't always as easy as it could be, but at least it's available so you can begin working with your system more fully today, rather than waiting for a third party product to arrive in the mail. In addition, these utilities are part of the operating system, so they're always available. Knowing they exist and understanding how to use them can help you overcome problems with systems even if they don't have your favorite third party product installed.

The utilities described in this chapter fall into two categories. The first are static utilities, such as DriverQuery, that provide good output for reports. These utilities take a snapshot of your system that you can use for comparison purposes later. The second are dynamic utilities, such as PerfMon, that provide constant output that you can use to monitor your system in real time. These utilities work well for diagnosing system problems. You can use them for troubleshooting or locating problems that only appear after long-term monitoring.

Getting System Status Information

Getting system status information, something static that you can view quickly to determine the state of your system, is an important part of tracking your system as a whole. For example, you might not know which drivers are running on your system right now, but you should. Knowing which drivers are running when your system's performing well can clue you into problems with your system later. Interestingly enough, some of the utilities that Microsoft provides for gamers are also your best friends for tracking hardware status.

Choosing between Command Line and Graphical Interfaces

A number of these utilities have graphical interfaces that this chapter doesn't discuss. For example, the DXDiag utility provides a very helpful graphical interface where you can interactively test a wealth of hardware on your system. Although this chapter concentrates on the command line interface for obtaining system status information, it's important to remember that the graphical interfaces have uses too.

Think about the graphical interface as the real-time, hands-on interface. You'll use it when you want to interact directly with the application. This is the mode to use when you're training someone. The graphical interface is easier for most people to understand, even when it isn't the most efficient way to use the application.

The command line interface is the one to use when efficiency and automation are the goals. In many cases, you'll use the command line interface for performing automated testing that you schedule with the Task Scheduler (see Chapter 10 for details on using the Task Scheduler). You can view the output later (when it's convenient) to check on the health of your system.

NOTE Windows has a number of older utilities included with it. One of those utilities is the PentNT utility. At one time, Intel released a version of its Pentium processor with a floating-point division flaw (learn more about this problem at `http://support.intel.com/support/processors/pentium/sb/CS-013008.htm`). The PentNT utility helps you overcome this particular problem. Most people have replaced their Pentium computers long ago, so this chapter doesn't provide detailed information about the PentNT utility. In most cases, Vista has eliminated these older utilities.

Obtaining Driver Information with the DriverQuery Utility

The DriverQuery utility displays a complete list of the drivers loaded on your system. Generally, you'll use this utility after you install the operating system to record the clean state of your system, and then after each major upgrade, including operating system service packs. By tracking the driver state of your system, you can determine when system errors are the result of faulty or incompatible drivers. This utility uses the following syntax:

```
DRIVERQUERY [/S system [/U username [/P [password]]]] [/FO format]
[/NH] [/SI] [/V]
```

The following list describes each of the command line arguments.

/S *system* Specifies the remote system that you want to check. In most cases, you'll also need to supply the /U and the /P command line switches when using this switch.

/U [*domain*\]*user* Specifies the username on the remote system. This name may not match the username on the local system. You'll need to supply a domain name when working with a domain controller.

/P [*password*] Specifies the password for the given user. You can provide the command line switch without specifying the password on the command line in cleartext. The system prompts you for the password. Using this feature can help you maintain the security of passwords used on your system.

/FO {TABLE | LIST | CSV} Defines the output provided by the utility. The table format is normally the easiest to view on screen. The table columns define the values for output, while each row contains one driver entry. The Comma Separated Value (CSV) output provides the best method for preparing the data for entry in a database. Use redirection (see the "Employing Data Redirection" section of Chapter 2 for details) to output the CSV data to a file and then import it to your database. The list format provides one data element per line. Each group of data elements defines one driver. The utility separates each driver by one blank line. Some people find the list format more readable when working in verbose mode since the table format requires multiple lines for each entry (the lines wrap).

/NH Forces the utility to display the data without a column header. You can only use this command line switch with the table and CSV formats. Omitting the header makes it easier to incorporate the data in a report or import it into a database.

/V Displays detailed data about each of the drivers. In addition to the standard output, the utility provides the driver description, start mode state, status, whether it accepts the stop command, whether it accepts the pause command, the size of the paged memory pool, the initial memory size, and the path to the driver file. This last column can provide you with helpful information about invasive drivers. Most standard drivers appear in the `\Windows\System32\` or `\Windows\System32\Drivers` directory. You can't use this switch with the `/SI` command line switch.

/SI Provides details about driver signing. The information includes the device name, the information (INF) filename, whether Microsoft signed the driver, and the device driver manufacturer.

When used by itself, the DriverQuery utility provides a report about the local system that includes the module name, the display name (the name the user sees), driver type, and the date the vendor built the driver. The output is in a tabular format. The command line switches give you a great deal of flexibility as to the form of output and the content.

Obtaining DirectX Status with the DXDiag Utility

Normally, you'll use the DirectX Diagnostic (DXDiag) utility in graphical mode because it provides a wealth of diagnostic tests and essential system information, at least for devices that you could possibly use for multimedia or gaming. The command line interface focuses more on recording the information in a permanent form for future reference. This utility uses the following syntax:

```
DXDiag [/X Outfile] [/T Outfile] [WHQL:{On | Off}]
```

The following list describes each of the command line arguments.

[/X *Outfile*] Outputs the DirectX data as XML. This feature works well for database import, but it isn't particularly easy to read directly by a human reader.

[/T *Outfile*] Outputs the DirectX data as text. This feature works well when you intend to read the DirectX data directly.

[WHQL:{On | Off}] Sets the Windows Hardware Quality Labs (WHQL) check on or off. This check verifies the digital signatures for the various drivers. You'll likely require an Internet connection to use this feature since the utility checks Microsoft's latest database of drivers.

NOTE The DXDiag utility returns immediately when you execute a command. The file may not appear for several minutes after the command completes execution. Consequently, don't execute the DXDiag utility several times because you don't see the output immediately.

Monitoring the File System with the FSUtil Utility

Many people take the file system for granted. After all, it just stores data on disk. However, the file system is a lot more complex than you might initially think. Not only does it have to read and write data, it also must create, delete, and edit files. The file system has to track directories and perform a number of other management tasks. It has to do all this without losing a single bit. It isn't until you start working with a utility such as File System Utility (FSUtil) that you begin to understand just how complex the file system is. FSUtil provides several modes of operation including:

- Behavior
- Dirty
- File
- FSInfo
- Hardlink
- ObjectID
- Quota
- ReparsePoint
- Sparse
- USN
- Volume

In addition to these modes, Vista offers a number of additional modes that support the special file system features it provides. Here's a list of the Vista-specific modes.

- Repair
- Resource
- Transaction

Each of these modes helps you manage a different aspect of the file system. For example, the behavior mode queries and sets the file system behavior parameters and controls how the file system reacts in a given situation. The following sections describe each of these operational modes in detail.

BEHAVIOR

The behavior mode controls how the file system works. For example, you can modify the use of the older DOS 8-character filename, with 3-character file extension. Vista adds a number of new options to this mode, all of which are marked by the special Vista icon. This mode uses the following syntax:

```
FSUtil Behavior Query [allowextchar] [disable8dot3]
   [disablecompression] [disableencryption] [disablelastaccess]
   [encryptpagingfile] [mftzone] [memoryusage] [quotanotify]
   [SymlinkEvaluation]
FSUtil Behavior Set [allowextchar {1 | 0}] [disable8dot3 {1 | 0}]
   [disablecompression {1 | 0}] [disableencryption {1 | 0}]
   [disablelastaccess {1 | 0}] [encryptpagingfile {1 | 0}]
```

```
[mftzone Zone] [memoryusage Value] [quotanotify Value]
[SymlinkEvaluation [L2L:{0|1}] | [L2R:{0|1}] | [R2R:{0|1}] |
[R2L:{0|1}]]
```

When querying a value, all you supply is the option name. However, when you set an option, you must also provide a new value. The following list describes each of the command line arguments.

allowextchar {1 | 0} Determines whether you can use extended characters, including diacritic characters used for languages other than English, in the short filenames on NTFS volumes. The default setting doesn't provide a value for this option. Setting the value to 1, or true, allows you to use the extended character set.

disable8dot3 {1 | 0} Determines whether Windows supports older DOS naming conventions or uses extended filenames exclusively. The older DOS naming conventions relied on an 8-character filename and a 3-character file extension. Disabling this support could cause some older applications to fail. The default value is 0, or false, which means that the older DOS naming convention is available.

disablecompression {1 | 0} Disables compression for the affected file system object. The default value is 0, or false, which means that compression is available.

disableencryption {1 | 0} Disables data encryption for the affected file system object. The default value is 0, or false, which means that encryption is available.

disablelastaccess {1 | 0} Determines whether Windows changes the last access time stamp for a directory or file each time you list the directory contents on an NTFS volume. The default setting doesn't provide a value for this option. Setting this option to 1, or true, will increase disk performance slightly, but then you'll lack last access time statistics when working with the drive.

encryptpagingfile {1 | 0} Encrypts the paging file to ensure third parties can obtain information about your system by reading it. For example, it may be possible to read passwords as part of the paging file under certain conditions. Using this setting incurs a significant performance penalty. The default value is 0, or false, which means that the paging file isn't encrypted.

mftzone *Zone* Changes the Master File Table (MFT) zone value. Learn more about the MFT at `http://www.microsoft.com/resources/documentation/Windows/XP/all/reskit/en-us/prkc_fil_rpjv.asp`. The Windows NT File System (NTFS) normally sets aside 12.5 percent of the disk (zone 1) to hold the MFT so that it doesn't become fragmented. Generally, this value provides more than sufficient space for data entries. Each zone (values 1 through 4) provides additional space for the MFT: 1 (12.5 percent), 2 (25 percent), 3 (37.5 percent), and 4 (50 percent). Any change to the MFT zone won't take effect until you reboot the system. Generally, you want to set this value before you do anything else with a new hard drive to ensure the MFT zone doesn't become fragmented.

memoryusage *Value* Controls the amount of paged memory used for file operations within Vista. The default value of 1 uses the default amount of paged memory for file operations. Setting the value to 2 increases the amount of paged memory available for file operations. However, this feature can have unwanted side effects. The added file operation memory only nets increased performance when you don't take paged memory away from other areas of the operation system. Generally, you'll need to experiment with this setting and monitor its effect on overall system performance before you make it permanent.

quotanotify *Value* Defines the interval between disk quota violation checks on an NTFS drive. The disk quota system ensures that a user doesn't use more resources than the administrator allows. The default setting is 3,600 seconds or 1 hour when you enable the quota system. You can supply any value between 1 second and 4,294,967,295 seconds. Longer intervals enhance system performance, but could result in more quota violations.

SymlinkEvaluation [L2L:{0|1}] | [L2R:{0|1}] | [R2R:{0|1}] | [R2L:{0|1}] Determines the use of symbolic links within the operating system. You can individually set the use of local-to-local (L2L), local-to-remote (L2R), remote-to-remote (R2R), and remote-to-local (R2L) links in Vista. The default value for L2L and L2R is 1, or true, which means that these symbolic links are enabled. The default value for R2R and R2L links is 0, or false, which means that you can't create these link types.

DIRTY

Use this mode to check or set the dirty bit for a volume. The system automatically performs an AutoChk whenever it detects the dirty bit during startup. The AutoChk utility looks for drive errors. This mode uses the following syntax:

```
FSUtil Dirty Query Volume
FSUtil Dirty Set Volume
```

The following describes the command line argument.

Volume Determines the NTFS volume to check during the next reboot. This utility only works with local volumes, so you can't query or set the dirty bit on a remote volume.

FILE

The file mode lets you perform tasks with files. Some of the tasks are quite mundane. For example, you can create a new file of a specific size. The file mode will even fill the file with zeros for you. Other tasks are unique. The `findbysid` argument lets you locate a file using its Security Identifier (SID). This mode uses the following syntax:

```
FSUtil File [findbysid UserName Directory] [queryallocranges
Offset=StartRange Length=RangeLength Filename] [setshortname Filename
ShortFilename] [setvaliddata Filename DataLength] [setzerodata
Offset=StartRange Length=RangeLength Filename] [createnew Filename Length]
```

The following list describes each of the command line arguments.

findbysid *UserName Directory* Locates a file based on the user's SID. The `username` argument contains a local user's name, which the operating system maps to the SID. FSUtil then locates the file based on this SID in the directory supplied. Unlike other command line utilities, this one lets you search for files that belong to specific users on an NTFS volume.

queryallocranges Offset=*StartRange Length=RangeLength Filename* Displays a list of allocated ranges within the specified file. The `Offset` argument defines the starting point of the search, while the `Length` argument specifies the length of the search. You can use this command to locate sparse regions within files. See the "Understanding Sparse Files" sidebar for additional information.

setshortname *Filename ShortFilename* Sets the short (DOS) filename for a file. The short filename must fall within the 8-character filename and 3-character extension limitations. The `Dir` command won't normally display the results of this command. However, using the `/X` command line switch with the `Dir` command displays both the long and the short filename.

`setvaliddata` ***`Filename DataLength`*** Sets the valid data length for a file. The Valid Data Length (VDL) is the length of the valid data within a file, rather than the actual file length as indicated by an End Of File (EOF) marker. The data between the VDL and the EOF may contain data, as in a download cache, but any query to that data returns a 0 since the data isn't valid. Because of the low-level nature of this particular argument, only administrators with the SetManageVolumePrivilege can execute it.

`setzerodata Offset=`***`StartRange`*** ***Length*=*`RangeLength`*** ***`Filename`*** Changes the data bits within a file to 0. This is an excellent method of clearing a file before deleting it for security reasons (deleting a file retains the data on disk; Windows only removes the directory entries, making the file recoverable). The start range determines the starting point within the file for writing zeros. The start of the file is 0, but you can use any range up to the size of the file in bytes. The range length determines how many zeros to write. This value must be less than or equal to the length of the file minus the start range value.

`createnew` ***`Filename Length`*** Creates a new file that FSUtil fills with zeros. You must include a filename and the length of the file. Because these files are zeroed, they make excellent test files for other file utilities.

UNDERSTANDING SPARSE FILES

It's possible for a file to contain some data in addition to large ranges of zeros (or null data). A cache file could fall into this category. You might allocate 1 MB for the cache, but the cache file could contain only a little data; the rest of the file contains zeros. The part of the file that contains zeros wastes disk space. There's no reason to allocate an entire 1 MB storage location for a file that contains 10 KB of data. The term for such a file is *sparse*. Generally, you want to manage sparse files so they use the minimum space necessary, yet continue to provide full functionality to the application that creates the sparse file.

The most common Windows application that uses sparse files is the indexing service. You define the size of the catalogs as part of creating a new catalog. However, the catalog might not actually contain that much information. Rather than waste the disk space, the indexing service uses a sparse file to hold the catalog.

Sparse files require special handling. The FSUtil utility provides a number of special commands to work with sparse files. For example, you can use the `queryallocranges` argument of the file mode to locate sparse files on the hard drive. Likewise, the `sparse` mode arguments help you manage sparse files. For example, you can use this mode to set a sparse range within a file. You can learn more about sparse files on the Microsoft Web site at `http://www.microsoft.com/resources/documentation/Windows/XP/all/reskit/en-us/prkc_fil_aixf.asp`.

FSINFO

This mode is one of the more interesting and immediately usable modes. It provides you with statistics regarding the file system. For example, you can use it to obtain a list of active drives on the current system. You could redirect this list to a text file for use with a script or output it to a batch file to perform a task on every attached drive. This mode uses the following syntax:

```
FSUtil FSInfo [drives] [drivetype Volume] [volumeinfo Volume]
[ntfsinfo Volume] [statistics Volume]
```

The following list describes each of the command line arguments.

drives Displays the current list of active drives on the system.

drivetype *Volume* Displays the drive information for the specified volume. The output is a generic term for the drive type such as Fixed Drive or CD-ROM Drive.

volumeinfo *Volume* Displays statistics about the specified volume including the volume name, volume serial number, maximum component length, and file system name. In addition, the output tells whether the drive supports case-sensitive filenames, Unicode in filenames, file-based compression, disk quotas, sparse files, reparse points, object identifiers, encrypted file system, and named streams. Finally, you can determine whether the volume preserves the case of filenames, and if it preserves and enforces Access Control Lists (ACLs).

ntfsinfo *Volume* Displays the low-level statistics about the NTFS volume. This information includes NTFS version, number of sectors, total clusters, free clusters, total reserved clusters, bytes per sector, bytes per cluster, bytes per file record segment, and clusters per file record segment. In addition, you can learn the following MFT statistics: valid data length, start location (MFT1 and MFT2), zone start, and zone end.

statistics *Volume* Displays a list of the operational statistics for the specified volume. The statistics include the following user information: UserFileReads, UserFileReadBytes, UserDiskReads, UserFileWrites, UserFileWriteBytes, and UserDiskWrites. These are all standard counters, so you can also access them using the Performance console. In addition to user information, you can obtain metadata, MFT, root file, and log file statistics.

HARDLINK

A hard link is a connection between two files. The new file that you create is a pointer to the existing file. In essence, you're creating another directory entry to a single file. The file continues to exist until you remove all of the directory entries pointing to it. Any change you make to the content of the new file also appears within the existing file, and vice versa. The main reason to use hard links is to create the same file in multiple locations on the hard drive. For example, you might need to use the same initialization file with multiple applications. Instead of copying the file multiple times, you can simply create multiple hard links to it. This mode uses the following syntax:

```
FSUtil Hardlink Create NewFilename Filename
```

The following list describes each of the command line arguments.

NewFilename The name of the new file to create from the existing file. The new file is simply a directory entry, not an actual copy of the file.

Filename The name of the existing file. You can include a drive and either relative or absolute path information to the file, along with the filename.

OBJECTID

Files on NTFS volumes have four identifiers: object, birth volume, birth object, and domain. Each of these identifiers is a 16-byte hexadecimal number in the form of `17e0b9211e61da11879e0013d4337d7d`. The first three identifiers always have a value; the fourth identifier (domain) isn't currently used. Generally, unless a file is damaged in some way, you should never need to change the identifiers. This mode uses the following syntax:

```
FSUtil ObjectID [query Filename] [set ObjectId BirthVolumeId
BirthObjectId DomainId Filename] [delete Filename] [create Filename]
```

The following list describes each of the command line arguments.

Filename Specifies the name of the file to query or modify.

ObjectId Contains a 16-byte hexadecimal number that uniquely identifies the file on a particular volume. This identifier is extremely important because the Distributed Link Tracking (DLT) Client service and the File Replication Service (FRS) use it to identify files. This identifier can change when you move a file from one volume to another. However, the BirthVolumeId and BirthObjectId values never change, so Windows can always identify a particular file using these values no matter where you move it.

BirthVolumeId Contains a 16-byte hexadecimal number that identifies the initial file volume. The DLT Client service uses this value to identify moved files.

BirthObjectId Contains a 16-byte hexadecimal number that reflects the file's initial ObjectID. The DLT Client service uses this value to identify moved files.

DomainId Contains a 16-byte hexadecimal value of all zeros. Windows doesn't currently use this identifier and you should always set it to 0.

query Displays the ObjectId, BirthVolumeId, BirthObjectId, and DomainId for the specified file.

set Changes the ObjectId, BirthVolumeId, BirthObjectId, and DomainId of the specified file.

delete Removes the ObjectId, BirthVolumeId, BirthObjectId, and DomainId from the specified file.

create Adds an ObjectId, BirthVolumeId, BirthObjectId, and DomainId to the specified file. Windows automatically generates unique identifiers for you.

QUOTA

Quotas help keep resource usage under control on systems with multiple users. Each user receives a specific amount of disk space to use for personal needs. Every file that has the user as an owner counts against the total. When the user exceeds their quota, the system informs both the user and the administrator (using a system of violation notifications). This mode uses the following syntax:

```
FSUtil Quota [disable Path] [track Path] [enforce Path]
[violations] [modify Path Threshold Limit User] [query Path]
```

The following list describes each of the command line arguments.

Path Specifies the target path (generally an entire volume) for a particular quota action. The path can include a drive specification. It can also rely on an absolute or relative path specification.

Threshold Defines the amount of space in bytes that the user can use on the drive before the system alerts the user to a possible limit violation. The user still has additional space on the drive, but the threshold is normally the point at which the user should consider cleaning up old files. The threshold is a warning point.

Limit Defines the amount of space in bytes that the user can access on the drive. Generally, the system begins issuing warnings for every disk activity at this point. Depending on the quota setup, the drive could prohibit additional drive use. The user must clean up old files on the hard drive after reaching the limit.

User Specifies the Windows account that has a quota attached to it.

disable Stops quota tracking and enforcement for the specified resource.

track Enables quota tracking for the specified resource. This option doesn't enable enforcement of any rules you have in place.

enforce Enables quota enforcement for the specified resource. This option doesn't enable tracking.

violations Displays a list of quota violations found in the event log. If the event log doesn't have any quota violations, the utility displays a "No quota violations detected" message. The utility checks both the System and Application logs for both quota threshold and quota limit violations.

modify Changes the quota settings for a particular user. You must supply the drive, threshold, limit, and user inputs when using this option.

query Displays the query settings for the specified resource. In addition to the actual quota settings, this command displays the per user settings. This information includes the user SID, change time, quota used, quota threshold, and quota limit.

VISTA

REPAIR

This is a new mode for Vista that lets you repair a file system object from the command line. This mode uses the following syntax:

```
FSUtil Repair [query Volume] [set Volume Flags] [wait FSObject]
[initiate Volume FileReference]
```

The following list describes each of the command line arguments.

query *Volume* Determines the repair status of the specified volume. The repair status defines what kinds of repairs you can perform on the volume. The status includes any of the following values.

1 The volume supports general repair.

8 The volume warns about potential data loss when performing a repair.

set *Volume Flags* Changes the repair status of the specified volume. The flag contains a number that specifies the repair status. See the query keyword for a list of acceptable values.

wait *FSObject* Tells the FSUtil to wait for the specified file system object repairs before performing any other tasks.

initiate *Volume FileReference* Performs a repair of the specified file on the referenced volume. To use this feature, you must provide the segment number of the file.

REPARSEPOINT

The ReparsePoint mode helps you manage Windows reparse points. A reparse point is a collection of user data, usually from a remote source. An application creates the reparse point by saving the data to a file along with some special configuration information. You can learn more about reparse points on the Microsoft Web site at `http://msdn.microsoft.com/library/en-us/fileio/fs/reparse_points.asp`. Normally, you'll rely on an application to create the reparse point. However, the Knowledge Base article at `http://support.microsoft.com/?kbid=205524` tells you how to create and manipulate them manually. In this case, the reparse point creates a link between another drive and a directory on the hard drive. To gain a better understanding of how you can use reparse points on an active system, read the Knowledge Base article at `http://support.microsoft.com/default`

`.aspx?scid=kb;en-us;Q262797`. Because of the way the system creates reparse points, you can only use FSUtil to query and delete them. This mode uses the following syntax:

```
FSUtil ReparsePoint [query Filename] [delete Filename]
```

The following list describes each of the command line arguments.

`Filename` Defines the path used as a junction or the filename of the user data storage. Whether the input defines a path or a filename (with an optional path) depends on the kind of reparse point in use.

`query` Requests information about the specified reparse point. The information includes the reparse tag created when the system defined the reparse point. The tag information varies, but can include the reparse tag value, one or more tag values, a Globally Unique Identifier (GUID), the data length, and the actual reparse data.

TIP Directories used as reparse points normally have a special icon attached to them, rather than using the standard folder icon. In the case of a drive, the icon is a special drive symbol. In other words, even though the entity is a directory, the system is treating it as a drive attached to that directory. If you delete the reparse point, the directory remains, but the icon changes back to a standard folder icon and the remote data is no longer available.

`delete` Removes the specified reparse point.

VISTA

Resource

This is a new mode for Vista that helps you interact with Transactional Resource Managers. A Transactional Resource Manager is a managed construct that provides a method of tracking and optionally reversing change to file system objects. You must use this mode to create, discover, and modify the folder used to hold the transaction information, including the transaction logs. Use the Transaction mode to work with the transactions contained in the log. This mode uses the following syntax:

```
FSUtil Resource [create Path] [info Path]
[setautoreset {True | False} RootPath] [setlog Options]
[start Path [RMLogPath TMLogPath]] [stop Path]
```

The setlog option requires additional explanation. The following list describes each of the other command line arguments.

`create` ***`Path`*** Creates a new folder that holds the logs for a Transactional Resource Manager. The path must not already exist. Creating the folder is the first step in defining a secondary Transactional Resource Manager. Once you create the folder, you must start the Transactional Resource Manager using the start option.

`info` ***`Path`*** Obtains information about any started Transactional Resource Manager. If the target system doesn't have any secondary Transactional Resource Managers running and you type this command without a path, then FSUtil reports the status of the default Transactional Resource Manager for the current drive. You can also access the default Transactional Resource Manager by providing the root directory for the target drive (such as C:\).

`setautoreset {True | False}` ***`RootPath`*** Changes the automatic reset feature for the default Transactional Resource Manager, which is always the root directory of the selected volume (such as C:\). This feature sets the default Transactional Resource Manager to reset all of its metadata each time you reboot the machine. The default setting retains the metadata across reboots to better track system state. You can use this feature to overcome problems with the transactional state of the file system.

start *Path* [*RMLogPath TMLogPath*] Starts the Transactional Resource Manager specified by path. You'll normally use this option to start a secondary manager, rather than the default. In addition to the Transactional Resource Manager folder, you can also specify the path to the log files that the manager uses to track file system transactions.

stop *Path* Stops the Transactional Resource Manager specified by path. You'll normally use this option to stop a secondary manager, rather than the default. While it's possible to stop the default manager, you can't restart it, so this action isn't advisable.

The setlog option of the resource mode lets you modify the log used to record transactions on the system. The log configuration affects just how much Vista can do when it comes to monitoring transactions on your system. This option uses the following syntax:

```
FSUtil Resource setlog
[growth {NumContainers containers Path | Percentage percent Path}]
[maxextents NumContainers Path] [minextents NumContainers Path]
[mode {full Path | undo Path}] [rename Path] [shrink Percentage Path]
[size NumContainers Path]
```

The following list describes the setlog option–specific command line arguments.

growth {*NumContainers* containers *Path* | *Percentage* percent *Path*} Changes the container growth increment. Each container holds a specific amount of data (the default is 10 MB). Every time the Transactional Resource Manager requires additional hard drive space to store transactions, it increases the number of containers. You can set the specific number of containers or grow the number of containers as a percentage of the current total log capacity. Consequently, if you set the value to 10 percent, the default container size is 10 MB, and the total log capacity is 200 MB, then the Transactional Resource Manager will add two containers. The default growth size is two containers.

maxextents *NumContainers Path* Defines the maximum number of containers that a Transactional Resource Manager can create. This setting helps you control hard drive usage by the Transactional Resource Manager. The default setting is 20 containers.

minextents *NumContainers Path* Defines the minimum number of containers that a Transactional Resource Manager can create (usually created at the beginning of a session). This setting can help improve performance by forcing the Transactional Resource Manager to create the full number of containers it requires at the outset, rather than taking time out to create them one or two at a time.

mode {full *Path* | undo *Path*} Determines the mode used to log transactions. The full logging method logs every activity as a transaction. However, this mode uses considerable hard drive space. The undo mode only records transactions required to undo permanent activities, such as erasing a file. The undo mode also appears as Simple when viewing the Transactional Resource Manager statistics.

rename *Path* Assigns a new GUID to the Transactional Resource Manager. The new GUID appears as part of the RM Identifier statistic. There isn't a good reason to use this option and many reasons you shouldn't when working with an application that may rely on the current GUID. In general, the application may cease working or work improperly.

`shrink` *`Percentage Path`* Determines the amount of hard drive space that the Transactional Resource Manager returns to the system when it no longer requires the space for transactions. The default setting doesn't return any hard drive space to the system, so the number of containers will only increase until the Transactional Resource Manager reaches the maximum number of containers.

`size` *`NumContainers Path`* Sets the number of containers available to the Transactional Resource Manager. You can use this option to manually return hard drive space to the system after performing a number of file system object changes.

Real World Scenario

Hard Drives as Databases

Hard drives have always been a kind of database, but operating systems typically don't treat them that way. Consequently, disk drives often suffer failures that databases would never encounter. However, Microsoft steadily adds database features to Windows. Vista is no exception. Although Microsoft's original plan for Vista included a considerable number of other database features that it later dropped, the use of transactions to support disk activities is a significant step forward.

In the real world, the hardware that comprises a hard disk isn't the valuable commodity—it's the data. By using transactions, Vista can reduce the possibility of damage to valuable data. However, transactions are more than a nice feature for Vista. The code for the Transactional Resource Manager actually appears as part of the .NET Framework and developers can rely on this technology to create robust applications. You can read about the developer view of transactions at `http://msdn.microsoft.com/library/en-us/dndotnet/html/introsystemtransact.asp`. Because the application code uses the same functionality as the operating system uses, you can also rely on the Resource and Transaction modes described in this chapter to work with application-specific Transactional Resource Managers.

Sparse

Some applications create large files that contain mostly with zeros. For example, an application may create a large cache to hold temporary data. Sparse file management compresses these files smaller than standard compression can. For a discussion of sparse files, see the "Understanding Sparse Files" sidebar. This mode helps you manage sparse files and uses the following syntax:

```
FSUtil Sparse [setflag Filename] [queryflag Filename]
[queryrange Filename] [setrange Filename Offset Length]
```

The following list describes each of the command line arguments.

`Filename` Specifies the file to manage.

`Offset` Defines the beginning of a sparse range.

`Length` Determines the number of bytes in the sparse range.

`setflag` Adds a sparse attribute to the file to mark it as a sparse file.

`queryflag` Displays status information as to the state of the sparse flag (attribute).

`queryrange` Displays any sparse ranges within the specified file. Each entry contains two numbers. The first number specifies the sparse range offset, while the second number defines the sparse range length.

setrange Sets a sparse range for the specified file. You must provide the offset (in bytes) for the beginning of the sparse range, as well as the number of bytes to include within the sparse range.

Transaction

The Transaction mode is new to Vista. It lets you interact with the transactions currently supported by a Transactional Resource Manager. See the "Resource" section of the chapter for additional details about working with a Transactional Resource Manager. This mode uses the following syntax:

```
FSUtil Transaction [commit GUID] [list] [fileinfo Filename]
[query [{files | all}] GUID] [rollback GUID]
```

The following list describes each of the command line arguments.

commit *GUID* Completes a transaction and makes all of the tasks specified by the entries in the log permanent. You must commit a transaction before the system considers the action completed, even though the file system objects will appear to have all of the changes.

list Displays a list of all of the current transactions.

fileinfo *Filename* Displays the transactional data about a particular file.

query [{files | all}] *GUID* Displays detailed information about the transaction specified by GUID. You can obtain just the file information or all of the transaction details. Use the list option to obtain a list of the current transactions and their associated GUIDs.

rollback *GUID* Undoes all of the changes made to file system objects within the current transaction since the start of the transaction. A rollback returns the file system objects to their prechange state.

USN

You use this mode to manage the Update Sequence Number (USN) for the system. The USN provides a persistent log of all of the changes made to the files on the system. As users add, delete, and modify files and directories, NTFS makes an entry in the USN. Each volume has a separate USN. The main use of the USN for administrators is to check the changes made to one or more files. Using the USN is more efficient than relying on time stamps and you'll receive more information as well. You can find a complete description of the USN on the Microsoft Systems Journal Web site at `http://www.microsoft.com/msj/0999/journal/journal.aspx`. This mode uses the following syntax:

```
FSUtil USN [createjournal m=MaximumSize a=AllocationDelta Volume]
[deletejournal [/D] [/N] Volume] [enumdata FileRef LowUSN HighUSN]
[queryjounral Volume] [readdata Filename]
```

The following list describes each of the command line arguments.

Volume Specifies the NTFS volume to manage. The journal always affects an entire volume. Consequently, even though you can query statistics for an individual file, you must work with a volume when creating or deleting the journal.

Filename Specifies the name of the file to manage. The filename can include both drive and path information.

m=*MaximumSize* Defines the maximum size of the USN journal in bytes. The journal can grow larger than this value, but NTFS truncates it during the next checkpoint to less than this size. The checkpoint size is the maximum size plus the allocation delta. Consequently, if you set the journal size to 1,000 bytes and the allocation delta to 100, then NTFS will automatically truncate the journal when it reaches 1,100 bytes to 900 bytes in size.

a=*AllocationDelta* Determines the delta between a full journal and a truncated journal.

/D Disables a USN journal (rather than deleting it) and returns control of the Input/Output (I/O) of the system immediately. NTFS continues to disable the journal in the background. This option takes more time to complete than the /N option, but lets the user continue working immediately.

/N Disables a USN journal (rather than deleting it) and maintains control of the I/O subsystem. The system won't read or write data to the hard drive while NTFS disables the USN journal. This option completes the process much faster, but requires that the user give up access to the system while the process completes.

FileRef Specifies the ordinal position of the file within the drive hierarchy. Each file has a unique number. This value specifies the starting point for the enumeration.

LowUSN Determines the lowest USN number within a range. Only USNs with numbers that are equal to or higher than this number appear within the range.

HighUSN Determines the highest USN number within a range. Only USNs with numbers lower than or equal to this number appear within the range.

createjournal Creates a new journal for the specified volume. If you set the m and a arguments to 0, Windows determines journal allocation sizes based on the size of the hard drive.

deletejournal Deletes or disables a USN journal. Deleting the journal removes it from the system permanently and could adversely affect applications such as Indexing Service, File Replication Service (FRS), Remote Installation Services (RIS), and Remote Storage that rely on it. Disabling the journal makes it inaccessible, but doesn't free the resources used by the journal.

enumdata Enumerates the change journal entries between two boundaries as specified by the LowUSN and HighUSN arguments for files starting with a specific reference number.

queryjournal Displays the USN journal statistics for the requested volume. This information includes the USN journal identifier, first USN number, next USN number, lowest valid USN, maximum valid USN, maximum size, and allocation delta.

readdata Displays data about the requested file. The information includes the major version, minor version, file reference number, parent file reference number, USN, time stamp, reason, source information, security identifier, file attributes, filename length, filename offset, and filename.

VOLUME

The Volume mode helps you work with volumes directly. This mode uses the following syntax:

```
FSUtil Volume [dismount Drive] [diskfree Drive]
```

The following list describes each of the command line arguments.

Drive Specifies the drive to query or dismount.

dismount Removes a drive from service. Dismounting a volume makes it unavailable for any activity.

diskfree Displays the amount of free space on the drive. The output includes the number of free bytes, the total number of bytes on the drive, and the available number of free bytes (after any allocations).

Managing Volume Labels with the Label Utility

The Label utility creates, deletes, or changes the volume label for a drive. The volume label appears at the top of the hierarchy in applications such as Windows Explorer and helps the user identify the drive. In addition to standard drives, this utility also works with mount points (see the "Reparse-Point" section of the chapter for details). This utility uses the following syntax:

```
LABEL [drive:][label]
LABEL [/MP] [volume] [label]
```

The following list describes each of the command line arguments.

drive: Specifies the letter of the drive to change.

label Defines the new volume label. If you leave the volume label blank, then the Label utility queries you for a volume label. Pressing Enter deletes any existing label. Type a new value and press Enter to change the volume label. Press Ctrl+C to abort the action without changing the label. Volume labels for FAT-formatted drives can only have 11 characters, while NTFS-formatted drives can have volume labels up to 32 characters. You can't use these characters in a label for a FAT-formatted drive: `* ? / \ | . , ; : + = [ ] < > "`.

/MP Specifies that the drive specification is a mount point or a volume, rather than a drive.

volume Defines the mount point or volume name. If you specify a volume name, then you don't need to provide the `/MP` command line switch.

Determining Memory Status with the Mem Utility

Many applications that execute at the command line have strict memory limitations. For example, you might try to run an old DOS application and find that it doesn't work as anticipated (or at all). In some cases, the application will tell you that it lacks sufficient memory, but in other cases, you need to diagnose the problem yourself using the Mem utility. This utility provides you with detailed information about the memory at the command prompt, which differs from the memory that Windows provides. The standard output shows the total amount of conventional memory, the amount of memory available to run applications, the amount of extended memory, and the amount of expanded memory. This utility uses the following syntax:

```
MEM [/PROGRAM | /DEBUG | /CLASSIFY]
```

The following list describes each of the command line arguments.

/PROGRAM or /P Displays the status of programs currently loaded into memory. Use this command line switch to identify applications that you can remove to free memory. Figure 3.1 shows typical output when using this command line switch. Notice that the output lists every memory usage, including the memory used by the command processor for requirements such as the file handles and drives. The size column shows the memory usage for the application or other element in hexadecimal. The `-- Free --` indicator in the Type column shows areas of free memory in the current command prompt.

NOTE The programs loaded into memory for the command prompt aren't the same programs that are loaded into the Windows environment. The list of applications that you see when you view the Applications tab of the Windows Task Manager won't match those shown at the command prompt. The environments are separate. Windows treats the command prompt as a single black box entity, even though it's running one or more applications.

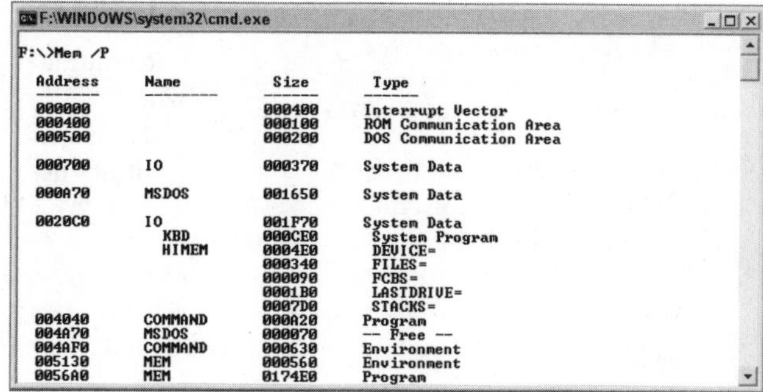

```
F:\WINDOWS\system32\cmd.exe
F:\>Mem /P

Address    Name       Size      Type
-------    ----       ----      ----
000000                000400    Interrupt Vector
000400                000100    ROM Communication Area
000500                000200    DOS Communication Area

000700     IO         000370    System Data

000A70     MSDOS      001650    System Data

0020C0     IO         001F70    System Data
             KBD      000CE0     System Program
             HIMEM    0004E0     DEVICE=
                      000340     FILES=
                      000090     FCBS=
                      0001B0     LASTDRIVE=
                      0007D0     STACKS=
004040     COMMAND    000A20    Program
004A70     MSDOS      000070    -- Free --
004AF0     COMMAND    000630    Environment
005130     MEM        000560    Environment
0056A0     MEM        0174E0    Program
```

FIGURE 3.1
The program mode of the Mem utility describes the way applications use memory.

`/DEBUG` or `/D` Displays the status of the programs, internal drivers, and other elements of the command prompt. Use this command line switch to identify potential problems at the command line prompt. The output from this command line switch looks like a very detailed version of the program output shown in Figure 3.1.

`/CLASSIFY` or `/C` Displays the programs based on memory usage. Categorizes the programs by size, provides a list of memory in use, and displays the largest memory block available. Use this command line switch to check for potential problems in memory allocation. As shown in Figure 3.2, the classify view is a little more readable than the other views and offers the memory allocation sizes in decimal. In addition, you can see the use of upper memory with greater ease.

TIP Not all older applications require more memory. A few older applications actually fail when they have too much memory. If your efforts to run the application fail when it has as much memory as possible, try reducing the available memory.

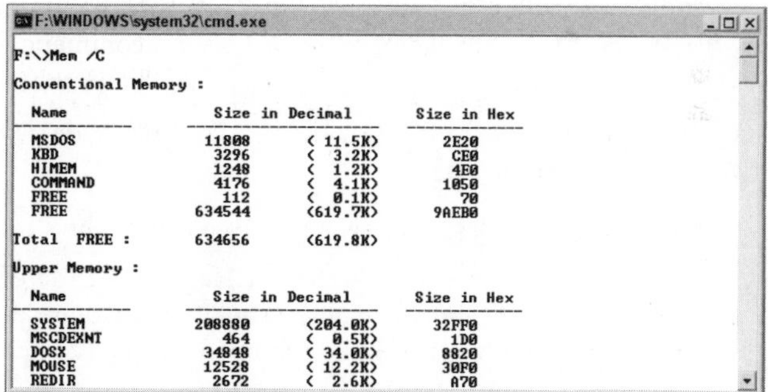

```
F:\WINDOWS\system32\cmd.exe
F:\>Mem /C

Conventional Memory :

  Name              Size in Decimal       Size in Hex
-------------     ---------------------   -------------
  MSDOS             11808     ( 11.5K)       2E20
  KBD                3296     (  3.2K)        CE0
  HIMEM              1248     (  1.2K)        4E0
  COMMAND            4176     (  4.1K)       1050
  FREE                112     (  0.1K)         70
  FREE             634544     (619.7K)      9AEB0

Total  FREE :      634656     (619.8K)

Upper Memory :

  Name              Size in Decimal       Size in Hex
-------------     ---------------------   -------------
  SYSTEM           208880     (204.0K)      32FF0
  MSCDEXNT            464     (  0.5K)        1D0
  DOSX              34848     ( 34.0K)       8820
  MOUSE             12528     ( 12.2K)       30F0
  REDIR              2672     (  2.6K)        A70
```

FIGURE 3.2
The classify mode of the Mem utility categorizes application use of memory.

Obtaining General System Information with the MSInfo32 Utility

The Microsoft Information 32-bit (MSInfo32) utility made an initial appearance with Office products. In fact, that's why you'll still find it in the `\Program Files\Common Files\Microsoft Shared\MSInfo` directory, rather than the more standard `\Windows\System32` directory. Newer versions of Windows also provide a copy of the utility in the `\WINDOWS\system32\dllcache` directory. Because the MSInfo utility doesn't appear in the standard directory, you might find that it won't execute correctly at the command prompt. You might need to add one of the MSInfo utility paths to your setup to execute the application from anywhere at the command prompt. Of course, the utility will always execute when you're in the appropriate directory.

CHOOSING THE CORRECT UTILITY

It's not always important to use the command line utilities that come with Windows. In some cases, you'll find that you really want and need the features provided by a third party application or by a utility that Microsoft has dropped. Many longtime Windows users will remember the WinMSD utility (see `http://support.microsoft.com/kb/q232848/` for details) that let you create system-level reports. The MSInfo32 utility replaces WinMSD. Even though the WinMSD executable still exists on your hard drive, it now displays a message telling you to use MSInfo32 instead.

Although Microsoft doesn't recommend that you download the actual WinMSD executable and use it with Windows XP and above, you'll find some substitutes on the Internet such as the WinMSDp command line utility found on the Petri.co.il Web site at `http://www.petri.co.il/download_free_reskit_tools.htm`. If you download this utility, make sure you address the security concerns in using it (see the Microsoft security bulletin at `http://www.microsoft.com/technet/security/bulletin/MS99-013.mspx` for details). The point is that using this utility might provide the interface that you really wanted to use instead of relying on Microsoft's choice for you, which is MSInfo32.

The main reason to use the MSInfo32 utility is to record a snapshot of the state of a system. The data includes everything from the kind of processor installed on the system to the applications running on it. In fact, you might be surprised at how much information this utility can record. Simply open the graphical portion of the utility, shown in Figure 3.3, to see the various information categories.

When you use the command line interface, the MSInfo32 utility records everything to a file on your system. You can use this file as an archive of the current system state and even use it to help set up another system to match the current system's setup. Administrators can use these snapshots to look for potential system problems by processing the resulting file through an application. This utility uses the following syntax:

```
MSInfo32 [Filename] [/pch] [/nfo Outfile] [/report Outfile]
[/category Catname] [/computer ComputerName] [/categories Catlist]
[/ShowCategories]
```

The following list describes each of the command line arguments.

`Filename` Defines the NFO file, PCHealth XML file, or CAB file containing system information that you want MSInfo32 to open. The utility displays the file using the graphical interface. However, you could use this option to open a number of files that you regularly collect for viewing at the same time.

`/pch` Opens the MSInfo32 utility in the history view. The history view displays changes to the system over time. For example, every time a piece of hardware experiences an address change, MSInfo32 records it for the history view.

`/nfo` ***`Outfile`*** Outputs the current system state to the specified NFO file. The NFO file is actually in an XML format that you can examine using any application designed to work with XML. In fact, the XML formatting makes it quite easy to create a custom utility to extract only the information you need for a particular purpose.

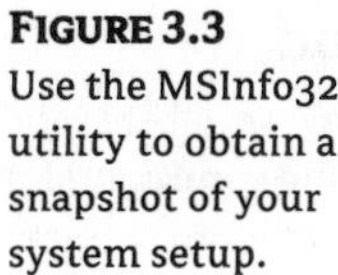

FIGURE 3.3
Use the MSInfo32 utility to obtain a snapshot of your system setup.

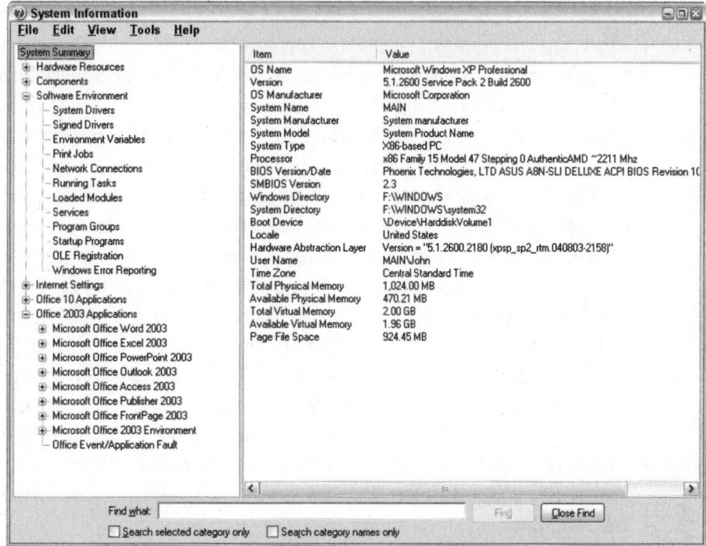

NOTE File output occurs in a silent mode. Even though the MSInfo32 utility returns immediately, that doesn't mean the output file is ready for use. MSInfo completes the task in the background so the user can continue working. Generally, you'll want to allow at least 10 minutes for the system to complete the task of outputting the file (more time is better).

`/report` ***`Outfile`*** Outputs the current system state to the specified text file.

`/category` ***`Catname`*** Opens MSInfo32 with the specified category selected. Use the `/ShowCategories` command line switch to open MSInfo with the category names displays, in place of the human readable categories shown in Figure 3.3.

`/computer` ***`ComputerName`*** Opens MSInfo32 with the information for the specified remote computer loaded in place of the local computer. You can also use this command line switch to generate reports for remote computers.

NOTE Remote systems must have the Windows Management Instrumentation (WMI) service running to collect information. Otherwise, MSInfo32 will simply report that it can't collect the information.

`/categories` ***`Catlist`*** Opens MSInfo32 with the specified categories in view. The utility hides all of the other categories. You can use this feature to reduce the amount of information you must wade through to locate the information you want. Add categories to the list by typing the category name with a plus sign (+) in front of it. A special category, All, displays all of the categories. Remove categories by typing the category name with a minus sign (-) in front of it. Use the `/ShowCategories` command line switch to open MSInfo with the category names displayed, in place of the human readable categories shown in Figure 3.3. You can also use this command line switch to generate reports with only the selected categories included.

`/ShowCategories` Opens MSInfo32 with the category names displayed in place of the standard human readable names.

Managing Environment Variables with the *Set* Command

The term *environment variable* is foreign to many users because environment variables work in the background to make life easier for both GUI users and those who work at the command line. Admittedly, someone working at the command line is more likely to see the effects of environment variables directly. For example, without a proper path environment variable, you can't execute many applications. The path points to the locations where the command processor should look for applications.

Windows supports two forms of environment variables: permanent and session. The session environment variables only affect the current command line session. As soon as you close the command window, these environment variables are gone. You create session environment variables using the `Set` command. Permanent environment variables exist for all Windows GUI applications as well as the command prompt. Unless you change them, permanent environment variables exist between reboots of your system as well. You set permanent environment variables using the Environment Variables dialog box shown in Figure 3.4. To access this dialog box, right-click My Computer and choose Properties from the context menu. Select the Advanced tab of the System Properties dialog box. Click Environment Variables to display the Environment Variables dialog box. Notice that this dialog box contains sections for user and system environment variables. The user environment variables only affect the current user, while the system environment variables affect everyone who uses the machine.

Figure 3.4 shows just the tip of the iceberg when it comes to environment variables. When you work at the command line, you often need environment variables in addition to those Windows uses. For example, the `COPYCMD` environment variable affects the Copy, Move, and XCopy utilities. You can set the command line switches you want to use with these utilities by setting the `COPYCMD` environment variable. Of course, you can always override your selections by specifying a different set of command line switches at the command line. For example, if you set the `/Y` command line switch in the `COPYCMD` environment variable, you can override it by specifying the `/-Y` command line switch.

Many environment variables only affect one application. For example, you can set the `MORE` environment variable to set the command line switches for the More utility. Every time you use the More utility, it searches for this environment variable and sets itself up accordingly.

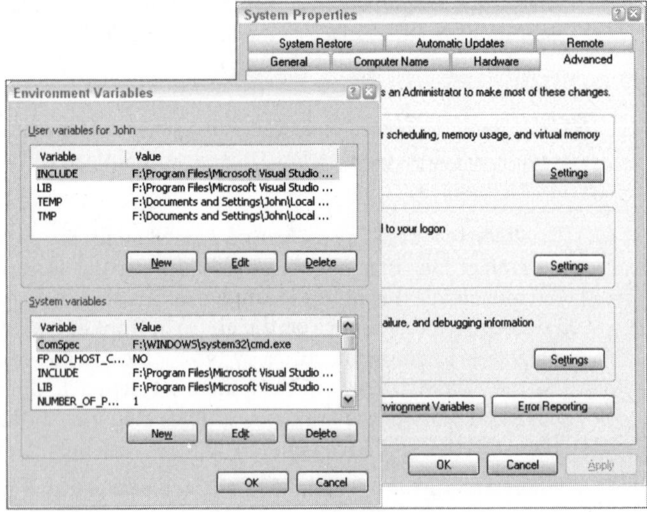

FIGURE 3.4
Use this dialog box to add new permanent environment variables to your system.

Command line environment variables need not impose on those used in Windows. Besides setting environment variables in the Environment Variables dialog box and at the command line using the `Set` command, you can add environment variables to the `AutoExec.NT` file. Windows executes the commands within AutoExec.NT every time it opens a command prompt for you. These environment variables appear every time you open a command prompt, but won't appear within Windows. You use the `Set` command within the AutoExec.NT file, just as you would at the command prompt. The "Modifying AutoExec.NT" section of Chapter 7 describes the AutoExec.NT file in more detail.

For all of the tasks that it performs, the `Set` command is relatively simple. This command uses the following syntax:

```
SET [variable[=[string]]]
SET /A expression
SET /P variable=[promptString]
SET "
```

The following list describes each of the command line arguments.

`variable` Specifies the environment variable name. The name can't contain spaces or most special characters. You can split words in a variable name using the underscore (_) or dash (-).

`string` Defines the value of the environment variable. If you type the environment variable, followed by an equals sign (=), but without a value, the `Set` command deletes the environment variable. Type the `Set` command followed by the environment variable without an equals sign to determine the current environment variable value. In fact, you can type as little as a single letter to see a list of environment variables and their associated values that begin with that letter.

`/A` ***`expression`*** Creates an environment variable based on an expression, such as a math equation or the concatenation of multiple environment variables, instead of a standard string.

`/P` ***`variable=[promptString]`*** Prompts the user to assign a value to an environment variable, rather than assigning the value directly. You must supply a variable name. The optional prompt string lets you provide a specific prompt to the user. Otherwise, the display doesn't show any prompt at all.

Windows XP comes with a number of standard environment variables, some of which you won't see in the Environment Variables dialog box. These hard-coded environment variables perform essential tasks, such as displaying the current directory for you. You can see a list of these environment variables on the Microsoft Web site at `http://www.microsoft.com/resources/documentation/windows/xp/all/proddocs/en-us/ntcmds_shelloverview.mspx`. Typing **`Set`** by itself and pressing Enter displays the list of environment variables set for your machine as shown in Figure 3.5. This list doesn't include the hard-coded environment variables such as CD.

You can use the `/A` command line switch to combine existing environmental variables or even perform math with them. For example, you could use the following `Set` command to create a new environment variable based on the existing `%NUMBER_OF_PROCESSORS%` environment variable.

```
SET /A TwiceTheProcessor=%NUMBER_OF_PROCESSORS% * 2
```

You can use any of the operators shown in Table 3.1 when creating your expression. The operators appear in order of precedence.

FIGURE 3.5
The Set command displays the list of environment variables defined for your machine.

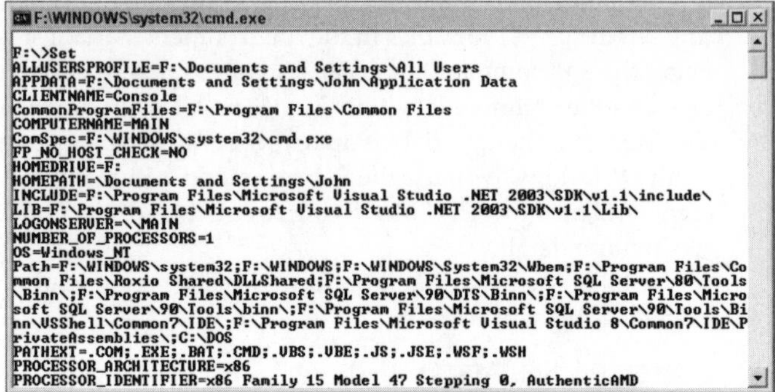

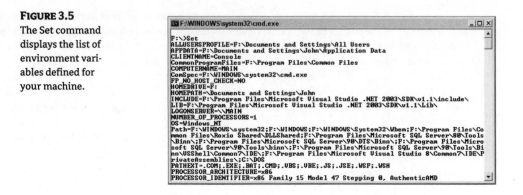

TABLE 3.1: Set Expression Operators

<table>
<tr><th>OPERATOR</th><th>DESCRIPTION</th></tr>
<tr><td>()</td><td>Group expression elements</td></tr>
<tr><td>! ~ -</td><td>Not, negate, and negative unary operators</td></tr>
<tr><td>* / %</td><td>Multiply, divide, and modulus arithmetic operators</td></tr>
<tr><td>+ -</td><td>Add and subtract arithmetic operators</td></tr>
<tr><td><< >></td><td>Right and left logical shift</td></tr>
<tr><td>&</td><td>Bitwise AND</td></tr>
<tr><td>^</td><td>Bitwise exclusive OR</td></tr>
<tr><td>|</td><td>Bitwise OR</td></tr>
<tr><td>= *= /= %= += -= &= ^= |= <<= >>=</td><td>Assignment operators</td></tr>
<tr><td>,</td><td>Expression separator</td></tr>
</table>

Any expressions you create can also contain octal, decimal, or hexadecimal numbers. All octal values begin with a 0 (zero) and hexadecimal values begin with a 0x. The Set command is quite handy when you create batch files, so you'll see additional coverage for it in the "Creating Batch Files" section of Chapter 7.

VISTA

Managing Environment Variables with the SetX Utility

The SetX utility is a new offering for Vista. It performs essentially the same tasks as the Set command described in the "Managing Environment Variables with the *Set* Command" section of the chapter. However, it offers considerably more flexibility because you can use SetX over a network to interact with variables on other machines. In addition, it offers considerable flexibility in setting variables, such as letting you choose between the current user and the system as a whole. Rather than repeat all of the common information for using SetX, please refer to the `Set` command as a starting point. This command uses the following syntax:

```
SETX [/S system [/U [domain\]user [/P [password]]]] var value [/M]
SETX [/S system [/U [domain\]user [/P [password]]]] var /K regpath [/M]
SETX [/S system [/U [domain\]user [/P [password]]]] /F file {var
   {/A x,y | /R x,y string}[/M] | /X} [/D delimiters]
```

The following list describes each of the command line arguments.

/S *system* Specifies the remote system that you want to check. In most cases, you'll also need to supply the `/U` and the `/P` command line switches when using this switch.

/U [*domain*\\]*user* Specifies the username on the remote system. This name may not match the username on the local system. You'll need to supply a domain name when working with a domain controller.

/P [*password*] Specifies the password for the given user. You can provide the command line switch without specifying the password on the command line in cleartext. The system prompts you for the password. Using this feature can help you maintain the security of passwords used on your system.

var Contains the name of the variable you wish to change.

value Sets the specified variable to the supplied value. You don't have to provide the equals sign (=) as you do when working with the `Set` command. Place values with spaces within double quotes.

/M Sets the value as a system-wide (machine-level) variable that appears in `HKEY_LOCAL_MACHINE`. The default setting places the variable within the current user's environment.

/K *regpath* Sets the specified variable using the content of a registry key. You must provide the fully qualified registry value (including all of the keys), such as `KEY_LOCAL_MACHINE\System\CurrentControlSet\Control\TimeZoneInformation\StandardName`.

/F *file* Specifies the name of a text file to use for settings. You must also provide the position of the setting within the file as an absolute or relative coordinate (line number and character position). In addition, if the setting is delimited, you must provide the delimiter used for it.

/A *x,y* Provides the absolute position of the setting within the file. You must provide the position as a line number and character number.

/R *x,y string* Provides a relative position of the setting within the file. SetX first searches for the string you specify within the file. It then moves relative to that string the number of lines and characters within the line that you specify.

/X Displays the file contents using x and y coordinates. This argument doesn't actually set any variables. What it does is display the position of each potential setting within the file so that you can use the `/A` and `/R` arguments with greater ease.

/D delimiters Defines the delimiters used to begin and end settings entries within the file. The default settings include space, tab, carriage return, and linefeed. You can use any ASCII character as a delimiter. The maximum number of delimiters, including the default delimiters, is 15.

Determining the Operating System Version with the *Ver* Command

The `Ver` command is one of the easier commands to use. It doesn't require any arguments and provides only one type of output. Whenever you use the `Ver` command, you receive the operating system version information. The version information contains the operating system name in human readable form, the major version number, the minor version number, and the build number. For example, the current Windows XP version at the time of this writing is Microsoft Windows XP [Version 5.1.2600].

Getting Volume Information with the *Vol* Command

The `Vol` command displays the volume information for the current or selected drive. The information includes the drive letter, the drive volume name, and the serial number. This command uses the following syntax:

```
VOL [drive:]
```

The following describes the command line argument.

`drive` Specifies the letter of the drive for which you want to obtain volume information. The default is the current drive.

Viewing the Volume Shadow Service Data with the VSSAdmin Utility

The VSSAdmin utility lets you view the status of the Volume Shadow Service (VSS), which is a method of providing a backup copy of Windows. (Learn more about how VSS works on the Microsoft Web site at `http://www.microsoft.com/technet/prodtechnol/windowsserver2003/library/TechRef/2b0d2457-b7d8-42c3-b6c9-59c145b7765f.mspx`.) VSSAdmin has only one accessible mode in Windows XP or before list, which displays information about the specified VSS feature. Vista adds a new resize mode. This utility uses the following syntax:

```
VSSAdmin list shadows [/set={shadow copy set guid}]
VSSAdmin list writers
VSSAdmin list providers
VSSAdmin list volumes
VSSAdmin resize storage /For=ForVolumeSpec /On=OnVolumeSpec
   [/MaxSize=MaxSizeSpec]
```

The following list describes each of the command line arguments.

`/set={shadow copy set guid}` Determines which shadow copy set to list based on the GUID provided as input.

`shadows` Lists all of the shadow copies on the system grouped by GUID.

`writers` Displays a list of shadow volume writers on the system. Common shadow writers include Internet Information Server (IIS), Windows Management Interface (WMI), and Microsoft Data Engine (MSDE). The information includes the writer name in human readable form, writer identifier as a GUID, the writer instance identifier as a GUID, and the current writer state.

`providers` Displays the current VSS provider information. This information includes the provider name, provider type, provider identifier as a GUID, and the version number.

`volumes` Displays a list of volumes eligible for shadow copies. In general, you can shadow any permanent hard drive on the system.

The new resize storage mode lets you change the amount of storage set aside for shadow copies on the specified volume. The following list describes each of the command line arguments.

`/For=`*`ForVolumeSpec`* Defines the volume for which you want to provide a shadow copy.

`/On=`*`OnVolumeSpec`* Defines the volume that will hold the shadow copy. This volume must be different from the `/For` argument volume.

`/MaxSize=`*`MaxSizeSpec`* Specifies the maximum size of the shadow copy. If you don't specify this value, then the shadow copy can be as large as the free space on the shadow drive. The minimum shadow copy size is 300 MB. You may include any of the following size definitions: KB, MB, GB, TB, PB, and EB. If you don't specify a size, then VSSAdmin assumes that you supplied the value in bytes.

Working with Plug and Play (PnP)

Vista provides a number of new utilities for working with plug and play. The purpose of these utilities is to make it easier for administrators to manage plug and play from a remote location and to provide greater accountability for driver installation. The following sections describe the new Vista plug and play utilities.

Performing Unattended Driver Installation with the PnPUnattend Utility

The PnPUnattend utility provides helper services for unattended installations. You can also execute it from the command line to obtain information about installation progress and to create a log file of the installation. This utility uses the following syntax:

```
PnPUnattend.exe [/auditSystem] [/s] [/L]
```

The following list describes each of the command line arguments.

`/auditSystem` Performs an unattended driver installation.

`/s` Searches for the required driver installation information, without performing an install.

`/L` Creates a log file of any installation.

Managing PnP Setups Using the PnPUtil Utility

You can use the PnPUtil utility to perform a driver installation from the command line. In addition, the options let you remove or edit driver information based on the content of an INF file, which you must always provide. This utility uses the following syntax:

```
PnPUtil.exe [-f | -i] [-a | -d | -e ] <INFname>
```

The following list describes each of the command line arguments.

`-f` Forces the utility to perform the specified action (add, edit, or delete).

`-i` Performs a standardized installation when used with `-a` based on the INF content.

`-a` Adds the device driver specified by the INF file to the system. However, adding the device driver simply makes it available for installation. You must combine this command line switch with the `-i` command line switch to actually install the driver.

`-d` Deletes the device driver specified by the INF file from the system. The INF file normally has oem, followed by a number, followed by INF, such as `oem0.inf`. Deleting an OEM (Original

Equipment Manufacturer) driver has the effect of uninstalling the device driver. You can obtain a list of OEM drivers using the `-e` command line switch.

`-e` Enumerates all of the third drivers currently installed on the system, but doesn't do anything with them. This is the only command line switch that doesn't require you to provide an INF filename.

`INFname` Provides the name of a file containing device driver information. You can use wildcard characters to specify multiple INF files.

Recording System Status Information

Making a permanent record of system status information is important, especially when an error occurs. Windows uses the term *event* to indicate a change. Events aren't necessarily errors. In fact, some events are informational, while others are simply warnings. Windows also provides a number of other events, such as security events where it performs an audit of the security on a system. Generally, though, you'll only consider three kinds of events: informational, warning, and errors.

Using Event Logs Effectively

Windows records all events in the event log. You can use the Event Viewer console in the Administrative Tools folder of the Control Panel to view the events. The standard logs for events are Application, Security, and System. Unfortunately, many users don't know the event logs exist and administrators don't find time to use them. In many cases, someone will call me in to look at their system and I find the answers I need to fix the error right in the event log that they failed to review. In fact, I'm amazed at how often the event log entry tells me what action to take or at least provides enough specifics that I can research the repair in the Microsoft Knowledge Base.

Educating yourself about the event log and understanding how to use it effectively is important. You can learn more about the event log in general on the Microsoft Web site at `http://www.microsoft.com/technet/prodtechnol/windows2000serv/maintain/monitor/03w2kadb.mspx`.

However, effective event log usage goes even further. As you begin writing your own applications (even batch file applications), consider adding event log entries to one of the standard logs or use a special log for the purpose. The Delphi Magazine article (`http://www.thedelphimagazine.com/samples/1655/article.htm`) shows how to add new event logs using registry entries. The following sections describe the utilities for working with system events.

Managing System Events with the EventCreate Utility

The EventCreate utility adds a new event log entry. You can send an event log entry to any current log, including any custom log that you create. In fact, this utility can create event log entries with the same complexity and level of information that any application can create. This utility uses the following syntax:

```
EVENTCREATE [/S system [/U username [/P [password]]]] /ID eventid
[/L logname] [/SO srcname] /T {ERROR | WARNING | INFORMATION} /D description
```

Notice that you must provide the `/ID`, `/T`, and `/D` command line switches. The following list describes each of the command line arguments.

`/S system` Specifies a remote system. You can use any connected system to store the event log entries. Some administrators send event log entries to a central location to ensure someone sees them. The remote system must allow the required access.

`/U [domain\]user` Defines the user context for executing the command. The user content is important because not every user has access to the event log. In addition, the user context appears as part of the event log entry.

`/P [password]` Provides a password for the user context. The utility prompts you for the password (when necessary) if you don't include it on the command line. In most cases, supplying the password when prompted is safer from a security perspective than including this information on the command line or as part of a batch file entry.

`/L logname` Determines the name of the log to use for the event entry. The three standard logs found on every Windows machine are Application, Security, and System. Many machines include additional event logs installed by applications that the system uses.

`/T {ERROR | WARNING | INFORMATION}` Specifies the kind of event to create. Even though the Windows event log accepts other event types, the only three acceptable types are error, warning, and information. These three types reflect three levels of severity, with information being the least severe and error being the most severe.

`/SO source` Defines the source of the event. You can use any string as the source. However, providing a meaningful application identifier is usually the best idea. Given that you'll use this feature from the command line, you might simply want to use "Command Line" as your source. When working with a batch file, use the batch filename as the source. Scripts and other forms of automation should use the script or application name.

`/ID id` Specifies the event identifier for the event. The identifier is a number between 1 and 1,000. Whenever practical, provide specific numbers for specific events. For example, you might assign a value of 500 to all file errors. The event identifier lets you sort the events in a manner other than type or source, so you should also keep this in mind when you create the event identifier list for your application.

`/D description` Provides an event description. The description should tell the viewer what happened to cause the event, the event effects, and any other pertinent information the viewer might need to resolve event problems caused by the event. Even informational events should include significant event information. For example, you might record that your application started, found no work to do, and terminated. Even though the application didn't experience an error, the information is still important to someone who expected your application to complete useful work.

NOTE The event log accepts several additional pieces of information that you can't add using the EventCreate utility. The event category requires that you register a specialized DLL to handle the category information. Given that you probably won't add the required DLL for a batch file application, Microsoft left this particular entry out. An event can also register data that amplifies the event description. The lack of support for this feature is regrettable because you could use it to create better event log entries. However, you can overcome this problem by providing a detailed description and possibly including the data as part of the description, rather than as a separate entry.

VISTA

Triggering System Events with the EventTriggers Utility

One of the problems with the event log is that it can quickly become clogged with a lot of information—more information than many network administrators want to wade through to locate a particular event of importance. Starting with Windows XP, you can set an event trigger on the event log. When an event log entry matching the criteria you specify appears, you can tell the EventTrigger utility to perform any number of tasks—anything from sending an email message to running a particular application (batch files included). Unfortunately, this utility is no longer available in Vista. However, Vista provides a counterpart in the form of the WEvtUtil utility. You can learn more about this utility in the "Managing Event Information with the WEvtUtil Utility" section of the chapter.

The interesting part about using event triggers is that you can track problems occurring on any system (local or remote) with greater ease. Although you might want to look at all of those informational messages in the event log at some point, the SQL Server error message is the one that you really want to know about the second it occurs. The SQL Server message is an example of an event log entry that you want to track using an event trigger. Of course, the entry could just as easily be from any other application. For example, you might want to know when the Windows Time service fails to find an online time synchronization source.

The EventTriggers utility provides three modes of operation: Create, Delete, and Query. Each one of these modes controls a particular aspect of working with event triggers. The following sections discuss these three modes of operation and show how you use them to manage event triggers on your system.

CREATE

Before you can use event triggers, you have to create them. The create mode helps you add new event triggers. Each event trigger reacts to a separate event in the event log, so you need one event trigger for each event log entry that you want to monitor. This mode uses the following syntax:

```
EVENTTRIGGERS /Create [/S system [/U username [/P [password]]]] /TR
triggername /TK taskname [/D description] [/L log] { [/EID id]
[/T type] [/SO source] } [/RU username [/RP password]]
```

The following list describes each of the command line arguments.

/S *system* Specifies a remote system. You can use any connected system to store the event log entries. Some administrators send event log entries to a central location to ensure someone sees them. The remote system must allow the required access.

/U [*domain*\]*user* Defines the user context for executing the command. The user content is important because not every user has access to the event log. In addition, the user context appears as part of the event log entry.

/P [*password*] Provides a password for the user context. The utility prompts you for the password (when necessary) if you don't include it on the command line. In most cases, supplying the password when prompted is safer from a security perspective than including this information on the command line or as part of a batch file entry.

/TR *triggername* Defines a human readable name to associate with the event trigger. Using names such as MyTrigger probably won't work well. It's important to create a descriptive name that you'll recognize easily. Make sure you make the name unique by adding some elements for the event log entry that it monitors. For example, WinMgmtWarning63 would be a good name for an event generated by the Windows management service at the warning level for event identifier number 63.

/L *log* Specifies the Windows event log to monitor. The three common logs include Application, System, and Security. The DNS Server and Directory logs commonly appear on servers. You can also specify any custom log. You can use wildcard characters to define the log name. The default value is "*" (without the quotes), which is all of the event logs on the specified machine.

/EID *id* Specifies which Event ID to monitor in the event log. This value is application specific, so you need to know which Event ID an application will use for a particular requirement.

/T *type* Specifies the Event Type to monitor in the event log. The valid values include `ERROR`, `INFORMATION`, `WARNING`, `SUCCESSAUDIT`, and `FAILUREAUDIT`. The `SUCCESSAUDIT` and `FAILUREAUDIT` only appear in security logs.

/SO *source* Specifies the Event Source to monitor in the event log. The Event Source varies by application and by entity performing a task. For example, the system can just as easily generate an event that a user can generate. Unless you want to monitor the activities of a specific entity, you should refrain from supplying this command line switch.

/D *description* Specifies the Description to monitor in the event log. Using this command line switch makes the event trigger very specific. In fact, the event trigger becomes so specific that you might miss events. Use this particular command line switch with caution and only in cases where you know exactly which message you want to receive.

/TK *taskname* Defines the name of the task to perform when the event trigger fires. Generally, this is the name of an application (including any required command line switches), batch file, script, or other executable entity. For example, you can tell Outlook to send you a message about the event using Outlook's command line switches to generate an email.

/RU *username* Defines the user account to use to run the task. Use `""` (two quotes) for the system account. The default username is the current username or the name used to access the remote system with the `/U` command line switch.

/RP *password* Defines the password for the task user account. The EventTriggers utility ignores this value when working with the system account. Supply a value of "*" (without the quotes) or none when you want the EventTriggers utility to prompt for a password.

Delete

Use the delete mode to remove any event triggers you no longer need. This mode uses the following syntax:

```
EVENTTRIGGERS /Delete [/S system [/U username [/P [password]]]] /TID id
[/TID id1 [...[/TID idn]]]
```

The following list describes each of the command line arguments.

/S *system* Specifies a remote system. You can use any connected system to store the event log entries. Some administrators send event log entries to a central location to ensure someone sees them. The remote system must allow the required access.

/U [*domain*\]*user* Defines the user context for executing the command. The user context is important because not every user has access to the event log. In addition, the user context appears as part of the event log entry.

/P [*password*] Provides a password for the user context. The utility prompts you for the password (when necessary) if you don't include it on the command line. In most cases, supplying the password when prompted is safer from a security perspective than including this information on the command line or as part of a batch file entry.

/TID *id* Specifies the Trigger Identifier to remove from the list of event triggers. Every time you create a new event trigger, the system assigns it an identifier. You can see this identifier by using the query mode. This command line switch accepts the * wildcard, which deletes all of the event triggers on the system.

QUERY

The query mode displays a list of all of the event triggers on a system. You can use this list for real-time work with the event triggers. However, by changing the format, you can also use this mode to add the event triggers to a database for later reference. This mode uses the following syntax:

```
EVENTTRIGGERS /Query [/S system [/U username [/P [password]]]] [/FO
{TABLE | LIST | CSV}] [/NH] [/V]
```

The following list describes each of the command line arguments.

/S *system* Specifies a remote system. You can use any connected system to store the event log entries. Some administrators send event log entries to a central location to ensure someone sees them. The remote system must allow the required access.

/U [*domain*\\]*user* Defines the user context for executing the command. The user content is important because not every user has access to the event log. In addition, the user context appears as part of the event log entry.

/P [*password*] Provides a password for the user context. The utility prompts you for the password (when necessary) if you don't include it on the command line. In most cases, supplying the password when prompted is safer from a security perspective than including this information on the command line or as part of a batch file entry.

/FO {TABLE | LIST | CSV} Defines the output format for this mode. The default output is a tabular view. The table columns define the values for output, while each row contains one event trigger entry. The CSV output provides the best method for preparing the data for entry in a database. Use redirection (see the "Employing Data Redirection" section of Chapter 2 for details) to output the CSV data to a file and then import it to your database. The list format provides one data element per line. Each group of data elements defines one event trigger. The utility separates each event trigger by one blank line. Some people find the list format more readable when working in verbose mode since the table format requires multiple lines for each entry (the lines wrap).

/NH Specifies that the EventTriggers utility shouldn't display the column headers. You can use this option when creating pure content for reports or other needs. The EventTriggers utility accepts this command line switch only when using the table and CSV formats.

/V Outputs additional information about each event trigger. The default output includes the trigger identifier, event trigger name, and the name of the task the event trigger performs. The additional information includes the host name, the event trigger query (the arguments used to trigger it), the description information, and the username used to run the task.

Managing Event Information with the WEvtUtil Utility

The WEvtUtil utility helps you monitor the event logs on a system. This utility replaces the other utilities provided in earlier versions of Windows. You might wonder about this change, until you begin looking at the Vista event log setup, which is very complex. (The new event logs are a significant change from past versions of Windows that have contained the same few logs.) The WEvtUtil utility has the flexibility required to work with Vista's complex event log setup. This utility uses the following syntax:

```
WEvtUtil COMMAND [ARGUMENT [ARGUMENT] ...] [/OPTION:VALUE [/OPTION:VALUE] ...]
```

It helps to discuss WEvtUtil command line arguments as commands and common options (with associated arguments). The following list describes each of the commands (the short name appears first, followed by the long name in parentheses).

`el (enum-logs)` Displays a list of all of the logs on the system.

`gl (get-log)` ***`Logname`*** Obtains configuration information about a specific log. You must provide the fully qualified name of the log that you want to work with. For example, if you want to know about the Backup log, you must provide the fully qualified name of Microsoft-Windows-Backup. Use the `el` command to obtain a list of fully qualified names.

`sl (set-log)` ***`Logname [/Option:Value [/Option:Value] ...]`*** Changes the configuration of a log file. You can supply option/value pairs or use an XML file to make the changes. The WEvtUtil utility accepts either short or long option names. When using an XML file, you must supply the `/c` option. The following list describes the option/value pairs used to configure a log (the long names appear in parentheses after the option).

`/e:{True | False} (enabled)` Enables or disables the log. The default value is true to enable the log.

`/i:{System | Application | Custom} (isolation)` Defines the log isolation mode: system, application, or custom. In addition, the mode identifies the other logs with which the log shares a session, which means these other logs have write permission for the target log. Use the system mode when a log affects that system as a whole. The resulting log shares a session with the System log. The Application mode is the option to use with general applications. Logs in this class share a session with the Application log. The Custom mode is for private logs that you don't want to share a session with any other log. You must use the `/ca` option to define security for custom logs.

`/lfn:`*`Value`* `(logfilename)` Provides the full path to the physical location of the log on the hard drive.

`/rt:{True | False} (retention)` Determines whether the log retains existing entries when the log becomes full. When you set the log retention mode to True, the log retains earlier entries when the log becomes full and discards all new entries. The default value of false discards older entries in favor of new ones.

`/ab:{True | False} (autobackup)` Performs an automatic backup of the log when it reaches maximum size. You must set the retention value to true using the `/rt` option when using this feature.

`/ms:`*`Value`* `(maxsize)` Specifies the maximum log size in bytes. The maximum log size in Vista is 1,048,576 bytes (1,024 KB). Log files are always multiples of 64 KB, so Vista rounds any value you provide to a multiple of 64 KB.

`/l:`*`Value`* `(level)` Defines the log level filter (normally critical, error, warning, information, or verbose). You may use any valid level value. This feature is only applicable to logs with a dedicated session (which means that the isolation mode is normally custom). You can remove a level filter by setting the value to 0.

/k:*Value* (keywords) Defines the log keyword filter (common keywords include Audit Failure, Audit Success, Classic, Correlation Hint, SQM, WDI Context, and WDI Diag). The value can include any valid 64-bit keyword mask. This feature is only applicable to logs with a dedicated session (which means that the isolation mode is normally custom).

/ca:*Value* (channelaccess) Defines the access permission for an event log. You must provide a valid security descriptor defined using the Security Descriptor Definition Language (SDDL). You can learn more about SDDL at `http://msdn2.microsoft.com/en-us/library/aa379567.aspx`.

/c:*Value* (config) Defines a path to a configuration file. The configuration file contains log file settings in the form of an XML file. When using this feature, you must not specify the `logname` command line argument because this value is ready as part of the configuration file. Here's a typical example of a configuration file.

```
<?xml version="1.0" encoding="UTF-8"?>
<channel name="Application" isolation="Application"
         xmlns="http://schemas.microsoft.com/win/2004/08/events">
  <logging>
    <retention>true</retention>
    <autoBackup>true</autoBackup>
    <maxSize>9000000</maxSize>
  </logging>
  <publishing>
  </publishing>
</channel>
```

Notice that the `<channel>` element includes the log filename as Application and an isolation level (`/i`) of Application. The logging options appear as part of the `<logging>` element. Each child element name is the long name for an option. For example, the `<retention>` element corresponds to the `/rt` command line argument. You can add other configuration options to the log, such as the publishing options.

ep (enum-publishers) Displays a list of event publishers. The list can be quite long, so you'll normally want to redirect the output to a text file.

gp (get-publisher) *PublisherName* [*/OPTION:VALUE* [*/OPTION:VALUE*] ...] Obtains specific event publisher configuration information. The output includes such helpful information as a publisher help link and the name of the DLL used to create event entries. This argument also supports the following options (the long names appear in parentheses after the option).

/ge:{True | False} (getevents) Obtains metadata for the events that this publisher will raise, in addition to the standard data.

/gm:{True | False} (getmessage) Obtains the actual messages that the event entries will use instead of the message ID.

/f:{XML | Text} (format) Determines the output format of the data. The default setting is Test. When you use XML, the output appears as an XML file that you can view using any XML viewer (making the output considerably easier to understand).

im (install-manifest) *Manifest* Installs an event manifest. The manifest can contain multiple publishers and logs. You can obtain an overview of event manifest instrumentation at `http://msdn2.microsoft.com/en-gb/library/aa385227.aspx`.

um (uninstall-manifest) *Manifest* Removes the specified event manifest from the system.

qe (query-events) *Path* [/*OPTION*:*VALUE* [/*OPTION*:*VALUE*] ...] Outputs event information from a log or log file. The path argument normally contains the name of the log. However, if you use the /lf option, then you must provide the physical path to the event log file. This argument also supports the following options (the long names appear in parentheses after the option).

> **/lf:{True | False} (logfile)** Specifies that the path argument contains a physical path to a log file, rather than a log filename.
>
> **/sq:{True | False} (structuredquery)** Specifies that the path argument contains a path to a file that contains a structure query.
>
> **/q:*Value* (query)** Provides an XPath query to filter the events read from the log. The utility returns all of the events when you don't provide this option. You can't use this option with the /sq option.
>
> **/bm:*Value* (bookmark)** Specifies a path to a file that contains a bookmark from a previous query. Using a bookmark lets you continue a previous query.
>
> **/sbm:*Value* (savebookmark)** Specifies a path to a file that the utility uses to store a bookmark for the current query. The bookmark file extension should be XML.
>
> **/rd:{True | False} (reversedirection)** Defines the direction in which the utility reads events. The default setting of true returns the most current events first.
>
> **/f:{XML | Text} (format)** Determines the output format of the data. The default setting is Test. When you use XML, the output appears as an XML file that you can view using any XML viewer (making the output considerably easier to understand).
>
> **/l:*LCID* (locale)** Provides a locale string that defines the locale used to output text information. This option is only available when you use the /f option to print events in text format.
>
> **/c:*Number* (count)** Defines the maximum number of events to read. If you combine this switch with the bookmark feature, you can read a segment of the event log at a time.
>
> **/e:*RootElementName* (element)** Defines a root element name to use to produce well-formed XML.

gli (get-log-info) *Path* Outputs information about the specified log. The path argument normally contains the name of the log. However, if you use the /lf option, then you must provide the physical path to the event log file. This argument also supports the following options (the long names appear in parentheses after the option).

> **/lf:{True | False} (logfile)** Specifies that the path argument contains a physical path to a log file, rather than a log filename.

epl (export-log) *Path TargetFile* [/*OPTION*:*VALUE* [/*OPTION*:*VALUE*] ...] Exports a log to the specified target file. The path argument normally contains the name of the log. However, if you use the /lf option, then you must provide the physical path to the event log file. This argument also supports the following options (the long names appear in parentheses after the option).

> **/lf:{True | False} (logfile)** Specifies that the path argument contains a physical path to a log file, rather than a log filename.
>
> **/sq:{True | False} (structuredquery)** Specifies that the path argument contains a path to a file that contains a structure query.

/q:*Value* (query) Provides an XPath query to filter the events read from the log. The utility returns all of the events when you don't provide this option. You can't use this option with the /sq option.

/ow:{True | False} (overwrite) Overwrites the contents in any existing target file without confirmation when set to True. The default setting is False.

al (archive-log) *LogFile* [/*OPTION*:*VALUE* [/*OPTION*:*VALUE*] ...] Archives an exported log—the log entries remain in place, but the utility outputs a copy of all existing log entries. You can create a log using either the export-log or clear-log commands. This argument also supports the following options (the long names appear in parentheses after the option).

/l:*LCID* (locale) Provides a locale string that defines the locale used to output text information. This option is only available when you use the /f option to print events in text format.

cl (clear-log) *LogName* [/*OPTION*:*VALUE*] Clears the specified log. This command differs from archiving in that the utility actually clears the log entries instead of leaving them in place. This argument also supports the following option (the long names appear in parentheses after the option).

/bu:*Filename* (backup) Creates a backup of the log before clearing it. You must specify a backup filename with an EVTX extension. (Don't use the EVT extension used with previous version of Windows because the file formats aren't compatible.)

Most of the commands use common options. The options are in addition to the special options discussed as part of the commands. The following list describes each of the options.

NOTE There are some differences between the WEvtUtil options and the options used by other utilities, even though many of them perform the same function. For example, the familiar /S command line switch (for remote system) is now the /r command line switch. Be careful when making assumptions about the options for this utility.

/r:*System* (remote) Specifies a remote system. You can use any connected system to store the event log entries. Some administrators send event log entries to a central location to ensure someone sees them. The remote system must allow the required access.

/u:[*domain*\]*user* (username) Defines the user context for executing the command. The user content is important because not every user has access to the event log. In addition, the user context appears as part of the event log entry.

/p:*Password* (password) Provides a password for the user context. The utility prompts you for the password (when necessary) if you don't include it on the command line. In most cases, supplying the password when prompted is safer from a security perspective than including this information on the command line or as part of a batch file entry.

/a:{Default | Negotiate | Kerberos | NTLM} (authentication) Specifies the kind of authentication to use for the remote location. The default value is Negotiate. Using a specific value can improve security when the remote machine offers multiple authentication options.

/uni:{True | False} (unicode) Specifies that the utility should display all output in Unicode when set to True.

Working with Performance Information

No matter what you do with your system, at some point, you'll want to know how it's performing. Performance data generally takes two forms. The static variety acts as a long-term record of the performance of your system as a whole. You can use it to track the performance of your system over time. The dynamic variety shows the current performance of your system. You can use it to check for changes in system status, look for positive gains after optimization, and even use it to troubleshoot your system (such as when a network card fails to deliver the throughput you anticipated).

UNDERSTANDING THE IMPORTANCE OF PERFORMANCE

Some people just aren't race fans; they don't care how well something is performing as long as it eventually gets the job done. They have no need for speed. However, performance monitoring is considerably more important than simply having bragging rights about your system speed. You don't need to be a race fan to gain something important from performance monitoring.

One of the tasks I perform after I set up a new system is to obtain and store a baseline performance evaluation. The purpose of this stored data is to provide a baseline for comparison later—after the system has operated for a while. When someone complains that their system no longer works as it did when it was new, I use the performance baseline I created to find out where the problem lies. For example, an inordinate level of network traffic might clue me into the activities of a cracker or a load of adware on the system. High error levels might tell me that a piece of hardware is beginning to fail. Both hard drives and network adapters are famous for providing this heads-up information before they become unusable. In short, performance isn't necessarily about speed; you can use performance statistics to learn more about your system and to fix it faster.

Unlike many of the utilities discussed in this chapter, you can perform setups using the command line utilities, but actual monitoring usually occurs using the Performance console found in the Administrative Tools folder of the Control Panel. This chapter focuses on the command line tasks—those parts of performance monitoring that other books tend to ignore. However, you'll need to augment this information with a usage guide for the Performance console. This book won't tell you how to use the graphical interface. The following sections describe the command line interface in detail.

Adding Performance Counters with the LodCtr Utility

Performance monitoring relies on the existence of counters. A counter is a special piece of code that counts something. The count might reflect the number of times a user accesses a file or makes a network request. No matter what the counter monitors, it provides output that the various performance monitoring applications can use to report performance data. In many cases, the performance counters appear as part of the application, so they're available from the moment you install the application. However, you can also obtain external counters in some cases. The LodCtr utility loads a counter into the system so that you can access it from performance monitoring software. This utility uses the following syntax:

```
LODCTR [\\computername] FileName
LODCTR /S:<IniFileName>
LODCTR /R:<IniFileName>
```

The following list describes each of the command line arguments.

computername Specifies the name of a remote computer. You must have access to the computer through Windows. This utility doesn't provide any means of specifying a username or password for the remote computer.

FileName Defines the name of a file that contains the initialization data for a counter. The INI file normally contains the name of the DLL with the counter code, counter definitions (such as the human readable name and any required help text), and the explanation text for an extensible counter DLL.

IniFileName Defines the name of an initialization file that contains counter registration information. This file lets you save and restore counter settings on a single machine or to move counter settings from one machine to another. The registration strings generally include the First Counter, First Help, Last Counter, and Last Help information for each of the counters. You'll also see a [PerfStrings_009] section that includes a list of all of the performance counter strings by number.

WARNING Even though the documentation for this utility seems to say that the utility produces a REG (registry) file, the file isn't a registry script. If you try to install the file using the RegEdit utility, the RegEdit utility displays an error. In fact, the file does appear in the INI file format and you should probably give it an INI file extension, rather than the REG file extension Microsoft recommends.

/S Saves the performance counter registry strings to the specified file.

/R Restores the performance counter registry string from the specified file.

Managing Performance Logs and Alerts with the LogMan Utility

The Windows performance monitoring software includes the capability of creating performance logs and of creating alerts. The logs act as a historical record of the data the performance monitoring software collects. The alerts can perform tasks based on the current system performance. For example, if a system is low on memory or other resources, you can use an alert to send a message to the administrator to fix the problem. This utility uses the following syntax:

```
LogMan VERB <collection_name> [options]
```

Notice that you must supply a verb, which is an action for the utility to perform. The verb has no slash as a command line switch would have; simply type the word by itself. The following list describes each of the verbs for this utility.

create {counter | trace} Creates a new counter or trace collection. The kind of entry you create determines its location in the Performance console. As shown in Figure 3.6, a counter appears within the Counter Logs folder, while a trace appears within the Trace Logs folder.

start Starts an existing collection. This action sets the begin time to manual.

stop Stops an existing collection. This action sets the end time to manual.

delete Deletes an existing collection. None of the collection information remains; you can't undo this action.

query {*collection_name* | *providers*} Queries a collection or provider. Typing **query** by itself displays a list of collections that includes the collection name, the collection type (counter or trace), and the collection status. When you supply a collection name, the display includes the name, type, status, start mode (normally manual), stop mode (normally manual), output filename, the run as information (username), and the counters monitored by the collection (such as `\Process(_Total)\% Processor Time`). If you use the provider's keyword, you'll see a list of registered providers and their associated GUID.

`update` Updates an existing collection of properties. You specify the existing collection name, along with the new properties that you want to use. Whenever an existing property conflicts with a new property, the new property overrides the existing property value.

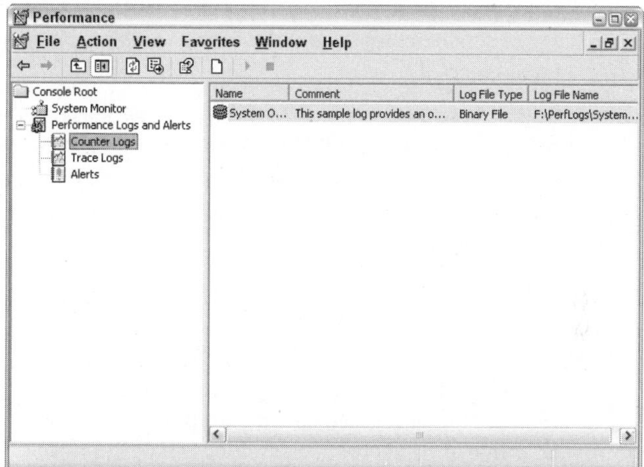

FIGURE 3.6
The kind of entry you create determines its location within the Performance console.

You combine verbs with a collection name and one or more command line switches to perform tasks with LogMan. The following list describes each of the command line arguments.

`collection_name` Defines the name of the collection to use. The collection name is the name that you assign to the counter or trace when you create it. This is the same name that appears in the Performance console shown in Figure 3.6.

`-s` ***`computer`*** Performs the task on a remote system. The default setting uses the local system.

`-config` ***`filename`*** Provides a file containing a list of settings to use in place of command line options. Using this feature lets you repeat setups with greater ease. In addition, creating the sometimes complex command line setups this utility requires is difficult. Using a configuration file reduces the work you'll need to perform at the command line.

`-b` ***`M/d/yyyy h:mm:ss[{ AM | PM }]`*** Defines the starting time for the collection. Collection continues until the specified ending time (see the `-e` command line switch) or you manually end the collection process using the stop verb. The default setting uses the current day and time. You can input times using a 24-hour clock. When specifying a time based on a 12-hour clock, add the AM or PM option.

`-e` ***`M/d/yyyy h:mm:ss[{ AM | PM }]`*** Defines the ending time for the collection. The default setting uses the current day and time. You can input times using a 24-hour clock. When specifying a time based on a 12-hour clock, add the AM or PM option.

`-m [start] [stop]` Modifies the collection to use a manual start or stop, rather than relying on a scheduled beginning or ending time.

`-[-]r` Repeats the collection daily at the specified begin and end time when used with a single dash. Using a double dash removes the daily collection feature. This command is only valid for begin and end times specified on the same day, month, and year.

-o { *Filename* | *DSN!Log* } Specifies the output information for the collection. You can use an output file by specifying a path and filename. As an alternative, you can specify a SQL database (for any vendor that supports SQL) by including the Open Database Connectivity (ODBC) DSN and the log set name within the SQL database. (See the "Working with ODBC Data Sources" section of Chapter 2 for information on configuring ODBC from the command line.) The default setting is to use a file with the same name as the performance collection and a BLG extension for counters or an ETL extension for traces.

-f { Bin | Bincirc | CSV | TSV | SQL } Defines the log format for the output. You can choose between binary, circular binary, CSV, Tab Separated Value (TSV), and Structure Query Language (SQL).

-[-]a Appends data to the existing log file when used with a single dash. Overwrites the existing log file when used with a double dash. The default setting is to overwrite the existing log file.

-[-]v [*nnnnnn* | *mmddhhmm*] Attaches versioning information (either a number or the current date) to the end of the log filename when used with a single dash. Removes the versioning information when used with a double dash.

-[-]rc *Filename* Runs a command after the system closes the log when used with a single dash. Disables running a command when used with a double dash. The commands always run in the foreground (so the user can see them).

-[-]max *Size* Defines the maximum log file size in megabytes when used with a single dash. When the log file exceeds the maximum size, the system stops collecting data even if other command line arguments specify a longer collection time. This command line switch specifies the number of records when used with a SQL output. Removes the log file size restriction when used with a double dash.

-[-]cnf [[[*hh*:]*mm*:]*ss*] Creates a new file when the specified time elapses or the file reaches the maximum file size when used with a single dash. Removes the collection time restriction when used with a double dash.

-c *CounterPath* [*CounterPath*...] Specifies one or more performance counters to collect. Each performance counter has a path that begins with the counter object, specific counter, and finally the instance. Consequently, the `\Process(_Total)\% Processor Time` counter path would collect the `_Total instance of the % Processor Time` counter found in the Processor object. Make sure you place each counter path in double quotes. The counter path can include wildcard characters. Here's a list of acceptable counter path formats.

```
\\machine\object(parent/instance#index)\counter

\\machine\object(parent/instance)\counter

\\machine\object(instance#index)\counter

\\machine\object(instance)\counter

\\machine\object\counter

\object(parent/instance#index)\counter

\object(parent/instance)\counter

\object(instance#index)\counter

\object(instance)\counter

\object\counter
```

-cf *Filename* Specifies a file containing a list of performance counters to collect. Each counter path must appear on a separate line.

-si [[*hh:*]*mm:*]*ss* Defines the sample interval (how often the system samples the counter) for the collection.

-ln *logger_name* Specifies the logger name for event trace sessions. The default logger name is the same as the collection name.

-[-]rt Runs the event trace session in real-time mode instead of a file when used with a single dash. Runs the event trace session using a log file.

-p *provider* [*flags* [*level*]] Defines a single provider to use as a source of data. The system providers usually include the Windows Kernel Trace and ACPI Driver Trace Provider. Installed providers commonly include ASP.NET Events, MSSQLSERVER Trace, and .NET Common Language Runtime. You can also specify nonsystem providers. Use the LogMan Query Providers option to obtain a list of providers for the current system.

-pf *Filename* Specifies a file containing a list of providers to use as part of an event trace. Each provider must appear on a separate line.

-[-]ul Runs the event trace session in user mode when used with a single dash. The system can only report on a single provider when running in user mode. Runs the event trace session in kernel mode when used with a double dash.

-bs *Value* Specifies the event trace session buffer size in kilobytes.

-ft <[[*hh:*]*mm:*]*ss*> Defines the interval for flushing the event trace session buffer from memory to disk.

-nb *Minimum Maximum* Defines the minimum and maximum number of event trace session buffers.

-fd Flushes all of the active buffers for an existing event trace session to disk.

-[-]u [*user* [*password*]] Defines a user account and password to use when running the collection. Using * as the password input causes the LogMan utility to prompt you for the password. Entering the password at a prompt means that other people won't see it at the command line or within a batch file.

-rf [[*hh:*]*mm:*]*ss* Runs the collection for the specified time.

-y Answers yes to all questions without prompting. This feature lets you set up counters and traces within a batch file without worrying about interruptions.

-ets Sends commands to event trace sessions without saving or scheduling.

-mode *trace_mode* [*trace_mode* ...] Specifies advanced event session logger mode values, which can include `globalsequence`, `localsequence`, or `pagedmemory`. The `globalsequence` option forces the event trace logger to add a sequence number to every event it logs even if the entries are in different logs. The `localsquence` option adds sequence numbers to every event logged to a specific event trace. The sequence number might appear in another log, but all sequence numbers within a specific log are unique. The `pagedmemory` option forces the event logger to use paged memory, rather than non-paged memory, for its internal buffer allocations. Although using paged memory can slow event logger performance, it can also enhance system performance as a whole.

Not all of the command line switches work with all of the verbs. You need to know which command line switches to use with each verb. With that requirement in mind, here are a few LogMan examples.

```
LogMan create counter perf_log -c "\Processor(_Total)\% Processor Time"
LogMan create trace trace_log -nb 16 256 -bs 64 -o c:\logfile
LogMan start perf_log
LogMan update perf_log -si 10 -f csv -v mmddhhmm
LogMan update trace_log -p "Windows Kernel Trace" (disk,net)
```

Viewing the Results of Changes with the PerfMon Utility

PerfMon was the performance monitoring utility of the past. Windows 2000 represents a sort of transition point where you can use PerfMon or the Performance console. However, starting with Windows XP, the Performance console is the main event and PerfMon has taken a background role. Now all that this utility will do for you is open the Performance counter with settings that you saved from Windows NT 4.0. In other words, you can see the same counters as you did in Windows NT 4.0, but the application displaying them differs. Consequently, the command line switches that you see here won't reflect what you used in the past. This utility uses the following syntax:

```
PerfMon [Filename] [/HTMLFILE:ConvFilename Filename]
```

The following list describes each of the command line arguments.

`Filename` Specifies a file containing Windows NT 4.0 PerfMon settings to adjust the display in the Performance console.

`ConvFilename` Specifies a file containing Windows NT 4.0 converted files. You may use the chart (.pmc), report (.pmr), alert (.pma), and log (.pml) files from a Windows NT 4.0 setup.

`/HTMLFILE` Displays the archived PerfMon files that you converted from a Windows NT 4.0 system. You must supply both the converted filename as well as the settings file used to configure the Performance console.

Reconfiguring Performance Logs with the ReLog Utility

Use this utility to create new performance logs from existing performance logs. The new logs can use a different sample rate. In addition, you can use this utility to convert a log from one format to another. You can use this utility to convert Windows NT 4.0 logs, including the compressed log format. This utility uses the following syntax:

```
ReLog <filename [filename ...]> [options]
```

The following list describes each of the command line arguments.

`filename` Specifies the names of one or more files that you want to convert.

`-a` Appends the output to an existing binary file.

`-c` *`CounterPath`* `[`*`CounterPath`* `...]` Defines one or more counters to filter from the input log. The output log will contain the remaining counters. Each performance counter has a path that begins with the counter object, specific counter, and finally the instance. Consequently, the `\Process(_Total)\% Processor Time` counter path would collect the `_Total instance of the % Processor Time` counter found in the Processor object. Make sure you place each counter path in double quotes. The counter path can include wildcard characters. Here's a list of acceptable counter path formats.

```
\\machine\object(parent/instance#index)\counter
\\machine\object(parent/instance)\counter
\\machine\object(instance#index)\counter
\\machine\object(instance)\counter
\\machine\object\counter
\object(parent/instance#index)\counter
\object(parent/instance)\counter
\object(instance#index)\counter
\object(instance)\counter
\object\counter
```

-cf *Filename* Specifies a file containing a list of performance counters to collect. Each counter path must appear on a separate line.

-f { Bin | Bincirc | CSV | TSV | SQL } Defines the log format for the output. You can choose between binary, circular binary, CSV, TSV, and SQL.

-t value Changes the sampling rate by writing every *n*th record into the output file. For example, if the original file contains one record for each second, specifying a value of two would change the sampling rate to one every other second. The default setting writes every record into the output.

-o { *Filename* | *DSN!Log* } Specifies the output information for the collection. You can use an output file by specifying a path and filename. As an alternative, you can specify a SQL database (for any vendor that supports SQL) by including the ODBC DSN and the log set name within the SQL database. (See the "Working with ODBC Data Sources" section of Chapter 2 for information on configuring ODBC from the command line.) The default setting is to use a file with the same name as the performance collection and a BLG extension for counters or an ETL extension for traces.

-b *M/d/yyyy h:mm:ss*[{ *AM* | *PM* }] Defines the starting time for the collection. Collection continues until the specified ending time (see the `-e` command line switch) or you manually end the collection process using the stop verb. The default setting uses the current day and time. You can input times using a 24-hour clock. When specifying a time based on a 12-hour clock, add the AM or PM option.

-e *M/d/yyyy h:mm:ss*[{ *AM* | *PM* }] Defines the ending time for the collection. The default setting uses the current day and time. You can input times using a 24-hour clock. When specifying a time based on a 12-hour clock, add the AM or PM option.

-config *Filename* Specifies a configuration filename that contains all of the command line options.

-q Lists all of the performance counters found in the input file. You can use this list to create input for the `-c` or `-cf` command line switches.

-y Answers yes to all questions without prompting. This feature lets you set up counters and traces within a batch file without worrying about interruptions.

Tracking Performance with the TypePerf Utility

You don't have to use the graphical interface to view performance data in real time. The TypePerf utility provides continuously updated performance data in a command window in text format. The display updates at the specified rate until you press Ctrl+C to stop it. This utility uses the following syntax:

```
TypePerf <counter [counter ...]> [options]
TypePerf -cf <filename> [options]
TypePerf -q [object] [options]
TypePerf -qx [object] [options]
```

The following list describes each of the command line arguments.

counter Specifies one or more performance counters to display. Each performance counter has a path that begins with the counter object, specific counter, and finally the instance. Consequently, the `\Process(_Total)\% Processor Time` counter path would collect the `_Total instance of the % Processor Time` counter found in the Processor object. Make sure you place each counter path in double quotes. The counter path can include wildcard characters. Here's a list of acceptable counter path formats.

```
\\machine\object(parent/instance#index)\counter

\\machine\object(parent/instance)\counter

\\machine\object(instance#index)\counter

\\machine\object(instance)\counter

\\machine\object\counter

\object(parent/instance#index)\counter

\object(parent/instance)\counter

\object(instance#index)\counter

\object(instance)\counter

\object\counter
```

-f { Bin | Bincirc | CSV | TSV | SQL } Defines the log format for the output. You can choose between binary, circular binary, CSV, TSV, and SQL.

-cf *Filename* Specifies a file containing a list of performance counters to collect. Each counter path must appear on a separate line. The default for the TypePerf utility is CSV.

-si [[*hh:*]*mm:*]*ss* Defines the sample interval (how often the system samples the counter) for the collection. The default is 1 second.

-o { *Filename* | *DSN!Log* } Specifies the output information for the collection. You can use an output file by specifying a path and filename. As an alternative, you can specify a SQL database (for any vendor that supports SQL) by including the ODBC DSN and the log set name within the SQL database. (See the "Working with ODBC Data Sources" section of Chapter 2 for information on configuring ODBC from the command line.) The default setting is to use a file with the same name as the performance collection and a BLG extension for counters or an ETL extension for traces. The default output is STDOUT (the display).

`-q [object]` Lists the installed counters. If you want to see the counters for a specific object, include the object name (such as Process). This command line switch doesn't list counter instances.

`-qx [object]` Lists the installed counters with instances. If you want to see the counters for a specific object, include the object name (such as Process).

`-sc samples` Defines the number of samples to collect. The default setting collects samples until you press Ctrl+C.

`-config Filename` Specifies a configuration filename that contains all of the command line options.

`-s computer` Performs the task on a remote system. The default setting uses the local system.

`-y` Answers yes to all questions without prompting. This feature lets you set up counters and traces within a batch file without worrying about interruptions.

Removing Performance Counters with the UnlodCtr Utility

The UnlodCtr utility unloads counters from memory. This utility uses the following syntax:

```
UNLODCTR [\\computername] driver
```

The following list describes each of the command line arguments.

`computername` Specifies the name of a remote computer. You must have access to the computer through Windows. This utility doesn't provide any means of specifying a username or password for the remote computer.

`driver` Defines the name of the driver that you want to unload. Unloading a driver removes all its entries from the registry.

VISTA

Assessing Your System with the WinSAT Utility

It's often hard to know whether your system passes the tests for using Vista. If you're an administrator and have hundreds (or even thousands) of systems to test, the question becomes even more difficult to answer. Fortunately, Vista comes with the Windows System Assessment Tool (WinSAT) utility that you can use to determine the suitability of a particular system for using Vista. This utility uses the following syntax:

```
WINSAT <assesment_name> [switches]
```

The following list describes each of the command line arguments.

`assesment_name` Defines what kind of assessment to perform on the system. The full assessment can require several minutes to run and you might only need to check whether the CPU will work. The following list describes the valid assessment types.

- **Formal** Performs the full set of assessment tests. This assessment provides a formal output file as well. You'll find the file in the `%systemroot%\windows\performance\datastore` folder. This is the only assessment that outputs data to a file.
- **Features** Performs a features assessment.
- **CPU** Performs the CPU assessment.
- **Mem** Performs the system memory assessment.

DWM Performs the Desktop Windows Manager (DWM) assessment. This particular assessment will produce less than perfect results if you don't have the compositor running. To check for the compositor, right-click Computer and choose Properties to display the System window. Click the Advanced System Settings link to display the System Properties dialog box. Click Settings in the Performance area to display the Visual Effects tab of the Performance Options dialog box. Check the Enable Desktop Composition option.

D3D Performs the Direct 3D assessment. This particular assessment will cause your screen to blank until the test completes. To stop the test, press Alt+Tab to display the command prompt, and then click Ctrl+C.

Media Performs the media assessment.

MFMedia Performs the Media Foundation Media (MFMedia) assessment.

Disk *`DiskNumber`* Performs the disk assessment on the specified disk.

`-v` Provides verbose assessment output. Unlike some commands, where verbose means a few extra lines, the output of this utility can go on for several pages. You may want to redirect the output to a text file when using this option.

`-xml` ***`Filename`*** Saves the output to the specified XML file.

`-eef` Enumerates any extra features that the assessment finds such as optical disks and memory modules.

Getting Started with Command Line Tasks

This chapter has discussed a number of utilities that provide system information in a variety of ways. These utilities all have one thing in common: they tell you something about your system. Some utilities provide static information, while others provide dynamic output. In addition, some utilities provide information about your hardware, some about the software, or some information about both. These utilities help you gain a better understanding of your system, which makes it harder for intruders to plant secret software on your system and helps you locate potential hardware problems before they shut you down.

An important consideration in working with these utilities is that you can become overwhelmed quite quickly. There are so many utilities that you could possibly spend your entire day monitoring your system, rather than using it for productive work. The important thing to remember about these utilities is that you should use them occasionally to improve your personal productivity, not as a means of impeding progress. One way to work around this problem is to create a schedule for checking out your system. A few minutes each morning with a different set of utilities will provide an amazing amount of information at an incredibly low cost in time.

Chapter 4 helps you look for things: files, hardware, and other resources of all types. Many industry pundits talk about the low cost of drive space today. All of that drive space hides a wealth of information. It's accessible, but it's hiding in plain sight. The purpose of Chapter 4 is to show you how to locate all of that missing data, those hidden utilities, the resources that you thought you had but now are lost. Consider this chapter an introduction to Microsoft's lost and found center for your computer.

Chapter 4

Locating Files and Other Resources

- Locating Files
- Monitoring Files
- Working with Other Resources

At one time, information overload was a new term and not many people suffered from it. As time progressed, the situation became worse until everyone suffers from information overload today. In fact, we really need to come up with a new term to express the nearly frantic nature of information overload today. Of course, you're wondering what this has to do with the topic of this chapter. Your hard drive is actually another source of information overload. I still remember when people considered a 30 MB hard drive huge. Today, a single application can easily consume 30 MB or more of space. In short, you have a lot more to wade through to locate the one file that you really need. Locating files and other resources on your system has become difficult because the system has too many items to track effectively—your system suffers from a different sort of information overload.

This chapter discusses utilities that fall into essentially three categories. The first category is utilities that locate files. They don't really do anything with the files; they just help you find them. The second category is utilities that take the next step; they help you manage the files in some way. The third category is utilities that work with resources other than files. These utilities could work with anything from your network connection to Terminal Server. You'll also find a few interesting utilities in the mix, such as the W32Tm utility that helps you manage the Windows clock.

Locating Files

Most people have probably spent more time than they care to admit trying to find a file on their hard drive. The fact that Windows Explorer does a poor job of locating some types of files, hides others, and generally performs poorly doesn't help matters. In fact, look on the market today and you'll find a whole list of third party utilities whose only claim to fame is that they can help you locate your files at least a little better than Windows Explorer does. However, if your only experience in finding files is using Windows Explorer and a collection of third party graphical utilities, then you'll be surprised at just how much the command line can help. This use of the command line benefits everyone. Even a complete novice can gain something by searching for files at the command prompt because the command prompt does the job faster, more efficiently, and without hiding anything from view.

FINDING DATA FILES QUICKLY

It's no secret that people have trouble finding their data files. You also won't find many people who will say that Microsoft has done a good job of making it easier to find data files. Third party utilities for locating information on your hard drive abound because Microsoft hasn't lived up to people's needs or expectations. Unfortunately, these third party utilities also come with hidden security problems, making people wary of using them. In short, it appears that you can choose between not finding what you need or turning the security of your system over to someone else. However, I have a third alternative, one that works well and doesn't compromise security.

At one time, Microsoft did do a reasonable job of helping you find the data files that you need. The only problem is that they never updated the utilities that performed these tasks with a graphical interface, so you must use them at the command line. For example, judicious use of the `Dir` command will help you locate any file that you can name or identify by its attributes. For example, if you can't find a file based on the name because you don't remember it, don't worry; the `Dir` command can help you locate it based on the date you created it or on the file size and I guarantee that it works far better than Windows Explorer.

Of course, sometimes you don't know anything about a file except that it contains a certain reference. That's when I use the FindStr utility. You can search any file with it, not just data files, and locate the strings you want. I've even used this utility to find executables on my hard drive based on a prompt I remembered. In short, you already have the tools you need to find anything on your hard drive.

Finding Files and Directories with the *Dir* Command

The `Dir` command offers a broad range of command line switches that makes looking for a file faster than you might think. Remembering all of the command line switches isn't necessarily easy, but you'll use some of them more often than you use others. In addition to command line switches, you can use wildcard characters to extend the functionally of the search. See the "Working with Wildcard Characters" sidebar in Chapter 2 for details on working with wildcard characters. This command uses the following syntax:

```
DIR [drive:][path][filename] [/A[[:]attributes]] [/B] [/C] [/D] [/L]
[/N] [/O[[:]sortorder]] [/P] [/Q] [/R] [/S] [/T[[:]timefield]] [/W]
[/X] [/4]
```

The following list describes each of the command line arguments.

/A[[:]*attributes*] Displays files with the specified attributes. An attribute defines the file system characteristics of a file. For example, a file with a hidden attribute isn't visible from the command prompt unless you use the `/AH` command line switch. You can also exclude a file with a specific attribute from the search by adding the minus (-) sign in front of the attribute. For example, specifying the `/-AD switch` would exclude directories from the output. See the sidebar titled, "Standard FAT and NTFS File Attributes" for a list of the command line attributes you can check from the command line.

/B Removes the heading and summary information from the output. You can use this feature to prepare a directory listing for a batch file or a script. It also comes in handy when you want to prepare a list of files for a report.

/C Displays the thousand separator in file sizes, which is the default for most systems. This feature makes the file sizes easier to read. Use the `/-C` command line switch to remove the thousand separator from the file sizes.

/D Displays the file output in a wide list format. Generally, this feature allows the display to hold more filenames at the expense of additional information, such as the file size. The `Dir` command sorts the list by column.

/L Displays the output using lowercase characters. Generally, the `Dir` command displays the filenames using uppercase or mixed case characters. A mixed case character display is standard for the Windows command window.

/N Displays files using the long list format where filenames appear on the far right of the display. This is the default setting for the Windows command window.

/O[[:]*sortorder*] Lists the directory in a sorted order. Generally, Windows sorts the directory by name. Normally, the `Dir` command sorts items in ascending order. You can sort in descending order by adding a minus (-) sign to the command line switch. For example, `/-AD` would sort the directory in descending date order. You can use any of the sort orders for the output.

- **E** By extension (alphabetic)
- **D** By date/time (oldest first)
- **G** Group directories first
- **N** By name (alphabetic)
- **S** By size (smallest first)

/P Pauses the output after each screen of information.

/Q Displays the file owner information in addition to the standard file output.

VISTA

/R Displays the alternate data streams in a file. Previously, Windows only displayed the main data stream. Vista lets you view the alternative data streams that many developers use to hide data from view.

/S Displays the files in the specified directory and all subdirectories. Each subdirectory has a separate header unless you specify the `/B` command line switch.

/T[[:]*timefield*] Determines which time field appears in the listing. The `Dir` command always uses the visible time field for sorting. The default setting shows the last modified date. Here are the time field values you can use.

- **C** Creation
- **A** Last Access
- **W** Last Written

/W Displays the file output in a wide list format. Generally, this feature allows the display to hold more filenames at the expense of additional information, such as the file size. The `Dir` command sorts the list by row.

/X Displays the short names generated for non-8.3 filenames (those used for DOS). The `Dir` command uses the same format as provided by the `/N` command line switch with the short name inserted in front of the long name. The display contains blanks for any long filenames that don't have an associated short filename.

/4 Displays the years with four digits. This is the default setting for the Windows command line.

Finding Files and Directories with the Where Utility

The Dir command provides you with a directory listing based on simple command line switches and wildcard characters. It's done the job for many years and is probably still the command of choice when you need to perform most file searches. The Where utility adds complex pattern matching to the search. The purpose of this command is to augment the features that Dir already provides. This command uses the following syntax:

```
WHERE [/R dir] [/Q] [/F] [/T] pattern...
```

The following list describes each of the command line arguments.

/R Searches all of the subfolders for a given pattern starting from the specified directory. This option works the same as the /S command line switch used with other versions of Windows.

/Q Performs the search in quiet mode. The utility only returns the exit code of the search. The valid exit codes include:

- 0: Search is successful
- 1: Search is unsuccessful
- 2: Other failures (such an incorrect syntax) caused the search to fail

/F Displays the matched filename in double quotes. This feature makes it easier to parse the output when you place it in a file using redirection, rather than display it on screen.

/T Displays the file size, last modified date, and time for all of the matched files. Normally, the Where utility displays only the filename.

pattern... The pattern can include the * (asterisk) and ? (question mark), just as you'd use them with the Dir command. In addition, you can use environment variables by using the $EnvVariable:SearchCriteria pattern and a specific path using the Path:SearchCriteria pattern. These alternative search patterns let you look for data in ways that you can't using the Dir command. Here are some examples of all four search techniques:

```
Search for all DLLs in the current folder:
Where *.DLL

Search for all four letter DLLs beginning with the A in the current
folder:
Where A???.DLL

Search for all DLLs in the Path environmental variable:
Where $Path:*.DLL

Search for all DLLs in the C:\Programs and C:\Windows\System32 folder:
Where "C:\Program Files;C:\Windows\System32:B*.DLL"
```

Detecting Shared Open Files with the OpenFiles Utility

The OpenFiles utility helps you track open shared files on any system of a network. This utility has a number of purposes, but the most important is to ensure that a system has no shared files open before shutting it down. Even though Windows performs an orderly shutdown on the server, the client may have data stored in a local cache that could get lost when the server shuts down. You could also use this utility to look for signs of unwanted intrusion (either locally or from a remote source). A shared file that you can't account for could indicate the activities of a cracker or a disgruntled employee. The OpenFiles utility has three modes of operation, Disconnect, Query, and Local, which are discussed in the sections that follow.

DISCONNECT

This mode disconnects a user or closes a file. You can use this mode to force a closure. In some cases, you might find this necessary when an application terminates abnormally and leaves the file in an uncertain state. This mode uses the following syntax:

```
OPENFILES /Disconnect [/S system [/U username [/P [password]]]]
{[/ID id] [/A accessedby] [/O {Read | Read/Write | Write}]}
[/OP openfile]
```

The following list describes each of the command line arguments.

WARNING **Always disconnect users or close files with care. Pursue every other possible means of disconnecting the user or closing the file before you use the disconnect mode. Disconnecting users or closing files using this technique may corrupt the data file or cause the application to lose data because this method doesn't consider any of the data that appears in the application cache.**

/S *system* Specifies the remote system that you want to check. In most cases, you'll also need to supply the /U and the /P command line switches when using this switch.

/U [*domain*\\]*user* Specifies the username on the remote system. This name may not match the username on the local system. You'll need to supply a domain name when working with a domain controller.

/P [*password*] Specifies the password for the given user. You can provide the command line switch without specifying the password on the command line in cleartext. The system prompts you for the password. Using this feature can help you maintain the security of passwords used on your system.

/ID *id* Specifies the identifier of the file to disconnect. You may use the * wildcard to disconnect all currently shared files by identifier. Use the OpenFiles /Query mode to obtain the list of files currently open on the system, including the file identifier.

/A *username* Disconnects all files opened by a particular user as specified by username. You can use the * wildcard to disconnect all currently shared files by username. Use the OpenFiles /Query mode to obtain the list of files currently open on the system, including the username.

/O {Read | Read/Write | Write} Closes all files opened in a particular mode. The valid values include read, read/write, and write. You can use the * wildcard to disconnect all currently shared files by open mode. Use the OpenFiles /Query /V mode to obtain the list of files currently open on the system, including the open mode. Note that the standard display doesn't include the open mode, so you must specify the /V command line switch.

/OP openfile Disconnects all open file connections created by a particular open filename. You can use the * wildcard to disconnect all currently shared files by filename. Use the OpenFiles /Query mode to obtain the list of files currently open on the system, including the name of the open file.

Query

Use this mode to obtain a list of the files currently open on a system. This mode uses the following syntax:

```
OPENFILES /Query [/S system [/U username [/P [password]]]]
[/FO {TABLE | LIST | CSV}] [/NH] [/V]
```

The following list describes each of the command line arguments.

/S *system* Specifies the remote system that you want to check. In most cases, you'll also need to supply the /U and the /P command line switches when using this switch.

/U [*domain*\\]*user* Specifies the username on the remote system. This name may not match the username on the local system. You'll need to supply a domain name when working with a domain controller.

/P [*password*] Specifies the password for the given user. You can provide the command line switch without specifying the password on the command line in cleartext. The system prompts you for the password. Using this feature can help you maintain the security of passwords used on your system.

/FO {TABLE | LIST | CSV} Defines the output provided by the utility. The table format is normally the easiest to view on screen. The table columns define the values for output, while each row contains one driver entry. The CSV output provides the best method for preparing the data for entry in a database. Use redirection (see the "Employing Data Redirection" section of Chapter 2 for details) to output the CSV data to a file and then import it to your database. The list format provides one data element per line. Each group of data elements defines one driver. The utility separates each driver by one blank line. Some people find the list format more readable when working in verbose mode since the table format requires multiple lines for each entry (the lines wrap).

/NH Forces the utility to display the data without a column header. You can only use this command line switch with the table and CSV formats. Omitting the header makes it easier to incorporate the data in a report or import it into a database.

/V Displays detailed file information. The standard display includes the file identifier, accessed by information, file type, and filename complete with path. The extended information provided by this command line switch includes the hostname (server), number of locks, and the mode used to open the file (read, read/write, or write).

Local

This mode uses the following syntax:

```
OPENFILES /Local [{ ON | OFF }]
```

The following describes the command line argument.

{ ON | OFF } Enables or disables the "maintain objects list" system global flag. The state of this flag determines whether the system tracks the state of local file handles. Enabling this flag adds overhead, which reduces performance, and also lets you track the status of shared files on your system. Calling the OpenFiles /Local mode without using this command line switch at all displays the current flag status, which is disabled on Windows systems.

Locating Information in Files with the Find and FindStr Utilities

The Find and FindStr utilities both locate files based on their content. The Find utility is less capable than FindStr, in most cases. The Find utility uses the following syntax:

```
FIND [/V] [/C] [/N] [/I] [/OFF[LINE]] "string"
   [[drive:][path]filename[...]]
```

The following list describes each of the command line arguments.

/V Displays all of the lines that don't contain the specified string.

/C Displays a count of the lines containing the specified string, but not the actual location.

/N Displays the line number of each occurrence of the specified string within the file.

/I Ignores the case of the characters when searching for the string. Normally, the Find utility will treat Cat, CAT, and cat as different strings.

/OFF[LINE] Processes all of the specified files, even if they have the offline attribute set.

string Defines the text string that you want to find. The Find utility doesn't allow the use of regular expressions, so you can only locate strings based on their actual content.

[drive:][path]*filename* Defines the files to search for the specified string. You can use wildcard characters to define the file specification.

NOTE If you don't specify a path, the Find utility searches the text typed at the prompt or piped from another command. This feature means that you could use Find to perform tasks such as locating a particular file based on size in a directory listing (as an example). You can use redirection to let Find locate particular data in the output of any command or utility.

There's one use for Find that isn't found in FindStr—you can use Find to determine just the number of occurrences of the search string in the target file using the /C switch. This particular feature and the smaller size of Find make it useful for scripting tasks where FindStr is overkill.

The easiest way to use FindStr is to define a simple string and make the call. FindStr will look in all of the files in the current folder for any words in the string. For example, typing **FindStr "Hello World" *.*** at the command prompt and pressing Enter causes the FindStr utility to look for the individual words *Hello* and *World* in all files in the current folder. The FindStr utility uses the following syntax:

```
FINDSTR [/B] [/E] [/L] [/R] [/S] [/I] [/X] [/V] [/N] [/M] [/O]
[/P] [/F:file] [/C:string] [/G:file] [/D:dir list] [/A:color
attributes] [/OFF[LINE]] strings [[drive:][path]filename[...]]
```

The following list describes each of the command line arguments.

/B Matches the search string against the beginning of the line.

NOTE Some of the FindStr features are line related. A line of text or other data ends when FindStr encounters a special carriage return (character number 13) and line feed (character number 10) combination. When looking at a text file, you see one line of text separated from another by white space. The carriage return and line feed combination causes the white space. In DLLs and other unreadable files, there's no need for lines of text, so the carriage return and line feed combination appear irregularly, if at all. This means the lines are much larger and could include the entire file.

/E Matches the search string against the end of the line.

/L Interprets the search strings literally. This means you no longer have access to regular expressions, and you also don't have to escape the special characters.

/R Defines the search string as a regular expression. See the "Using Regular Expressions at the Command Prompt" sidebar for additional information.

/S Looks for the search string in the specified files in the current directory and all subdirectories. When you use this command line switch in the root directory of a hard drive, you can search the entire hard drive for a search string. Because FindStr actually looks in every file, you'll find this process can take a long time.

/I Performs a case-insensitive search. Normally, FindStr differentiates between *Hello* and *hello*—using this command line switch changes that behavior so the two capitalizations are treated the same.

/X Prints only the lines that match the search string exactly.

/V Prints only the lines that don't contain an exact match.

/N Prints the line number before each line that matches. This option helps you find the line faster in a text editor that supports line numbering.

/M Prints only the filenames of files that contain a match. You can redirect the output from FindStr to a file to use as an input for a script or other additional processing.

/O Prints the character offset of the matching text in each line. This option helps you find the text faster in text editors that provide column number support.

/P Tells FindStr to skip files that contain nonprintable characters, such as executable files. Given that most data files now contain nonprintable characters, you should probably avoid using this option unless you know the data appears in pure text files.

/F:*File* Reads the list of files to process from a file. You can also supply a value of "/" to type the names of the files to check at the command line.

/C:*String* Performs a literal search with the search string. For example, normally when you type **"Hello World"** as the search string, FindStr looks for the words separately—lines containing either *Hello* or *World* will match. However, when you specify this option, FindStr only matches lines that contain the whole term, *Hello World*.

/G:*File* Reads the list of search strings to look for from a file. You can also supply a value of "/" to type the search strings at the command line.

/D:*Directories* Defines a list of directories to search. You must separate each directory entry with a semicolon.

/A:*ColorAttribute* Tells FindStr to display the filenames using colors. You must provide two hexadecimal (base 16) values from 0 through F (these values are the same as 0 through 15 decimal). The first value is the background color and the second is the text color. This switch doesn't affect display of the matching text color, which relies on the current background and foreground colors of the command prompt.

/OFF[LINE] Processes all of the specified files, even if they have the offline attribute set.

strings Defines one or more text strings that you want to find. Use regular expressions (the /R command line switch) to locate text based on wildcards.

[drive:][path]*filename*[...] Defines one or more files to search for the specified string. You can use wildcard characters to define the file specification.

USING REGULAR EXPRESSIONS AT THE COMMAND PROMPT

The true power of FindStr and other advanced text manipulation command line utilities is that you can create specialized strings using a concept called regular expressions. A regular expression defines how to look for a string, rather than precisely which string to find. Regular expressions can contain the special characters described in the following list.

. (Period) Provides a placeholder for any single character. For example, "w.ll" could represent the words *wall*, *well*, or *will*.

*** (Asterisk)** Represents 0 or more occurrences of the previous character or class. For example, "to*" could represent the words *to* or *too*, or simply the letter *t*.

^ (Circumflex) Represents a character or class at the beginning of a line. For example, "^Hello" would find the word in the line *Hello World*, but not in the line *George said, Hello*.

$ (Dollar sign) Represents a character or class at the end of the line. For example, "World$" would find the word in the line *Hello World*, but not in the line *World Peace*.

[Characters] Contains a character class (set of characters) from which FindStr selects. For example, "w[ai]ll" will match the words *wall* and *will*, but won't match *well*.

[^Characters] Contains a character class (set of characters) that FindStr won't select. For example, "w[^ai]ll" will match the word *well*, but won't match the words *wall* or *will*.

[Character-Character] Specifies a range of characters that FindStr will use for selection. For example, "[a-z]" selects all characters *a* through *z*, but not numbers or special symbols.

\Character Tells FindStr to use the character literally, rather than as a special character. Programmers call this process escaping the character. For example, "z**" locates terms that begin with *z* followed by 0 or more asterisks within the file.

\<Characters Locates the characters when they appear at the beginning of a word. For example, "\<we" locates the words *welcome* and *well*, but not the word *owe*.

Characters\> Locates the characters when they appear at the end of a word. For example, "we\>" locates the word *owe*, but not the words *welcome* and *well*.

Using regular expressions lets you create complex search patterns that reduce search time and ensure good results. For example, you could create a telephone number search pattern using the search string "(...)...-...." assuming that your telephone numbers always include an area code and are formatted using the method shown. I've actually used this search pattern to locate telephone numbers hidden in DLLs.

Monitoring Files

Finding files—knowing that they exist and where you can find them—isn't always enough. Sometimes you need to monitor the files and manage them using low-level utilities. These utilities aren't your run-of-the-mill editor that modifies the content of the file. Instead, these utilities perform some type of monitoring action with the file as a whole. For example, you can check the current attributes used to define a file for the operating system using the Attrib utility. The following sections describe these monitoring utilities in detail.

UNDERSTANDING THE NEED TO MONITOR FILES

I often check my customers' files for unexpected changes. Not only do I check executables, but data files as well. Sometimes a customer will ask why I perform this particular task and the answer is simple: the customer isn't the only one changing those files. Many people have the mind-set that once they change a file, the change stays put. However, this conception of Windows is seldom true. Even if your system is completely clean, the operating system, device drivers, update programs, and other external forces all modify the files on your system. In some cases, these automated changes don't work as expected and you could actually end up with an old version of a file on your system that will cause it to perform poorly (or perhaps, not at all).

Of course, there are also the unexpected changes made by crackers, adware, spyware, and viruses. A sudden change to a data file you haven't modified for months could provide a pointer to other nasty changes on your machine. Only by monitoring your files will you ever learn about these changes and be able to act on them. In short, monitoring is required when you want to ensure your system will remain functional.

Changing File and Directory Attributes with the Attrib Utility

The Attrib (attribute) utility lets you discover the attributes attached to a given file in an unambiguous way. Attributes are special notations that the file system makes about the folder or file. For example, when you modify a file, the file system sets the archive attribute, which tells your backup program that the file has changed. When the backup program makes a copy of the file, it resets the archive attribute. See the "Standard FAT and NTFS File Attributes" sidebar for additional details about attributes. This utility uses the following syntax:

```
ATTRIB [{+R | -R}] [{+A | -A }] [{+S | -S}] [{+H | -H}]
[drive:][path][filename] [/S [/D] [/L]]
```

The following list describes each of the command line arguments.

`+` Sets an attribute.

`-` Clears an attribute.

`R` Modifies the read-only file attribute.

`A` Modifies the archive file attribute.

`S` Modifies the system file attribute.

`H` Modifies the hidden file attribute.

`[drive:][path]`*`filename`* Defines one or more files to modify or query. You can use wildcard characters to define the file specification. Specifying a file specification without any attribute changing command line switches displays the attributes for those files. Using Attrib by itself, without any file specification, displays the attributes for all files in the directory. This technique even displays system and hidden files.

`/S` Processes files that match the file specification in the current directory and all subdirectories.

`/D` Processes the directories as well as the files that match the file specification.

`/L` Processes the attributes of a symbolic link, rather than the symbolic link's target.

You can also use the Attrib utility to locate files with a specific attribute. It works much the same as the `Dir` (directory) command at the command prompt, but the focus is on the attributes, rather than other file or folder information. To test this command, open a command prompt in the root directory (the uppermost directory) of your C drive, type **`Attrib *.*`** at the command prompt, and press Enter. You'll see a list of all of the files in the root directory, along with their associated attributes. For example, many of the files will have an `A` for archive next to them. Some files, such as `ntldr`, will have the `S` (system), `H` (hidden), and `R` (read-only) attributes.

It's possible to view and change the attributes (except system) for a file using Windows Explorer. To change an attribute, right-click the file and choose Properties from the context menu. You'll see the file Properties dialog box. The Read-only and Hidden options on the General tab modify these attributes on the file. Click Advanced and you'll see the Advanced Attributes dialog box that contains the File Is Ready for Archiving option that controls the archive attribute. Although this method is aesthetically pleasing, you have to change the files one at a time. Using Attrib, you can change a number of files using a single command. For example, if you want to remove the system, hidden, and read-only attributes from every executable in a particular folder, you'd type:

```
Attrib -h -r -s *.EXE
```

Real World Scenario

STANDARD FAT AND NTFS FILE ATTRIBUTES

Everyone categorizes the data they create. For example, you might make a differentiation between data and executable files, and then further categorize the data by the application that created it. Categorizing files is important because the categorization process helps you define the file and specify what it does for you. The operating system categorizes files, too, and in a way that you can use to your advantage. By knowing how to use attributes, you can differentiate between files that the system uses (ones that you normally don't need to worry about) and those that you use.

A friend of mine was relating a story about another use for attributes. You use attributes as a means of determining how the operating system interacts with files. Many companies now enforce a policy of setting hidden files so they remain hidden, even in Windows. Otherwise, users will delete files they shouldn't, which is where this story began. It seems that one user deleted all of the "extraneous" files on her system to make room for more data files, files such as Command.COM, Config.SYS, and AutoExec.BAT. The next morning, the user complained that the system wouldn't boot. After restoring the system, the network administrator warned the user not to delete any more files. The next month, the user did the same thing all over again. It wasn't long before the company had a new "no delete" policy in place, which remains in force today for Windows users.

The File Allocation Table (FAT) file system used with DOS and older versions of Windows, the File Allocation Table 32-bit (FAT32) file system used with Windows 95 and above, and the Windows NT File System (NTFS) used with versions of Windows starting with Windows NT, rely on file attributes to identify particular file conditions. For example, the archive attribute shows that the file has changed since the last full backup. The command line utilities described in this book can't access all of these attributes directly. For example, even though some utilities can perform a task based on the offline attribute, none of them can manipulate this attribute in any significant way. All of the inaccessible attributes appear as part of NTFS. The following list describes the attributes that you can access using the command line utilities.

A The operating system sets this attribute whenever a file or directory experiences a change. The attribute alerts backup applications to the need for creating a backup of the file under specific conditions. However, you can also use the attribute to monitor the system for unexpected changes. For example, unless you've recently updated a particular Windows DLL, the archive attribute should remain clear (unset). A change in the attribute status could indicate the activities of a cracker.

D The directory attribute indicates that a file system entry is a directory, a container for other files and directories. You can use the directory in a number of ways—everything from mapping the structure of your hard drive to locating hidden entities on the hard drive. Many viruses now rely on hidden directories to store their data.

H The hidden file attribute indicates that you normally can't see the file as part of a directory listing. The file still exists and the operating system can still access it. The original intent of the hidden attribute was to keep system and other sensitive files hidden from users who might accidentally modify or delete them. Windows generally makes this feature obsolete by showing all files, hidden or not, unless you set the operating system not to display them by selecting the "Do not show hidden files and folders" option on the View tab of the Folder Options dialog box. However, the hidden attribute still keeps files hidden from the view of command line utilities, so you need to know it exists.

R The read-only attribute ensures that you can't change, delete, or even move a file without seeing an error message. The read-only attribute commonly appears as part of operating system files. However, developers also use it with read-only data for applications and you might even see it in use for other purposes, such as license files. Windows does honor the read-only attribute, so you can't easily override the effects of this attribute no matter how you access the file.

S The system attribute marks a file as one that the operating system relies on to perform essential tasks. Generally, you don't want to change, delete, or modify files marked with this attribute—doing so could cause the operating system to freeze, refuse to boot, or behave erratically.

L Symbolic links are essentially pointers to a physical file or folder somewhere else on the drive, another local drive, or even a network drive. The symbolic link makes it unnecessary to track where a file or folder exists. Instead, you focus on the data itself. A directory entry marked as a symbolic link has no real content—just the pointer to the actual file or folder.

VISTA

Changing File and Directory Access with the CACLs Utility

The Check Access Control Lists (CACLs) utility verifies the security settings of a file or directory. Windows attaches an Access Control List (ACL) to every directory and file on the system. The ACL defines rights to the file or directory; it can also remove rights to the file or directory based on the security setup for your system. Each ACL contains multiple entries called Access Control Entries (ACEs). A user can have multiple entries, one for each right that the administrator grants or denies. This utility uses the following syntax:

```
CACLS filename [/T] [/E] [/C] [/G user:{R | W | C | F}]
[/R user [...]] [/P user:{N | R | W | C | F} [...]] [/D user [...]]
```

The following list describes each of the command line arguments.

NOTE Even though Vista still lets you use the CACLs utility, Microsoft has marked this utility as deprecated. In other words, this utility will cease to exist in any form in a future version of Windows. Use the new ICACLs utility to change file and directory access in Vista instead. The "Changing File and Directory Access with the ICACLs Utility" section of the chapter explains this new utility.

filename Specifies the file to query or manage.

/T Changes the ACLs of the specified files or directories in the current directory and all subdirectories.

/E Edits the ACL instead of replacing it. Normally, the system writes a new ACL. However, the system can require a lot of time to perform the task when you change a large number of files that have complex ACLs. Unfortunately, editing the ACL can result in odd conditions where the user ends up with rights they shouldn't have or lacks needed rights due to the order of the entries in the ACL. It's normally a good idea to rewrite the ACL, rather than create a security hole.

/C Ignores access denied errors by moving to the next file or next action.

/G *user*:*{R | W | C | F}* Grants the specified user read, write, change, or full control over a file or directory.

/R *user* Revokes the user's access rights to the file or directory. You must use this command line switch with the /E command line switch because this task requires editing the ACL, rather than creating a new ACL. The use of /E is safe, in this case, because you're removing ACEs from the list, rather than adding new ones.

/P *user*:*{N | R | W | C | F}* Replaces the specified user's access rights with new rights that include none (no access), read, write, change, or full control.

/D *user* Denies file or directory access to the specified file or directory. This action is different from the /R command line switch. When using the /R command line switch, the user's access becomes undefined or defined by other Windows elements such as a parent directory. In this case, you specifically deny access to the user. Consequently, even if a user should have access based on access rights in a parent directory, this command line switch removes that access.

The CACLs utility doesn't provide fine control over file and directory access. For example, using the full set of Windows ACEs, you can set a file to disallow changes in ownership, even if the user otherwise has full control. Figure 4.1 shows a CACLs utility output that has a mixture for fine and coarse entries.

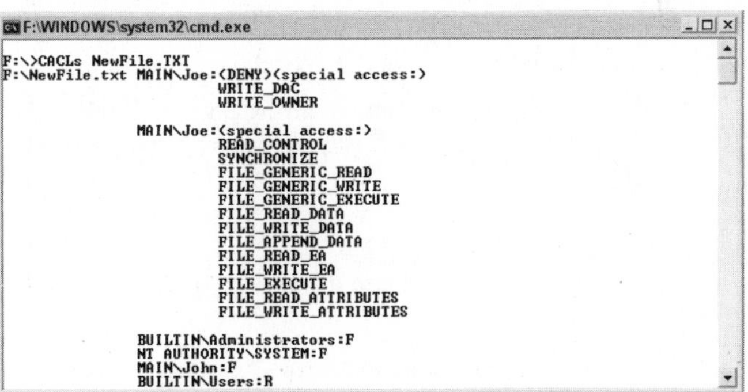

F:\WINDOWS\system32\cmd.exe
F:\>CACLs NewFile.TXT
F:\NewFile.txt MAIN\Joe:(DENY)(special access:)
WRITE_DAC
WRITE_OWNER
MAIN\Joe:(special access:)
READ_CONTROL
SYNCHRONIZE
FILE_GENERIC_READ
FILE_GENERIC_WRITE
FILE_GENERIC_EXECUTE
FILE_READ_DATA
FILE_WRITE_DATA
FILE_APPEND_DATA
FILE_READ_EA
FILE_WRITE_EA
FILE_EXECUTE
FILE_READ_ATTRIBUTES
FILE_WRITE_ATTRIBUTES
BUILTIN\Administrators:F
NT AUTHORITY\SYSTEM:F
MAIN\John:F
BUILTIN\Users:R

FIGURE 4.1
The CACLs utility lets you make coarse adjustments to the file and directory security.

NOTE The CACLs utility relies on a number of abbreviations to convey information. The container inherit (CI) abbreviation signifies that this particular user inherited the Access Control Entry (ACE) from a parent directory. The object inherit (OI) signifies that the ACE reflects a right inherited by the file and not a user. The inherit only (IO) abbreviation shows that the ACE doesn't apply to the current file or directory.

As shown in Figure 4.1, the Administrators group, the system, and user John have full access to the file. The Users group has read-only access to the file. However, Joe has a mixture of rights that demonstrates the fine control that Windows can provide. Even though user Joe has most rights to the file, he can't change the file ownership or the Discretionary Access Control List (DACL). Figure 4.1 demonstrates that even though you can use the CALCs utility in a batch file or script to automate setting security on a system, the resulting setup may require additional changes to bring it into full conformance with company policy.

VISTA

Changing File and Directory Access with the ICACLs Utility

Vista places a significant new emphasis on security. Given the current computing environment, the emphasis is welcome. However, the new emphasis requires a new security utility as well. The ICACLs utility replaces the older CACLs utility used in previous versions of Windows. This new utility has an interesting array of command line syntaxes as shown here:

```
ICACLS Name /Save ACLFile [/T] [/C] [/L] [/Q]

ICACLS Directory [/Substitute SidOld SidNew [...]] /Restore ACLFile
[/C] [/L] [/Q]

ICACLS Name /SetOwner User [/T] [/C] [/L] [/Q]

ICACLS Name /FindSID SID [/T] [/C] [/L] [/Q]

ICACLS Name /Verify [/T] [/C] [/L] [/Q]

ICACLS Name /Reset [/T] [/C] [/L] [/Q]

ICACLS Name [/Grant[:r] SID:Permission[...]]
       [/Deny SID:Permission [...]]
       [/Remove[:g|:d]] SID[...]] [/T] [/C] [/L] [/Q]
       [/SetIntegrityLevel Level[...]]
```

The following list describes each of the command line arguments.

Name Provides the name of an ACL to work with when using the ICACLs utility.

/Save Stores all of the ACLs for the matching names into an ACL file for later use with the /Restore option.

ACLFile Provides the name of a file used to store all of the ACLs.

/T Changes the ACLs of the specified files or directories in the current directory and all subdirectories.

/C Ignores access denied errors by moving to the next file or next action.

/Q Performs the task in quiet mode. The utility doesn't display any success messages.

/L Processes the ACLs of a symbolic link, rather than the symbolic link's target.

Directory Defines a directory used to perform a task.

/Substitute *SidOld SidNew* [...] Specifies that the command should substitute an old Security Identifier (SID) with the value of a new SID.

/Restore Restores the content of an ACL file to either an old or new SID.

/SetOwner Changes the owner of the specified items.

User Defines the name of a user who is the subject of a particular task.

/FindSID Locates all of the names that contain an ACL that mentions the specified SID.

SID Specifies an SID to used to perform a task. The SID may appear in either friendly name form or numerical form. Append an asterisk (*) to the beginning of the SID when you use the numerical form.

/Verify Locates all of the files that have security problems. The two specific checks verify that the file doesn't have an ACL that isn't in canonical form and that the ACL lengths are consistent with ACE counts. The ICACLs utility preserves the canonical order of the ACEs within an ACL. It follows this form:

- Explicit denials
- Explicit grants
- Inherited denials
- Inherited grants

/Reset Replaces any custom file ACLs with the default inherited ACL. This action resets the file's security to a known state of accessibility.

/Grant[:r] ***SID:Permission*** Grants the specified user the rights defined by the combination of an SID and associated permission. When you include the `:r` argument, the granted rights replace those the user currently holds. Otherwise, the new rights are in addition to those that the user already possesses. The `Permission` variable is actually a mask that you can specify in one of two forms: simple and specific. You can't mix the types in a single use of the utility. Here's the list of simple rights that you can assign.

- F (full access)
- M (modify access)
- RX (read and execute access)
- R (read-only access)
- W (write-only access)

Here's a list of the specific rights that you can assign.

- D (delete)
- RC (read control)
- WDAC (write DAC)
- WO (write owner)
- S (synchronize)
- AS (access system security)
- MA (maximum allowed)
- GR (generic read)

- GW (generic write)
- GE (generic execute)
- GA (generic all)
- RD (read data/list directory)
- WD (write data/add file)
- AD (append data/add subdirectory)
- REA (read extended attributes)
- WEA (write extended attributes)
- X (execute/traverse)
- DC (delete child)
- RA (read attributes)
- WA (write attributes)

When working with directories, you may also assign inheritance rights to the security settings. Inheritance rights apply to either simple or specific rights. Here's the list of inheritance rights.

- (OI) (object inherit)
- (CI) (container inherit)
- (IO) (inherit only)
- (NP) (don't propagate inherit)

`/Deny` ***`SID`*****`:`*****`Permission`*** Defines the specified user the rights defined by the combination of an SID and associated permission. When the system adds the specified deny ACE, it also removes any associated grant ACE that may appear in the user's list of rights. See the `/Grant` command line switch for an explanation of permissions.

`/Remove[:[g|d]]` ***`SID`*** Removes all occurrences of the specific SID within an ACL. When you add the `:g` argument, the system removes all grant ACEs associated with the SID. When you add the `:d` argument, the system removes all deny ACEs associated with the SID. The default action removes both grant and deny ACEs.

`/SetIntegrityLevel` ***`Level`*****`[...]`** Adds an integrity ACE to all of the matching files. You specify the integrity level as L (low), M (medium), or H (high). This option also accepts the inheritance options of CI (container inherit) and OI (object inherit) when working with directories.

Determining File and Directory Status with the ChkDsk Utility

The ChkDsk utility has been around in various forms from the days of DOS—before Windows appeared on the scene. Of course, Microsoft keeps adding features to this utility and it now runs as part of Windows, instead of part of DOS, but the concept remains the same. You use ChkDsk to perform a basic check of the hard drive. In addition, you can optionally use it to recover lost clusters and attempt repairs on damaged clusters. This utility uses the following syntax:

```
CHKDSK [volume[[path]filename]]] [/F] [/V] [/R] [/X] [/I] [/C] [/L[:size]] [/B]
```

The following list describes each of the command line arguments.

/F Adds fixing media errors to the list of tasks to perform. This switch differs from /R, which recovers clusters lost when an application terminates unexpectedly.

/R Adds recovering lost clusters to the list of tasks to perform. Using this switch also adds the /F switch automatically.

/V Displays the full path and name of every file on the disk. Use this switch only on FAT or FAT32 formatted drives.

/L [*Size*] Outputs the current size of the log file used to track drive activity when you use the /L switch alone. Including the optional log file size modifies the size of the log for the current drive. Theoretically, a larger log could help improve drive reliability, but in practice, the default size normally works well. Use this switch only on NTFS-formatted drives.

/X Forces the operating system to dismount a drive before performing a check. Dismounting the drive makes all drive resources unavailable, but also ensures uninterrupted access by ChkDsk, which can help improve the results of any tasks performed. The operating system must mount a drive before you can access the drive contents again. Use this switch only on NTFS formatted drives.

/I Performs a less robust check of the drive indexes (the portion of the drive used to locate files). Normally, you won't use this switch when you want to check a drive for optimum performance. However, you can use this switch to reduce the time required to check the drive. Use this switch only on NTFS-formatted drives.

/C Skips checking cycles within the drive folders. When a folder contains cyclical references, damage to the files can result. Consequently, even though this switch does reduce the time to check the drive, you want to avoid using it because ChkDsk doesn't thoroughly check the drive otherwise. Use this switch only on NTFS-formatted drives.

/B Reevaluates bad clusters on the hard drive. If the cluster is readable, ChkDsk places it back into service. This option is only available on NTFS drives and using it also includes the /R command line switch.

To use ChkDsk to perform a basic check, type **ChkDsk** at the command prompt and press Enter. ChkDsk always assumes that you want to check the current drive. When you want to check a different drive, add the drive letter to the command. In addition, when you're working a FAT-formatted drive, you can specify a specific file. For example, you could type **ChkDsk C:\DRVSPACE.BIN** to check the DRVSPACE.BIN file on drive C.

NOTE You can't use ChkDsk directly on the Windows (boot) drive with either the /F or /R options because Windows needs access to specific files at all times. Use the ChkNTFS utility to repair the Windows drive. It's possible to use ChkDsk in the read-only mode to look for potential errors without fixing.

Performing Boot Time Disk Checks with the ChkNTFS Utility

Most of the hard drives used with Windows today rely on NTFS because it's more robust. It provides data encryption, extra security, and built-in file compression. In addition, NTFS is more reliable than the older FAT file system. However, NTFS also requires a little more care at times because it's more complex than FAT. The following sections describe how to use the ChkNTFS utility and how the associated AutoChk application enhances ChkNTFS at boot time.

Using the ChkNTFS Utility

The ChkNTFS utility works with ChkDsk to ensure your system remains problem free. You won't see the effects of this utility right away in most cases. This utility sets up your drive to use ChkDsk during the boot process, rather than after Windows has booted, to ensure you can gain full access to the drive. The drive repair can occur without Windows interference. When you select a drive for a scan, ChkNTFS says that it's dirty. Therefore, when you see that the drive isn't dirty, that means ChkNTFS hasn't scheduled it for a check. A drive can also become dirty when Windows detects an error on it. This utility uses the following syntax:

```
CHKNTFS volume [...]
CHKNTFS /D
CHKNTFS /T[:time]
CHKNTFS /X volume [...]
CHKNTFS /C volume [...]
```

To use ChkNTFS, you must provide a drive argument or one of the command line switches at a minimum. When you supply a drive argument, ChkNTFS tells you the drive format and determines whether Windows has scheduled it for a check. The following list describes each of the command line arguments.

`volume` Determines the volume to check for errors. You can specify the volume using a drive letter followed by a colon, a mount point, or a volume name.

`/D` Places all of the drives in the default state. You can use this switch to remove a drive from the checklist when you schedule the check. This switch won't reverse a mandatory check due to an error detected by Windows.

`/T[:Time]` Tells how much time the utility allows before it begins the check sequence during boot time when you use this switch by itself. The automatic countdown lets you decide at boot time whether to run ChkDsk as planned. Supplying the optional time value modifies the countdown timer to give the user more or less time to make the ChkDsk decision. The default automatic countdown value is 10 seconds.

`/X Volume` Excludes one or more drives from a check. You use this option when you set up the system to perform ChkDsk every time it boots. This is a one time switch—Windows excludes the drive for one boot cycle.

`/C Volume` Schedules a drive for a check during the next boot cycle.

TIP You don't have to use ChkNTFS to perform some tasks. For example, when you want to set up a drive for a scan, right-click the drive in Windows Explorer and choose Properties from the context menu. Select the Tools tab and click Check Now. You'll see a Check Disk dialog box. Check both of the repair options and click Start. When working with a boot drive, Windows Explorer displays an error saying that it couldn't complete the check. It then offers the chance to perform the check later during the next boot. Click Yes and Windows Explorer sets up the check.

Understanding How AutoChk Works with ChckNTFS

AutoChk is a non-Windows application; you can't run it from the command prompt. However, the utility does run during the boot process, which is when you'll see it at work. The AutoChk utility determines which volumes to check at boot time based on entries it finds in the registry. The `HKEY_LOCAL_MACHINE\SYSTEM\CurrentControlSet\Control\Session Manager` key normally contains a value that indicates that AutoChk should check all volumes for the dirty bit (attribute), which means that they require a boot time check.

The dirty bit is an indicator. You can manually set the dirty bit by using the ChkNTFS utility or request that the system set it when using the ChkDsk utility on a drive that is locked. In addition, the system sets the dirty bit whenever one of a number of errors occurs. Finally, you can modify the registry so that AutoChk performs specific tasks whenever you boot the system. The Microsoft Knowledge Base article at `http://support.microsoft.com/kb/q218461/` provides additional information on this topic.

It's important to note the correspondence between commands you enter at the command prompt using ChckNTFS and the corresponding change to the registry that results in AutoChk running during the boot process. For example, if you enter **`ChkNTFS D: E: /X`** at the command prompt, the system actually enters **`Autocheck AutoChk /k:D /k:E *`** into the registry. The `/k AutoChk` command line switch excludes the specified drive from checks during the boot process.

Encrypting Data with the Cipher Utility

The Cipher utility provides encryption status information about files and directories on your hard drive. It relies on the encryption capabilities built into NTFS and doesn't work with FAT-formatted drives. Windows registers encrypted files in the name of the current user, so the encryption is seamless. The only time you actually see the encryption at work is when you try to open files or directories encrypted by someone else. This utility uses the following syntax:

```
CIPHER [/E | /D | /C] [/S:directory] [/A] [/I] [/F] [/Q] [/B] [/H]
   [pathname [...]]
CIPHER /K
CIPHER /R:filename [/Smartcard]
CIPHER /U [/N]
CIPHER /W:directory
CIPHER /X[:efsfile] [filename]
CIPHER /Y
CIPHER /ADDUSER [/CERTHASH:hash | /CERTFILE:filename] [/S:directory]
   [/B] [/H] [pathname [...]]
CIPHER /REMOVEUSER /CERTHASH:hash [/S:directory] [/B] [/H]
   [pathname [...]]
CIPHER /REKEY [pathname [...]]
```

The following list describes each of the command line arguments.

NOTE Even though Vista adds a number of new command line switches, it may not support all of the command line switches older versions of Windows support. For example, Vista doesn't appear to support the /A command line switch. Consequently, you may need to rewrite some scripts to accommodate the new Cipher command line under Vista.

`pathname` Defines the location of a file to encrypt or query. The pathname includes the drive, path, and filename. The pathname can include multiple files or directories; separate each file or directory with a space. You may also use wildcard characters with a pathname.

`directory` Defines an absolute or relative directory path. The directory can contain a drive when you use an absolute path. You can't specify a filename as part of the directory argument.

`filename` Defines a filename without a file extension. You can't include a drive or path as part of the filename. The filename can't contain wildcard characters.

`efsfile` Defines an Encrypting File System (EFS) path that can include a drive, path, and filename.

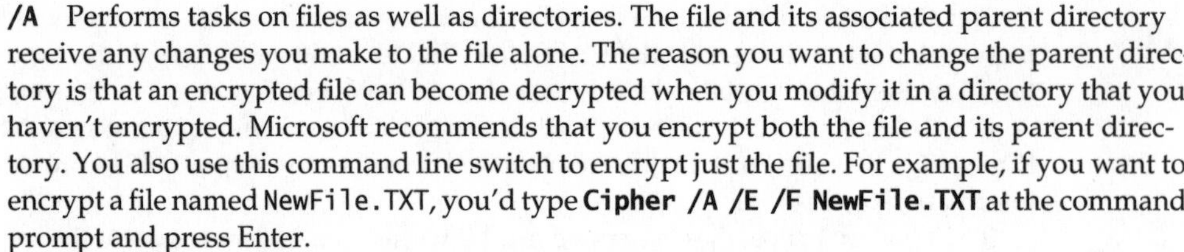

/A Performs tasks on files as well as directories. The file and its associated parent directory receive any changes you make to the file alone. The reason you want to change the parent directory is that an encrypted file can become decrypted when you modify it in a directory that you haven't encrypted. Microsoft recommends that you encrypt both the file and its parent directory. You also use this command line switch to encrypt just the file. For example, if you want to encrypt a file named `NewFile.TXT`, you'd type **`Cipher /A /E /F NewFile.TXT`** at the command prompt and press Enter.

/ADDUSER Adds a user as someone who can access an encrypted file. You must provide a credential for the user to use when accessing the file. Cipher makes it possible to use a certificate hash or a certificate file. When using a certificate file, Cipher accesses the certificate hash in the file and records it.

/B Aborts the encryption when encountering an error. By default, Cipher attempts to continue the encryption.

/C Displays information about the encrypted file.

/CERTFILE:*filename* Specifies the name of file that contains a hash for the user.

/CERTHASH:*hash* Provides the actual hash used to define security access for the user.

/D Decrypts the specified directories or files. When working with a directory, the directory is marked so the system won't encrypt files added to it afterward. You must include the `/A` command line switch to work with files.

/E Encrypts the specified directories or files. When working with a directory, the directory is marked so that the system automatically encrypts any files added to it afterward. You must include the `/A` command line switch to work with files.

/F Forces the encryption operation on all specified objects, even those that the system has already encrypted. Normally, the system skips any files that are already encrypted. You may have to use this switch when working with files in some instances.

/H Forces the system to work with files (encrypt, decrypt, or query) that have the hidden or system attributes. Normally, the system skips files with these attributes.

/I Forces Cipher to continue performing tasks even after it experiences an error. Normally, Cipher stops performing tasks when it encounters an error. Using this command line switch would allow a batch file to continue processing files, even when some of the files failed to react as anticipated. You should redirect the output to a log file when using this option to track the errors and take any required remedial action when the task completes.

/K Defines a new encryption key for the user running Cipher. You can't use any other command line switches with this command line switch. The system displays a message that includes the new key when you use this option. Save this thumbprint to a file so that you can use it to open files encrypted on one machine on another machine. The Microsoft Knowledge Base article at `http://support.microsoft.com/default.aspx?scid=kb;en-us;295680&sd=tech` describes this process in detail. Never let anyone see or use your encryption key because they can use the key to access your encrypted files.

/N Prevents the system from updating keys used to encrypt files. Use this command line switch with the `/U` switch to locate all encrypted files on a local drive without actually performing any updates. Use redirection to place the list of encrypted files in a text file for later use.

/Q Reports only essential information, such as errors, rather than general information including success messages.

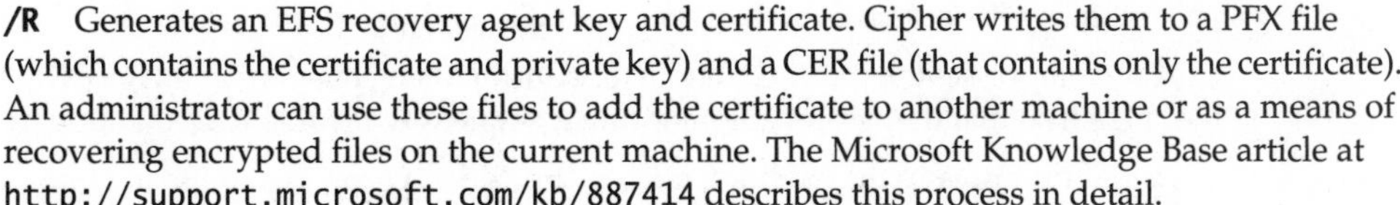

/R Generates an EFS recovery agent key and certificate. Cipher writes them to a PFX file (which contains the certificate and private key) and a CER file (that contains only the certificate). An administrator can use these files to add the certificate to another machine or as a means of recovering encrypted files on the current machine. The Microsoft Knowledge Base article at `http://support.microsoft.com/kb/887414` describes this process in detail.

/REKEY Updates the specified files to use the current configured EFS key. This option uses the key associated with the current user account. The user must have the required access using the old key and also have a new current key. You use this option to update files before discarding an old key.

/REMOVEUSER Removes a user from the list of users who can share a common encrypted file. You must supply the actual security hash value for the user. In addition, you must supply the Secure Hashing Algorithm 1 (SHA1) hash value for the certificate.

/S Performs the requested tasks in the current directory and all subdirectories.

/Smartcard Writes the recovery key and certificate to a smart card, rather than writing the information to a file. You use this option with the `/R` command line switch. This option requires that you install special hardware on your system, including a device for writing to smart cards.

/U Touches all of the encrypted files on local drives. This action updates the user's encryption key or recovers the agent's key to the current keys if you've changed them using any of the techniques described in this section (such as using the `/K` command line switch). This command line switch fails with encrypted files that don't belong to the current user. However, it does list all of the encrypted files even if they belong to another user. Use this command line switch with the `/N` switch if you want to list the encrypted files without changing them.

/W Removes (wipes) data from the available unused disk space on the entire volume. You must use this option alone. You can specify any directory on the local hard drive. When working with a mount point, the Cipher utility removes the data from the remote drive. Use this option with care since it wipes out all data from deleted files, making recovery with most recovery tools impossible. The Microsoft Knowledge Base article at `http://support.microsoft.com/default.aspx?scid=kb;en-us;315672&sd=tech` provides details on how to perform this task safely.

/X Creates a backup of the current EFS certificate and keys into the specified file. If you supply the EFSFile input, the utility only backs up the current user's certificate. Otherwise, the utility backs up both the EFS certificate and any required keys.

/Y Displays your current EFS certificate thumbnail on the local PC.

When used by itself, the Cipher utility displays the current encryption state of files in the current directory. You can supply a directory without any other arguments to see the encryption state of files in other directories. The utility shows all encrypted files with an `E` and all unencrypted files with a `U`.

Compressing Data with the Compact Utility

One of the advantages of using NTFS is the file compression feature that it includes. Using file compression means that you can store more information on a single hard drive. In addition, due to the manner in which hard drives work, you can experience a small performance gain by using compression (compaction). This utility uses the following syntax:

```
COMPACT [/C | /U] [/S[:dir]] [/A] [/I] [/F] [/Q] [filename [...]]
```

The following list describes each of the command line arguments.

/C Compresses the specified files or directories. Using this command line switch on a directory marks it so that the system automatically compresses any files added afterward.

/U Uncompresses the specified files or directories. Using this command line switch on a directory marks it so that the system doesn't compress any files added afterward.

/S[:*dir*] Performs the specified tasks on the current directory or the directory included as an argument and all subdirectories. The default is the current directory.

/A Forces the system to work with files (compress, uncompress, or query) that have the hidden or system attributes. Normally, the system skips files with these attributes.

/I Forces Compact to continue performing tasks even after it experiences an error. Normally, Compact stops performing tasks when it encounters an error. Using this command line switch would allow a batch file to continue processing files, even when some of the files failed to react as anticipated. You should redirect the output to a log file when using this option to track the errors and take any required remedial action when the task completes.

/F Forces the compression operation on all specified objects, even those that the system has already compressed. Normally, the system skips any files that are already compressed. You may have to use this switch when working with files in some instances.

/Q Reports only essential information such as errors, rather than general information including success messages.

filename Specifies the file or directory name to work with. You can use all of the standard wildcard combinations to specify multiple files or directories. See the "Working with Wildcard Characters" sidebar in Chapter 2 for details.

When used by itself, the Compact utility displays the current compaction state of files in the current directory, as shown in Figure 4.2. You can supply a directory without any other arguments to see the compaction state of files in other directories. The utility shows all compacted files with a C; all normal files have a space in place of the C. In addition to the compaction state, the standard output includes the actual file size, the compacted file size, and the compaction ratio. Unlike other utilities, Compact doesn't use a tabular format—each line contains a continuous entry that shows the information used to determine the compaction ratio. The bottom of the display shows the statistics for the directory including the number of compacted files, the actual and compacted size of all of the files, and the compaction ratio for the directory as a whole.

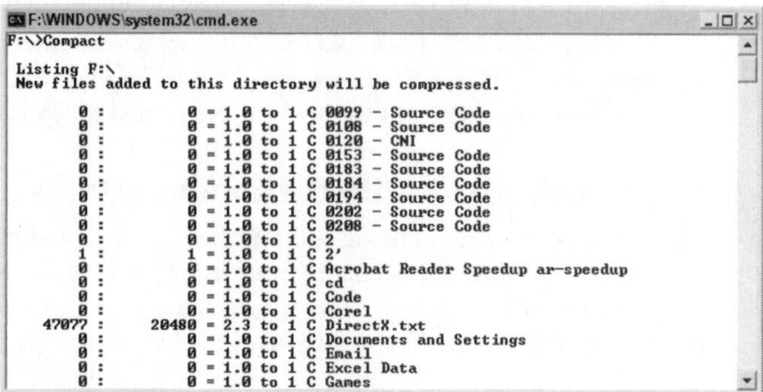

FIGURE 4.2
Use the Compact utility to discover how much space you save by using this feature.

Working with Other Resources

Even though you'll spend a lot of time working with files, your system has many other resources to manage. Some of these resources refer to physical devices, such as the power configuration used to control a UPS. Other resources include the security features of your system. One of the major resources in the other category is Terminal Server. The following sections describe these other resources in detail.

Converting Program Groups with the GrpConv Utility

A very long time ago (think Windows 3.*x*), Windows relied on an application named Program Manager, instead of the current Windows Explorer interface. Program Manager stored applications in groups, rather than in folders as Windows currently does. In fact, older versions of Windows included the ProgMan application, which is the Program Manager. You can still find `ProgMan.EXE` in the `\Windows\System32` folder, but it doesn't do anything (Windows 9*x* users could actually start the Program Manager interface for compatibility purposes). As with many older utilities, you won't find either GrpConv or `ProgMan.EXE` when working with Vista.

The GrpConv utility converts the groups originally used by the Program Manager into folders for use with Windows Explorer. Generally, you'll never need to use this utility unless you have some very old systems to manage. The Knowledge Base article at `http://support.microsoft.com/default.aspx?scid=kb;en-us;119941` discusses this utility in full detail.

Managing Power Settings with the PowerCfg Utility

Some people associate the power configuration settings with how long their monitor stays on or how their UPS reacts to a power failure. However, power configuration encompasses a lot more ground that these simple configuration tasks. Even though you can change any power configuration using the graphical interface, the settings appear in disparate locations. Using the PowerCfg utility to manage the power configuration puts everything in one place. Of course, given the enormous job this utility has, it also has a complex command line. This utility uses the following syntax:

```
POWERCFG /LIST
POWERCFG /QUERY [name] [/NUMERICAL]
POWERCFG /CREATE name
POWERCFG /DELETE name [/NUMERICAL]
POWERCFG /SETACTIVE name [/NUMERICAL]
POWERCFG /CHANGE name settings [/NUMERICAL]
POWERCFG /EXPORT name [/FILE filename] [/NUMERICAL]
POWERCFG /IMPORT name [/FILE filename] [/NUMERICAL]
POWERCFG /HIBERNATE {ON|OFF}
POWERCFG /GLOBALPOWERFLAG {ON|OFF} /OPTION {BATTERYICON |
   MULTIBATTERY | RESUMEPASSWORD | WAKEONRING | VIDEODIM}
POWERCFG /AVAILABLESLEEPSTATES
POWERCFG /BATTERYALARM {LOW|CRITICAL} [settings]
POWERCFG /DEVICEQUERY queryflags
POWERCFG /DEVICEENABLEWAKE devicename
POWERCFG /DEVICEDISABLEWAKE devicename
```

Vista adds so many new features to the PowerCfg utility that you'll probably want to review them as a group.

```
POWERCFG /CHANGENAME GUID name [scheme_description]
POWERCFG /DUPLICATESCHEME GUID DESTINATION_GUID
```

```
POWERCFG /DELETESETTING SUB_GUID SETTING_GUID
POWERCFG /GETACTIVESCHEME
POWERCFG /SETACVALUEINDEX SCHEME_GUID SUB_GUID SETTING_GUID
   SettingIndex
POWERCFG /SETDCVALUEINDEX SCHEME_GUID SUB_GUID SETTING_GUID
   SettingIndex
POWERCFG /LASTWAKE
POWERCFG /ALIASES
POWERCFG /SETSECURITYDESCRIPTOR {GUID | ACTION} SDDL
POWERCFG /GETSECURITYDESCRIPTOR {GUID | ACTION}
```

The following list describes each of the command line arguments.

/LIST, /L Lists the names of existing power schemes. You can see the same list in the Power Schemes tab of the Power Options Properties dialog box accessible through the Power Options applet of the Control Panel. This command line switch varies from the `/Query` command line switch that you can use to see the actual power scheme settings.

/QUERY [*name*], /Q [*name*] Displays the configuration information for a specified power scheme. If you don't supply a power scheme, the utility displays the current power scheme and its settings. The command line switch supplies the Name, Numerical ID, Turn off monitor (AC), Turn off monitor (DC), Turn off hard disks (AC), Turn off hard disks (DC), System standby (AC), System standby (DC), System hibernates (AC), System hibernates (DC), Processor Throttle (AC), and Processor Throttle (DC) fields as output. The AC fields specify the operating time when the system is on standard line current, while the DC fields specify the operating time when the system is on battery.

NOTE Command line arguments for the PowerCfg utility work like arguments for other utilities. Always enclose any power scheme name with spaces in double quotes or the command will fail.

/CREATE *name*, /C *name* Creates a new power scheme with the specified name. The new scheme inherits the properties of the currently active scheme. Use the `/Change` command line switch to configure the new scheme after you create it.

/DELETE *name*, /D *name* Deletes the power scheme with the specified name.

/SETACTIVE *name*, /S *name* Changes the active power scheme to the specified power scheme.

/CHANGE *name settings*, /X *name settings* Modifies the settings for the specified power scheme. Changing a setting value to 0 disables that feature. You can change any of the power scheme settings individually using the command line switches that follow.

/monitor-timeout-ac *minutes* Sets the monitor power-down time in minutes when the system is on AC power.

/monitor-timeout-dc *minutes* Sets the monitor power-down time in minutes when the system is on battery.

/disk-timeout-ac *minutes* Sets the hard drive power-down time in minutes when the system is on AC power.

/disk-timeout-dc *minutes* Sets the hard drive power-down time in minutes when the system is on battery.

/standby-timeout-ac *minutes* Sets the system standby time in minutes when the system is on AC power.

/standby-timeout-dc *minutes* Sets the system standby time in minutes when the system is on battery.

/hibernate-timeout-ac *minutes* Sets the system hibernation time in minutes when the system is on AC power.

/hibernate-timeout-dc *minutes* Sets the system hibernation time in minutes when the system is on battery.

/processor-throttle-ac {NONE | CONSTANT | DEGRADE | ADAPTIVE} Sets the processor-throttling feature when the system is on AC power.

/processor-throttle-dc {NONE | CONSTANT | DEGRADE | ADAPTIVE} Sets the processor-throttling feature when the system is on battery.

/EXPORT *name [/FILE filename], /E name [/FILE filename]* Exports the specified power scheme to a file. A file can contain only one power scheme, so you must always include the power scheme name. The `/File` command line switch defines the name of the file to use for storage. If you don't include this command line switch, the PowerCfg utility uses a default filename of `Scheme.POW`.

/IMPORT *name [/FILE filename], /I name [/FILE filename]* Imports the specified power scheme from a file. The file doesn't include a power scheme name, so you can give the power scheme any appropriate name. The `/File` command line switch defines the name of the file that contains the power scheme. If you don't include this command line switch, the PowerCfg utility uses a default filename of `Scheme.POW`.

/HIBERNATE {ON¦OFF}, /H {ON|OFF} Enables the hibernate feature when you select the On argument. Disables the hibernate feature when you select the Off argument. Some systems don't support the hibernate feature, so changing this setting may not have any effect. This command line switch always affects the currently active power scheme. Use the `/Query` command line switch to determine the state of the hibernate setting for the currently active power scheme.

/NUMERICAL, /N Sets the PowerCfg utility to use a numerical power scheme identifier, in place of the more common name. When you use this command line switch, specify the power scheme using its associated number, in place of the name for any of the commands that support it. You can use this command line switch with the `/Query`, `/Delete`, `/SetActive`, `/Change`, `/Export`, and `/Import` command line switches. The standard power configurations include:

0: Home/Office

1: Portable/Laptop

2: Presentation

3: Always On

4: Minimal Power Management

5: Max Battery

/GLOBALPOWERFLAG {ON|OFF} /OPTION {BATTERYICON | MULTIBATTERY | RESUMEPASSWORD | WAKEONRING | VIDEODIM}, /G {ON|OFF} /OPTION {BATTERYICON | MULTIBATTERY | RESUMEPASSWORD | WAKEONRING | VIDEODIM} Turns one of the global power flags on or off. The global power flags affect all of the power schemes, so any change you make affects the system as a whole and not a specific power setup. The global power flags include the following options.

BATTERYICON Controls the battery meter icon in the system tray.

MULTIBATTERY Controls the multiple battery display in the system power meter. You only need to set this feature on when your UPS contains multiple batteries.

RESUMEPASSWORD Prompts the user for a password when the system resumes operation after being in standby or hibernation.

WAKEONRING Controls wake-on-ring support for systems that provide this feature.

VIDEODIM Controls the video dimming support for systems such as laptops that operate on battery most of the time.

/AVAILABLESLEEPSTATES, /A Reports the sleep states available on the system. The PowerCfg utility supports four sleep states: S1 is a light sleep, S2 is a deeper sleep, S3 is the deepest sleep, and S4 is hibernation. Each successive sleep state reduces the power requirements of the system or device. However, deeper levels of sleep usually require longer wake-up periods as well. The PowerCfg utility tries to report the reason a system doesn't support a particular sleep state, but usually fails.

/BATTERYALARM {LOW|CRITICAL} [*settings*], /B {LOW|CRITICAL} [*settings*] Configures the battery alarm. Using this command line switch with just the Low or Critical value displays the current settings, as shown in Figure 4.3.

Notice the hierarchy of settings defined in Figure 4.3. You use additional command line switches to configure these settings. The following list describes each of the additional command line switches.

/activate {on | off} Enables or disables the alarm.

/level *percentage* Determines when the system actives the alarm. The percentage must be within the range of 0 to 100.

/text {on | off} Controls text notification. Setting text notification on displays a message to the user when power fails, the power level reaches the low alarm, and when the power level reaches the critical alarm.

/sound {on | off} Controls audible notification. Setting audible notification on sounds an audible alarm for the user when power fails, the power level reaches the low alarm, and when the power level reaches the critical alarm.

/action {none | shutdown | hibernate | standby} Specifies the action the system takes when an alarm occurs. The actions the system can take depends on the system capability. For example, to place the system in a hibernate state, the system must support hibernation.

/forceaction {on | off} Forces the action defined by the `/action` command line switch even if a program stops responding when set to on. Using this feature ensures the system shuts down promptly, but could result in data loss.

/program {on | off} Specifies that the system should run an application when an alarm sounds. However, you can't set the application using this utility. You must use the SchTasks utility described in the "Managing Tasks with the SCHTasks Utility" section of Chapter 10.

/DEVICEQUERY *queryflags* Displays a list of devices that meet the criteria specified by the `queryflags` argument. You may use more than one query flag to narrow the list of returned devices. The number of devices that support particular power off and wake-up features on a modern system is amazing. However, you usually need to know how the devices will react when setting up a power critical device such as a laptop. For example, it doesn't help to place the devices in an S1 sleep level when most of them don't support that mode. The following list describes the query flags.

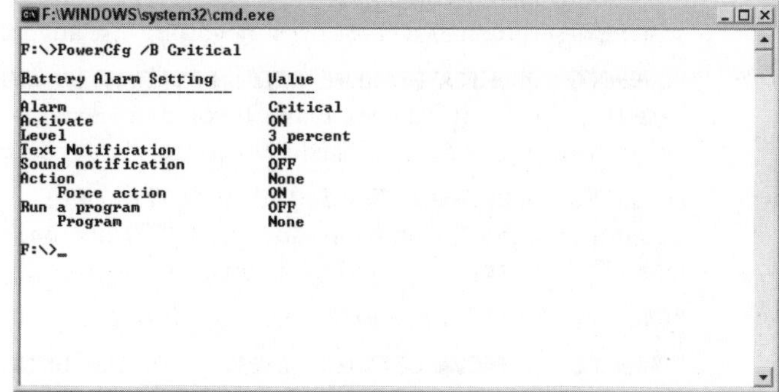
F:\WINDOWS\system32\cmd.exe
F:\>PowerCfg /B Critical
Battery Alarm Setting Value
Alarm Critical
Activate ON
Level 3 percent
Text Notification ON
Sound notification OFF
Action None
Force action ON
Run a program OFF
Program None
F:\>_

FIGURE 4.3
Display the low or critical battery alarm settings as needed to locate required changes.

`wake_from_S1_supported` Returns all devices that support waking the system from a light sleep.

`wake_from_S2_supported` Returns all devices that support waking the system from a deeper sleep.

`wake_from_S3_supported` Returns all devices that support waking the system from the deepest sleep state.

`wake_from_any` Returns all devices that support waking the system from any sleep mode.

`S1_supported` Lists devices that support light sleep states.

`S2_supported` Lists devices that support deeper sleep states.

`S3_supported` Lists devices that support the deepest sleep states.

`S4_supported` Lists devices that support hibernation.

`wake_programmable` Lists devices that a user can configure to wake from a sleep state.

`wake_armed` Lists devices that are currently configured to wake from any sleep state.

`all_devices` Returns a list of devices present in the system, even if they don't support any sleep mode or hibernation. This list only contains the device name.

`all_devices_verbose` Returns a verbose list of devices, even if they don't support any sleep mode or hibernation. This list contains a wealth of information that varies by device. As a minimum, you'll receive the device name, the device identifier, and the sleep, wake, and hibernation modes it supports. Optional information includes whether you can program the device or configure it in some way.

`/DEVICEENABLEWAKE` *`devicename`* Enables the specified device to wake the system from a sleep state. The device must provide programmable functionality. You can obtain a list of these devices using the `/DEVICEQUERY wake_programmable` command line switch.

V
VISTA

`/DEVICEDISABLEWAKE` *`devicename`* Disables a device from waking the system from a sleep state. You can obtain a list of devices currently set to wake the system using the `/DEVICEQUERY wake_armed` command line switch.

The following list describes each of the Vista-specific command line arguments.

`POWERCFG /CHANGENAME` *`GUID name`* `[`*`scheme_description`*`]` Modifies the name of the power scheme specified by GUID. Use the `PowerCfg /List` command to obtain a list of existing GUIDs.

The name argument contains the new power scheme name. You can optionally change the power scheme description as well. Make sure you enclose any value that contains spaces in quotes.

POWERCFG /DUPLICATESCHEME *GUID [DESTINATION_GUID]* Creates a new power scheme based on an existing power scheme. If you don't provide a destination GUID, the utility creates one for you automatically. Use the `PowerCfg /List` command to obtain a list of existing GUIDs.

POWERCFG /DELETESETTING *SUB_GUID SETTING_GUID* Removes the specified power setting. You must provide the both the subgroup GUID and the setting GUID as part of this call. Use the `PowerCfg /Query` command to obtain a list of both subgroup GUIDs and setting GUIDs.

POWERCFG /GETACTIVESCHEME Displays the name and the GUID of the active power scheme.

POWERCFG /SETACVALUEINDEX *SCHEME_GUID SUB_GUID SETTING_GUID SettingIndex* Sets a value associated with a particular power scheme when the system is powered by AC power. You must provide the power scheme GUID, subgroup GUID, setting GUID, and a setting value (normally a numeric or Boolean value). Use the `PowerCfg /List` command to obtain a list of power scheme GUIDs. Use the `PowerCfg /Query` command to obtain a list of both subgroup GUIDs and setting GUIDs.

POWERCFG /SETDCVALUEINDEX *SCHEME_GUID SUB_GUID SETTING_GUID SettingIndex* Performs the same task as the `/SETACVALUEINDEX` command line switch, except when using DC power.

POWERCFG /LASTWAKE Reports data about the last time the system returned from the sleep state. If the system hasn't ever returned from the sleep state, the call returns: `Wake History Count - 0`.

POWERCFG /ALIASES Displays all power system aliases and their associated GUIDs. These entries aren't associated with the power scheme, subgroup, or setting, but generally refer to state information such as `HIBERNATEIDLE` or `BATLEVELCRIT`.

POWERCFG /SETSECURITYDESCRIPTOR {*GUID* | *ACTION*} *SDDL* Sets the security descriptor associated with a particular power system component. Provide a GUID when you want to work with a power scheme. Use `ActionSetActive`, `ActionCreate`, or `ActionDefault` when you want to modify a power system action. The SDDL variable must contain a security descriptor. You can learn more about SDDL at `http://msdn2.microsoft.com/en-us/library/aa379567.aspx`. Use the `PowerCfg /GetSecurityDescriptor` call to see an example of an SDDL.

POWERCFG /GETSECURITYDESCRIPTOR {GUID | ACTION} Obtains the security descriptor associated with a particular power system component. Provide a GUID when you want to work with a power scheme. Use `ActionSetActive`, `ActionCreate`, or `ActionDefault` when you want to view a power system action.

Working with Terminal Server

Microsoft originally released Terminal Server with Windows NT 4.0, and it's been around in various forms ever since. Terminal Server provides Windows functionality by using a mainframe model. The client acts as a terminal for the server that has all of the applications the client needs to run. Using this model, the client can run Windows even if it doesn't provide the functionality required to do so. You can find a good write-up of how Terminal Server can help you run applications centrally at `http://www.microsoft.com/technet/prodtechnol/windowsserver2003/library/ServerHelp/af49a8bc-9fa0-48c3-a5cf-0ff77e698fd0.mspx`.

Make sure you check out the new Query utility if you're using Vista. This new utility helps you discover details about Terminal Server and its associated users, processes, and sessions.

This chapter doesn't teach you how to use Terminal Server. However, it does show you how to use a number of utilities to access, query, and manage this important resource. The following sections describe the command line utilities that you'll use when working with Terminal Server.

TIP When you display help for many of the utilities described in this section, you'll see the Terminal Server command that the utility executes. For example, the QAppSrv utility executes the `QUERY TERMSERVER` command. The utilities don't provide access to all of the Terminal Server commands because you don't need to use all of them from the command line. However, you can find an easy-to-use list of these commands on the Web site at `http://www.robvanderwoude.com/index.html`.

Locating Terminal Servers with the QAppSrv Utility

The QAppSrv utility displays a list of all of the application terminal servers on a network. If you use this utility without any arguments, it searches the network for a terminal server and displays its name. Running this utility is the same as using the `QUERY TERMSERVER` command from within Terminal Server. This utility uses the following syntax:

```
QAppSrv [servername] [/DOMAIN:domain] [/ADDRESS] [/CONTINUE]
```

The following list describes each of the command line arguments.

servername Specifies the Terminal Server to query.

/DOMAIN:*domain* Displays information for the specified domain. The default setting displays information for the current domain.

/ADDRESS Displays the network and node addresses for the Terminal Servers on the network.

/CONTINUE Forces the utility to display all of the servers without pausing after each screen of information.

Obtaining Processes with the QProcess Utility

The QProcess utility displays information about Terminal Server processes. It's the same as running the `QUERY PROCESS` command from within Terminal Server. The output of this utility includes the username, session name, session identifier, process identifier, and user. This utility uses the following syntax:

```
QProcess [* | processid | username | sessionname | /ID:nn |
programname] [/SERVER:servername] [/SYSTEM]
```

Notice that you may only specify one of the process identifiers. For example, if you include a session name, you can't include the program name. The following list describes each of the command line arguments.

* Displays all of the visible processes.

processid Displays the specified process.

username Displays all processes that belong to a particular user.

sessionname Displays all of the processes running within a particular session name.

/ID:*nn* Displays all of the processes running within a particular session identifier.

programname Displays all of the processes associated with a particular application.

/SERVER:*servername* Specifies the terminal server to query. The default is the current server.

/SYSTEM Displays process information for system purposes.

Getting Session Information with the QWinSta Utility

Use this utility to obtain information about the various sessions running on a system. It's the same as running the QUERY SESSION command from within Terminal Services. The utility outputs the session name, username, session identifier, session state, session type, and the device used to create the session. The device information is blank for the local session. This utility uses the following syntax:

```
QWinSta [sessionname | username | sessionid] [/SERVER:servername]
[/MODE] [/FLOW] [/CONNECT] [/COUNTER]
```

Notice that you may only specify one of the session identifiers. If you provide a session name, then you can't provide a username as well. The following list describes each of the command line arguments.

sessionname Specifies the name of the session to query.

username Specifies the name of the user to query.

sessionid Specifies the numeric identifier of the session to query.

/SERVER:*servername* Specifies the terminal server to query. The default is the current server.

/MODE Displays the current line settings. In this case, the output changes to show the session name, session state, device used to access the system, session type, device baud rate, device parity, device data bits, and device stop bits.

/FLOW Displays the current flow control settings. In this case, the output changes to show the session name, session state, device used to access the system, session type, and the flow control settings.

/CONNECT Displays the current connect settings. In this case, the output changes to show the session name, session state, device used to access the system, session type, and the connection settings.

/COUNTER Displays the current Terminal Services counters information. In addition to the standard information, the output includes the total sessions created, total sessions disconnected, and total sessions reconnected.

Terminating a Session with the Reset Utility

Use this utility to reset a session. In this case, the system disconnects the user from the system and receives a message to that effect. If you simply want to reset the session to a known good state, use the RWinSta utility instead. This utility uses the following syntax:

```
RESET [sessionname | sessionid] [ /server:server_name] /v
```

Notice that you may only specify one of the session identifiers. If you provide a session name, then you can't provide a session identifier as well. The following list describes each of the command line arguments.

sessionname Specifies the name of the session to reset.

sessionid Specifies the numeric identifier of the session to reset.

/SERVER:*servername* Specifies the terminal server to reset. The default is the current server.

/v Displays additional information about every action that the utility takes to reset the session. This information varies by session.

Resetting the Hardware and Software with the RWinSta Utility

This utility resets the subsystem hardware and software to a known state. You use it when a session has experienced non-recoverable errors. It's the same as running the `RESET SESSION` command from within Terminal Services. This utility uses the following syntax:

```
RWinSta {sessionname | sessionid} [/SERVER:servername] [/V]
```

Notice that you may only specify one of the session identifiers. If you provide a session name, then you can't provide a session identifier as well. The following list describes each of the command line arguments.

sessionname Specifies the name of the session to reset.

sessionid Specifies the numeric identifier of the session to reset.

/SERVER:*servername* Specifies the terminal server to reset. The default is the current server.

/V Displays additional information about every action that the utility takes to reset the session. This information varies by session.

Monitoring Other Sessions with the Shadow Utility

Use this utility to monitor another Terminal Server session. This utility uses the following syntax:

```
SHADOW {sessionname | sessionid} [/SERVER:servername] [/V]
```

Notice that you may only specify one of the session identifiers. If you provide a session name, then you can't provide a session identifier as well. The following list describes each of the command line arguments.

sessionname Specifies the name of the session to monitor.

sessionid Specifies the numeric identifier of the session to monitor.

/SERVER:*servername* Specifies the terminal server to monitor. The default is the current server.

/V Displays additional information about every action that the utility takes to monitor the session. This information varies by session.

Attaching a User Session with the TSCon Utility

Use this utility to attach a user session to an existing Terminal Server session. This utility uses the following syntax:

```
TSCON {sessionid | sessionname} [/DEST:sessionname] [/PASSWORD:pw] [/V]
```

Notice that you may only specify one of the session identifiers. If you provide a session name, then you can't provide a session identifier as well. The following list describes each of the command line arguments.

sessionname Specifies the name of the session to monitor.

sessionid Specifies the numeric identifier of the session to monitor.

/DEST:*sessionname* Connects the current user session to the specified destination Terminal Service session.

/PASSWORD:*pw* Specifies the password of the user who owns the identified session.

/V Displays additional information about every action that the utility takes to connect to the Terminal Services session. This information varies by session.

Disconnecting an Active Session with the TSDiscon Utility

Use this utility to disconnect from an existing Terminal Services session. The Terminal Services session continues to run after you disconnect from it. This utility uses the following syntax:

```
TSDISCON [sessionid | sessionname] [/SERVER:servername] [/V]
```

Notice that you may only specify one of the session identifiers. If you provide a session name, then you can't provide a session identifier as well. The following list describes each of the command line arguments.

sessionname Specifies the name of the session to disconnect.

sessionid Specifies the numeric identifier of the session to disconnect.

/SERVER:*servername* Specifies the terminal server to disconnect from. The default is the current server.

/V Displays additional information about every action that the utility takes to disconnect from the session. This information varies by session.

Ending Processes with the TSKill Utility

Use this utility to end a Terminal Services process. This utility uses the following syntax:

```
TSKILL processid | processname [/SERVER:servername] [/ID:sessionid | /A] [/V]
```

Notice that you may only specify one of the process identifiers. If you provide a process name, then you can't provide a process identifier as well. The following list describes each of the command line arguments.

processid Specifies the numeric identifier of the process to terminate.

processname Specifies the name of the process to terminate.

/SERVER:*servername* Identifies the server that is running the process. The default setting is the current server. You must include either the /ID or /A command line switch when using this command line switch and a process name to terminate a session.

/ID:*sessionid* Identifies the session under which the process is running.

/A Ends this process for all sessions.

/V Displays detailed information about the processes that the utility terminates.

Shutting the Terminal Server Down with the TSShutDn Utility

Use this utility to shut down Terminal Server in a controlled manner. The users receive a message stating the server shutdown time. In addition, you can use this utility to reboot the server. For some odd reason, Vista doesn't support this utility. Unfortunately, Microsoft doesn't provide an alternative for the TSShutDn utility. This utility uses the following syntax:

```
TSSHUTDN [wait_time] [/SERVER:servername] [/REBOOT] [/POWERDOWN]
[/DELAY:logoffdelay] [/V]
```

The following list describes each of the command line arguments.

wait_time Determines the number of seconds the system waits after user notification to terminate all user sessions and shut down the Terminal Server. The default setting is 60 seconds.

/SERVER:*servername* Specifies the name of the server to shut down. The default setting shuts down the current server.

/REBOOT Reboots the server after all the user sessions terminate. The server restarts and ends up in a known good state.

/POWERDOWN Powers the Terminal Server down. The host system remains running.

/DELAY:*logoffdelay* Specifies the number of seconds to wait after logging all connected sessions off. The delay provides time for applications to complete any required tasks. The default setting is 30 seconds.

/V Displays detailed information about all of the actions the utility performs to shut down the Terminal Server.

Obtaining Session Status Information with the Query Utility

Query is a new utility supplied with Vista. It provides four different modes that help you discover information about Terminal Server. This utility falls more in line with Microsoft's latest strategy for working with Terminal Server, so you should use it whenever possible in new scripts and batch files. The following sections tell you about the process, session, user, and Terminal Server (TermServer) modes.

PROCESS

The Process mode helps you discover information about Terminal Server processes. Every application creates a process when it runs, so this information focuses on the applications that Terminal Server is running. The output information includes the user name, session name, session identifier (ID), Process Identifier (PID), and image (application) name. This mode uses the following syntax:

```
QUERY PROCESS [* | processid | username | sessionname | /ID:nn |
programname] [/SERVER:servername]
```

The following list describes each of the command line arguments.

* Displays all of the visible processes.

processid Displays process information for the specified PID.

username Displays all of the processes belonging to a particular user. You'll always find processes belonging to your personal account, local account, network service account, and local service account.

sessionname Displays all of the processes running in a particular session. The two default sessions are console and services.

/ID:*nn* Displays all of the processes running within a particular session. You'll always see two sessions. Session 0 works with the services sessions and session 1 works with the console sessions.

programname Displays all of the sessions associated with a particular program name. If multiple people are using the same application, you'll see one session for each user.

/SERVER:servername Enumerates the specified processes on a particular Terminal Server. If you don't have rights to access the Terminal Server, you'll see a security error message. If the server isn't running Vista, you'll likely see an "Error Enumerating Processes" message.

SESSION

The Session mode tells you about the sessions running on Terminal Server. Depending on what command line options you use, you can obtain a wealth of session information. The default settings provide the session name, username, session identifier, session state, connection type, and connection device. This mode uses the following syntax:

```
QUERY SESSION [sessionname | username | sessionid] [/SERVER:servername]
[/MODE] [/FLOW] [/CONNECT] [/COUNTER]
```

The following list describes each of the command line arguments.

sessionname Displays all of the processes running in a particular session. The two default sessions are console and services.

username Displays all of the processes belonging to a particular user. You'll always find processes belonging to your personal account, local account, network service account, and local service account.

sessionid Displays all of the processes running within a particular session. You'll always see two sessions. Session 0 works with the services sessions and session 1 works with the console sessions.

/SERVER:servername Enumerates the specified processes on a particular Terminal Server. If you don't have rights to access the Terminal Server, you'll see a security error message. If the server isn't running Vista, you'll likely see an "Error Enumerating Processes" message.

/MODE Displays the current line settings. The output changes to include several new columns including the session name, state, device, type, baud, parity, data bits, and stop bits.

/FLOW Displays the current flow control settings. The output changes to include several new columns including the session name, state, device, type, and flow control.

/CONNECT Displays the current connection mode. The output changes to include several new columns including the session name, state, device, type, and connection type.

/COUNTER Displays three counter settings that include total sessions created, total sessions disconnected, and total sessions reconnected.

USER

The User mode displays information about users logged into Terminal Server. The output information includes the username, session name, session identifier, session state, idle time, and logon time. This mode uses the following syntax:

```
QUERY USER [username | sessionname | sessionid] [/SERVER:servername]
```

The following list describes each of the command line arguments.

username Displays all of the processes belonging to a particular user. You'll always find processes belonging to your personal account, local account, network service account, and local service account.

sessionname Displays all of the processes running in a particular session. The two default sessions are console and services.

sessionid Displays all of the processes running within a particular session. You'll always see two sessions. Session 0 works with the services sessions and session 1 works with the console sessions.

/SERVER:servername Enumerates the specified processes on a particular Terminal Server. If you don't have rights to access the Terminal Server, you'll see a security error message. If the server isn't running Vista, you'll likely see an "Error Enumerating Processes" message.

TERMSERVER

The TermServer mode outputs information about Terminal Server. The information you receive depends on the Terminal Server you query and the command line options you select. This mode uses the following syntax:

```
QUERY TERMSERVER [servername] [/DOMAIN:domain] [/ADDRESS] [/CONTINUE]
```

The following list describes each of the command line arguments.

servername Specifies the name of the Terminal Server. The system must be running Terminal Server. The Query utility won't return any information, even if you have Terminal Server installed, unless Terminal Server is running at the time of the query.

/DOMAIN:*domain* Specifies the domain to search for Terminal Servers. The Query utility assumes that you want to query the current domain.

/ADDRESS Adds network and node address information to the output.

/CONTINUE Displays all of the Terminal Server information as continuous output, rather than pausing after each screen. Use this option when you plan to redirect the output to a file.

Working with Remote Access Server

The Remote Access Server (RAS) provides dial-up connectivity to your server from a remote location. Some people might think that dial-up connectivity and the other services that RAS provides belong to a bygone age, but most large organizations actually rely on a mixed environment in which dial-up is still an essential part of the picture. For example, the ComputerWorld article at `http://www.computerworld.com/hardwaretopics/hardware/story/0,10801,106776,00.html?source=NLT_AM&nid=106776` points out some amazing mixed environment statistics. Microsoft also takes this need seriously by providing a special area on their Web site for general networking and RAS needs at `http://www.microsoft.com/technet/community/en-us/networking/default.mspx`.

TIP Even though the Windows NT resources that Microsoft provides might seem outdated, RAS really hasn't changed much from that early version of Windows. For example, the vast majority of the information in the RAS Reference at `http://www.microsoft.com/resources/documentation/windowsnt/4/server/reskit/en-us/net/sur_ras.mspx` is just as useful today as when Microsoft first put it together. (Modems have admittedly gotten faster, but the concepts remain the same.)

The following sections describe the RAS-specific tools included with Windows. However, these utilities aren't the end of the story. To manage RAS functionality you must become familiar with the NetSH utility. You'll find a discussion of this utility in the "Scripting Networking Solutions with the NetSH Utility" section of Chapter 8. Finally, Microsoft provides many tools such as RASSrvMon (RAS Server Monitor) that aren't available with Windows. You can download these tools at `http://www.microsoft.com/downloads/details.aspx?FamilyID=9d467a69-57ff-4ae7-96ee-b18c4790cffd&displaylang=en`.

Dialing Out with the RASDial Utility

You use the RASDial utility to determine the current RAS status, as well as dial out to a RAS server. Use the RASDial utility by itself to determine the current RAS status. The output displays any connections you've made. This utility uses the following syntax:

```
RASDial entryname [username [password|*]] [/DOMAIN:domain]
   [/PHONE:phonenumber] [/CALLBACK:callbacknumber]
   [/PHONEBOOK:phonebookfile] [/PREFIXSUFFIX]
RASDial [entryname] /DISCONNECT
RASDial
```

The following list describes each of the command line arguments.

entryname Specifies an entry from the RAS phonebook (PBK file) entry. The utility uses the default PBK file located in the `\Windows\System32\RAS` directory unless you specify a different PBK file using the `/PHONEBOOK` command line switch. Always place entry names that contain spaces in quotes. You may also elect to use a telephone number that doesn't appear in the phonebook by using the `/PHONE` command line switch.

username[{ password | *}] Specifies the username used to connect to the remote system. In many cases, you'll also need to supply a password to create the connection. If you supply an asterisk (*) for the password, RAS will prompt you for the password. Using this technique reduces the possibility of someone compromising your password. Instead of seeing the password in plain text at the command prompt, anyone viewing your display will simply see a series of asterisks in the prompt dialog box.

/Domain:*domain* Specifies the user's domain on the remote machine. If you don't specify a domain, the system uses the last value of the Domain field in the Connect To dialog box.

/Phone:*phonenumber* Substitutes the specified telephone number for the one in the RAS phonebook entry. You can use this feature to dial one-time telephone numbers for support or other reasons.

/Callback:*callbacknumber* Substitutes the specified callback telephone number for the one in the RAS phonebook. The callback number is the one that the server calls to re-create a connection after it verifies your user information. Many remote systems use callbacks as a security measure to ensure they reach a valid user. Your user account must allow you to specify a different callback number in order for this feature to work.

/Phonebook:*phonebookfile* Specifies an alternative RAS phonebook (PBK) file. You can use this alternative phonebook to hold personal or specialized numbers. The default phonebook appears in the `\Windows\System32\RAS` directory under your username.

/PrefixSuffix Applies the current Telephony Application Programming Interface (TAPI) location dialing settings to the telephone number. You set up these options using the Phone and Modem Options applet found in the Control Panel. The system doesn't use these options by default; you must specifically turn them on for dialing outside of your current location.

/Disconnect Disconnects an existing RAS connection. You may optionally specify a particular entry name when you have multiple RAS connections in use.

Accessing Dial-up Networking with the RASPhone Utility

You use the RASPhone utility to create entries in your RAS phonebook. Each entry specifies a kind of connection. The four major connection types include dial-up to a private network, connecting to a private network through the Internet using a Virtual Private Network (VPN), connecting directly to another computer using a serial, parallel, or infrared port, and connecting to a network using broadband. The discussion in this section doesn't tell you how to use the graphical utilities to create such a connection; it concentrates on the command line interface. Using RASPhone by itself displays the graphical interface. This utility uses the following syntax:

```
RASPhone [-f file] [[{-e | -d | -h | -r}] entry]
RASPhone [-f file] -a [entry]
RASPhone [-f file] -l{a | d | e | h | r} [link]
```

The following list describes each of the command line arguments.

-f *file* Defines the full path to the RAS phonebook (PBK) file. The path can include a drive, relative or absolute path, and a filename.

-e Displays the dialog box required to edit the specified entry. The dialog box varies by entry type.

-d Displays the dial-up dialog box for creating a connection to the remote resource.

-h Disconnects the specified remote connection without displaying a dialog box.

-r Deletes the specified entry from the RAS phonebook without displaying a dialog box. Note that this task is permanent; you can't undelete a RAS phonebook entry and must create it from the beginning it you accidentally delete it.

entry Specifies an entry from the RAS phonebook (PBK file) entry. The utility uses the default PBK file located in the `\Windows\System32\RAS` directory unless you specify a different PBK file using the `/PHONEBOOK` command line switch. Always place entry names that contain spaces in quotes. You may also elect to use a telephone number that doesn't appear in the phonebook by using the `/PHONE` command line switch.

-a Displays the New Connection Wizard that you use to create a new entry. This wizard relies on a graphical interface; you can't create entries at the command line.

-l{a | d | e | h | r} Performs any of the specified command line tasks to a dial-up shortcut file instead of the RAS phonebook.

link Specifies the full path to the dial-up link shortcut file. The path can include a drive, relative or absolute path, and a filename.

Setting Up a Telephony Client with the TCMSetup Utility

Use this utility to set up or disable the TAPI client. Despite its name, TAPI helps the system create a number of connection types, so correct setup is important. For example, this setup can define physical connectivity to the corporate Private Branch Exchange (PBX). You must use this utility to perform some setups, such as designating a Windows 2000 server as a resource for TAPI clients. This utility uses the following syntax:

```
tcmsetup [/r] [/q] [/x] /c Server [Server...]
tcmsetup [/q] /c /d
```

The following list describes each of the command line arguments.

/r Disables automatic server discovery. Only the servers that you specify with this command appear as TAPI resources.

/q Prevents the utility from displaying message boxes. Use this feature with batch files to prevent the system stopping to wait for user input.

/x Specifies that TAPI relies on connection-oriented callbacks. Use this feature on heavy traffic networks where packet loss is high. The default setting uses connectionless callbacks, which offer better efficiency at the expense of reliability.

/c Defines this request as a client setup. You must include this command line switch.

Server Specifies one or more remote servers to use as TAPI service providers. You must specify a minimum of one server. The client uses the server's lines and telephones for communication. The client must appear within the same domain as the server or in a domain that has a two-way trust relationship with the client's domain. Separate each of the servers in a multiple server listing with a space.

/d Clears the list of remote TAPI servers. Disables the TAPI client by preventing it from using TAPI service providers that appear on remote servers. The command also prevents automatic discovery of TAPI servers. You must use this utility to re-enable TAPI services on the client.

Communicating with Telnet

Telnet provides low-level access to other machines using a standardized protocol and connection. This section describes the command line interface for the Windows version of Telnet, which varies a little from the interface other platforms use. This section won't tell you how to perform management tasks.

NOTE Vista doesn't install any Telnet support by default. You must open the Programs and Features applet and choose the Turn Windows Features On or Off link to display the Windows Features dialog box. Near the bottom of the list, you'll find separate entries for Telnet Client and Telnet Server. You must install both to obtain the full set of utilities described in this section of the chapter. Depending on your setup, you might also need to make both security and firewall adjustments before the utilities will work at all.

Real World Scenario

OLD DOESN'T MEAN OUTDATED

Some people will view the utilities in some parts of this book as antiquated relics from an earlier time. However, these time-tested utilities are often your best means of managing a system, especially when you can use your knowledge on multiple machines. Telnet is an older utility that predates Windows. In addition to your Windows installation, you'll find Telnet on just about every other operating system. The utility is low level, but quite useful. Many administrators rely on this tool to perform configuration tasks, access a frozen server from a remote location, check routers, and generally perform tasks that you can't easily perform using a graphical utility.

You'll find a number of Telnet-related files that don't include any type of user interface in the `\Windows\System32` folder. These support files provide additional Telnet functionality. For example, the `TlNtSess.EXE` file controls the Telnet session. You can obtain an overview of how these other files affect Telnet under Windows on the Microsoft site at `http://www.microsoft.com/technet/prodtechnol/windowsserver2003/library/TechRef/566bc823-b916-40cf-a0c0-1dedffaebeb1.mspx`.

ADMINISTRATING TELNET WITH THE TLNTADMN UTILITY

The Telnet Administrator utility helps you control Telnet sessions on your machine. You access it using the TLNTAdmn utility. If you use TLNTAdmn alone, you'll see a display of the current server status, as shown in Figure 4.4. Adding start, stop, pause, or continue to the command line controls the Telnet service state. Note that these commands only work if you set Telnet to manual or automatic mode—the command fails if you disable the Telnet service.

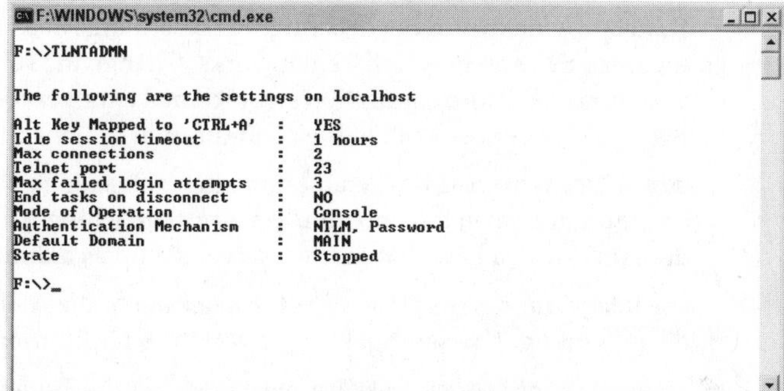
F:\WINDOWS\system32\cmd.exe
F:\>TLNTADMN
The following are the settings on localhost
Alt Key Mapped to 'CTRL+A' : YES
Idle session timeout : 1 hours
Max connections : 2
Telnet port : 23
Max failed login attempts : 3
End tasks on disconnect : NO
Mode of Operation : Console
Authentication Mechanism : NTLM, Password
Default Domain : MAIN
State : Stopped
F:\>_

FIGURE 4.4
Use the TLNTAdmn utility to display the status of your Telnet server.

The TLNTAdmn utility includes three user-specific commands. Use the `-s` switch with an optional session identifier to display the user status information. Each user entry includes the user ID, name, remote connection point, and logon time. The idle time column is a good indicator of who has gone to lunch with their Telnet connection intact. Use the `-m` switch with a session identifier to send the user a message. The third user option is the `-k SessionIdentifier` switch. Use it to end a user session. This utility uses the following syntax:

```
TLNTAdmn [ComputerName] [-u user [-p password]] start | stop | pause |
continue | -s sessionid | -k sessionid | -m sessionid message | config
config_options
```

The following list describes each of the command line arguments.

ComputerName Specifies the name of a remote computer. The default setting uses the local computer.

-u *user* Specifies the name of the user account used to execute command. The default setting relies on the user account for the currently logged in user.

-p *password* Specifies the user password.

start Starts the Telnet service. This option only works when the service is set to automatic or manual. You can't start a disabled service.

stop Stops the Telnet service.

pause Pauses the Telnet service. A pause is temporary when compared to a stop. Don't use pause when you actually mean to stop the service.

continue Continues the service from a pause.

-s *sessionid* Lists information about the specified session.

-k *sessionid* Terminates the specified session. Exercise care in using this option since a terminated session could cause data loss. Generally, you'll use this as a last resort. Try sending a message to the user first to shut down the session from the client side or physically end the session from the client terminal yourself.

-m *sessionid message* Sends a message to the specified session. Make sure you place any message within quotes. Otherwise, the utility sends just the first word of the message to the remote terminal and then displays an error message.

config *config_options* Changes the server configuration. Use one or more configuration options to change the way in which the server works.

Telnet provides a number of configuration options. Each of these configuration options controls an aspect of the way in which Telnet works. Change the server configuration carefully because some options can cause connection errors or make the server unavailable to users who need it. The following list describes each of the configuration options.

dom = *Domain* Sets the default domain for checking usernames. If you're using a peer-to-peer configuration, then the only domain is your machine. The only time you can set this to another domain is if you have a Windows server set up as a domain controller.

ctrlakeymap = <Yes|No> Sets the mapping of the ALT key to Ctrl+A when on. This is the default setting. This setting doesn't affect the VTNT terminal, but does affect other terminal types.

timeout = *hh:mm:ss* Determines how long the Telnet server waits before it logs out a user automatically. You must include the colons between the hours, minutes, and seconds. In addition, if you want to set a value to 0, then include a 0 on the command line. For example, if you want to set the timeout value to 30 minutes, type **TLNTADMN config timeout = 0:30:00** at the command line.

timeoutactive = {Yes | No} Enables idle session timeout counter. Whenever a session reaches the timeout value, the Telnet server disables it automatically.

maxfail = *Attempts* Sets the maximum number of login failure attempts before disabling the user account. Telnet won't allow disabled user accounts to connect.

maxconn = *Connections* Determines the maximum number of connections the Telnet server accepts. Note that the Microsoft documentation states that you can accept a maximum of two sessions. This is incorrect. Using this configuration option allows you to accept the maximum number of connections your machine can handle.

port = *Number* Changes the connection port number. It's always a good idea to change this number to something other than the default to help thwart crackers. Of course, if you leave the port open and use poor security, someone will still get in.

sec = [+/-]NTLM [+/-]PASSWD Determines the acceptable security (authentication) mechanisms. Allowing NTLM enables the user to log in using their default Windows username and password.

mode = {Console | Stream} Controls how the server reacts to control character input. Always use console mode to ensure users can use applications such as EDIT.

Executing Commands Remotely with the Telnet Utility

The Telnet utility manages Telnet sessions at the command prompt. You'll start the Telnet client at a command prompt by typing **Telnet** and pressing Enter. Telnet displays a Welcome message, the escape character, and a Microsoft Telnet prompt. This utility uses the following syntax:

```
TELNET [-a][-e escape char][-f log file][-l user][-t term][host [port]]
```

The following list describes each of the command line arguments.

-a Performs an automatic logon using the currently logged on username and password. This option works about the same as the `-l` option except you don't have to specify the username. Windows XP and above ignore this option if you have NTLM security enabled. It automatically logs on using the currently logged on username and password.

NOTE The Windows XP and above version of Telnet sets Windows NT LAN Manager (NTLM) authentication on by default. This means that it will always attempt to log on using the currently logged on username and password. Using this option makes access somewhat automatic. All you need to do is type **`Telnet HostName`** at the command prompt and Telnet connects you, if you have proper rights. However, this option has two unfortunate side effects. The first is that you can't specify another username and password to log onto the system. The second is that the NTLM option appears to interfere with operation of some Telnet clients. You can turn off this feature using the TLNTAdmn utility described in the "Administrating Telnet with the TLNTAdmn Utility" section of the chapter.

-e Modifies the escape character used to enter the Telnet client prompt from a remote session. Telnet defaults to Ctrl+], which is a good choice because it isn't used by anything else.

-f *Filename* Sets the filename for client side logging. Using this option also turns client-side logging on. Client-side logging doesn't track the commands you type at the Telnet prompt; they only record what you've done at the remote terminal connection. For example, if you type a `Dir` command at the remote prompt, you'll see the `Dir` command and results in the log. However, you won't see the command used to open the connection because that occurs at the Telnet prompt.

-l *Username* Specifies the username to log in with on the remote system. You can't specify a password at the command line, so you still have to provide a password before the session will start. Windows XP and above ignores this option if you have NTLM security enabled. It automatically logs on using the currently logged on username and password.

-t *TerminalType* Specifies the terminal type used for command processing and text display. Telnet supports the VT100, VT52, ANSI, and VTNT terminal types. The terminal type determines the characteristics of the session. It dates back to a time when people accessed mainframes using utilities such as Telnet. Using the default ANSI terminal usually works fine. Telnet remembers your preferred terminal type from session to session.

TIP The default terminal type of ANSI does work fine for most connections, especially those with a mainframe. However, the ANSI terminal type causes problems when you run certain Windows XP character mode utilities. Any utility that has a display and a functional menu system will likely require you to use the VTNT terminal. For example, if you normally use the `EDIT` command to work with text files, you'll want to use the VTNT terminal.

HostName [PortNumber] Specifies the hostname or IP address of the remote computer. You may optionally specify a service name or port number. The only time you need to specify a port number is to access a service other than Telnet or if the Telnet administrator changes the port number.

Managing the System Time with the W32Tm Utility

Time is a critical resource for most people and not just because there's too little of it. When your computer lacks proper time synchronization, your applications might not work as expected.

Entries you make into remote databases suddenly bear the wrong timestamp. It's more than just inconvenient. The W32Tm utility helps you manage time on your system. You use it to set how Windows reacts to time events and to set your system up as a timeserver. This utility uses the following syntax:

```
w32tm [/register | /unregister ]
w32tm /monitor [/domain:<domain name>]
   [/computers:<name>[,<name>[,<name>...]]] [/threads:<num>]
   [/ipprotocol:<4|6>] [/nowarn]
w32tm /ntte <NT_time_epoch>
w32tm /ntpte <NTP_time_epoch>
w32tm /resync [/computer:<computer>] [/nowait] [/rediscover] [/soft]
w32tm /stripchart /computer:<computer> [/period:<refresh>] [/dataonly]
   [/samples:<count>] [/packetinfo] [/ipprotocol:<4|6>]
w32tm /config [/computer:<computer>] [/update]
   [/manualpeerlist:<peers>] [/syncfromflags:<source>]
   [/LocalClockDispersion:<seconds>] [/reliable:(YES|NO)]
   [/largephaseoffset:<milliseconds>]
w32tm /tz
w32tm /dumpreg [/subkey:<key>] [/computer:<computer>]
w32tm /query [/computer:<computer>] {/source | /configuration | /peers
   | /status} [/verbose]
w32tm /debug {/disable | {/enable /file:<name> /size:<bytes>
   /entries:<value> [/truncate]}}
```

The following list describes each of the standard command line arguments.

register Registers the current machine to run as a time service and adds the default configuration to the registry.

unregister Unregisters the current machine as a time service and removes all configuration information from the registry.

monitor Monitors a remote computer for time changes. This command line switch sets the local time to match the remote timeserver when you specify a domain. When used alone, this command switch reports monitoring statistics.

domain:*domain_name* Specifies which domain to monitor. If you don't supply a domain name or you haven't used the /computers command line switch, then the system uses the default domain. You may include this option more than once at the command line to create multiple time sources.

/computers:*name[,name[,name...]]* Specifies the computers you want to use for monitoring purposes on the domain. The command line switch may include multiple computers from the same domain. Separate each computer with a comma without a space between names. Prefix Primary Domain Controller (PDC) names with an asterisk (*). You may include this option more than once at the command line to create multiple time sources (once for each domain).

threads:*num* Determines the number of computers to analyze simultaneously. The default value is 3. You may specify any value between 1 and 50.

ntte *NT_time_epoch* Converts the specified Windows system time into a human readable form.

/ntpte NTP_time_epoch Converts the specified Windows Network Time Protocol (NTP) time into a human readable form.

/resync Causes a remote computer to resynchronize its clock. This command line switch also forces the remote computer to discard all error statistics and begin creating new ones.

/computer:*computer* Specifies the name of the target. If you don't specify this command line switch, the Win32Tm utility interacts with the local computer.

/nowait Forces the utility to return control of the command prompt immediately. Normally, the Win32Tm utility waits for the resynchronization process to complete before returning.

/rediscover Forces the utility to rediscover timeservers on the network before it performs the resynchronization process. Always use this command line switch when you've added a new timeserver to the network.

/soft Resynchronizes the system's clock without discarding the error statistics. Don't use this command line switch because Microsoft has disabled it. Keeping the current error statistics could cause the affected machine to update its clock incorrectly. Microsoft only provided this command line switch for compatibility purposes.

/stripchart Displays text output showing the time differential between the local computer and the specified computer. The display updates every 2 seconds unless you specify a different interval using the /period command line switch. The output never includes graphics, despite the presence of the /dataonly command line switch. The display continues to update with one entry per line at the command prompt until you press Ctrl+C. Using the /samples command line switch sets a specific number of updates so you don't have to press Ctrl+C to stop the utility.

/period:*refresh* Defines the strip chart update frequency in seconds.

/dataonly Displays only data in the output (this is the default and only output for Windows).

/samples:*count* Determines the number of samples to take before ending the strip chart.

/config Configures the specified computer to use a particular time source. You can only use this command line switch to change the Windows time setup. Using the /config command line switch alone displays an error message. Contrast this command with the Net /Time utility described in the "Managing the Network with the Net Utility" section of Chapter 5.

/update Notifies the target computer that the changes are complete and it should update the Windows time service. You must perform this configuration change for any of the settings discussed in this section to take effect.

/manualpeerlist:*peers* Specifies one or more time service peers. Use spaces to define multiple peers. You may use a Domain Name System (DNS) name or an IP address to describe a peer. When using this command line switch with multiple peers, you must place the entire command line switch within quotes, not just the peer list.

/syncfromflags:*source* Defines the sources to use for synchronization. You may specify multiple sources. The two valid sources include MANUAL (the list of peers supplied as part of a /manualpeerlist command line switch) and DOMHIER (relies on a domain controller, DC, within the domain hierarchy).

NOTE Windows 2003 users have access to two additional command line switches for the W32Tm utility. The first, /Reliable:{YES | NO}, lets you identify reliable time sources for the computer. The operating system will always use a reliable time source first, and unreliable time sources when no reliable time source is present. The second, /largephaseoffset:milliseconds, sets a time difference between the local and the network time. This differential lets the system compensate for spikes (uncharacteristic changes) in time management.

/LocalClockDispersion:*seconds* Defines the accuracy of the local clock. Windows uses this rating as a means of compensating for errors when it can't locate a remote source.

/tz Displays the local time zone settings. The output includes the time bias information, as well as settings for both standard and daylight savings time.

/dumpreg Displays the Windows time settings located in the HKEY_LOCAL_MACHINE\SYSTEM\CurrentControlSet\Services\W32Time key.

/subkey:key Displays values associated with the specified subkey of the HKEY_LOCAL_MACHINE\SYSTEM\CurrentControlSet\Services\W32Time key.

Vista adds a number of additional command line options. The following list describes each of the Vista command line arguments.

/ipprotocol:{4|6} Chooses the IP version to use for the utility. You can choose between IP version 4 or IP version 6.

/nowarn Prevents the display of warning messages. This feature is useful when you want to redirect the output to a file.

/packetinfo Displays the NTP packet response message so that you can perform troubleshooting as required.

/reliable:{YES | NO} Specifies whether this machine is a reliable time source. This setting only applies to domain controllers.

/largephaseoffset:*milliseconds* Defines the difference between local and network time that W32Tm considers a spike. The utility registers errors whenever it encounters a large time spike and also attempts to correct the time differential.

/query Displays information about the target computer's time source. You control the output by including one of the specific output command line switches (/source, /configuration, /peers, or /status) and the /verbose command line switch.

/source Outputs the time source information for the specified computer. The default setting when not using an external time source is Local CMOS Clock.

/configuration Outputs a considerable range of time source information including such specifics as the time source DLL.

/peers Outputs a list of time source peers and their status.

/status Outputs the Windows Time Service status. This information includes such useful statistics as the time of the last update and the poll interval.

/verbose Augments the time service status information.

/debug Enables or disables output of Windows Time Service information to a log.

/disable Disables time service logging.

/enable Enables time service logging.

/file:*name* Specifies the name of a file to use for logging purposes.

/size:*bytes* Specifies the maximum size of the time service log. When the log is full, Vista begins removing the oldest entries and adding new entries. The time service uses a circular logging system so the log will never overflow.

`/entries:`*`value`* Defines the list of entries that the log will contain as numeric values. Unfortunately, Microsoft doesn't document these values, but the range is within the values from 0 to 300. Fortunately, the debugging mode works fine without this command line switch.

`/truncate` Truncates an existing log file before making new entries. This command line switch ensures that the log doesn't contain any old entries when you start the debugging process.

Getting Started with Command Line Tasks

Now that you know about the utilities at your disposal for managing files and other resources on your system, you might wonder why you've played around with the graphical utilities all this time. The graphical utilities have a task to fulfill as well. In many cases, the graphical utilities focus on ease of use, while the command line utilities offer flexibility and power. You might find times where ease of use really is a significant advantage and want to stick with the graphical utilities that you've relied on up to this point. However, the command line utilities add the extra bit of power you need to locate files that Windows Explorer won't even admit exist.

I'm not a proponent of memorization—possibly because my memory has failed me so often. However, some of the utilities in this chapter fall into the category of "must memorize to use effectively." For example, you can't drop everything to locate this book every time you want to use the `Dir` command. Memorizing the `Dir` command and its common command line switches is the only way to gain the level of efficiency that most people demand today. Of course, you don't have to memorize everything. You do have this book for reference whenever you need it. The memorization process is only important for the utilities that you use often.

Chapter 5 shows a special category of utilities that are especially important in today's highly connected environment—security. These utilities won't stop the next virus or phishing attack on your machine, but they can help you with security in a number of ways. For example, you can use file verification to determine whether a virus has compromised any of the files on your system. Monitoring the system setup can help you ensure that you only have the Windows features you actually need installed, reducing the number of security holes you have to consider. You can use various diagnostic aids to check your TCP/IP connection. Even though Chapter 5 won't turn you into a security specialist, being aware of these security and monitoring aids is a first step toward making your system truly secure.

Chapter 5

Securing and Monitoring a System

- Working with the Network
- Managing FTP Servers with the FTP Utility
- Working with Users
- Virus and External Intrusion Protection
- Configuring the System Setup
- Interacting with the Internet
- Working with General Applications
- Converting Event Trace Logs with the TraceRpt Utility

It's easy to think that system protection ends with a firewall, virus checker, and adware blocker. However, these tools are fallible. Yes, you can keep them updated and use them faithfully, but they won't catch every virus or every piece of adware, or prevent information you really wanted to keep local from going out. All you need to do is search the archives of any trade press magazine to find the failures of every vendor out there. The only way to ensure the security of your system is to monitor it yourself. You still need these tools, but the monitoring is the human supervision required to help them fulfill their tasks faithfully.

Even if your only purpose for monitoring a system is to thwart the efforts of the nefarious individuals seeking entry into your system, monitoring has other useful effects. By monitoring your system, you can begin seeing hardware and software failures long before they become a problem that will ruin your day. Monitoring can help locate potential network problems as well. You'll also find that you pay better attention to your system. For example, you'll begin to wonder what that hidden directory is holding, rather than simply assume that it has a purpose. In short, monitoring has all kinds of useful benefits and there aren't many negatives to consider unless you use the information you gain carelessly.

NOTE For the purposes of this book, the term *cracker* refers to an individual who's breaking into a system on an unauthorized basis. It also refers to someone who places software on your system without obtaining your permission first. *Cracking* includes any form of illegal activity on the system such as stealing your identity. On the other hand, the term *hacker* refers to someone who performs authorized (legal) low-level system activities, including testing system security. Hackers also help find undocumented solutions for many computer needs and create workarounds for both hardware and software problems. In some cases, you need to employ the services of a good hacker to test the security measures you have in place, or suffer the consequences of a break-in.

Working with the Network

Networks are complex combinations of hardware and software that link systems together so they can work interactively and share data. A network can consist of static or dynamic connections. People use networks for work and play. In most cases, businesses would find it difficult or impossible to perform useful work without networks of some kind in place. Generally, all networks follow the same rules or protocols. A protocol is simply a kind of rule that everyone has agreed to follow, usually through a standards organization. The most famous of these rules is the International Standards Organization/Open Systems Interconnection (ISO/OSI) seven-layer network model discussed at `http://en.wikipedia.org/wiki/OSI_model`.

This section isn't going to help you configure your network or provide you with advice on how to create a network. Many other books can help you through that process. However, the following sections do describe the many useful utilities that Microsoft provides for navigating all seven layers of the network model. In many cases, these utilities provide you with insights about the construction of your network and how to prevent outside intrusion (or at least keep it at bay). The utilities you use depend, in part, on the combination of hardware and software you use, so you need to have some idea of what your network uses before these sections will become completely useful.

Managing the ATM Call Manager with the ATMAdm Utility

VISTA

The Asynchronous Transfer Mode Administrator (ATMAdm) utility helps you work with Asynchronous Transfer Mode (ATM) networks. Vista doesn't provide support for this utility and there isn't a replacement utility. If you don't have an ATM network, then you won't have to worry about any of the ATM subjects in this book. However, if you're interested in ATM, you can find a good basic discussion at `http://en.wikipedia.org/wiki/Asynchronous_Transfer_Mode`. The ATMAdm utility helps you monitor the ATM network. This utility uses the following syntax:

```
ATMAdm [-c] [-a] [-s]
```

The following list describes each of the command line arguments.

-c Lists all of the ATM connections on your system.

-a Lists all of the registered ATM addresses for your system.

-s Displays the ATM network statistics.

Getting the Media Access Control Information with the GetMAC Utility

Every network adapter has a Media Access Control (MAC) address. The address is unique for every network adapter across all vendors. The output from this utility consists of the network adapter MAC address and the transport name associated with it. You don't gain much in the way of additional information. However, the MAC address is central to all kinds of monitoring activity, including sniffing packets on your network (the act of filtering the packets and viewing the ones of interest). This utility uses the following syntax:

```
GETMAC [/S system [/U [domain\]user [/P [password]]]]
[/FO {TABLE | LIST | CSV}] [/NH] [/V]
```

The following describes the command line arguments.

/S *system* Specifies the remote system that you want to check. In most cases, you'll also need to supply the `/U` and the `/P` command line switches when using this switch.

/U [*domain*\]*user* Specifies the username on the remote system. This name may not match the username on the local system. You'll need to supply a domain name when working with a domain controller.

/P [*password*] Specifies the password for the given user. You can provide the command line switch without specifying the password on the command line in cleartext. The system prompts you for the password. Using this feature can help you maintain the security of passwords used on your system.

/FO {TABLE | LIST | CSV} Defines the output provided by the utility. The table format is normally the easiest to view on screen. The table columns define the values for output, while each row contains one driver entry. The Comma Separated Value (CSV) output provides the best method for preparing the data for entry in a database. Use redirection (see the "Employing Data Redirection" section of Chapter 2 for details) to output the CSV data to a file and then import it to your database. The list format provides one data element per line. Each group of data elements defines one driver. The utility separates each driver by one blank line. Some people find the list format more readable when working in verbose mode since the table format requires multiple lines for each entry (the lines wrap).

/NH Forces the utility to display the data without a column header. You can only use this command line switch with the table and CSV formats. Omitting the header makes it easier to incorporate the data in a report or import it into a database.

/V Displays detailed data about each of the network adapters. In addition to the standard output, the utility provides the human readable connection name and network adapter name. Using this command line switch makes it a lot easier to associate a particular MAC address with a specific network adapter (making monitoring easier as well).

Getting the NetWare Routing Information with the IPXRoute Utility

VISTA

NetWare servers have access to a special protocol, Internet Packet eXchange (IPX). Because this protocol has special features, you need a different utility to work with it. Unfortunately, Vista doesn't appear to support this utility and there isn't a replacement for it. (You can learn more about the special features of IPX at `http://www.rhyshaden.com/ipx.htm`.) Generally, most NetWare servers now use Transmission Control Protocol/Internet Protocol (TCP/IP), so you won't have to consider the IPX protocol even if you have a NetWare server installed. The IPXRoute utility helps you manage the routing tables used to direct NetWare packets. When you use the IPXRoute utility by itself, it displays the default settings for packets that NetWare sends to unknown, broadcast, and multicast addresses. This utility uses the following syntax:

```
ipxroute servers [/type=x]
ipxroute ripout network
ipxroute resolve {GUID | name} {GUID | AdapterName}
ipxroute board=n [def] [gbr] [mbr] [remove=xxxxxxxxxxxx]
ipxroute config
```

The following list describes each of the command line arguments.

servers [/type=*x*] Displays the Service Access Point (SAP) table for the specified server type. If you don't specify a type, then the utility displays all servers. The server type must be an integer that defines a particular server. The following list defines the valid server types.

0000 Unknown

0003 Print Queue

0004 File Server

0005 Job Server

0007 Print Server

0009 Archive Server

0024 Remote Bridge Server

0047 Advertising Print Server

>8000 Reserved

ripout ***network*** Discovers whether the network is readable by consulting the IPX routing table. The utility sends a Routing Information Protocol (RIP) request to the network if necessary. The network argument contains the IPX network segment number. Use the `config` command line option to determine the network segment number.

resolve {GUID | ***name*****} {GUID |** ***AdapterName*****}** Resolves (changes) a Globally Unique Identifier (GUID) to its friendly name, or the friendly name to its GUID.

board=*n* Specifies the network adapter that you want to query or for which you want to set parameters. The input argument is an integer specifying the board number.

def Sends packets to the ALL ROUTES broadcast. When the system transmits a packet to a unique MAC address that isn't in the source routing table, the IPXRoute utility sends the packet to the SINGLE ROUTES broadcast.

gbr Sends packets to the ALL ROUTES broadcast. When the system transmits a packet to the FFFFFFFFFFFF address, the IPXRoute utility sends the packet to the SINGLE ROUTES broadcast.

mbr Sends packets to the ALL ROUTES broadcast. When the system transmits a packet to the C000xxxxxxxx multicast address (where xxxxxxxx is any valid hexadecimal number), the IPXRoute utility sends the packet to the SINGLE ROUTES broadcast.

remove=*xxxxxxxxxxxx* Removes the specified node from the source routing table.

config Displays the statistics for all of the currently configured IPX bindings. The configuration information includes the workstation network segment attachments, the workstation node address, and the frame type.

Managing WinHTTP Proxy Configuration with the ProxyCfg Utility

V VISTA

Use the ProxyCfg utility to configure the Windows HyperText Transfer Protocol (WinHTTP) proxy on a system. The WinHTTP proxy controls client access to Web servers. Unfortunately, Vista doesn't support this utility and there isn't a replacement for it. You can learn more about this technology on the Microsoft Web site at `http://msdn2.microsoft.com/en-us/library/aa382925.aspx`. This utility uses the following syntax:

```
proxycfg [-d] [-p <server-name> [<bypass_list>]]
proxycfg -u
```

The following list describes each of the command line arguments.

-d Sets the client to use direct server access.

-p ***server-name*** Sets the client to use one or more proxy servers to access a Web server. The proxy server sits between the client and the Web server.

bypass_list Defines a list of proxy servers to bypass.

-u Imports the user's manual proxy configuration settings from Internet Explorer. These settings appear as part of the LAN Settings on the Connections tab of the Internet Properties applet found in the Control Panel.

Managing the Network with the Net Utility

The Net utility represents one of the most flexible and comprehensive means of controlling all aspects of your network. Given all that it does, it's not surprising that the Net utility relies on several operating modes to perform tasks. For example, you manage user accounts using the Accounts mode. The Net utility modes include Accounts, Computer, Config, Continue, File, Group, Help, HelpMsg, LocalGroup, Name, Pause, Print, Send, Session, Share, Start, Statistics, Stop, Time, Use, User, and View. Vista doesn't support the Name and Send modes. The following sections describe each of these modes.

NOTE If you find that you need help with the Net utility, you can't use the standard practice of typing `/?`. The `/?` command line switch provides extremely limited help. Instead, you need to type **`Net Help`** Mode at the command line and press Enter. For example, to obtain help on using the Accounts mode, type **`Net Help Accounts`** and press Enter.

Accounts

Use the Accounts mode to modify all user accounts on a system with specific settings. For example, you can define all user accounts to have a maximum password age of so many days. This mode only affects existing user accounts—not user accounts that you create in the future. Typing `Net Accounts` by itself displays the current settings. This mode uses the following syntax:

```
NET ACCOUNTS [/FORCELOGOFF:{minutes | NO}] [/MINPWLEN:length]
[/MAXPWAGE:{days | UNLIMITED}] [/MINPWAGE:days] [/UNIQUEPW:number]
[/DOMAIN]
```

The following list describes each of the command line arguments.

/FORCELOGOFF:{*minutes* | NO} Sets the number of minutes before the system forces a user to log off after the user's account or valid logon hours expire. The default setting of NO prevents forced logoff.

/MINPWLEN:*length* Sets the minimum number of characters in a password. The default setting is 6 characters. You may use any value between 0 and 14 characters.

/MAXPWAGE:{*days* | UNLIMITED} Sets the maximum number of days between password changes. You may define no password change requirement by using the `UNLIMITED` argument. The `/MAXPWAGE` setting must always exceed the `/MINPWAGE` setting. The default setting is 90 days. You may use any value between 1 and 999 days.

/MINPWAGE:*days* Sets the minimum number of days that must pass before a user can change their password. A value of 0 sets non-minimum time. The `/MAXPWAGE` setting must always exceed the `/MINPWAGE` setting. The default setting is 0 days. You may use any value between 0 and 999 days.

/UNIQUEPW:*number* Specifies that the user must provide a unique password for each password change through the number specified. For example, if you specify 5, then the system will track five of the user's passwords and allow the user to reuse a password on the sixth change. The maximum value is 24.

/DOMAIN Performs the task on a domain control for the current domain. Otherwise, any task affects only the local computer.

COMPUTER

Use the Computer mode to add a computer to the domain database or delete it from the database. You can only use this mode on a server. This mode uses the following syntax:

```
NET COMPUTER \\computername {/ADD | /DEL}
```

The following list describes each of the command line arguments.

computername Specifies the Universal Naming Convention (UNC) name of the computer to add or delete. Always use the computer's name as it appears to the network.

/ADD Adds the specified computer to the domain.

/DEL Removes the specified computer from the domain.

CONFIG

Use the Config mode to discover network configuration information for the current machine. When used alone, this mode displays the configurable services on a machine. This mode uses the following syntax:

```
NET CONFIG [SERVER | WORKSTATION]
```

The following list describes each of the command line arguments.

Server Displays information about the configuration of the server service. This information includes the server name, server comment, software version, network node information, whether the server is hidden, the maximum number of users that can log in, the maximum number of available file handles per session, and the idle session time.

Workstation Displays information about the configuration of the workstation service. This information includes computer UNC name, full computer name, username, network node information, software version, workstation domain, workstation Domain Name Service (DNS) name, logon domain, and COM statistics.

Config Server

You can use the Config Server mode to adjust a few, but not all, of the server configuration features. This mode uses the following syntax:

```
NET CONFIG SERVER [/AUTODISCONNECT:time] [/SRVCOMMENT:"text"] [/HIDDEN:{YES | NO}]
```

The following list describes each of the command line arguments.

/AUTODISCONNECT:*time* Sets the maximum number of minutes that a user's session remains inactive before the server disconnects it. Use a value of –1 to force the system to remain connected indefinitely. You may use any value from –1 to 65,535 minutes. The default setting is 15 minutes.

/SRVCOMMENT:"*text*" Adds a comment to the server information. The comment appears in all graphical displays and in the Net View mode. You may use up to 48 characters for the comment. Always enclose comments in quotes.

/HIDDEN:{YES | NO} Determines whether the server appears in the display listing for servers. Using this feature can prevent unauthorized users from finding a server on your network since the user would need to know the server name to access it. However, this setting doesn't change the server security. You still have to set security aggressively to protect your server. The default setting is NO.

CONTINUE

Use this mode to reactivate a service that you suspended using the Net Pause mode or the Services console located in the Administrative Tools folder of the Control Panel. This mode uses the following syntax:

```
NET CONTINUE service
```

The following list describes each of the command line arguments.

service Specifies the name of the service to reactivate. Always enclose services that contain a space in their name in quotes. The following list contains typical service names.

NET LOGON

NT LM SECURITY SUPPORT PROVIDER

SCHEDULE

SERVER

WORKSTATION

FILE

Use this mode to control shared files on a system. When used alone, the File mode displays a list of active files on the current system. This mode uses the following syntax:

```
NET FILE [id [/CLOSE]]
```

The following list describes each of the command line arguments.

id Specifies a particular open file. Queries information about a specific file when used alone.

/CLOSE Closes the specified file and removes any file locks.

GROUP

Use the Group mode to query, add, delete, and modify Windows groups. Use this mode alone to display a list of groups on the domain controller. This command only works on Windows domain controllers. Use the LocalGroup mode for local workstations instead. This mode uses the following syntax:

```
NET GROUP [groupname [/COMMENT:"text"]] [/DOMAIN]
NET GROUP groupname /ADD [/COMMENT:"text"] [/DOMAIN]
NET GROUP groupname /DELETE [/DOMAIN]
NET GROUP groupname username [...] /ADD [/DOMAIN]
NET GROUP groupname username [...] /DELETE [/DOMAIN]
```

The following list describes each of the command line arguments.

groupname Defines the name of the group that you want to query, add, delete, or modify. Providing just the group name displays the list of users in that group. You also see the group alias and comment (the comment normally indicates the purpose of the group).

/COMMENT:"*text*" Adds or modifies a comment for a new or existing group. You may use up to 48 characters to describe a group. Always enclose comments within quotes.

/DOMAIN Performs the specified task on the domain controller for the current domain. Using this command line switch lets you use a workstation for making changes to groups and users on the domain controller. The default setting performs tasks on the local machine, which means that the utility will fail unless you're working at the domain controller.

***username*[...]** Defines one or more usernames to add or remove from a group. Separate multiple entries with a space.

/ADD Adds a group or a username to a group.

/DELETE Removes a group or a username from a group.

HELP

The Help mode displays detailed help about the other modes. This mode uses the following syntax:

```
NET HELP command
```

The following describes the command line argument.

command Specifies the command (mode) for which you want help. The Help mode provides `NET HELP SERVICES` to show the services that you can start and stop using the Net utility. Use `NET HELP SYNTAX` to see help on using the various Help mode screens. Enter **`NET HELP HELP`** at the command line to see a complete list of Help mode screens.

HELPMSG

The Net utility displays a wealth of messages to provide information, warnings, and error indications. In addition, you can run into these messages when using Windows. For example, the event log often contains network-specific messages. Often, these messages appear as a number. The HelpMsg mode accepts a number as input and outputs the information in human readable form. This mode uses the following syntax:

```
NET HELPMSG MessageNumber
```

The following describes the command line argument.

MessageNumber Specifies a four-digit error number that Windows displays for information, warning, or error indication. Type only the four-digit number. You don't need to provide the NET prefix that Windows displays with some messages. For example, one common error is NET2182. You'd type **`Net HelpMsg 2182`** and press Enter at the command prompt to display the human readable message of "The requested service has already been started."

LOCALGROUP

Use the LocalGroup mode to query, add, delete, and modify Windows groups on the local machine. Use this mode alone to display a list of groups on the local machine. This mode uses the following syntax:

```
NET LOCALGROUP [groupname [/COMMENT:"text"]] [/DOMAIN]
NET LOCALGROUP groupname /ADD [/COMMENT:"text"] [/DOMAIN]
NET LOCALGROUP groupname /DELETE [/DOMAIN]
NET LOCALGROUP groupname name [...] /ADD [/DOMAIN]
NET LOCALGROUP groupname name [...] /DELETE [/DOMAIN]
```

The following list describes each of the command line arguments.

groupname Defines the name of the group that you want to query, add, delete, or modify. Providing just the group name displays the list of users in that group. You also see the group alias and comment (the comment normally indicates the purpose of the group).

/COMMENT:"*text*" Adds or modifies a comment for a new or existing group. You may use up to 48 characters to describe a group. Always enclose comments within quotes.

/DOMAIN Performs the specified task on the domain controller for the current domain. Using this command line switch lets you use a workstation for making changes to groups and users on the domain controller. The default setting performs tasks on the local machine.

***username*[...]** Defines one or more usernames to add or remove from a group. Separate multiple entries with a space.

/ADD Adds a group or a username to a group.

/DELETE Removes a group or a username from a group.

NAME

The Name mode adds and deletes aliases for users of the Windows Messenger service. Administrators commonly use this service to send network messages and other important information. Sources of aliases for messages include names added with the Net Name utility, the computer name (added as a name when the workstation service starts), and a username (added when you log into the computer). You can't delete the workstation name as a destination for messages. This mode uses the following syntax:

```
NET NAME [name [/ADD | /DELETE]]
```

The following list describes each of the command line arguments.

name Specifies the alias (name) to receive messages. The name can contain up to 15 characters.

/ADD Adds the name of the list of aliases for a computer. The use of this command line switch is optional. Typing **`Net Name`** name and pressing Enter will automatically add the name to the list.

/DELETE Removes the name for the list of aliases for the computer.

WARNING The Net Name mode relies on the Windows Messenger service. This isn't the same as Microsoft Messenger, the online utility. Windows Messenger sends messages between machines on the network. Microsoft recommends disabling this particular service because crackers commonly target it as a way to spread a virus on a network. In general, you don't want to use this service in place of more common methods of sending messages, such as email. You can discover how to disable this service on the About Web service site at `http://antivirus.about.com/cs/tutorials/ht/msgsvc.htm`. As one example of what can happen with Windows Messenger, see the Microsoft Knowledge Base article at `http://support.microsoft.com/kb/883261`.

PAUSE

Use the Pause mode to suspend a service temporarily. Use Net Stop when you wish to stop a service long term. Pausing a service maintains its presence in memory and therefore preserves the service's state information. Stopping a service removes it from memory and frees the resources that the service is using. This mode uses the following syntax:

```
NET PAUSE service
```

The following describes the command line argument.

service Specifies the name of the service to pause. Always enclose services that contain a space in their name in quotes. The following list contains typical service names.

NET LOGON

NT LM SECURITY SUPPORT PROVIDER

SCHEDULE

SERVER

WORKSTATION

You can't pause some services. The Net utility displays an error when you try to stop some services. Here's a list of common services that you can't pause.

DCOM Server Process Launcher

Event Log

Plug and Play

Remote Procedure Call (RPC)

Security Accounts Manager

PRINT

The Print mode controls printing on the local machine. Used with just the sharename, the `Net Print` command displays the status of the print queue. You can also use this mode to manage the existing print jobs. This mode uses the following syntax:

```
NET PRINT \\computername\sharename [\\computername] job#
[/HOLD | /RELEASE | /DELETE]
```

The following list describes each of the command line arguments.

computername Specifies the name of the computer providing the print services as a queue.

sharename Specifies the name of the print queue. The print queue name is the same as the sharename for the printer.

job# Specifies the job number to modify. The system assigns the print job number when the user submits the print job. The computer provides each job with a unique number across printer queues.

/HOLD Prevents a job from printing. All of the other jobs in the printer queue will bypass a job on hold and print. The job stays in the printer queue until the user releases the job or deletes it.

/RELEASE Releases a job that a user previously placed on hold.

/DELETE Removes a job from the printer queue.

SEND

Use the Send mode to send a message to other users on the network with the Windows Messenger service. Unlike email, the message appears immediately on the remote system as a popup. The utility displays an error when you attempt to send a message to someone who's not active on the network. Use the Net Name utility to determine which users or systems are available to receive messages. This mode uses the following syntax:

```
NET SEND {name | * | /DOMAIN[:name] | /USERS} message
```

The following list describes each of the command line arguments.

name Specifies the username, computer name, or messaging name to receive the message you send. Always enclose names that include spaces in quotes.

* Sends the message to all of the names in your group. A group might only include the names in a workgroup and not the entire organization.

/DOMAIN[:*name*] Sends the message to all of the names in a domain. The default is to use the current system's domain. You may also specify a domain name to send messages to other domains.

/USERS Sends the message to all users connected to a particular server, regardless of the user workgroup and domain boundaries. Use this option when you intend to perform tasks such as shutting a server down.

message Defines the message to send. Always enclose the message in quotes (even though the command line help for this utility doesn't mention the requirement to use quotes).

Session

Whenever your system acts as a server (the Server service is started) and someone uses a shared resource, the activity creates a session. The Session mode lists and deletes sessions associated with the specified computer. When used alone, it displays sessions for the local computer. Note that you must have the Server service started to use this mode. This mode uses the following syntax:

```
NET SESSION [\\computername] [/DELETE]
```

The following list describes each of the command line arguments.

computername Specifies the name of a computer to work with when listing or deleting sessions.

/DELETE Ends the session between the local computer and the specified computer. The utility closes all open files on the local computer for the ended session and frees any resources that the session uses. If you use this command line switch without specifying a computer, the utility ends all of the existing sessions.

Share

Use the Share mode to define resources available to other users or machines on the network. For example, you can choose to share a hard drive with other users on the network. When used alone, the Share mode displays a list of shared items on the local computer. Each shared item entry includes the device name, the pathname, and a descriptive comment. You must start the Server service to use this mode. This mode uses the following syntax:

```
NET SHARE sharename
NET SHARE sharename=drive:path [/USERS:number | /UNLIMITED]
[/REMARK:"text"] [/CACHE:Manual | Documents | Programs | None ]
NET SHARE sharename [/USERS:number | /UNLIMITED] [/REMARK:"text"]
 [/CACHE:Manual | Documents | Programs | None]
NET SHARE {sharename | devicename | drive:path} /DELETE
```

The following list describes each of the command line arguments.

sharename Specifies the network name (the UNC name) of the shared resource. Type **Net Share sharename** alone and press Enter to display information about the shared resource including the sharename, path, remark, maximum users, users, and caching.

drive:*path* Specifies the absolute path of the drive or directory to share. The path must contain a drive letter and colon as a minimum. You share a directory by combining the drive information with an absolute path on that drive.

/USERS:*number* Defines the maximum number of users who can simultaneously access the shared resource.

/UNLIMITED Specifies that an unlimited number of users can simultaneously access the shared resource.

/REMARK:"*text*" Provides a descriptive comment about the shared resource. Always enclose the comment in quotes. It's a good idea to include a comment about the shared resource that specifies why you're sharing it. The more descriptive you make the comment, the easier it becomes for users who need the resource to find it.

devicename Defines one or more printers (LPT1: through LPT9:) by sharename.

/DELETE Stops sharing the resource.

/CACHE:Manual Enables manual client caching of programs and documents from this share. Using this option leaves the decision of whether to cache up to the user. Caching generally improves performance at the expense of local resources. Some devices might not have enough local resources to perform caching effectively.

/CACHE:Documents Enables automatic caching of documents from this share.

/CACHE:Programs Enables automatic caching of documents and programs from this share.

/CACHE:None Disables caching from this share.

START

Use this mode to start a service. You can also perform this task using the Services console located in the Administrative Tools folder of the Control Panel. Using `Net Start` alone displays a list of the services that are currently active on the local machine. This mode uses the following syntax:

```
NET START [service]
```

The following describes the command line argument.

service Specifies the name of the service to start. Always enclose services that contain a space in their name in quotes. The following list contains typical service names.

```
NET LOGON
NT LM SECURITY SUPPORT PROVIDER
SCHEDULE
SERVER
WORKSTATION
```

STATISTICS

The statistics mode displays the service statistics for the local workstation or Server service. When used alone, the mode displays the services for which you can obtain statistics. This mode uses the following syntax:

```
NET STATISTICS [WORKSTATION | SERVER]
```

The following list describes each of the command line arguments.

SERVER Displays the Server service statistics, which include sessions accepted, sessions timed out, sessions errored out, kilobytes sent, kilobytes received, mean response time (msec), system errors, permission violations, password violations, files accessed, communication devices accessed, print jobs spooled, and times buffers exhausted (both big buffers and request buffers).

WORKSTATION Displays the Workstation service statistics, which include bytes received, Server Message Blocks (SMBs) received, bytes transmitted, SMBs transmitted, read operations, write operations, raw reads denied, raw writes denied, network errors, connections made, reconnections made, server disconnects, sessions started, hung sessions, failed sessions, failed operations, use count, and failed use count.

STOP

Use this mode to stop a service that you started using the Net Start mode or the Services console located in the Administrative Tools folder of the Control Panel. This mode uses the following syntax:

```
NET STOP service
```

The following describes the command line argument.

service Specifies the name of the service to stop. Always enclose services that contain a space in their name in quotes. The following list contains typical service names.

`NET LOGON`

`NT LM SECURITY SUPPORT PROVIDER`

`SCHEDULE`

`SERVER`

`WORKSTATION`

You can't stop some services. The Net utility displays an error when you try to stop some services. Here's a list of common unstoppable services.

DCOM Server Process Launcher

Event Log

Plug and Play

Remote Procedure Call (RPC)

Security Accounts Manager

TIME

Use the Time mode to access a time service. The essential task of this mode is to synchronize the local computer with a timeserver. Contrast this mode with the W32Tm utility discussed in Chapter 4. While the W32Tm utility interacts with the timeserver (and even creates it), the Time mode interacts with the client and uses the timeserver as a resource. Read the Microsoft Knowledge Base article at `http://support.microsoft.com/kb/q224799/` for additional Windows time service information. This mode uses the following syntax:

```
NET TIME [\\computername | /DOMAIN[:domainname]
| /RTSDOMAIN[:domainname]] [/SET] [\\computername] /QUERYSNTP
[\\computername] /SETSNTP[:ntp server list]
```

The following list describes each of the command line arguments.

\\computername Specifies the name of the computer to check or use for synchronization.

/DOMAIN[:*domainname*] Specifies the domain of the PDC to use for synchronization purposes. The default is the client's current domain.

/RTSDOMAIN[:*domainname*] Specifies the domain of the Reliable Time Server (RTS) to use for synchronization purposes. The default is the client's current domain.

/SET Synchronizes the specified system's time (the default is the local system) with the time on the configured time source (a specific computer or domain).

/QUERYSNTP Displays the currently configured National Time Protocol (NTP) server for this computer.

/SETSNTP[:*ntp server list*] Sets the NTP timeservers that this computer relies on for synchronization. You may specify more than one server using IP addresses or DNS names separated by spaces. When working with multiple timeservers, you must surround the entire command line switch with quotes. Three common servers include `tick.usno.navy.mil`, `tock.usno.navy.mil`, and `ntp2.usno.navy.mil`.

USE

The Use mode connects a computer to a shared resource, disconnects a computer from a shared resource, or lists the shared resources. When used by itself, this mode displays the status, local drive letter, remote UNC source, and the network type of any drives the local system uses. This mode uses the following syntax:

```
NET USE [devicename | *] [\\computername\sharename[\volume]
[password | *]] [/USER:[domainname\]username] [/USER:[dotted
domainname\]username] [/USER:[username@dotted domainname] [/SMARTCARD]
 [/SAVECRED] [[/DELETE] | [/PERSISTENT:{YES | NO}]]
NET USE {devicename | *} [password | *] /HOME
NET USE [/PERSISTENT:{YES | NO}]
```

The following list describes each of the command line arguments.

NOTE There's a lack of consistency between Windows and the Net Use utility when working with printers. If you create a connection to a drive using the standard Windows techniques, you'll see it in the list when you use the `Net Use` command. However, if you create a connection to a printer, the printer doesn't show up in the list, even if you ensure the printer has an LPT port connection. Any printer connections that you create using Net Use do show up in the list, but these connections don't show up in the Printers and Faxes folder. Generally, you'll want to work with printers in Windows unless you have a need for a printer connection in a batch file for script.

devicename Specifies a name to connect to the resource or specifies the device that you want to connect. The two device types are disk drives (D: through Z:) and printers (LPT1: through LPT3:). (It's theoretically possible to create printer connections up to LPT9: even though Microsoft only documents connections up to LPT3:.) Type an asterisk (*) instead of a specific device name to assign the next available device name to a device.

\\computername Specifies the name of the computer that controls the shared resource. Make sure you enclose the computer name, including the backslashes, in double quotes when the computer name has a space in it. You may use any computer name from 1 to 15 characters long.

\sharename Specifies the sharename for the resource you want to use. This entry is the same as the name that appears in Network Neighborhood.

\volume Specifies a NetWare volume on the server. You must have the correct software installed on your system to access the NetWare volume. In most cases, this means you'll have Client Services for NetWare or Gateway Services for NetWare installed to connect to the NetWare servers.

password Defines the password used to access the shared resource, which isn't necessarily the same as the local password.

***** Produces a prompt for the password. The system displays a dialog box that shows the password as a series of asterisks instead of using cleartext at the command line. Using this feature can help you maintain the security of passwords used on your system.

/USER Specifies that the utility uses a different username than the current username to make the connection. The username can take a number of forms as shown by the command line syntax. In addition, you can provide alternative credentials, such as smart cards.

domainname Defines the domain name to use for the logon. If you omit the domain name, then the utility uses the currently logged in domain. You may also use a dotted form of the domain name, which looks much like the domain names for the Internet, when working with Active Directory.

username Specifies the username to use to log into the remote system.

/SMARTCARD Specifies that the connection relies on the credentials stored on a smart card.

/SAVECRED Specifies that the connection should save the username and password. The utility ignores this command line switch unless the connection requires a username and password for access. This option isn't available with versions of Windows older than Windows XP, including Windows XP Home Edition.

/HOME Connects the user to their home directory. This command line switch only works when the user account has a home directory specified.

/DELETE Deletes the connection from the list of persistent connections. The connection becomes unusual as soon as the command completes.

/PERSISTENT:{YES | NO} Sets the state of the persistent network connection. When set to YES, the utility saves all connections as you make them and restores them at the next logon. When set to NO, the utility doesn't save any new connections. However, the utility still restores any existing connections during the next logon even if you set this command line switch to NO. Use the `/DELETE` command line switch to remove any persistent connections you no longer need.

User

The User mode works with user accounts on the network. You can change local user accounts or specify that you want to change the user information on the domain. The utility displays a list of current users when you use the User mode alone. The names appear in three columns and the output doesn't include any additional information. The User mode only works on servers (machines that have the Server service running). This mode uses the following syntax:

```
NET USER [username [password | *] [options]] [/DOMAIN]
NET USER username {password | *} /ADD [options] [/DOMAIN]
NET USER username [/DELETE] [/DOMAIN]
NET USER username [/TIMES:{times | ALL}]
```

The following list describes each of the command line arguments.

username Specifies the name of the user account that you want to add, delete, modify, or view. The user account name can contain up to 20 characters.

password Specifies the password used to access the user account. A password must satisfy all logon requirements for the machine, including the minimum and maximum length requirements set with the `Net Accounts` command. A password can contain up to 14 characters.

* Produces a prompt for the password. The system displays a dialog box that shows the password as a series of asterisks instead of using cleartext at the command line. Using this feature can help you maintain the security of passwords used on your system.

/DOMAIN Performs the requested task on the domain controller of the current domain instead of the local machine. You must have the rights required to make user account changes on the domain controller to use this command line switch.

/ADD Adds the user account to the user accounts database.

/DELETE Removes the user account from the user accounts database.

/TIMES:{*times* | ALL} Specifies the times that the user can log into the system. The option requires specific intervals or the keyword ALL, which means that the user has no time restriction.

options Specifies one or more specialized options that the mode uses when working with a particular user.

The options require a little more explanation. You use the options to change the way that the User mode handles specific users. The following list describes each of the options.

/ACTIVE:{YES | NO} Activates or deactivates the account. The user can't access the server when the account is inactive. The default setting is YES.

/COMMENT:"*text*" Provides a comment for the user's account. You can use a maximum of 48 characters to describe the user or the user's role. Always enclose the comment in quotes.

/COUNTRYCODE:*nnn* Defines a three-digit country code for the user. The country code tells applications how to implement language support for the user. In addition, the country code affects how Windows displays help and error message. Use a value of 0 to signify the default country code. You can find a list of standard three-digit country codes at `http://www.unicode.org/onlinedat/countries.html`.

/EXPIRES:{*date* | NEVER} Defines an expiration date for the user account. The default setting of NEVER keeps the account active forever. The form of the date depends on the country code; it's usually mm/dd/yy or dd/mm/yy. You can use a number for months, abbreviate them with three letter codes, or spell them out. The year can appear as a two- or four-digit number. Always use slashes and not spaces to separate the date elements.

/FULLNAME:"*name*" Specifies the user's full name for the account. The full name is the user's given name, rather than the account name used for logging into the system. Enclose the name in quotes.

/HOMEDIR:*pathname* Defines a home directory for the user. The path must exist. You must supply an absolute path and it's always a good idea to include the drive letter.

/PASSWORDCHG:{YES | NO} Specifies whether the user can change their own password. The default setting is YES.

/PASSWORDREQ:{YES | NO} Specifies whether the user account must have a password associated with it. The default setting is YES. Creating a user account without a password, even on a stand-alone machine, is an invitation to invasion by a cracker. In fact, you should change your password relatively often to ensure that crackers have short-term use of your machine even if they do guess your password.

/PROFILEPATH[:*path*] Sets the path for the user's logon profile. You can learn more about user logon profiles at `http://www.kellys-korner-xp.com/win_xp_logon.htm`.

/SCRIPTPATH:*pathname* Defines the location of the user's logon script. The logon script controls actions the machine takes as part of setting Windows up for the user after the user logs into the system.

/TIMES:{*times* | ALL} Defines the user's logon hours. A user can't log onto the system outside of these hours. You express the times as starting day, ending day, starting time, and ending time. The system limits you to using one-hour increments for the time. You can spell days out or abbreviate them. The times can appear in 12- or 24-hour format. Supplying a value of ALL as input means that the user can always log into the system. Likewise, a blank value means the user can never log into the system. Separate the day and time values using commas. Create multiple entries by separating the day and time groups with semicolons.

/USERCOMMENT:"*text*" Defines a user comment for the user account. The comment should describe the user or the user's role within the organization. Create useful comments that describe the user in such a way that it's easier to identify the user in a large organization.

/WORKSTATIONS:{*computername*[...] | *} Defines up to eight computers that the user can use for login purposes. If this command line switch doesn't include a list, or the list is an asterisk (*), then the user can log in from any computer.

VIEW

The View mode displays a list of shared resources on a computer. When you use this mode without any command line switches, it displays all of the machines on a network or domain. This mode uses the following syntax:

```
NET VIEW [\\computername [/CACHE] | /DOMAIN[:domainname]]
NET VIEW /NETWORK:NW [\\computername]
```

The following list describes each of the command line arguments.

computername Specifies the computer whose resources you want to view. The default output includes the sharename, resource type, used as information, and comment.

/DOMAIN:*domainname* Specifies the domain for which you want to view the available computers. The utility displays the current domain or local network when you omit this command line switch.

/NETWORK:NW Displays the list of available servers on a NetWare network. The utility displays the resources available on a particular computer when you include the `computername` argument.

/CACHE Displays the offline client caching settings for the resources on the specified computer. The output includes the sharename, resource type, used as information, and the caching setting.

Sharing Folders Using the SHRPubW Utility

Your hard drive is probably loaded with a wealth of undocumented utilities. In many cases, these undocumented utilities are gold for anyone working at the command line. The SHRPubW is one of those undocumented Microsoft utilities that can make a difference in many cases. The command line interface for this utility is `SHRPubW /s` *`ComputerName`*, where *`ComputerName`* is the name of a computer on the network. You must always include the `/s` command line switch, which causes the utility to share a folder on the target computer. In all cases, this utility starts the Create a Shared Folder Wizard. Follow the prompts and you'll end up with a shared folder on your machine or any other machine you designate.

This utility has a number of interesting uses. One of the most interesting uses is sharing a folder on Windows XP Home machines. The graphical interface doesn't provide any means of performing this task. However, Windows XP Home does include this utility, so you can still share folder with this operating system.

Another interesting use for this utility is to share folders on other machines. For example, if you're a network administrator and want to share a folder on your server without walking over to it, you can start this utility with that server's name. The utility helps you set basic share security and the user will see the new share immediately.

Discovering TCP/IP Diagnostic Tools

In most respects, TCP/IP isn't a complex protocol for communicating between computers. However, the ways in which networks use TCP/IP does complicate matters. The same protocol that connects machines on the network can also connect you to any machine worldwide on the Internet. In addition to the broad usage that TCP/IP enjoys, the protocol also appears on most platforms. Unfortunately, each platform seems to have its own little oddities in dealing with TCP/IP. Finally, TCP/IP has evolved over time. In general, some of the utilities you'll see in the sections that follow are remakes of utilities that appear on other systems. The utilities of early UNIX still appear as part of TCP/IP. Consequently, the following sections may have a few surprises for you because they include a wide variety of utilities that have a single purpose, diagnosing problems with TCP/IP connections.

Managing the Address Resolution Protocol with the ARP Utility

V VISTA

The Address Resolution Protocol (ARP) utility displays and modifies the IP to physical address translation tables that ARP relies on to make connections. Vista doesn't support the `-g` command line switch, but does add the `-v` command line switch. This utility uses the following syntax:

```
ARP -a [inet_addr] [-N if_addr] [-v]
ARP -g [inet_addr] [-N if_addr]
ARP -d inet_addr [if_addr]
ARP -s inet_addr eth_addr [if_addr]
```

The following list describes each of the command line arguments.

-a Displays the current ARP entries by requesting the current protocol data. The output includes the interface address, Internet address, physical address, and type of connection. When used alone, the table includes all entries for all tables. If you specify the internet address, the utility displays the IP and physical addresses for the specified computer. When more than one network interface uses ARP, the utility displays entries for each ARP table.

-g Performs the same task as `-a`.

inet_addr Defines an Internet address. Generally, this value is the computer that hosts the ARP table, which might not be the local computer. This utility doesn't currently support IP version 6, so the addresses are all in the form of 192.168.0.1.

-N *if_addr* Displays a list of ARP entries for the specified network interface. The `N` is case sensitive and the utility ignores a lowercase `n`.

if_addr Specifies the Internet address of the interface that the utility will modify. If you don't include this argument, the utility modifies the first applicable interface. You can normally obtain the information required for this entry using the IPConfig utility.

-d Deletes the host specified by the Internet address. You may delete just a specific interface by including the interface address. Delete all of the hosts by using the asterisk (*) wildcard.

-s Adds a new host to the ARP table and associates the Internet address with the physical (Ethernet) address. The resulting entry is permanent; you must manually delete it using the `-d` command line switch.

eth_addr Specifies a physical address as 6 hexadecimal bytes separated by hyphens in the form 00-AA-00-4F-2A-9C. You can obtain the physical address using the GetMac utility.

VISTA

-v Displays information in verbose mode. In addition to the standard entries, the output also includes all loopback interface entries.

Discovering User Information with the Finger Utility

Use the Finger utility to obtain information about a user with access to a remote system. The remote computer must run the Finger service or daemon, which means that it's normally a Linux or UNIX system. The standard output includes the login name, the username, the user's Terminal Type (TTY), the amount of idle time, when the user logged in, and where the user logged in. This utility uses the following syntax:

```
finger [-l] [User] [@host] [...]
```

The following list describes each of the command line arguments.

-l Displays the user information in long list format, with one item per output line. This option makes room for long entries. However, it only displays the user's login name and username.

User Specifies the login name of the user to check. When you omit the `user` argument, Finger displays information about all of the users on the specified computer.

@host Specifies the identity of the remote computer running the Finger service. You must have proper rights to make the request on the remote computer. The host information can appear as a computer name or IP address.

Getting the Local Hostname with the Hostname Utility

The Hostname utility can both set and query the hostname on many operating systems. However, when using Windows, the Hostname utility can only obtain the name of the host; the utility ignores the `-s` command line switch. Use this utility by typing **`Hostname`** at the command prompt and pressing Enter. The utility still lets you query the current host when working with batch files or scripts.

MANAGING THE INTERNET PROTOCOL WITH THE IPCONFIG UTILITY

The IPConfig utility displays information about the configuration of the IP stack (software) on the local machine. You can also use it to renew the IP address for a particular adapter, which includes both the Dynamic Host Configuration Protocol (DHCP) and Domain Name System (DNS) settings. Vista adds Internet Protocol Version 6 (IPv6) support to this utility. This utility uses the following syntax:

```
ipconfig [/? | /all | /renew [adapter] | /release [adapter]
| /flushdns | /displaydns | /registerdns | /showclassid adapter
| /setclassid adapter [classid] | /renew6 [adapter] | /release6
[adapter]]
```

The following list describes each of the command line arguments.

adapter Specifies the name of the connection. The connection name is the one that appears in the Network Connections window (accessed by right-clicking My Network Places and choosing Properties from the context menu). A common connection name for a single adapter machine is "Local Area Connection." Enclose the connection name in quotes.

/all Displays complete configuration information for all of the adapters. The information includes all of the Windows IP configuration information, plus the Ethernet information. For example, you can use the output to discover both the physical and IP address of the connection. In addition, you can see the adapter's description (human readable name) and both DNS and DHCP information.

/release Releases the IP address for the specified adapter.

/release6 Releases the IPv6 address for the specified adapter.

TIP You'll find that Vista provides support for a wide range of IPv6 commands and utilities. These new features only support IPv6. You still use the older commands to work with Internet Protocol Version 4 (IPv4), which is the current standard. You can learn more about IPv6 at `http://www.ipv6.org/`.

/renew Renews the IP address for the specified adapter.

/renew6 Renews the IPv6 address for the specified adapter.

/flushdns Purges (clears) the DNS Resolver Cache. The cache is a memory location that stores DNS information about other machines. This cache can become corrupted, making purging the only way to clear it and start fresh. Generally, you won't need to purge the cache unless you move machines around on the network and change their IP address.

/registerdns Refreshes all of the DHCP leases and re-registers the DNS names.

/displaydns Displays the contents of the DNS Resolver Cache. The content depends on the machine type. For example, a server might contain a wealth of addresses for machines across the network and even machines on the Internet. A workstation might only contain the DNS information for Localhost.

/showclassid Displays the DHCP class identifiers allowed for the adapter. In many cases, you won't find any classes defined. Use the asterisk (*) wildcard to obtain class identifiers for all of the adapters on the local machine.

/setclassid Modifies or sets the DHCP class identifier for the specified adapter. Use the asterisk (*) wildcard to set the class identifier for all adapters on the local machine. Using this command line switch without specifying a class identifier clears the class identifier information for the specified adapter.

The IPConfig utility replaces the WinIPCfg utility found in older versions of Windows. However, it doesn't include the graphical interface of WinIPCfg. To obtain the same functionality that the WinIPCfg utility provides, right-click the network connection of interest and choose Status from the context menu. Select the Support tab shown in Figure 5.1. The Support tab provides an overview of the connection data. Click Repair to renew the connection. Click Details to obtain that same information graphically that you can obtain using the `/All` command line prompt.

Obtaining Multicast Router Information with the MRInfo Utility

The MRInfo utility provides information about the multicast routers on a system. The output includes both the multicast router interfaces and a list of the neighboring machines. This utility uses the following syntax:

```
mrinfo [-n?] [-i address] [-t secs] [-r retries] destination
```

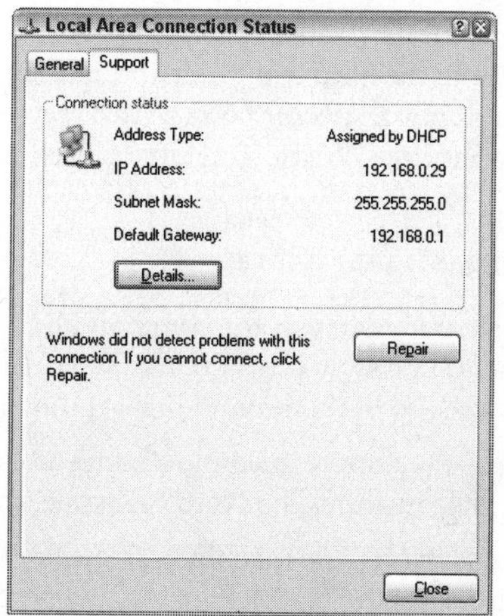

Figure 5.1
Use the connection Status dialog box to discover the information found in the graphical interface of WinIPCfg.

The following list describes each of the command line arguments.

-n Displays the IP addresses in numeric format. The output normally contains the IP addresses as DNS names.

-i *address* Defines the address of the local interface to query. The utility sends this interface information to the destination.

-t *seconds* Defines the timeout in seconds for Internet Group Multicast Protocol (IGMP) queries. The default setting is 3 seconds, which might not be long enough on large networks. You can learn more about the IGMP standard at `http://www.ietf.org/rfc/rfc1112.txt`.

-r *retries* Defines the extra number of times to send the Simple Network Management Protocol (SNMP) queries. The utility always sends the SNMP query at least once. The default number of extra tries is 0. You can find the SNMP specification at `http://www.ietf.org/rfc/rfc1157.txt`.

destination Specifies the IP address or the DNS name of the destination.

Each of the interface entries in the output contains a series of informational entries placed within square brackets and separated by slashes like this: `[1/0/pim/querier/leaf]`. A parent node may contain only the first three entries, but leaf nodes normally include all five pieces of data. The entries always appear in the same order and the node never skips information. The following list describes the entries in order of appearance.

Metric Defines the cost of the link in hops. This value is used in routing calculations.

TTL *Threshold* Defines the Time-to-Live (TTL) threshold for the multicast datagram. The router forwards the datagram when the TTL in the IP header is greater than the TTL threshold for the interface. This value limits the distances that packets can travel.

PIM Defines the Protocol Independent Multicast (PIM) the interface uses. The PIM defines the type of routing the server uses.

Querier Defines the designated multicast router that sends the IGMP Host Membership queries.

Leaf Indicates that this router is on the edge of the network—that it doesn't have any child nodes.

Getting NetBIOS over TCP/IP Status with the NBTStat Utility

The NBTStat utility displays a number of NetBIOS statistics about a network, including the NetBIOS over TCP/IP (NetBT) protocol status. You can also receive information about NetBIOS name tables for both the local computer and remote computers, and the NetBIOS name cache. The utility helps you perform specific tasks such as refreshing the local NetBIOS cache or the Windows Internet Name Service (WINS). This utility uses the following syntax:

```
NBTSTAT [ [-a RemoteName] [-A IP_address] [-c] [-n] [-r] [-R]
[-RR] [-s] [-S] [interval] ]
```

It's important to note that the command line switches for this utility are case sensitive. Using the `-a` command line switch isn't the same as using the `-A` command line switch. The following list describes each of the command line arguments.

-a Lists the remote machine's name table when you provide a machine name as input. The name table includes the NetBIOS name, the type, and the status.

-A Lists the remote machine's name table when you provide an IP address as input. The name table includes the NetBIOS name, the type, and the status.

-c List the NetBIOS Table (NBT) cache of remote machine names and their IP addresses. The table contents include the NetBIOS name, type, host address, and life in seconds.

-n Lists the local NetBIOS names. The resulting table includes the NetBIOS name, type, and status.

-r Lists the NetBIOS names resolved or registered by broadcast and using WINS. The output includes the resolved by broadcast, resolved by name server, registered by broadcast, and registered by name server statistics. In addition, you'll see a listing of NetBIOS names.

-R Purges and reloads the remote cache name table.

-S Lists the sessions table with the destination IP addresses. The resulting table includes the local name, state, whether the destination is used for input or output, the remote host IP address, the input buffer size in megabytes, and the output buffer size in megabytes.

-s Lists the sessions table with the destination IP addresses converted to NetBIOS names. The resulting table includes the local name, state, whether the destination is used for input or output, the remote host NetBIOS name, the input buffer size in megabytes, and the output buffer size in megabytes.

-RR Sends the name release packets to WINS, and then starts the refresh process.

RemoteName Specifies the remote host machine name.

IP_address Specifies the remote host IP address.

interval Redisplays the selected statistics at the specified interval in seconds. Press Ctrl+C to stop the output.

Performing Network Diagnostics with the NetDiag Utility

V VISTA

The NetDiag helps you research a number of networking problems by using specific tests. Each test outputs data about a particular network feature, and you can use the tests to assess the general health of the network. Vista doesn't provide support for this utility by default. However, you can download a copy of the utility from `http://www.microsoft.com/downloads/details.aspx?familyid=1EA70814-7E6C-46E5-8C8C-3C439A732E9F`. This utility uses the following syntax:

```
netdiag [/q] [/v] [/l] [/debug] [/d: DomainName]
[/fix] [/DcAccountEnum] [/test: TestName] [/skip: TestName]
```

The following list describes each of the command line arguments.

/q Outputs only error information.

/v Outputs verbose information, which includes testing, general, and error information.

/l Sends the output to `NetDiag.LOG`. The utility creates the log file in the same directory as the `NetDiag.EXE` file.

/debug Outputs debugging information, which includes all of the verbose output (the /v command line switch) and detailed information required to diagnose networking errors.

/d:*DomainName* Locates a domain controller within the specified domain.

/fix Locates and fixes minor problems.

/DcAccountEnum Enumerates (lists) the domain controller computer accounts.

/test:*TestName* Executes only the requested test or tests. Generally, the utility performs all tests in an attempt to locate all networking problems on the first pass. You must bind TCP/IP to one or more adapters before running any of the tests. The utility runs any non-skippable tests. Use this feature when you already have a good idea of which problems the utility will locate. The valid tests for this command line switch include:

Autonet	Automatic Private IP Addressing (APIPA) address test
Bindings	Bindings test
Browser	Redir and Browser test
DcList	Domain controller list test
DefGw	Default gateway test
DNS	DNS test
DsGetDc	Domain controller discovery test
IpConfig	IP address configuration test
IpLoopBk	IP address loopback ping test

IPX	IPX test
Kerberos	Kerberos test
Ldap	LDAP test
Member	Domain membership test
Modem	Modem diagnostics test
NbtNm	NetBT name test
Ndis	Netcard queries test
NetBTTransports	NetBT transports test
Netstat	Netstat information test
Netware	Netware test
Route	Routing table test
Trust	Trust relationship test
WAN	WAN configuration test
WINS	WINS service test
Winsock	Winsock test

/skip:*TestName* Skips the requested test or tests. (See the `/test` command line switch for additional details.) The tests that you can skip include:

Autonet	Automatic Private IP Addressing (APIPA) address test
Bindings	Bindings test
Browser	Redir and browser test
DcList	Domain controller list test
DefGw	Default gateway test
DNS	DNS test
DsGetDc	Domain controller discovery test
IpConfig	IP address configuration test
IpLoopBk	IP address loopback ping test
IPX	IPX test
Kerberos	Kerberos test
Ldap	LDAP test
Modem	Modem diagnostics test
NbtNm	NetBT name test
Netstat	Netstat information test
Netware	Netware test

Route	Routing table test
Trust	Trust relationship test
WAN	WAN configuration test
WINS	WINS service test
Winsock	Winsock test

Getting Network Statistics with the NetStat Utility

The NetStat utility outputs statistics about the network. You can use this utility in a number of ways. For example, changes in a statistic could indicate the activities of a cracker or the imminent failure of a piece of hardware. The statistics can also indicate the success of performance modifications you make or the impact of security features that you install. Vista doesn't support the `-v` command line switch, but it does support a number of additional command line switches including `-f` and `-t`. This utility uses the following syntax:

```
NETSTAT [-a] [-b] [-e] [-f] [-n] [-o] [-p proto] [-r] [-s] [-t] [-v]
[interval]
```

The following list describes each of the command line arguments.

-a Displays all connections and listening ports for the current machine. The output includes both TCP and User Datagram Protocol (UDP) connections. The table includes the protocol, local address, foreign address, and state of the connection.

-b Displays the application that created each connection or listening port. This feature is actually one of the better ways to locate spyware, adware, and viruses on your system because these applications usually communicate outside your machine. In most cases, the cracker doesn't write the application in such a way that it disguises this information, so you can see the applications you don't want on your machine quite quickly. The output table includes the protocol, local address, foreign address, state, and Process Identifier (PID). The PID includes both the number and the translated application name in square brackets ([]). Using this feature can be time consuming and usually fails unless you're part of the Administrators group.

-e Displays the Ethernet statistics, which include the amount of data sent and receive for general data bytes, unicast packets, non-unicast packets, discards, errors, and unknown protocols. You can combine this command line switch with the `-s` switch to receive a complete picture of the Ethernet status.

-f Displays the Fully Qualified Domain Names (FQDN) for foreign addresses, which means you have better access to other domain information.

-n Displays addresses and port numbers in numerical form. The default setting displays the addresses as DNS names whenever possible.

-o Displays the owning PID for each connection.

-p *proto* Displays the connections for the specified protocol. You may use TCP, UDP, TCPv6, or UDPv6 as the protocol names. When you use this command line switch with the `-s` switch to display per-protocol statistics, you may use IP, IPv6, ICMP, ICMPv6, TCP, TCPv6, UDP, or UDPv6 as the protocol name.

-r Displays the routing table. The output includes the interfaces, as well as the active and persistent routes. The routing information includes the network destination, netmask, gateway, interface, and metric.

-s Displays per-protocol statistics for the current machine. By default, the statistics include the for IP, IPv6, ICMP, ICMPv6, TCP, TCPv6, UDP, and UDPv6 protocols. You can reduce the size of the list by using the `-p` command line switch to select a specific protocol. The statistics that the utility will output vary by protocol.

-t Displays the current offload state for the connection. The default offload state is InHost. The offload state is part of the network protocol offload that Microsoft has introduced as part of scalable networking. The operating system actually offloads certain tasks to the Network Interface Card (NIC). Of course, your NIC has to support these features. To see the offload settings for your NIC, right-click its entry in the Network Connections window and choose Properties. Click Configure in the network connection's Properties dialog box and choose the Advanced tab. You'll see the offload settings in the list of settings that your NIC supports.

-v Displays the sequence of components used to create a connection or listening port for all executables. Generally, you'll use this switch with the `-b` command line switch to displays complete statistics for each application with a network connection. Figure 5.2 shows typical output. Notice how the utility tells you not only the application name but the specific DLL involved in creating the connection as well.

interval Redisplays the selected statistics at the specified interval in seconds. Press Ctrl+C to stop the output.

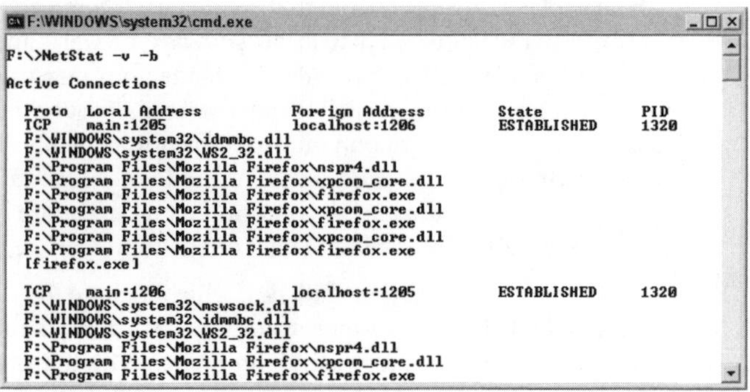

FIGURE 5.2
Combine the -v and -b command line switches to learn specifics about connections on your machine.

TRACKING SERVERS WITH THE NSLOOKUP UTILITY

The NSLookup utility provides information about the DNS setup on your network. You can use this utility to perform tasks such as diagnosing DNS errors. The NSLookup utility has two modes. The interactive mode provides access a number of subcommands that you can't access from the command prompt. For example, you can't access the exit subcommand at the command prompt because you have already exited the interactive mode by being at the command prompt. You can access the `QueryType` and `Set` subcommands. This utility uses the following syntax:

```
nslookup [-Query=QueryType] [-SetOption=Value]
[-QueryType=QueryType QueryData] [ComputerToFind | [-Server]}]
```

Note that if you find the command line version of NSLookup a tad difficult to follow, you can find an online version at `http://www.kloth.net/services/nslookup.php` that employs an easier-to-use Web interface. In fact, using this online version can significantly ease the learning process for the command line version since you'll see how the various commands work. The following list describes each of the command line arguments.

-Query=*QueryType* Sets the type of query that the NSLookup utility performs for all subsequent commands. This command line switch affects the kind of data you must provide for the `ComputerToFind` argument. NSLookup supports the following query types.

A Specifies a computer's IP address.

ANY Specifies all types of data.

CNAME Specifies a canonical name for an alias.

GID Specifies a group identifier of a group name.

HINFO Specifies a computer's CPU and type of operating system.

MB Specifies a mailbox domain name.

MG Specifies a mail group member.

MINFO Specifies mailbox or mail list information.

MR Specifies the mail rename domain name.

MX Specifies the mail exchanger.

NS Specifies a DNS name server for the named zone.

PTR Specifies a computer name if the query is an IP address; otherwise, specifies the pointer to other information.

SOA Specifies the start of authority for a DNS zone.

TXT Specifies the text information.

UID Specifies the user identifier.

UINFO Specifies the user information.

WKS Describes a well-known service.

-SetOption=*Value* Most versions of NSLookup use an actual `-set` command line switch. However, when using the Windows version of NSLookup, specify the set option as part of the command line switch. When required, you must also supply a value for the option. The timeout option requires a value as part of the input, so you might type **`nslookup -timeout=30 mit.edu`** and press Enter to give MIT additional time to answer a query. Some options are simply on or off values that you don't need to set specifically. For example, type **`nslookup -d2 mit.edu`** and press Enter to receive extensive information about the DNS configuration at MIT. If you use this feature without specifying either a query or a computer to find, then NSLookup starts in interactive mode using the settings you provided. Here's a list of standard NSLookup options.

-all Displays a list of the option settings, current server, and the current host.

-[no]debug Specify debug to display debugging information with the query. The `nodebug` option is the default. The debugging information includes the header, any queries you made, and the authority records from the computer. In some cases, the output includes an additional records section.

-[no]d2 Specify `d2` to display additional debugging information with the query. The `nod2` option is the default. The additional debugging information includes the header and queries for the send request, and the header, queries, and authority records for the get request.

-[no]defname Specify `nodefname` when you want to refrain from sending your domain name with the query. The default setting is `defname`, which sends the domain name.

-[no]recurse Specify `norecurse` to receive just the first answer to a query. Otherwise, the NSLookup utility makes multiple requests to obtain all of the information from the server. The default setting is `recurse`.

-[no]search Specify `nosearch` to refrain from using the domain search list. The default setting is search.

-[no]vc Specify `novc` when you don't want to use a virtual circuit. The default setting is `novc`. A virtual circuit can improve performance by providing a set path for data transmission. However, you must set up this feature on the server before it becomes available.

-domain=*NAME* Sets the default domain name to the specified value. The default setting uses the current domain.

-srchlist=*N1*[/*N2*/.../*N6*] Defines a search list. The first member of the search list also acts as the domain, unless you specify some other value using the `-domain` command line switch. The Windows version of NSLookup allows up to six search list elements.

-root=*NAME* Defines the root server.

-retry=X Sets the number of retries for a particular query. The default setting is 1.

-timeout=*X* Sets the initial timeout interval (the amount of time that passes before NSLookup considers a query to fail) to the specified value. The default setting is 2 seconds.

-type=*X* or -querytype=*X* Sets the query type as specified. See the `-Query` command line switch for a listing of valid query types.

-class={IN | CHAOS | HESIOD | ANY} Sets the query class. The query class can be any of the following classes: `IN` (specifies the Internet class), `CHAOS` (specifies the Chaos class), `HESIOD` (specifies the MIT Athena Hesiod class), and `ANY` (specifies any of the previously listed classes).

-[no]msxfr Specify `nomsxfr` when you want to perform a standard query using standardized techniques. The default is to use the Microsoft Fast Zone Transfer (MSXFR).

-ixfrver=*X* Specifies the current version to use in the IXFR transfer request. The default value is 1.

-QueryType=*QueryType QueryData* Performs a query of the specified type (see the `-Query` command line switch for details) using the specified data. For example, if you want to determine all of the types of data that MIT handles, you would type **`NSLookup -QueryType=ANY mit.edu`** and press Enter.

ComputerToFind Specifies the computer to interact with when making queries. The computer name relies on the current DNS server when you don't specify a server name. Append a period to the name to view information for a computer not in the current DNS domain. Specifying an IP address displays the name of the computer based on the DNS entry. Using a hyphen (`-`) in place of the DNS name places the NSLookup utility in interactive mode.

TIP Some NSLookup commands can require an inordinate amount of time to complete due to distances and machine configurations. Press Ctrl+B to interrupt any interactive command. To exit interactive mode at any time, type `Exit` and press Enter.

The NSLookup utility relies on commands to perform various tasks. Consequently, it's important to know which commands to use to perform diagnostics or query the DNS system for some other purpose. The following list contains the NSLookup commands that Windows supports (which aren't necessarily the same as the UNIX commands for the same utility—see `http://publib16.boulder.ibm.com/pseries/en_US/cmds/aixcmds4/nslookup.htm` for an example of an alternative form of this utility).

Tracing Transmission Paths with the PathPing Utility

The Path Packet Internet Groper (PathPing) utility serves an important function by showing you the path between your machine and a remote machine. In addition, it provides communication statistics for each host in the communication path.

Using the PathPing utility can tell you when your communication is taking an unusual route. A communication disruption and network congestion can cause a message to take an unusual route, but so can someone using a "man in the middle" attack. The man in the middle attack is one in which a cracker intercepts any communication you make, records the information for future use, and then passes the information along to the intended recipient so you don't suspect what's happening.

The PathPing utility can also tell you where communications are breaking down (so you know whether you need to call your ISP) and can help you diagnose a number of connection problems. At the very least, the PathPing utility can tell you why communications are so slow on a given day.

Vista doesn't support the `-P`, `-R`, and `-T` options (however, it does support the `-p period` option, and be sure you don't confuse lowercase with uppercase `-P`). This utility uses the following syntax:

```
pathping [-g host-list] [-h maximum_hops] [-i address] [-n] [-p period]
  [-q num_queries] [-w timeout] [-P] [-R] [-T] [-4] [-6] target_name
```

The following list describes each of the command line arguments.

-g ***host-list*** Specifies that the Echo Request messages used as part of defining the path between one point and another use the `Loose Source Route` option in the IP header with the set of intermediate destinations. The PathPing utility creates the list of servers that it outputs by extending the path between the source and destination by one machine for each call. The target machine, the one that's at the end of the line, receives an Echo Request message that requests that machine's name, which is why you receive a list of hosts as part of the output. This option lets the command use a number of intermediate routers to speed the process of defining the path between one machine and another. The results are less accurate, but you receive them faster. The host list must use the standard dotted notation for the IP addresses and you must separate each of the hosts with a space. The PathPing utility allows a maximum of nine hosts in the host list. You can find a diagram of the affected IP header data at `http://www.networksorcery.com/enp/protocol/ip/option003.htm`. You can find a good discussion of this topic in the "Loose Source and Record Route" section of the Web page at `http://www.freesoft.org/CIE/Course/Section3/7.htm`.

-h ***maximum_hops*** Defines the maximum number of hops the utility uses to search for the target. A hop is an individual jump from one host to another. For example, when you communicate with the server on your network, the direct communication between client and server normally requires one hop or one connection between client and host. The PathPing utility automatically stops tracing the path when it reaches the specified number of hops. Using this option reduces the wait for long paths when you only need some of the path between your machine and the target.

-i *address* Defines a specific starting address for the path search. The default starting location is the current machine. However, by starting the path search on your ISP's machine or even further down the path, you reduce the search time. Theoretically, you can also use this command line switch to determine the path from a completely different machine to a destination. In practice, this technique tends to produce inaccurate results.

Overcoming Documentation Errors

If you haven't run into a documentation error at some point in your career, consider yourself lucky. You'll encounter documentation problems with the PathPing utility. Depending on where you go, you might find what appear to be interesting additional command line switches, but in fact turn out to be documentation errors. Like many Windows utilities, Microsoft has made changes and documented some items inaccurately. The best place to go when you suspect a documentation error is the Microsoft Knowledge Base. For example, you can find an update for this utility at `http://support.microsoft.com/default.aspx?scid=KB;EN-US;Q244602`.

It's important to realize that the documentation you're viewing might not always match the utility you're using. For example, the Windows 2000 version of a utility will often contain less functionality than its Windows XP or Windows 2003 counterpart. In addition, Microsoft often includes undocumented command line switches or discontinues a command line switch without removing it from the documentation. When you can't find what you need in the Microsoft Knowledge Base or are unsure whether you're reviewing materials for the right version of the utility, check third party resources as well. For example, you'll find a third party resource for the PathPing utility at `http://www.pchelper.com/modules.php?name=News&file=article&sid=81&POST-NUKESID=d18f99f92e500ee411dea29a2beabd11`.

-n Displays only the IP addresses of the hosts in the path, rather than displaying the hostnames. Using this technique produces faster results because the utility doesn't have to make two queries for each intermediate location. In addition, using this approach can help you trace a complete path when some intermediaries have disabled the Request Echo message handling code.

-p *period* Defines the number of milliseconds to wait between pings (or requests for information). Using a shorter ping period improves performance, but could result in a failure of PathPing to resolve the entire path. The default setting is 250 milliseconds.

-q *num_queries* Defines the maximum number of Request Echo messages per hop. Normally, the PathPing utility uses 100 requests to determine path statistics for each hop. A higher number produces statistics that are more accurate. However, if you're mainly interested in the path, then you should set this value to 1.

-w *timeout* Specifies the number of milliseconds to wait for each reply. The default setting is 3,000 milliseconds.

-P Specifies that the utility test for Resource ReSerVation Protocol (RSVP) PATH connectivity. RSVP is a protocol for requesting a specific amount of bandwidth for an application. For example, many IP phones rely on an RSVP setup to ensure a specific level of voice quality. However, if the entire IP path doesn't support RSVP, then your IP phone call quality will suffer. The party at the other end will think you're talking from within a tunnel or, worse, will simply miss some of the information you provide during the call. Using this command line switch can help you locate problems with a communication path for a bandwidth-sensitive application such as an IP phone.

Microsoft follows the RFC 2205 standard for RSVP in Windows. You can learn more about this standard at `http://www.faqs.org/rfcs/rfc2205.html`.

-R Specifies that the utility test that each hop is RSVP aware. Essentially, this is a less aggressive version of the `-P` command line switch that you can use to test for minimal RSVP adherence.

-T Performs a detailed check on specific communication features within the path. The Layer-2 priority tags help improve performance by working with the Data Link layer. You can learn more about this topic at `http://www.microsoft.com/technet/prodtechnol/windowsserver2003/library/TechRef/2464f7e3-f420-4702-a1a9-55c03f913cd6.mspx`.

-4 Forces PathPing to use Internet Protocol Version 4 (IPv4) calls, even when the system normally uses IPv6.

-6 Forces PathPing to use Internet Protocol Version 6 (IPv6) calls, even when the system normally uses IPv4. Even though newer versions of Windows include some level of IPv6 support (see the "Working with IP Version 6" section of the chapter for details), most systems still use IPv4 and will do so for several more years.

NOTE The path from one location to another will likely vary every time you issue the `PathPing` command. That's because the Internet makes connections on an as needed basis. For example, try typing **`PathPing microsoft.com`** at the command line and pressing Enter. Depending on your ISP and conditions on the Internet, the path might require 11 hops the first time, 17 hops the second time, and 15 hops the third time. The path varies because of the way that the Internet works. However, if you keep noticing the same host every time you issue the `PathPing` command and it's not your ISP, then you might have a problem (or it could simply be random chance). The point is that `PathPing` can help you understand trends and see potential problems, but don't depend on it as a precise tool that will display a blinking error message telling you something is wrong.

Checking Connections with the PING Utility

The Packet Internet Groper (PING) utility helps you diagnose problems on your network by sending a series of messages of a specific length from one computer to the other. You can vary a number of the PING utility features to produce specific results. In addition, you can use it to see a number of difficult to find problems, such as messages that end up going through too many intermediaries to reach a destination. This utility uses the following syntax:

```
ping [-t] [-a] [-n count] [-l size] [-f] [-i TTL] [-v TOS]
[-r count] [-s count] [[-j host-list] | [-k host-list]]
[-w timeout] [-R] [-S srcaddr] [-4] [-6] target_name
```

The following list describes each of the command line arguments.

-t Forces the utility to continue pinging the specified host until stopped. Use this feature for diagnostic tasks so you don't have to restart the PING utility continuously. You can stop the utility in two ways. Press Ctrl+Break to stop pinging the host and generate the statistics that normally appear at the end of the PING session. Press Ctrl+C to stop the utility immediately without generating the statistics.

-a Resolves address to hostnames. Using this command line switch can require additional pings to perform a given check, but also means that the output is more readable.

-n *count* Defines the number of Echo Request messages to send. The default setting is 4.

-l ***size*** Defines the size of the buffer used to create the data field of the message. The default size is 32 bytes. The maximum size is 65,527 bytes. Larger buffers tend to reduce performance, but also create a more realistic test. Generally, you should test with the same size buffer that your application will use.

-f Sets the Don't Fragment flag in the packets. Routers generally break packets down into smaller sizes to improve performance. In addition, some routers don't accommodate the same size packet, so the packet becomes fragmented to meet the needs of a specific router. Using this command line switch lets you check for Path Maximum Transmission Unit (PMTU) problems between machines. You can learn more about PMTU at `http://www.microsoft.com/technet/community/columns/cableguy/cg0704.mspx`.

-i ***TTL*** Defines the Time-to-Live field of the message. A larger TTL value can let the packet travel a longer distance. However, a larger value also increases the time you must wait to discover an error on the network. The default value is 128. You may set this value to a maximum of 255.

-v ***TOS*** Defines the type of service (level of quality) the message should receive. The default value is 0. You may use a value up to 255. You can learn more about the TOS field of the message in the standards document at `http://www.ietf.org/rfc/rfc0791.txt` in the "Type of Service" section and the standards document section at `http://www.freesoft.org/CIE/RFC/1812/111.htm`.

-r ***count*** Specifies that the system use the Record Route option in the IP header to record the path the message will follow from one machine to another. This option lets you record the path and display it as part of the output. The *count* argument defines how many hops the system records. Every hop negatively affects performance, but you also obtain additional path information. The minimum value of count is 1 and the maximum value is 9.

-s ***count*** Specifies that the system record the timestamp in the Internet Timestamp option in the IP header for each hop. The minimum value of count is 1 and the maximum value is 4.

-j ***host-list*** Specifies that the Echo Request messages used as part of defining the path between one point and another use the `Loose Source Route` option in the IP header with the set of intermediate destinations. The PING utility creates the list of servers that it outputs by extending the path between the source and destination by one machine for each call. The target machine—the one that's at the end of the line—receives an Echo Request message that requests that machine's name, which is why you receive a list of hosts as part of the output. This option lets the command use a number of intermediate routers to speed the process of defining the path between one machine and another. The results are less accurate, but you receive them faster. The host list must use the standard dotted notation for the IP addresses and you must separate each of the hosts with a space. The PING utility allows a maximum of nine hosts in the host list. You can find a diagram of the affected IP header data at `http://www.networksorcery.com/enp/protocol/ip/option003.htm`. You can find a good discussion of this topic in the "Loose Source and Record Route" section of the Web page at `http://www.freesoft.org/CIE/Course/Section3/7.htm`.

-k ***host-list*** Specifies that the Echo Request messages used as part of defining the path between one point and another use the Strict Source Route option in the IP header with the set of intermediate destinations. When using this command line switch, PING queries the servers in the path using the precise host list that you provide. The result is more accurate than a standard path ping. However, using this technique also means that the utility will display an error and exit immediately if one of the host isn't directly reachable. The maximum number of hosts in the list is nine.

-w ***timeout*** Specifies the number of milliseconds to wait for each reply. The default setting is 4,000 milliseconds.

-R Tests the reverse route (from the target to your machine) as well by adding a special routing header. You can only use this option with IPv6.

-S ***srcaddr*** Specifies a source address to use so that you can test from a different client to the specified target. You can only use this option with IPv6. The default source address is the current machine.

-4 Forces PING to use Internet Protocol Version 4 (IPv4) calls, even when the system normally uses IPv6.

-6 Forces PING to use Internet Protocol Version 6 (IPv6) calls, even when the system normally uses IPv4. Even though newer versions of Windows include some level of IPv6 support (see the "Working with IP Version 6" section of the chapter for details), most systems still use IPv4 and will do so for several more years.

Real World Scenario

USING PING FOR DIAGNOSTICS

Many network administrators know the benefits of using PING, and those that don't often learn quite quickly. For example, a recent client call presented a problem where the network almost worked, but not quite. Using a Time Domain Reflectometer (TDR) showed that the cables were good. The diagnostics for the network card didn't show any unusual results and the systems had all of the correct setup information. By using PING, it was possible to diagnose an intermittent timing problem with the network card, which isn't a hard error and is extremely difficult to locate without the right tools.

You'll use this utility more often than you think. This command line tool helps you test TCP/IP connections with another computer, so the diagnostic benefits are apparent the first time you use it. The two command lines you'll commonly use for PING in a diagnostic mode are:

```
PING <HostName>
PING <IP Address>
```

Therefore, if you want to contact a machine named AUX, you'd type **`PING AUX`** and press Enter. PING outputs four messages of 32 bytes and tells you about the response to each one. You can modify the size of the packet sent to the remote computer using the `-l Size` command line switch. To test the computer at 192.168.0.1 with 1,024-byte packets, you can type **`PING -l 1024 192.168.0.1`** and press Enter. Using a different packet size often reveals problems the standard packet size won't show. The maximum packet size is 65,500 bytes.

You can also use the `-n Count` switch to change the number of packets sent to the other computer. You might suspect that an error won't occur until you send the fifth or sixth packet, so you can adjust the count to 5 or 6. If you use a value of –1, PING continues sending packets until you press Ctrl+C (using Ctrl+Break won't work).

MANAGING FILES WITH THE RCP UTILITY

The Remote Copy Protocol (RCP) utility copies files between a Windows system and a system running the Remote Shell Daemon (RSHD) service. Windows doesn't provide support for this service, so you can't use this utility for connecting with a Windows machine. However, the RCP utility does come in handy for transferring data to UNIX systems and UNIX -based operating systems. Vista doesn't provide support for the RCP utility and there isn't any alternative utility available. This utility uses the following syntax:

```
RCP [-a | -b] [-h] [-r] [host][.user:]source [host][.user:] path\destination
```

The following list describes each of the command line arguments.

-a Specifies that RCP use ASCII transfer mode. This mode converts the End of Line (EOL) characters to a carriage return for UNIX and a carriage return/line feed combination for personal computers. This is the default transfer mode. Use this mode to transfer text files.

-b Specifies that RCP use binary image transfer mode. This mode transfers all of the data in the file precisely, including all control characters. Use this mode to transfer nontext data such as graphics.

-h Transfers hidden files.

-r Copies the contents of all subdirectories at the source. You must specify a directory as the destination when using this command line option.

host Specifies the local or remote host. When you specify the host as an IP address or when the hostname relies on a dot notation, you must specify the user.

.user: Specifies the username to use on the remote machine. The default relies on the current username. Notice that you must include a dot as a prefix and a colon as a postfix for this argument.

source Specifies which files to copy. You may use wildcard characters to define the file specification.

path\destination Defines the destination relative to the logon directory on the remote host. The path is normally relative to the logon directory and not an absolute path. When working with multiple files, the destination is always a directory. Use escape characters (\ , ", or ') in the remote paths to use wildcard characters on the remote host.

EXECUTING COMMANDS REMOTELY WITH THE REXEC UTILITY

The Remote Execution (RExec) utility executes a command on a remote server that runs the RExec daemon service. Windows doesn't provide support for this service, so you can't use this utility for communicating with a Windows machine. However, you can use RExec to control some UNIX systems. Vista doesn't provide support for the RExec utility and there isn't any alternative utility available. This utility uses the following syntax:

```
REXEC host [-l username] [-n] command
```

The following list describes each of the command line arguments.

host Specifies the remote host on which to run the command.

-l *username* Specifies the user account on the remote host.

-n Redirects the input of RExec to NULL (nothing or no device). Use this option to prevent the local computer from displaying the results of the command.

command Specifies the command that you want to run on the remote system.

MANIPULATING THE NETWORK ROUTING TABLES WITH THE ROUTE UTILITY

The Route utility displays the current IP routing information for the local machine and lets you change the routing table as needed. The routing table includes a number of entries, but the most important are the active routes and the permanent routes. An active route is one that's currently connected, but might not be permanent. A permanent route is always available, even when it isn't connected (active). This utility uses the following syntax:

```
ROUTE [-f] [-p] [-4 | -6] [command [destination] [MASK netmask]
[gateway] [METRIC metric] [IF interface]
```

The following list describes each of the command line arguments.

-f Clears the routing table of all gateway entries. Using this command line switch with one of the commands clears the routing table before the utility executes the command. For example, if you add a new entry, then the routing table will contain just that entry when the utility finishes its work. This command line switch doesn't affect host routes (those with a netmask of 255.255.255.255), loopback routes (those with an IP address of 127.0.0.0), or multicast routes (those with an IP address of 224.0.0.0 and a netmask of 240.0.0.0).

-p Makes a route persistent across boots of the system when used with the `ADD` command. The system normally doesn't preserve routes when you restart the system and rediscovers the routes during the boot process. The Route utility ignores this command line switch for all other commands. You can't use this command line switch with older versions of Windows (most notably, Windows 95). Windows stores permanent routes in the `HKEY_LOCAL_MACHINE\SYSTEM\CurrentControlSet\Services\Tcpip\Parameters\PersistentRoutes` registry key.

command Performs the required IP routing task. The Route utility supports the following four commands.

PRINT Prints (displays) one or more routes.

ADD Adds a new route to the routing table. You can add an IP network address (where the host bits of the network address are set to 0), an IP address for a host route (those with a netmask of 255.255.255.255), or 0.0.0.0 for the default route.

DELETE Removes a route from the routing table. You can't remove host routes (those with a netmask of 255.255.255.255), loopback routes (those with an IP address of 127.0.0.0), or multicast routes (those with an IP address of 224.0.0.0 and a netmask of 240.0.0.0).

CHANGE Modifies an existing routing table entry.

destination Specifies the destination for the route. Windows supports three route types that include an IP network address (where the host bits of the network address are set to 0), an IP address for a host route (those with a netmask of 255.255.255.255), or 0.0.0.0 for the default route.

MASK *netmask* Specifies the subnet mask value for this route entry. The default subnet mask is 255.255.255.255.

gateway Specifies the next host in the communication path. The gateway is the forwarding IP address; it defines how to reach the IP address specified by this route. When working with locally attached subnet routes, the gateway address is the IP address assigned to the interface attached to the subnet. When working with a remote route, the gateway address is a directly reachable IP address assigned to a neighboring router.

IF *interface* Defines the interface to use to reach the destination. You can obtain a list of interfaces using the `Route Print` command. The Route utility lets you define interfaces using decimal or hexadecimal values. Precede the number with 0x when working with a hexadecimal number. When you don't provide this command line switch, the utility relies on the gateway information to determine the interface.

METRIC *metric* Defines the cost of using a particular route. When the system needs to transfer information, it begins with the lowest cost route and moves to the next higher cost route as needed (for example, when an error occurs). The metric value is in the range from 1 to 9,999. There aren't any absolute metric values. Generally, you determine the metric value in relation to other routes on the system and by considering the number of hops, the speed of the path, path reliability, path throughput, and administrative properties.

-4 Forces Route to use Internet Protocol Version 4 (IPv4) calls, even when the system normally uses IPv6.

-6 Forces Route to use Internet Protocol Version 6 (IPv6) calls, even when the system normally uses IPv4. Even though newer versions of Windows include some level of IPv6 support (see the "Working with IP Version 6" section of the chapter for details), most systems still use IPv4 and will do so for several more years.

CHECKING CONNECTIONS USING RPC WITH THE RPCPING UTILITY

The Remote Procedure Call (RPC) Ping (RPCPing) utility is new for Vista. It lets you check RPC connections to a server with the same efficiency as other ping variants described in this chapter. Most people associate the RPC protocol with the Component Object Model (COM). However, in today's computing environment, it's better to view RPC as application-to-application communication. For example, you might want to test the connectivity between a local copy of Outlook and Exchange Server. This utility uses the following syntax:

```
RPCPing [-t <protseq>] [-s <server_addr>] [-e <endpoint>
|-f <interface UUID>[,MajorVer]] [-O <Object_UUID]
[-i <#_iterations>] [-u <security_package_id>] [-a <authn_level>]
[-N <server_princ_name>] [-I <auth_identity>] [-C <capabilities>]
[-T {Static | Dynamic}]
[-M {Anonymous | Identify | Impersonate | Delegate}]
[-S <server_sid>] [-P <proxy_auth_identity>] [-F <RPCHTTP_flags>]
[-H <RPC/HTTP_authn_schemes>] [-o <binding_options>]
[-B <server_certificate_subject>] [-b]
[-R {None | Default | <Proxy_Name>}] [-E] [-q] [-c]
[-A <http_proxy_auth_identity>] [-U <HTTP_proxy_authn_schemes>]
[-r <report_results_interval>] [-v {1 | 2 | 3}] [-d]
```

The following list describes each of the command line arguments.

-t *protseq* Defines the protocol sequence to use. The standard protocol sequences include `ncacn_ip_tcp`, `ncacn_np`, and `ncacn_http`. You can find a list of all of the protocol sequences at `http://support.microsoft.com/kb/325930`. The default protocol sequence is `ncacn_ip_tcp`.

-s *server_addr* Specifies the server address. The default setting is the local machine.

-e *endpoint* Specifies the endpoint to ping. The endpoint is the target of the test. The default setting is the endpoint mapper on the local machine. You can't use this option with the `-f` command line switch.

Real World Scenario

Watch for RPC Security Issues

One possible outcome of an RPC check is that you'll find an unexpected problem. For example, the RPC service might not be running or you might not have sufficient rights to access RPC using this utility. Unfortunately, Vista tends to provide the same error for all error sources and you need to review the output information when testing locally. The output information includes the following fields (with sample error data included).

```
Exception 5 (0x00000005)
 Number of records is: 1
 ProcessID is 3452
 System Time is: 11/13/2006 18:26:0:60
 Generating component is 2
 Status is 0x5, 5
 Detection location is 1750
 Flags is 0
 NumberOfParameters is 1
 Long val: 0x5
```

This error message tells you that you don't have the required credentials to perform the test. It's possible to overcome this particular error by including the required credentials as part of the RPCPing call. In real-world testing, it's easy to forget that Vista locks just about everything down so tightly that running even simple tests is nearly impossible. For example, it's unlikely that you'd see this error information when working with Windows 2000 as long as you have an administrator account.

-o *binding_options* Defines the RPC binding options to use during testing. This feature relies on the `RpcStringBindingCompose()` function of the Windows API. You can learn more about this function at `http://msdn.microsoft.com/library/en-us/rpc/rpc/rpcstringbindingcompose.asp`. The article at `http://msdn2.microsoft.com/en-us/library/aa378705.aspx` provides an example of the `RpcStringBindingCompose()` function. The option strings appear at `http://msdn.microsoft.com/library/en-us/rpc/rpc/string_binding.asp`. See the article at `http://msdn2.microsoft.com/en-us/library/aa375384.aspx` to learn more about how the binding options affect a real-world environment.

-f *interface_UUID*[,*MajorVer*] Specifies which interface to ping. You identify the interface by providing its Universal Unique Identifier (UUID). The default interface version is 1.0, which you can override by providing a major version number. When you use this option, the RPCPing utility queries the endpoint mapper on the specified machine to locate the interface endpoint. The utility then uses the interface endpoint for testing purposes.

-O *Object_UUID* Specifies the object UUID to ping. The object must register an object UUID (generally, using RegSvr32 or an equivalent utility) to use this feature.

-i *#_iterations* Defines the number of calls to make. The RPCPing utility uses a default value of 1, which is sufficient to test connectivity. If you want to test for other kinds of errors, you'll normally need to specify more iterations.

-u *security_package_id* Determines which security provider RPCPing uses to make the call. You specify the security provider as a number or a name. If you use a number, then it must match the numbers used for the `RpcBindingSetAuthInfoEx()` function (see `http://msdn.microsoft.com/library/en-us/rpc/rpc/rpcbindingsetauthinfoex.asp` for details on this function). You must specify an authentication level other than none when using this option (otherwise, RPCPing won't use security for the test). Here's a list of the standard security providers and their associated numbers.

Negotiate 9 (You can also provide values of `nego`, `snego`, or `negotiate`.)

NTLM 10

SChannel 14

Kerberos 16

-a *authn_level* Determines the authentication level that RPCPing uses to make the calls during the test. You must provide the `-u` command line option when using this option. RPCPing doesn't provide a default value for this option. You can use any of the following authentication levels.

- connect
- call
- pkt (packet)
- integrity
- privacy

-N *server_princ_name* Defines the server principal name. You use the same arguments as you would when using the `RpcBindingSetAuthInfoEx()` function (see `http://msdn.microsoft.com/library/en-us/rpc/rpc/rpcbindingsetauthinfoex.asp` for details on this function). You can only use this option when you also specify the `-a` and `-u` options.

-I *auth_identity* Specifies an alternative identity to use to connect to the server. You specify the identity as a string in the form `"user,domain,password"`. Always enclose the identity information in double quotes when it contains spaces or other special characters that can cause problems at the command line. Use the asterisk (*) instead of the password when you want the system to prompt you for the identification information. Using this approach reduces the risk that someone will see your password or other identification in plain text. The default for this option is the identification of the current user. You can only use this option when you also specify the `-a` and `-u` options.

-C *capabilities* Identifies the security services the application requires. The RPCPing call requires that you provide a hexadecimal bitmask of flags. You can find these flags in the `Capabilities` field of the RPC_SECURITY_QOS data structure described at `http://msdn2.microsoft.com/en-us/library/aa378647.aspx`. You can only use this option when you also specify the `-a` and `-u` options.

-T {Static | Dynamic} Defines the type of identity tracking that the call uses. The default value is dynamic tracking. You can only use this option when you also specify the `-a` and –u options. This option is the same as the `IdentityTracking` field of the RPC_SECURITY_QOS data structure described at `http://msdn2.microsoft.com/en-us/library/aa378647.aspx`.

-M {Anonymous | Identify | Impersonate | Delegate} Defines the impersonation type. The default value is impersonate. You can only use this option when you also specify the `-a` and `-u` options. This option is the same as the `ImpersonationType` field of the RPC_SECURITY_QOS data structure described at `http://msdn2.microsoft.com/en-us/library/aa378647.aspx`.

-S ***Server_SID*** Provides the expected Security Identifier (SID) of the server. This option is only usable with Windows .NET Server 2003 or higher. You can only use this option when you also specify the `-a` and `-u` options. The intended purpose of this option is to prevent a cracker from tricking the server into a Denial of Service (DoS) attack.

-P ***proxy_auth_identity*** Provides the identity of the RPC/HTTP proxy to use for authentication purposes. This value has the same format as the `-I` option. You can only use this option when you also specify the `-a`, `-u`, and `-H` options.

-F ***RPCHTTP_flags*** Specifies the flags to pass to the RPC/HTTP front-end authentication. The flags can appear as names or numbers. You can only use this option when you also specify the `-a` and `-u` options. This option is the same as the `Flags` field of the RPC_HTTP_TRANSPORT_CREDENTIALS data structure described at `http://msdn2.microsoft.com/en-us/library/aa378624.aspx`. The following list describes the flags you can use.

Use SSL 1 (You can also provide `ssl` or `use_ssl` as values.)

Use first auth scheme 2 (You can also provide `first` or `use_first` as values.)

-H ***RPC/HTTP_authn_schemes*** Specifies the authentication scheme to use for the RPC/HTTP front-end authentication. The flags can appear as names or numbers. You can only use this option when you also specify the `-a` and `-u` options. The following list describes the authentication schemes you can use.

Basic 1

NTLM 2

Certificate 65536 (You can also abbreviate this value as Cert.)

-B server_certificate_subject Defines the server certificate subject. This entry has the same value as the ServerCertificateSubject of the RPC_HTTP_TRANSPORT_CREDENTIALS data structure described at `http://msdn2.microsoft.com/en-us/library/aa378624.aspx`. This option only works when you use Secure Sockets Layer (SSL) authentication. You can only use this option when you also specify the `-a` and `-u` options.

-b Prints the server certificate subject on screen. The utility retrieves this value from the certificate sent by the server. This option only works when you use SSL authentication. You can only use this option when you also specify the `-a`, `-u`, and `-E` options.

-R {None | Default | ***Proxy_Name*****}** Specifies the HTTP proxy to use for a call. When you set this option to None, RPCPing attempts to contact the RPC proxy directly. An input value of Default uses the Internet Explorer settings on the client machine. RPCPing treats any other value as the name of a specific HTTP proxy. The utility relies on a standard value of Default. You can only use this option when you also specify the `-a`, `-u`, and `-E` options. In addition, you must set the `-t` option to `ncacn_http` protocol. The RPCPing utility ignores this command line switch when you specify the HTTP proxy as part of the `-o` option.

-E Restricts the test to using the RPC/HTTP proxy only. The ping doesn't reach the server. Use this option when you want to test the proxy, rather than the server. You can only use this option when you also specify the `-a` and `-u` options. Use the `-R` option when you want to specify the HTTP proxy, rather than using the default settings.

-q Places the RPCPing utility in quiet mode. The utility won't issue any prompts except for password and it assumes a response of Y (yes) for all other queries. This option is useful for batch files where you don't want to make the user aware of all of the underlying prompts. However, use this option with care since the default response is yes.

-c Forces the RPCPing utility to rely on a smart card certificate in place of standard credentials. The utility will prompt the user to provide a smart card for authentication purposes.

-A *http_proxy_auth_identity* Specifies the credentials to use when authenticating with the HTTP proxy. This value has the same format as the `-I` option. You can only use this option when you also specify the `-a`, `-u`, and `-U` options.

-U *HTTP_proxy_authn_schemes* Defines the authentication schemes to use for HTTP proxy authentication. The flags can appear as names or numbers. You can only use this option when you also specify the `-a` and `-u` options. The following list describes the authentication schemes you can use.

Basic 1

NTLM 2

-r report_results_interval Indicates the reporting interval in seconds when you specify multiple testing iterations. The default reporting interval is 15 seconds.

-v {1 | 2 | 3} Determines the amount of information the RPCPing utility provides as output. The default value is 1, which provides basic test information. Increasing the value enhances the amount of output information.

-d Launches the RPC network diagnostic user interface.

Executing Commands Remotely with the RSH Utility

The Remote Shell (RSH) utility runs commands on remote hosts running the RSH daemon service. Windows doesn't provide support for this service, so you can't use this utility for communicating with a Windows machine. However, you can use RSH to control UNIX and Linux systems (and other operating systems with UNIX roots). You can install this service on Windows systems using the instructions at `http://www.microsoft.com/technet/interopmigration/unix/sfu/sfu35rsh.mspx`. However, you need a separate product to obtain the required software. Vista doesn't provide support for the RSH utility and there isn't any alternative utility available. This utility uses the following syntax:

```
RSH host [-l username] [-n] command
```

The following list describes each of the command line arguments.

host Specifies the remote host on which to run the command.

-l *username* Specifies the user account on the remote host.

-n Redirects the input of RExec to NULL (nothing or no device). Use this option to prevent the local computer from displaying the results of the command.

command Specifies the command that you want to run on the remote system.

Managing Files with the TFTP Utility

The Trivial File Transfer Protocol (TFTP) utility transfers data from one computer to another. The host must have the TFTP daemon service installed. Workstation versions of Windows (such as Windows XP) don't provide support for this service. Server versions of Windows provide a limited version of the TFTP daemon service, but you can only use it for booting Windows workstations. However, you can use TFTP to transfer data to UNIX and Linux systems (and other operating systems with UNIX roots). The standard at `http://spectral.mscs.mu.edu/RFC/rfc1350.html` describes this protocol in detail. Vista doesn't provide support for the TFTP utility and there isn't any alternative utility available from Microsoft. However, you can find third party alternatives in places such as Windows Vista Software Archive (`http://tftp.vista-files.org/`). This utility uses the following syntax:

```
TFTP [-i] host [GET | PUT] source [destination]
```

The following list describes each of the command line arguments.

-i Specifies binary transfer mode (also called octet mode). This mode moves data byte by byte and doesn't perform any control character translation. Use binary mode to transfer non-text data such as graphics. The default mode, ASCII, converts the End of Line (EOL) characters to a carriage return for UNIX and a carriage return/line feed combination for personal computers. Use ASCII mode to transfer text files.

host Specifies the host (remote) computer.

GET Obtains a file from the host. This command transfers the file destination on the remote host to the file source on the local computer.

PUT Sends a file to the host. This command transfers the file source on the local computer to the file destination on the remote host.

source Specifies the file that you want to transfer.

destination Specifies where to transfer the file.

Tracking the Network Path with the TraceRt Utility

The Trace Route (TraceRt) utility serves an important function by showing you the path between your machine and a remote machine. Essentially, this is a simpler form for the PathPing utility described in the "Tracing Transmission Paths with the PathPing Utility" section of the chapter. Unlike the PathPing utility, the TraceRt utility doesn't provide any network statistics. It does have one advantage: it keeps trying to find a route even through multiple errors, which makes it valuable with troublesome routes. This utility uses the following syntax:

```
tracert [-d] [-h maximum_hops] [-j host-list] [-w timeout]
[-R] [-S srcaddr] [-4] [-6] target_name
```

The following list describes each of the command line arguments.

-d Specifies that the utility not resolve addresses to hostnames. Using this command line switch can reduce the time required to trace a route. In addition, it can help you trace stubborn routes (those that won't provide a hostname). However, the information provided is less readable.

-h *maximum_hops* Defines the maximum number of hops the utility uses to search for the target. A hop is an individual jump from one host to another. For example, when you communicate with the server on your network, the direct communication between client and server normally requires one hop or one connection between client and host. The PathPing utility automatically stops tracing the path when it reaches the specified number of hops. Using this option reduces the wait for long paths when you only need some of the path between your machine and the target.

-j ***host-list*** Specifies that the Echo Request messages used as part of defining the path between one point and another use the `Loose Source Route` option in the IP header with the set of intermediate destinations. The PING utility creates the list of servers that it outputs by extending the path between the source and destination by one machine for each call. The target machine, the one that's at the end of the line, receives an Echo Request message that requests that machine's name, which is why you receive a list of hosts as part of the output. This option lets the command use a number of intermediate routers to speed the process of defining the path between one machine and another. The results are less accurate, but you receive them faster. The host list must use the standard dotted notation for the IP addresses and you must separate each of the hosts with a space. The PING utility allows a maximum of nine hosts in the host list. You can find a diagram of the affected IP header data at `http://www.networksorcery.com/enp/protocol/ip/option003.htm`. You can find a good discussion of this topic in the "Loose Source and Record Route" section of the Web page at `http://www.freesoft.org/CIE/Course/Section3/7.htm`.

-w ***timeout*** Specifies the number of milliseconds to wait for each reply. The default setting is 4,000 milliseconds.

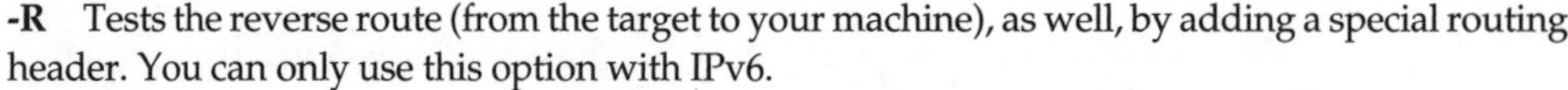

-R Tests the reverse route (from the target to your machine), as well, by adding a special routing header. You can only use this option with IPv6.

-S ***srcaddr*** Specifies a source address to use so that you can test from a different client to the specified target. You can only use this option with IPv6. The default source address is the current machine.

-4 Forces PING to use Internet Protocol Version 4 (IPv4) calls, even when the system normally uses IPv6.

-6 Forces PING to use Internet Protocol Version 6 (IPv6) calls, even when the system normally uses IPv4. Even though newer versions of Windows include some level of IPv6 support (see the "Working with IP Version 6" section of the chapter for details), most systems still use IPv4 and will do so for several more years.

Managing FTP Servers with the FTP Utility

The File Transfer Protocol (FTP) utility is one of the easiest ways of transferring files to literally any system. FTP is a standardized protocol that just about every operating system platform supports. In addition, FTP appears in more forms than just about any other protocol. For example, you can use FTP from Internet Explorer or Firefox with equal ease. However, the FTP utility lets you perform file transfers at the command prompt, so you can use it even if the host system isn't operating quite right. This utility uses the following syntax:

```
FTP [-v] [-n] [-i] [-d] [-g] [-s:<Filename>] [-a] [-w:<Buffer_Size>]
    [-x:sendbuffer] [-r:recvbuffer] [-b:asyncbuffers] [-A] [-?]
    [<Host>]
```

FTP uses case-sensitive switches. For example, `-A` isn't the same as `-a`. In addition, you must use the - (minus) sign and not the / (slash) when typing command line arguments. You need to type the command with these requirements in mind. Most of these switches also appear in the interface, so you can modify the behavior after you start the application. The following list describes each of the command line arguments.

-v This switch disables the display of remote server responses. It comes in handy if you want the download to progress in the background without disturbing your foreground task.

-n Use this switch to disable auto-logon on initial connection.

-i Use this switch to remove interactive prompting during multiple file transfers. This enables you to automate the file transfer process.

-d Use this switch to display all FTP commands passed between the client and server. This enables you to debug script files.

-g This switch disables filename globbing (essentially, wildcard expansion), which permits the use of wildcard characters in local filenames and pathnames.

-s:*Filename* Replace `<Filename>` with the name of a text file containing FTP commands. In essence, this switch enables you to create a script for your FTP download. Use this switch instead of redirection (>).

-a This switch tells FTP to use any available interface when creating a connection to the host.

-w:*Buffer_Size* Use this switch to change the data transfer buffer size. The default size of 4,096 bytes normally works well. However, you might want to decrease the buffer size if you experience errors on a connection or use a larger buffer size for local connections. A large buffer is more efficient, but you lose less data for each damaged packet when working with a small buffer.

-A Use this switch to log in as an anonymous user. Note that this is the only switch typed in uppercase.

-? Use this switch to display online help. Note that, at the time of this writing, there are typos in both the Help and Support Center document and the application-supplied help.

V VISTA **-x:sendbuffer** Overrides the default send buffer size of 8,192 bytes.

V VISTA **-r:recvbuffer** Overrides the default received buffer size of 8,192 bytes.

V VISTA **-b:asyncbuffers** Overrides the default number of asynchronous buffers (3 is the default).

Host Replace this parameter with the name or address of the host you want to connect to for a file download.

The FTP utility provides a surprising array of commands you can use after you run the utility. There really are too many to list here, but you can get a list easily enough. All you need to remember is one command: the question mark (?). If you type a question mark, you see a list of all the things you can do with FTP.

Working with Users

Users require security to ensure they don't attempt to access files or perform tasks that would be harmful to the system. In addition, you need to protect users from themselves to a certain extent by ensuring they can't perform tasks that would tend to reduce productivity, such as damaging data files. Some users are less than honorable, so most users require some level of monitoring as well. You don't want to become "big brother" by watching the user's every move, but it's also prudent to exercise some level of proactive supervision to ensure you network, data, and other users remain safe. Fortunately, the command line has a lot to offer in the way of user utilities that you can automate through batch files and scripts. The following sections tell you about these user utilities.

Monitoring Users with the AuditUsr Utility

The Audit User (AuditUsr) utility helps you set the auditing policy for a specific user. Auditing helps you see what the user is doing without actually observing the user. For example, you can detect when a user is having trouble logging into the system by auditing the login failures. All of the audit entries determine the contents of the audit log and don't product output as such from this command. You can, however, export and import user entries.

Vista no longer provides access to the AuditUsr utility and there isn't any replacement. In fact, this utility has been missing since Windows 2003 SP1. Microsoft changed the way that auditing worked. You can read about the changes at `http://blogs.msdn.com/ericfitz/archive/2004/12/20/327478.aspx`. For a near equivalent to this utility, see the AuditPol utility described in the "Auditing User Access with the AuditPol Utility" section of the chapter. This utility uses the following syntax:

```
AuditUsr /is <security_principal>:<categories>
AuditUsr /if <security_principal>:<categories>
AuditUsr /es <security_principal>:<categories>
AuditUsr /ef <security_principal>:<categories>
AuditUsr /r <security_principal>
AuditUsr /ra
AuditUsr /e <filename>
AuditUsr /i <filename>
```

The following list describes each of the command line arguments.

/is ***security_principal:categories*** Adds or changes a successful completion entry in the audit log. The security principal is the name of the person you want to change. The category determines the success event that the audit log entry includes. The following list contains the valid categories of success entries.

System Event Audits system events including shutdown and startup. The system events also include security log entries and any system changes that would affect the security system.

Logon/Logoff Audits when the user logs onto or off the system. This setting also affects remote access, where the user logs into the local system from a remote system, even if the user doesn't perform this task directly (such as when an application performs the task for the user).

Object Access Audits when the user accesses specific objects including files, folders, registry keys, the printer, or any other system object that has its own Security Access Control List (SACL) defined. You define the SACL using the Auditing tab of the Advanced Security Settings dialog box for the target object. Consequently, the audit log entries for this particular setting depend on other changes you make to the system.

Privilege Use Audits every user change of a user right to override specific system behaviors. For example, the user might change the system time or define a new security setting for a file. Windows doesn't track these user rights uses: bypass traverse checking, debug programs, create a token object, replace process-level token, generate security audits, backup files and directories, and restore files and directories.

Detailed Tracking Audits user activity at a detailed level. The user actions include program activation, process exit, handle duplication, and indirect object access. Another name for this level of auditing is process tracking because you're tracking individual processes. The log can become quite large when you use this level of auditing.

Policy Change Audits every user change to user rights assignment policies, audit policies, or trust policies.

Account Management Audits account management tasks performed by the user. The tasks include creating, changing, or deleting a user account or group, renaming, disabling, or enabling a user account, and setting or changing a password.

Directory Service Access Audits when the user accesses any directory service object that has its own SACL defined. As with objects, you must define the SACL separately for the directory service object.

Account Logon Audits user logon or logoff from another system where Windows relies on this computer to validate the account.

/if ***security_principal:categories*** Adds or changes an include failure entry in the audit log. The security principal is the name of the person you want to change. The category determines the success event that the audit log entry includes. See the `/is` command line switch for a list of valid categories.

/es ***security_principal:categories*** Adds or changes an exclude success entry in the audit log. The security principal is the name of the person you want to change. The category determines the success event that the audit log entry includes. See the `/is` command line switch for a list of valid categories.

/ef ***security_principal:categories*** Adds or changes an exclude failure entry in the audit log. The security principal is the name of the person you want to change. The category determines the success event that the audit log entry includes. See the `/is` command line switch for a list of valid categories.

/r ***security_principal*** Removes all per-user auditing entries for the specified security principal.

/ra Removes all per-user auditing entries for all users.

/e ***filename*** Exports the current per-user auditing settings for the local computer to a file.

/i ***filename*** Imports the per-user auditing settings from a file and makes them the current settings.

Configuring Profiles the CMStP Utility

Use this utility to install or remove a Connection Manager Service Profile (CMStP). The Connection Manager provides access to a number of specialized user connections. For example, the Connection Manager could allow access to a Virtual Private Network (VPN). You can find a description of this and related technologies at `http://www.windowsitpro.com/Windows/Article/ArticleID/4981/4981.html`. This utility uses the following syntax:

```
ServiceProfileFileName.exe /q:a /c:"cmstp.exe
ServiceProfileFileName.inf [/nf] [/ni] [/ns] [/s] [/su] [/u]"
cmstp.exe [/nf] [/ni] [/ns] [/s] [/su] [/u]
"[Drive:][Path]ServiceProfileFileName.inf"
```

The two syntaxes are completely different. This utility allows these two forms of access for managing profiles. The following list uses Syntax 1 and Syntax to reference these two command line syntaxes since the command line arguments differ for each and describe each of the command line arguments.

ServiceProfileFileName.exe Specifies the name of the installation package that contains the profile that you want to install. This argument appears as part of Syntax 1. Notice that Syntax 1 actually relies on the installer package to call this utility, rather than calling the utility directly.

/q:a Specifies that the installer package should install the profile without prompting the user. The CMStP utility still displays the installation succeeded message. This argument appears as part of Syntax 1.

[*Drive*:][*Path*]*ServiceProfileFileName*.INF Specifies the configuration file that contains instructions for installing the profile. The CMStP utility assumes the information (INF) file appears in the same directory as the installer package when using Syntax 1, so you can't use the drive and path arguments as part of Syntax 1.

/nf Prevents the CMStP utility from installing the support files.

/ni Prevents the CMStP utility from creating a desktop icon. All newer versions of Windows ignore this command line switch since they create a desktop shortcut (see the `/ns` command line switch); it's only valid with Windows NT 4.0 and the Windows 9*x* versions.

/ns Prevents the CMStP utility from creating a desktop shortcut. All newer versions of Windows use this command line switch.

/s Specifies that the installer package should install or uninstall the profile without prompting the user. In addition, the installer package won't display verification or success messages.

/su Specifies that the installer package should install the profile for a single user (the currently logged in user) rather than for all users. You can only use this command line switch with versions of Windows XP and newer.

/u Uninstalls the service profile.

Obtaining Group Policy Results with the GPResult Utility

Use this utility to obtain the Resultant Set of Policy (RSoP) for a particular user on a system. This utility considers all of the security settings for both the computer and the user and creates a resultant policy—the policy that actually affects the user's security setup on the system. Microsoft provides a wealth of articles on RSoP. For example, you can see how RSoP affects Internet Protocol Security (IPSec) assignments at `http://www.microsoft.com/technet/prodtechnol/windowsserver2003/library/ServerHelp/35675107-c728-47cd-8ad9-bfd2d5e7fe0a.mspx`. You'll find a good overview on this topic at `http://www.microsoft.com/technet/prodtechnol/windowsserver2003/library/BookofSP1/a940a24d-34c2-471c-89e5-d9f1500374c9.mspx`. You'll also find an excellent article on planning and logging RSoP at `http://www.windowsnetworking.com/articles_tutorials/Resultant-Set-Policy-Planning-Logging.html`. This utility uses the following syntax:

```
GPRESULT [/S system [/U [domain\]user [/P [password]]]]
[/SCOPE {USER | COMPUTER}] [/USER [domain\]targetuser] [/V | /Z]
```

The following list describes each of the command line arguments.

/S *system* Specifies the remote system that you want to check. In most cases, you'll also need to supply the `/U` and the `/P` command line switches when using this switch.

/U [*domain*\\]*user* Specifies the username on the remote system. This name may not match the username on the local system. You'll need to supply a domain name when working with a domain controller.

/P [*password*] Specifies the password for the given user. You can provide the command line switch without specifying the password on the command line in cleartext. The system prompts you for the password. Using this feature can help you maintain the security of passwords used on your system.

/USER [*domain*\]*targetuser* Displays RSoP data for the specified user. You can check the information of users in other domains by including the user domain.

/SCOPE {*USER* | *COMPUTER*} Specifies the scope of the output. You can display the user or computer information separately. The utility displays both user and computer information when you omit this command line switch.

/V Displays verbose information about the user or computer. The amount of additional information you receive varies by system. The utility displays details specific settings that have a precedence of 1.

/Z Displays super-verbose information about the user or computer. The amount of additional information you receive varies by system. The utility displays details specific settings that have a precedence of 1 or higher. Using this command line switch lets you see whether a setting is set in multiple places.

TIP Much of the Microsoft documentation leads you to believe that this utility is useless without having Active Directory installed. However, even without Active Directory, you can discover security information about a user with this utility. For example, you can verify that the system views the workstation as stand-alone, check the user's group participating, and verify local policies for the user.

Managing Group Policies with the GPUpdate Utility

The Group Policy Update (GPUpdate) utility lets you update the group policies on a computer. Use this utility as a replacement for the now obsolete `/refreshpolicy` command line switch for the SecEdit utility. Using this utility ensures that essential group policy changes appear on a computer, especially systems that are on 24 hours per day. This utility uses the following syntax:

```
GPUpdate [/Target:{Computer | User}] [/Force] [/Wait:<value>]
[/Logoff] [/Boot] [/Sync]
```

The following list describes each of the command line arguments.

/Target:{*Computer* | *User*} Specifies that the utility updates only user or computer policy settings. The default is to refresh both user and computer policy settings.

/Force Reapplies all policy settings, even those that haven't changed. Normally, the utility only applies new settings. This command line switch ensures that the system has all of the current policies, even if a policy was accidentally changed.

/Wait:*value* Determines the number of seconds the utility waits for policy processing to finish. The default setting is 600 seconds. You can cause the utility to end immediately by using a value of 0. A value of –1 forces the utility to wait indefinitely for the policy processing to complete. Use the –1 option when you want to ensure the policies are in place before rebooting the system. Policy processing continues in the background even if the utility ends.

/Logoff Forces the system to log off after the utility finishes refreshing the system policies. Using this option ensures the user sees the new policy settings. You must use this feature to install client-side extension policies that don't refresh in the background, but do refresh when the user logs in. For example, you'll need to use this technique for software installation and folder redirection policies. The utility ignores the command line switch when there aren't any policies that require a logoff to implement.

/Boot Forces a reboot for situations similar to the `/Logoff` command line switch. However, this command line switch affects those policy updates that require a reboot, rather than a simple logoff. As with the `/Logoff` command line switch, the utility ignores this command line switch when there aren't any policies that require a reboot.

/Sync Performs the next foreground policy application synchronously (possibly reducing the update time required for group policies). Foreground policy applications occur at computer boot and during user logon. You can specify this command line switch with the `/Target` command line switch to synchronize updates for just the user or just the computer policies. The utility ignores the `/Force` and `/Wait` command line switches when you use this command line switch.

Sending Messages with the Msg Utility

The message (Msg) utility sends a message to the specified users or session. Vista no longer supports the Msg utility due to the security problems that it causes. This utility relies on the Windows Messenger service, which most administrators disable by default now because of the security problems of using this service. If you receive a 1702 error when using this utility, it likely means that the Messenger service isn't running. This utility uses the following syntax:

```
MSG {username | sessionname | sessionid | @filename | *}
     [/SERVER:servername] [/TIME:seconds] [/V] [/W] [message]
```

The following list describes each of the command line arguments.

username Specifies the login name of the user to receive the message.

sessionname Specifies the name of the session to receive the message.

sessionid Specifies the numeric identifier of the session to receive the message.

@filename Specifies the name of a file containing a list of usernames, session names, or session identifiers to receive the message. Always precede the filename with the at sign (@).

* Sends the message to all sessions on the specified server.

/SERVER:*servername* Specifies the server to handle the message. Sending a message to remove server requires access to Terminal Server in addition to the Messenger service.

/TIME:*seconds* Specifies the wait period in seconds for the recipient to acknowledge the message.

/V Displays information about the actions the utility performs.

/W Waits for a response from the user. This option is very useful when using the `/V` command line switch because it helps ensure that you receive complete information about the actions the utility performs.

message Specifies the message to send. The utility prompts for this information if you don't supply it or requests the information from the standard input device.

Auditing User Access with the AuditPol Utility

The AuditPol utility helps you manage audit policies. Auditing is the process of monitoring user or other object successes and failures with the current system. For example, you could monitor every time the user fails to log into the system properly. The AuditPol utility supports the following modes of operation .

Get Displays the current audit policy.

Set Modifies the audit policy.

List Displays a list of selectable audit policies.

Backup Saves the current audit policy to a file.

Restore Restores a saved audit policy from a file.

Clear Restores the audit policy to a known state (no audit policy at all).

Remove Removes the per-user audit policy for the specified user.

The following sections describe each of these modes in detail.

GET

The Get mode displays the audit policy for the current or specified user. This mode uses the following syntax:

```
AuditPol /Get [/user:<username>|<{sid}>]
[/category:*|<name>|<{guid}>[,:<name>|<{guid}>...]]
[/subcategory:<name>|<{guid}>[,:<name>|<{guid}>...]]
[/option:{CrashOnAuditFail | FullPrivilegeAuditing | AuditBaseObjects |
AuditBaseDirectories}] [/sd] [/r]
```

The following list describes each of the command line arguments.

/user:{*username* | *SID*} Specifies the user account to query. You can provide either the username or the SID. Add the domain (`domain\username`) to qualify the username in a domain setting. You must use either the `/category` or `/subcategory` option with this option. The utility queries the system audit policy when you don't supply a username.

/category:{* | *name* | *GUID*}[, {*name* | *GUID*}...] Specifies one or more categories to query. You can query all of the categories by using an asterisk (*) in place of a specific category name. The utility lets you identify a category using its name or GUID. Separate multiple category entries using commas and enclose any category name with a space or other special symbol in double quotes. An example of a category is System.

/subcategory:{*name* | *GUID*}[, {*name* | *GUID*}...] Specifies one or more subcategories to query. The utility lets you identify a subcategory using its name or GUID. Separate multiple subcategory entries using commas and enclose any category name with a space or other special symbol in double quotes. You don't have to specify both category and subcategory—using subcategory alone is sufficient. An example of a subcategory is Security System Extension.

/sd Retrieves the security descriptor used to delegate access to the audit policy. You can't use this option with any other option—it must appear separately.

/option:{CrashOnAuditFail | FullPrivilegeAuditing | AuditBaseObjects | AuditBaseDirectories} Retrieves the state (policy) for the specified option. You can't use this option with any other option—it must appear separately.

/r Displays the output in CSV format.

SET

The Set mode changes the audit policy for the current or specified user. This mode uses the following syntax:

```
AuditPol /set
[/user[:<username>|<{sid}>][/include][/exclude]]
```

```
[/category:<name>|<{guid}>[,:<name>|<{guid}>...]]
   [/success:<enable>|<disable>][/failure:<enable>|<disable>]
[/subcategory:<name>|<{guid}>[,:<name>|<{guid}>...]]
   [/success:<enable>|<disable>][/failure:<enable>|<disable>]
[/option: {CrashOnAuditFail | FullPrivilegeAuditing | AuditBaseObjects |
AuditBaseDirectories} /value:<enable>|<disable>]
```

The following list describes each of the command line arguments.

/user:{*username* | *SID*} Specifies the user account to set. You can provide either the username or the SID. Add the domain (`domain\username`) to qualify the username in a domain setting. You must use either the `/category` or `/subcategory` option with this option. The utility queries the system audit policy when you don't supply a username.

/include Forces the system to generate an audit as part of the per-user policy even if the audit isn't specified by the system audit policy. This option is the default. You use this option with the `/user` option.

/exclude Forces the system to suppress an audit as part of the per-user policy even if the audit is specified by the system audit policy. This option isn't honored for users who are members of the Administrators local group. You use this option with the `/user` option.

/category:{*name* | *GUID*}[, {*name* | *GUID*}...] Specifies one or more categories to set. The utility lets you identify a category using its name or GUID. Separate multiple category entries using commas and enclose any category name with a space or other special symbol in double quotes. An example of a category is System.

/subcategory:{*name* | *GUID*}[, {*name* | *GUID*}...] Specifies one or more subcategories to set. The utility lets you identify a subcategory using its name or GUID. Separate multiple subcategory entries using commas and enclose any category name with a space or other special symbol in double quotes. You don't have to specify both category and subcategory—using subcategory alone is sufficient. An example of a subcategory is Security System Extension.

/success {Enable | Disable} Sets the success auditing for the associated category or subcategory. Use Enable or Disable to start or end success auditing.

/failure {Enable | Disable} Sets the failure auditing for the associated category or subcategory. Use Enable or Disable to start or end failure auditing.

/option:{CrashOnAuditFail | FullPrivilegeAuditing | AuditBaseObjects | AuditBaseDirectories} /value {Enable | Disable} Sets the state (policy) for the specified option. You can't use this option with any other option—it must appear separately. Always include the `/value` option to enable or disable the option.

/sd Sets the security descriptor used to delegate access to the audit policy. You can't use this option with any other option—it must appear separately. The security descriptor must include a Discretionary Access Control List (DACL) specified using the Security Descriptor Definition Language (SDDL).

LIST

Use the List mode to obtain a list of possible users, categories, or subcategories, rather than the audit settings. For example, if you use the `/user` option alone, you'll see a list of users that have audit policies set, rather than the user's settings. This mode uses the following syntax:

```
AuditPol /list
[/user|/category|/subcategory[:<categoryname>|<{guid}>|*] [/v] [/r]
```

The following list describes each of the command line arguments.

/user Displays a list of users who have audit policies set.

/category Displays a list of categories whether or not they have audit policies set.

/subcategory[:{*categoryname* | *GUID* | *} Displays a list of subcategories when you supply a category name or associated GUID. Use the asterisk (*) to display a list of all subcategories regardless of category.

/v Outputs additional information depending on the list you display. This option displays the SID for users and the GUID for both categories and subcategories.

/r Displays the output in CSV format.

Backup

The Backup mode lets you make a backup of the current audit policy. This mode uses the following syntax:

```
AuditPol /backup /file:<filename>
```

The following describes the command line argument.

/file:*Filename* Specifies the name of the file you want to use for the backup.

Restore

The Restore mode restores an audit policy you previously saved to a file. This mode uses the following syntax:

```
AuditPol /restore /file:<filename>
```

The following describes the command line argument.

/file:*Filename* Specifies the name of the file you want to restore.

Clear

The Clear mode clears the audit policies for all users on the system. This mode uses the following syntax:

```
AuditPol /clear [/y]
```

The following describes the command line argument.

/y Suppresses the prompt that asks whether you're sure you want to clear all of the audit policies.

WARNING Use the Clear mode with care because you'll remove all the audit policies and the process isn't reversible. The best policy is to make a backup before you use this option.

Remove

The Remove mode clears the per-user audit policy for the specified users. This mode uses the following syntax:

```
AuditPol /remove [/user[:<username>|<{sid}>]] [/allusers]
```

The following list describes each of the command line arguments.

/user:{*username* | *SID*} Specifies the user account to change. You can provide either the username or the SID. Add the domain (`domain\username`) to qualify the username in a domain setting. You must use either the `/category` or `/subcategory` option with this option. The utility queries the system audit policy when you don't supply a username.

/allusers Removes the per-user audit policies for all users. This option is equivalent to using the Clear mode from a user perspective. However, the audit policy options remain intact.

Obtaining User Login Information with the QUser Utility

The QUser utility provides quick access to user login information. The information you receive includes the username, session name, session identifier, state, amount of idle time, and the login time. You can use this utility to quickly find orphaned logins (sessions that are started, but never ended even though the user has stopped using the session). This utility uses the following syntax:

```
QUSER [username | sessionname | sessionid] [/SERVER:servername]
```

The following list describes each of the command line arguments.

username Specifies the login name of the user you want to query.

sessionname Specifies the name of the session you want to query. The default session name is Console.

sessionid Specifies the number of the session you want to query.

/SERVER:*servername* Provides the name of a server. The default setting queries the local machine.

Discovering User Identity with the WhoAmI Utility

Discovering who you are in relation to other elements of the system is important. A username is only part of your identity. For example, the system also knows about an SID and your group affiliations. The WhoAmI utility provides information about the current user based on input criteria. Using this utility alone displays just the username. This utility uses the following syntax:

```
WHOAMI [/UPN | /FQDN | /LOGONID]
WHOAMI { [/USER] [/GROUPS] [/PRIV] } [/FO {TABLE | LIST | CSV}] [/NH]
WHOAMI /ALL [/FO {TABLE | LIST | CSV}] [/NH]
```

The following list describes each of the command line arguments.

/UPN Displays the user's name in User Principle Name (UPN) format. Use this option in a domain setting.

/FQDN Displays the user's name in Fully Qualified Distinguished Name (FQDN) format. Use this option in a domain setting.

/USER Displays the username and SID.

/GROUPS Displays the user's group affiliations. Each group entry includes the group name, type (such as well-known group or alias), group SID, and group attributes (such as mandatory group, enabled by default, and enabled group).

/PRIV Displays the user's privileges. Each privilege entry includes the privilege name, description, and state (enabled or disabled).

/LOGONID Displays the SID that represents the user's logon identification.

/ALL Displays the username, user's group affiliations, user's privileges, and logon identifier.

/FO {TABLE | LIST | CSV} Defines the output provided by the utility. The table format is normally the easiest to view on screen. The table columns define the values for output, while each row contains one driver entry. The CSV output provides the best method for preparing the data for entry in a database. Use redirection (see the "Employing Data Redirection" section of Chapter 2 for details) to output the CSV data to a file and then import it to your database. The list format provides one data element per line. Each group of data elements defines one driver. The utility separates each driver by one blank line. Some people find the list format more readable when working in verbose mode since the table format requires multiple lines for each entry (the lines wrap).

/NH Forces the utility to display the data without a column header. You can only use this command line switch with the table and CSV formats. Omitting the header makes it easier to incorporate the data in a report or import it into a database.

Virus and External Intrusion Protection

VISTA

Before you read anything else in this section, it's important to understand that most versions of Windows don't provide a virus checker in the purest sense of the term, but the MRT comes very close. You won't find any utility to block spyware or adware in earlier versions of Windows either. Vista does provide rudimentary virus, spyware, and adware protection.

In addition, even though Windows XP SP2 and above do provide a firewall, some industry pundits consider it weak at the very least. For one thing, the firewall doesn't do a good job checking both incoming and outgoing data. The firewall in Vista is significantly stronger and includes two-way protection.

In some people's minds, these three items are the end of any virus and intrusion protection requirement on a system and they'll stop reading this section immediately. However, virus and intrusion protection only begins with these three types of utilities; you really do need more protection and you need to perform some tasks manually if you want to keep your system safe, rather than constantly cleaning up the aftermath of a successful attack.

The utilities in the sections that follow represent a next step. They aren't the final word in virus and external intrusion detection, but they help. You'll want to combine these utilities with other utilities described throughout the book. The point of these particular utilities is that they specialize in helping you maintain better control over your system. These utilities are relatively easy to use and complement the functionality of the three major applications that most people rely on exclusively to safeguard their systems.

VERIFYING DRIVER SAFETY WITH THE SIGVERIF UTILITY

Many people aren't overly concerned about the unsigned drivers on their systems. After all, the driver seems to do its job. However, drivers work at the lowest level of the operating system and you can't judge their performance solely on how they work from a user perspective. You must hold drivers to a higher standard than applications if you want to keep your system safe. A signed driver might not provide absolute safety from the vagaries of viruses and external intrusion, but it's generally better equipped to keep your system safe. At least a third party has verified that the driver meets specific standards of construction.

The SigVerif utility helps you locate drivers that lack a signature. It uses a graphical interface, so you won't find detailed coverage of it in this book. However, you can start this utility at the command prompt and store the results in a file for later analysis. The point is that this utility locates any unsigned driver on your system so you can request signed versions from the hardware vendors that put your system together. You can read more about this utility at `http://www.windowsitpro.com/Article/ArticleID/7918/7918.html`.

Removing Viruses with the BlastCln Utility

The Blast Clean (BlastCln) utility helps you locate two common viruses on your system, Blaster and Nachi. Microsoft updates BlastCln the utility monthly through the Windows Update service. In fact, you've probably run this utility every time you visited Windows Update without really knowing it because this utility appears on the list every month. However, you might want to check your machine more often than once a month to ensure it remains clean. In addition, running the utility as part of Windows Update doesn't provide you with a detailed report of any potential infestations on your system. Running the utility from the command prompt using the /V command line switch does provide additional information. You can learn a little more about this utility from the Knowledge Base article at `http://support.microsoft.com/?kbid=833330`. Vista doesn't provide support for the BlastCln utility—possibly because of the other protections that this operating system provides. This utility uses the following syntax:

```
BlastCln [/v] [/u] [/f] [/z] [/q]
```

The following list describes each of the command line arguments.

/v Displays additional information about the virus checking process. Generally, the output tells you that the utility is checking services, processes, the registry, and the hard drive for specific filenames. When the utility doesn't find any evidence of either Blaster or Nachi, it tells you that it's stopping the tool.

/u Performs the virus check using unattended mode. The user doesn't see any evidence that the utility is running.

/f Forces other applications to quit when the computer shuts down after the utility has cleaned up either a Blaster or Nachi infection.

/z Prevents a restart of the system after BlastCln utility installation is complete.

/q Performs the virus check using quiet mode. The user doesn't see any evidence that the utility is running and the utility doesn't request any user interaction when it detects a virus.

Managing the File System with the FltMC Utility

The Filter Manager Control (FltMC) utility tracks minifilters attached to your hard drive or other storage system (such as a DVD drive). You'll often see this utility included as part of a Windows service pack. However, it usually does its work and ends. A minifilter controls what a drive sees, which means that a minifilter could help control viruses by rejecting virus content. Here are the types of filters that Microsoft provides support for in storage applications.

- Activity Monitor
- Undelete
- Antivirus
- Replication
- Continuous Backup
- Content Screener
- Quota Management
- System Recovery
- Cluster File System
- Hierarchical Storage Manager (HSM)
- Compression
- Encryption
- Physical Quota Management
- Open File
- Security Enhancer
- Copy Protection

Generally, you won't need to use this utility unless you want to see which minifilters are running on your system or your storage vendor provides an update that you must install manually. You can use the FltMC in several modes to load, unload, attach, detach, and list filters. The following sections describe the modes that FltMC supports.

LOAD

Use this mode to load a filter driver. Loading the driver doesn't activate it. This mode uses the following syntax:

```
FltMC Load [driverName]
```

The following describes the command line argument.

driverName Specifies the name of the file that contains the driver that you want to load.

UNLOAD

Use this mode to unload an inactive driver. The utility won't unload a driver that's in use. This mode uses the following syntax:

```
FltMC Unload [driverName]
```

The following describes the command line argument.

driverName Specifies the name of the file that contains the driver that you want to unload.

FILTERS

Use this mode to list the filters installed on your machine. These filters are loaded, but not necessarily active. Use the Instances mode to see which filters are active. This mode uses the following syntax:

```
FltMC Filters
```

INSTANCES

Use this mode to list the active filters on your machine. These filters are loaded and have at least one instance attached to a particular volume. A filter may have multiple instances. This mode uses the following syntax:

```
FltMC Instances
```

VOLUMES

Use this mode to list the volumes that have a filter instance attached. This mode uses the following syntax:

```
FltMC Volumes
```

ATTACH

Use this mode to attach a filter that you've loaded into memory to a particular volume. You can assign the instance (the attachment of a filter to a volume) a specific name. In addition, you can also specify an altitude when you obtain this information from the minifilter vendor. The altitude determines the minifilter's order in the minifilter attachment stack, which determines when the minifilter sees data sent to the storage device. This mode uses the following syntax:

```
FltMC Attach [filterName] [volumeName] [[-i instanceName ][-a altitude]]
```

The following list describes each of the command line arguments.

filterName Specifies the name of the filter that's been loaded into memory using the Load mode.

volumeName Specifies the name of the volume, such as C:, that will have the filter attached.

-i *instanceName* Specifies the name of the instance. When the utility is successful in attaching the minifilter to the volume, it displays the resulting instance name.

-a *altitude* Specifies the altitude of the minifilter when compared to other minifilters in the stack. Microsoft controls the altitude information and you'll receive this information (when required) from the minifilter vendor. Normally, this information appears as part of the registry entries for the minifilter.

DETACH

Use this mode to detach a minifilter from a storage device that you previously attached using the Attach mode. This mode uses the following syntax:

```
FltMC detach [filterName] [volumeName] [instanceName]
```

The following list describes each of the command line arguments.

filterName Specifies the name of the filter that's been loaded into memory using the Load mode.

volumeName Specifies the name of the volume, such as C:, that will have the filter detached.

instanceName Specifies the name of the instance to remove. If you don't supply an instance, the utility removes the default instance.

Detect and Remove Malicious Software with the MRT Utility

The Malicious [Software] Removal Tool (MRT) helps you remove common malicious software from your system. You can find a description of this utility in the Knowledge Base article at `http://support.microsoft.com/?id=890830`. It's important to review this Knowledge Base article relatively often because Microsoft updates it each month with the list of viruses that MRT can detect. If you're an administrator, make sure you check the deployment instructions in the Knowledge Base article at `http://support.microsoft.com/kb/891716`. When used alone, the MRT utility displays a graphical interface the user can use to clean a system. This utility uses the following syntax:

```
MRT [/Q] [/N] [/F] [/F:Y]
```

The following list describes each of the command line arguments.

/Q Forces the utility to run in quiet mode, which means the user won't see the usual graphical interface.

/N Performs virus detection only; the utility doesn't clean up any viruses that it finds.

/F Forces the utility to perform an extended scan of the system. The extended scan requires considerably more time, but can help you locate virus files, registry settings, and hidden directories in addition to the usual memory check.

/F:Y Forces the utility to perform an extended scan of the system. In addition, the utility automatically cleans up any viruses that it finds.

Verifying System Files with the SFC Utility

The System File Scan (SFC) utility can help you keep viruses at bay by ensuring you have the correct version of the system files on your system. Viruses often replace system files with patched versions that contain the virus code. Hitchhiking on an existing system file makes it less likely that someone will remove the virus and ensures the virus gets a chance to run, so virus writers are motivated to use system files whenever they think they can. This utility uses the following syntax:

```
SFC [/SCANNOW] [/SCANONCE] [/SCANBOOT] [/REVERT] [/PURGECACHE]
    [/CACHESIZE=x]
```

The following list describes each of the command line arguments.

/SCANNOW Scans all of the protected system files immediately and repairs any damage it finds. The utility normally relies on the content of the `\WINDOWS\system32\dllcache` folder to make repairs to the system files. However, it can also use the Windows XP CD, the content of service pack folders, or even online sources when necessary.

/SCANONCE Scans all of the protected system files one time during the next boot. Using this option is the best way to ensure that the SFC utility runs when most of the files are accessible (not loaded in memory).

/SCANBOOT Scans all of the protected system files during every boot cycle. Although this command line switch can improve system security, it also noticeably increases system boot time.

/REVERT Sets SFC to use the default settings.

/PURGECACHE Purges (removes) the files in the `\WINDOWS\system32\dllcache` folder. Use this option when you think that the files in this backup folder are corrupted.

/CACHESIZE=x Sets the file cache size. The `\WINDOWS\system32\dllcache` folder can become huge. Limiting the size of the cache can help your system use disk space more efficiently. However, a smaller cache size also means that you might not have a backup of important DLLs when you need them.

Sometimes Microsoft does something interesting with a utility. The SFC utility in Vista performs the same task as it does in other versions of Windows, but most of the command line switches are different. The Vista version of this utility uses the following syntax:

```
SFC [/SCANNOW] [/VERIFYONLY] [/SCANFILE=<file>] [/VERIFYFILE=<file>]
[/OFFWINDIR=<offline windows directory>
/OFFBOOTDIR=<offline boot directory>]
```

The following list describes each of the command line arguments.

/SCANNOW Scans all of the protected system files immediately and repairs any damage it finds. The utility normally relies on the content of the `\WINDOWS\system32\dllcache` folder to make repairs to the system files. However, it can also use the Windows XP CD, the content of service pack folders, or even online sources when necessary.

/VERIFYONLY Verifies all of the protected system files immediately and works much the same as the `/SCANNOW` option. However, this option doesn't perform any repairs.

/SCANFILE=*File* Scans the specified file and repairs any damage. You must provide the full path to the file.

/VERIFYFILE=*File* Verifies the specified file, but doesn't repair any damage. You must provide the full path to the file.

/OFFBOOTDIR=*Directory* Performs offline repair of the specified boot directory.

/OFFWINDIR=*Directory* Performs offline repair of the specified Windows directory.

Verifying Drivers with the Verifier Utility

The Verifier utility performs general driver verification on your system through the Driver Verifier. Driver vendors are supposed to use this utility to ensure their drivers don't make illegal system calls or cause system corruption. You can use Verifier to ensure you do have good drivers loaded on your system and that a virus hasn't modified the driver files on your machine. Most of the drivers on your machine appear in the \WINDOWS\system32\drivers folder and have a SYS file extension. This utility uses the following syntax:

```
verifier /standard /driver NAME [NAME ...]
verifier /standard /all
verifier [/disk] [ /flags FLAGS ] /driver NAME [NAME ...]
verifier [/disk] [ /flags FLAGS ] /all
verifier /querysettings
verifier /volatile /flags FLAGS
verifier /volatile /adddriver NAME [NAME ...]
verifier /volatile /removedriver NAME [NAME ...]
verifier /reset
verifier /query
verifier /log LOG_FILE_NAME [/interval SECONDS]
```

The following list describes each of the command line arguments.

/standard Performs a standard check of the specified drivers during the next boot cycle. The standard check includes the Special Memory Pool, Forcing IRQL Checking, Memory Pool Tracking, I/O Verification (but not the enhanced version), Deadlock Detection, and DMA Verification checks. Technically, every driver on your machine should be able to pass a standard check. The driver vendor should provide you with information about any drivers that won't pass the Verifier checks.

/driver *NAME* [*NAME* ...] Checks one or more drivers with a specific name during the next boot cycle. Use this command line option to check one or two specific drivers, rather than checking all of the drivers on the machine. Separate each driver name with a space. You can't use wildcard characters to define a filename specification.

/all Verifies all of the drivers on the machine.

/flags *FLAGS* Performs a specific check using the tests defined by the supplied bit flags. For example, if you want to check both special pool checking and force IRQL checking, then you would supply a flag value of 00000011b (binary) or 3 (decimal). You can specify the flag values in hexadecimal by preceding the flag value with 0x. The following list describes each of the flags.

- **Bit 0** Special Pool Checking
- **Bit 1** Force IRQL Checking
- **Bit 2** Low Resources Simulation
- **Bit 3** Pool Tracking
- **Bit 4** I/O Verification
- **Bit 5** Deadlock Detection
- **Bit 6** Enhanced I/O Verification
- **Bit 7** DMA Verification

/querysettings Displays a summary of the nonvolatile Driver Verifier settings. These options include the options you have selected and the list of drivers selected for verification.

/volatile Forces a change to the Driver Verifier volatile settings. These changes take effect immediately, rather than during the next boot cycle. The settings last until you reboot the machine, so they aren't permanent. You can only perform the Special Memory Pool, Forcing IRQL Checking, and Low Resources Simulation checks when using volatile settings.

/adddriver *NAME* [*NAME* ...] Adds the specified driver to the volatile driver list. Separate each driver name with a space. You can't use wildcard characters to define a filename specification.

/removedriver *NAME* [*NAME* ...] Removes the specified driver from the volatile driver list. Separate each driver name with a space. You can't use wildcard characters to define a filename specification.

/reset Clears all of the Driver Verifier settings. The Driver Verifier won't verify any drivers during the next boot cycle.

/query Displays a list of the current Driver Verifier activity.

/log *LOG_FILE_NAME* [**/interval** *SECONDS*] Creates a log file with the specified name. At specific intervals, the log records the Driver Verifier statistics. The default logging interval is 30 seconds. You can specify the logging interval using the `/interval` command line switch. The utility won't stop when you issue this command at the command prompt. To stop the recording process and regain control of the command prompt, press Ctrl+C.

/disk Enables the Disk Integrity Verification option after the next system boot. This option is only available for Windows 2003 and above.

Configuring the System Setup

Your system setup helps define how your system works and interacts with you and your applications. For example, the boot configuration controls what you see as options when you boot your system. In addition, the boot configuration can control the way the system boots. Knowing how to change the boot configuration is important and you might find that you want to copy a boot configuration to another machine. You'll find a lot of system setup information in other parts of the book. However, the following sections describe utilities specifically devoted to system setup tasks.

Managing the Boot Configuration with the BootCfg Utility

At one time, the Boot Configuration (BootCfg) utility helped you manage your boot options and that was it. Sometime between the release of Windows XP and Windows 2003, Microsoft decided the utility should do a lot more. Consequently, you'll find that you can now perform tasks such as debugging your 1394 (Firewire) port as part of the boot process. This utility uses the following syntax:

NOTE Due to changes in the way Vista works, you won't find the BootCfg utility available any longer. Use the BCDEdit utility instead. This new utility takes features such as BitLocker into account.

```
BootCfg /Copy [/S system [/U [domain\]user [/P password]]]
     [/D description] /ID bootid
BootCfg /Delete [/S system [/U [domain\]user [/P password]]] /ID bootid
BootCfg /Query [/S system [/U [domain\]user [/P password]]]
BootCfg /Raw [/S system [/U [domain\]user [/P password]]]
     osoptions [/A] /ID bootid
BootCfg /Timeout [/S system [/U [domain\]user [/P password]]]
     timeoutvalue
BootCfg /Default [/S system [/U [domain\]user [/P password]]] /ID
     bootid
BootCfg /EMS [/S system [/U [domain\]user [/P password]]]
     {ON | OFF | EDIT} [/port {COM1 | COM2 | COM3 | COM4 | BIOSSET}]
     [/baud {9600 | 19200 | 38400 | 57600 | 115200}] [/ID bootid]
```

```
BootCfg /Debug [/S system [/U [domain\]user [/P password]]]
     {ON | OFF | EDIT} [/port {COM1 | COM2 | COM3 | COM4 | BIOSSET}]
     [/baud {9600 | 19200 | 38400 | 57600 | 115200}] [/ID bootid]
BootCfg /Addsw [/S system [/U [domain\]user [/P password]]]
     [/MM val] [/BV] [/SO] [/NG] /ID bootid
BootCfg /Rmsw [/S system [/U [domain\]user [/P password]]]
     [/MM val] [/BV] [/SO] [/NG] /ID bootid
BootCfg /Dbg1394 [/S system [/U [domain\]user [/P password]]]
     {ON | OFF} [/CH channel] /ID bootid
```

The following list describes each of the command line arguments.

/Copy Makes a copy of an existing boot entry from the [Operating Systems] section of the boot configuration (`Boot.INI` file) that you can use to add operating system options.

/S *system* Specifies the remote system that you want to check. In most cases, you'll also need to supply the `/U` and the `/P` command line switches when using this switch.

/U [*domain*\\]*user* Specifies the username on the remote system. This name may not match the username on the local system. You'll need to supply a domain name when working with a domain controller.

/P [*password*] Specifies the password for the given user. You can provide the command line switch without specifying the password on the command line in cleartext. The system prompts you for the password. Using this feature can help you maintain the security of passwords used on your system.

/D *description* Provides a description of the new boot entry made as a result of copying the specified boot entry.

/ID *bootid* Specifies the identifier of the boot entry to copy, delete, or manage in some other way. You can obtain a list of boot entries using the `BootCfg /Query` command.

/Delete Removes an existing boot entry from the [Operating Systems] section of the boot configuration file.

/Query Displays the current boot entries and their settings.

/Raw Specifies a command line switch to add to any of the current boot entries. Changing the command line switches modifies how the operating system boots. The Knowledge Base article at `http://support.microsoft.com/default.aspx?scid=kb;en-us;833721` tells you which command line switches Windows XP and Windows 2003 support.

osoptions Defines the command line switches you want to use for the operating system boot cycle.

[/A] Appends the new operating system command line switches to the existing switches. The default setting overwrites any existing settings with the new settings you specify.

/Timeout Modifies the timeout value (the time the system waits to boot the default operating system entry).

timeoutvalue Specifies the time the system waits before it uses the default operating system selection to boot the system. The default setting is 30 seconds. You can choose any value between 0 and 999 seconds.

/Default Modifies the default boot entry.

/EMS Allows the user to configure the `/Redirect` command line switch for the Emergency Management Services (EMS). Using this option adds a `redirect=Port#` entry to the [Boot Loader] section of the configuration file. Essentially, the entry makes it possible for the system to connect to another location if it can't boot for any reason. This service is only available on servers.

{ON | OFF | EDIT} Configures the EMS redirection, Debug, or 1394 Firewire debug setting. Setting the value to ON adds a `/Redirect` command line switch to the [Boot Loader] section, a `/Debug` command line switch to the specified boot entry, or a `/DBG1394` command line switch to the specified boot entry. Setting the value to OFF removes the entry. Setting the value to EDIT changes an existing entry to use a different port or baud setting. The 1394 Firewire debug setting doesn't allow use of the EDIT option.

/port {COM1 | COM2 | COM3 | COM4 | BIOSSET} Sets the EMS port value. The utility accepts the four standard serial ports. In addition, you can use the BIOS setting for EMS. Make sure you configure the BIOS when using the BIOSSET option.

/baud {9600 | 19200 | 38400 | 57600 | 115200} Sets the baud (data transfer) rate for the specified port.

/Debug Sets the port and baud rate of the port used for remote debugging of the specified boot entry.

/Addsw Adds a command line switch to the specified boot entry. This command line switch only allows specific switches, rather than the full list of switches described in the Knowledge Base article at `http://support.microsoft.com/default.aspx?scid=kb;en-us;833721`.

/MM *val* Specifies the maximum amount of memory that the operating system can use. This command line switch can help you locate memory-related problems that affect the operating system as a whole.

/BV Adds the `/BaseVideo` command line switch, which directs the operating system to use standard VGA for display purposes.

/SO Adds the `/SOS` command line switch, which forces the operating system to show the name of every device driver as it loads.

/NG Adds the `/NoGUIBoot` command line switch, which prevents the operating system from showing the progress bar as it boots the system.

/Rmsw Removes a command line switch from the specified boot entry.

/Dbg1394 Sets the system to use a 1394 Firewire port to debug the specified boot entry.

/CH *channel* Selects one of the Firewire channels, 1 through 64, to use for debugging.

Managing the Boot Configuration with BCDEdit in Vista

VISTA

The Boot Configuration Data Store Editor (BCDEdit) utility is a powerful replacement for the BootCfg utility provided with previous versions of Windows. The main reason for the replacement is that Microsoft has significantly changed the boot cycle to accommodate new technologies such as BitLocker. The BCDEdit utility relies on commands, as do many utilities in Windows, but you access the commands from the command line, rather than using an interactive environment as you would when working with other utilities such as Telnet. You specify one or more commands in sequence to obtain specific results from BCDEdit. Consequently, this utility doesn't use a precise command line syntax, nor do the commands appear in any specific order. Here are the commands that you can use with their associated options.

/bootdebug [*ID*] {On | Off} Turns boot debugging on or off. When you specify an identifier, the switch affects the specified application. You can use this command on any entry, but it only affects boot applications. If you specify this command without an identifier, the system sets boot debugging for the operating system loader.

NOTE You can obtain a list of common identifiers by typing **`BCDEdit /? ID`** at the command line. The resulting list shows the common identifiers that could appear in the boot configuration, not those that actually do appear. Use the `BCDEdit /enum` command to display the identifiers that do appear as part of the configuration.

/bootems [*ID*] {On | Off} Turns Emergency Management Services (EMS) for the specified entry on or off. When you specify an identifier, the switch affects the specified application. You can use this command on any entry, but it only affects boot applications. If you specify this command without an identifier, the system sets EMS for the operating system loader.

/bootsequence *ID* [...] [{/addfirst | /addlast | /remove}] Modifies the boot sequence. Use a single identifier with the `/addfirst` and `/addlast` options to add an identifier to the beginning or end of the boot sequence. Use the `/remove` option to remove the identifiers from the boot sequence.

[/store *Filename*] /copy *ID* /d *Description* Copies the specified identifier. The `/d` option specifies the description that you want assigned to the copy of the identifier. You may optionally store the copy in a different file using the `/store` option, which must appear in front of the `/copy` command.

/create [*ID*] /d *Description* [{/application *AppType* | /inherit [*AppType*] | /inherit DEVICE | /device}] Creates a new identifier. You can optionally specify an identifier for the new entry. The `/d` option provides a description of the new entry. The `/application` option creates a new application entry of one of the following types: BOOTSECTOR, OSLOADER, RESUME, or STARTUP. The `/inherit` option creates an inherit entry, one that's inherited by other entries. If you don't specify an application type, then any application can inherit the entry. The allowable inherit entry types include BOOTMGR, BOOTSECTOR, FWBOOTMGR, MEMDIAG, NTLDR, OSLOADER, and RESUME. The `/inherit DEVICE` option creates a special inherit entry that's only inherited by device options. The `/device` option creates a new device options entry.

NOTE The type information associated with the data store defines the format of the entry and how it affects the boot process. For example, an OSLOADER entry lets you load other operating systems. These options appear as part of the boot menu. Use the `BCDEdit /? TYPES` command to display a complete list of entry types. Add the type name to the command line and you'll see specific help for that type.

/createstore *Filename* Creates a new file that contains a boot configuration data store.

/dbgsettings [*DebugType* [DEBUGPORT:<port>] [BAUDRATE:*BAUD*] [CHANNEL:*Channel*] [TARGETNAME:*TargetName*] /start *StartPolicy* /noemux] Changes the debugger settings. Don't confuse this setting with `/bootdebug`, which chooses the items to debug. This setting affects the specified debugger type: SERIAL, 1394, or USB. Use the DEBUGPORT and BAUDRATE settings for serial port debugging, the CHANNEL setting for 1394 debugging, and the TARGETNAME setting for USB debugging. The `/start` option defines how the device starts and you can use these settings: ACTIVE, AUTOENABLE, or DISABLE. The `/noemux` option tells the kernel mode debugger to ignore any user-mode exceptions.

/debug [*ID*] {On | Off} Turns kernel mode debugging on or off. When you specify an identifier, the switch affects the specified Windows boot loader. You can use this command on any entry, but it only affects Windows boot loader entries. If you specify this command without an identifier, the system sets kernel mode debugging for the current boot loader.

/default *ID* Specifies the entry to use as the default boot manager. When the timer runs out, Vista automatically boots the selected entry.

[/store *Filename*] /delete *ID* [/f] [/cleanup | /nocleanup] Deletes the specified entry from the data store. Use the `/f` option to ensure BCDEdit deletes the entry; otherwise, it won't delete well-known entries. The `/cleanup` option ensures that the deleted item is removed from the display order. This option also removes any entries that reference the deleted entry. The `/cleanup` option is the default—you must specify `/nocleanup` when you don't want the deleted entry removed from the display order. You may optionally delete entries in a different file using the `/store` option, which must appear in front of the `/delete` command.

[/store *Filename*] /deletevalue [*ID*] *DataType* Deletes a data element from an entry in the boot configuration. The data type corresponds to one of the standard types you obtain using the `BCDEdit /? TYPES` command. When you specify an identifier, the switch affects the specified entry. If you specify this command without an identifier, the system deletes an entry for the current boot loader. You may optionally delete entries in a different file using the `/store` option, which must appear in front of the `/deletevalue` command.

/displayorder *ID* [...] [{/addfirst | /addlast | /remove}] Modifies the entry display order. Use a single identifier with the `/addfirst` and `/addlast` options to add an identifier to the beginning or end of the display order. Use the `/remove` option to remove the identifiers from the display order.

/ems [*ID*] {On | Off} Turns Emergency Management Services (EMS) for the specified boot entry on or off. When you specify an identifier, the switch affects the specified boot entry. You can use this command on any entry, but it only affects boot entries. If you specify this command without an identifier, the system sets EMS for the current boot entry.

/emssettings {BIOS | EMSPORT:*Port* EMSBAUDRATE:*BAUDRate*} Defines the global EMS settings. This command doesn't enable or disable EMS for any particular boot entry—it simply defines how EMS communicates. The `BIOS` option lets EMS rely on the BIOS configuration to determine how to react. This setting only works when your BIOS provides EMS support. The EMSPORT and EMSBAUDRATE settings affect serial port support and you shouldn't use them with the `BIOS` option.

[/store *Filename*] /enum [{*EntryType* | *ID*}] [/v] Lists the contents of the data store. The `/enum` command can list all of the entries, a specific entry, or entries of a particular type. The types you can list include ACTIVE, FIRMWARE, BOOTAPP, BOOTMGR, OSLOADER, RESUME, INHERIT, and ALL. The `/v` option displays the entry GUIDs, rather than the well-known values. You may optionally list entries in a different file using the `/store` option, which must appear in front of the `/enum` command (see Figure 5.3).

/export *Filename* Exports the system's data store to an external file.

/import *Filename* Imports the entries found in an external file into the system data store.

[/store *Filename*] /set [*ID*] *DataType Value* Changes the value of an entry to a new value. When you specify an identifier, the command affects the specified entry. If you specify this command without an identifier, the system sets values for the current boot entry. You may optionally change entries in a different file using the `/store` option, which must appear in front of the `/set` command.

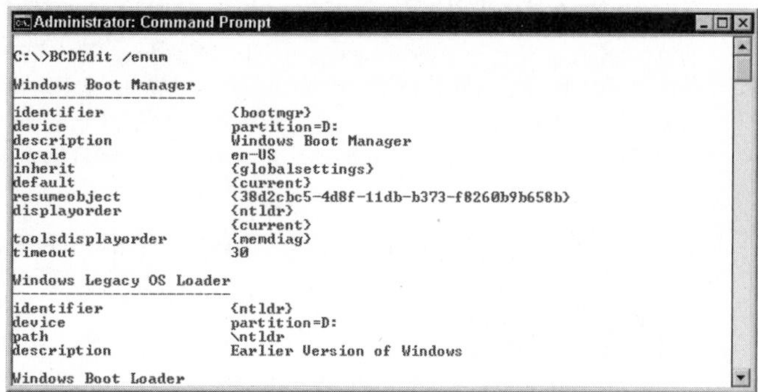

FIGURE 5.3
The /enum command outputs the contents of the current data store.

/store [*Filename*] Defines the data store to which other commands in the stream apply. You can't use this command with the `/createstore` command. If you don't include a filename, the commands affect the system store.

/timeout *Timeout* Changes the time that the boot manager waits for the user to make a selection before booting the default entry. The default setting is 30 seconds.

/toolsdisplayorder *ID* [...] [{/addfirst | /addlast | /remove}] Modifies the tools display order when displaying the tools menu during the boot sequence. Use a single identifier with the `/addfirst` and `/addlast` options to add an identifier to the beginning or end of the tools display order. Use the `/remove` option to remove the identifiers from the tools display order.

Now that you have a better idea of the commands you can use with BCDEdit, it's time to look at what passes for command line syntax. This utility uses the following syntax:

```
BCDEdit <Command> [<Command>...] [/? [TOPICS] [ID] [TYPES [{BOOTAPP |
BOOTMGR | BOOTSECTOR | CUSTOMTYPES | FWBOOTMGR | MEMDIAG | NTLDR |
OSLOADER | RESUME}]] [FORMATS]] [/enum] [/v]
```

The following list describes each of the command line arguments.

/? Obtains help about the specific command.

TOPICS Displays a list of detailed help topics, which includes the commands, standard identifiers, data types, and other command line options.

ID Displays a list of well-known identifiers for the operating system. For example, the `{bootmgr}` entry refers to the Windows Boot Manager entry.

TYPES [{BOOTAPP | BOOTMGR | BOOTSECTOR | CUSTOMTYPES | FWBOOTMGR | MEMDIAG | NTLDR | OSLOADER | RESUME}] Displays help information about configuration entry types. Using TYPES alone displays a list of the available types. Using TYPES with a specific entry, such as TYPES BOOTAPP, displays the type information for that entry.

FORMATS Displays information about the type information formatting rules.

/enum Lists the entries in a store.

/v Displays verbose information for the specified command. The amount of additional information varies by command.

Accessing the WinPE Network Installer with the NetCfg Utility

The NetCfg utility provides access to the Windows Pre-installation Environment (WinPE). Using this deployment environment can save you considerable time and effort as described at `http://www.microsoft.com/licensing/sa/benefits/winpe.mspx`. Learn more about WinPE at `http://www.microsoft.com/technet/windowsvista/deploy/winpe.mspx`. This utility uses the following syntax:

```
netcfg [-v] [-e] [-winpe] [-l <full-path-to-component-INF>]
   -c {p | s | c} -i <comp-id>
netcfg [-v] -winpe
netcfg [-v] -q <comp-id>
netcfg [-v] [-e] -u <comp-id>
netcfg [-v] -s {a | n}
netcfg [-v] -b <comp-id>
```

The following list describes each of the command line arguments.

WARNING You must pass the arguments in the order shown in the syntax or the command may fail. It's always a good idea to use the order shown in the syntax examples, but when using the NetCfg utility the order is essential.

-v Displays verbose information about the specified task. The amount and type of information depends on the command that you're executing.

-e Uses servicing environment variables during package installation and uninstallation.

-winpe Installs the TCP/IP, NetBIOS, and Microsoft Client for Windows pre-installation environment.

-l *Full-Path-To-Component-INF* Specifies the location of the INF file that contains the package installation instructions.

-c {p | s | c} Defines the class of the package you want to install: protocol, service, or client.

-i *CompID* Installs the specified package. Use the `-s` command line switch to obtain a list of component identifiers.

-q *CompID* Queries the installation status of the specified package. Use the `-s` command line switch to obtain a list of component identifiers.

-u *CompID* Uninstalls the specified package. Use the `-s` command line switch to obtain a list of component identifiers.

-s {a | n} Displays the specified component types where `a` is adapters and `n` is network components.

-b *CompID* Shows the binding paths for the specified component. Use the `-s` command line switch to obtain a list of component identifiers.

Accessing the Windows Package Manager with the PkgMgr Utility

The PkgMgr helps you service the operating system by installing and uninstalling both new packages and package updates. This utility uses the following syntax:

```
PkgMgr /ip [/m:Directory] /p:PackageName [/o:[BootPath]WinDirectory]
   [/n:Filename] [/s:Sandbox] [/quiet] [/norestart] [/l:LogFile]
```

```
PkgMgr /up [/m:Directory] /p:PackageName [/o:[BootPath]WinDirectory]
   [/n:Filename] [/quiet] [/norestart] [/l:LogFile]
PkgMgr /up PackageName [, PackageName...] [/o:[BootPath]WinDirectory]
   [/n:Filename] [/quiet] [/norestart] [/l:LogFile]
PkgMgr /iu PackageName [, PackageName...] [/o:[BootPath]WinDirectory]
   [/n:Filename] [/s:Sandbox] [/quiet] [/norestart] [/l:LogFile]
PkgMgr /uu PackageName [, PackageName...] [/o:[BootPath]WinDirectory]
   [/n:Filename] [/quiet] [/norestart] [/l:LogFile]
```

The following list describes each of the command line arguments.

PackageName Specifies the name of the package that you want to work with.

/m:*Directory* Specifies the location of the package. The default location is the current directory.

/p Specifies the name of a single package.

/o:[*BootPath*]*WinDirectory* Performs an offline action on the Windows image.

/n:*Filename* Provides the name of a file that contains automated responses to installation requirements.

/s:*Sandbox* Provides the name of a sandbox directory on the system where the application should extract files prior to checking them for viruses and other problematic code.

/quiet Performs the required task without a user interface.

/norestart Suppresses the restart at the end of the installation.

/l:*LogFile* Logs all actions to the specified log file.

/ip Installs one or more packages.

/up Uninstalls one or more packages.

/iu Installs a package update. The package must exist on the system or this command generates an error.

/uu Uninstalls a package update. The original package and the package update must exist on the system or this command generates an error.

Configuring Local Security Policies with the SecEdit Utility

The Security Edit (SecEdit) utility helps you analyze and manage security policies on your system. This utility uses the following syntax:

```
secedit /analyze /db FileName [/cfg FileName] [/overwrite]
[/log FileName] [/quiet]
secedit /configure /db FileName [/cfg FileName ] [/overwrite]
[/areas Area1 Area2 ...] [/log FileName] [/quiet]
secedit /export [/db FileName] [/cfg FileName]
[/mergedpolicy] [/areasArea1 Area2 ...] [/log FileName] [/quiet]
secedit /import /db FileName.sdb /cfg FileName [/overwrite]
[/areas Area1 Area2 ...] [/log FileName] [/quiet]
secedit /validate FileName
secedit /GenerateRollback /CFG FileName /RBK SecurityTemplatefilename
 [/log FileName] [/quiet]
```

The following list describes each of the command line arguments.

/analyze Performance analysis of the security policy on a system by comparing it to the settings in a database.

/db ***FileName*** Specifies the database used to perform the analysis, configuration, or other tasks.

/cfg ***FileName*** Specifies a security template to import into the database before the utility performs a task. You can create a security template using the Security Template Microsoft Management Console (MMC) snap-in.

/overwrite Overwrites any existing database entries before the utility imports the security template. Otherwise, the utility adds the settings in the security template to the existing database.

/log ***FileName*** Specifies the file to use for logging purposes. The log receives the status of the configuration process. If you don't specify this command line switch, the utility uses the `SCESrv.LOG` file located in the `\WINDOWS\security\logs` folder.

/quiet Performs the analysis without displaying any comments.

/configure Performs a security configuration based on the content of the specified security database.

/areas ***Area1 Area2 ...*** Specifies the security areas to manage. If you don't include this command line switch, the utility manages all security areas. You can specify multiple areas by separating each area with a space. The following list contains the valid security areas.

SECURITYPOLICY Defines the user security policy, which includes account policies, audit policies, event log settings, and security options.

GROUP_MGMT Defines the restricted group settings.

USER_RIGHTS Defines the user rights assignments to system objects.

REGKEYS Defines the registry permissions.

FILESTORE Defines the file system permissions.

SERVICES Defines the system service settings.

/export Exports the security settings to a database file.

/mergedpolicy Creates a merged database file that includes both local and domain security settings.

/import Imports the security settings from a database file. You can use a template file to provide overrides for settings in the database.

/validate ***FileName*** Validates the contents of a security template. Use this option to reduce syntax-induced errors.

/GenerateRollback Generates a security rollback based on the content of a security rollback template. The system offers you the opportunity to create a rollback template when you apply a security update to the system. This rollback template will return the system to the state it was in before the security update.

/RBK SecurityTemplatefilename Specifies the name of the file that contains the security rollback template.

Adding and Removing Applications with the SysOCMgr Utility

The SysOCMgr utility helps you install a limited set of system components. The Knowledge Base article at `http://support.microsoft.com/?kbid=222444` shows how to use this utility to manage Windows components. Vista replaces this utility with the OCSetup utility. See the "Adding and Removing Applications with the OCSetup Utility" section of the chapter for details. However, you can use the utility to install any software that relies on an INF file and can use an answer file. This utility uses the following syntax:

```
sysocmgr /i:InfFile.inf [/u:AnswerFilePathAndName [/q][/w]] [/r] [/z]
[/n] [/f] [/c] [/x] [/l]
```

The following list describes each of the command line arguments.

/i:*InfFile.inf* Specifies the INF file that contains the information required to install the optional component. The utility views this file as the master information file.

/u:*AnswerFilePathAndName* Specifies the path and filename of an optional answer file that contains arguments for unattended installation of the component. You can see an example of an answer file at `http://www.microsoft.com/technet/prodtechnol/WindowsServer2003/Library/IIS/efefcb53-b86e-4cac-9b4b-fcf5f1145aa9.mspx`.

/q Performs an unattended installation of the component. An unattended installation suppresses all user interface elements.

/w Prompts the user for permission to reboot the system when the new component requires a reboot.

/r Suppresses a reboot of the system even if the new component requires a reboot to function properly. The utility ignores this command line switch when the new component doesn't require a reboot.

/z Specifies that the arguments that follow this command line switch aren't optional arguments and that the utility should pass them to the component.

/n Forces the utility to treat the master information file as a new file instead of relying on a cached version in the `\WINDOWS\inf` folder.

/f Forces the utility to install the component so that it's initialized as if the installer hasn't run. This command line switch can help you overcome the effects of an incorrect installation by resetting the component configuration information.

/c Disallows user cancellation of the installation during the final installation phase.

/x Suppresses the initializing banner.

/l Performs a multi-language aware installation.

Adding and Removing Applications with the OCSetup Utility

The Optional Component Setup (OCSetup) utility replaces the SysOCMgr utility found in previous versions of Windows. This utility performs precisely the same tasks as SysOCMgr; it simply uses a different interface. This utility uses the following syntax:

```
OCSetup Component [/uninstall] [/passive] [/unattendfile:File] [/quiet] [/
norestart] [/log:File] [/x:Parameters]
```

The following list describes each of the command line arguments.

Component Specifies the name of the component to install or uninstall.

/uninstall Uninstalls the specified component.

/passive Performs the installation in unattended mode. The system only provides progress messages.

/unattendfile:*File* Provides the name of a file that contains answers to installation questions. You'll need to examine the component documentation to determine how to construct the unattended installation file.

/quiet Performs the installation in unattended mode. The system doesn't provide any output.

/norestart Completes the installation without restarting the system.

/log:*File* Creates a log that contains the actions performed by the utility.

/x:*Parameters* Provides optional arguments to the component you want to install. You'll need to examine the component documentation to determine which parameters to provide.

Getting System Configuration Information with the SystemInfo Utility

The SystemInfo utility lets you query the system for configuration information. The purpose of this utility is to provide a quick overview of the system configuration, not the detailed information that other utilities, such as MSInfo32 (described in Chapter 3) provide. One of the more important outputs of this utility is the hot fixes section, which provides you with a complete list of the hot fixes applied to the system (something you can't easily find out using other utilities). This utility uses the following syntax:

```
SYSTEMINFO [/S system [/U username [/P [password]]]] [/FO
{TABLE | LIST | CSV}] [/NH]
```

The following list describes each of the command line arguments.

/S *system* Specifies the remote system that you want to check. In most cases, you'll also need to supply the `/U` and the `/P` command line switches when using this switch.

/U [*domain*\]*user* Specifies the username on the remote system. This name may not match the username on the local system. You'll need to supply a domain name when working with a domain controller.

/P [*password*] Specifies the password for the given user. You can provide the command line switch without specifying the password on the command line in cleartext. The system prompts you for the password. Using this feature can help you maintain the security of passwords used on your system.

/FO {TABLE | LIST | CSV} Defines the output provided by the utility. The table format is normally the easiest to view on screen. The table columns define the values for output, while each row contains one driver entry. The CSV output provides the best method for preparing the data for entry in a database. Use redirection (see the "Employing Data Redirection" section of Chapter 2 for details) to output the CSV data to a file and then import it to your database. The list format provides one data element per line. Each group of data elements defines one driver. The utility separates each driver by one blank line. Some people find the list format more readable when working in verbose mode since the table format requires multiple lines for each entry (the lines wrap).

/NH Forces the utility to display the data without a column header. You can only use this command line switch with the table and CSV formats. Omitting the header makes it easier to incorporate the data in a report or import it into a database.

Interacting with the Internet

The sections that follow consider two Windows features that provide Internet support outside of the other discussions in this chapter (such as the TCP/IP tools discussed in the "Discovering TCP/IP Diagnostic Tools" section). The first area of concern is managing Internet Information Server (IIS). The IIS utilities don't let you perform standard management tasks, such as adding a new Web application. These utilities focus more on mundane tasks, such as converting IIS logs so you can use them for administrative tasks. The second area of concern is discovering how Microsoft plans to adapt Windows to work with Internet Protocol Version 6 (IPv6). This new version of IP greatly extends the number of addresses the Internet can support and provides a wealth of new (and needed) features. You can see a list of IPv6 standards at `http://www.ipv6.org/specs.html`.

NOTE Sometimes you'll find utilities that don't have any apparent use any longer. Microsoft often includes these utilities for compatibility purposes so that batch files and scripts don't fail. One such Internet-related utility is IISSync. Even though this utility had a purpose at one time, it no longer does anything useful.

Converting IIS Logs with the ConvLog Utility

VISTA

The ConvLog utility converts IIS logs from any format to the National Center for Supercomputing Applications (NCSA) format. You might need the logs in one format for a reporting utility and another format for storage in your database. Use this utility to make the transition between formats easier. Vista doesn't support the ConvLog utility and there isn't a replacement for it. This utility uses the following syntax:

```
ConvLog [-i{i | n | e}] [-t {ncsa[:GMTOffset] | NONE}]
[-o OutputDirectory] [-x] [-d] [-l{0 | 1 | 2}] [-c] LogFile
```

The following list describes each of the command line arguments.

LogFile Specifies the name of the log to convert. You can use wildcard characters to convert more than one log.

-i{i | n | e} Defines the input log file type. The input file can use any of these formats.

- **i** Microsoft Internet Standard Log File Format
- **n** NCSA Common Log File format
- **e** World Wide Web Consortium (W3C) Extended Log File Format

-t {ncsa[:*GMTOffset*] | NONE} Defines the time zone information for the file. The default is to use the NCSA Greenwich Mean Time (GMT) offset value in the form +0800 where the time zone is 8 hours ahead of GMT.

-o *OutputDirectory* Defines the output directory for the converted file.

-x Saves non-www entries to a dump (DMP) log file.

-d Converts the IP addresses to DNS entries.

-l{0 | 1 | 2} Specifies the local format for the time data. Specify the formats by number. Here are the valid format specifications.

- **0** MM/DD/YY (U.S.)
- **1** YY/MM/DD (Japan)
- **2** DD.MM.YY (Germany)

-c Forces the utility to continue the conversion even when it locates an incorrectly formatted entry.

Monitoring and Managing IIS with the IISReset Utility

• VISTA

Use the IISReset utility to change the status of the IIS service on the specified computer. Vista doesn't support the IISReset utility and there isn't a replacement for it. This utility uses the following syntax:

```
iisreset [computername] [/RESTART] [/START] [/STOP] [/REBOOT]
[/REBOOTONERROR] [/NOFORCE] [/TIMEOUT:val] [/STATUS] [/ENABLE]
[/DISABLE]
```

The following list describes each of the command line arguments.

computername Specifies the name of the computer to manage.

/RESTART Stops and then restarts all Internet services.

/START Starts all Internet services.

/STOP Stops all Internet services.

/REBOOT Reboots the computer.

/REBOOTONERROR Reboots the computer when the system experiences an error starting, stopping, or restarting the Internet services.

/NOFORCE Specifies that the utility shouldn't force the Internet services to stop when stopping them gracefully fails.

/TIMEOUT:*val* Specifies the time (in seconds) that the system should wait for a successful stop of Internet services. When the wait time expires, the system can reboot when you specify the `/REBOOTONERROR` command line switch. The default wait settings are 20 seconds for a restart, 60 seconds for a stop, and 0 seconds for a reboot.

/STATUS Displays the status of all Internet services. The output includes the service name and its current state (such as stopped).

/ENABLE Enables restarting of IIS on the local system.

/DISABLE Disables restarting of IIS on the local system.

Working with IP Version 6

The IPv6 update is in the planning stages on the Internet, but you probably won't get to work with it just yet. The update includes many new features that developers have wanted. However, the big issues are more addresses and better security. This chapter doesn't delve into the intricacies of IPv6, but it does discuss two new utilities for IPv6 and updates of some existing TCP/IP tools.

Managing the IPv6 Policies and Security with the IPSec6 Utility

Use the IPSec6 utility to change IP policies and security on the local machine. Vista doesn't require the IPSec6 utility because all of the required functionality is implemented as part of the various standard utilities. You'll find the IPv6 changes added to utilities throughout the book. This utility uses the following syntax:

```
ipsec6 sp [Interface]
ipsec6 sa
ipsec6 l FileName
ipsec6 s FileName
ipsec6 d [{sp | sa}] [Index]
ipsec6 m [{on | off}]
```

The following list describes each of the command line arguments.

sp [*Interface*] Displays the active security policies. You can limit the output to a specific interface by including the interface argument.

sa Displays a list of active security associations.

l *FileName* Loads the security policies from the `FileName.spd` file and the security associations from the `FileName.sad` file. Don't include an extension for the filename; the utility adds the SPD and SAD extensions for you.

s *FileName* Saves the current security policies to `Filename.spd` and the current associations to `Filename.sad`. You can use this command line switch to create security files for later use. When the system doesn't have any security policies or associations, the utility creates template SPD and SAD files that you can edit to create security policies and associations using a standard text editor.

ipsec6 d [{sp | sa}] [*Index*] Deletes the specified security policy or association. Use the `sp` argument to delete a policy and the `sa` argument to delete an association. The utility deletes both the policy and association when you don't provide an option. The index number references a specific security policy or association. When you omit the index number, the utility deletes all of the entries.

ipsec6 m [{on | off}] Specifies whether IP security protects the binding updates used for mobile IPv6. The default setting enables IP security.

Managing the IPv6 Service with the IPV6 Utility

Vista doesn't require the IPV6 utility because all of the required functionality is implemented as part of the various standard utilities. You'll find the IPv6 changes added to utilities throughout the book.

All IPv6 configuration and management in previous versions of Windows takes place with the IPv6 command line tool. Some of the tasks you can perform include installing and uninstalling IPv6 support. You can also change the IPv6 routing tables and control the size of the cache, among other tasks. This utility isn't stable as of the time of writing. However, Microsoft documents the utility online at `http://msdn.microsoft.com/library/en-us/wcetcpip/html/cmconIPv6exe.asp`.

An Overview of IPv6 Counterparts to Older TCP/IP Utilities

Older versions of Windows support updated versions of a number of other TCP/IP utilities. (Vista doesn't use these utilities because it supports IPv6 natively.) These utilities have the same functionality as the IPv4 utilities discussed in this chapter. The only difference is that they work with IPv6. Refer to the IPv4 utility descriptions in this chapter for further information. Here's a list of IPv6-compatible utilities currently supplied with Windows.

- PING6
- TraceRt6

Working with General Applications

Most users live for general applications. Word processors, spreadsheets, graphics, productivity enhancers, and other applications all serve the user's needs in some way. Of course, the operating system also runs applications and you'll find more than a few services and other low-level tasks running. In fact, even a well-maintained system will run 25 or more tasks and most run far more. Most users have no idea of which applications are running on their systems, but using the utilities in this book, you can discover what those applications are, who's running them, and what the application is supposed to do. The following sections describe three helpful utilities for managing applications on your system.

Terminating Tasks with the TaskKill Utility

You have a number of ways to kill tasks on a system, but sometimes you have to kill a task by remote control or use the command line to do it. The TaskKill utility fulfills both needs. It lets you maintain control over a system, even if you have to use a network connection to do it. This utility uses the following syntax:

```
TASKKILL [/S system [/U username [/P [password]]]] { [/FI filter]
[/PID processid | /IM imagename] } [/F] [/T]
```

The following list describes each of the command line arguments.

/S *system* Specifies the remote system that you want to check. In most cases, you'll also need to supply the `/U` and the `/P` command line switches when using this switch.

/U [*domain*\\]*user* Specifies the username on the remote system. This name may not match the username on the local system. You'll need to supply a domain name when working with a domain controller.

/P [*password*] Specifies the password for the given user. You can provide the command line switch without specifying the password on the command line in cleartext. The system prompts you for the password. Using this feature can help you maintain the security of passwords used on your system.

/FI *Filter* Filters the output information from the utility. The filters can become complex, so read the text that appears after this list for additional information. Table 5.1 describes the filter criteria.

/PID *processid* Specifies the Process Identifier (PID) of the process that you want to terminate.

/IM *imagename* Specifies the image name (application name) of the process that you want to terminate. You can use wildcard characters to terminate multiple applications.

/F Forces the process to terminate. Using this option can cause data loss by terminating an application before it has saved any changes the user had made.

/T Terminates the process and any processes started by the process. The TaskKill utility removes all of the processes that the application creates. This is the best option to use for an application that has frozen because there isn't any guarantee the application will clean up after itself.

TABLE 5.1: An Overview of TaskKill and TaskList Filters

FILTER	DESCRIPTION	COMPARISON OPERATORS	VALID VALUES
STATUS	This filter can help you locate any applications that are no longer responding so that you can manually end them.	eq, ne	Running or Not Responding
IMAGENAME	Use this filter to locate a particular application in the list based on its filename.	eq, ne	The executable filename
PID	Use this filter to locate a particular instance of an application when there's more than one copy of the application running.	eq, ne, gt, lt, ge, le	Process Identifier
SESSION	Unless you're using a sharing application such as Terminal Services, this filter is useless because every application running is for the current session.	eq, ne, gt, lt, ge, le	The session number
SESSIONNAME	Unless you're using a sharing application such as Terminal Services, this filter is useless because every application running is for the current session.	eq, ne	The name of the session
CPUTIME	This filter can help you locate applications that have just started or have been running a long time. For example, you might notice a sudden drop in system performance and can use this filter to locate applications that have just started to help determine which application might have caused the performance problem.	eq, ne, gt, lt, ge, le	The amount of time that the application has used the CPU in hours, minutes, and seconds since the session has started
MEMUSAGE	Sometimes you have more applications loaded than the system can comfortably support. This filter helps you locate applications that you can end or possible candidates for removal from the system.	eq, ne, gt, lt, ge, le	The amount of memory the application uses in kilobytes
USERNAME	Use this filter to separate applications that the user starts from those the system starts.	eq, ne	The name of the user who started the application

TABLE 5.1: An Overview of TaskKill and TaskList Filters *(CONTINUED)*

FILTER	DESCRIPTION	COMPARISON OPERATORS	VALID VALUES
SERVICES	Use this filter to locate the application hosting a particular service on the system.	eq, ne	A service name
WINDOWTITLE	This filter can help you locate a particular application based on the name it displays to the user.	eq, ne	The name the application displays to the user on the title bar
MODULES	This filter can help you locate applications based on the modules they use. You can use this filter to help locate a variety of problems, including DLL conflicts (when two applications use the same DLL, but they each need a different DLL version).	eq, ne	The filenames of any modules that an application uses

Listing Applications and Services with the TaskList Utility

The TaskList utility provides a lot more information than Task Manager, but it's also harder to use. You can use TaskList to find specific information about services and applications running on your system. For example, you can determine which services are running or perhaps locked up (not responding). To get a display similar to the one shown in Task Manager, type **TaskList** at the command prompt and press Enter. This utility uses the following syntax:

```
TASKLIST [/S system [/U username [/P [password]]]] [/M [module] | /SVC
| /V] [/FI filter] [/FO format] [/NH]
```

The following list describes each of the command line arguments.

/S *system* Specifies the remote system that you want to check. In most cases, you'll also need to supply the /U and the /P command line switches when using this switch.

/U [*domain*\\]*user* Specifies the username on the remote system. This name may not match the username on the local system. You'll need to supply a domain name when working with a domain controller.

/P [*password*] Specifies the password for the given user. You can provide the command line switch without specifying the password on the command line in cleartext. The system prompts you for the password. Using this feature can help you maintain the security of passwords used on your system.

/M [*Module*] Displays a list of applications that require the specified support module. Most applications require use of one or more modules (usually DLLs) for support. When you use this switch alone, TaskList displays a list of every module used by every loaded application. It's quite a list, so you'll probably want to redirect the output to a file using the > or >> redirection symbols and adding a filename. The switch also lets you optionally specify a specific module name. You can use this option to determine which applications require a specific module to execute. Often, this process can help you understand why a particular application glitches when another application is loaded (sometimes they rely on a shared module, but each application requires a different version of that module).

/SVC Displays a list of services supported by each of the `SVCHOST.EXE` entries in the task list. You'll find that each `SVCHOST.EXE` entry supports one or more services.

/V Displays additional application information including the application status, name of the user running the process, the amount of processor time the application is using, and the name of the application window. You might be surprised at how many of the applications listed are run by the system on your behalf or to maintain Windows. One of the most useful columns for optimization purposes is Window Title, which tells you the human readable name of the application. The connection between the executable and window names can help you locate viruses, adware, and spyware on your system.

/FI *Filter* Filters the output information from the utility. The filters can become complex, so read the text that appears after this list for additional information. Table 5.1 describes the filter criteria.

/FO {TABLE | LIST | CSV} Defines the output provided by the utility. The table format is normally the easiest to view on screen. The table columns define the values for output, while each row contains one driver entry. The CSV output provides the best method for preparing the data for entry in a database. Use redirection (see the "Employing Data Redirection" section of Chapter 2 for details) to output the CSV data to a file and then import it to your database. The list format provides one data element per line. Each group of data elements defines one driver. The utility separates each driver by one blank line. Some people find the list format more readable when working in verbose mode since the table format requires multiple lines for each entry (the lines wrap).

/NH Forces the utility to display the data without a column header. You can only use this command line switch with the table and CSV formats. Omitting the header makes it easier to incorporate the data in a report or import it into a database.

Converting Event Trace Logs with the TraceRpt Utility

The TraceRpt utility converts the binary data in the event trace logs for the system into a format that you can use for permanent database storage or other needs. This utility uses the following syntax (the first syntax is for data stored in files, while the second is for real-time data conversion):

```
TraceRpt filename [filename ...] [options]
TraceRpt -rt <session_name [session_name ...] [options]
```

The following list describes each of the command line arguments and options.

filename Specifies one or more Event Trace Log (ETL) files to process.

-rt Performs real-time processing instead of converting a file.

session_name Specifies the session to track in real time.

-o [*filename*] Specifies the output file for the ETL data. The output is in CSV format. The default filename is `dumpfile.csv`.

-summary [*filename*] Specifies a summary report text file. The output is in CSV format. The default filename is `summary.txt`.

-report [*filename*] Specifies a text output report file for the ETL data. The default filename is `workload.txt`.

-config *filename* Specifies the name of a settings file that contains the required command options.

-y Answers yes to all of the utility questions without prompting the user.

Vista supports a number of new command line options. Most of these additions support new event log features not found in previous versions of Windows, so it wouldn't even make sense to add them to previous Windows versions unless Microsoft retrofitted the entire event log structure. The following list tells you about these additional command line options and arguments.

-f {XML | HTML} Defines the output format of the report. The output format defines what you see on screen.

-of {CSV | EVTX | XML} Specifies the dump format (the format when outputting to a file). The default output is XML.

-df *Filename* Provides a Microsoft-specific counting and reporting schema file.

-int *Filename* Specifies the name of a file to use to dump the interpreted event structure.

-rts Places a raw timestamp in the event trace header. You can use this option with the `-o` option, but not with the `-report` or `-summary` options.

-tmf *Filename* Specifies the name of a Trace Message Format (TMF) definition file. The TMF file contains instructions for parsing and interpreting binary data. You can discover more about the structure and contents of the TMF definition file at `http://msdn2.microsoft.com/en-gb/library/ms797950.aspx`.

-tp *Value* Defines the TMF file search paths. As with any other path, you can separate multiple paths using the semicolon (;).

-i *Value* Defines the provider image path. A provider is the originator of an event log. Learn more about providers at `http://msdn2.microsoft.com/en-gb/library/ms797953.aspx`. The Program Database (PDB) file that matches the provider is located in the symbol server. Details of the PDB appear at `http://msdn2.microsoft.com/en-gb/library/ms797956.aspx`. As with any other path, you can separate multiple paths using the semicolon (;).

-pdb *Value* Defines the symbol server path. As with any other path, you can separate multiple paths using the semicolon (;).

-gmt Converts that Windows Software Trace Preprocessor Payload (WPP) timestamps to Greenwich Mean Time (GMT) time. You can learn more about the WPP at `http://msdn2.microsoft.com/en-gb/library/ms793164.aspx`.

-rl {1 | 2 | 3 | 4 | 5} Sets the system report level. The default level is 1. A higher report level includes more information in the report.

-lr Creates a less restrictive report. The utility uses a best match system for events that don't match the event schema.

-export [*Filename*] Exports the event schema to a file. The default filename is `Schema.MAN`. You can optionally provide a different filename.

Perform System Diagnostics with DispDiag

The DispDiag utility performs diagnostics on your display. It creates a file that contains information such as the display adapter type, the current operating system version, and registry settings for the display adapter. This utility uses the following syntax:

```
dispdiag [-testacpi] [-d]
```

The following list describes each of the command line arguments and options.

-testacpi Performs a diagnostic test to check application hot keys. The command line displays the code and scan code for each key you press. Using this feature helps you diagnose application hot key problems. The DispDiag utility won't create an output file when you use this feature.

-d Creates a dump file in addition to the data file. The dump file contains the contents of memory to aid in diagnosis of display problems.

Getting Started with Command Line Tasks

This chapter has discussed the utilities you can use to monitor and secure your system. Of course, these are just the utilities that naturally fall into the monitoring category. Your hard drive is literally packed with utilities that might help you monitor your system in some way. For example, many of the utilities you have discovered in the book so far have diagnostic and reporting functions that can alert you to potential problems. All you really need is a willingness to look at the output in a new way—one that meets your requirements.

As with many of the utilities in this book, you can easily become a slave to running them without gaining much of a benefit. You have to ask the question of where you draw the line in monitoring your system. At some point, you have to decide that you have done everything possible and don't really have time to do anything more. Of course, you'll also want to use your newfound knowledge to build up those fallen walls that a cracker is very happy to breach. The bottom line is that you need to create some type of threat analysis and determine how much protection you need from that threat before you begin using the utilities in this chapter. Also, consider how long it takes you to use a utility and discover methods of automating any tasks that you can.

Chapter 6 discusses some of the most dangerous utilities in the book. Developers and administrators employ these utilities to perform low-level work with the system. In many cases, you could simply skip this chapter unless you have a specific need. The discussions in Chapter 6 move beyond simple system configuration and monitoring. Utilities in Chapter 6 can perform tasks such as converting a FAT drive into an NTFS drive or perform system-level debugging of an application such as a service or device driver. In short, Chapter 6 isn't for the faint of heart or those light of skills.

Chapter 6

Using Developer and Low-Level Utilities

- ◆ Working with Automated System Recovery
- ◆ Using the Start Command
- ◆ Performing Disk Maintenance
- ◆ Employing Low-Level Utilities
- ◆ Accessing Functions within DLLs
- ◆ Uninstalling the Operating System with the OSUninst Utility
- ◆ Controlling Services with the SC Utility
- ◆ Shutting Down the System with the ShutDown Utility
- ◆ Replicating COM+ Applications with the COMRepl Utility
- ◆ Managing Type Libraries with the RegTLib Utility
- ◆ Saving and Restoring System Restore Data with the SRDiag Utility
- ◆ Performing Web-Based Enterprise Management Tasks
- ◆ Understanding Windows Side-by-Side (WinSxS) Behavior with SxSTrace

In all of the previous chapters, you saw utilities that just about anyone could use. These utilities represent the kinds of tasks that everyone from an average user to an administrator might need at various times. Needless to say, anyone working at the command line has to have a certain level of Windows knowledge—novices need not apply. However, the utilities in this chapter fall into a different class. The utilities in this chapter present a significant opportunity to harm your system when used incorrectly. In fact, some of the utilities are best left in the hands of experienced administrators and developers. Even a power user should think twice before employing some of them.

The utilities in this chapter also differ from the others in the book because they do things that you probably won't do every day. For example, it's unlikely that you'll need to use Automated System Recovery (ASR) from the command line every day. In fact, this feature works more or less automatically (as its name implies) in the background, so you might never interact with it directly. Likewise, you won't have to convert a disk from the File Allocation Table (FAT) to Windows NT File System (NTFS) format every day. A few of the utilities could help the power user. For example, this chapter shows how to defragment your hard drive from the command line.

Working with Automated System Recovery

The ASR functionality in Windows can make a significant difference when you need to get a system up and running again after a major problem. The emphasis of ASR is automation. Yes, you still have to produce a floppy, but the automation is noticeable during the recovery phase. The Microsoft TechNet article at `http://www.microsoft.com/technet/prodtechnol/winxppro/maintain/asr.mspx` tells how to use ASR with the graphical interface for backup and at the recovery console for recovery. The only problem is that you can't depend on users to use ASR and the graphical interface doesn't lend itself to maintaining several machines efficiently. Normally, you'd use a command line setup to ensure that the system saves ASR information. The problem is that the manual method requires that you sit in front of the machine and feed it a floppy when requested to save the ASR information—hardly an effective method for the administrator with hundreds of machines to maintain.

VISTA

Vista uses an entirely different method of performing system recovery. First, system files are significantly better protected in Vista. In fact, all files receive additional protection. Second, you can create a shadow copy of a file using a restore point, or back it up using the Back Up Files Wizard or the WBAdmin utility (see the "Performing Backups with the WBAdmin Utility" section of Chapter 2 for details). This action creates a version of the file that you can later restore if necessary. To restore a previous version, right-click the file, select the Previous Versions tab, highlight the version you want to restore, and click Open, Copy, or Restore. Third, you also have System Restore to rely on, which means you can move the system back to a previous state as needed. Consequently, Vista doesn't support the ASR utilities.

Unlike most of the utilities in this book, you'll find that working with the ASR utilities is frustrating at best. Use the `/?` command line switch and you'll find that two of the three utilities `ASR_Fmt` and `ASR_LDM` display a tantalizing list of command line options, none of which appears to work on first glance. Microsoft Knowledge Base articles such as the one at `http://support.microsoft.com/?kbid=262006` provide clues that you might be able to access the ASR utilities from the command line through NTBackup, but none of the available command line switches appear to perform this task. In addition, many users, such as the one at `http://forums.techarena.in/archive/index.php/t-56551.html`, find it impossible to create the required files at the command line. It turns out that the sticking point is figuring out what Microsoft means by a context for the `/Backup` form of the command. You must provide a context in order to use the command. The context appears to be a file handle, but Microsoft certainly doesn't document this information and after a lot of experimentation I was unable to document it as fact. Here's is a list of the Knowledge Base articles that Microsoft does provide, none of which actually documents the utilities (you can access the Microsoft Knowledge Base at `http://support.microsoft.com/default.aspx?scid=fh;EN-US;KBHOWTO`).

- 299044: How to Install Additional Files During Automated System Recovery
- 314058: Description of the Windows XP Recovery Console
- 314470: Definition of System Partition and Boot Partition
- 314686: ASR Cannot Restore System Disk to Replacement Disk of Identical Size
- 314688: A "Logical Disk Manager ASR Utility Error" Message When You Use ASR to Restore Disks That Are in a RAID Set
- 316484: "The Files for the Recovery Diskette Could Not Be Created" Error Message Occurs When You Use Ntbackup for Automated System Recovery

Unlike the `/Backup` option, the `/Restore` option does appear to work from the command line. Microsoft doesn't document the `/Restore` option any better than it does the `/Backup` option, but at least you can find a Microsoft document that shows usage. After you create an ASR backup using the manual method, check the \WINDOWS\Repair folder of your system and you'll notice it contains a nu including the ASR.SIF file shown in Figure 6.1. Notice that you must provide the /Restore command line switch as a minimum and optionally provide the /SIFPath command line switch as well. After testing this feature out on several machines, it's apparent that you can successfully automate this particular feature of working with the ASR utilities. Always use the /SIFPath command line switch when restoring from a hard drive instead of a floppy (Microsoft doesn't recommend hard drive restoration).

The bottom line is that the ASR utilities represent an instance where Microsoft has failed completely to provide a utility that the administrator can use to leverage a useful system feature to protect users from themselves. Although ASR represents a viable option for individuals and small networks, it's unlikely that anyone with many machines will use it to create a viable emergency restoration. The alternatives include using products such as Norton Ghost to create a local backup of the system. You could also create a bootable Windows CD to assist in setting up a machine after a failure. Microsoft does help in these areas. Consider reading Microsoft-provided articles such as the Microsoft Windows XP Service Pack 1 Installation and Deployment Guide at http://www.microsoft.com/windowsxp/downloads/updates/sp1/spdeploy.mspx#the_integrated_installation_fmay and the Help with Windows article titled, "Slipstreaming Windows XP Service Pack 2 and Create Bootable CD" at http://www.helpwithwindows.com/WindowsXP/winxp-sp2-bootcd.html.

The following sections tell how you may be able to perform the same tasks that the graphical ASR utilities perform, but from any location using the command line. In addition, you need to know about the command line utilities when working with other products. For example, the IBM Tivoli Storage Manager for Windows requires that you know something about these command line utilities (see the details at http://publib.boulder.ibm.com/tividd/td/TSMC/GC32-0788-04/en_US/HTML/ans60000559.htm).

FIGURE 6.1 You can definitely use the \Restore option from the command line.

```
asr.sif - Notepad
File  Edit  Format  View  Help
[COMMANDS]
1=1,3000,0,"%SystemRoot%\system32\asr_fmt.exe","/restore"
2=1,2000,1,"%SystemRoot%\system32\asr_ldm.exe","/restore"
3=1,4990,1,"%SystemRoot%\system32\asr_pfu.exe","/restore"
4=1,4000,1,"ntbackup","recover /1"
```

WARNING Although it's unlikely that you'll run into the ASR limitations on a modern system, you can't use ASR with hard drives formatted in certain ways. Even though the Microsoft documentation isn't very clear, drives formatted using the FAT32 (32-bit File Allocation Table) file system should work fine (see the Microsoft Knowledge Base article at http://support.microsoft.com/kb/q154997/ for details on FAT32). Theoretically, you can create FAT32 drives up to 2 TB in size. However, drives formatted using the older 16-bit FAT have significant limits. ASR only supports FAT16 volumes up to 2.1 GB. It doesn't support drives formatted with large cluster sizes. Microsoft recommends converting these older volumes to NTFS, which is certainly the least work-intensive option. However, it's possible that you can't use NTFS for some reason. In this case, try reformatting the drive using FAT32.

Backing Up and Restoring System Data with the ASR_Fmt Utility

The Automated System Recovery Format (ASR_Fmt) utility performs the basic tasks of backing up and restoring system information on your machine. This utility uses the following syntax:

```
ASR_Fmt /Backup /Context=ASRContext
ASR_Fmt /Restore [/SIFPath=Path]
```

Real World Scenario

USING ASR FOR MAJOR SYSTEM RECOVERY

A customer of mine recently suffered a devastating virus attack. The helpful staff at a major computer company was just about ready to have him format his hard drive. However, he felt that he really didn't want to give up his system without making some kind of an effort. He told me afterward that he could practically hear the support person shrug their shoulders as he hung up; they obviously didn't care.

Unlike many customers, this one actually had the two things needed to restore his system. First, we did a full recovery of the system using ASR (yes, it does work for some viruses, but not for others—we were lucky this time). The system came up, but the virus had damaged some data files. Before we did anything else, I quickly restored his data (with full overwrite) from the backup made the day before. Using a full overwrite ensured that the data didn't remain lurking in the background, hidden in some file.

Using just ASR and the backup, we were able to recover his system completely. Total time expended was just over 2 hours. Yes, that's a lot of time to spend recovering the system, but imagine the time required to format the drive, set up Windows again, reinstall all of those applications, and finally restore the data. Spending 2 hours to get the system up and running again was a bargain.

The following list describes each of the command line arguments.

/Backup Performs a backup of the required ASR information. This feature is undocumented and you probably won't get it to work outside of the automated environment.

/Context=*ASRContext* Specifies the backup context. Unfortunately, this command line switch is completely undocumented. Precisely what Microsoft means by an ASR context is unknown. Some people have ventured the opinion that the context is a handle to a file or other Windows resource. Without Microsoft documentation or a successful experiment using other methods, however, it's impossible to know.

/Restore Recovers the ASR information. When using a floppy, the default setup, the `/SIFPath` command line switch is apparently optional.

/SIFPath=*Path* Specifies the location of the `ASR.SIF` file. This file normally appears on the ASR floppy or within the `\Windows\Repair` folder of the hard drive.

Working with Logical Disks Using the ASR_LDM Utility

The Automated System Recovery Logical Disk Manager (ASR_LDM) utility provides logical disk management support such as setting the hard drive partition. This utility uses the following syntax:

```
ASR_LDM /Backup /Context=ASRContext
ASR_LDM /Restore [/SIFPath=Path]
```

The following list describes each of the command line arguments.

/Backup Performs a backup of the required ASR information. This feature is undocumented and you probably won't get it to work outside of the automated environment.

/Context=*ASRContext* Specifies the backup context. Unfortunately, this command line switch is completely undocumented. Precisely what Microsoft means by an ASR context is unknown. Some people have ventured the opinion that the context is a handle to a file or other Windows resource. Without Microsoft documentation or a successful experiment using other methods, however, it's impossible to know.

/Restore Recovers the ASR information. When using a floppy, the default setup, the /SIFPath command line switch is apparently optional.

/SIFPath=*Path* Specifies the location of the ASR.SIF file. This file normally appears on the ASR floppy or within the \Windows\Repair folder of the hard drive.

Working with Protected Files Using the ASR_PFU Utility

The Automated System Recovery Protected Files Utility (ASR_PFU) ensures that you have access to all protected files, such as the registry. This utility doesn't provide any form of command line help, so the syntax provided in this section is based on working with the other utilities and the scant documentation provided by Microsoft and third parties. This utility probably uses the following syntax:

```
ASR_PFU /Backup [/Context=ASRContext]
ASR_PFU /Restore /SIFPath=Path
```

The following list describes each of the command line arguments.

/Backup Performs a backup of the required ASR information. This feature is undocumented and you probably won't get it to work outside of the automated environment.

/Context=*ASRContext* Specifies the backup context. Unfortunately, this command line switch is completely undocumented. Precisely what Microsoft means by an ASR context is unknown. Some people have ventured the opinion that the context is a handle to a file or other Windows resource. Without Microsoft documentation or a successful experiment using other methods, however, it's impossible to know.

/Restore Recovers the ASR information. When using a floppy, the default setup, the /SIFPath command line switch is apparently optional.

/SIFPath=*Path* Specifies the location of the ASR.SIF file. This file normally appears on the ASR floppy or within the \Windows\Repair folder of the hard drive.

Using the *Start* Command

Many of the commands and utilities discussed so far in this book will wait until they complete a task before they return control of the command prompt to the user. A common way to handle this problem, when the application supports it, is to ask it to return immediately and continue working in the background. The only problem with this approach is that you aren't sure that the command or utility completed successfully. The Start command helps you overcome this problem by creating a new window for the command or window to run in. The command or utility still controls the command prompt until it completes, but since it runs in another window, the user can continue working.

Another use for this utility is to start the command or utility in a window with a specific title. You can apply settings to a window that rely on the window title (see the "Configuring the Command Window" section of Chapter 1 for details). Whenever you open a window with that title, it also has the special formatting that you specified. In short, you can create custom environments in which to run a utility. This utility uses the following syntax:

```
START ["title"] [/Dpath] [/I] [/MIN] [/MAX] [/SEPARATE | /SHARED] [/LOW
   | /NORMAL | /HIGH | /REALTIME | /ABOVENORMAL | /BELOWNORMAL] [/WAIT]
   [/B] [{command | program}] [parameters]
```

The following list describes each of the command line arguments.

"*title*" Defines the title of the command window title bar.

path Specifies the starting directory for the command window. This value doesn't have to be the same as the path for the command that you want to execute. For example, it might be the path to the data directory for the command.

/B Starts the application without creating a new window. The application executes as a background task and doesn't display a user interface. The lack of user interface means that the application won't provide Ctrl+C handling, so you would need to stop the application using the Task Manager or an application such as the TaskKill utility described in the "Terminating Tasks with the TaskKill Utility" section of Chapter 5. Some applications may also allow termination using Ctrl+Break.

/I Passes the standard command environment to the new window, rather than using any changes made to the command environment by the current command window. Using this command line switch ensures that the application won't run in a contaminated environment where an environmental setting could adversely affect the way the application runs.

/MIN Starts the application with the command window minimized.

/MAX Starts the application with the command window maximized.

/SEPARATE Starts 16-bit Windows applications in a separate memory space. Normally, Windows uses a separate memory space for all 32-bit applications, but a single memory space for all 16-bit applications. Older applications don't always use memory correctly, resulting in memory corruption that can cause other applications to fail. Using this command line switch eliminates shared memory corruption problems. However, this feature comes at the cost of performance and overall system resource usage. Unlike 32-bit memory spaces, 16-bit memory spaces remain fixed in memory, which uses the memory inefficiently and causes memory fragmentation. Memory fragmentation can cause Windows to perform inefficiently, leading to performance problems. In short, use this command line switch only when you actually experience problems.

/SHARED Starts the 16-bit Windows application in a shared memory space. This is the default setting and you should normally use it unless you experience memory corruption problems while running the application.

/LOW Starts the application in the IDLE priority class. Use this priority setting for applications that only run when other applications don't require the processor. This command line switch helps the system function more efficiently when you want to run the application as a background task and don't care when it completes its work.

/BELOWNORMAL Starts the application in the BELOWNORMAL priority class. Use this priority setting for background applications that you want to complete in a timely manner, but not at the expense of foreground applications.

/NORMAL Starts the application in the NORMAL priority class. This is the default setting. Foreground applications normally start at this priority. You should only use this setting for applications that you want to complete at a normal pace. This setting does affect all foreground application responsiveness.

/ABOVENORMAL Starts the application in the ABOVENORMAL priority class. This setting places the application at a slightly higher priority than standard applications. The other foreground tasks continue to run, but at a noticeably slower pace. Use this setting for priority applications that must complete tasks quickly.

/HIGH Starts the application in the HIGH priority class. You won't normally have a good reason to use this priority for any application. Using this priority level can affect system functionality and definitely slows other foreground applications to a crawl. Always use this setting with extreme caution.

/REALTIME Starts the application in the REALTIME priority class. Using this priority level stops execution of other foreground tasks and some system tasks as well. In addition, system functionality degrades noticeably. In some circumstances, the system could actually freeze and require a reboot. Generally, you don't want to use this priority for any reason.

/WAIT Starts the application and waits for it to terminate. This setting ensures that you know when an application completes its task.

{*command* | *program*} Specifies the internal command/batch file or the external utility/application to run. The command window remains visible after you run an internal command or batch file because the system executes the command processor (CMD.EXE) with the /K switch. (See the "Using the CMD Switches" section of Chapter 7 for details on the CMD.EXE command line switches.) The system runs external utilities and applications in a window or in a full screen console. Unless you change the default behavior using a command line switch, the window or full screen console closes when the application completes execution.

parameters Specifies the parameters (arguments) passed to the command or program.

Performing Disk Maintenance

At one time, computer systems had just two kinds of disks—the hard disks used for large, fixed storage needs, and floppy disks used for smaller, portable storage needs. Today, users need to work with a vast array of storage formats. A user might rely on RAM drive storage or memory cards. The storage might not even appear in the same physical area because many users rely on online storage for some needs. However, because of the early use of the term *disk* within the computing community, most people refer to these other forms of storage as disks. The following sections discuss various disk maintenance utilities, even if the storage used doesn't necessarily take the form of a physical disk.

Managing Removable Storage with the RSM Utility

The Removable Storage Management (RSM) utility helps you manage any portable media for your machine. Microsoft provides this utility so you can manage resources for applications that don't support the Removable Storage Application Programming Interface (API) through scripts or batch files. Early versions of the RSM utility relied on a simple command line and didn't provide much functionality. The following sections reflect the modes supported by newer versions of the utility.

NOTE Like many utilities, the command line for RSM is case insensitive when you type actual arguments. However, this utility differs in that the Media Objects, which include media, drives, changers, libraries, media types, and slots, are case sensitive. If you have a drive named MyDrive and want to refer to it by its friendly name, then you must observe the actual case of the name when typing the command. In addition, unlike many utilities, you must type the arguments for a command line switch directly after the switch. For example, /MMyPool will work, but /M MyPool won't because it has a space between the command line switch and the argument.

Vista does provide support for the RSM utility. However, you won't find it in the same location as previous versions of Windows. Depending on your system configuration, you'll likely find this utility in the \Windows\winsxs\x86_microsoft-windows-r..emanagement-service_31bf3856ad364e35_6.0.5744.16384_none_21ccd2c119fdb6d5 folder of your hard drive. In addition, you might see complaints about a missing NTMSAPI.DLL file that you'll find in the \Windows\winsxs\x86_microsoft-windows-r..management-apilayer_31bf3856ad364e35_6.0.5744.16384_none_cb8fdf31cbc6c1a7 folder. Theoretically, Microsoft will eventually work out all of these issues. In the meantime, you may have to spend some time getting the RSM utility to work. All you need to do is create a new folder and place all of the files from both directories into it to make RSM work under Vista. Make sure you have full rights to the new folder or the copy process will fail.

ALLOCATE

Use the allocate mode to allocate existing media for a specific use. This mode uses the following syntax:

```
RSM ALLOCATE /M<MediaPoolName> [/L[G|F]<LogicalMediaID> |
   /P[G|F]<PartitionID>] /O[{ERRUNAVAIL | NEW | NEXT}] [/T{<timeout> |
   INFINITE}] [/LN<LogicalMediaName>] [/LD<LogicalMediaDescription>]
   [/PN<PartitionName>] [/PD<PartitionDescription>] [/B]
```

The following list describes each of the command line arguments.

/M*MediaPoolName* Specifies the name of the media pool to use for the allocation.

/LG*LogicalMediaIdentifier* Defines the logical media identifier as a GUID.

/LF*LogicalMediaIdentifier* Defines the logical media identifier as a friendly name.

/PG*PartitionID* Defines the partition identifier as a GUID.

/PF*PartitionID* Defines the partition identifier as a friendly name.

/O[{ERRUNAVAIL | NEW | NEXT}] Defines the removable storage allocation options. You may use more than one command line switch to define multiple options, but each option must appear as a separate command line switch. The ERRUNAVAIL option specifies that the utility submit a request for new media to the operator when the allocation fails due to a lack of media. The NEW option allocates media in such a way that another application can't use the media. You can use this option to reserve the second side of two-sided media for exclusive use of a single application. Once you set the media aside, you must actually allocate it with the NEXT option. The NEXT option allocates the next partition of media previously allocated using the NEW option.

/T{timeout | INFINITE} Specifies the timeout value for a drive in milliseconds. The timeout value determines how long the utility waits for the media allocation to succeed. The default setting is INFINITE.

/LN*LogicalMediaName* Defines the friendly name that the utility assigns to the LogicalMedia object of the allocated media.

/PN*PartitionName* Defines the friendly name that the utility assigns to the Partition object of the allocated media.

/LD*LogicalMediaDescription* Defines the description that the utility assigns to the LogicalMedia object of the allocated media.

/LD*PartitionDescription* Defines the description that the utility assigns to the Partition object of the allocated media.

/B Specifies the bare option that you can use with scripts. The utility displays only the GUIDs of the allocated media. You can redirect this output to another utility to perform additional media processing.

DEALLOCATE

Use the deallocate mode to deallocate previously allocated media. This mode uses the following syntax:

```
RSM DEALLOCATE /L[G|F]<LogicalMediaID> | /P[G|F]<PartitionID>
```

The following list describes each of the command line arguments.

/LG*LogicalMediaID* Defines the logical media to deallocate as a GUID.

/LF*LogicalMediaID* Defines the logical media to deallocate as a friendly name.

/PG*PartitionID* Defines the partition to deallocate as a GUID.

/PF*PartitionID* Defines the partition to deallocate as a friendly name.

MOUNT

Use the mount mode to make removable media available for use. This mode uses the following syntax:

```
RSM MOUNT /L[G|F]<LogicalMediaID> /O[{ERRUNAVAIL | READ | WRITE |
   OFFLINE}] [/R[{NORMAL | HIGH | LOW | HIGHEST | LOWEST}]
   [/T{timeout | INFINITE}]]
RSM MOUNT /P[G|F]<PartitionID> /O[{ERRUNAVAIL | READ | WRITE |
   OFFLINE}] [/R[{NORMAL | HIGH | LOW | HIGHEST | LOWEST}]
   [/T{timeout | INFINITE}]]
RSM MOUNT /S[G|F]<SlotID> /O[{ERRUNAVAIL | READ | WRITE | OFFLINE}]
   [/R[{NORMAL | HIGH | LOW | HIGHEST | LOWEST}] [/T{timeout | INFINITE}]]
RSM MOUNT /C[G|F]<ChangerID /O[{ERRUNAVAIL | READ | WRITE | OFFLINE}]
   [/R[{NORMAL | HIGH | LOW | HIGHEST | LOWEST}] [/T{timeout | INFINITE}]]
RSM MOUNT /D[G|F]<DriveID> /O[{ERRUNAVAIL | DRIVE | READ | WRITE |
   OFFLINE}] [/R[{NORMAL | HIGH | LOW | HIGHEST | LOWEST}]
   [/T{timeout | INFINITE}]]
```

The following list describes each of the command line arguments.

/LG*LogicalMediaID* Defines the logical media to mount as a GUID.

/LF*LogicalMediaID* Defines the logical media to mount as a friendly name.

/PG*PartitionID* Defines the partition to mount as a GUID.

/PF*PartitionID* Defines the partition to mount as a friendly name.

/SG*SlotID* Defines the slot identifier to mount as a GUID.

/SF*SlotID* Defines the slot identifier to mount as a friendly name.

/CG*ChangerID* Defines the changer identifier to mount as a GUID.

/CF*ChangerID* Defines the changer identifier to mount as a friendly name.

/DG*DriveID* Defines the drive identifier to mount as a GUID.

/DF*DriveID* Defines the drive identifier to mount as a friendly name.

/O[{ERRUNAVAIL | DRIVE | READ | WRITE | OFFLINE}] Defines the removable storage allocation options. You may use more than one command line switch to define multiple options, but each option must appear as a separate command line switch. The ERRUNAVAIL option tells the utility to generate an error if either the media or the drive isn't available. The error normally notifies an operator of the need to fix the drive. The READ option mounts the drive for read access. The WRITE option mounts the drive for write access. This option fails when you try to mount media that's marked as completed (non-writeable). The DRIVE option is required when you use the /DG or /DF options. The OFFLINE option tells the utility to generate an error if the media isn't online.

/T{timeout | INFINITE} Specifies the timeout value for a drive in milliseconds. The timeout value determines how long the utility waits for the media allocation to succeed. The default setting is INFINITE.

[/R[{NORMAL | HIGH | LOW | HIGHEST | LOWEST}] Specifies the mount priority of the media. The system mounts higher priority media first. The default priority is NORMAL.

DISMOUNT

Use the dismount mode to remove media from service. This mode uses the following syntax:

```
RSM DISMOUNT /L[G|F]<LogicalMediaID> | /P[G|F]<PartitionID> [/O[DEFERRED]]
```

The following list describes each of the command line arguments.

/LG*LogicalMediaID* Defines the logical media to dismount as a GUID.

/LF*LogicalMediaID* Defines the logical media to dismount as a friendly name.

/PG*PartitionID* Defines the partition to dismount as a GUID.

/PF*PartitionID* Defines the partition to dismount as a friendly name.

/O [DEFERRED] Defines the removable storage allocation options. The DEFERRED option marks the media as dismountable, but keeps the media in the drive. The default setting dismounts the media immediately and ejects it from the drive.

EJECT

Use the eject mode to eject media from the device. When the media is virtual, then the utility performs the equivalent of ejecting the media from the device; the bottom line is that the media is no longer available for use. This mode uses the following syntax:

```
RSM EJECT /P[G|F]<PhysicalMediaID> [/A[{START | STOP | QUEUE}]]
   [/O<EjectOperation>] [/B]
RSM EJECT /S[G|F]<SlotID> /L[G|F]<LibraryID> [/A[{START | STOP |
   QUEUE}]] [/O<EjectOperation>] [/B]
RSM EJECT /D[G|F]<DriveID> /L[G|F]<LibraryID> [/A[{START | STOP |
   QUEUE}]] [/O<EjectOperation>] [/B]
```

The following list describes each of the command line arguments.

/PG*PhysicalMediaID* Defines the physical media identifier to eject as a GUID.

/PF*PhysicalMediaID* Defines the physical media identifier to eject as a friendly name.

/SG*SlotID* Defines the slot identifier to eject as a GUID.

/SF*SlotID* Defines the slot identifier to eject as a friendly name.

/DG*DriveID* Defines the drive identifier to eject as a GUID.

/DF*DriveID* Defines the drive identifier to eject as a friendly name.

/LG*LibraryID* Specifies the library to eject as a GUID. Use a GUID with the /SG and /DG options. The library identifier is the specific media to eject from the drive.

/LF*LibraryID* Specifies the library to eject as a friendly name. Use a friendly name with the /SF and /DF options. The library identifier is the specific media to eject from the drive.

/A[{START | STOP | QUEUE}] Defines the ejection action to perform. The default action is START. The START action begins the ejection process. The system ejects the media until a timeout occurs (the timeout value appears as part of the library object for all ejects in the library) or you call this command with a STOP action. The STOP action terminates the eject operation. You must use the GUID returned when you start the ejection to perform a STOP action. The QUEUE action queues the media for ejection. The system ejects the media in turn. You can use this action to group media for multi-slot Inputs/Exports (IEPorts). The discussion at http://www.osronline.com/ddkx/storage/05chgr_59nr.htm provides IEPort details.

/O*EjectOperation* Obtains the GUID when you use eject with the START action (or switch). Use the resulting GUID with the STOP action (or switch) to stop the eject process.

/B Specifies the bare option that you can use with scripts. You can redirect this output to another utility to perform additional media processing.

EJECTATAPI

Use the eject ATAPI mode to eject media from an Advanced Technology Attachment Packet Interface (ATAPI) device. This mode uses the following syntax:

```
RSM EJECTATAPI /N<AtapiChangerNumber>
```

The following describes the command line argument.

/N*AtapiChangerNumber* Specifies the number found at the end of the device name for the changer. For example, CdChanger0 has a changer number of 0. The number uniquely identifies the device.

CREATEPOOL

Use the create pool mode to create a new media pool. This mode uses the following syntax:

```
RSM CREATEPOOL /M<MediaPoolName> [/T[G|F]<MediaPoolTypeID>]
   /A[{EXISTING | ALWAYS | NEW}] [/D] [/R]
```

The following list describes each of the command line arguments.

/M*MediaPoolName* Specifies the name of the media pool that you want to create.

/TG*MediaPoolTypeID* Defines the media pool type identifier as a GUID.

/TF*MediaPoolTypeID* Defines the media pool type identifier as a friendly name.

/A[{EXISTING | ALWAYS | NEW}] Defines the pool creation action to perform. The EXISTING action opens an existing media pool. It returns an error when an existing media pool doesn't exist. The ALWAYS action opens an existing media pool or creates a new media pool when one doesn't exist. The NEW action always creates a new media pool. It returns an error when a media pool already exists.

/D Specifies that the media pool can draw media from the free pool.

/R Specifies that the media pool can return media to the free pool.

DELETEPOOL

Use the delete pool mode to remove a media pool. This mode uses the following syntax:

```
RSM DELETEPOOL /M<MediaPoolName>
```

The following describes the command line argument.

/MMediaPoolName Specifies the name of the media pool that you want to delete.

VIEW

Use the view mode to display one of the RSM objects on screen. You can use this mode to discover any information you need to use any of the other modes described for this utility. This mode uses the following syntax:

```
RSM VIEW /T[{DRIVE | LIBRARY | CHANGER | STORAGESLOT | IEDOOR | IEPORT
   | PHYSICAL_MEDIA | MEDIA_POOL | PARTITION | LOGICAL_MEDIA |
   MEDIA_TYPE | DRIVE_TYPE | LIBREQUEST}] [/CG<ContainerID>] [/GUIDDISPLAY] [/B]
```

The following list describes each of the command line arguments.

/T[{DRIVE | LIBRARY | CHANGER | STORAGESLOT | IEDOOR | IEPORT | PHYSICAL_MEDIA | MEDIA_POOL | PARTITION | LOGICAL_MEDIA | MEDIA_TYPE | DRIVE_TYPE | LIBREQUEST}] Defines the kind of information you want the utility to return. You may only request one media object at a time. The output always contains the object's friendly name data unless you specify the /GUIDDISPLAY command line switch. You must specify a particular object; using /T alone displays an error message.

/CGContainerID Specifies the container identifier for an object as a GUID.

/GUIDDISPLAY Specifies that the output should appear as a GUID, rather than as a friendly name.

/B Specifies the bare option that you can use with scripts. You can redirect this output to another utility to perform additional media processing.

REFRESH

Use the refresh mode to refresh the library, physical media, or all devices of a particular media type. The refresh cycle obtains the latest device information. This mode uses the following syntax:

```
RSM REFRESH /L[G|F]<LibraryID>
RSM REFRESH /P[G|F]<PhysicalMediaID>
RSM REFRESH /TG<MediaTypeID>
```

The following list describes each of the command line arguments.

/LGLibraryID Specifies the library to eject as a GUID. Use a GUID with the /SG and /DG options. The library identifier is the specific media to eject from the drive.

/LFLibraryID Specifies the library to eject as a friendly name. Use a friendly name with the /SF and /DF options. The library identifier is the specific media to eject from the drive.

/PGPhysicalMediaID Defines the physical media identifier to eject as a GUID.

/PFPhysicalMediaID Defines the physical media identifier to eject as a friendly name.

/TGMediaTypeID Defines the media type identifier as a GUID.

INVENTORY

Use the inventory mode to create an inventory of the specified library. The system queues the request, so it might not execute immediately. This mode uses the following syntax:

```
RSM INVENTORY /L[G|F]<LibraryID> /A[{FULL | FAST | DEFAULT | NONE | STOP}]
```

The following list describes each of the command line arguments.

/LG*LibraryID* Specifies the library to inventory as a GUID.

/LF*LibraryID* Specifies the library to inventory as a friendly name.

/A[{FULL | FAST | DEFAULT | NONE | STOP}] Defines an action to perform for the inventory. You may only choose one of the options. The FULL action performs a complete on-media inventory. The FAST action performs a differential inventory of the media (to look for changes between this inventory and a previous inventory) unless the library has a bar code reader installed. When a bar code reader is present, the utility performs a bar code inventory. The DEFAULT action uses the inventory method specified as part of the library object. The NONE action doesn't perform any inventory. The STOP action causes the current inventory, if any, to terminate.

Converting FAT Partitions to NTFS with the Convert Utility

At some point, you may need to convert a hard drive formatted using the FAT format into one that uses NTFS. However, this task is becoming less common as people move from Windows 9*x* to Windows NT–based operating systems. Newer machines usually come with NTFS installed. In fact, the number of existing systems with FAT installed diminishes every day, so you'll eventually be able to forget about the Convert utility as a relic of some bygone era. However, for now, you'll still need to convert hard drives from one format to another.

The Convert utility is unique in that it relies on three other utilities to perform its work: AutoConv (automates the file system conversion during reboots), AutoFmt (automates the file formatting process during reboots), and AutoLfn (automates the conversion of long filenames). These executables exist in the `\Windows\System32` directory, but you can't use them at the command prompt. When you try to execute them, you'll see an error message such as, "The C:\WINDOWS\system32\autolfn.exe application cannot be run in Win32 mode." The reason you need to know about these three utilities, even though you'll never use them from the command line, is that some misguided individuals have marked them as viruses and will attempt to tell you that these files are a source of infection. Not all of the utilities in the `\Windows\System32` directory execute from the command line.

NOTE Convert can't update the boot drive of your system immediately because the drive is locked by the operating system. However, the Convert utility will offer to mark the drive for conversion during the next boot cycle when the system hasn't locked the drive. Your system must have access to the AutoConv, AutoFmt, and AutoLfn utilities to perform the conversion during a boot or the conversion will fail. The system normally recovers from this error, but it's better to check for the presence of the required utilities at the outset.

You actually control the activities of the AutoConv, AutoFmt, and AutoLfn utilities through the Convert utility. The Convert utility helps you set up everything, and then you let the system handle the details automatically. This utility uses the following syntax:

```
CONVERT volume /FS:NTFS [/V] [/CvtArea:filename] [/NoSecurity] [/X]
```

The following list describes each of the command line arguments.

volume Specifies the drive letter (include the colon), mount point, or volume name to convert.

/FS:NTFS Specifies that you want the volume converted to NTFS.

/V Performs the conversion in verbose mode. Normally, the utility only displays initialization and error messages. The verbose mode provides a number of supplemental messages.

/CvtArea:*filename* Specifies a contiguous file (one that isn't fragmented) in the root directory that you want to use as a placeholder for the NTFS system files. Using this technique can help avert some of the performance degradation that normally occurs with a converted drive.

/NoSecurity Sets the converted files and directories to give the Everyone group full access. This setting means that everyone can access the files and circumvents the security features that NTFS can provide. Make sure you set security to reasonable levels of access after the conversion.

/X Forces the volume to dismount (become inaccessible) prior to conversion if necessary. The system closes all handles to the volume, which means any open files become inaccessible as well.

Converted drives don't always perform as well as drives that you created as NTFS drives from the outset. The main problem is that the Convert utility may not be able to place the MFT in the same location as it would appear on a drive that's formatted with NTFS at the outset. The additional head movement causes the drop in performance. The converted drive security setup may differ from the original drive as well. Make sure you read the Knowledge Base article at `http://support.microsoft.com/kb/237399` for additional information about security changes that can occur as the result of a conversion.

Improving Disk Access Performance with the Defrag Utility

As your hard drive processes files, it becomes fragmented; a file may appear in several segments on the hard drive. Moving the disk head to read each of these file segments is time consuming and hurts the performance of your system. Windows does provide a graphical interface for defragmenting your hard drive, but using the command line interface can be more efficient, especially when you automate the process so that it starts automatically. This utility uses the following syntax:

```
defrag <volume> [-a] [-f] [-v] [-?]
```

Vista supports these forms for the Defrag utility:

```
defrag <volume> -a [-v]
defrag <volume> [{-r | -w}] [-f] [-v]
defrag        -c [{-r | -w}] [-f] [-v]
```

The following list describes each of the command line arguments.

volume Specifies the drive letter or mount point to defragment.

-a Performs an analysis of the drive only. The analysis tells you whether the drive requires defragmentation, but doesn't actually perform the task. The output information includes the fragmentation percentage, which you can use as an indicator of drive condition. Don't use this command line option when you want to automate the defragmentation process.

-f Forces a defragmentation, even if the drive or mount point free space is low. Normally, the Defrag utility requires 15 percent free space to perform a complete defragmentation. Using this command line switch lets you perform a partial defragmentation when the free space is less than optimal.

-v Displays additional information about the defragmentation process.

VISTA

The following list describes the Vista-specific command line arguments.

-r Performs a partial defragmentation, which runs faster, but doesn't assure the hard drive will run at peak efficiency. Defrag only consolidates fragments smaller than 64 MB. This is the default setting under Vista.

-w Performs a full defragmentation of the drive regardless of fragment size. Although this option can improve performance on heavily fragmented drives, you pay a penalty in additional defragmentation time.

-c Performs defragmentation of all drives on the system. Combine this command line switch with the `-w` or `-r` command line switch to specify the level of defragmentation.

Compressing Files with the Diantz and MakeCAB Utilities

Most people assume that you need to use a third party compression product to create file archives with Windows. Of course, the ZIP file format is the most popular solution, but there are other alternatives, such as the RAR format supported by WinRAR (`http://www.rarlab.com/`). However, you can use the cabinet (CAB) file format without buying a third party utility. The only utility provided with newer Windows versions is MakeCAB. An older utility, Diantz, appears on the hard drive, but it calls MakeCAB. The CAB file appears in many places in Windows. For example, you'll find that Microsoft uses CABs to compress many application files on setup disks. In fact, there's even a Microsoft Cabinet Software Development Kit discussed at `http://support.microsoft.com/kb/310618/`. This utility uses the following syntax:

```
MAKECAB [/V[n]] [/D var=value ...] [/L dir] source [destination]
MAKECAB [/V[n]] [/D var=value ...] /F directive_file [...]
```

The following list describes each of the command line arguments.

source Specifies the name of the file you want to compress. Unlike many Windows utilities, you can't use wildcards to create a file specification. Provide a source filename when you want to compress a single file or a directive file when you want to compress multiple files.

destination Specifies the name of the destination file. When you specify a source file without a destination filename, the utility creates a file with an underscore that replaces the last letter of the file extensions. For example, when you type **`MakeCAB NewFile.txt`** and press Enter, the utility produces an output file with the name `NewFile.tx_`.

/F *directive_file* Specifies the name of a Diamond Directive File (DDF) that contains instructions for creating complex archives. You can specify multiple files, some of which are compressed and others that aren't. Using a DDF, you can create an archive that spans multiple disks. The `MAKECAB.DOC` file in the `\cabsdk\DOCS` directory of the Microsoft Cabinet Software Development Kit tells how to create a DDF.

/D *var=value* Defines variable settings for the MakeCAB utility. These variables control how MakeCAB works. For example, you can tell MakeCAB to create an archive without compressing any of the files by using the `COMPRESS=OFF` directive. You can find a complete list of variables and their associated values in section "4.2.2. Variable Summary" of the Microsoft Cabinet Software Development Kit.

/L *dir* Specifies the directory to use to store the archive. The default setting uses the current directory.

/V[*n*] Specifies a level of verbosity for the compression messages. The utility accepts any value between 1 and 3. The default setting is 1, which provides major messages and a completion message. The second verbosity level provides a list of files in the archive as the utility compresses them. The third verbosity level includes compression levels and other activities.

Managing Partitions with the DiskPart Utility

The DiskPart utility lets you manage partitions on your hard drive without relying on the graphical utilities. In some cases, this utility is your only resource when the graphical environment isn't running and you need to make a repair. You can use DiskPart with direct command line input, or supply a text file containing a script of actions for DiskPart to perform. You'll usually have a better experience with DiskPart if you create a script to perform the required tasks. Using a script reduces the potential for error. To use a script, type **`DiskPart /s`** ***`ScriptName`*** and press Enter. Otherwise, start the command line version of DiskPart by typing **`DiskPart`** and pressing Enter. You'll see the `DISKPART>` prompt where you enter the specific subcommands described in the following list.

`active` Marks the partition with focus as active. Making a partition active informs the Basic Input/Output System (BIOS) or Extensible Firmware Interface (EFI) that the partition is a valid system partition that the system can use to boot. If you mark a partition that doesn't contain system files active, the system may not boot. DiskPart doesn't check your partition selection for accuracy.

`add disk=`*`n`* *[noerr]* Mirrors a simple volume with the focus set to the specified disk. The disk must contain enough unallocated space to match the size of the simple volume that you want to mirror.

NOTE Use the `noerr` option only with scripts. Normally, a script will end when it encounters an error. Using the `noerr` option lets the script continue running.

`assign [{letter=D | mount=Path}] [noerr]` Assigns a drive letter or mount point to the volume with focus. If you don't specify a drive letter or mount point, the utility uses the next available drive letter. The utility generates an error when you attempt to assign an existing drive letter to the volume. The system won't allow you to assign drive letters to system volumes, boot volumes, or volumes that contain the paging file. In addition, you can't assign a drive letter to an Original Equipment Manufacturer (OEM) partition or any GUID Partition Table (GPT) partition other than a basic data partition.

`attributes` ***`volume`*** *[{set | clear}] [{hidden | readonly | nodefaultdriveletter | shadowcopy}] [noerr]* Displays, sets, or clears attributes on the specified volume. This command is only available on Windows 2003 and above systems. Use attributes with a volume specification alone to see the attributes for that volume. The set option adds an attribute, while the clear option removes the attribute. The `hidden` attribute hides the volume from view, while the `readonly` attribute makes it impossible for the user to write to the volume. The `nodefaultdriveletter` attribute prevents the drive from receiving a drive letter during the boot cycle. Generally, there isn't a good reason to use this feature unless you want to create an invisible drive for a specific reason, such as a ghost backup of the system. The `shadowcopy` attribute defines the drive as a shadow copy of another drive. You can obtain a good overview of the Windows VSS at `http://computerperformance.co.uk/w2k3/disaster_volume_shadow.htm`.

`automount [enable] [disable] [scrub] [noerr]` Defines the automatic mounting functionality that Windows provides. Normally, Windows automatically mounts any new basic disks that it finds during the boot cycle. The enable option enables automatic basic disk mounting. The disable option disables the automatic mounting feature. The scrub object removes any mount point directories and registry settings for volumes that are no longer in the system. This feature ensures that each new drive that you mount or remount receives a clean setup and that Windows doesn't attempt to use old and possibly incorrect settings. This command is only available on Windows 2003 and above systems.

break disk disk=*N* *[nokeep] [noerr]* Breaks mirrored volumes into two simple volumes. You can only use this command with dynamic disks. The first disk in the set retains the current drive letter and any mount points. The second disk receives the focus so that you can assign it a new drive letter. The nokeep option tells the utility to free any data on the second disk. The second disk becomes a new empty disk that you can format and use as a simple volume.

clean [all] Removes the partition and volume formatting on the disk with focus. The system overwrites the Master Boot Record (MBR) partitioning information and hidden section information on MBR disks. The system overwrites the GPT partitioning information, including the Protective MBR, on GPT disks. A GPT disk doesn't include hidden sector information. The system completely erases the disk when you use the all option.

convert basic [noerr] Converts an empty dynamic disk into a basic disk.

NOTE The system won't convert a disk that has data on it. Back up the hard drive data and remove the partitions and volumes before you perform a conversion. This same note holds true for any conversion you want to perform.

convert dynamic [noerr] Converts an empty basic disk into a dynamic disk.

convert gpt [noerr] Converts an empty basic disk that relies on the MBR partition style into an empty basic disk that relies on the GPT partition style.

TIP The GPT partition style has significant advantages over the MBR partition style. See the Microsoft article at `http://www.microsoft.com/resources/documentation/Windows/XP/all/reskit/en-us/prkb_cnc_ywwc.asp` for a comparison of the two technologies.

convert mbr [noerr] Converts an empty basic disk that relies on the GPT partition style into an empty basic disk that relies on the MBR partition style.

create partition efi [size=*N*] *[offset=N] [noerr]* Creates an EFI partition on a GPT disk. You must have an Itanium computer to use this feature. The utility gives the new partition the focus once the system creates it. The size argument defines the size of the partition in megabytes. The utility uses all of the free space on the disk when you don't specify this option. The offset argument defines the byte offset of the new partition. If you don't specify an offset, the utility creates the partition at the beginning of the first disk extant that's large enough to hold it.

create partition extended [size=*N*] *[offset=N] [noerr]* Creates an extended partition on the current drive. The utility gives the new partition the focus once the system creates it. A disk can only have one extended partition. You must create an extended partition before you can create logical drives. The size argument defines the size of the partition. For example, if you specify a size of 500 MB, the system rounds the size of the partition up to 504 MB. The system uses all of the free space on the disk when you don't define a partition size. The offset only affects MBR disks. The offset defines the byte offset of the partition. If you don't specify an offset, the partition begins at the beginning of the free space on the disk. The system snaps the partition size to the cylinder size; it rounds the offset to the closest cylinder boundary. For example, if you specify an offset that's 27 MB and the cylinder size is 8 MB, the system rounds the offset to the 24 MB boundary.

create partition logical [size=*N*] [offset=*N*] [noerr] Creates a logical disk within an extended partition. The utility gives the new partition the focus once the system creates it. The system snaps the partition size to the cylinder size. For example, if you specify a size of 500 MB, the system rounds the size of the partition up to 504 MB. The system uses all of the free space on the disk when you don't define a partition size. The offset only affects MBR disks. The offset defines the byte offset of the partition. If you don't specify an offset, the partition begins at the beginning of the extended partition. The offset you specify must allow enough room for the partition defined by the size argument. If the offset won't allow enough space, the system changes the offset so that the logical disk can fit within the extended partition.

create partition msr [size=*N*] *[offset=N] [noerr]* Creates a Microsoft Reserved (MSR) partition on a GPT disk. The size argument defines the size of the partition in MB. The utility uses all of the free space on the disk when you don't specify this option. The offset argument defines the byte offset of the new partition. If you don't specify an offset, the utility creates the partition at the beginning of the first disk extant that's large enough to hold it. The offset is sector snapped. The system rounds up the value of the offset to fill an entire sector.

WARNING MSR partitions can cause a number of problems. The most significant problem is that Itanium computers won't mount an MSR partition. This means you can't store data on the partition or delete it; the partition ends up wasting space on the disk. In addition, GTP disks require a specific partition layout. Adding an MSR partition could disrupt the layout and make the disk unreadable. On GPT disks used to start Windows XP 64-bit Edition (Itanium), the EFI System partition is the first partition on the disk, followed by the MSR partition. GPT disks used only for data storage don't have an EFI System partition; the MSR partition is the first partition.

create partition primary[size=*N*] *[offset=N] [ID={***Byte** | ***GUID***}*] [align=N] [noerr]* Creates a primary partition on a disk. The utility gives the new partition the focus once the system creates it. The system snaps the partition size to the cylinder size. For example, if you specify a size of 500 MB, the system rounds the size of the partition up to 504 MB. The system uses all of the free space on the disk when you don't define a partition size. The offset only affects MBR disks. The offset defines the byte offset of the partition. If you don't specify an offset, the partition begins at the beginning of the extended partition. The offset you specify must allow enough room for the partition defined by the size argument. Microsoft sets the ID argument aside for OEMs. Never specify an ID for a GPT disk. Use the create partition EFI and create partition MSR as needed to set up GPT disks. When working with an MBR disk, you can use the ID to set the disk type. The MBR values include C12A7328-F81F-11D2-BA4B-00A0C93EC93B (EFI system partition), E3C9E316-0B5C-4DB8-817D-F92DF00215AE (MSR partition), EBD0A0A2-B9E5-4433-87C0-68B6B72699C7 (basic data partition), 5808C8AA-7E8F-42E0-85D2-E1E90434CFB3 (LDM Metadata partition on a dynamic disk), and AF9B60A0-1431-4F62-BC68-3311714A69AD (LDM Data partition on a dynamic disk). The `align` argument specifies the alignment of the primary partition on a disk that isn't cylinder aligned. You normally use this value for hardware Redundant Array of Inexpensive Disks (RAID) setups to improve performance. The value is the number of kilobytes from the beginning of the disk to the closest alignment boundary.

create volume raid [size=*N*] *disk=N,N,N[,N,...] [noerr]* Creates a RAID-5 volume based on three or more dynamic disks. The utility automatically changes focus to the new volume once the system creates it. The `size` argument specifies the amount of space that the RAID-5 volume consumes on each drive. When you don't specify the size, the utility creates the largest possible RAID-5 volume by using the maximum space on the smallest volume (or the maximum available space when the drives are the same size). The RAID-5 volume consumes the same amount of space on each disk. The `disk` argument defines which disks to use in the RAID-5 volume. The volume must contain at least three drives simply because of the way that RAID-5 works (you can find an overview of the various RAID levels at `http://www.microsoft.com/technet/prodtechnol/exchange/guides/E2k3HighAvGuide/02ed19b2-d2b3-4f77-8835-b4b0dd2f68f5.mspx`).

`create volume simple [size=`*`N`*`] [disk=`*`N`*`] [noerr]` Creates a simple volume. The utility automatically changes focus to the new volume once the system creates it. The size argument defines the size of the volume in megabytes. The utility uses the entire free space on the disk when you don't specify the size argument. The disk argument specifies the disk to receive the new volume. The utility uses the current disk when you don't specify the disk option.

`create volume stripe [size=`*`N`*`] disk=`*`N,N[,N,...]`*` [noerr]` Creates a striped volume using two or more dynamic disks. The utility automatically changes focus to the new volume once the system creates it. The `size` argument defines the amount of space the volume consumes on each drive. Every drive provides precisely the same amount of space toward the total volume size. The system uses all of the free space on the smallest drive when you don't provide the size argument. The `disk` argument specifies the drives to use to create the striped set. You must provide a minimum of two drives for a striped set.

`delete disk [noerr] [override]` Removes a missing dynamic disk from the disk list. The override option enables DiskPart to remove all of the simple volumes on a disk. When the disk contains half a mirrored volume, the system removes the half of the mirrored volume. This command fails on RAID-5 volumes.

`delete partition [noerr] [override]` Removes the partition with focus from the drive. You can't delete the system partition, boot partition, or any partition that contains the active paging file or crash dump (memory dump). Use the override argument to allow DiskPart to remove partitions of any type on a drive. Normally, DiskPart removes only data partitions from the drive.

WARNING Deleting a partition on a dynamic disk could delete all of the volumes on the disk and leave the disk in an unusable state. Always remove volumes on a dynamic disk using the `delete volume` command.

`delete volume [noerr]` Deletes the volume with focus from the drive. You can't delete the system volume, boot volume, or any volume that contains the active paging file or crash dump (memory dump).

`detail disk` Displays the properties of the disk with focus. In addition, this command shows any volumes on the disk.

`detail partition` Displays the properties of the partition with focus.

`detail volume` Displays the disks on which the current volume resides. You can use this command with a volume that spans multiple disks, such as a mirrored, striped, or RAID-5 volume.

`exit` Terminates the DiskPart session.

`extend [size=`*`N`*`] [disk=`*`N`*`] [noerr]` Extends the currently selected volume into the next contiguous unallocated space. The unallocated space must appear on the same disk. The unallocated space must also appear after the current partition; the sector number of the unallocated space must be higher than the sector number of the currently selected volume. This command only works for NTFS-formatted volumes. The `size` argument defines the amount of space to add to the current partition. If you don't specify the `size` argument, the system uses all of the contiguous unallocated space. The `disk` argument applies to dynamic disks. Use this argument to specify the dynamic disk to use to extend the volume. If you don't specify the `disk` argument, the system uses the current disk.

`gpt attributes=`*`N`* Applies the specified attributes to a GPT disk. The GPT attribute field is 64-bits long and contains two subfields. The higher subfield applies only to partition identifiers; the lower subfield applies to all identifiers. Currently, the file system only supports two attributes. The 0x0000000000000001 attribute defines a required partition. Adding this attribute means that disk utilities won't delete the partition for any reason. The 0x8000000000000000 attribute tells the system not to automatically assign the drive a drive letter. The main purpose for this attribute is to ensure the system won't automatically assign a drive letter when you move the drive to another machine. Using this feature allows the user of the other machine to assign a drive letter based on that machine's configuration. This command is only available on Windows 2003 and above systems.

`help` Displays a list of DiskPart commands.

`import [noerr]` Imports a foreign disk group into the local computer's disk group. This command imports every disk that's in the same group as the disk that has focus.

`inactive` Marks the current MBR disk partition inactive, which means you can no longer boot from the partition. When the computer reboots, the system will start using the next available boot option specified in the BIOS, such as a CD-ROM drive or a Pre-Boot eXecution Environment (PXE)–based boot environment. A PXE can include Remote Installation Services (RIS). Some computers won't restart without an active partition, so use this command with care. If you're unable to start your computer after marking the system or boot partition as inactive, insert the Setup CD in the CD-ROM drive, restart the computer, and repair the partition using the FixMBR and FixBoot utilities from the Recovery Console.

`list disk` Lists the disks installed and detected for the current machine. The output includes the disk number, disk status, total disk size, amount of free space, whether the disk is basic or dynamic, and the GPT style. The disk with the asterisk (*) is the one with focus.

`list partition` Lists the partitions for the currently selected disk. The output includes the partition number, the partition size, the partition type, and the offset of the partition from the beginning of the disk. On dynamic disks, these partitions may not correspond to the dynamic volumes on the disk. This discrepancy occurs because dynamic disks contain entries in the partition table for the system volume or boot volume (if present on the disk). The partition with the asterisk (*) is the one with focus.

`list volume` Lists the volumes on all disks for the current machine. The output includes the volume number, the volume drive letter, the volume label, the file system used to support the volume, the volume type (such as partition, DVD-ROM, or CD-ROM), the volume size, the volume status, and information about the volume purpose (such as a system or a boot drive). The volume with the asterisk (*) is the one with focus.

`online [noerr]` Brings the offline volume with focus online. This command also resynchronizes the mirrored or RAID-5 volume.

`rem` Provides a means for making comments in scripts. You won't use this command in interactive mode.

`remove [{letter=`*`D`* | *mount=*`Path` | *all}] [dismount] [noerr]* Removes a drive letter or mount point from the drive with focus. If you don't specify a drive letter or mount point, the utility removes the first drive letter or mount point that it encounters. The letter option specifies the drive letter that you want to remove. The mount option specifies the path of the mount point that you want to remove. Use the all option to remove all of the drive letters and mount paths for a drive. The dismount option takes the drive offline when it no longer has any drive letters or mount points assigned to it. You can't access a dismounted drive. You can't remove the drive letters on system, boot, paging volumes, OEM partition, any GPT partition with an unrecognized GUID, or any of the special, nondata, GPT partitions such as the EFI system partition.

`repair disk=N` *[noerr]* Repairs the RAID-5 volume with focus by replacing a failed RAID-5 member with the specified dynamic disk. The new disk must have free space equal to or greater than the disk that it replaces.

`rescan` Locates any new disks that you've added to the computer.

`retain` Prepares an existing simple volume for use as a boot or system volume. When working with an MBR disk, the utility adds the partition entry to the MBR. The dynamic system volume must begin at a cylinder-aligned offset and be an integral number of cylinders in size. When working with a GPT disk, the utility creates a partition entry in the GPT.

`select disk[=n]` Selects the specified disk and gives it focus. If you don't provide a number, the utility lists the drive that has the focus.

`select partition[=n]` Selects the specified partition and gives it focus. If you don't provide a number, the utility lists the partition that has the focus.

`select volume[={n | d }]` Selects the specified volume and gives it focus. You may provide either a volume number or a drive letter as input. If you don't provide a number or letter, the utility lists the volume that has the focus.

Mounting a Volume with the MountVol Utility

The MountVol utility helps you create, delete, and list mount points. You can use this utility to manage mount points without using a drive letter. Windows 2003 provides functionality that older versions of Windows don't provide. You can't use the Windows 2003 version of the utility on older Windows versions since these older versions won't provide the required support as part of the file system. This utility uses the following syntax:

```
MOUNTVOL [drive:]path VolumeName
MOUNTVOL [drive:]path /D
MOUNTVOL [drive:]path /L
```

VISTA

Windows 2003 and Vista support some additional syntax options that include:

```
MOUNTVOL [drive:]path /P
MOUNTVOL /R
MOUNTVOL /N
MOUNTVOL /E
MOUNTVOL drive:/S
```

Vista doesn't support the /S command line switch. The following list describes each of the command line arguments.

`[drive:]path` Specifies the existing NTFS directory to use for the mount point. When you don't specify the drive, the utility assumes you want to use the current drive. You can use an absolute or relative path.

`VolumeName` Specifies the name of the volume that you want to make the target of the mount point.

/D Removes the volume mount point from the specified directory.

/L Lists the mounted volume name for the specified directory. If the directory doesn't include a mount point, the utility displays an "The file or directory is not a reparse point." error message.

/P Removes the volume mount point from the specified directory. The system dismounts the basic volume at this point and takes the volume offline, which makes it unmountable. When other processes are using the volume, the system closes any open handles before dismounting the volume. The system marks volumes dismounted using this technique with the `NOT MOUNTED UNTIL A VOLUME MOUNT POINT IS CREATED` attribute. If the volume has additional mount points, remove them first using the `/D` command line switch. You can recreate the basic volume by assigning the volume a mount point.

/R Removes the volume mount point directories. In addition, this command line switch removes the registry settings for volumes that are no longer in the system. This approach prevents the system from mounting new volumes automatically and using the previously assigned mount points.

/N Disables automatic mounting of new basic volumes. After you use this command line switch, the system won't automatically mount new volumes when you add them to the system.

/E Enables automatic mounting of new basic volumes. This is the default setting for a new system.

/S Mounts the EFI system partition on the specified drive. You can use this command line switch only on Itanium-based computers.

Managing Disk Performance with the DiskPerf Utility

The original purpose of the DiskPerf utility was to help you control monitoring of disk performance on your computer. However, systems later than Windows 2000 keep the counters used to monitor performance enabled permanently. Consequently, the main purpose this utility serves on later systems is to let you see which performance counters Windows provides, which is still a useful function when you want to monitor these counters at the command line.

The DiskPerf utility can also temporarily disable the performance counters. You can use this feature with older applications that rely on the Windows API `IOCTL_DISK_PERFORMANCE()` function to retrieve raw counter information (see the description of this function at `http://msdn2.microsoft.com/en-us/library/aa365183.aspx`). Don't reboot the system when you disable the counters because the effect is temporary; rebooting the machine will simply remove the effect. This utility uses the following syntax:

```
DISKPERF [-Y[D|V] | -N[D|V]] [\\computername]
```

The following list describes each of the command line arguments.

-Y Sets the system to start all performance counters when you start the system on older systems. This command line switch restarts all of the disk performance counters on Windows 2000 and above systems. The performance counters always start automatically on these systems after a reboot.

-YD Enables the disk performance counters for physical drives when you start the system.

-YV Enables the disk performance counters for logical drives or storage volumes when you start the system.

-N Sets the system to disable all performance counters when you start the system on older systems. This command temporarily disables all of the disk performance counters on Windows 2000 and later systems.

-ND Disables the performance counters for physical drives.

-NV Disables the disk performance counters for logical drives.

computername Specifies the name of the computer. Using this argument alone lets you see the list of disk performance counters. Adding a command line switch changes the performance counter setting.

Managing RAID Setups Using the DiskRAID Utility

VISTA

The DiskRAID utility helps you work with any Redundant Array of Inexpensive Disks (RAID) hardware on your system. However, there are some caveats for using this utility. The biggest problem is that your system must have the appropriate Virtual Disk Service (VDS) drivers installed—something that isn't supported by all vendors. In addition, except for the command line syntax, the VDS software apparently has vendor-specific commands. Consequently, you'll need to refer to the vendor documentation to use this utility fully. This utility uses the following syntax:

```
DISKRAID [/? | [/s <file-path>] [/v]]
```

The following list describes each of the command line arguments.

/? Displays the DiskRAID usage instructions.

/s *file-path* Specifies the location of a file containing commands that DiskRAID should execute. The instructions found in this script file depend on the vendor implementation.

/v Executes all DiskRAID commands in verbose mode. You'll see additional output. The amount and type of information depends on the vendor implementation.

Employing Low-Level Utilities

The low-level utilities that Windows provides affect the system in some way. You might use one to shut down a system or to view the internal workings of an executable program. The point is that these low-level utilities won't see daily use and novice users definitely shouldn't use them for any reason. Even though most of these utilities won't damage your system permanently, they can cause enough of a disruption that you could lose many hours fixing the problems they cause. In short, use these utilities only when you need to and then only when you understand what they do.

Examining, Modifying, and Debugging Files with the Debug Utility

Microsoft originally intended the Debug utility to help developers debug assembly language applications. You can still use the utility for that purpose, but the number of assembly language programs still in use is very small. In fact, it's likely that you'll never see an application originally written in assembler.

Fortunately, the Debug utility does have other purposes. For example, you can use it to view hidden information in executable files. Application developers leave many notes inside applications and it's often helpful to view these messages when deciding on the alternative uses of a utility. You can also locate copyright information in files when you want to know more about the file. Sometimes, you can also use the Debug utility to locate information in data files or make quick fixes to damaged data files. Most people refer to this other use for Debug as hex (short for hexadecimal) editing. However, the Debug utility interface is archaic and many people find it hard to use. If you need low-level access to files regularly, you might want to invest in a third party utility for the task such as XVI32 (see the "Using XVI32 to View Files in Depth" section of Chapter 12 for details). This utility uses the following syntax:

```
DEBUG [[drive:][path]filename [testfile-parameters]]
```

The following list describes each of the command line arguments.

[drive:][path]filename Specifies the name of the file that you want to view, edit, or debug.

testfile-parameters Specifies the command line arguments required by the application you want to test. You never use this second argument to simply view or edit a file.

Converting Executables with the Exe2Bin Utility

The Exe2Bin utility converts an application from the Portable Executable (PE) format to the binary format. The main difference is in how the executable loads. At some time in the past, you needed to use this utility quite often to convert executable files because the linkers of the time didn't provide the required functionality, but now it's a relic that you might never use. The resulting binary file is smaller than the executable and may execute slightly faster. At a time when developers counted individual bits, this utility served an important purpose. This utility uses the following syntax:

```
EXE2BIN [drive1:][path1]input-file [[drive2:][path2]output-file]
```

The following list describes each of the command line arguments.

[drive1:][path1]input-file Specifies the location and name of the EXE file you want to convert. If you don't provide drive and path information, the utility assumes that you want to use the current drive and path.

[drive1:][path1]output-file Specifies the location and name of the binary file (usually with a COM extension) that you want to output. If you don't provide drive and path information, the utility assumes that you want to use the current drive and path.

Ensuring Proper Application Execution with the ForceDOS Utility

VISTA

The ForceDOS utility is a compatibility program. You use it to start DOS applications in the MS-DOS subsystem that Windows provides. The only time you need to use this utility is when Windows consistently attempts to start a DOS application in Windows mode. Note that this utility isn't available in the 64-bit versions of Windows, but it's hardly likely that the applications that ForceDOS addresses will run in this environment anyway. Likewise, Microsoft has discontinued the ForceDOS utility for all versions of Vista. This utility uses the following syntax:

```
FORCEDOS [/D directory] filename [parameters]
```

The following list describes each of the command line arguments.

/D directory Specifies the working directory that the specified application will use. The working directory information helps the application find ancillary files.

filename Specifies the name of the application that you want to start.

parameters Specifies the command line arguments to pass to the application.

Terminating a Session Using the Logoff Utility

The Logoff utility ends a user session and logs off the user. The advantage of this utility is that you can find it in older versions of Windows, so you can use the same script on just about any machine. The disadvantage of this utility is that it provides limited functionality. The ShutDown utility, described in the "Shutting Down the System with the ShutDown Utility" section of the chapter, is far more capable and you should use it whenever possible. This utility uses the following syntax:

```
LOGOFF [sessionname | sessionid] [/SERVER:servername] [/V]
```

The following list describes each of the command line arguments.

sessionname Defines the name of the session that you want to log off. Older versions of the tool don't provide this argument. The default is to log off the current session.

sessionid Defines the identifier of the session that you want to log off.

/SERVER:*servername* Specifies the server containing the user session to log off. Some documentation implies that you need Terminal Server to use this command line switch, but it appears to work just as well without it.

/V Displays detailed information about the actions the system performs during the logoff cycle.

Performing System-Level Debugging with the NTSD Utility

The New Technology Symbolic Debugger (NTSD) is the Windows form of the Debug utility in that you can use it to debug Windows applications. However, that's where the similarities end. Unlike DOS applications, Windows applications require a lot of support from the operating system. Consequently, you can use this utility to perform a number of non-debugging tasks on applications. For example, you can use it to determine which DLLs an application requires to run. Try typing **NTSD Notepad.EXE** in the `\Windows` directory at the command prompt and press Enter. You'll see a display similar to the one shown in Figure 6.2. Notice that the utility begins by loading all of the required modules for `Notepad.EXE`. The list begins with `Notepad.EXE` of course, but then moves on to `NTDLL.DLL` and other DLLs that the application requires. Type **Q** and press Enter to exit the debugger. Unfortunately, Vista seems to lack support for this utility.

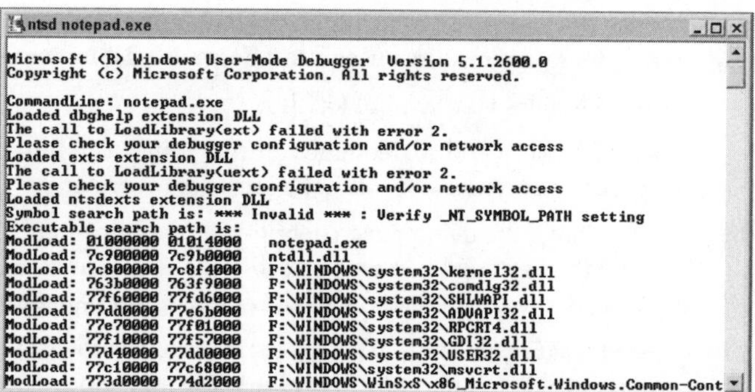

FIGURE 6.2
The NTSD utility can help you debug a Windows application or simply learn which DLLs it uses.

This chapter can't provide you with a tutorial on using NTSD. You'll find a good overview of this utility at `http://www.codeproject.com/debug/cdbntsd.asp`. Note that Microsoft doesn't provide the CDB and WinDbg debuggers mentioned in the article with Windows, so you can't try them out. The advantage of NTSD is that Microsoft does supply it with Windows, so it's always available for use. The article at `http://www.debuginfo.com/articles/ntsdwatson.html` tells how you can use NTSD as an alternative to Dr. Watson. In many cases, NTSD will lead you to a solution to the problem that Dr. Watson won't provide. This utility uses the following syntax:

```
ntsd [-?] [-2] [-d] [-g] [-G] [-myob] [-lines] [-n] [-o] [-s] [-v] [-w]
    [-r BreakErrorLevel]  [-t PrintErrorLevel] [-hd] [-pd] [-pe] [-pt #]
    [-pv] [-x | -x{e|d|n|i} <event>] [-- | -p pid | -pn name | command-
    line | -z CrashDmpFile] [-zp CrashPageFile] [-premote transport]
    [-robp] [-aDllName] [-c "command"] [-i ImagePath] [-y SymbolsPath]
    [-clines #] [-srcpath SourcePath] [-QR \\machine] [-wake <pid>]
    [-remote transport:server=name,portid] [-server transport:portid]
    [-ses] [-sfce] [-sicv] [-snul] [-noio] [-failinc] [-noshell]
```

Notice that this syntax contains multiple instances of some letters. NTSD treats uppercase and lowercase letters differently, so make sure you use the proper case when you type a command line switch. The following list describes each of the command line arguments.

-2 Creates a separate console window for the debuggee (the application you're debugging).

-d Sends all of the debugger output to the kernel mode debugger using the DbgPrint debugger extension. You can't use this command line switch with debugger remoting. In addition, you can only use this command line switch when you've enabled the kernel mode debugger.

-g Ignores the initial breakpoint in the debuggee. Normally, this means you'll see the interface for any graphical application.

-G Ignores the final breakpoint at process termination. Normally, this means that you won't see all of the cleanup activities that the application performs before it exits.

-myob Ignores version mismatches in the `DBGHELP.DLL` file.

-lines Displays line number information when the application's debugging files provide this information.

-n Enables verbose output from the symbol handler. Using this command line switch can provide you with additional information about variables used in the application.

-o Debugs all of the processes launched by the debuggee. Using this command line switch not only lets you see all of the interactions between the application and the processes it launches, it also increases resource usage and degrades debugger performance.

-s Disables lazy symbol loading.

-v Enables verbose debugger output, which can improve the amount of information you receive, but can also result in information overload.

-w Forces the debugger to debug 16-bit applications in a separate Virtual DOS Machine (VDM). Normally, you won't need to use this command line switch with newer versions of Windows since these versions don't have 16-bit applications loaded.

-r *BreakErrorLevel* Defines the error level at which the debugger pauses application execution (break). You may use any value between 0 and 3. A higher value breaks application execution at more critical errors.

-t *PrintErrorLevel* Defines the error level at which the debugger displays an error message. You may use any value between 0 and 3. A higher value breaks application execution at more critical errors.

-hd Forces the debugger to avoid using the debug heap for created processes. This option only works on Windows XP and above.

-pd Forces the debugger to detach from the created process automatically.

-pe Specifies that any attachment to a process should use an existing debug port.

-pt # Specifies the interrupt timeout value.

-pv Specifies that the debugger should use noninvasive methods to attach to a process.

-x Sets the second-chance break on Access Violation (AV) exceptions. You can find a discussion of this technique IIS applications at `http://www.microsoft.com/technet/archive/interopmigration/linux/mvc/debugdst.mspx`.

-x{e|d|n|i} event Sets the break status for a specified event. You must supply the event value, which is a two or three letter event name. For example, `wos` is the WOW64 single step event and `cc` is the Control-Break exception continue event. The command line switches are as follows: `-xe` enables the event, `-xd` disables the event (usually sets it as a second-chance break), `-xn` sets the event as output; and `-xi` sets the event as ignored.

-- Using this command line switch is the same as issuing the `-G`, `-g`, `-o`, `-p`, `-1`, `-d`, and `-pd` command line switches.

-p *pid* Specifies the Process Identifier (PID) (as a decimal number) of the running application that you want to attach to and debug.

-pn *name* Specifies the name of the process that you want to attach to and debug.

command-line Specifies the name of the application that you want to start and debug. Make sure you specify any command line arguments that the application requires as part of the command line.

-z *CrashDmpFile* Specifies the name of the crash dump file that you want to debug.

-zp *CrashPageFile* Specifies the name of a page dump file that you want to use with a crash dump file during debugging.

-premote *transport* Specifies the name of a process server to use to process transport arguments used with remoting.

-robp Allows the debugger to set breakpoints within read-only memory.

-a *DllName* Sets the default extension DLL.

-c "*command*" Executes the specified debugger command. Because most of the debugger commands include spaces, be sure to enclose the command in quotes.

-i *ImagePath* Specifies the location of the executables that generated the fault that you want to debug. You can also set this value using the `_NT_EXECUTABLE_IMAGE_PATH` environment variable.

-y *SymbolsPath* Specifies the symbol file search path. You can also set this value using the `_NT_SYMBOL_PATH` environment variable.

-clines # Specifies the number of lines of output history that a remote client retrieves.

-srcpath *SourcePath* Specifies the source file search path.

-QR *machine* Queries the specified machine for remote servers.

-wake *pid* Wakes the sleeping debugger identified by the specified process identifier and exits.

-remote *transport:server=name,portid* Defines a remote connection to a server. You must use this as the first argument when present. The transport arguments can include `tcp`, `npipe`, `ssl`, `spipe`, `1394`, or `com`. The `server` argument is the server that you want to use for debugging. The `name` argument is the name of the machine on which the debug server is running. The `portid` argument is the port that the debugger server is using for communication. When working with the TCP protocol, use the port number. The `npipe` transport relies on the name of the pipe. A `1394` (FireWire) connection relies on the channel number. A `com` transport requires the COM port number, the baud rate, and channel number. See the vendor documentation when creating an `ssl` or `spipe` transport connection.

-server *transport:portid* Creates a debugger session that other people can access from a remote location. You must use this as the first argument when present. The transport arguments include `tcp`, `npipe`, `ssl`, `spipe`, `1394`, or `com`. The `portid` argument is the port that the debugger server is using for communication. When working with the TCP protocol, use the port number. The `npipe` transport relies on the name of the pipe. A `1394` (FireWire) connection relies on the channel number. A `com` transport requires the COM port number, the baud rate, and channel number. See the vendor documentation when creating an `ssl` or `spipe` transport connection.

-ses Enables strict symbol loading.

-sfce Fails critical errors that the debugger encounters during file searching.

-sicv Ignores the Compiler Violation (CV) record when symbol loading.

-snul Disables automatic symbol loading for unqualified names.

-noio Disables all I/O for dedicated remoting servers.

-failinc Forces incomplete symbol and module loads to fail.

-noshell Disables the shell (!!) command.

Unlike many other utilities described in this book, the NTSD utility includes a number of specialized features. One of those features is the ability to change NTSD performance using environment variables. Other utilities such as the `Copy` command do have this feature, but not to the extent that NTSD has used it. Here's a list of environment variables that you can use.

_NT_SYMBOL_PATH=[*Drive:*][*Path*] Defines the symbol image path.

_NT_ALT_SYMBOL_PATH=[*Drive:*][*Path*] Defines an alternate symbol image path.

_NT_DEBUGGER_EXTENSION_PATH=[*Drive:*][*Path*] Specifies the path that the debugger should search first for extensions DLLs.

_NT_EXECUTABLE_IMAGE_PATH=[*Drive:*][*Path*] Specifies the path the debugger should use when searching for an executable image to debug.

_NT_SOURCE_PATH=[*Drive:*][*Path*] Defines the search path for the source code files associated with the application you want to debug.

_NT_DEBUG_LOG_FILE_OPEN=*filename* Specifies a file to use for all output from the debugging session. The debugger always overwrites the file and begins at offset 0.

_NT_DEBUG_LOG_FILE_APPEND=*filename* Specifies a file to use for all output from the debugging session. In this case, the output is appended to the file, which preserves data from previous debugging sessions.

_NT_DEBUG_HISTORY_SIZE=*size* Specifies the size of the debugging server's output history in kilobytes.

You'll also want to know about some of the control key combinations the NTSD utility provides. The following list is the most commonly used control key combinations.

Ctrl+B, Enter Quit the debugger

Ctrl+C Break into the target application.

Ctrl+F, Enter Break into the target application (same as Ctrl+C).

Ctrl+P, Enter Debug the current remote debugger.

Ctrl+V, Enter Toggle the verbose display mode.

Ctrl+W, Enter Print version information.

Managing Compatibility Databases with SDBInst

The SDBInst utility helps you manage and maintain application databases. In fact, these databases often support application patches. Microsoft often uses the SDBInst utility to provide patches for all their products including Office and Windows. As an example of one of these patches (and there are many) check the Knowledge Base article at `http://support.microsoft.com/?kbid=328597`. Lest you think that this utility is a Microsoft invention, check the MySQL Web site at `http://dev.mysql.com/doc/maxdb/en/1f/906b3c12904d04e10000000a114084/content.htm`. You'll notice that not only does SDBInst have a place in other vendor application deployments, it exists on both the Windows and the Linux platforms (as shown by the instructions for both platforms on the Web site) as well.

The SDBInst program supports a special Solution Database (SDB) (or Support Database) file. Many vendors provide utilities for creating these files. For example, you'll find the instructions for producing SDB files using a utility from SoftwareBisque at `http://www.bisque.com/thesky/tom/whatisdb.asp`.

You can use SDBInst to install and uninstall SDB files. Uninstalling an SDB usually results in removing the patch that you applied to an application or operating system. This utility uses the following syntax (the first syntax installs a file, while the second uninstalls it):

```
SDBInst [-q] SDBFilename
SDBInst [-q] [-u SDBFilename] [-g GUID] [-n "Name"]
```

Vista supports this extended version of SDBInst (the basic functionality is the same):

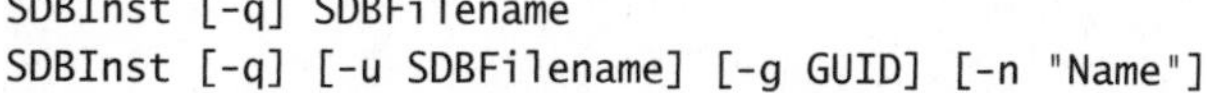

```
SDBInst [-q] [-u SDBFilename] [-g GUID] [-p] [-n "Name"] SDBFilename
```

The following list describes each of the command line arguments.

-q Forces the utility to rely on quiet mode. The utility doesn't display any dialog boxes to the user.

SDBFilename Specifies the name of the SDB file that you want to install on the system.

-u *SDBFilename* Specifies that you want to uninstall an SDB patch using a reference to the original SDB file.

-g *GUID* Specifies that you want to uninstall an SDB patch using the GUID of the patch as defined in the registry.

-n "*Name*" Specifies that you want to uninstall an SDB patch using the patch name. The patch name often appears in the Add or Remove Programs dialog box that you can access using the Add or Remove Programs applet in the Control Panel.

VISTA

The following list describes the Vista-specific command line arguments.

-p Allows SDB files to contain patches.

Accessing Functions within DLLs

It's easy to think of a command as a built-in function within CMD.EXE and a utility as an external application that you run. However, the command line presents a third alternative, one that you might not have ever considered. The RunDLL32.EXE file is a utility that you can't run directly. Instead, you feed it a DLL that contains one or more externally accessible functions and add any arguments that the function requires as part of your input. For example, let's say you want to add a beep to your batch file. You can use the MessageBeep() function found in the User32.DLL file by adding this command to a batch file or script.

```
RunDLL32 User32.DLL,MessageBeep
```

Notice that you type the utility name, **RunDLL32**, followed by the name of the DLL, **User32.DLL**, and the name of the function, **MessageBeep()**. Note that the capitalization of the function you call is important; MessageBeep isn't the same as messagebeep.

You have many resources for learning how to use this particular command line feature. The best place to begin learning is the Registry. Simply open the RegEdit utility and search for RunDLL32 entries by selecting the Edit ➤ Find command and typing **RunDLL32** in the Find What field. Figure 6.3 shows a typical entry. In this case, the example shows how to create a new LNK file using the RunDLL32 command.

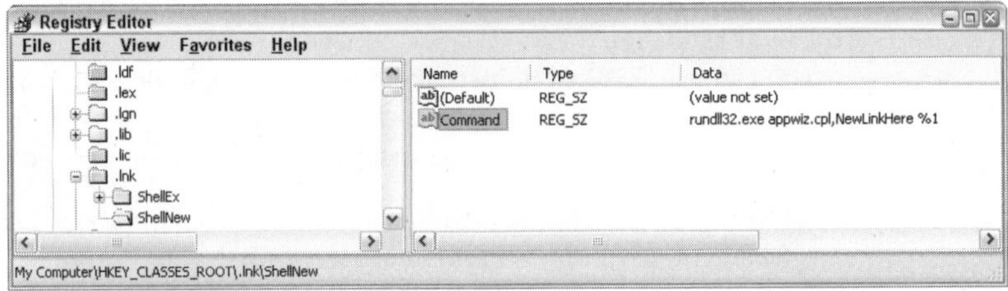

FIGURE 6.3 DLLs provide a lot of hidden functionality that you can access with RunDLL32.

This case is interesting in that you're not using what most people would consider a DLL file to accomplish the task. The AppWiz.CPL file is actually a Control Panel applet for the Add or Remove Programs applet. It just happens to provide the functionality needed to create a link. Notice that in this case you pass the name of the link to the function. Replace any variable entries, %1 in this case, with the actual variable you want to use when working at the command line. You'll find a wealth of RunDLL32 tips online, including suggested command lines. Make sure you always understand what a command will do and verify its functionality before you actually use it. Some wannabe comedians will use their Web sites to get you to do odd and dangerous things to your computer. One of the better Web sites to try is Using Rundll at http://www.ericphelps.com/batch/rundll/.

The registry might not contain a solution for every need. You can look at the DLLs directly using an application such as Depends (Dependency Walker). This particular utility is used so often by developers that it has its own Web site at http://www.dependencywalker.com/ with appropriate download links for various platforms. Figure 6.4 shows a typical view of a DLL opened in the Depends utility. Most of the information displayed in this figure has nothing to do with the command line and you can ignore it. However, the second window on the right side of the display shows the list of functions in the DLL. Notice that Figure 6.4 shows the MessageBeep() function highlighted.

Of course, Depends won't tell you what task the function performs or how to use it. To an extent, you're left on your own on usage details and you'll definitely want to spend time online looking for suggestions. However, you can get complete details on the function when working with any Microsoft DLL on the MSDN Library Web site at `http://msdn.microsoft.com/library/`. Simply type the function name in the Search For field and click Search. Other vendors usually provide similar documentation that you can use to learn more about the functions on their Web sites within DLLs.

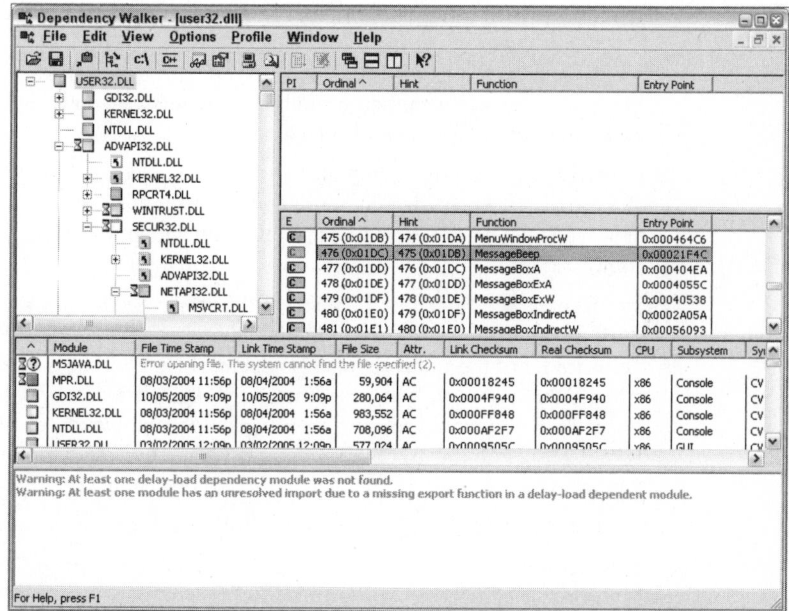

FIGURE 6.4
Look for interesting functions to run in DLLs using the Depends utility.

WARNING Vista places significant security restrictions on users. Consequently, some RunDLL32 solutions that worked in the past might not work today. Always test a RunDLL32 solution using the same privileges as the anticipated user, rather than your own privileges, which are very likely more inclusive.

Uninstalling the Operating System with the OSUninst Utility

If you've ever wondered how to remove Windows from a system, the OSUninst utility answers the question. Vista, however, doesn't provide any means of uninstall, so you won't find the OSUninst utility when using Vista. The OSUninst utility is one of the few that doesn't have a command line as such. You don't need to type any command line switches to make this utility work. In fact, you can't even execute this utility while Windows is running. Microsoft provides a simple message telling you that you can't remove Windows and that's it. To use this utility, you start the machine in the Recovery Console by using your installation CD, or you can start the machine in Safe Mode at the command prompt. Don't start the GUI.

Once the system starts, locate the `\Windows\System32` directory. Type **`OSUninst`** at the command prompt and press Enter. Follow the directions to remove Windows from your machine.

Controlling Services with the SC Utility

The Service Control (SC) utility helps you control services on your machine. The control is at a low level. Although you can start, stop, pause, and continue services using other utilities, this utility lets you perform additional tasks, such as query the service for detailed status information, send it a change of configuration message, or enumerate the services that the target service depends on. This utility uses the following syntax:

```
sc [\\server] [command] [service name] [<option1> [<option2>...]]
```

The following list describes each of the command line arguments.

`\\server` Specifies the server that runs the service you want to manage. The default assumes that you want to use the local machine.

`command` Specifies the command you want to execute. For example, if you want to stop a service, you issue the `stop` command. Some commands can work alone or with a service name. To obtain a list of all of the services installed on a machine, type **`SC Query`** and press Enter at the command line.

`service_name` Specifies the name of the service that you want to manage. This name isn't the same as the name that you see displayed in the Services console located in the Administrative Tools folder of the Control Panel. The name also isn't the executable name for the service. This entry is the name that the service used for registration purposes. For example, to access the Event Log, you would use the eventlog service. However, the display name for this service is Event Log and the executable name is `Services.EXE`. Use the `SC Query` command to obtain a list of registered service names on the target system.

`option1 [option2...]` Provides additional information required by some commands.

The focus of this is the command that you issue to a service. The command determines what tasks the service performs. For example, when you issue a stop command, the service stops whatever it's doing at the time. The following list describes the common commands for all services. Theoretically, a vendor could (and many do) introduce custom commands for a particular service. You'll need to refer to the vendor documentation to discover these custom commands.

`query` Queries the status of a service or enumerates the services installed on the computer. The output from this command includes service name, type, state, Win32 exit code, service exit code, checkpoint, and wait hint. You don't need to provide a service name with this command. You can filter the output of this command by adding optional information described in the following list (make sure you include the space between the equals sign (=) and the setting).

`type={driver | service | all}` Specifies the kind of service to query. The default setting is a service.

`state={inactive | all}` Defines the state of the service to enumerate. The default setting is active.

`bufsize=`*`size`* Defines the size of the enumeration buffer in bytes. The default size is 4,096 bytes.

`ri=`*`index`* Specifies the resume index at which to begin the enumeration. This number starts the enumeration at a location other than the first entry. The default setting is 0.

`group=`*`group`* Defines which service groups to enumerate. The default setting is all groups.

queryex Queries the extended status of a service or enumerates the services installed on the computer. You can filter the output of this command by adding optional information as explained for the query command. The output from this command includes service name, type, state, Win32 exit code, service exit code, checkpoint, wait hint, PID, and flags. You don't need to provide a service name with this command.

start Starts the specified service.

pause Pauses the specified service. Pausing the service differs from stopping it. When you stop a service, the service returns all resources to the operating system and removes itself from memory. Pausing the service lets it maintain status information and the service remains in memory.

interrogate Queries the status of a specific service. The output from this command includes service name, type, state, Win32 exit code, service exit code, checkpoint, and wait hint.

continue Restarts the service after a pause. You can't issue this command for a stopped service; use the start command instead.

stop Stops the requested service. Stopping the service differs from pausing it. When you stop a service, the service returns all resources to the operating system and removes itself from memory. Pausing the service lets it maintain status information and the service remains in memory.

config Changes the service configuration. You must specify these changes using the options in the following list. Make sure you include the space between the equals sign (=) and the value.

> **type={own | share | interact | kernel | filesys | rec | adapt}** Defines the service type. Change this setting only if the vendor requests that you do so.
>
> **start={boot | system | auto | demand | disabled}** Defines the method the system uses to start the service. The auto option always starts the service when the system starts, while the disabled option prevents the service from ever starting.
>
> **error={normal | severe | critical | ignore}** Defines the method used to report service errors in the event log. Using the ignore option means that the system never reports errors for the service.
>
> **binPath=*BinaryPathName*** Specifies the location of the service's executable on the hard drive.
>
> **group=*LoadOrderGroup*** Specifies the service's group, which defines the order in which the service loads, among other things.
>
> **tag={yes | no}** Specifies whether the system obtains a tag identifier from the `CreateService()` function call. The system only uses tag identifiers for the boot-start and system-start drivers.
>
> **depend=*Dependencies*** Defines one or more dependencies for this service to start. The requested service must start before this service can start. Separate each of the dependencies with a slash (/).
>
> **obj=*AccountName* | *ObjectName*** Specifies an account name or a driver object name to use to run the service. This entry defines the security for the service. The default setting is the LocalSystem driver object.
>
> **DisplayName=*display_name*** Defines the name that the user sees in the Services console.
>
> **password=*password*** Specifies a password the service must use to log into the system. You don't need to provide a password for the LocalSystem driver object.

description Changes the description of a service.

failure Specifies the action the system should take in case of a service failure. You specify these actions using the following options.

reset=*interval* Defines the length of time that the service must wait in seconds before the system can reset the failure count to 0. You may specify a value of INFINITE to keep the failure count from ever resetting. Use this setting with the actions option.

reboot=*message* Defines the message to broadcast before rebooting the system due to a failure.

command=*command* Defines the command you want to run after a failure.

actions={run | reboot | restart}/delay Specifies an action to take, along with the delay time, for executing the action in milliseconds. For example, `run/5000` would attempt to run the service again after 5,000 milliseconds. You must also specify a reset interval when using an action.

failureflag [*ServiceName*] [*Flag*] Modifies the failure flag to a new value. You can use this command to set special failure flags that define the special circumstances of a failure (such as environmental factors). The default value of 0 tells the Service Control Manager (SCM) to use the configured failure actions on the service only when the service terminates in a state other than `SERVICE_STOPPED`. When you set this value to 1, the SCM performs the configuration failure actions whenever the service terminates with an exit code other than 0 (in addition to the actions performed with a flag value of 0). The system ignores this flag when the service lacks configured failure actions.

sidtype [*ServiceName*] [{Unrestricted | Restricted | None}] Changes the service Security Identifier (SID) type of the service. This change affects the service's ability to interact with the system by increasing or decreasing its privileges. In all three cases, the setting affects the content of the process token. When you specify a value of Unrestricted, the service's SID appears as part of the process token without restrictions. You can only use this level for Win32 user mode services. The Restricted setting also places the service's SID in the process token, but as a restricted token. You can learn more about restricted tokens at `http://msdn2.microsoft.com/en-us/library/aa379316.aspx`. Finally, the None setting doesn't add the service's SID to the process token.

privs [*ServiceName*] [*Privileges*] Modifies the privileges required to run the service. This command can keep unwary users from starting the service (even accidentally or through an application). You can see a listing of common privilege constants at `http://msdn2.microsoft.com/en-us/library/aa375728.aspx`.

qc Queries the specified service for configuration information. The output from this command includes service name, type, start type, error control, binary path name, load order group, tag, display name, dependencies, and service start name.

qdescription [*BufferSize*] Queries the description for a service. You can specify an optional buffer size argument for this command that defines the size of the buffer you've set aside for the description. When the buffer is too small, the utility returns a value that tells you the minimum buffer size.

qfailure [*BufferSize*] Queries the actions taken by a service when a failure occurs. You can specify an optional buffer size argument for this command that defines the size of the buffer you've set aside for the description. When the buffer is too small, the utility returns a value that tells you the minimum buffer size.

qfailureflag [*ServiceName*] Queries the failure actions flag of the service. You use this option for diagnostic purposes.

qsidtype [*ServiceName*] Queries the service's SID type.

qprivs [*ServiceName*] [*BufferSize*] Queries the privileges required to run the service. You can see a listing of common privilege constants at `http://msdn2.microsoft.com/en-us/library/aa375728.aspx`.

delete Removes a service from the registry, which means that the system won't activate it and that the service won't appear in the Services console.

create *ServiceName* *binPath=* Path Creates a service by querying the executable and adding any required entries to the registry. The creation process requires that you supply a service name and the path to the binary (executable) file. In addition, you can provide configuration options for the service as defined in the following list. Make sure you include the space between the equals sign (=) and the value.

- **type={own | share | interact | kernel | filesys | rec | adapt}** Defines the service type. Change this setting only if the vendor requests that you do so.
- **start={boot | system | auto | demand | disabled}** Defines the method the system uses to the start the service. The auto option always starts the service when the system starts, while the disabled option prevents the service from ever starting.
- **error={normal | severe | critical | ignore}** Defines the method used to report service errors in the event log. Using the ignore option means that the system never reports errors for the service.
- **binPath=*BinaryPathName*** Specifies the location of the service's executable on the hard drive.
- **group=*LoadOrderGroup*** Specifies the service's group, which defines the order in which the service loads, among other things.
- **tag={yes | no}** Specifies whether the system obtains a tag identifier from the `CreateService()` function call. The system only uses tag identifiers for the boot-start and system-start drivers.
- **depend=*Dependencies*** Defines one or more dependencies for this service to start. The requested service must start before this service can start. Separate each of the dependencies with a slash (/).
- **obj={*AccountName* | *ObjectName*}** Specifies an account name or a driver object name to use to run the service. This entry defines the security for the service. The default setting is the LocalSystem driver object.
- **DisplayName=*display_name*** Defines the name that the user sees in the Services console.
- **password=*password*** Specifies a password the service must use to log into the system. You don't need to provide a password for the LocalSystem driver object.

control *Value* Sends a control code to a service. Control codes generally ask the service to perform a task. The control code can be a standard value such as `paramchange`, `netbindadd`, `netbindremove`, `netbindenable`, or `netbinddisable`. Many services also provide custom control codes. You must obtain these custom codes from the vendor documentation.

sdshow Displays the security descriptor for a service in Security Descriptor Definition Language (SDDL) format. You can learn more about SDDL at `http://msdn2.microsoft.com/en-us/library/aa379567.aspx`.

sdset *SD* Sets the service's security descriptor. You must provide the security descriptor in SDDL format. You can learn more about SDDL at `http://msdn2.microsoft.com/en-us/library/aa379567.aspx`.

showsid *Name* Displays the SID string associated with a service based on the arbitrary name you provide as input. The name can be of an existing service or a service that doesn't exist on the local machine. The resulting string lets you query the security of a service.

GetDisplayName *KeyName [BufferSize]* Obtains the display name (the one shown in the Services console) for a service based on its key name. For example, when you enter a key name of eventlog, you receive a display name of Event Log. You can specify an optional buffer size argument for this command that defines the size of the buffer you've set aside for the description. When the buffer is too small, the utility returns a value that tells you the minimum buffer size.

GetKeyName "*DisplayName*" *[BufferSize]* Obtains the key name (the one used for most SC utility commands) for a service based on its display name. For example, when you enter a display name of Event Log, the utility returns a key name of event log. Make sure you enclose the display name in quotes. You can specify an optional buffer size argument for this command that defines the size of the buffer you've set aside for the description. When the buffer is too small, the utility returns a value that tells you the minimum buffer size.

EnumDepend *[BufferSize]* Enumerates the dependencies (the list of services that must be running before the service can start) for a service. You can specify an optional buffer size argument for this command that defines the size of the buffer you've set aside for the description. When the buffer is too small, the utility returns a value that tells you the minimum buffer size.

The SC utility has three special commands that affect the services as a whole, so they don't require a service name. The following list describes the three commands.

boot {ok | bad} Determines whether the system saves the last boot information into the last-known-good boot configuration.

Lock Locks the SCManager database. The command line will display a prompt that shows that the system has locked the database. The database remains locked until you press **u** to remove the lock.

QueryLock Returns the locked status of the SCManager database.

Shutting Down the System with the ShutDown Utility

The ShutDown utility lets you shut down a system in a controlled manner. In addition, the utility helps you document the reason for the shutdown and can even provide the user with a specific level of control over the shutdown process. You can even shut down other machines on the network, such as after the completion of an application installation. This utility uses the following syntax:

```
shutdown [/i | /l | /s | /r | /g | /a] [/f] [/m \\computername] [/t xx]
   [/c "comment"] [/d [u][p:]xx:yy]
shutdown [/i | /l | /s | /r | /g | /a | /p | /h | /e] [/f] [/m
   \\ComputerName] [/t XXX] [/d [p:] XX:YY/c"Comment"]
```

The first version is for Windows XP users, while the second is for Windows 2003 users. The following list describes each of the command line arguments.

/i Displays the GUI version of the utility. You must supply this command line switch as the first option.

/l Logs off, rather than rebooting the system. You can't use this command line switch with the -m switch.

/s Shuts down the computer. In most cases, this means turning off the computer.

/r Shuts down and restarts the computer. This command line switch performs a soft boot of the system, which is all you need to ensure application changes take place as intended.

/g Shuts down and restarts the computer. After the system reboots, Vista automatically restarts any registered applications.

/a Aborts the system shutdown. Although you can stop a pending shutdown, it's usually difficult to stop a shutdown that's already in progress.

/m *computername* Specifies a remote computer to shut down, restart, or abort. You must have the rights required to perform these actions on the remote computer.

/t *xx* Specifies a timeout to perform the shutdown. The system defaults to a value of 30 seconds.

/c "*comment*" Provides a shutdown comment for the event log that details why you shut the system down. The comment can contain a maximum of 127 characters. You must use this command line switch with the -d switch. Always place the comment in quotes.

/f Forces any running applications to close without warning. Normally, the system warns the user of the shutdown and provides time for the user to react. Use this option with extreme caution because it can result in data loss.

/d [u][p]:*xx*:*yy* Specifies a reason for the shutdown. This reason appears as part of the event log entry. The u argument defines the shutdown as user related. If you don't provide the u argument, the system assumes that the shutdown somehow relates to a system need. The p argument defines the shutdown as planned. If you don't provide the p argument, the system assumes the shutdown was unplanned—part of an emergency. The p argument is important because it affects whether the ShutDown utility is successful. If you provide the p argument and then use an unplanned reason code, the utility registers an error. Likewise, if you omit the p argument and use a planned reason code, the utility registers an error. The xx argument is the major reason code. You may use any value between 0 and 255. The yy argument is the minor reason code. You may use any value between 0 and 65,535. Unfortunately, Microsoft doesn't document reason codes for this utility. However, your reason codes should match those of System Shutdown Reason Codes Web page at http://msdn2.microsoft.com/en-us/library/aa376885.aspx. If you want to use some other reason for shutting a system down, you must register the reason in the registry so the ShutDown utility can provide the correct text within the registry entry.

/p Turns off a local computer (you can't use this command line switch with a remote system) without a timeout period of user warning. You can only use this command line switch with the /d command line switch. If your computer doesn't support power off functionality, the system will shut down, but the computer will remain running.

/h Places the computer in the hibernation state when you have hibernation enabled. You can only use this command line switch with the /f switch. Since hibernation isn't the same as shutting the computer down, the utility doesn't allow you to provide a reason code using the /d command line switch or a comment using the /c command line switch.

/e Enables you to document the reason for an unexpected shutdown on the target computer. You must be part of the administrators group to document an unexpected shutdown.

TIP Many users complain about the amount of time spent waiting for Windows to shut down. You can greatly improve the shutdown speed by creating a new shortcut and adding this entry to the Target field, `%windir%\System32\shutdown.exe -s -t 0`. Set the Start In field to `%windir%` as well. Using this command line doesn't affect the shutdown in any way whatsoever. You won't lose data or anything of that nature. The only change is that Windows won't wait for applications to end before it begins the shutdown process. Since the default wait period is 30 seconds (even if the computer isn't doing anything), you can save 30 seconds by using this technique.

Replicating COM+ Applications with the COMRepl Utility

Use the COMRepl utility to replicate all of the COM+ applications on the current machine to one or more remote machines. This utility doesn't replicate system applications, COM+ utilities, COM+ QC Dead Letter Queue Listener, IIS in-process applications, IIS utilities, or all applications created for isolated or pooled virtual roots. You won't find this utility in the normal `\Windows\System32` directory. To add this command to the path, use the `path = %PATH%;%windir%\system32\Com` set command. This utility uses the following syntax:

```
COMREPL <source> <targetList> [/n [/v]]
```

The following list describes each of the command line arguments.

source Specifies the name of the source computer.

targetList Specifies the names of the target computers. Separate each target computer with a space.

/n Performs the replication without displaying any confirmation prompts.

/v Echoes the log output to the console so that you can see every event that occurs during replication.

Managing Type Libraries with the RegTLib Utility

Use the RegTLib utility to register a type library on your system. You won't find this utility in the normal `\Windows\System32` directory. To add this command to the path, use the `path = %PATH%;%windir%\system32\URTTemp` set command. Vista doesn't support this utility and there isn't any replacement provided. This utility uses the following syntax (the first form registers a type library; the second form unregisters a type library):

```
RegTLib [-q] Library
RegTLib [-q] -u Library
```

The following list describes each of the command line arguments.

-q Performs a quiet registration or unregistration of a type library. The user doesn't see any prompts.

Library The drive, path (absolute or relative), and filename of the type library you want to register.

-u Unregisters the type library by removing its entries from the registry.

Saving and Restoring System Restore Data with the SRDiag Utility

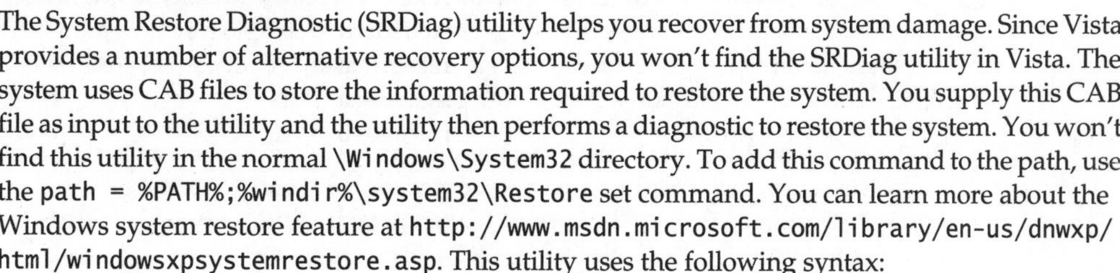

The System Restore Diagnostic (SRDiag) utility helps you recover from system damage. Since Vista provides a number of alternative recovery options, you won't find the SRDiag utility in Vista. The system uses CAB files to store the information required to restore the system. You supply this CAB file as input to the utility and the utility then performs a diagnostic to restore the system. You won't find this utility in the normal `\Windows\System32` directory. To add this command to the path, use the `path = %PATH%;%windir%\system32\Restore` set command. You can learn more about the Windows system restore feature at `http://www.msdn.microsoft.com/library/en-us/dnwxp/html/windowsxpsystemrestore.asp`. This utility uses the following syntax:

```
SrDiag [/CabName: cab] [/CabLoc:"path"]
```

The following list describes each of the command line arguments.

/CabName:*cab* Specifies the full name of the CAB file that you wish to use for system restoration. When you don't supply a CAB file as input, the system creates a CAB file that uses the following format: `<machine_name>_mmddyy_hhss.cab`. This file appears in whatever directory you choose to use for restoration file storage.

/CabLoc:"*path*" Specifies the location of the CAB file on disk. The path must include a final backslash (\). The default setting is the current directory.

Performing Web-Based Enterprise Management Tasks

Microsoft has worked hard to introduce more techniques for remote management of systems on large networks, including use of the Internet. Web-Based Enterprise Management (WBEM) is one of several attempts to make Windows friendlier for large organizations. You'll find that WBEM is the term that many vendors use for this kind of management and there are some defacto standards for implementing it.

WMI is Microsoft's technology for implementing WBEM on Windows. Consequently, you'll often see the two terms used almost interchangeably in the Microsoft documentation. The Windows Management Instrumentation service provides the server functionality for working with WMI on a computer system. Although the following sections tell you about the command line utilities that you can use to work with both WBEM and WMI, they don't provide you with administration information for these technologies. You'll find a good overview of both WBEM and WMI on the Microsoft Web site at `http://www.microsoft.com/whdc/system/pnppwr/wmi/WMI-intro.mspx`. If you must maintain older systems and want to use the WMI functionality described in this chapter, make sure you download the update at `http://www.microsoft.com/downloads/details.aspx?displaylang=en&FamilyID=AFE41F46-E213-4CBF-9C5B-FBF236E0E875`.

TIP One of the newer graphical utilities that Microsoft has introduced to make working with WMI easier is the Windows Management Instrumentation Tester. Microsoft also calls this utility Web-Based Enterprise Management Test in some literature. (Realizing the confusion they were causing, some Microsoft documentation actually uses both terms now.) You can get an overview of this utility, along with usage instructions, at `http://www.microsoft.com/technet/prodtechnol/windowsserver2003/library/ServerHelp/ae5ecb63-eb4d-4857-a742-41902fd5e6e4.mspx`.

Administering Managed Object Format Files with the MOFComp Utility

The Managed Object Format (MOF) Compiler (MOFComp) utility parses files that contain WMI scripting information and adds the result to the WMI repository where you can access the classes. You can see an example of a script that relies on MOF to add Simple Network Management Protocol (SNMP) functionality to a computer system at `http://msdn2.microsoft.com/en-us/library/aa393621.aspx`. This utility uses the following syntax:

```
mofcomp [-check] [-N:<Path>] [-class:updateonly|-class:createonly]
   [-instance:updateonly|-instance:createonly] [-B:<filename>]
   [-P:<Password>] [-U:<UserName>] [-A:<Authority>] [-WMI] [-AUTORECOVER]
   [-MOF:<path>] [-MFL:<path>] [-AMENDMENT:<Locale>]
   [-ER:<ResourceName>] [-L:<ResourceLocale>] <MOF filename>
```

The following list describes each of the command line arguments.

-check Performs a syntax check of the script only.

-N:*path* Loads the result into the specified namespace.

-class:updateonly Performs class updates, rather than creating a new class.

-class:safeupdate Performs a class update only when there aren't any conflicts.

-class:forceupdate Forces the system to update the class by resolving conflicts if possible.

-class:createonly Creates new classes only; the compiler won't update existing classes.

-instance:updateonly Performs instance updates, rather than creating new instances.

-instance:createonly Creates new instances only; the compiler won't update existing instances.

-U:*UserName* Specifies the username.

-P:*Password* Specifies the user password.

-A:*Authority* Specifies the authority for verifying the account information. For example, you might specify a domain using `NTLMDOMAIN:Domain`, where `Domain` is the domain name of the system.

-B:*filename* Creates a MOF file as output, rather than adding the compiled result to the database.

-WMI Performs the Windows Driver Model (WDM) checks on the results. You must use the `-B` command line switch with this switch.

-AUTORECOVER Adds MOF to the list of files compiled during a database recovery.

-Amendment:*LOCALE* Divides the MOF into language-neutral and language-specific versions.

-MOF:*path* Specifies the name of the language-neutral output.

-MFL:*path* Specifies the name of the language-specific output.

-ER:*ResourceName* Extracts a binary MOF from the named resource.

-L:*ResourceLocale* Specifies the number of the locale you want to extract from a named resource when using the `-ER` switch.

Interacting with the WBEM Server with the WinMgmt Utility

The WinMgmt utility is a special application for interacting with the Windows Management Instrumentation service. It provides better management than the SC utility because it addresses specific WMI requirements. This utility uses the following syntax:

```
Winmgmt [/exe] [/kill] [/regserver] [/unregserver] [/backup <filename>]
   [/restore <filename><mode>] [/resyncperf <winmgmt service process
   id>] [/clearadap]
```

The following list describes each of the command line arguments.

/exe Runs `WinMgmt.EXE` as an application, rather than as a service. The Windows Management Instrumentation entry won't appear in the Services console. The main reason to use this command line switch is to allow debugging of providers using the standard Microsoft debuggers. When you run `WinMgmt.EXE` as an application, it runs in the user's security context. Normally, you should run this program as a service so that it receives the proper rights.

/kill Terminates all instances of `WinMgmt.EXE` on the local system including any processes started as a service by the Service Control Manager. You must have administrative rights to use this command line switch.

/regserver Registers the Windows Management Instrumentation service by adding entries to the registry.

/unregserver Removes the registry entries for the Windows Management Instrumentation service. This act makes the service unavailable for use, which can result in a loss of operating system functionality.

/backup *filename* Backs up the WMI repository to the specified filename. The filename argument can contain a drive and path specification, along with the actual backup filename. The backup process requires a write lock on the repository, which means that the operating system suspends any write operations to the repository until the backup process completes.

/restore *filename mode* Restores the WMI repository from the specified file. The filename argument can contain a drive and path specification, along with the actual backup filename. The utility deletes the existing repository when you restore a backup. It writes the specified backup file to the automatic backup file, and then connects to WMI to perform the restoration. The restoration process requires exclusive access to the repository, which means that the utility will disconnect any existing clients from WMI before it begins the restoration process. You must set the mode argument to 1 to force user disconnection and begin the restoration or 0 to restore only when there aren't any users connected. Newer versions of Windows ignore the mode argument and always disconnect users to perform the restoration.

/resyncperf *winmgmt_service_process_id* Invokes the WMI AutoDiscovery/AutoPurge (ADAP) mechanism.

/clearadap Removes all of the ADAP information from the registry. This effectively resets the state of each performance library. The ADAP utility stores state information about the system performance libraries in the registry.

Tracing WinSxS Behavior with the SxSTrace Utility

The SxSTrace utility helps you trace side-by-side execution on Vista systems. The side-by-side execution feature lets you maintain multiple versions of DLLs. Each application can use its own DLL to perform tasks, which means you'll encounter fewer problems. However, the `WinSxS` folder can eventually become full of DLLs that you don't use, which is why tracing application DLL use is so helpful. This utility uses the following syntax:

```
SxSTrace Trace -logfile:FileName [-nostop]
SxSTrace Parse -logfile:FileName -outfile:ParsedFile
   [-filter:AppName]]
SxSTrace StopTrace
```

The following list describes each of the command line arguments.

`Trace` Begins the trace of side-by-side DLL usage on the system.

`Parse` Transforms the log file created during a trace into output. The standard method is to output the data to a file. You can then supply the name of a filter application to view the data.

`StopTrace` Stops the current trace and closes the log file.

`-logfile:`*`FileName`* Defines the name of the file to use for logging purposes.

`-nostop` Specifies that the utility shouldn't prompt you before it stops a trace. Normally, the utility asks whether you're sure that you want to stop a trace.

`-outfile:`*`ParsedFile`* Defines the name of an output file that contains the translated log file data.

`-filter:`*`AppName`* Specifies the name of an application to filter the data. The data is in a specific text format, which makes it relatively easy to parse by third party applications.

Getting Started with Command Line Tasks

This chapter provided you with information about the last of the major utilities that Windows supports. You've discovered all kinds of interesting new technologies and techniques. For example, when you need to ensure the archive you create today is accessible tomorrow, you might want to use the MakeCab utility. No need for third party software here—Windows comes with support for CABs built in. However, most of the utilities in this chapter fall into the category of things that you'll use once or twice, or perhaps not at all.

The utilities in this chapter are easy to forget because you won't use them often. I often include such utilities in my troubleshooting notebook. A troubleshooting notebook comes in handy because it tells me what I've done to fix problems in the past or provides suggestions on how to fix them in the future. If you don't already have a troubleshooting notebook of your own, you should put one together now and begin filling it with solutions and ideas. I maintain my notebook in an Access database so I can sort it by topic, date, or other criteria as needed. A little time spent putting such a notebook together now can save you a weekend in the office later.

Chapter 7 begins looking at automation. It explores what you can to do make working at the command line easier. You'll discover two forms of automation in Chapter 7. The first involves making the command line more useful by changing the files that control how the command line appears to you when you open it. The second shows how to work with batch (BAT) and command (CMD) files. Even though these files may seem like old technology best relegated to the days of DOS, you'll be surprised at how much you can actually do with them. These low-tech solutions to automation are easy to put together, easy to understand, and don't require any special tools.

Part 2

Using Windows Automation

In This Section:

Chapter 7

Creating CMD and BAT Files

- Starting the Command Interpreter
- Working at the Command Prompt
- Creating Batch Files

All of the preceding chapters of the book introduced you to commands and utilities. You can use them at the command prompt in an interactive mode by typing them, along with their command line switches and arguments, one at a time. However, when you use the command line with any frequency, you quickly tire of entering all of this information by hand. It's a lot better to automate the commands you use most often, in some way, so that you can enter one command to get a lot of work done. The CMD (Command) and BAT (Batch) files discussed in this chapter let you do just that and with only a modicum of work.

Users have relied on batch files for various sorts for many years because they're quick to create, easy to understand, and painless to modify. Testing a batch file is simple—you don't need any fancy tools or a debugger. In fact, as far as any kind of programming goes, working with batch files represents the least difficult way to get started. You literally enter the commands in the same order as you do at the command prompt. With a little effort in Windows, you can cut and paste your way to a completed batch file.

One of the most interesting uses of batch files are the `AutoExec.NT` and `Config.NT` files used to configure the command line. These two files represent a significant opportunity to configure the command environment to meet specific needs without doing much more than selecting a menu option, yet most people miss this opportunity. This chapter demonstrates that a little code mixed with some simple instructions really can do a lot to make the command line environment a pleasure to work with.

Starting the Command Interpreter

The command interpreter is a special kind of application. When you open a command window, what you're really doing is starting the command interpreter. The command interpreter accepts your commands and does something with them. The command interpreter for Windows is `CMD.EXE`. This application is responsible for creating the command window, accepting your configuration commands, and providing access to the built-in commands such as the `Dir` command.

You can configure the command interpreter using five techniques in Windows. The first is to add command line switches to the `CMD.EXE`. This approach configures the command interpreter as a whole and you don't have much control over this particular change once the command interpreter is running. Of course, you can have a shortcut for each occasion that relies on different command line switch setups for each task.

The second configuration method is to change the content of `Config.NT`. The `Config.NT` file appears in the `\Windows\System32` directory and the command interpreter calls on it to configure the command window environment. The `Config.NT` file changes the device drivers, number of files, the loading of the Virtual DOS Machine into upper memory, and other configuration issues.

The third configuration method is to change the content of `AutoExec.NT`. This file is actually a batch file that you can modify as you would any other batch file. All of the techniques described in the "Creating Batch Files" section of the chapter apply to this file. You can create any environment you want using the proper programming techniques. In fact, you could present the user with choices and act on those choices as part of configuring the environment.

The fourth configuration method is the Program Information File (PIF). The configuration information you provide for DOS applications using this file directly affect their execution. In fact, the PIF provides a means of specifying alternative `Config.NT` and `AutoExec.NT` files. Consequently, when your command line application requires a special environment in which to run, you can create it.

The fifth configuration method is manual command line changes. The "Managing Environment Variables with the *Set* Command" section of Chapter 3 discusses some of the changes you can make. However, you can make other changes using common command line utilities that you'll find in the sections that follow.

Using the CMD Switches

The command interpreter, `CMD.EXE`, is the most important part of the command line because it affects everything you do at the command line. A small change in the command interpreter can make a significant change in the way your applications run. The default command prompt setup assumes that you don't want to use any of the command line switches and that you want to start in your home directory.

If you used the Disk Operating System (DOS) at some point, it's important to remember that the command line switches that Windows supplies for the `CMD.EXE` command interpreter in no way match what you used in the past. Microsoft does make some command line switches available for compatibility purposes. For example, the `/X` command line switch is the same as `/E:ON`, `/Y` is the same as `/E:OFF`, and `/R` is the same as `/C`. The command interpreter ignores all other old switches; you need to use the command line switches described in this section instead.

You might also remember a few convenience features from the days of DOS that no longer appear as part of Windows. For example, at one time you could create a setup menu by using the `[MENU]` entry in `Config.SYS`. The `Config.NT` file doesn't support this setup. The only alternative is to create multiple `Config.NT` files and assign them to applications as needed. In short, even though the command interpreter does many of the same things that the DOS version does, this command interpreter is different and you need to proceed with caution about any assumptions you want to make. This application uses the following syntax:

```
CMD [{/A | /U}] [/Q] [/D] [/E:{ON | OFF}] [/F:{ON | OFF}] [/V:{ON |
   OFF}] [[/S] [{/C | /K}] string] [/T:FG]
```

The following list describes each of the command line arguments.

/C *string* Performs the command specified by *string* and then terminates the command interpreter session. Generally, you won't get to see any application output using this technique unless the application provides graphical output or you use redirection to save the results in a file.

NOTE When using either the `/C` or `/K` command line switches, you can specify multiple commands by creating a single string that contains all of the commands. Separate each command using a double ampersand (&&). You must enclose the entire string in double quotes. For example, `"Dir *.DOC&&Dir *.TXT"` would perform two `Dir` commands. The first would search for any file with a DOC extension, while the second would search for any file with a TXT extension.

/K *string* Performs the command specified by *string*. The command window remains after execution ends so that you can see the application results.

/S Modifies the treatment of the command string used with the `/C` and `/K` command line switches. The command interpreter provides two methods for processing the command string. When you use the `/S` command line switch, the command processor views the string associated with the `/C` and `/K` command line switch. It verifies that the first character is a quote and removes it from the string. The command processor then looks for the closing quote and removes it as well. You can use this option when the presence of quotes causes problems executing the command. The command interpreter also strips the quotations marks when you:

- Use any of the following special characters within the string: &<>( ) @ ^ |
- Include one or more white space characters
- Include an executable filename as part of the string
- Use more than one set of quotes in the string

/Q Turns echo off. Echo is the output of the command interpreter that tells you which command is running.

/D Disables the execution of `AutoRun` commands from the registry. This registry entry appears later in this section of the chapter.

/A Specifies the output of internal commands to a pipe or file using American National Standards Institute (ANSI) characters.

/U Specifies the output of internal commands to a pipe or file using Unicode characters.

/E:ON Enables the command extensions. The command extensions provide added functionality for these commands: `Assoc`, `Call`, `ChDir (CD)`, `Color`, `Del (Erase)`, `EndLocal`, `For`, `FType`, `GoTo`, `If`, `MkDir (MD)`, `PopD`, `Prompt`, `PushD`, `Set`, `SetLocal`, `Shift`, and `Start` (also includes changes to external command processes). The "Understanding Command Extensions" section of the chapter tells you how the command extensions affect these commands.

NOTE You might notice that some commands appear in parentheses. For example, the `ChDir` command appears before the (CD) command in parentheses. The two commands are equivalent. You can use whichever form you want. The parentheses don't show a preference, simply an alternative.

/E:OFF Disables command extensions.

/F:ON Enables file and directory name completion characters. File and directory completion allow speed typing at the command line. For example, if you want to type `Dir Temp`, using directory or file completion, you could type `Dir T`, and then press Ctrl+D (for a directory) or Ctrl+F (for a file). The command interpreter automatically completes the directory or filename for you. If you type in a partition string that doesn't match any entries, the command interpreter beeps to signify that the entry is incorrect. When the command interpreter sees multiple entries that could match the entry you provide, it displays the first entry in the list. You cycle through the entries by pressing Ctrl+D or Ctrl+F again. Use the Shift+Ctrl+D and Shift+Ctrl+D control key combinations to move backward through the list of choices. You can change the control characters that this feature uses by changing the associated registry entry. You must enclose any file or directory names that begin with special characters in quotes. These characters include <space> &()[]{}^=;!'+,`~.

/F:OFF Disables file and directory name completion characters (see the `/F:ON` command line switch for details).

/V:ON Enables delayed environment variable expansion. The expansion relies on the exclamation mark (!) as the delimiter. Consequently, supplying `!MyVar!` at the command line would expand (display the value of) `MyVar` at execution time.

/V:OFF Disables delayed environment variable expansion.

NOTE Vista continues to support the /T command line switch, even though it doesn't appear with the CMD executable help. It's important to realize that Microsoft often gets rid of undocumented command line switches, so you might not have access to this feature in a future release.

/T:FG Sets the foreground (F) and background (G) colors. You must place the values together, without any space between. The following list tells you which colors you can use at the command prompt, along with their associated color number.

0—Black

1—Blue

2—Green

3—Aqua

4—Red

5—Purple

6—Yellow

7—White

8—Gray

9—Light blue

A—Light green

B—Light aqua

C—Light red

D—Light purple

E—Light yellow

F—Bright white

Working with the Command Interpreter in the Registry

Many of the command line behaviors depend on registry settings. You can find these settings in the `HKEY_CURRENT_USER\Software\Microsoft\Command Processor` key for the local user and `HKEY_LOCAL_MACHINE\SOFTWARE\Microsoft\Command Processor` for everyone using the same machine.

The command interpreter looks for these registry settings when you don't provide an appropriate command line switch. If you don't see the registry entry, then the command interpreter uses a default setting. Local user settings always override the machine settings, and command line switches always override the registry settings. Here are the registry settings and their meanings.

AutoRun Defines the command that you want the command interpreter to run every time you open a command prompt. This value is of type `REG_SZ` or `REG_EXPAND_SZ`. Simply provide the executable name along with any command line switches that the executable may require. As with the string for the `/C` and `/K` command line switches, you can separate multiple commands using a double ampersand (&&).

EnableExtensions Specifies whether the command interpreter has extensions enabled. See the `/E:ON` command line switch description for a list of the applications that this entry affects. This value is of type `REG_DWORD`. Set it to enabled using a value of 0x1 and disabled using a value of 0x0.

CompletionChar Defines the file completion character (see the `/F:ON` command line switch for details). The default character is Ctrl+F (0x06). Use a value of a space (0x20) to disable this feature since the space isn't a valid control character. This value is of type `REG_DWORD`.

PathCompletionChar Defines the directory completion character (see the `/F:ON` command line switch for details). The default character is Ctrl+D (0x04). Use a value of a space (0x20) to disable this feature since the space isn't a valid control character. This value is of type `REG_DWORD`.

DelayedExpansion Specifies whether the command interpreter uses delayed variable expansion. See the `/V:ON` command line switch description for additional information. This value is of type `REG_DWORD`. Set it to enabled using a value of 0x1 and disabled using a value of 0x0.

UNDERSTANDING COMMAND EXTENSIONS

Command extensions are additional processing that the command interpreter provides for certain commands. The effects vary by command, but generally, the commands receive additional functionality. In some cases, such as the `del (erase)` command, the extensions simply change the way the command works. The following list describes the command extension changes to each of the affected commands.

Assoc Microsoft hasn't documented how command extensions change the `Assoc` command. Even though Microsoft lists it as one of the commands that changes with command extensions, there isn't any obvious difference at the command line.

Call Accepts a label as the target for a call (rather than a filename as normal). This feature means that you can transfer control from one portion of a batch file to another. Using extensions means that you can call the label using `call :Label Arguments`. Notice that you must precede the label with a colon.

Chdir (CD) Displays the directory names precisely as they appear on your hard drive. For example, if a directory name has a space, you'll see the space when you change directories. Capitalization is also the same. A directory name that appears with an initial capital letter in Windows Explorer will also appear that way at the command prompt. In addition, when you turn the command extensions off, the command doesn't treat spaces as delimiters. Consequently, you don't need to surround directory names with spaces or with quotes in order to obtain the correct results from this command.

Color Microsoft hasn't documented how command extensions change the `Color` command. Even though Microsoft lists it as one of the commands that changes with command extensions, there isn't any obvious difference at the command line.

Del (Erase) Changes the way the /S command line switch works. The command shows you just the files that it deletes, rather than showing you all of the files, including those that it couldn't find.

EndLocal Restores the command extension settings to their state before calling the `SetLocal` command. Normally, the `SetLocal` command doesn't save the state of the command extensions.

For Implements an expanded number of `For` command options. When working with directories, you process directories, rather than a list of files within a directory, using this call: `for /D {%% | %}Variable in (Set) do Command [CommandLineOptions]`. You can also perform recursive processing of a directory tree. Using this feature means that a single command can process an entire tree, rather than using individual commands to process a branch. Use the `for /R [[Drive:]Path] {%% | %}Variable in (Set) do Command [CommandLineOptions]` command line syntax to perform recursion. It's also possible to iterate through a range of values, similar to the functionality of the `For` loop used in higher level languages, using this command syntax: `for /L {%% | %}Variable in (Start#,Step#,End#) do Command [CommandLineOptions]`. Variable substitution is another useful feature that using command extensions provides (see the "Using Variable Substitution" section of the chapter for details). Finally, you can perform complex file parsing and iteration with the command extension in place (see the "Performing Complex File Iteration" section of the chapter for details).

NOTE Vista provides support for the ForFiles utility. This utility overcomes the need for use of some types of extensions. Learn more about this utility in the "Using the ForFiles Utility" section of the chapter.

FType Microsoft hasn't documented how command extensions change the `FType` command. Even though Microsoft lists it as one of the commands that changes with command extensions, there isn't any obvious difference at the command line.

Goto Defines a special label called `:EOF`. If you define a `Goto` command in a batch file with the `:EOF` label, the system transfers control to the end of the current batch file and exits. You don't need to define the label in the batch file to make this feature work.

If Defines additional comparison syntax that makes the `If` command considerably more flexible. See the "Using the *If* Command" section of the chapter for details.

MkDir (MD) Lets you create intermediate directories with a single command. For example, you could define an entire subdirectory structure using `MD MyDir/MySub1/MySub2`. If `MyDir` doesn't exist, the system creates it first, then `MySub1`, and, finally, `MySub2`. Normally, you'd need to create each directory separately and use the `CD` command to move to each lower level to create the next subdirectory.

PopD Removes any drive letter assignment made by the `PushD` command.

Prompt Supports additional prompt characters. The `$+` character adds one or more plus signs (+) to the command prompt for every level of the `PushD` command. Using this feature lets you know how many levels of redirection the `PushD` command has saved on the stack and how many more times you can use the `PopD` command to extract them. The `$m` character adds the remote name associated with a drive to the command prompt. The command prompt doesn't display any additional information for local drives.

PushD Allows you to push network paths onto the stack as well as local drive letters and path information.

Set Displays all currently defined environment variables when you use the `Set` command alone. Displays the specified environment variable when you supply an environment variable name, but not an associated value. If you supply only a partial variable name, the `Set` command displays all of the variables that could match that name.

SetLocal Allows the `SetLocal` command to enable or disable command extensions as needed to meet specific language requirements.

Shift Supports the `/N` command line option, which lets the `Shift` command shift variables starting with the *n*th variable. For example, if you use `Shift /2` at the command line, then variables %0 and %1 are unaffected by the shift, but variables %3 through %9 receive new variable input.

Start Microsoft hasn't documented how command extensions change the `Start` command. Even though Microsoft lists it as one of the commands that changes with command extensions, there isn't any obvious difference at the command line.

Modifying *Config.NT*

The `Config.NT` file contains a number of entries that affect how the system works at the command prompt. At one time, the configuration file contained a wealth of device drivers and statements that defined how the command prompt used files and buffers. However, the `Config.NT` file rarely contains device drivers and these driver entries are normally defined by third party software for you. One of the more common driver entries provides NetWare connectivity at the command prompt. (However, in many cases, all you need are some entries in the `AutoExec.NT` file to provide NetWare support.) The following sections describe common additions you can make to the `Config.NT` file.

NOTE Some people may remember `Config.SYS`, the file that DOS uses to perform the same configuration that Windows performs with `Config.NT`. In fact, some people try to move `Config.SYS` to the Windows environment. Fortunately, the 32-bit version of Windows accepts many older DOS commands even when it doesn't use them. For example, the FastOpen utility provides a caching feature in DOS to make directory searches faster. Even though Windows provides this file too, it doesn't actually use the functionality and FastOpen doesn't actually perform any task. Once you move to the 64-bit versions of Windows, much of this functionality is missing completely. For example, you can't create a `Config.NT` file that contains a reference to the FastOpen utility.

Using *ANSI.SYS* to Control the Environment

The `ANSI.SYS` device driver provides added functionality for applications at the command prompt. By using special escape codes, you can create a character-based user interface for your batch files. You can find a good listing of ANSI escape codes at `http://www.evergreen.edu/biophysics/technotes/program/ansi_esc.htm` and on the Microsoft Web site at `http://www.microsoft.com/technet/archive/msdos/comm1.mspx?mfr=true`. This utility uses the following syntax:

```
device=[Drive:][Path]ANSI.SYS [/X] [/K] [/R]
```

As with all device drivers that you add to the `Config.NT` file, you begin the `ANSI.SYS` entry using `device= entry`, followed by the drive and path to the `ANSI.SYS` file. The following list describes each of the command line arguments.

/X Remaps the extended keys on 101-key keyboards independently. Actually, this feature works no matter how many extra keys your keyboard has.

/K Forces `ANSI.SYS` to treat a 101-key (or more) keyboard like an 84-key keyboard by ignoring the extended keys.

/R Changes the line scrolling functionality to improve readability when working with screen reader programs. A screen reader program interprets the screen content and presents it using some other form of output. Normally, screen reader applications say what's on screen to help those with special sight needs understand the content.

SETTING THE DOS LOCATION

This utility uses the following syntax:

```
DOS=[{HIGH | LOW}] [{,UMB | ,NOUMB}]
```

The following list describes each of the command line arguments.

HIGH | LOW Determines whether the command environment attempts to load part of itself into the High Memory Area (HMA) (HIGH) or keep all of the code in conventional memory (LOW). The default setting is LOW. Generally, you want to load the command environment into high memory to preserve more conventional memory for applications.

UMB | NOUMB Determines whether the command environment should manage the Upper Memory Blocks (UMBs) created by a UMB provider. Windows provides a UMB provider as a default. DOS users used to rely on a special program named `EMM386.EXE` to perform this task. The UMB argument tells the command environment to manage the UMBs, which frees additional memory for loading applications in areas other than conventional memory. The default setting is `NOUMB`.

RUNNING DOS APPLICATIONS ONLY

You can execute any kind of application you want from the command prompt. If you want to start Notepad, simply type Notepad and press Enter. However, mixing Windows and older DOS applications can sometimes cause problems. Developers wrote DOS applications with the expectation that these applications controlled the entire machine, which can cause myriad problems with Windows applications. If you have one of these older applications (and they're quite rare), you can help the DOS application execute properly by adding the `NTCMDPROMPT` entry to `Config.NT`. This entry tells the operating system to disallow Windows application execution at the command prompt, which means that the DOS application will continue to feel that it owns the machine. Of course, you can start your Windows applications from another command prompt or by using any of the usual techniques, such as the Start menu.

NOTE Some people have asked whether the NTCMDPROMPT entry really does stop all applications from interrupting the DOS application. For example, does this entry stop an Instant Messaging (IM) application from interfering with your game of Tank Wars? Every application I tested seemed to abide by the rules. However, Microsoft doesn't always play by the rules. When other vendors learn Microsoft's tricks, they use them to avoid abiding by the rules too. Consequently, there's no guarantee that your IM application won't interfere with your Tank Wars game, but there's good reason to believe that you'll normally have success using the NTCMDPROMPT entry.

DISPLAYING THE *CONFIG.NT* COMMANDS

Normally, you won't see any information about the commands that execute before the command window opens; all you see is a command prompt. Adding an `ECHOCONFIG` to the `Config.NT` file displays each of the commands as they execute. Using this feature can help you diagnose problems with the `Config.NT` file contents.

Controlling Expanded Memory EMM Entry

Older applications, especially character mode (DOS) games, rely on the Expanded Memory Specification (EMS) memory to overcome command prompt memory limitations. It's important to remember that the command line effectively limits the amount of memory available to DOS applications to 640 KB minus any memory that the operating system uses. Normally, you set the amount of this memory as part of the application's PIF. However, the PIF doesn't let you control the Expanded Memory Manager (EMM), which is the application that actually makes the memory accessible. The `EMM` entry lets you change how the EMM works. This option uses the following syntax:

```
EMM = [A=AltRegSets] [B=BaseSegment] [RAM]
```

The following list describes each of the command line arguments.

A=AltRegSets Defines how many alternative mapping register sets the EMM has available for mapping memory between extended memory and conventional memory. You can provide any value between 1 and 255. The default setting of 8 works fine in most cases. Check your application documentation for additional requirements.

B=BaseSegment Defines the base segment, the location where the EMM places code within the DOS conventional memory area from extended memory as needed. Generally, any setting you choose works fine. However, some applications use specific segments for their use. Using the same memory segment for two purposes causes memory corruption and can cause the application to fail. The application documentation should tell you about any requirements. You can set the base segment to any hexadecimal value between 0x1000 and 0x4000. The default setting is 0x4000.

RAM Specifies that the EMM should only use 64 KB of address space from the UMB area for the EMM page. Normally, the EMM uses the entire UMB for the EMM page to improve EMM performance. However, your application may require more conventional memory than this practice allows. Using the RAM option reduces the EMM page size, which makes it easier for the command environment to load more applications in upper memory—freeing conventional memory for application use.

Setting the Number of Accessible Files

The Files setting may not seem very important, but every file handle you provide to the command environment uses conventional memory. Remember that conventional memory is already quite small and many older applications barely load in the space provided. The default Files=40 setting usually provides a good compromise. This setting means that the command environment can open 40 files, which is more than sufficient for most older applications. You can increase the number to as many as 255 when your application complains that it's out of file handles or decrease the number to as little as 8 when the application complains about a lack of memory.

Controlling Extended Memory with *HIMEM.SYS*

The `HIMEM.SYS` driver provides extended memory support at the command prompt. The eXtended Memory Specification (XMS) is a method that applications use to overcome the DOS memory limitations. You set the amount of available XMS using the PIF for the application. However, you can further refine XMS functionality by relying on the command line switches described in this section. As with all device drivers that you add to the `Config.NT` file, you begin the `HIMEM.SYS` entry using the device= entry, followed by the drive and path to the HIMEM.SYS file. This driver uses the following syntax:

```
DEVICE=[drive:][path]HIMEM.SYS [/HMAMIN=m] [/INT15=xxxx]
    [/NUMHANDLES=n] [/TESTMEM:{ON|OFF}] [/VERBOSE]
```

The following list describes each of the command line arguments.

NOTE **HIMEM.SYS includes a number of command line switches, many of which are archaic. For example, even though HIMEM.SYS still supports the /A20CONTROL command line switch, you'd have to have a very old computer (over 10 years old) to need it. In short, unless you have a very old system, you'll never have a use for these older command line switches. In addition to the /A20CONTROL command line switch, I haven't discussed the /CPUCLOCK, /EISA,/ MACHINE, and /SHADOWRAM command line switches. This section contains descriptions of the command line switches that are still useful.**

/HMAMIN=*m* Specifies how many kilobytes of HMA memory an application must request in order for HIMEM.SYS to fulfill the request. Some applications ask for small pieces of the HMA area, which fragments an already small memory area and makes it unavailable for other applications. It becomes a question of efficient memory use. An application that can use a larger piece of the HMA will likely free more conventional memory for use by other applications. You can specify any value between 0 and 63. The default value is 0. Setting this command line switch to 0 or omitting it from the command line lets HIMEM.SYS allocate the HMA memory to the first application that requests it, regardless of how much HMA memory that application will use.

/INT15=*xxxx* Specifies the amount of extended memory in kilobytes that HIMEM.SYS should reserve for the Interrupt 15h interface. You may wonder what the Interrupt 15h interface is all about; it's the method that applications use to interact with XMS. The only time you need to use this command line switch is if you have an older DOS application, very likely a game or graphics application, that relies on XMS memory. The application will very likely display a nebulous error message that specifically mentions the Interrupt 15h interface. Make sure you set the amount of XMS memory to 64 KB larger than the amount required by the application. You can specify any value from 64 KB to 65,535 KB. However, you can't specify more memory than your system has installed. When you specify a value less than 64, HIMEM.SYS sets the value to 0. The default value is 0.

/NUMHANDLES=*n* Specifies the maximum number of Extended Memory Block (EMB) handles that the system can use simultaneously. Every time an application requests more memory, it needs a handle to access that memory. Generally, you don't need to provide this command line switch unless you have an older graphics-intensive application. You can specify a value from 1 to 128. The default setting is 32, which is more than enough for most applications. Changing the number of handles uses more memory for housekeeping chores, so you'll want to use this command line switch with care.

/TESTMEM:{ON | OFF} Determines whether HIMEM.SYS performs a memory check when you open the command prompt. Most people don't actually know whether the memory they're using is good, so checking it from time to time is a way to reduce unwelcome surprises. However, running the test takes time. You'll see a noticeable delay in displaying the command prompt when you use this command line switch. In most cases, it's far better to test your memory using a third party diagnostic program that works outside of Window's influence. Otherwise, you can't be sure that you're testing all of the memory and won't know which surprises Windows has hidden from view. The HIMEM.SYS test is more thorough than the test that runs when you start your computer, so you can use it when you don't have any other means of testing available.

/VERBOSE Displays additional status and error messages while HIMEM.SYS is loading. The system normally doesn't display any messages unless it encounters a problem loading or initializing HIMEM.SYS. Adding this command line switch can point out potential problems in your system setup and aid in diagnosing application problems that you wouldn't normally detect. You can abbreviate this command line switch as /V. Unfortunately, despite the documentation for HIMEM.SYS online, you can't display the verbose messages by pressing the Alt key as the system loads HIMEM.SYS into memory; you must use the /VERBOSE command line switch to see the extended messages.

Modifying *AutoExec.NT*

Although Config.NT offers some interesting low level methods of changing the command line environment, the AutoExec.NT file provides far more opportunities. Any application that you can access from the command line is also a candidate for inclusion in the AutoExec.NT file. Adding applications that you always use can set up the command line from the outset, so you see what you need without entering any commands at all. You can also program the AutoExec.NT file as you would any other batch file. This means you can add menus to your setup so you can choose the options you want to see. See the "Creating Batch Files" section of the chapter for details on creating a programmed interface to your AutoExec.NT file. The sections that follow describe some utilities that you'll use most often from within the AutoExec.NT file. These utilities tend to configure the command environment, in some way, to make your computing experience better. However, don't limit yourself to these selections—any command or utility described in the book is a candidate for inclusion.

NOTE You'll find some older utilities that Windows installs for compatibility purposes, and then doesn't support. The KB16 utility should provide keyboard support, but you'll find that the command line provides this support automatically, so you don't actually need to use the KB16 utility. Even though the KB16 utility loads into memory and appears to perform a task, it doesn't do anything. In addition to the KB16 utility, you'll find that Windows doesn't support the MSCDex utility. This chapter doesn't discuss these compatibility commands and utilities.

SET THE CODE PAGE NUMBER WITH THE CHCP UTILITY

A code page defines language support at the command prompt. In the days of DOS, you needed to provide a code page to obtain proper language support at the command prompt, but Windows doesn't usually require you to set a code page. You might need to set a code page for older character-mode applications. Only the OEM font you installed as part of Windows displays properly when you use a raster font in a windowed command prompt. However, you can use any of the supported code pages in full screen mode or with a TrueType font. This utility uses the following syntax:

```
CHCP [nnn]
```

The following describes the command line argument.

nnn Defines the code page to use. The standard code page numbers appear in Table 7.1. Code pages 874 through 1258 are both OEM and ANSI implementations that are only available in Windows. You can install additional code pages as needed. The Web site at http://www.i18nguy.com/unicode/codepages.html#msftdos shows how these code pages appear.

TABLE 7.1: Standard OEM and OEM/ANSI Code Pages

CODE PAGE	COUNTRY OR LANGUAGE
437	United States
850	Multilingual (Latin I)
852	Slavic (Latin II)
855	Cyrillic (Russian)
857	Turkish
860	Portuguese
861	Icelandic
863	Canadian-French
865	Nordic
866	Russian
869	Modern Greek
874	Thai
932	Japanese Shift-JIS
936	Simplified Chinese GBK
949	Korean
950	Traditional Chinese Big5
1258	Vietnam

ADDING DPMI SUPPORT USING THE DOSX UTILITY

The DOS Protected Mode Interface (DPMI) is one method for a DOS application to access more than the 640 KB that DOS (the command line) typically allows. In addition, this interface provides protected memory access, so the DOS application doesn't interfere with Windows operation. You can read about DPMI at `http://whatis.techtarget.com/definition/0,,sid9_gci213913,00.html`. To use this interface, an application developer needs to provide special support in the application; usually as part of a third party add-on library. All you need to know is whether the application (typically a game) supports DPMI to use this feature. This utility uses the following syntax:

```
DosX
```

As you can see, this utility doesn't require any command line switches and it doesn't display any messages after you install it. You can use the MEM utility described in the "Determining Memory Status with the Mem Utility" section of Chapter 3 to determine whether the utility loaded into memory as anticipated.

Enable Graphics Character Support with the GrafTabl Utility

Normally, the system displays any extended characters your application needs to display as plain text. In some cases, this means the extended characters won't display correctly because your system may lack the capability required to display the extended characters properly. The GrafTabl utility helps Windows display extended characters as graphics, which means they always display correctly as long as you have the proper code page support loaded. The GrafTabl utility only affects extended character display; you need to use the Mode or CHCP utilities to change the console input. This utility uses the following syntax:

```
GRAFTABL [xxx]
GRAFTABL /STATUS
```

The following list describes each of the command line arguments.

xxx Specifies the code page number to use for display purposes. Table 7.1 lists the common code pages for Windows.

/STATUS Displays the code page that the GrafTabl has loaded for display purposes. This command line switch doesn't reflect the Mode or CHCP utility settings.

NOTE The GrafTabl utility won't work with Windows Itanium or Windows 64-bit versions.

Printing Command Line Graphics with the Graphics Utility

Windows XP isn't supposed to do anything when you try to use the Graphics utility, according to the Windows help file. However, the Graphics utility does load and apparently has some functionality. With this in mind, using the Graphics utility is an "at your own risk" kind of utility that you should only try as a last resort to obtain required application functionality. The `\WINDOWS\system32` directory contains the `GRAPHICS.COM` and `GRAPHICS.PRO` files mentioned in the Knowledge Base article at `http://support.microsoft.com/default.aspx?scid=kb;en-us;Q78123`.

WARNING Using the Graphics utility can produce some unexpected side effects when working at the command prompt. For example, you may find that the command history buffer no longer works. In addition, you might not be able to scroll through the buffer to see older information. The Graphics utility tends to restrict you to a single command mode and only one screen at a time.

Use the Graphics utility to load support for printing graphics at the command line. Some older applications may require this support, but generally, you don't need to load the Graphics utility. For example, you may need to load the graphics utility to print a screenshot of an older game. Press Shift+Print Screen to print a graphics image with this utility loaded. This utility uses the following syntax:

```
GRAPHICS [type] [[drive:][path]filename] [/R] [/B] [/LCD]
   [/PRINTBOX:STD | /PRINTBOX:LCD]
```

The following list describes each of the command line arguments.

type Specifies the printer type. In most cases, you'll want to use the default type unless you experience problems getting the default type to work. The printer types include: COLOR1, COLOR4, COLOR8, HPDEFAULT, DESKJET, GRAPHICS, GRAPHICSWIDE, LASERJET, LASERJETII, PAINTJET, QUIETJET, QUIETJETPLUS, RUGGEDWRITER, RUGGEDWRITERWIDE, THERMAL, and THINKJET.

[drive:][path]filename Specifies a file containing printer support information. You must obtain this file from the printer vendor in most cases.

/R Prints the output as white letters on a black background as normally displayed on screen. Normally, the utility reverses the colors to save ink.

/B Prints the background in color for the COLOR4 and COLOR8 printers.

/LCD Outputs the screen using the Liquid Crystal Display (LCD) aspect ratio so the output looks like the screen.

/PRINTBOX:STD | /PRINTBOX:LCD Displays a print box around the output. The options specify the print box size. You can choose between the standard (STD) or LCD aspect ratios.

Saving Memory Using the *LH* Command

The `Load High (LH)` command attempts to load a utility into high memory, instead of using application memory. Loading the utility high saves memory that memory-hungry applications can use to load. Generally, you should try to load high all of the utilities that you can, including DosX and ReDir. Windows 64-bit editions don't support this command. This command uses the following syntax:

```
LH
```

You don't need to provide any command line switches with this command. Simply add the command or utility that you want to load high after `LH` on the command line. The system won't display an error message if the command fails. However, you can verify the utility's location in memory using the Mem utility.

Adding CD Support with the MSCDexNT Utility

Windows provides all of the CD and DVD support that you need. The name of this support under DOS is Microsoft Compact Disk (or CD-ROM) Extensions (MSCDEX). However, you still need access to this support from the command prompt. Loading the MSCDexNT utility loads several additional applications including `VCDEX.DLL`, which is the 32-bit MSCDEX Virtual Device Driver. This utility uses the following syntax:

```
MSCDexNT
```

You don't need to supply any command line switches when using this utility.

Installing the Network Redirector Using the ReDir Utility

Use this utility to load the VDM Virtual Device Driver (VDD) redirector. The redirector provides virtual device access from the command prompt. Essentially, it provides network access. This utility uses the following syntax:

```
ReDir
```

You don't need to supply any command line switches when using this utility.

Adding NetWare Support with the NW16 and VWIPXSPX Utilities

If you're using a NetWare server and want to access applications on the server from the command prompt, you must install special NetWare utilities. In fact, Microsoft normally takes care of this requirement for you when you install NetWare client support. The Novell software also performs this task, but using the special Novell client software instead of the Microsoft counterparts discussed in this section. You may find that you need to verify and troubleshoot NetWare support. For example, the Knowledge

Base article at `http://support.microsoft.com/default.aspx?scid=kb;en-us;Q136199` tells how to diagnose problems when NetWare applications refuse to run. These utilities use the following syntax:

```
NW16
VWIPXSPX
```

Make sure you load the two utilities in the order shown. In addition, you must load these two utilities after you load the ReDir and DosX utilities. You don't need to supply any command line switches when using these utilities.

Vista doesn't provide full support for the old NetWare IPX/SPX protocols. In fact, you won't find them offered as an installation option, but Vista apparently installs the required support when it detects a NetWare server. Generally speaking, you'll want to configure your NetWare system to use the TCP/IP protocols to avoid a wealth of NetWare connectivity issues with Vista. Installing TCP/IP makes these utilities unnecessary.

Modifying Application Behavior Using a PIF

The PIF is an addition to a DOS application that controls how Windows interacts with the application. You don't start the application using the PIF (although double-clicking the PIF will start the application), but the PIF always affects how Windows works with the application. From a command line perspective, you can use a PIF to perform two special tasks. First, you can create custom `AutoExec.NT` and `Config.NT` for the application so you can control the application environment. Second, you can add command line switches to the application command line so that the application starts with the features you want to use. The following sections describe these two configuration techniques.

Real World Scenario

MAKING APPLICATIONS WORK AT THE COMMAND LINE

Many people wonder how I get older applications to work so often at the command line. The basic principle that you must grasp is that Windows isn't going to turn over any control of the command prompt, its resources (such as memory), or environment. However, many older applications assume they have full control of the system. The result is a crash where the older application fails because Windows has a firm grasp of everything. Consequently, you need to make the older application think that it has full control over the system even when it doesn't.

The PIF is one of the most important tools you have for making older applications work at the command prompt. By creating a custom `AutoExec.NT` and `Config.NT` file for the application, you can control the environment and make it more accessible to the application. You can even create a custom command prompt by calling a batch file and using the `CMD.EXE` command line switches described in the "Using the CMD Switches" section of this chapter. Changing the environment in this way can turn an application that doesn't work into one that does.

Fortunately, Windows also provides some help. Check the options on the Compatibility tab of the PIF's Properties dialog box. Using these options, you can force Windows to use different color options or run in a compatibility mode. The Misc tab contains options that control how Windows interacts with the application; you can even give the application exclusive access to the mouse. The Screen tab contains useful settings for changing the way that Windows handles the application window. For example, you can set the application to run in full screen mode when it fails to run in a window. Finally, if you haven't noticed already, older applications often require special memory setups. The Memory tab contains the options you can use to change the memory environment to anything the application needs.

USING A CUSTOM *AUTOEXEC.NT* AND *CONFIG.NT*

Every time you open a command prompt from Windows, even as part of executing an application, Windows uses the `AutoExec.NT` and `Config.NT` files in the `\Windows\System32` directory to create the application environment. The only problem with this approach is that a setup that works for most applications is unlikely to work for every application. Consequently, you might run into situations where you end up tinkering with the `AutoExec.NT` and `Config.NT` files to make a specific application work. Of course, you don't want to change the files that are already working for other applications on your system. Instead, create custom versions of these two files in the application directory. Copying the existing files is a good way to start because you'll have the mandatory entries in place.

A custom `AutoExec.NT` or `Config.NT` file can contain anything that the standard files contain. Any command or utility that you need to configure the environment can appear in the `AutoExec.NT` file. Of course, you can't include ancient DOS drivers in the `Config.NT` file because Windows won't use them and this particular issue can cause problems in resurrecting some older applications. If your application has such a need, it might be time to replace it.

Once you have a new `AutoExec.NT` or `Config.NT` file (or both) for your application, you need to set the PIF so that it uses the custom files, rather than the general files that every application uses. To assign a custom setup, begin by right-clicking the DOS executable in Windows and choosing Properties from the context menu. This act performs two tasks. First, it displays the properties for the application. Second, it creates the PIF file. The PIF has the same name as the application executable, but it uses a PIF extension instead of EXE or COM. Select the Program tab and you'll see the command line interface for the application as shown in Figure 7.1. Figure 7.1 shows the Windows XP version of this dialog box on the left and the Vista version of this dialog box on the right. Vista's security adds constraints to the whole compatibility issue that will make it considerably more difficult for you to make the application work. Make certain that you change any required security settings on the Security tab as part of configuring your application.

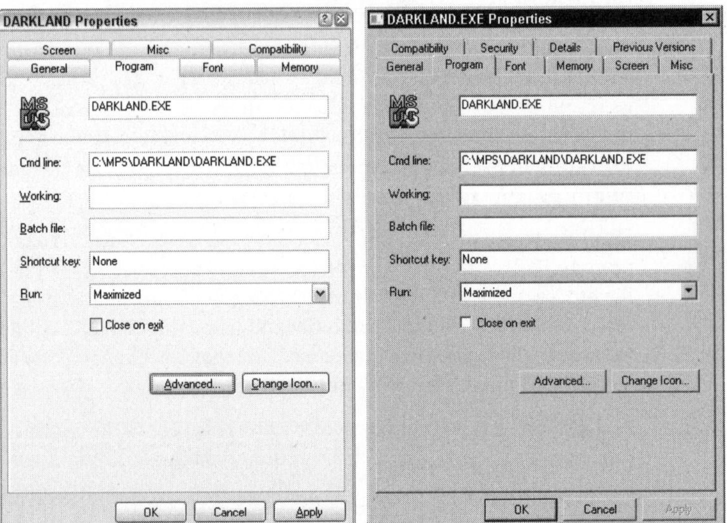

FIGURE 7.1
The Program tab is a point of focus for working with the command line in a PIF.

The "Customizing Windows Explorer with Command Line Switches" section of the chapter describes how to work with the Cmd Line field. Click Advanced and you'll see the Windows PIF Settings dialog box shown in Figure 7.2. Because this particular application is a game with settings common to all of the games on my system, I placed the alternative `AutoExec.NT` file in the `\Windows\System32` directory. To add a custom `AutoExec.NT` or `Config.NT` file to the application, all you need to do is type the location into the appropriate field as shown.

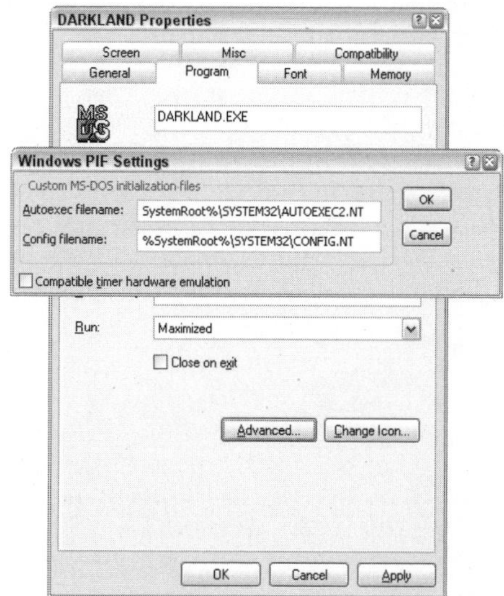

FIGURE 7.2
Change the Autoexec Filename and Config Filename fields to match your custom files.

NOTE Changes to `AutoExec.NT` and `Config.NT` may not be enough to make your application run under Vista. In many cases, you'll also need to check the Run this Program as an Administrator option on the Compatibility tab of the application's Properties dialog box as well. In the past, all applications assumed that you were the sole owner of the system and therefore its administrator. Vista changes that perception by making all users standard users with limited rights. Checking the Run this Program as an Administrator option reduces the change that the application will fail outright do to a limit on rights.

CUSTOMIZING WINDOWS EXPLORER WITH COMMAND LINE SWITCHES

You can create a shortcut or PIF for any application on your system that includes custom command line switch settings. In fact, you can create a custom setup for every potential need as long as the command line switches won't change. (If you have arguments that will change, you should use a batch file or script instead of a PIF or shortcut file.) One application that nearly everyone will want to change is Windows Explorer, so this section looks at Windows Explorer as a command line customization option.

Windows Explorer isn't a DOS or a command line application, so you can change the command line settings for it using the technique described in the "Using a Custom *AutoExec.NT* and *Config.NT*" section of the chapter. In this case, you'll begin by locating `Explorer.EXE` in the `\Windows` directory. Right-click the file in Windows Explorer and choose Create Shortcut from the context menu. Windows creates a shortcut with precisely the same name as the original file. Rename the file to something else by right-clicking it and choosing Rename from the context menu. The example uses My Explorer.

At this point, you can right-click the file and choose Properties from the context menu. You'll see a Properties dialog box similar to the one shown in Figure 7.3. The Target field contains the information you want to change for this application. Depending on the command line switches the application supports, you can modify the application behavior. The following list describes the command line switches that Windows Explorer uses.

FIGURE 7.3
Modify the command line for any application to meet specific needs.

/n Opens Windows Explorer in single-pane mode. The pane displays the default selection, which is usually the root drive where Windows is installed.

/e Starts Windows Explorer using the default view.

/e, *Directory* Starts Windows Explorer using the default view with the focus on the specified folder. When using this option, you can still access the root folder, along with any other directories on the system.

/root, *Directory* Starts Windows Explorer using the specified directory as the root folder. You can't access parent directories, but you can access any subdirectories.

/select, *Object* Opens a window view with the specified folder, file, or application selected.

Windows Explorer normally opens with My Computer selected, which means that it isn't ready for use by most people. You can change this behavior by using a different command line. For example, changing the command line to `%SystemRoot%\explorer.exe /e, C:\` forces Windows Explorer to open with the C drive on your system selected so you can get right to work.

Once you finish setting the shortcut settings, close the dialog box by clicking OK. Drag and drop the new shortcut wherever you need it for quick access. For example, placing the shortcut in the Start ➤ Programs ➤ Startup folder means that your system will start with a copy of Windows Explorer opened to the correct location every time you restart your machine.

Defining Application Compatibility with the SetVer Utility

Some older applications expect a specific version of DOS (the command interpreter) when they execute and won't execute with any other version. Usually, these applications won't even start; they simply display an error message telling you to get the right version of DOS. You can overcome this particular problem by adding an entry for the application to the Set Version (SetVer) utility table. When you try to execute the application, the command interpreter tells it that it's executing with the specific version of DOS that the application needs. This utility uses the following syntax:

```
Display the SetVer Information
      SETVER [drive:path]
Add a New Application
      SETVER [drive:path] filename n.nn
Delete an Application
      SETVER [drive:path] filename /DELETE [/QUIET]
```

The following list describes each of the command line arguments.

[drive:path] Specifies the location of the `SetVer.EXE` file.

filename Specifies the name of the program to add to or delete from the SetVer table.

n.nn Specifies the DOS version to report to the application.

/DELETE or /D Deletes the application listing from the SetVer table.

/QUIET Performs the specified task without displaying any prompts. Use this option when working with batch files to prevent the utility from interrupting the user.

NOTE You must load `SetVer.EXE` as a device driver in `Config.NT` to obtain the version-setting feature that it provides. You can check the SetVer status at the command prompt by typing `SetVer` and pressing Enter. The command displays a list of applications that appear in the SetVer table, and then display the SetVer status. You'll see an error message when the device isn't loaded into memory.

Using Common DOS Utilities

You'll find a number of common DOS utilities on your hard drive. Most of these utilities appear with every version of DOS, even those that Microsoft didn't produce (such as the IBM version). For the most part, these utilities perform maintenance tasks that you could perform in a batch file. For example, many people had batch files for working with the DiskCopy utility when floppy disks were popular. The following sections describe these utilities in detail.

Comparing the Contents of Disks with the DiskComp Utility

You can use this utility to compare the contents of two floppy disks. Because of the way the utility works, the two floppies must have precisely the same format and you can't compare two newer forms of media, such as CDs. A better alternative for modern media is the FC utility described in the "Performing Advanced File Comparison with the FC Utility" section of Chapter 2. This utility uses the following syntax:

```
DISKCOMP [drive1: [drive2:]]
```

The following list describes each of the command line arguments.

drive1: Specifies the source drive.

drive2: Specifies the destination drive. If you don't specify a destination drive, the utility assumes that you'll use one drive for the comparison and will prompt you to replace the source disk with the destination disk as needed.

Copying One Disk to Another with the DiskCopy Utility

You can use this utility to copy the contents of one floppy disk to another floppy disk. Because of the way the utility works, the two floppies must have precisely the same format. A better alternative for modern media is the XCopy utility described in the "Performing Bulk File Transfers with the XCopy Utility" section of Chapter 2. This utility uses the following syntax:

```
DISKCOPY [drive1: [drive2:]] [/V]
```

The following list describes each of the command line arguments.

drive1: Specifies the source drive.

drive2: Specifies the destination drive. If you don't specify a destination drive, the utility assumes that you'll use one drive for the comparison and will prompt you to replace the source disk with the destination disk as needed.

/V Verifies that the files copied correctly. Always use this option to ensure maximum copy reliability.

Modifying Data Files with the Edit Utility

The Edit utility is a very useful application to know about because it works when most other editors don't. The Edit utility is quite small, so you can place it on a floppy if you want or a CD that contains your diagnostic software. In addition, you don't need a graphical interface to use Edit, so it works at the DOS prompt, the Windows recovery console, or just about anywhere else you might need an editor. However, even with these limits, Edit supports a robust interface for a text editor, as shown in Figure 7.4.

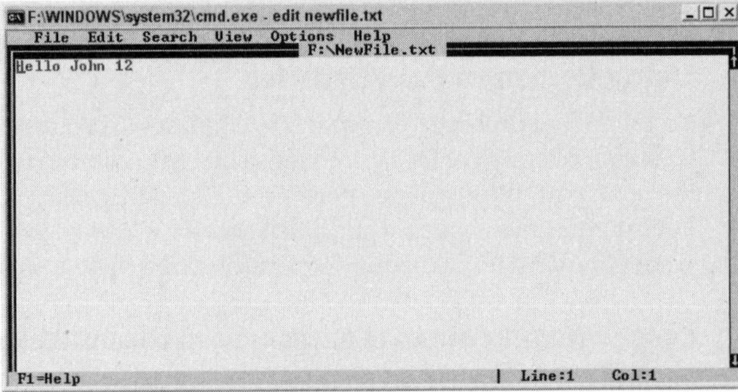

Figure 7.4
Use Edit wherever you need a fully functional text editor.

As you can see, the utility sports many of the same features as Notepad, but without the Notepad requirements. This utility uses the following syntax:

```
EDIT [/B] [/H] [/R] [/S] [/<nnn>] [/?] [file(s)]
```

The following list describes each of the command line arguments.

/B Sets Edit to start in monochrome mode.

/H Sets Edit to start with the maximum number of lines of text for your hardware. The default setup displays 25 lines of text.

/R Loads files in read-only mode. Use this option when you want to view the file content without accidentally changing it.

/S Forces Edit to use short filenames.

/nnn Loads a binary file and displays the content by wrapping any long lines to the specified number of characters.

file Specifies the name of the file to load. You can use wildcard characters and multiple file specifications to load multiple files. This argument must appear as the last argument on the command line.

FORMATTING A DISK WITH THE FORMAT UTILITY

The Format utility formats a drive and prepares it for use. The utility removes any existing data from the volume you select. This section discusses the command line version of the Format utility. The recovery console offers a slightly different version of this utility. You must be a member of the Administrators group to use this utility. The utility always displays a warning message before it formats a hard drive; you must specifically accept the warning message content before the format will start. This utility uses the following syntax:

```
FORMAT volume [/FS:file-system] [/V:label] [/Q] [/A:size] [/C] [/X]
   [/P:Passes]
FORMAT volume [/V:label] [/Q] [/F:size] [/P:Passes]
FORMAT volume [/V:label] [/Q] [/T:tracks /N:sectors] [/P:Passes]
FORMAT volume [/V:label] [/Q] [/P:Passes]
FORMAT volume [/Q]
```

The following list describes each of the command line arguments.

WARNING **The Format utility has caused more people more woe than any other utility ever created. Simply stated, the Format utility will format your hard drive. In many cases, you can recover files that the Format utility removes from the hard drive using a special utility, but the process is time consuming and error prone at best. Use this utility with extreme caution.**

volume Specifies the drive letter, mount point, or volume name to format. Always include this argument because the default value is the current drive.

/FS:*filesystem* Specifies the file system to use to format the volume. You have the option of using the FAT (older 16-bit), FAT32, or NTFS file systems when working with a hard drive. Floppy media only accepts the FAT file system.

/V:[*label*] Specifies the volume name. If you use this command line switch without specifying a volume name, the Format utility prompts you for a volume name upon completion of the format.

/Q Performs a quick format of the media. A quick format deletes the file table and the root directory of the media. It doesn't perform a sector-by-sector scan of the media to locate bad sectors. You should only use this option with known good media.

/C Creates an NTFS volume that the system compresses by default. Consequently, you won't need to perform this step separately later.

/X Forces the system to dismount the drive before formatting if necessary. Dismounting the drive closes all open handles.

/A:*size* Overrides the default allocation unit size for the hard drive. You can use this feature to optimize storage for specific tasks. For example, if you plan to store many small files, you might want to use a small allocation size. The size argument can include 512 bytes, 1024 bytes, 2048 bytes, 4096 bytes, 8192 bytes, 16 KB, 32 KB, and 64 KB cluster sizes for NTFS drives. You can't use compression on NTFS drives with a cluster size larger than 4096. A FAT or FAT32 formatted drive can use cluster sizes of 512 bytes, 1024 bytes, 2048 bytes, 4096 bytes, 8192 bytes, 16 KB, 32 KB, 64 KB, 128 KB, and 256 KB. You can only use the 128 K and 256 K options for a sector size greater than 512 bytes.

NOTE FAT and FAT32 file systems impose a limit on the number of clusters per volume. A FAT-formatted drive can have 65,526 or fewer clusters. A FAT32-formatted drive can have any number of clusters between 65,526 and 4,177,918. The Format utility stops immediately when it detects that a drive can't meet the number of cluster requirements using the specified cluster size.

/F:*size* Specifies the size of the floppy disk to format. The default setting is 1.44 MB. You can specify this value as 1440, 1440k, 1440kb, 1.44, 1.44m, or 1.44mb. The Format utility will also format 720 KB floppies. None of the Microsoft documentation specifies whether the utility formats 2.88 MB floppies. Theoretically, you can also format the very old 5½-inch floppies with sizes of 640 KB and 1.2 MB. Use this option, whenever possible, instead of the `/T` and `/N` command line switches.

/T:*tracks* Specifies the number of tracks per side of the disk.

/N:*sectors* Specifies the number of sectors per track.

The format command provides a number of exit codes that you can use when working with batch files. The following list describes each of the exit codes.

0 The format completed successfully.

1 The format failed because you provided incorrect arguments.

4 A fatal error occurred. For example, the utility couldn't format the drive because the system has it locked for use. The Format utility uses this error when the 0, 1, or 5 codes don't apply.

5 The user pressed `N` when the utility asked whether it should proceed with the disk format. Pressing `N` always stops the formatting process.

/P:*Passes* Zeroes every sector on the hard drive the number of times defined by `Passes`. This is a new security feature for Vista. The /P command line switch makes it possible for you to erase the data on a hard drive more completely. However, the only certain way to ensure the data is gone is to destroy the hard drive completely and magnetically erase the media.

Load Older DOS Applications with the LoadFix Utility

Some older applications don't load correctly. You'll see a "Packed file corrupt" error message when you try to load them. The LoadFix utility modifies the loading process for these applications so they load above the 64 KB area of memory used for operating system needs. This utility uses the following syntax:

```
LOADFIX [drive:][path]filename
```

The following describes the command line argument.

[drive:][path]filename Specifies the name and location of the file to modify.

CONFIGURING SYSTEM DEVICES WITH THE MODE UTILITY

The Mode utility configures system devices for use. In addition, you can use it to display the status of a single device or all devices in the system. To display the status of all accessible devices type `Mode` and press Enter. If you want the status of just one device, type `Mode` followed by the device name, such as LPT1:, and press Enter. This utility uses the following syntax:

```
Serial Port
       MODE COMm[:] [BAUD=b] [PARITY=p] [DATA=d] [STOP=s] [to={on |
          off}] [xon={on | off}] [odsr={on | off}] [octs={on | off}]
          [dtr={on | off | hs}] [rts={on | off | hs | tg}] [idsr={on |
          off}]
Device Status
       MODE [device] [/STATUS]
Redirect Printing
       MODE LPTn[:]=COMm[:]
Select Code Page
       MODE CON[:] CP SELECT=yyy
Code Page Status
       MODE CON[:] CP [/STATUS]
Display Mode
       MODE CON[:] [COLS=c] [LINES=n]
Typematic Rate
       MODE CON[:] [RATE=r DELAY=d]
```

The following list describes each of the command line arguments.

COM*m*[:] Defines the COM port to configure. The Mode utility recognizes any COM port for which it can find a device name. Generally, this means it will support COM1: through COM9: unless you have special hardware to make additional COM ports available.

NOTE As you work with utilities at the command prompt, you'll find that different utilities support different numbers of ports. Most utilities support at least LPT1: through LPT3:, but you'll find a few that support up to LPT9:. Support for the COM (serial) ports is even more diverse. A few utilities only support COM1: through COM3:. More common is support for COM1: through COM4: for utilities. However, you'll find a few that support up to COM9: and a few that support as many COM ports as your machine has installed. One device is a constant: every workstation supports the CON: (console) device.

BAUD=*b* Determines the transmission rate of the COM port in bits per second (bps). Note that bps isn't always equivalent to baud; see the definition at `http://webopedia.internet.com/TERM/B/baud.html` for details. Table 7.2 shows numbers you must use to specify a desired rate.

TABLE 7.2: Baud Rates Supported by the Mode Utility

NUMERIC VALUE	EQUIVALENT BAUD RATE
11	110 baud
15	150 baud

TABLE 7.2: Baud Rates Supported by the Mode Utility *(CONTINUED)*

NUMERIC VALUE	EQUIVALENT BAUD RATE
30	300 baud
60	600 baud
12	1,200 baud
24	2,400 baud
48	4,800 baud
96	9,600 baud
19	19,200 baud

PARITY=*p* Determines how the system checks for transmission errors. The mode command supports the values shown in Table 7.3.

TABLE 7.3: Parity Types Supported by the Mode Utility

PARITY VALUE	PARITY CHECKING TYPE
`n`	none
`e`	even
`o`	odd
`m`	mark
`s`	space

DATA=*d* Specifies the number of data bits per character. You may use any value between 5 and 8. The default setting of 7 provides support for standard ASCII characters. Use 8 for extended ASCII characters (the 256-character set). Not all computers support 5 or 6 bits per character.

STOP=*s* Specifies the number of stop bits after each character. You may specify 1, 1.5, and 2 as stop bit values. The default setting for 110 baud is 2. All other data transfer rates use 1 as a default value. Not all computers support 1.5 stop bits.

to={on | off} Specifies whether the computer uses infinite time out processing. The default value is off. Setting this value to on means that the computer will wait literally forever to receive a response from a host or client computer.

xon={on | off} Specifies whether the system enables XON/XOFF protocol. The XON/XOFF protocol provides flow control for serial communications, making them more reliable, but also exacting a performance penalty. You can learn more about the XON/XOFF protocol at `http://docs.hp.com/en/32022-90051/ch09s08.html`.

odsr={on | off} Specifies whether the system enables the Data Set Ready (DSR) output handshaking.

octs={on | off} Specifies whether the system enables the Clear to Send (CTS) output handshaking.

dtr={on | off | hs} Specifies whether the system enables the Data Terminal Ready (DTR) output handshaking. The on mode provides a constant signal showing the terminal is ready to receive data. The hs mode provides a handshaking signal between the two terminals.

rts={on | off | hs | tg} Specifies whether the system enables the Request to Send (RTS) output handshaking. The on mode provides a constant signal showing the terminal is ready to send data. The hs mode provides a handshaking signal between the two terminals. The tg mode provides a toggling feature between ready and not ready states.

idsr={on | off} Specifies whether the system enables DSR sensitivity. You must enable this feature to use DSR handshaking.

device Defines the name of the device that you want to work with. Standard names include LPT1: through LPT3:, COM1: through COM9:, and CON:.

/STATUS Specifies that you want to obtain the status of a specified device or of all accessible devices on the system.

LPT*n*[:] Defines the number of the LPT port to configure. Generally, this means supplying a name from LPT1: through LPT3: unless your system includes special parallel port support.

CON[:] Defines the console as the target for configuration or a status check.

NOTE The Mode utility only supports physical devices. You can't use it to configure virtual devices. For example, if you redirect a network printer to use LPT1:, the Mode utility won't display any status information about it and you won't be able to configure the device in any way. However, if you have a physical LPT1 port on your machine, you can use the Mode utility to configure it. Because every workstation computer has a physical console, you can always use the Mode utility to configure the CON device and obtain status information about it.

CP Configures or queries the code page information for the selected device. Table 7.1 contains a list of the code pages that Windows supports natively. You can add support for additional code pages.

SELECT=*yyy* Determines the number of the code page to use with the selected device.

COLS=*c* Determines the number of columns displayed on screen. The default setting is 80 columns. Although you can configure the number of columns to any value, other standard values include 40 and 135. Using a nonstandard value can result in command line application problems.

LINES=*n* Determines the number of lines in the screen buffer. The default value is 25 (the other standard value is 50). You can use any value for the number of lines.

RATE=*r* Determines the typematic rate for the keyboard. The typematic rate determines how fast Windows will repeat a character when you press the associated key on the keyboard. You may use any value in the range from 1 through 32. The default setting is 20 characters per second. If you set the typematic rate, you must also set the delay.

DELAY=*d* Determines the delay between the time you press a key and the time Windows begins repeating the associated character on screen. Valid values for d are 1 (0.25 seconds), 2 (0.50 seconds), 3 (0.75 seconds), and 4 (1 second). The default value is 2.

Working at the Command Prompt

Some commands and utilities help you create a better working environment at the command prompt. In many cases, these commands are aesthetic; they don't do any useful work in the sense of modifying a file or the system state. The following sections describe these efficiency commands and utilities.

Real World Scenario

CREATING A NICE WORK ENVIRONMENT

You might wonder why you would spend time learning about commands and utilities that don't do any useful work. For me, it's the same reason for having carpeting on the floor or a remote for the television; it's all about comfort. For example, you'll find that the display buffer eventually becomes full of extraneous data you don't really want to see any longer. Sure, you could ignore the garbage on your screen, but it's a lot better to get rid of it so you can work in comfort. Using the CLS command will clear the display buffer for you so you can continue working efficiently.

Users of your batch file and script applications want a nice working environment too. You'll often use these commands and utilities in your batch files to provide special effects. The CLS command clears the display so the user viewing the output of the batch file doesn't become confused.

Redirecting Command Line Output to the Clipboard with the Clip Utility

The Clip utility is an interesting addition to Vista. Anyone who has used redirection knows the benefits of sending output data to another location, such as a file, or getting input from another location, such as the COM port. The Clip utility lets you perform redirection using the Windows Clipboard. You use redirection or the pipe command as you normally do. For example, `Dir | Clip` sends the output for the directory command to the clipboard. This command uses the following syntax:

```
Clip
```

You don't need to supply any command line switches when using this command.

Clearing the Display with the *CLS* Command

The `Clear Screen (CLS)` command clears the screen buffer and presents you with a clean display. All that remains is the command prompt. This command uses the following syntax:

```
CLS
```

You don't need to supply any command line switches when using this command.

Managing User Names and Passwords with CmdKey

The CmdKey utility is a new addition to Vista that helps you manage username and passwords. Using this utility, you can display, create, and delete credentials as needed. However, this utility only works with the current user. In other words, the credentials you manage are for the current user, not for another user on the same system. To work with other users, you must first log in as that user. Consequently, this command works well with login batch files that perform tasks on the user's behalf, but not necessarily as a good tool for administering users at the command line.

A system can have two kinds of passwords managed by CmdKey. The first is generic passwords that you can use anywhere. For example, you might create a username and password to access a remote system using a Virtual Private Network (VPN). The second is domain passwords that you use to access a domain server. These password types appear in the Type field output when you list credentials for your system.

Displaying

The /list command line switch lets you list all of the credentials associated with the current account. This mode uses the following syntax:

```
cmdkey /list
cmdkey /list:targetname
```

The following list describes each of the command line arguments.

/list Displays all of the entries or only those that you specify with a target name.

targetname Defines a target credential. You use the name of the credential as the target. This command line argument doesn't allow wildcard characters, so you can only use it to list one credential at a time.

Creating

Creates a new domain or generic credential based on a username and password. Use the /add command line switch to create domain credentials and the /generic command line switch to create generic credentials. This mode uses the following syntax:

```
cmdkey /add:targetname /user:username /pass:password
cmdkey /add:targetname /user:username /pass
cmdkey /add:targetname /user:username
cmdkey /add:targetname /smartcard
cmdkey /generic:targetname /user:username /pass:password
cmdkey /generic:targetname /user:username /pass
cmdkey /generic:targetname /user:username
cmdkey /generic:targetname /smartcard
```

The following list describes each of the command line arguments.

/add Creates a domain credential.

/generic Creates a generic credential.

targetname Defines a target credential. You use the name of the credential as the target. This command line argument doesn't allow wildcard characters, so you can only use it to list one credential at a time.

/user:*username* Specifies the username used for login purposes. The username can include any qualifiers required to perform the login.

/pass or /pass:*password* Specifies the password used for login purposes. If you specify /pass without the password, the system prompts you for a password to use on the remote system. Unlike many password prompts, this prompt doesn't display the password characters as asterisks (*), so it's easy to make mistakes. Make sure you type the password carefully.

/smartcard Creates a password based on the content of a smartcard. The system prompts you to provide the smartcard as part of the input.

DELETING

You can't change a credential using the CmdKey utility. To change a credential, you must first delete the old credential and then create a new one. In addition, you'll likely find that you need to delete old credentials when you don't need them any longer. This mode uses the following syntax:

```
cmdkey /delete:targetname
cmdkey /delete /ras
```

The following list describes each of the command line arguments.

/delete:*targetname* Removes the specified credential. You must provide a target name unless you're deleting a Remote Access Server (RAS) credential.

/ras Specifies that you want to remove a RAS credential.

Changing Screen Colors with the *Color* Command

The `Color` command changes the foreground (text) and background colors of the command window. This command uses the following syntax:

```
COLOR [FG]
```

The following describes the command line argument.

FG Sets the foreground (F) and background (G) colors. You must place the values together, without any space between. If you use the `Color` command without specifying color values, the command changes the colors to the default values used when you opened the command window. The following list tells you which colors you can use at the command prompt, along with their associated color number.

0—Black

1—Blue

2—Green

3—Aqua

4—Red

5—Purple

6—Yellow

7—White

8—Gray

9—Light blue

A—Light green

B—Light aqua

C—Light red

D—Light purple

E—Light yellow

F—Bright white

Working with the System Date Using the *Date* Command

The `Date` command displays or sets the system date. This command uses the following syntax:

```
DATE [{/T | date}]
```

The following list describes each of the command line arguments.

/T Displays the date without prompting for a new date. This command line switch only works when you enable command extensions.

date Specifies the new system date.

Tracking Command Line Actions with the DosKey Utility

The DosKey utility performs three tasks. First, it provides the history feature that most people use to scroll through existing command line entries. Press Down Arrow to see the next command, Up Arrow to see the previous command, Page Down to see the most recent command, and Page Up to see the oldest command in the history.

Second, you can use this command to edit previous commands. The following list describes the editing features.

LEFT ARROW Moves to the previous character in the command.

RIGHT ARROW Moves to the next character in the command.

CTRL+LEFT ARROW Moves to the previous word in the command.

CTRL+RIGHT ARROW Moves to the next word in the command.

HOME Moves to the beginning of the line.

END Moves to the end of the line.

ESC Clears the command from the display.

F1 Copies the next character from the same column in the command that you previously issued.

NOTE The system places the previous command in a special area of memory called the template and lets you work with that command based on the current column position. For example, if you typed `Dir *.BAK` as the previous command, executed it, and then typed `Dir` at the command line, pressing F1 would type a space. Pressing F1 again would type the asterisk (*) and so on. Using the same example, pressing F2 and then the letter A would display `Dir *.BA` at the command prompt. Using the combination of the template and function keys helps you reduce the number of keystrokes you make to type a command.

F2 Searches forward in the previous command for the next key you type after pressing F2.

F3 Copies the remainder of the previous command to the command line.

F4 Deletes characters from the current cursor position up to a character you specify. For example, if the command line currently displays `Dir *.BAK` and the cursor is blinking under the asterisk (*), pressing F4 and the letter B would change the command prompt to read `Dir BAK`.

F5 Copies the previous command into the current command line.

F6 Places an end-of-file character (Ctrl+Z) at the current cursor position. You typically use this feature when using the console to create a file.

F7 Displays all of the commands stored in the command history in a dialog box. Select a command using the Up Arrow and Down Arrow. Press Enter to select the command. DosKey will type the selected command at the command prompt. Press Enter again to execute the command. You can also note the sequential number in front of the command and use this number with the F9 key.

ALT+F7 Deletes all commands stored in the current command history buffer.

F8 Displays a single command from the command history that starts with the characters in the current command. Press F8 multiple times to cycle through the list of matching commands.

F9 Prompts you for a history buffer command number, and then displays the command associated with the number you specify. Press Enter to run the command. Press F7 to display a list of commands in the command history buffer, along with their associated command number.

ALT+F10 Deletes all macro definitions.

Third, you can use this command to create macros. The macros automate some command line tasks, similarly to batch files, but far more inconveniently. You can also use these macros to interact with applications. However, the number of applications that can use DosKey macros is extremely limited. For example, you could use a DosKey macro with the FTP utility described in the "Managing FTP Servers with the FTP Utility" section of Chapter 5. To qualify for use with the DosKey utility, the application must run at the command prompt and provide buffered input. Because of the limitations posed by DosKey macros, this book won't discuss them. However, you can find many examples of DosKey macros online. For example, the Web page at `http://www.palmtoppaper.com/ptphtml/17/pt170037.htm` shows a number of helpful macros you can create. You'll find a good how-to article at `http://www.atarimagazines.com/compute/issue137/S18_How_to_create_keyboa.php`. The article at `http://www.melbpc.org.au/pcupdate/9405/9405article7.htm` provides step-by-step creation process for DosKey macros. This utility uses the following syntax:

```
DOSKEY [/REINSTALL] [/LISTSIZE=size] [/MACROS[:ALL | :exename]]
  [/HISTORY] [/INSERT | /OVERSTRIKE] [/EXENAME=exename] [/MACROFILE=filename]
  [macroname=[text]]
```

The following list describes each of the command line arguments.

/REINSTALL Installs a new copy of DosKey. Use this feature when your current copy has become corrupted or simply filled with extraneous data.

/LISTSIZE=size Determines the number of commands that will fit within the command history buffer. The default setting is 10.

/MACROS Displays a list of all of the DosKey macros. The output includes command line macros, as well as those associated with an application.

/MACROS:ALL Displays a list of all the DosKey macros for all executables that have DosKey compatibility. For example, if you create a DosKey macro for the FTP utility, this command line switch would display it.

/MACROS:*exename* Displays a list of all the DosKey macros associated with the specified application.

/HISTORY Displays a list of all of the commands in the command history buffer.

/INSERT Places DosKey in insert mode. Any new text you type at the command line will appear in addition to the existing text.

/OVERSTRIKE Places DosKey in overstrike mode. Any new text you type at the command line will replace (overwrite) existing text.

/EXENAME=*exename* Specifies the name of an executable to use when creating a macro. The resulting macro will run within that application. The application must support DosKey to use this functionality. If you don't specify this command line switch, any macro you create or install will run at the command line and not as part of an application.

/MACROFILE=*filename* Specifies a file containing macros that you want to install.

macroname Specifies the name for a macro you create. Typing the macro name, followed by an equals sign, and pressing Enter deletes a macro from the list.

text Contains the text of the macro you want to record. You must include a macro name, followed by an equals sign, followed by the macro text to use this argument. For example, you can define a macro named MyDir that displays a directory by typing `DosKey MyDir=Dir *.* /P` and pressing Enter. After you create this macro, you can type `MyDir` at the command prompt, press Enter, and DosKey will execute the MyDir macro.

Obtaining Command Line Help with the Help Utility

In most cases, you'll type the name of a utility, followed by the /? command line switch to learn more about it. However, Microsoft decided to make things difficult in some cases. For example, some utilities require that you use the `/Help` command line switch instead or you might have to use the Help utility to learn more about the command or utility in question. To see a list of commands and utilities that Help supports, type `Help` and press Enter. This utility uses the following syntax:

```
HELP [command]
```

The following describes the command line argument.

command Specifies the name of the command for which you want to obtain more information. If you type **`Help`** by itself and press Enter, you'll see a list of all of the available commands. You can then choose a specific command to learn more about with the Help utility.

Working with the System Time Using the *Time* Command

The Time command displays or sets the system time. This command uses the following syntax:

```
TIME [/T | time]
```

The following list describes each of the command line arguments.

/T Displays the date without prompting for a new time. This command line switch only works when you enable command extensions.

time Specifies the new system time.

Changing the Command Window Title with the *Title* Command

The title that a command window displays might not seem important at first, but the title can be important for two reasons. First, if you have multiple command windows open, using a descriptive title can make it easier to locate the correct command window on the Windows Taskbar. Second, it's important to remember that Windows associates settings changes you make with the command window title. Changing the title affects how Windows stores the settings changes you make. The `Title` command can change the title of a command window. This command uses the following syntax:

```
TITLE [string]
```

The following describes the command line argument.

string Contains the text for the command window.

Creating Batch Files

Batch files are a type of simple programming that can help you store a series of commands that you want to execute more than once. The batch file normally appears within a file with a BAT extension. In most cases, you won't need to perform any programming to create a batch file; simply create a file that contains the commands you want to execute one after the other.

NOTE Windows doesn't support the `Break` command found in many older batch files. The original purpose of the `Break` command was to provide control over the Ctrl+Break key. Setting `Break ON` would let someone press Ctrl+Break to stop execution of a batch file. Windows ignores this command line switch. In addition, Vista changes support for some batch commands from previous versions of Windows and adds new commands. Consequently, batch files that worked fine in Windows XP may suddenly stop working in Vista.

Even with the limitations of a batch file, however, you might be surprised at the number of ways that people use them. For example, if you find that you're constantly forgetting how to perform tasks at the command line, create a menu system with your favorite commands. That way, you only have to look up the command information one time. The following sections describe the programming features of batch files and provide you with some sample batch files.

FINDING CODE ONLINE

I'm a code hound. I have more links to online code than I care to think about because all of these links are useful in some way. This chapter contains batch file examples that help you understand basic principles and perform some essential tasks at the command line. However, if you're like me, you'll want more; you'll want examples that show you how to perform more tasks than I could ever include in a single book. You can find a wealth of batch files for performing administrative or other essential tasks at the Rob van der Woude Web site at `http://www.robvanderwoude.com/batexamples_0c.html`. If you want to see some very complex examples, including using math within a batch file (something most people will say you can't do) then go to Tom Lavedas' Batch File Applications Web site at `http://members.cox.net/tglbatch/`.

Using the *Call* Command

You use the Call command to call another location with the current batch file or to start another batch file. When you want to call another location in the same batch file, you use the label formatting shown here.

```
Call :MyLabel
```

Calling another batch file is similar. You provide the drive, path, and filename of the batch file. In addition, you can provide command line arguments for the external batch file as shown here.

```
Call C:\MyBatchFiles\MyBatch.BAT CommandArg1
```

A call is different from going to another location. When a call completes, the batch file returns to the calling location and executes the next instruction. In contrast, when you use the Goto command, the batch file actually transfers control to the new location. The return feature of the Call command lets you create an advanced programming construct called recursion. Recursion occurs when a batch file calls itself. You must provide an exit strategy, however, or the batch file will enter an endless loop.

The easiest way to see the effect of the Call command is to create two batch files named Batch1.BAT and Batch2.BAT. Here's the content for Batch1.BAT.

```
@ECHO OFF
Call Batch2.BAT
Call Batch2.BAT Passed %1 %PATH%
ECHO In Batch 1
GOTO :EOF
ECHO Goodbye
```

Here's the content for Batch2.BAT.

```
ECHO In Batch 2, Goodbye
IF NOT [%1]==[] ECHO String: %1
IF NOT [%2]==[] ECHO Batch 1 Input: %2
IF NOT [%3]==[] ECHO Environment Variable: %3
```

Looking at the Batch1.BAT content, the example begins by turning echo off. You'll normally add this code to your batch files so the user doesn't see a lot of confusing text that has nothing to do with the current task. Preceding the ECHO command with the @ symbol tells the system not to display the ECHO command either. The first call to Batch2.BAT doesn't pass any information, so Batch2.BAT only displays the message, "In Batch 2, Goodbye." The second call to Batch2.BAT passes the three kinds of information you can include with a batch file: a string, a local variable (argument), and a global variable. The code then proceeds to display "In Batch 1," and then it exits. The GOTO :EOF statement is special; it tells the batch file to end now. You don't have to define a label, in this case, because EOF is built into the command process. (See the "Using the *Goto* Command" section of this chapter for details.)

The Batch2.BAT file always echoes "In Batch 2, Goodbye." In this case, the IF statements verify that the caller has passed information to the batch file. When the caller doesn't pass the required variables, then the batch file doesn't display any information for that input. The [%1]==[] construct is one way to check for an empty input. Figure 7.5 shows the output from this application. Notice the sequence of events. The first batch file calls the second batch file. When the second batch file is finished, execution continues with the next statement in the first batch file.

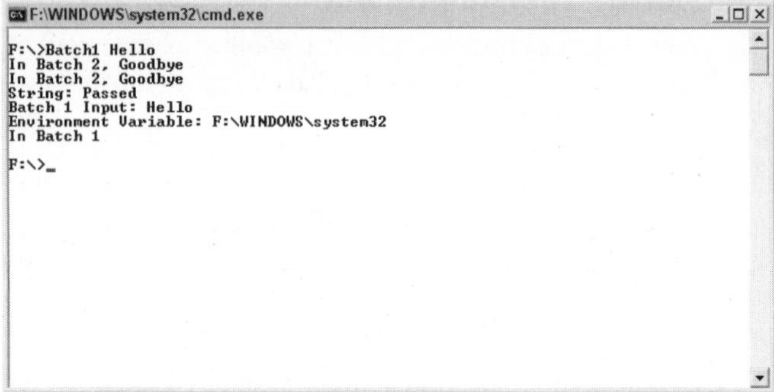

F:\WINDOWS\system32\cmd.exe
F:\>Batch1 Hello
In Batch 2, Goodbye
In Batch 2, Goodbye
String: Passed
Batch 1 Input: Hello
Environment Variable: F:\WINDOWS\system32
In Batch 1
F:\>_

FIGURE 7.5
Calls provide a means of performing subtasks in a batch file and then continuing with the main task.

Windows provides enhanced methods of working with variables in batch files. These enhanced expansions help you pass specific variable information to a callee from your batch files. See the "Using Variable Substitution" section of the chapter for details on using this technique.

Using the *Choice* Command

VISTA

The `Choice` command lets you add interactive processing to batch files. Whether you use this option depends on the kind of automation you want to add to your processing tasks. Most of the automation you create for optimization tasks won't require any kind of interactivity because you already know how you want the task performed based on experience you obtained performing the task manually. However, sometimes you do need to add some interactivity. For example, you might run the command one way on Friday and a different way the rest of the week. The `Choice` command can also help you add safeguards that ensure the user understands the ramifications of performing a certain task before they actually do it. Vista changes the Choice command significantly, breaking many batch files. Consequently, you'll find the Vista form of the Choice command later in this section. The Windows XP and earlier version of the `Choice` command provides the following optional arguments.

Text Provides text that the `Choice` command displays to explain the choice to the user. This is the same as combining the `Choice` and `Echo` commands, but only requires one line of code.

/C:*Keys* Defines the single character response the user can type. The default values are Y (for yes) and N (for no). The valid input values appear within brackets. For example, when you use `/C:ABC`, the `Choice` command displays them as `[A,B,C]` on the command line. You can override this option using the `/N` switch—the keys remain, but `Choice` doesn't display them.

/N Tells `Choice` not to display the valid keys at the command prompt. The choices appear as a list of letters without explanation, which might work in some cases (a numeric list), but not in others (a series of letters). One reason to use this option is to display a custom list of options. Many batch files will list the choice letters with a fuller explanation of the choice, such as (Q)uit. The user presses Q to quit, but having the fuller explanation reduces potential confusion.

/S Makes the inputs case-sensitive—normally `Choice` treats uppercase and lowercase letters the same. Using case-sensitive input doubles the number of letter choices, but can also create user confusion.

/T:Character,NumberOfSeconds Provides an automatic selection feature. `Choice` automatically types the character for the user after the number of seconds elapses. The number of seconds can range from 0 to 99, where a value of 0 makes the choice automatically without pausing for user input. Some batch files use the 0 option where the user would normally have a choice, but doesn't in a specific case, such as installing an application.

When you use `Choice` by itself, it displays a simple `[Y,N]` prompt that doesn't accomplish much unless you also provide an Echo command to describe what the user should say yes or no to. Normally, you'll combine the `Choice` command with one or more arguments. Listing 7.1 shows a simple example of the `Choice` command at work.

LISTING 7.1: Using the *Choice* Command

```
Echo Off

REM Keep repeating until the user enters E.
:Repeat

REM Display the choices.
Choice /C:DCE /N /T:E,10 Choose an option (D)isplay, (C)opy, or (E)nd.

REM Act on the user choice.
If ErrorLevel 3 Goto End
If ErrorLevel 2 Goto Copy
If ErrorLevel 1 Goto Display

REM Copy the file.
:Copy
Echo You chose to copy the file.
Goto Repeat

REM Display the file.
:Display
Echo You chose to display the file.
Goto Repeat

REM End the batch processing.
:End
Echo Goodbye
Echo On
```

The code begins by creating a repeat label so the batch file continues working until the user specifically stops it. Next, the code uses the `Choice` command to display the choices to the user. The `/C` switch tells `Choice` that the valid options are D, C, or E instead of the default Y or N. Because the text specifically defines the characters that the batch file expects, the batch file uses the `/N` switch to suppress displaying the valid key choices on the command line. The `/T` command line switch tells `Choice` to automatically choose E after 10 seconds.

Although this batch file doesn't actually do anything with a file, it shows how you'd set up the batch file to process the user choice. Notice that the batch file uses the ErrorLevel clause of the `If` statement to detect the user choice. The ErrorLevel clause detects every choice lower than the user selection, so you must place the values in reverse order, as shown. In addition, you must specifically set the batch file to go to another location because it will process all other statements after the current error level.

The processing code simply displays a string telling you what choice the user made. Normally, you'd add tasks that the batch file should perform based on the user's selection. Notice that the copy and display selections tell the batch file to go back to the Repeat label. This is the most common technique for creating a menu loop in a batch file. The batch file ends by telling the user goodbye and turning echo back on.

The Vista form of the Choice command differs not in arguments, but in how you combine those arguments at the command line. Here's the command line for Vista:

```
CHOICE [/C choices] [/N] [/CS] [/T timeout /D choice] [/M text]
```

The changes make the command clearer, but they break existing batch files in a way that you can't easily fix. The new /CS command line switch lets you make choices case sensitive, so you can have 26 additional menu choices. However, notice that /T no longer takes both a default option and a timeout value. The new form requires that you provide a choice using the /D command line switch instead. You must also provide the /M command line switch to specify optional text. The following sample code performs the same task, but the first form works in Windows XP and earlier, while the second form works in Vista.

```
Old Choice Command Form
CHOICE /C:N /N /T:N,15
Vista Choice Command Form
CHOICE /C N /N /T 15 /D N
```

NOTE Vista provides alternatives for the Choice command. The TimeOut utility provides a specific timeout value without requiring the user to make a choice. You can learn more about this utility in the "Using the TimeOut Utility" section of the chapter. The WaitFor utility lets you use signaling between systems or applications on the same system. One application sends a signal and another reacts when it receives the signal. You can learn more about this utility in the "Using the WaitFor Utility" section of the chapter.

Using the *Echo* Command

The command line uses the term *echo* to describe the process where the system echoes (repeats) every command in a batch file to the command line. Echo provides a means of seeing which command the system is processing. However, echo can become confusing for users who aren't aware of or don't care about the commands that are executing. In addition, echo can disrupt visual effects, such as menu systems, that you create. The Echo command has two forms. The first form

```
ECHO [{ON | OFF}]
```

displays the echo status when you don't include any arguments. The ON argument turns on echo so you can see the commands and the OFF argument turns off echo so you can create visual effects. You can precede the Echo command with the @ sign so it doesn't appear as one of the commands. @Echo OFF would turn echo off without displaying the echo command at the command prompt.

The second form of Echo

```
ECHO [message]
```

lets you display a message. Simply type the text you want to see after the Echo command. In this case, the system won't display the Echo command, just the message you want to display. Don't use the @ sign with this form of the Echo command or the user won't see the message.

Using the *Exit* Command

Most people associate the `Exit` command with closing the current command window. Using `Exit` alone will close the command window. However, you can also use this command within a batch file to exit the batch file. To perform this task, you must use one or both of the following optional `Exit` arguments.

/B Specifies that you want to exit a batch file, rather than the current command line session. If you don't specify this command line switch, the command window closes, even when you issue the `Exit` command from a batch file.

ExitCode Defines an exit code for the batch file. The default exit code is 0, which normally signifies success. You can use exit codes to alert the caller to errors or special conditions. The exit codes aren't defined by the system, so you can define any set of exit codes that you deem necessary for your application.

Using the *ForFiles* Utility

VISTA

The ForFiles utility provides a means of looping through a list of files and performing actions on those files one at a time. For example, you might want to process all files that someone has changed since a certain date. In most respects, this loop method works precisely the same as the For command described in the "Using the *For* Command" section of the chapter. This command uses the following syntax:

```
FORFILES [/P pathname] [/M searchmask] [/S] [/C command]
[/D [+ | -] {MM/dd/yyyy | dd}]
```

The following list describes each of the command line arguments.

/P *pathname* Specifies the starting point for a search. The path is the starting folder in the search. The default setting uses the current directory as the starting point.

/M *searchmask* Defines a search mask for the files. You can use the asterisk (*) and question mark (?) as wildcard characters, just as you would when using the Directory command. The default setting searches for all files in the target directory.

/S Searches all of the subdirectories of the specified directory.

/C *command* Specifies the command you want to execute for each file. Always wrap the command in double quotes to ensure it isn't interpreted as part of the ForFile command. The default command is `"cmd /c echo @file"`. Always precede internal command processor command by typing cmd /c. The following list describes the variables that you can use as part of the command.

@file Returns the name of the file, including the file extension.

@fname Returns the name of the file without the extension.

@ext Returns only the file extension.

@path Returns the full path of the file. This information includes the drive as well as the actual path.

@relpath Returns the relative path of the file. The relative path begins at the starting folder.

@isdir Specifies whether the file type is a directory. True indicates a directory entry.

@fsize Indicates the size of the file in bytes.

@fdate Indicates the date that someone last modified the file.

@ftime Indicates the time that someone last modified the file.

TIP You can include special characters in a command by using the 0xHH format where HH is a hexadecimal number. For example, you can specify a tab by typing 0x09.

/D *date* Selects files that have a last modified date within the specified range. You specify a specific date using the month/day/year (mm/dd/yyyy) format. Add a plus sign if you want files after the specified date or a minus sign if you want files before the specified date. For example, /D -01/01/2008 would select all files modified before January 1st, 2008. You can also specify a relative date by providing a positive or negative number. For example, /D -7 would select all files modified within the last seven days. The /D command line switch will accept any number between 0 and –32,768.

Using the *For* Command

The For command fulfills a special niche in batch file programming. You know from the "Working with Wildcard Characters" sidebar in Chapter 2 that you can use wildcard characters to make multiple file selections when needed. Unfortunately, using wildcard characters won't always work. Sometimes you need to know the name of the file. A command line utility might not support wildcard characters or the file argument doesn't easily fit within the wildcard method of description. That's where the For statement comes into play for batch files. This command takes the form:

```
FOR %%variable IN (set) DO command [command-parameters]
```

You can also use this command at the command prompt to process files manually. Instead of using a single percent (%) symbol, you use two in front of the variable. Here's a sample of how you can use this command in a batch file.

```
Echo Off
For %%F In (*.BAT *.TXT) Do Dir %%F /B
Echo On
```

In this case, the For command processes all of the files that have a BAT or TXT extension in the current directory. The command processes the files in the order in which they appear in the directory and you have no guarantee what the order is. The %%F variable contains the name of an individual file. The Dir command is called once for each file with the %%F variable as an input. In this case, the command outputs the filenames using the bare format, so you could use this batch file to create a text file containing a list of files that match the criteria. Additional processing could archive the files or do anything else that you might like. The For command provides the following arguments.

{%*Variable* | %%*Variable*} Specifies a replaceable parameter; the argument that will receive the individual members of a set. The replaceable parameter takes two forms. Use the %Variable form when you want to use the replaceable parameter as input to another command or utility. Use the %%Variable form when you want to use the replaceable parameter for activities within the batch file. The variable names are case-sensitive, so %f isn't the same as %F. In addition, you must use an alphabetical variable name, such as %A, %B, or %C.

(*Set*) Defines the set to process. The set can include one or more files, directories, range of values, or text strings that you want to process with the specified command. For example, you can use environment variables as the set. The command For %%P In (%PATH%) Do ECHO %%P would display the members of the PATH environment variable as individual strings.

Command Specifies the command you want to perform for each entry in the set.

CommandLineOptions Defines the command line options for the command that you want to perform for each entry in the set. The command line options are command or utility specific; see the other entries in this book for details.

Performing Complex File Iteration

You can use the For command to process command output, strings, and the content of files. In this case, the For command begins by breaking the input into individual lines of content and discarding any blank lines. It then breaks whatever input you provide into specific tokens based on the rules you specify. A token can be a control character, a special word, or anything else you can define as part of the simple syntax for this command. The For command passes the token to a command you specify as input. Here's the command line syntax for this form of the For command.

```
for /F ["ParsingKeywords"] {%% | %}Variabe lin (FileNameSet) do Command
   [CommandLineOptions]
for /F ["ParsingKeywords"] {%% | %}Variable in ("LiteralString") do
   Command [CommandLineOptions]
for /F ["ParsingKeywords"] {%% | %}Variable in ('Command') do Command
   [CommandLineOptions]
```

Notice that you need to use a different command line syntax for each kind of input. A filename appears without quotes, while a string appears in double quotes and a command appears in single quotes. The small differences in command format determines how the For command views the input.

The ParsingKeywords input is a quoted string that specifies the rules for parsing the input into tokens. These keywords always appear in double quotes, as shown. The following list describes the keywords you can use.

eol=*c* Specifies an end of line character. The For command only allows you to specify one character.

skip=*N* Specifies the number of lines to skip at the beginning of the file.

delims=*xxx* Specifies a delimiter set. The delimiter set defines which characters the For command views as elements between tokens. The default setting relies on the space and tab. Consequently, the For command produces a new token every time it sees a space or tab within the input.

tokens=*X,Y,M-N* Defines which tokens to retrieve from each line of text to pass to the For command body for each iteration. The For command allocates one variable for each of the tokens. The M-N format defines a range of tokens to use as input. Whenever the last character in a processed string is an asterisk (*), the For command creates an additional variable to receive the additional text on the line after the For command parses the last token.

usebackq Specifies that you can use quotation marks to quote filenames in FileNameSet, a back quoted string is executed as a command, and a single quoted string is a literal string command.

You need to use a slightly different command line syntax with the For command when you rely on the usebackq keyword. Here are the three command lines using this syntax.

```
for /F ["usebackqParsingKeywords"] {%% | %}Variable in ("FileNameSet")
   do Command [CommandLineOptions]
for /F ["usebackqParsingKeywords"] {%% | %}Variable in
   ('LiteralString') do Command [CommandLineOptions]
for /F ["usebackqParsingKeywords"] {%% | %}Variable in ('Command') do
   Command [CommandLineOptions]
```

USING VARIABLE SUBSTITUTION

Variable substitution is the act of exchanging a variable name for the content of that variable. However, unlike expansion, you don't necessarily use all of the variable content. For example, instead of using the entire path for a file, you might just use the drive letter, the path, or the filename. The following list describes the basic forms of variable substitution available with the `For` command. (The list assumes that you're using a variable named `I`, which translates into `%I` at the command line.)

%~I Removes any surrounding quotation marks from the variable content.

%~fI Expands `%I` to a fully qualified path name.

%~dI Expands `%I` to a drive letter only.

%~pI Expands `%I` to a path only.

%~nI Expands `%I` to a filename only.

%~xI Expands `%I` to a file extension only.

%~sI Creates a path variable, and then changes any long directory names into their short name equivalents.

%~aI Obtains the file attributes of the input file.

%~tI Obtains the date and time of the input file.

%~zI Obtains the size of the input file.

%~$PATH:*I* Searches the directories listed in the `PATH` environment variable for the file specified by I. The system then expands the first match that it finds to a fully qualified filename, which includes the drive, path, and filename. This variable substitution returns an empty string when the `PATH` environment variable is undefined or if the system can't find a match for the filename.

You can use these variable substitutions in combination to produce specific results. For example, you might want to create a directory-like listing of files. The following list provides some ideas on how to use the variable substitution arguments in combination.

%~dpI Outputs just the drive letter and path of a file, without including the filename.

%~nxI Outputs the filename and extension, but leaves out the drive letter and path.

%~fsI Outputs the file information using the short name (8.3 format) form only.

%~dp$PATH:*I* Locates the file using the `PATH` environment variable. The system outputs just the drive letter and path of the first match found.

%~ftzaI Creates the same output as the `Dir` command. However, the output is different from the `Dir` command because the file listing could span multiple directories. The focus of the listing is different.

Using the *Goto* Command

The `Goto` command transfers control from one part of a batch file to another. You can't use the `Goto` command to transfer control to other batch files. For this task, you use the `Call` command described in the "Using the *Call* Command" section of the chapter. The `Goto` command takes a simple form: `Goto Label`, where `Label` is a keyword used to define the transfer point in the batch file. Labels are always preceded by a colon, such as `:MyLabel`. Listings 7.1 and 7.2 both show the `Goto` command in action.

Using the *If* Command

To write any reasonably complex batch file, you need to perform flow control—the active selection of code to run based on current conditions. For example, you might want to know that the previous task succeeded before you begin the next task. In some cases, you'll look for a specific file or act on user input to the batch file. You can also verify that the user provided a certain input string. The point is that you can exercise some control over how the batch files react to system and environmental conditions. Batch files don't provide extensive decision-making support, but you can use these three forms of the `If` statement to increase the flexibility of your batch files.

```
If [Not] ErrorLevel number command
If [Not] string1==string2 command
If [Not] Exist filename command
```

In all three cases, you can add the word "Not" to perform the reverse of the check. For example, you can perform a task when a given file doesn't exist, rather than when it does exist. By combining both versions of the `If` statement, you can create the equivalent of an `If...Else` statement found in most programming languages.

The `ErrorLevel` argument requires special consideration. Whenever you run an application, batch file, or script, the system provides a numeric error level as output. By convention, an error level of 0 always represents success. Other numbers represent an error or special condition. A special condition isn't always an error; it's simply not complete success. In fact, you might expect an application, batch file, or script to exit with a special condition. For an example of a command that exits with special conditions, review the `Choice` command in the "Using the *Choice* Command" section of the chapter. Error conditions can represent a user, system, or application failure. For example, consider the XCopy error levels shown in Table 7.4.

TABLE 7.4: XCopy Error Levels

ERROR LEVEL	MEANING
0	Success, no error occurred.
1	The system didn't find any files to copy.
2	The user stopped XCopy by pressing Ctrl+C.
4	The application experienced an initialization error. The system doesn't have enough memory or disk space. You may have entered an invalid drive name or used invalid syntax at the command line.
5	The system experienced a disk write error.

As you can see, the cause of an error varies greatly depending on conditions. In all cases, you could rightfully say that the application has experienced an error. However, notice that error level 2 could actually occur by design. The user recognizes an error and presses Ctrl+C to stop the copying process before it completes. In this case, you have to consider whether the error level defines a special condition or an error by prompting the user and handle it appropriately. Listing 7.2 shows examples of the various `If` statement forms at work.

LISTING 7.2: Using the *If* Statement in Batch Files

```
Echo Off

REM Verify the user has provided an action.
If %1Err==Err GoTo ProcessError

REM Simulate an error when the file doesn't exist.
Copy MyFile.TXT MyFile2.TXT
If Not ErrorLevel 1 Goto CheckFile
   Echo The File doesn't exist so the batch file can't copy it.

REM Check for a specific file and process it when it does exist.
:CheckFile
If Exist MyFile.TXT Goto ProcessFile

REM If the file doesn't exist then create it. Display a message with
REM instructions and then let the user type the text.
Echo Type some text for the test file. Press Ctrl+Z when you finish.
Pause
Copy CON MyFile.TXT

REM This is a label for processing the file.
:ProcessFile

REM Determine whether the user wants to display the file.
If Not %1==display Goto Process2
   Echo MyFile.TXT Contains:
   Type MyFile.TXT
   Goto TheEnd

REM Determine whether the user wants to delete the file.
:Process2
If Not %1==delete Goto ProcessError
   Erase MyFile.TXT
   Echo Deleted MyFile.TXT
   Goto TheEnd

REM The user didn't define a processing action.
:ProcessError
Echo You didn't tell the batch file what to do!
Echo Type UseIf Display to display the file or
Echo UseIf Delete to delete the file.

:TheEnd
Echo On
```

The first line of this example demonstrates a principle that you should always use in batch files that you expect someone else will use—check for errors within the limits of the batch file to do so. In this case, the batch file expects the user to provide an input value of `delete` or `display`. When the user doesn't provide any input value, then the first input value, `%1`, is blank so the string `Err` equals `Err` and the code goes to a label named `ProcessError`. Batch files can work with up to nine input values at a time using `%1` through `%9` as variables. The `Goto` statement always tells the code to go to a label within the batch file. You define a label by preceding the label name with a colon such as `:ProcessError`.

The next segment of code attempts to copy a temporary file to another file. The operation results in an error that you can trap using the `ErrorLevel` statement when the file doesn't exist. When the `ErrorLevel` value matches the value you provide, then the `If` statement executes the command. In this case, because the code uses the `Not` clause, the reverse is true, the `If` statement only executes the `Goto` command when the error level is not 1. Notice that, in this case, the code uses the `Echo` command to display an error message to the user—`Echo` works not only for turning messages on or off, but for displaying custom messages to the user that the `Echo` setting doesn't hide as well.

Once the code performs these initial steps, it determines whether the `MyFile.TXT` file does exist using the `Exit` clause of the `If` statement. When the file exists, the code immediately begins processing it. Otherwise, the code displays a message prompting the user to type information for such a file. Notice the `Pause` command, which pauses the batch file execution until the user presses a key. The `Copy` command sends whatever the user types at the console (`CON`) to the `MyFile.TXT` file until it detects an end of file character, which the user creates by pressing Ctrl+Z.

Now that you know the file exists, the batch file can process it. This batch file provides two options: displaying the file and deleting it. The problem with batch files is that they use case-sensitive string comparisons—the word `delete` is different from the word `Delete` so error trapping can cause false problems. Some developers resolve this problem by using single character command line switches for batch files. That way, all you need to do is perform two checks, one for uppercase and another for lowercase. The example uses a full word for the purpose of demonstration. To see how this works, type `Delete` at the command line instead of `delete`—the code will display a failure message. When the user does type `delete`, the batch file erases the file and displays a success message. Likewise, when the user types `display`, the code sends the content of `MyFile.TXT` to the display. In both cases, the code goes to `TheEnd` where the batch file turns `Echo` back on.

So far, the chapter has discussed the standard form of the `If` command that you can execute even at the DOS prompt. The `If` command has the following additional syntax forms when you use command line extensions.

```
if [/i] String1 CompareOp String2 Command [else Expression]
if CMDEXTVERSION Number Command [else Expression]
if DEFINED Variable Command [else Expression]
```

The following list describes each of the command line arguments.

/I Performs a case-insensitive comparison of the two strings. This feature is handy when you expect the user to input a string, but don't know how the user will capitalize it. These comparisons are generic, in that if both `String1` and `String2` are composed of numbers, the system converts the strings to numbers and performs a numeric comparison.

String1 Specifies the input string; the first half of the comparison.

CompareOp Defines the comparison operator. Each three-letter comparison operator performs a different comparison as described in the following list.

  EQU Equal to

  NEQ Not equal to

LSS Less than

LEQ Less than or equal to

GTR Greater than

GEQ Greater than or equal to

String2 Specifies the comparison string—the second half of the comparison.

Command Specifies the command that you want to execute when the comparison is true.

else *Expression* Defines the else expression for the `If` command. When you use this syntax, you must surround the `If` and `Else` portions of the statement in parentheses. In addition, the entire statement must appear on a single line. You can't separate the various elements to provide a neater appearance. Here's an example of this form of the `If` command.

```
IF [%1] EQU [] (ECHO String Empty) ELSE (ECHO String Has Data)
```

In this case, the `If` command checks whether the input has a string for the first variable. When the input is available, the output tells the user that the string has data. Otherwise, the input displays, "String Empty" as output.

CMDEXTVERSION *Number* Tests for a specific version of the command extensions feature. When the command extension version number is equal to or greater than the specified number, the condition is true. This form of `If` command never returns true when you disable command extensions.

DEFINED *Variable* Tests whether you have a specific environment variable defined. The `DEFINED` argument works just like the `EXISTS` argument. The `If` command returns true when the variable is defined.

Using the *Pause* Command

The `Pause` command stops batch file execution to give the user time to react to a particular need. For example, if you need the user to change media to complete the batch file, you could use the `Echo` command to tell the user about the need and then use the `Pause` command to tell the user to press any key when the media exchange is complete.

Using the *Prompt* Command

The `Prompt` command changes the command line prompt. For example, instead of the usual drive letter, directory, and greater than sign, you could use the time and date as a prompt. In fact, the prompt can contain any text you want. To change the prompt, simply type `Prompt`, followed by the text you want to display, and press Enter. The following list defines the special characters you can use as part of the command prompt.

$A & (Ampersand)

$B | (Pipe)

$C ((Left parenthesis)

$D Current date

$E Escape code (ASCII code 27)

$F) (Right parenthesis)

$G > (Greater than sign)

$H Backspace (erases previous character)

$L < (Less than sign)

$N Current drive

$P Current drive and path

$Q = (Equals sign)

$S (Space)

$T Current time

$V Windows version number

$_ Carriage return and linefeed

$$ $ (Dollar sign)

You can access two additional formatting characters when you have command extensions enabled. The following list describes these two additions.

$+ Displays zero or more plus sign characters depending on the depth of the PushD utility directory stack. The display shows one character for each level you've pushed onto the stack.

$M Displays the remote name associated with the current drive letter. If this is a local drive, then the system displays an empty string.

Using the *Rem* Command

The `Rem (Remark)` command lets you add comments to your batch files. Given that batch files often use difficult to read coding sequences and that you'll probably want to modify them at some point, lots of comments are advisable. In fact, you'll want to add at least one comment for each complex line of code in your batch file. Many people have lost use of interesting and helpful batch files because they contain complex code that becomes unreadable after the initial writer forgets what the code means.

Using the *Shift* Command

A batch file supports a maximum of 10 command line arguments numbered %0 through %9. However, you might run into situations where you need more than 10 command line arguments. The `Shift` command can help you shift in these additional arguments. The new arguments replace existing arguments. In fact, all of the arguments are shifted one position, so the argument in %1 now appears in %0. Unfortunately, the argument in %0 is shifted out so that it's no longer accessible.

You can retain some older arguments in memory when you have command extensions enabled. The `Shift` command will accept a numeric argument that tells where to begin shifting arguments. For example, when the command appears as `Shift /2`, the values in %0 and %1 are unaffected. However, `Shift` will shift the arguments starting with %2 so that %2 now contains the value from %3.

Using the TimeOut Utility

The TimeOut utility provides a unique feature in that you can tell it to wait for a specified time period no matter what the user does. Consequently, unlike the Choice command, when you tell TimeOut to wait 30 seconds, it waits the entire time period even if the user presses a key. In addition, the TimeOut utility doesn't display a message for the timeout, so you can use this utility where silence is necessary (such as a background task). This command uses the following syntax:

```
TIMEOUT [/T] timeout [/NOBREAK]
```

The following list describes each of the command line arguments.

/T *timeout* Specifies the timeout value. The command line switch is optional. You may specify any value from -1 to 99999 seconds. A value of -1 means that the utility waits indefinitely for a key press. The utility won't allow you to combine a value of -1 with the /NOBREAK command line switch since that would effectively lock the system.

/NOBREAK Prevents the utility from recognizing key presses. The TimeOut utility waits for the specified time period before it exits.

Using the WaitFor Utility

The WaitFor utility enables communication between processes. You can send a signal from one application to another. In fact, you can use this feature for signaling between batch files. When using this utility, you start the receiving application first and tell it to wait for the signal. The sender then sends the signal when it's ready. This command uses the following syntax:

```
Sender Syntax:
WAITFOR [/S system [/U [domain\]user [/P [password]]]] /SI signal

Receiver Syntax:
WAITFOR [/T timeout] signal
```

The following list describes each of the command line arguments.

/S *system* Specifies the remote system that you want to check. In most cases, you'll also need to supply the /U and the /P command line switches when using this switch.

/U [*domain*\\]*user* Specifies the username on the remote system. This name may not match the username on the local system. You'll need to supply a domain name when working with a domain controller.

/P [*password*] Specifies the password for the given user. You can provide the command line switch without specifying the password on the command line in clear text. The system prompts you for the password. Using this feature can help you maintain the security of passwords used on your system.

/SI Sends the requested signal across the network.

signal Specifies the signal to send or receive. The signal is a simple string value such as StartSetup. A system can wait for multiple unique signals. The maximum signal name length is 255 characters. You may use a-z, A-Z, 0-9, and any ASCII character code in the range 128-255 for the string value. The string value can't contain special characters or spaces.

/T timeout Defines the amount of time to wait for the signal. You can specify any value from 1 to 99,999 seconds. The default setting waits an infinite amount of time.

Getting Started with Command Line Tasks

This chapter has demonstrated the functionality that batch files can provide. If you work at the command line very often, you should have a full set of batch files to augment your toolkit. Batch files are a very simple form of programming that can produce dramatic results because they rely on the power of the commands that Windows provides at the command prompt. In fact, you'll find a wealth of tools that can make the command line use of batch files even more powerful in Chapters 12, 13, and 14 of the book. This chapter introduces what anyone can do with batch files because everyone has access to these features. Batch files can be quite powerful.

It's your turn to try writing batch files. Start simply. Try writing batch files to configure the command line to meet specific needs. You might try something as simple as changing the color of the command line to match your mood on a given day. The point is to try simple concepts first and work your way up to more complex goals. With the right tools, you can automate a considerable number of the tasks you need to perform each day to administrate a network or even work with a single machine.

As powerful as batch files can be in the right hands, they can't perform some basic programming tasks. A batch file limits you to the resources of the commands and utilities available from the command prompt. Chapter 8 shows the next step in automating the command prompt—the use of scripts. A script can provide better programming support and you can even obtain a certain level of debugging for scripts. A script also provides an essential that a batch file can't—a nice user interface. Although batch files work just fine for experienced users and administrators, they aren't a very good choice for novice users. The scripting techniques demonstrated in Chapter 8 help you improve the command line experience for everyone, even—with the proper additions—novice users.

Chapter 8

Working with Scripts

- Understanding Scripting Languages
- Executing Scripts
- Scripting Networking Solutions with the NetSH Utility
- Creating a Basic Script
- Using the Scripting Objects
- Impersonating a User with the RunAs Utility
- Changing the Environment

The batch files described in Chapter 7 do provide a reasonable amount of flexibility and they're very easy to produce. However, batch files aren't the same as using an actual programming language. Scripts provide a happy medium between the complexity of a full-fledged programming language that you can compile into an executable and the ease of using batch files. You gain access to more of the system functionality through scripts and have better access to programming constructs, such as flow control. Error trapping is also better with scripts. In fact, you'll be amazed at what scripts can do. People have even developed games in them and most of the Web pages on the Internet rely on scripts to perform tasks in the background.

This chapter isn't going to make you a scripting guru. In fact, it assumes that you already know something about scripting or are willing to look at online resources if you don't. However, you'll discover how scripting can make you extremely effective at the command line. The following sections help you understand script languages, learn how to execute them at the command line, and then create scripts under a variety of conditions. Finally, you'll learn how to overcome security problems that using scripts might incur in today's complex workstation environment.

Understanding Scripting Languages

There are many scripting languages on the market today. Space won't allow me to discuss them all, even if I knew them all. The following sections discuss JavaScript and VBScript for one reason—they're the languages that Windows supports out of the box so you don't need to install anything special to use them. Of the two, JavaScript enjoys greater popularity and you can use it on more than one platform. Consequently, the scripting examples in the book rely on JavaScript.

 **Real World Scenario**

SCRIPTS, NOT JUST FOR THOSE WHO TINKER

There's a perception that script languages are so limited that you can only use them to create small programs and that only people who like to tinker need consider using them. However, script languages today are more powerful that you might think. For example, it's quite easy to write applications that interact with Web services using scripts. I've personally written scripts to interact with all of the major online Web services including Amazon.com, Google, and eBay. Of course, Web service support is really just the tip of the iceberg and not everyone is working with Web services today.

Script languages provide access to a number of the features that developers consider essential for complex applications. For example, you can access most COM controls and components using a script language. The ability to create objects means that you can rely on code other developers created to produce complex applications. For example, most developers would argue that eXtensible Markup Language (XML) support is essential today. You can gain access to XML by creating the correct objects using a script language. In fact, the "Using the Scripting Objects" section of the chapter describes specialized scripting objects you can use.

Don't get the idea that scripting languages are a replacement for full-fledged programming languages, however. They do have limitations. For example, you'll find that debugging, while available, is limited. You also won't gain access to all of the features that an Integrated Development Environment (IDE) can provide. Scripts are procedural and many developers feel that classes are the best way to approach some programming problems. In short, scripts really are that halfway point between batch files and full-fledged programming languages.

NOTE You'll find that JavaScript comes in several slightly different forms and names. Besides JavaScript, you'll see this language as LiveScript, JScript, and ECMAScript. You can find an interesting language history at `http://www.webmasterworld.com/forum91/68.htm` (may require a log in).

Learning the Basics of JavaScript

This chapter doesn't provide a nuts and bolts discussion of JavaScript. I'm assuming you have some experience using this language. Because this language is used in so many ways, you can find great JavaScript resources online. Many sites include tutorials, a reference, and sample code. If you want to be sure your code runs in as many environments as possible, make sure you download a copy of European Computer Manufacturer's Association (ECMA) standard 262 from `http://www.ecma-international.org/publications/standards/Ecma-262.htm`, which is the standard for JavaScript.

If you've never used JavaScript before, you'll need a good tutorial. The W3Schools.com site at `http://www.w3schools.com/js/default.asp` provides an excellent tutorial for first-time users. Webmonkey provides several JavaScript tutorials including a basic tutorial at `http://www.webmonkey.com/98/03/index0a.html` and an advanced tutorial at `http://www.webmonkey.com/98/29/index0a.html`. You might also want to view their crash course index at `http://www.webmonkey.com/programming/javascript/tutorials/jstutorial_index.html`.

It's important to have a good JavaScript reference. One of the best places to find a JavaScript reference is at `http://www.mozilla.org/js/language/`. If you want to learn about the Microsoft perspective on JavaScript, the Microsoft Windows Script Technologies site at `http://www.script-info.net/jsvbs/msscript/misc/vtorimicrosoftwindowsscripttechnologies.php` contains a wealth of helpful information.

Real World Scenario

VERIFYING YOUR JAVASCRIPT SETUP

You may run into a problem where the scripts in this book don't work. Double-clicking the script file doesn't work and it appears that you can't do anything else with the file either. In fact, Windows might not know anything about the file at all. Although it does happen with VBScript, most people have problems getting their JavaScript (JS) files to run correctly after they install certain kinds of software or perform actions with virus detection software. If you double-click on a JS file and nothing happens, the problem might be in the registry. For whatever reason (and I wasn't able to verify a single specific reason), sometimes people find Windows or another external application removes their JavaScript settings.

The main problem is that the registry lacks entries for the .JS extension handler. Verify that you have the handler installed by viewing the `HKEY_CLASSES_ROOT\.JS` key first. This key should say JSFile as the (Default) value. Now, look at the `HKEY_CLASSES_ROOT\JSFile` entry. It should have JScript Script File as the (Default) value and `@%SystemRoot%\System32\wshext.dll,-4804` as the FriendlyTypeName value. You should see two open verbs. The first is at `HKEY_CLASSES_ROOT\JSFile\Shell\Open\Command` and should have a (Default) value of `%SystemRoot%\System32\WScript.exe "%1" %*`. The second is at `HKEY_CLASSES_ROOT\JSFile\Shell\Open2\Command` and should have a (Default) value of `%SystemRoot%\System32\CScript.exe "%1" %*`. If you're not seeing these entries, it means that something has gone awry with your registry. When this problem occurs, you can usually restore your JavaScript and VBScript settings by typing **`RegSvr32 WSHExt.DLL`** in the `\Windows\System32` folder and pressing Enter.

Learning the Basics of VBScript

As with JavaScript, this chapter doesn't provide a VBScript tutorial. Unfortunately, VBScript is also less popular than JavaScript, so you won't find as many resources online for using it. However, a few developers still use VBScript for their application needs. The main VBScript Web site is at `http://msdn.microsoft.com/library/en-us/script56/html/0a8270d7-7d8f-4368-b2a7-065acb52fc54.asp`. This Web site includes a VBScript user's guide and language reference. You can find another good reference on the W3Schools Web site at `http://www.w3schools.com/vbscript/vbscript_ref_functions.asp`.

You can find a number of good tutorials online. One of the better tutorials is at `http://www.w3schools.com/vbscript/vbscript_intro.asp`. Make sure you try the Learn by Example resource on the W3Schools Web site at `http://www.w3schools.com/vbscript/vbscript_examples.asp`. A basic tutorial appears on the IntranetJournal Web site at `http://www.intranetjournal.com/corner/wrox/progref/vbt/` and `http://www.intranetjournal.com/corner/aitken/vbs-1.shtml`. Once you learn the basics, try the tutorials on the ComputerTechnicalTutorials Web site at `http://www.techtutorials.info/vbscript.html`. You can find a browser perspective of VBScript tutorial at `http://www.tizag.com/vbscriptTutorial/`.

Sometimes you need additional help using VBScript. The VisualBasicScript.com Web site at `http://www.visualbasicscript.com/` provides a forum for asking questions about VBScript. You also find a complete, albeit somewhat outdated, book on VBScript at `http://docs.rinet.ru/`

`VB/`. If you haven't found what you wanted in this section, try the centralized Web site of VBScript links at `http://www.cetus-links.org/oo_vbscript.html`. If you don't find what you want with one of the sources listed in this section, try the list of resources found at `http://searchvb.techtarget.com/generic/0,295582,sid8_gci1158017,00.html?track=NL-283&ad=539962`.

Executing Scripts

All you need to create a script is a text editor, such as Notepad, and a little time. You can also use script-specific tools such as the Visual Basic Editor or Microsoft Script Editor provided with Microsoft Office. A number of third parties also produce products that can help you create and even compile your script. Chapter 14 discusses a few of these products and you'll find more online. No matter what you do to create your script, however, it's useless unless you can run it. Windows provides two interpreters—applications that run scripts—for you to use. The first, CScript, works at the command line and the second, WScript, works from within Windows. The following sections describe both options.

Running Scripts with the CScript and WScript Utilities

Windows supports two methods of starting scripts. The CScript application works at the command prompt, while the WScript application works from within the graphical user environment. Both applications accomplish the same task—they provide a means for interpreting a script file you create.

CScript and WScript use the same command line. You must provide a script name as the first command line argument. Most scripts have a VBE or JS file extension, but any extension is acceptable. For example, you can still use VBS files with Windows Script Host (WSH), but the icon won't look right, in some cases, and you can't double-click it to start the execution with newer Windows products. The VBS extension is the right choice for older versions of Windows. The icon is yellow for VBE files and blue for JS files. These utilities use the following syntax:

```
CScript <Script Name> [<WSH Command Line Switches>] [<Script Arguments>]
WScript <Script Name> [<WSH Command Line Switches>] [<Script Arguments>]
```

The following list describes each of the command line arguments.

`//?` Displays the currently documented command line switches. The newest versions of WSH tend to reject older switches, even those of the undocumented variety.

`//B` Limits user interaction with the script. Batch mode suppresses all non–command line console user interface requests from the script. It also suppresses error message display (a change from previous versions).

`//D` Activates debugging mode so you can fix errors in a script.

`//E:`*`Engine`* Specifies the engine to use to execute the script. You use this feature when a script has something other than the default extension (such as `.JS` or `.VBS`). The common settings are `//E:JScript` for JavaScript and `//E:VBScript` for VBScript. However, you can use any compatible scripting engine.

`//H:CScript` Makes `CSCRIPT.EXE` the default application for running scripts. (WScript is the default engine.)

`//H:WScript` Makes `WSCRIPT.EXE` the default application for running scripts.

`//I` Allows full interaction with the user. Any pop-up dialog boxes will wait for user input before the script continues.

`//Job:JobName` Executes a WSH job. A WSH job has a Windows Script File (WSF) extension. This file enables you to perform tasks using multiple scripting engines and multiple files. Essentially, this allows you to perform a "super batch" process. Creating WSF files is an advanced technique not discussed in this book because it isn't very useful in most cases. You can learn more about this topic at `http://msdn.microsoft.com/archive/en-us/wsh/htm/wsAdvantagesOfWs.asp`.

`//Logo and //NoLogo` WSH normally prints out a logo message. You'd use the `//NoLogo` switch to prevent WSH from displaying this message.

`//S:` This command line switch allows you to save current command line options for a user. WSH will save the following options: `//B`, `//I`, `//Logo`, `//Nologo`, and `//T:n`.

`//T:TimeLimit` Limits the maximum time the script can run to the number of seconds specified. Normally, there isn't any timeout value. You'd use this switch in situations where a script might end up in a continuous loop or is unable to get the requested information for other reasons. For example, you might use this switch when requesting information on a network drive.

`//X` Starts the script in the debugger. This allows you to trace the execution of the script from beginning to end.

`//U` Outputs any console information using Unicode instead of pure ASCII. You use this switch on systems where you need to support languages other than English. This is a CScript-only option.

Notice that all of these command line switches start with two slashes (`//`) to differentiate them from switches you may need for your script. WSH passes script arguments to your script for processing. Script arguments can be anything including command line switches of your own or values needed to calculate a result.

NOTE Users of older versions of CScript and WScript may remember the `//C` and the `//W` switches used to switch the default scripting engines. Newer versions of CScript and WScript replace these switches with the `//H` switch. You'll also find the `//R` (reregister) and`//Entrypoint` switches missing from WSH because script developers no longer need the functionality. Always use the correct command line switches for the version of Windows and WSH installed on your machine.

You can work with WSH in either interactive or batch mode. Use batch mode when you need to perform tasks that don't require user input. For example, you might want to run Scan Disk every evening, but use different command line switches for it based on the day. You could use Task Scheduler to accomplish this task, but using it in conjunction with a WSH script improves the flexibility you get when running the task.

Another kind of batch processing might be to send log files to your supervisor or perhaps set up a specific set of environment variables for a character-mode application based on the current user. On the other hand, interactive mode requires user interaction. You'd use it for tasks such as cleaning the hard drive because you don't always know whether the user needs a particular file. Such a script could ask the user a set of general questions, and then clean excess files from the hard drive based on the user input. The cleaning process would follow company guidelines and save the user time.

TIP Because batch processing doesn't require any form of user input, it's usually a good idea to include the `//T` switch with the `//B` switch. This combination stops the script automatically if it runs too long. In most cases, using this switch setup stops an errant script before it corrupts the Windows environment or freezes the machine. However, you can't time some tasks with ease. For example, any Web-based task is difficult to time because you can't account for problems with a slow connection. In this case, you'll need to refrain from using the `//T` switch or provide a worst-case scenario time interval.

The next set of command line switches to consider is //Logo and //NoLogo. There isn't any right or wrong time to use these switches, but you usually use the //Logo switch when testing a script and the //NoLogo switch afterward. The reason is simple. During the testing process, you want to know about every potential source of problems in your script environment, including an old script engine that might cause problems. On the other hand, you don't want to clutter your screen with useless text after you debug the script. Using the //NoLogo switch keeps screen clutter to a minimum.

Configuring the Host and Property Page Options

You don't have to rely exclusively on command line switches to configure WSH; you can configure two WSH options from the Windows Script Host Settings dialog box shown in Figure 8.1. Run WScript by itself and you'll see the Windows Script Host Settings dialog box.

FIGURE 8.1
Configure WSH to meet specific needs.

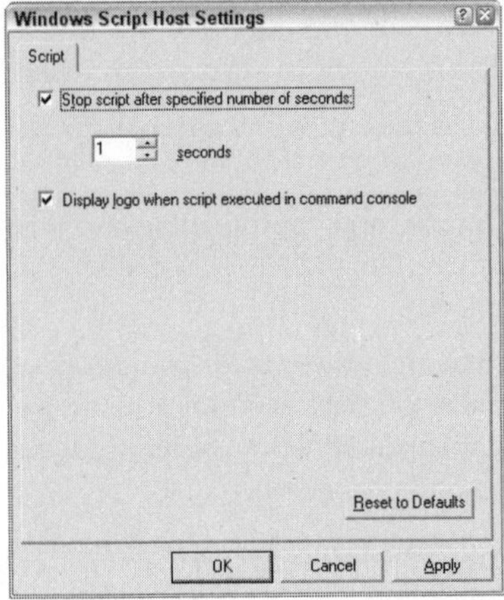

The Stop Script after Specified Number of Seconds check box tells WSH to stop executing a script after a certain time interval has elapsed. The edit box below it contains the number of seconds to wait. Setting this option is like adding the //T command line switch to every script that you run.

The Display Logo When Script Executed in Command Console check box determines whether WSH displays WSH logo when running scripts from the DOS prompt. Normally, Windows checks this option, which is the same as adding the //Logo command line switch to every script that you run. Clearing this option tells WSH that you don't want to display the logo, which is the same as using the //NoLogo command line switch.

You can also display the Windows Script Host Settings dialog box for individual scripts. Simply right-click the script file and select Properties from the context menu. Select the Script tab to see the options. These settings only affect the individual script file; the options for WSH in general remain the same.

Scripting Networking Solutions with the NetSH Utility

Many of the utilities discussed in this book are mini-command processors. For example, the FTP utility described in the "Managing FTP Servers with the FTP Utility" section of Chapter 5 describes such an environment. The Network Command Shell (NetSH) utility extends this idea by providing an extensible command processor. You access the functionality that this utility provides by loading a helper DLL. Each helper DLL places the NetSH utility into a different context. The use of helper DLLs theoretically makes it possible for third party vendors to add NetSH functionality as part of their network product installation. One of the essential commands to know for NetSH, since it's so flexible, is NetSH Show Helper. This command displays a list of helper DLLs installed on your machine, which may differ from the list shown in Figure 8.2 based on the operating system features you have installed.

FIGURE 8.2
Obtain a list of helper DLLs for your setup using the NetSH Show Helper command.

```
F:\WINDOWS\system32\cmd.exe
F:\>NetSH Show Helper
Helper GUID                             DLL Filename   Command
--------------------------------------  -------------  -------
{00770721-44EA-11D5-93BA-00B0D022DD1F}  HNETMON.DLL    bridge
{CC41B21B-8040-4BB0-AC2A-820623160940}  DGNET.DLL      diag
{8B3A0D7F-1F30-4402-B753-C4B2C7607C97}  FWCFG.DLL      firewall
{0705ECA1-7AAC-11D2-89DC-006008B0E5B9}  IFMON.DLL      interface
{89D00931-1E00-11D3-8738-00600837C775}  IFMON.DLL        ip
{05BB0FE9-8D89-48DE-B7BB-9F138B2E950C}  IPV6MON.DLL      ipv6
{F1EFA7E5-7169-4EC0-A63A-9B22A743E19C}  IPV6MON.DLL        6to4
{F1EFA7E5-7169-4EC0-A63A-9B22A743E19C}  IPV6MON.DLL        isatap
{86A3A33F-4D51-47FF-B24C-8E9B13CEB3A2}  IPV6MON.DLL      portproxy
{0705ECA2-7AAC-11D2-89DC-006008B0E5B9}  RASMONTR.DLL   ras
{42E3CC21-098C-11D3-8C4D-00104BCA495B}  RASMONTR.DLL     aaaa
{E0C5D007-D34C-11D2-9B76-00104BCA495B}  RASMONTR.DLL     appletalk
{13D12A78-D0FB-11D2-9B76-00104BCA495B}  RASMONTR.DLL     ip
{6FB90155-D324-11D2-9B76-00104BCA495B}  RASMONTR.DLL     ipx
{69F21BC3-D349-11D2-9B76-00104BCA495B}  RASMONTR.DLL     netbeui
{65EC23C0-D1B9-11D2-89E4-006008B0E5B9}  IPMONTR.DLL    routing
{0705ECA0-7AAC-11D2-89DC-006008B0E5B9}  IPMONTR.DLL      ip
{0705ECA3-7AAC-11D2-89DC-006008B0E5B9}  IPPROMON.DLL       autodhcp
{0705ECA3-7AAC-11D2-89DC-006008B0E5B9}  IPPROMON.DLL       dnsproxy
{0705ECA3-7AAC-11D2-89DC-006008B0E5B9}  IPPROMON.DLL       igmp
{0705ECA3-7AAC-11D2-89DC-006008B0E5B9}  IPPROMON.DLL       nat
{0705ECA3-7AAC-11D2-89DC-006008B0E5B9}  IPPROMON.DLL       ospf
```

Notice the hierarchy of contexts displayed in Figure 8.2. To access the IP context at the command line, you must type NetSH Interface IP and then the command you wish to use. Likewise, if you want to access the 6To4 context, you must type **`NetSH Interface IPv6 6To4`** at the command line. Typing any context by itself (or followed by a question mark (?) or Help) displays the list of commands for that context.

VISTA

Type a command to see the list of subcommands or the instructions for using that command. Type a subcommand to see the instructions for using that subcommand. For example, to discover how to add a new IP address, type **`NetSH Interface IP Add Address`** at the command prompt and press Enter. You'll see a help display explaining the command, as shown in Figure 8.3. Figure 8.3 shows the Vista view of the help for this command. If you're familiar with previous versions of Windows, you'll notice that the Vista help is an improvement.

FIGURE 8.3
The multilevel command structure provided by NetSH provides you with help at each step.

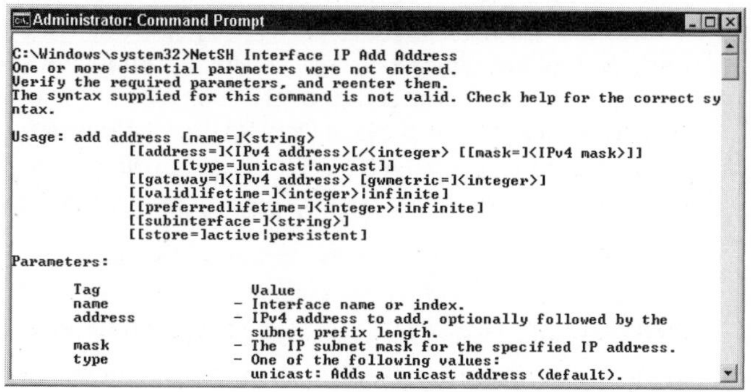

```
Administrator: Command Prompt

C:\Windows\system32>NetSH Interface IP Add Address
One or more essential parameters were not entered.
Verify the required parameters, and reenter them.
The syntax supplied for this command is not valid. Check help for the correct sy
ntax.

Usage: add address [name=]<string>
             [[address=]<IPv4 address>[/<integer>] [[mask=]<IPv4 mask>]]
                 [[type=]unicast|anycast]]
             [[gateway=]<IPv4 address> [gwmetric=]<integer>]
             [[validlifetime=]<integer>|infinite]
             [[preferredlifetime=]<integer>|infinite]
             [[subinterface=]<string>]
             [[store=]active|persistent]

Parameters:

       Tag              Value
       name           - Interface name or index.
       address        - IPv4 address to add, optionally followed by the
                        subnet prefix length.
       mask           - The IP subnet mask for the specified IP address.
       type           - One of the following values:
                        unicast: Adds a unicast address (default).
```

NOTE This chapter doesn't discuss the specifics of each context because they vary according to operating system version and the helpers you have installed. Unfortunately, there isn't any documented resource from Microsoft for standard contexts in Windows 2000, but you can use the Windows XP resource as a guideline. You can obtain a free reference sheet for the Windows 2000 version of the NetSH utility at `http://techrepublic.com.com/5139-1035-729370.html` (the Web site does require a one-time registration). The contexts for Windows XP appear at `http://www.microsoft.com/resources/documentation/windows/xp/all/proddocs/en-us/ntcmds.mspx` and the contexts for Windows 2003 appear at `http://technet2.microsoft.com/WindowsServer/en/Library/552ed70a-208d-48c4-8da8-2e27b530eac71033.mspx`. As of this writing, Microsoft hasn't provided contexts for Vista, but you can use the Windows 2003 contexts as a starting point. You can find additional NetSH utility documentation in the Microsoft Knowledge Base article at `http://support.microsoft.com/?kbid=242468` and The Cable Guy article at `http://www.microsoft.com/technet/community/columns/cableguy/cg1101.mspx`.

The NetSH utility provides access to a broad range of networking functionality using contexts. Each context represents a different functional network area such as configuring the firewall or modifying security. You can interact with NetSH at the command line, in an interactive environment, and using scripts. In this case, a script file is simply a list of commands that you want NetSH to perform. You place these commands in a text file and pass them to NetSH to execute. This utility uses the following syntax:

```
netsh [-a AliasFile] [-c Context] [-r RemoteMachine]
[-u [DomainName\]UserName] [Command | -f ScriptFile]
```

The following list describes each of the command line arguments.

-a *AliasFile* Specifies the alias file to use. An alias file contains a set of strings and their associated NetSH equivalents. You can use the alias in place of the corresponding NetSH command. This feature also allows you to map older commands to the appropriate NetSH command.

-c *Context* Defines the context of the command that you want to run. A context refers to a specific helper DLL.

Command Specifies the NetSH command to execute. The command is helper DLL specific.

-f *ScriptFile* Specifies the name of a file that contains NetSH commands. A script file is simply a text file that contains NetSH commands one after another. You can use the pound (#) symbol followed by text to create script file comments. Use the NetSH `Dump` command to display a sample script. Because the script is long, you might want to use redirection to send the output to a file (see the "Employing Data Redirection" section of Chapter 2 for details).

-r *RemoteMachine* Defines the name or IP address of a remote machine to use to execute NetSH commands. This feature helps you manage remote systems.

VISTA

-u [*DomainName*\]*UserName* Specifies the credentials to use to log into a system. Vista prompts you for a password when logging into another system.

The various helper DLLs provide contexts that you can use to perform specific tasks. You can access some of these contexts directly from the command line using a command. Table 8.1 describes each of the top-level contexts.

TABLE 8.1: Standard NetSH Contexts

CONTEXT NAME	WINDOWS VERSION	DESCRIPTION
Bridge	Windows XP and above	Shows configuration information for network adapters that are part of a network bridge. You can also use this context to enable or disable Level 3 compatibility mode.
Diag	Windows XP and above	Performs network diagnostic commands. For example, you can use this context to display network service status information or perform diagnostics similar to the Ping utility described in the "Checking Connections with the Ping Utility" section of Chapter 5. A special NetSH Diag GUI command displays a Web page in the Help and Support Center that provides access to the network diagnostics.
Firewall	Windows XP and above	Provides complete access to the Windows firewall. You can use this context to add and remove configuration information, as well as display the current firewall state.
Interface	Windows 2000 and above	Provides access to the network interfaces installed on your machine, which normally include IP, IPV6 (Windows XP and above), and standard port proxies. You can use this context to configure the TCP/IP protocol including addresses, default gateways, DNS servers, and WINS servers.
RAS	Windows 2000 and above	Provides access to the Remote Access Server (RAS) and all of its configuration information. For example, this context provides access to the Authentication, Authorization, Accounting, and Auditing (AAAA) subcontext where you perform security setups.
Routing	Windows 2000 and above	Helps you configure the routing features of the system using a command line interface, rather than rely on the Routing and Remote Access console. The biggest advantage of the command line interface, in this case, is speed. You can access and manage remote servers over a large network, especially wide area networks (WANs) much faster using NetSH than you can the graphical equivalents. In addition, since these configuration tasks can become quite complex, you gain the advantage of scripting them once, rather than going through every required step each time you perform the task.
WinSock	Windows XP and above	Shows Windows Socket (WinSock) information for the current system. You can also use this context to dump the WinSock configuration script.

The default context is the root context, the NetSH utility itself. You can use specific commands from this context to perform configuration tasks or access other contexts. The following list describes the command line arguments, which differ according to the version of Windows that you use and the networking features you have installed.

add Adds a configuration entry to the list of entries. When working at the root context, you can add new helper DLLs to the list.

delete Deletes a configuration entry from the list of entries. When working at the root context, you can remove a helper DLL from the list.

dump Displays a configuration script. The script is quite long, so you'll want to use redirection to store the script to a file.

exec Executes the specified script file.

interface Sets NetSH to use the interface context.

ras Sets NetSH to use the RAS context.

routing Sets NetSH to use the routing context.

set Updates the configuration settings. Most versions of NetSH only allow you to set the machine name when working at the root context.

show Displays NetSH configuration information. Most versions of NetSH provide commands to display both the list of aliases and the list of helpers installed on the system.

Windows XP (and above) provides additional functionality to support items such as the firewall. Here are the Windows XP additions.

bridge Sets NetSH to use the bridge context.

diag Sets NetSH to use the diag context.

firewall Sets NetSH to use the firewall context.

winsock Sets NetSH to use the winsock context.

Windows 2003 and above supports still more commands. The following list describes the Windows 2003 additions.

cmd Creates a command window where you can enter NetSH commands manually.

comment Executes any commands accumulated in offline mode.

flush Discards the commands accumulated in offline mode.

online Sets the current mode to online. In online mode, which is the default for all previous versions of NetSH, the utility executes immediately any command you issue. Use the `show mode` command to display the current mode.

offline Sets the current mode to offline. In offline mode, which was new for Windows 2003, the utility accumulates any commands you issue and executes them as a batch. Using this second approach on remote servers can greatly enhance performance without any loss of functionality. Use the `show mode` command to display the current mode.

pushd Pushes a context onto the NetSH stack. Earlier versions pushed context onto the system stack by using the `PushD` command described in the "Storing and Retrieving the Current Directory with the *PushD* and *PopD* Commands" section of Chapter 2.

Real World Scenario

NEWER UTILITIES CAN REPLACE OLDER EQUIVALENTS

One of the tricks of the trade when working at the command line is to look for efficient replacements of old bulky commands. The NetSH utility is such a replacement. You can use it in place of a number of older utilities and graphical tools. For example, the NetSH utility replaces the older RouteMon utility. Even though you'll find the RouteMon executable on Windows XP and newer systems, the executable now tells you to use NetSH instead.

As part of keeping track of utility functionality, you must also monitor the services that Microsoft supports. For example, Windows 2000 supports the ReSerVation Protocol (RSVP), but Microsoft no longer supports this service on Windows XP and newer systems. The loss of this service affects the method you use to reserve network resources and, consequently, the use of utilities. See the MSDN article at `http://msdn2.microsoft.com/en-us/library/aa374137.aspx` for details. Of course, even if the latest version of Windows supports a particular service, you'll want to ensure the service runs automatically. As an example, Windows XP originally enabled the TelNet service, but disabled it for the SP2 release. You'll often need to rely on third party resources, such as the Web site at `http://www.ss64.com/ntsyntax/services.html`, to obtain information about services because Microsoft tends to hide this information (or not publish it at all).

popd Removes a context from the NetSH stack. Earlier versions popped the context from the system stack using the PopD command described in the "Storing and Retrieving a Previous Directory with the *PushD* and *PopD* Commands" section of Chapter 2.

Creating a Basic Script

Scripts can make the command line significantly easier to automate and can improve the reliability of command line tasks by helping you perform tasks in the same sequence every time. This section shows how to create basic scripts in both VBScript and JavaScript so you can see the differences between the two languages. You'll also see how to use some of the objects described in the "Using the Scripting Objects" section of the chapter. The following code shows a basic example in VBScript.

```
' Test1.VBS shows how to use functions and subprocedures
' within a WSH script.

WScript.Echo("The value returned was: " + CStr(MyFunction(1)))

function MyFunction(nSomeValue)
    WScript.Echo("Function received value of: " + CStr(nSomeValue))
    Call MySubprocedure(nSomeValue + 1)
    MyFunction = nSomeValue + 1
end function

sub MySubprocedure(nSomeValue)
    WScript.Echo("Subprocedure received value of: " + CStr(nSomeValue))
end sub
```

As you can see, the sample code uses the WScript object to send information to the screen. The WScript object is always available at the command line, even though you have probably never used it as part of a browser application. As shown in the example, it's important to know how to use both functions and subs, the two building blocks of VBScript. The following code shows a similar example for JavaScript.

```
// Test1.JS shows how to use functions within a WSH script.

WScript.Echo("The value returned was: " + MyFunction(1));

function MyFunction(nSomeValue)
{
   WScript.Echo("The value received was: " + nSomeValue);
   return nSomeValue + 1;
}
```

JavaScript only provides functions, so that's all this example demonstrates. It's also important to notice that VBScript requires you to convert numeric values to a string, while JavaScript performs the conversion automatically. The following sections show how to perform certain command line–oriented tasks using scripting.

Scripting the Command Line and System Environment

Many of your scripts require access to the command line. The command line is where you type switches to modify the behavior of the script, as many of the utilities described in this book do. The system environment contains user, application, and operating system values, such as the user's name or the version of the operating system. The JavaScript code in Listing 8.1 retrieves information from the command line. It also retrieves information about the application environment.

LISTING 8.1: Working with the Command Line and System Environment

```
// ProgInfo.JS determines the specifics about your program and then
// displays this information on screen.

// Create some constants for display purposes (buttons and icons).
var intOK = 0;
var intOKCancel = 1;
var intAbortRetryIgnore = 2;
var intYesNoCancel = 3;
var intYesNo = 4;
var intRetryCancel = 5;
var intStop = 16;
var intQuestion = 32;
var intExclamation = 48;
var intInformation = 64;

// Create some popup return values.
var intOK = 1;
var intCancel = 2;
```

```
var intAbort = 3;
var intRetry = 4;
var intIgnore = 5;
var intYes = 6;
var intNo = 7;
var intClose = 8;
var intHelp = 9;

// Create a popup display object.
var WshShell = WScript.CreateObject("WScript.Shell");

// Create a variable for holding a popup return value.
var intReturn;

// Get the program information and display it.
WshShell.Popup("Full Name:\t" + WScript.Fullname +
        "\r\nInteractive:\t" + WScript.Interactive +
        "\r\nName:\t\t" + WScript.Name +
        "\r\nPath:\t\t" + WScript.Path +
        "\r\nScript Full Name:\t" + WScript.ScriptFullName +
        "\r\nScript Name:\t" + WScript.ScriptName +
        "\r\nVersion:\t\t" + WScript.Version,
        0,
        "Program Information Demonstration",
        intOK + intInformation);

// Ask if the user wants to display the argument list.
intReturn = WshShell.Popup("Do you want to display the argument list?",
            0,
            "Argument List Display",
            intYesNo + intQuestion);

// Determine if the user wants to display the argument list and
// display an appropriate message.
if (intReturn == intYes)

    // See if there are any arguments to display.
    DisplayArguments();
else
    WScript.Echo("Goodbye");

function DisplayArguments()
{

    // Create some variables.
    var strArguments = "Arguments:\r\n\t";    // Argument list.
    var intCount = 0;                 // Loop counter.

    // See if there are any arguments, if not, display an
```

```
    // appropriate message.
    if (WScript.Arguments.Length == 0)
        WshShell.Popup("There are no arguments to display.",
            0,
            "Argument List Display",
            intOK + intInformation);

    // If there are arguments to display, then create a list
    // first and display them all at once.
    else
    {
        for (intCount = 0;
             intCount < WScript.Arguments.Length;
             intCount++)

            strArguments = strArguments +
                           WScript.Arguments.Item(intCount) + "\r\n\t";

        WshShell.Popup(strArguments,
                       0,
                       "Argument List Display",
                       intOK + intInformation);
    }
}
```

When you run this script, you'll see a dialog box containing all of the information about the script engine. When you click OK, the program asks if you want to display the command line arguments. If you say yes, then you'll see anything you typed at the command line. Otherwise, the script displays a Goodbye message.

You should notice a few things about this example. First, I created an object in this code. You need access to the `WshShell` object for many of the tasks you'll perform with scripts. The code also shows how to use the `Popup()` method to obtain information from the user. Finally, the code uses the `Arguments` object to access the command line information. Notice the object hierarchy used in this example.

Scripting the Registry

Many of the utilities described in this book rely on the registry to store and retrieve data about the machine, the operating system, the user, and the application itself. Knowing how to access the registry from your script is important because you also need to access these values in order to discover how a particular utility will react or how the user had configured the system. You can also use the registry to store and retrieve values for your script. The example in Listing 8.2 shows how to use VBScript to access information in the registry. You don't want to change information unless you have to, but seeing what's available in the registry is a good way to build your knowledge of both scripting and the registry. Note that this example uses the command line argument to determine which file extension to look for in the registry. The example will use the .TXT file extension when you don't supply one.

LISTING 8.2: Working with the Registry

```
' RegRead.VBE will display the application extension information
' contained in the registry.

' Create an icon and button variable for Popup().
intOK = 0
intInformation = 64

' Create a popup display object.
set WshShell = WScript.CreateObject("WScript.Shell")

' Create variables to hold the information.
strExtension = ""     ' File extension that we're looking for.
strFileType = ""      ' Holds the main file type.
strFileOpen = ""      ' File open command.
strFilePrint = ""     ' File print command.
strDefaultIcon = ""   ' Default icon for file type.

' See if the user provided a file extension to look for.
' If not, assign strExtension a default file extension.
if (WScript.Arguments.Length > 0) then
    strExtension = WScript.Arguments.Item(0)
else
    strExtension = ".txt"
end if

' Get the file type.
strFileType = WshShell.RegRead("HKEY_CLASSES_ROOT\" +_
                strExtension + "\")

' Use the file type to get the file open and file print
' commands, along with the default icon.
strFileOpen = WshShell.RegRead("HKEY_CLASSES_ROOT\" +_
                strFileType +_
                "\shell\open\command\")
strFilePrint = WshShell.RegRead("HKEY_CLASSES_ROOT\" +_
                strFileType +_
                "\shell\print\command\")
strDefaultIcon = WshShell.RegRead("HKEY_CLASSES_ROOT\" +_
                strFileType +_
                "\DefaultIcon\")

' Display the results.
WshShell.Popup "File Type:" + vbTab + vbTab + vbTab + strFileType +_
       vbCrLf + "File Open Command:" + vbTab + strFileOpen +_
       vbCrLf + "File Print Command:" + vbTab + vbTab + strFilePrint +_
       vbCrLf + "Default Icon:" + vbTab + vbTab + strDefaultIcon,_
       0,_
       "RegRead Results",_
       intOK + intInformation
```

When you run this script, it reads the command line. If you haven't supplied a value, the script will assign a default extension of .TXT. The script uses the extension to locate information in the registry such as the file open and print commands. Finally, the script uses the `Popup()` method to display the output.

You should notice several differences between this example and the JavaScript example in Listing 8.1. First, the method for creating an object requires the use of a `set`—you can't simply assign the object to a variable. You'll also notice that VBScript has access to all of the standard Visual Basic constants such as `vbTab` and `vbCrLf`. Finally, VBScript handles many of the method calls as subs, not as functions. You need to exercise care when working in a mixed environment.

Using the Scripting Objects

A section of a chapter can't provide you with a complete tutorial on scripting. Some developers require months to learn everything there is to know about the scripting language and the objects the language controls. This section helps you understand the various objects that WSH supports. You won't become a guru overnight, but you could create some simple scripts immediately after you work through this chapter. As you learn more, you'll be able to create scripts of increasing complexity. Scripting isn't hard to learn, but you need to take your time and learn it a bit at a time.

TIP Windows XP and above doesn't include any sample scripts. However, earlier versions of Windows do include a samples directory for scripts that you can use to learn more about the scripting process. You can still download the script samples from Microsoft's site at `http://msdn2.microsoft.com/en-us/library/ms950396.aspx`.

WSH depends on objects that Microsoft supplies as part of Windows to perform tasks such as outputting text to the display. This chapter demonstrates the latest version of WSH. Every version of Windows has similar objects, but you might not find some objects in older versions of Windows.

NOTE An object consists of three elements: properties, methods, and events. A property describes the object and determines its functionality. For example, you can say an apple is red. In this case, red is a property of the apple. However, you can also paint the apple blue. In this case, you changed the color property of the apple to another value. Methods are actions you can perform with an object. For example, looking at an apple again, you can say that it has a grow method. As the tree applies the grow method, the apple becomes larger. Events are responses to specific object actions. For example, when the apple becomes mature, it raises the "color" event to tell you that it's ripe.

Writing scripts in Windows means knowing the object you want to work with, the properties that object provides, and the methods you can use with that object. You don't have to know about every object. In fact, you'll find it easier to learn about one object at a time. The following sections will tell you about the main scripting object, WScript, and some of the supporting objects it contains.

TIP The combination of WSH and a scripting engine form an interpreter that accepts a script file as input and outputs application data from the computer. Of course, WSH and its associated scripting engines are more complex than any previous interpreter. You can read about Microsoft's original vision for WSH at `http://www.microsoft.com/mind/0698/cutting0698.htm`. The Internet includes many useful WSH resource sites. Of the more interesting sites is the Scripting Guide for Windows site at `http://www.winguides.com/scripting/`. You can find books about WSH at `http://ourworld.compuserve.com/homepages/Guenter_Born/WSHBazaar/USBook.htm`. You'll find quite a few other resource sites throughout the sections. Make sure you check them out to get the most out of the material presented in this chapter.

Working with the WScript Object

The WScript object is the main object for WSH. You'll access every other object through this one. The following list tells you about the properties that the WScript object supports.

Application Provides you with access to a low level interface for WScript. An interface is a pointer to a list of functions that you can call for a particular object. Only advanced programmers will need this property because WSH exposes all of the basic functions for you.

Arguments Provides a complete list of the arguments for this script. Applications pass arguments on the command line. WSH passes the argument list as an array. You create a variable to hold the argument list, and then access the individual arguments as you would any array. The `Arguments.Count` property contains the total number of array elements.

FullName Contains the full name of the scripting engine along with the fully qualified path to it. For example, if you were using CScript, you might get `C:\WINDOWS\SYSTEM32\CSCRIPT.EXE` as a return value.

Interactive Returns true if the script is in interactive mode.

Name Returns the friendly name for WScript. In most cases, this is Windows Script Host.

Path Provides just the path information for the host executable. For example, if you were using CScript, you may get a return value of: `C:\WINDOWS\SYSTEM32\`.

ScriptFullName Contains the full name and path of the script that's running.

ScriptName Provides just the script name.

Version Returns the WSH Version number.

Remember that all of these properties tell you about the WScript object. You can also use methods to perform tasks with the WScript object. The following list provides a brief overview of the more important methods you'll use with the WScript object. Note that most of these methods require you pass one or more parameters as input. A parameter is a piece of data the method uses to perform a task.

`CreateObject(`*`strProgID`*`)` Create the object specified by `strProgID`. This object could be WSH specific like `"WScript.Network"` or application specific like `"Excel.Application"`.

`GetObject(`*`strPathname [, strProgID]`*`)` Retrieves the requested object. `strPathname` contains the filename for the object you want to retrieve. In most cases, this is going to be a data file, but you can retrieve other kinds of objects as well. As soon as you execute this command, WSH will start the application associated with that object. For example, if you specified `C:\MyText.TXT` as the `strPathname`, then WSH may open Notepad to display it. The optional `strProgID` argument allows you to override the default processing of the object. For example, you may want to open the text file with Word instead of Notepad.

`Echo(`*`AnyArg`*`)` Displays text in a window (WScript) or to the console screen (CScript). `AnyArg` can contain any type of valid output value. This can include both strings and numbers. Using `Echo` without any arguments displays a blank line.

`GetScriptEngine(`*`strEngineID`*`)` Registers an alternative script engine such as PerlScript (see the PerlScript site at `http://www.xav.com/perl/Components/Windows/PerlScript.html` or the Windows Script Host Resources site at `http://labmice.techtarget.com/scripting/WSH.htm` for details on this alternative). `strEngineID` contains the identifier for the script engine that you want to retrieve. You'll need to register the engine using the `GetScriptEngine.Register()` method before you can actually use it. A script engine also requires you to provide a default extension.

Real World Scenario

WORKING WITH OBJECTS

Scripts have a definite advantage over batch files because you can use objects in scripts. An object can be anything. For example, you can create an object that contains an Excel worksheet and use the functionality of Excel to perform tasks at the command line. A worksheet could hold a directory listing and you can use the database features of Excel to perform a customized sort. All you need to do is create the object using the `WScript.CreateObject()` method. If you already have a data file available to use for your application, then use the `WScript.GetObject()` method to open the data file directly. In most cases, you don't even need to worry about which application to use because the system will use the correct application by default.

Applications are an obvious kind of object. Your machine contains literally thousands of objects, all of which are available for use. For example, you can load an XML document by using the Msxml2.DOMDocument.5.0 object. Once you create this object, you can load the XML document using the `Load()` method and then process it using the various methods that the object provides. For example, use the `TransformNode()` method to use XSLT to transform the XML from one presentation to another.

Make sure you spend time looking at all of the objects described in the script resource Web pages provided in this chapter. You might be surprised at how much work a script can perform with only a modicum of work on your part. Even though the WScript objects described in this section are your most important resource, don't neglect the other resources at your fingertips.

`Quit(`*`intErrorCode`*`)` Exits the script prematurely. The optional `intErrorCode` argument returns an error code if necessary. You can test for this value using the `ErrorLevel` clause in batch files.

Working with the WScript.WshArguments Object

Whenever you start a script, you have the option of passing one or more arguments to it on the command line. That's where the WshArguments object comes into play. It helps you determine the number of arguments, and then retrieve them as needed. You'll always use the WScript.Arguments property to access this object; it's not directly accessible. The following list describes the properties for this object.

`Item(`*`intIndex`*`)` Retrieves a specific command line argument. `intIndex` contains the index of the argument that you want to retrieve. The array used to hold the arguments is 0 based, so the first argument number is 0.

`Count()` Returns the number of command line arguments.

`Length()` Returns the number of command line arguments. WSH provides this property for JScript compatibility purposes.

Working with the *WScript.WshShell* Object

You'll use the `WScript.WshShell` object to access the Windows shell (the part of Windows that interacts with applications and creates the user interface) in a variety of ways. For example, you can use this object to read the registry or to create a new shortcut on the desktop. This is an exposed

WSH object, which means you can access it directly. However, you need to access it through the WScript object like this: `WScript.WshShell`. The following list describes the WshShell methods.

`CreateShortcut(`*`strPathname`*`)` Creates a WSH shortcut object. `strPathname` contains the location of the shortcut, which will be the Desktop in most cases.

`DeleteEnvironmentVariable(`*`strName [, strType]`*`)` Deletes the environment variable specified by `strName`. The optional `strType` argument defines the type of environment variable to delete. Typical values for `strType` include `System`, `User`, `Volatile`, and `Process`. The default environment variable type is `System`.

`GetEnvironmentVariable(`*`strName [, strType]`*`)` Retrieves the environment variable specified by `strName`. Default environment variables include `NUMBER_OF_PROCESSORS`, `OS`, `COMSPEC`, `HOMEDRIVE`, `HOMEPATH`, `PATH`, `PATHEXT`, `PROMPT`, `SYSTEMDRIVE`, `SYSTEMROOT`, `WINDIR`, `TEMP`, and `TMP`. The optional `strType` argument defines the type of environment variable to delete. Typical values for `strType` include `System`, `User`, `Volatile`, and `Process`. The default environment variable type is `System`.

`Popup(`*`strText [,intSeconds] [,strTitle] [,intType]`*`)` Displays a message dialog box. The return value is an integer defining which button the user selected including the following values: OK (1), Cancel (2), Abort (3), Retry (4), Ignore (5), Yes (6), No (7), Close (8), and Help (9). `strText` contains the text that you want to display in the dialog box. `intSeconds` determines how long WSH displays the dialog box before it closes the dialog box and returns a value of –1. `strTitle` contains the title bar text. The `intType` argument can contain values that determine the type of dialog box you'll create. The first `intType` argument determines button type. You have a choice of OK (0), OK and Cancel (1), Abort, Retry, and Ignore (2), Yes, No, and Cancel (3), Yes and No (4), and Retry and Cancel (5). The second `intType` argument determines which icon Windows displays in the dialog box. You have a choice of the following values: Stop (16), Question (32), Exclamation (48), and Information (64). Combine the `intType` argument values to obtain different dialog box effects.

`RegDelete(`*`strName`*`)` Removes the value or key specified by `strName` from the registry. If `strName` ends in a backslash, then `RegDelete` removes a key. You must provide a fully qualified path to the key or value that you want to delete. In addition, `strName` must begin with one of these values: `HKEY_CURRENT_USER`, `HKEY_LOCAL_MACHINE`, `HKEY_CLASSES_ROOT`, `HKEY_USERS`, `HKEY_CURRENT_CONFIG`, or `HKEY_DYN_DATA`.

`RegRead(`*`strName`*`)` Reads the value or key specified by `strName` from the registry. If `strName` ends in a backslash, then `RegRead` reads a key. You must provide a fully qualified path to the key or value that you want to read. In addition, `strName` must begin with one of these values: `HKEY_CURRENT_USER`, `HKEY_LOCAL_MACHINE`, `HKEY_CLASSES_ROOT`, `HKEY_USERS`, `HKEY_CURRENT_CONFIG`, or `HKEY_DYN_DATA`. `RegRead` can only read specific data types including `REG_SZ`, `REG_EXPAND_SZ`, `REG_DWORD`, `REG_BINARY`, and `REG_MULTI_SZ`. Any other data types will return an error.

`RegWrite(`*`strName, anyValue [, strType]`*`)` Writes the data specified by `anyValue` to a value or key specified by `strName` to the registry. If `strName` ends in a backslash, then `RegWrite` writes a key. You must provide a fully qualified path to the key or value that you want to write. In addition, `strName` must begin with one of these values: `HKEY_CURRENT_USER`, `HKEY_LOCAL_MACHINE`, `HKEY_CLASSES_ROOT`, `HKEY_USERS`, `HKEY_CURRENT_CONFIG`, or `HKEY_DYN_DATA`. `RegRead` can only write specific data types including `REG_SZ`, `REG_EXPAND_SZ`, `REG_DWORD`, and `REG_BINARY`. Any other data types will return an error.

Run(*strCommand* [, *intWinType*] [*lWait*]) Runs the command or application specified by strCommand. You can include command line arguments and switches with the command string. intWinType determines the type of window that the application starts in. You can force the script to wait for the application to complete by setting lWait to True; otherwise, the script begins the next line of execution immediately.

SetEnvironmentVariable(*strName*, *strValue* [, *strType*]) Sets the environment variable named strName to the value specified by strValue. The optional strType argument defines the type of environment variable to create. Typical values for strType include System, User, Volatile, and Process. The default environment variable type is System.

Working with the *WScript.WshNetwork* Object

The WshNetwork object works with network objects such as drives and printers that the client machine can access. This is an exposed WSH object, which means you can access it directly using the WScript.WshNetwork object. The following list describes properties associated with this object.

ComputerName Returns a string containing the client computer name.

UserDomain Returns a string containing the user's domain name.

UserName Returns a string containing the name that the user used to log on to the network.

As with any other WSH object, the WshNetwork object uses methods to work with network resources. The following list describes the methods associated with this object.

AddPrinterConnection(*strLocal*, *strRemote* [, *lUpdate*] [, *strUser*] [, *strPassword*]) Creates a new printer connection for the local machine. strLocal contains the local name for the printer specified by strRemote. The strRemote value must contain a locatable resource and usually uses a UNC format such as \\Remote\Printer. Setting lUpdate to True adds the new connection to the user profile, which means Windows will make the connection available each time the user boots their machine. strUser and strPassword contain optional username and password values required to log onto the remote machine and create the connection.

EnumNetworkDrives() Returns a WshCollection object containing the list of local and remote drives currently mapped from the client machine. A WshCollection object is essentially a 0-based array of strings.

EnumPrinterConnections() Returns a WshCollection object containing the list of local and remote printers currently mapped from the client machine. A WshCollection object is essentially a 0-based array of strings.

MapNetworkDrive(*strLocal*, *strRemote* [, *lUpdate*] [, *strUser*] [, *strPassword*]) Creates a new drive connection for the local machine. strLocal contains the local name for the drive specified by strRemote. The strRemote value must contain a locatable resource and usually uses a UNC format such as \\Remote\Drive_C. Setting lUpdate to true adds the new connection to the user profile, which means Windows will make the connection available each time the user boots their machine. strUser and strPassword contain optional username and password values required to log onto the remote machine and create the connection.

RemoveNetworkDrive(*strName* [, *lForce*] [, *lUpdate*]) Deletes a previous network drive mapping. If strName contains a local name, Windows only cancels that connection. If strName contains a remote name, then Windows cancels all resources associated with that remote name.

Set `lForce` to True if you want to disconnect from a resource whether that resource is in use or not. Setting `lUpdate` to True will remove the connection from the user profile so that it doesn't appear the next time that the user logs onto the machine.

`RemovePrinterConnection(`*`strName`* *[, `lForce`] [, `lUpdate`]*`)` Deletes a previous network printer connection. If `strName` contains a local name, Windows only cancels that connection. If `strName` contains a remote name, then Windows cancels all resources associated with that remote name. Set `lForce` to True if you want to disconnect from a resource whether that resource is in use or not. Setting `lUpdate` to True will remove the connection from the user profile so that it doesn't appear the next time that the user logs onto the machine.

Impersonating a User with the RunAs Utility

It's important to set security on your machine to prevent outside sources, especially those from email or Web sites, to run scripts on your machine. Of course, setting security to prevent others from executing virus-laden code also tends to keep your scripts from running—at least with the credentials of the current user. The RunAs utility provides a way for you to have great security and still allow script execution too. You use this utility to run a particular application with credentials other than those used by the current user. This utility uses the following syntax:

```
RUNAS [ [/noprofile | /profile] [/env] [/netonly] ] /user:<UserName> program
RUNAS [ [/noprofile | /profile] [/env] [/netonly] ] /smartcard
   [/user:<UserName>] program
```

The following list describes each of the command line arguments.

`/noprofile` Specifies that you don't want to load the RunAs user's profile when running the application. The benefit of using this setting is that the application loads more quickly. In addition, this setting acts as a safety feature because the application you want to run is less likely to corrupt the RunAs user's settings. However, using this feature can prevent some applications from running, especially when they rely on settings in the user profile to perform certain tasks.

`/profile` Specifies that you want to load the RunAs user's profile when running the application. This is the default setting.

`/env` Specifies that you want to use the current environment, instead of the RunAs user's environment, to run the application. This feature is useful when the local environment is different from the environment that the RunAs user normally relies on to run applications.

`/netonly` Specifies the credentials supplied for the RunAs user apply to remote access only.

`/savecred` Uses the credentials previously saved by the RunAs user, rather than obtaining a new copy of the credentials. This option isn't available when using Windows XP Home Edition and the utility will ignore it.

`/smartcard` Specifies that the RunAs user credentials appear on a smart card.

`/user:`*`UserName`* Specifies the username. You must supply the username in one of two forms, `User@Domain` or `Domain\User`.

`program` Specifies the application you want to run as well as any command line switches the application requires to run.

A WORD ABOUT SECURITY

Anyone who spends time reading the trade press knows that there are individuals out there who would just love to take over your computer. In fact, you don't even have to read the trade press, just look at your local newspaper for articles. However, despite all of the warnings and the how-to articles describing how to avoid viruses, computers are still picking them up. The problem, as I see it, is the desire of most people not to have any limits. After all, isn't that what most commercials tell us today? There are no limits, advertisers tell us, yet viruses provide a real world example of limits that technology places on us. No one wants to get a virus, yet I still see people loading into their browser every gizmo ever created so they can see that little animation that someone sent them. They won't remember the animations 10 minutes from now, but the virus they pick up from the animation can last for weeks.

I'm not going to tell you yet again what you already know. Locking your system down is your responsibility. However, as I've been telling clients for years, you still have work to do and lockdowns tend to inhibit work too. That's why the RunAs utility is possibly the most important security feature on your system. Using the RunAs utility, you can lock your system down to the point of paranoia and still run the utilities, batch files, and scripts that you need to run, all without logging into and out of your system multiple times. Don't give in to the desire to run applications without protection; you do have a real alternative that works well.

Changing the Environment

Vista provides the means to control the user's environment with greater accuracy through command line utilities. You can define whether the user can install applications, enable or disable session logons, and modify port configurations. The Change utility is the most powerful of the three because you can use it to perform any of these tasks. The remaining three utilities provide subsets of the Change functionality. The following sections describe these environment-changing utilities.

Changing Logons, Ports, and Users with the Change Utility

The Change utility helps you control the user's ability to install applications, enable or disable session logons, and control ports. You could consider each of these actions a specific utility mode, but the utility is quite simple, so this section describes all three tasks. This utility uses the following syntax:

```
CHANGE USER {/EXECUTE | /INSTALL | /QUERY}
CHANGE LOGON {/QUERY | /ENABLE | /DISABLE}
CHANGE PORT [portx=porty | /D portx | /QUERY]
```

The following list describes each of the command line arguments.

`USER {/EXECUTE {Enable | Disable} | /INSTALL {Enable | Disable} | /QUERY}` Specifies whether the user has execute or install privileges. Follow the privilege with the word *enable* to enable the privilege or *disable* to disable the privilege. Use the `/Query` command line switch to determine the user's current capabilities.

`LOGON {/QUERY | /ENABLE | /DISABLE}` Determines whether Vista enables or disables session logons. The `/Query` command line switch displays the current session logon status.

PORT [portx=porty | /D portx | /QUERY] Redefines the port configuration. You can assign a port to a particular device. Use the /D command line switch to remove the port assignment. The /Query command line switch displays the current port assignments.

Enabling or Disabling Session Logons with the ChgLogon Utility

Use the ChgLogon utility to enable or disable session logons. This utility uses the following syntax:

```
CHGLOGON {/QUERY | /ENABLE | /DISABLE}
```

Usage is the same as the CHANGE LOGON {/QUERY | /ENABLE | /DISABLE} utility form described in the "Changing Logons, Ports, and Users with the Change Utility" section of the chapter.

Listing COM Port Mappings Using the ChgPort Utility

The ChgPort utility controls port assignments on the current system. This utility uses the following syntax:

```
CHANGE PORT [portx=porty | /D portx | /QUERY]
```

Usage is the same as the CHANGE PORT [portx=porty | /D portx | /QUERY] utility form described in the "Changing Logons, Ports, and Users with the Change Utility" section of the chapter.

Modifying the Install Mode with the ChgUsr Utility

The ChgUsr utility controls the user's execute and install privileges on the system. This utility uses the following syntax:

```
CHGUSR {/EXECUTE | /INSTALL | /QUERY}
```

Usage is the same as the CHANGE USER {/EXECUTE | /INSTALL | /QUERY} utility form described in the "Changing Logons, Ports, and Users with the Change Utility" section of the chapter.

Getting Started with Command Line Tasks

This chapter has shown you how to work with scripts at the command prompt. Of course, this is merely the tip of the iceberg. Scripting can become quite addictive and profitable as well, because it represents an easy way to create applications that run on multiple platforms. In short, if this chapter is your introduction to scripting, it's a good one, but you can do a lot more. Of course, what you've seen might seem like quite a lot already because scripting at the command line gives you complete access to your system in a way that batch file programming can't.

It's your turn. If you don't already know how to work with scripting languages, make sure you use the resources at the beginning of the chapter to learn. These tutorials and online references will greatly enhance your ability to begin working with scripts immediately. Of course, you'll want to go slowly when scripting anything that could cause damage to your system. The best general rule is to try one thing at a time, perfect your knowledge, and go on to the next item you want to learn.

Chapter 9 helps you get to the next step with scripting, at least if you're an administrator on a larger network. Active Directory is the means by which larger networks track machines and users (among other things). Learning to script Active Directory can save you considerable time performing maintenance tasks on a network. Because Active Directory is centralized and uses a well-defined format for entries, learning how to perform one task well usually translates into knowing how to perform a lot of other tasks as well. The scripting techniques and tips in Chapter 9 will get you headed in the right direction.

Chapter 9

Scripting for Active Directory

- Discovering Helpful Active Directory Utilities
- Working with Objects
- Working with Users, Groups, and Computers

Active Directory is the data storage container for modern Windows networks of any size. One or more domain controllers provide support for the Active Directory database, which is a hierarchical, object-based data store. Using Active Directory has centralized data storage needs for most companies by providing a single replicated data store for all settings of any type. The data need not appear on a single machine, but you access it as if it did appear in one location. Active Directory contains all settings for every kind of object on the network—everything from users to workstations. By knowing which objects to access, you can learn anything you want about the network and perhaps more than you knew was available before you began your search. Of course, you need the proper rights to access the data. Unlike previous storage technologies, Active Directory does provide a significant amount of security to protect the vast store of data it contains.

NOTE The Active Directory support you can expect from Windows varies by the version that you're using. None of the workstation versions of Windows, including Windows XP and Vista, ships with Active Directory tools, but you can use many of the tools in these environments. See the article at `http://www.microsoft.com/technet/prodtechnol/windowsserver2003/library/TechRef/767c4008-46c1-4684-85a8-ff7f25cd6d55.mspx` for the workstation support details on these tools. When working with Windows 2000, you basically receive support using ADSIEdit, DSQuery, and NTDSUtil. All of the other tools discussed in this chapter require a Windows 2003 setup, access to a Windows 2003 machine, or that you download and install the Active Directory tools supplied with Windows 2003.

Because of everything it does, Active Directory is quite complex. You don't want to make a mistake when editing it, which means performing actions consistently. Microsoft provides a number of utilities to help you maintain Active Directory. This chapter doesn't discuss the graphical utilities, but in this case, you'll actually find that the command line utilities are more powerful and provide better access to Active Directory than the graphical utilities in most cases. More importantly, the command line utilities in this chapter let you script Active Directory actions so that you can perform a number of tasks using simple command line entries that are difficult to use incorrectly. You can perform Active Directory automation equally well using batch files, scripts, or even full-fledged applications.

Vista users will have to observe a few additional precautions when working with these utilities. First, you must open an administrator command prompt to use these utilities. The "Vista Changes for the Command Line" section of Chapter 1 describes the command line changes, all of which apply when working with Active Directory. To open an administrator command line, right-click the Start ➤ Programs ➤ Accessories ➤ Command Prompt entry and choose Run as Administrator from the context menu. Second, you must ensure you have full access to the server. Remember that Vista treats any network drive as the Internet zone until such time as you change the zone to the Trusted zone. You typically need to have Trusted zone access to the network drive to work with Active Directory. Third, as with any other version of Windows, you must have administrative privileges to work with Active Directory in Vista. In some cases, you might have to provide access to a resource specifically in your name to manipulate it.

The sections that follow begin with descriptions of a few helpful command line utilities. The chapter progresses to looking at specific kinds of objects and showing how you can manipulate them. Finally, the chapter discusses how you can work with users, groups, and computers.

GRAPHICS AND THE COMMAND LINE OFTEN WORK TOGETHER

Just because you're focusing on the command line doesn't mean you won't ever need to work with a graphical utility. This book doesn't discuss the main graphical utility for editing Active Directory, the Active Directory Services Interface Editor (ADSIEdit). The ADSIEdit utility can come in quite handy, though, even when you're working at the command line. For example, you can use it when you're creating a script to ensure you get the Lightweight Directory Access Protocol (LDAP) statement for selecting an object correct. Instead of figuring out the LDAP by hand, you can simply copy and paste it for the object you want to select from ADSIEdit.

I've been using ADSIEdit for a wealth of needs over the years. For example, it appears in my book, *.NET Development Security Solutions* (Sybex, 2003), because it's a necessary tool for developers. You can find a number of articles, tutorials, and reference guides for ADSIEdit online. For example, you can find a great overview of ADSIEdit on Microsoft TechNet at `http://technet2.microsoft.com/WindowsServer/en/Library/ebca3324-5427-471a-bc19-9aa1decd3d401033.mspx`. You'll find a great tutorial article about ADSIEdit on the ExhangeIS Web site at `http://www.exchangeis.com/blogs/exchangeis/archive/2005/08/09/48.aspx`. If you're working with Windows 2003, make sure you check out the Windows 2003-specific information about ADSIEdit at `http://www.computerperformance.co.uk/w2k3/utilities/adsi_edit.htm`.

Discovering Helpful Active Directory Utilities

Active Directory comes with a number of useful utilities that make working with Active Directory fast. Because Active Directory relies on a highly hierarchical structure, using a graphical utility can prove time consuming; using a command line utility saves time. Of course, saving time doesn't always mean reduced complexity or easier use. The graphical utilities have the advantage when you don't know very much about Active Directory and need help making the right decisions. The command line utilities provided are for advanced users who already know how Active Directory works.

The following sections describe several command line utilities. Each of these utilities helps you manage a different aspect of Active Directory from the command line. In some cases, you can perform everything you need to do with Active Directory using just one utility, but in many cases, you'll need to combine several utilities to achieve a desired effect.

WARNING Never use any of these utilities for the first time on a production machine—one that you rely on to perform your daily work. A seemingly insignificant change or a change made in error can result in significant network damage. Always set up a test system, work with the utilities for a while, and then move on to the production systems when you know precisely how a particular change will affect the system.

Managing Active Directory with the DSQuery Utility

The Directory Services Query (DSQuery) utility helps you to obtain information about Active Directory content. For example, you can obtain a complete list of the computers attached to the network or the names of the users who rely on the network. Each kind of data requires that you use a specific object type or the asterisk (*) for all object types. The following list shows the most common objects (those supported by the utility).

- computer
- contact
- group
- ou (organizational unit)
- site
- server
- user
- quota
- partition
- * (all objects)

All of these objects require some basic input to obtain the data. For example, you can expect to provide a username. The following list provides the common inputs for each of the objects.

{*StartNode* | *forestroot* | *domainroot* | *ObjectDN*} Determines the node where the search starts. You can specify a node's distinguished name, or use one of the default starting nodes that include forestroot (forest root) or domainroot (domain root). Searching in the forest root means that the utility performs a global catalog search of all the domain controllers. Only the quota object uses the Object Distinguished Name variable, which defines the distinguished name of the object to use as a starting point for searches. The default setting is domainroot.

-o {dn | rdn | samid | upn} Specifies the output format for the list of entries the search obtains. Not every object can use every output format. For example, when you search the contact object, you can't use the `samid` output. See the individual object descriptions for additional details. The default setting relies on the `dn` format. The following list describes the common formats.

dn Displays the distinguished name for each entry.

rdn Displays the relative distinguished name for each entry. A relative distinguished name only shows the path from the starting point to the current location in the Active Directory hierarchy.

samid Displays the Security Access Manager (SAM) account name for each entry.

upn Displays the User Principal Name (UPN) for each entry. This output only applies to the user object.

-scope {subtree | onelevel | base} Defines the scope of the search. The scope determines how far down the hierarchy the utility searches for the specified object. The subtree option searches the subtree root and the specified start node. The `onelevel` option searches the immediate children (one level down the hierarchy) of the start node only. The `base` option searches the single object represented by the start node. When working with the forest root node, you can only perform a subtree search. The default search scope is `subtree`.

-name *Name* Searches for the object with the specified name. You can use the asterisk (*) to signify wildcard searches. For example, `A*` would search for all objects beginning with the letter A, while `*ing` would search for objects that end with "ing." You can also combine wildcards. For example, `A*ing` would search for objects that begin with "A" and end with "ing."

-desc Description Searches for an object with a specific description. As with the `-name` argument, you can use wildcard characters as part of the search criteria. Always enclose arguments that contain spaces within quotes. Because most descriptions contain spaces, you can reduce errors by always enclosing descriptions in quotes.

{-s *Server* | -d *Domain*} Connects to the specified remote server or domain (not both). You must have the required rights to access the server or domain. The default settings rely on the domain controller for the logon domain. If you aren't logged into a domain, the utility attempts to use the logon server. When a logon server isn't available, the utility uses the local machine or registers an error that Active Directory isn't installed.

-u *UserName* Specifies the name of the user account to use to log onto a remote server. The default setting relies on the user account of the currently logged on user. The username can take several forms as shown in the following list.

UserName The account name such as GeorgeS.

Domain\UserName The domain name combined with the username such as `MyDomain\GeorgeS`.

User Principal Name (UPN) The UPN version of the username that includes the fully qualified domain such as `GeorgeS@MyDomain.MyCompany.com`.

-p {*Password* | *} Specifies the user password. The utility prompts you for a password when you provide the asterisk (*) in place of the actual password. Using this second option is actually better from a security perspective because the prompt dialog box will replace your password with asterisks. Using the command line option displays your password in plain text.

-q Places the utility in quiet mode. The utility doesn't output any information to the command line.

-r Searches using recursive techniques. A recursive search follows all referrals in children of the starting object, which means that you'll see all potential results for a particular search. However, recursive searches can consume considerable resources and require additional time to complete. The default setting doesn't perform a recursive search.

-gc Performs the search using the Active Directory global catalog, which means searching the entire forest. The default search only searches the current domain. A global catalog search locates objects that meet the search criteria across the entire network, but requires more resources and additional time to complete.

-limit *NumberOfObjects* Determines the number of objects that the utility returns for the specified search. Limiting the number of objects that the utility returns can enhance performance and use resources more efficiently. Setting this argument to 0 returns all of the objects. The default setting returns the first 100 objects.

{-uc | -uco | -uci} Forces the utility to output the results or input arguments in Unicode. The following list describes each of these Unicode options.

-uc Specifies a Unicode format for both input and output when using a pipe (|).

-uco Specifies a Unicode format for output when using a pipe (|) or file.

-uci Specifies a Unicode format for input when using a pipe (|) or file.

TIP **Use the pipe (|) to transfer data between Active Directory utilities. In fact, you can use the output of one search as input to a second search to create complex searches.**

Even though the basic concepts are the same for each object, the individual objects present small differences in the manner in which you query them. The following sections describe these common objects and tell how you can access them.

COMPUTER

The computer object locates computers on the network that match the search criteria. A computer can serve any purpose in this case—everything from a server to a workstation. This object uses the following syntax:

```
dsquery computer [{StartNode | forestroot | domainroot}]
   [-o {dn | rdn | samid}] [-scope {subtree | onelevel | base}]
   [-name Name] [-desc Description] [-samid SAMName]
   [-inactive NumberOfWeeks] [-stalepwd NumberOfDays] [-disabled]
   [{-s Server | -d Domain}] [-u UserName] [-p {Password | *}] [-q]
   [-r] [-gc] [-limit NumberOfObjects] [{-uc | -uco | -uci}]
```

The following list describes each of the special command line arguments.

-samid SAMName Searches for computers that have the specified SAM account name.

-inactive *NumberOfWeeks* Searches for computers that have been inactive for the specified number of weeks. In this case, the system measures activity by logons to the domain. Consequently, even if someone uses a computer daily, the system considers it inactive until the user logs into the domain.

-stalepwd *NumberOfDays* Searches for computers that have not changed their password for the specified number of days.

-disabled Searches for computers that have disabled accounts. The reason the system disabled the account isn't important.

CONTACT

The contact object locates all contacts in Active Directory that match the specified search criteria. Note that this object doesn't support the `samid` option for the `-o` command line switch. This object uses the following syntax:

```
dsquery contact [{StartNode | forestroot | domainroot}] [-o {dn | rdn}]
   [-scope {subtree | onelevel | base}] [-name Name]
```

```
    [-desc Description] [{-s Server | -d Domain}] [-u UserName]
    [-p {Password | *}] [-q] [-r] [-gc] [-limit NumberOfObjects]
    [{-uc | -uco | -uci}]
```

This object doesn't support any specialized command line arguments.

GROUP

Use the group object to locate all groups that match the specified search criteria. In some cases, this object fails to find the group because you haven't specified the group criteria correctly. Use the asterisk (*) object when group searches fail to locate the groups you want to find. This object uses the following syntax:

```
dsquery group [{StartNode | forestroot | domainroot}]
   [-o {dn | rdn | samid}] [-scope {subtree | onelevel | base}]
   [-name Name] [-desc Description] [-samid SAMName]
   [{-s Server | -d Domain}] [-u UserName] [-p {Password | *}] [-q]
   [-r] [-gc] [-limit NumberOfObjects] [{-uc | -uco | -uci}]
```

The following describes the special command line argument.

`-samid` ***`SAMName`*** Searches for groups that have the specified SAM account name.

OU (ORGANIZATIONAL UNIT)

The ou object locates all organizational units that match the specified search criteria. In some cases, this object fails to find the organizational unit because you haven't specified the group criteria correctly. Use the asterisk (*) object when ou searches fail to locate the organizational unit you want to find. Note that this object doesn't support the `samid` option for the `-o` command line switch. This object uses the following syntax:

```
dsquery ou [{StartNode | forestroot | domainroot}] [-o {dn | rdn}]
   [-scope {subtree | onelevel | base}] [-name Name]
   [-desc Description] [{-s Server | -d Domain}] [-u UserName]
   [-p {Password | *}] [-q] [-r] [-gc] [-limit NumberOfObjects]
   [{-uc | -uco | -uci}]
```

This object doesn't support any specialized command line arguments.

SITE

The site object searches for a site that matches the specified search criteria. A site normally specifies a location or region versus the domain used to provide a logical separation of computers despite location. Note that this object supports a limited range of command line arguments. It doesn't support a starting node selection or a scope. In addition, it doesn't support the `samid` option for the `-o` command line switch. This object uses the following syntax:

```
dsquery site [-o {dn | rdn}] [-name Name] [-desc Description]
   [{-s Server | -d Domain}] [-u UserName] [-p {Password | *}] [-q]
   [-r] [-gc] [-limit NumberOfObjects] [{-uc | -uco | -uci}]
```

This object doesn't support any specialized command line arguments.

SERVER

The server object locates all servers (rather than all machines) that match the specified search criteria. This object doesn't support a starting node selection or a scope. In addition, it doesn't support the samid option for the -o command line switch. This object uses the following syntax:

```
dsquery server [-o {dn | rdn}] [-forest] [-domain DomainName]
   [-site SiteName] [-name Name] [-desc Description]
   [-hasfsmo {schema | name | infr | pdc | rid}] [-isgc]
   [{-s Server | -d Domain}] [-u UserName] [-p {Password | *}] [-q]
   [-r] [-gc] [-limit NumberOfObjects] [{-uc | -uco | -uci}]
```

The following list describes each of the command line arguments.

-forest Searches for all domain controllers (server objects) that are part of the current forest.

-domain *DomainName* Searches for all server objects that are part of the specified domain. You must use the DNS name of the domain controller. Don't use this command line switch when you want to display all of the domain controllers within the current domain since this is the default setting.

-site *SiteName* Searches for all of the domain controllers (server objects) that appear as part of the specified site.

-hasfsmo {schema | name | infr | pdc | rid} Searches for the domain controller that holds the requested operations master role. The following list describes each role.

- **schema** Specifies the schema master of the forest.
- **name** Specifies the domain-naming master of the forest.
- **infr** Specifies the infrastructure master of the forest.
- **pdc** Specifies the PDC of the domain specified by the -domain command line switch or the current domain when you don't specify a domain.
- **rid** Specifies the Relative Identifier (RID) master of the domain specified by the -domain command line switch or the current domain when you don't specify a domain.

-isgc Searches for all Global Catalog (GC) servers in the scope specified by the -forest, -domain, or -site command line switches. If you don't specify any of the command line switches that the utility uses to define a scope, the utility locates all GC servers in the current domain.

USER

The user object locates all users in Active Directory that match the specified search criteria. In some cases, this object fails to find the group because you haven't specified the group criteria correctly. Use the asterisk (*) object when group searches fail to locate the groups you want to find. This object uses the following syntax:

```
dsquery user [{StartNode | forestroot | domainroot}]
   [-o {dn | rdn | upn | samid}] [-scope {subtree | onelevel | base}]
   [-name Name] [-desc Description] [-upn UPN] [-samid SAMName]
   [-inactive NumberOfWeeks] [-stalepwd NumberOfDays] [-disabled]
   [{-s Server | -d Domain}] [-u UserName] [-p {Password | *}] [-q]
   [-r] [-gc] [-limit NumberOfObjects] [{-uc | -uco | -uci}]
```

The following list describes each of the command line arguments.

-upn *UPN* Searches for users with the specified UPN.

-samid *SAMName* Searches for users that have the specified SAM account name.

-inactive *NumberOfWeeks* Searches for users that have been inactive for the specified number of weeks. In this case, the system measures activity by logons to the domain. Consequently, even if someone uses a computer daily, the system considers the user inactive until they log into the domain.

-stalepwd *NumberOfDays* Searches for users that have not changed their password for the specified number of days.

-disabled Searches for users that have disabled accounts. The reason the system disabled the account isn't important.

QUOTA

The quota object locates quota specifications that match the specified search criteria. The quota specification determines the maximum number of directory objects a given security principal can own in a particular directory partition. Note that this object doesn't support the `samid` option for the `-o` command line switch. Use spaces to separate multiple distinguished names in an argument. In addition, you can't specify a scope or name. This object uses the following syntax:

```
dsquery quota {domainroot | ObjectDN} [-o {dn | rdn}] [-acct Name]
   [-qlimit Filter] [-desc Description] [{-s Server | -d Domain}]
   [-u UserName] [-p {Password | *}] [-q] [-r] [-gc]
   [-limit NumberOfObjects] [{-uc | -uco | -uci}]
```

The following list describes each of the command line arguments.

-acct *Name* Forces the utility to locate quota specifications assigned to the specified security principal (user, group, computer, or InetOrgPerson). You may use a distinguished name as input for this command line argument. The command line argument also accepts the security principal information in the form `Domain\SAMAccountName`.

-qlimit *Filter* Defines the search in terms of a quota specification. This command line argument tends to filter the output and reduce the number of responses you must search to locate a particular entry. The utility reads any filter you provide with this argument as a string. Always use quotes around the argument. Any range values you provide must also appear within the quotes, such as `-qlimit "=99"`. Use a value of `"-1"` to locate quotas without any limit.

PARTITION

The partition object locates partitions within Active Directory that match the specified search criteria. The search features of this object are somewhat limited. You don't have access to the starting node, the `samid` option for the `-o` command line switch, the scope, the object name, or object description. This object uses the following syntax:

```
dsquery partition [-o {dn | rdn}] [-part Filter]
   [{-s Server | -d Domain}][-u UserName] [-p {Password | *}] [-q] [-r]
   [-gc] [-limit NumberOfObjects] [{-uc | -uco | -uci}]
```

The following describes the command line argument.

-part *Filter* Defines a filter for partition objects by specifying a Common Name (CN).

*** (ALL OBJECTS)**

The * object is different from all of the other objects discussed in this section. First, you can use the * object to search for any other object in Active Directory. Second, this object relies on the LDAP to locate items in Active Directory, rather than using the more direct approach provided by the other objects. Some of the arguments are still the same as for other objects. For example, you can still choose a starting point for the search and access remove systems. This object uses the following syntax:

```
dsquery * [{ObjectDN | forestroot | domainroot}]
   [-scope {subtree | onelevel | base}] [-filter LDAPFilter]
   [-attr {AttributeList | *}] [-attrsonly] [-l]
   [{-s Server | -d Domain}] [-u UserName] [-p {Password | *}] [-q]
   [-r] [-gc] [-limit NumberOfObjects] [{-uc | -uco | -uci}]
```

The following list describes each of the command line arguments.

`-filter` ***`LDAPFilter`*** Defines a search filter that relies on LDAP. The utility searches for the specified object using the LDAP filter in place of directly accessible values, such as an object name. The default filter of `(objectClass=*)` returns all Active Directory objects. An LDAP filter consists of object name and value pairs. For example, a filter value of `(&(objectCategory=Person) (sn=smith*))` locates a person with any form of the name of smith.

`-attr` ***`{AttributeList | *}`*** Defines the attributes that should appear as part of the result set. For example, you might want to know the first and last names of persons that you locate in Active Directory, but not their addresses. Separate each attribute name in the list using a semicolon. Make sure you surround the attribute list with quotes. If you specify an asterisk (*), the utility returns all attributes for the requested object. The utility automatically outputs the data in a list format when you use this option, even if you don't specify the `-l` command line switch. The default attribute list value is the distinguished name of the selected object.

`-attrsonly` Outputs only the attribute types present for the objects in the result set. The utility doesn't output any of the object values. The default setting displays both the attribute type and the associated value.

`-l` Displays the output in a list format. The default setting displays the output in a tabular format.

Managing the Active Directory Database with the NTDSUtil Utility

The Windows NT Directory Services Utility (NTDSUtil) is an interactive utility, for the most part, so you won't use it with a batch file very often. However, by entering the correct command at the command prompt, you can get to the correct area of this utility quickly. This utility uses the following syntax:

```
NTDSUtil [{Command | Stream}]
```

The following list describes each of the command line arguments.

NOTE Because this is an interactive command-processing environment, the chapter won't discuss NTDSUtil in detail. However, you can find a wealth of tutorials online for this utility. For example, you'll find an excellent tutorial for the novice on the ComputerPerformance site at `http://www.computerperformance.co.uk/w2k3/utilities/windows_ntdsutil.htm`.

Command Specifies an optional starting point for executing commands in the interactive environment. Here's a list of standard commands that NTDSUtil understands.

`Authoritative restore` Restores the Directory Information Tree (DIT) database.

`Domain management` Prepares the system to create a new domain.

`Files` Manages the NTDS database files.

`Help` Displays help information about the selected management function. The help you see depends on the commands you issued previously. See the `Stream` command line argument entry for details.

`IPDeny List` Manages the LDAP IP deny list. This list determines the machine that can access Active Directory remotely.

`LDAP policies` Manages the LDAP protocol policies.

`Metadata cleanup` Removes old metadata from the system. This feature includes removing old objects off decommissioned servers.

`Popups {On | Off}` Enables or disables popups.

`Quit` Ends a particular command level. You must issue multiple `Quit` commands, one for each level. See the `Stream` command line argument entry for an example. Entering the `Quit` command at the NTDSUtil prompt always exits the application.

`Roles` Manages the NTDS role owner tokens.

`Security account management` Manages the security account database. This command line switch also searches for and removes duplicate SID entries in the security account database.

`Semantic database analysis` Analyzes the database looking for semantic errors.

`Stream` Specifies multiple commands that NTDSUtil should execute as a stream. The commands must appear as a single string with each command separated with a space. For example, you can obtain help about the roles task by typing **`NTDSUtil Roles Help Quit Quit`** at the command line and pressing Enter. Figure 9.1 shows the effect of using this command. Notice that NTDSUtil processes each command separately. First, the NTDSUtil prompt appears, where the utility enters the `Roles` command. Second, at the Flexible Single Master Operations (fsmo) maintenance prompt, the utility enters the `Help` command. Third, the utility enters the `Quit` command to exit the fsmo maintenance prompt. Fourth, the utility enters `Quit` again to exit the NTDSUtil and the command prompts.

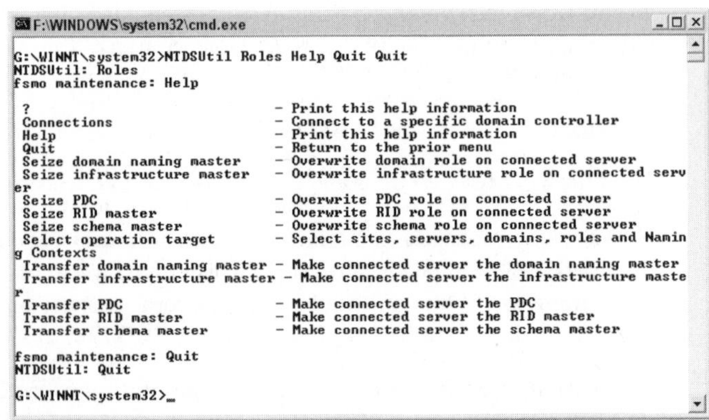

FIGURE 9.1
NTDSUtil is one of the few command line utilities that processes command streams successfully.

Working with Objects

The focus of data storage within Active Directory is the object. Each object includes a unique set of attributes used to define the object. For example, a person object will include the user's name and password, along with other essential user data such as their address. The following sections describe utilities specifically designed to work with Active Directory objects in a particular way. While you can use these utilities at the command line, you'll often use them in batch files and scripts to automatic management tasks at the command line.

Creating New Objects Using the DSAdd Utility

The DSAdd utility adds new objects to Active Directory. Each object requires different input to create the object. The DSAdd utility supports the following common objects.

- computer
- contact
- group
- ou (organizational unit)
- user
- quota

All of these objects require some basic input to obtain the data. For example, you can expect to provide a username. The following list provides the common inputs for each of the objects.

`ObjectDN` Specifies the distinguished name for the object that you want to add. In most cases, the command line syntax for the objects will appear with the object name, such as `ComputerDN` for the computer object's distinguished name. Every object requires a distinguished name so the distinguished name is one of the few pieces of required information you must provide. If you don't supply the distinguished name on the command line, the utility will attempt to obtain the distinguished name using the standard input (StdIn) device, which can include the keyboard, a redirected file, or as piped output from another command. Always end the standard input with the Ctrl+Z character.

`-desc` ***`Description`*** Determines the object description. Always enclose arguments that contain spaces within quotes. Because most descriptions contain spaces, you can reduce errors by always enclosing descriptions in quotes.

`{-s` ***`Server`*** **`|`** ***`-d Domain`*** **`}`** Connects to the specified remote server or domain (not both). You must have the required rights to access the server or domain. The default settings rely on the domain controller for the logon domain. If you aren't logged into a domain, the utility will attempt to use the logon server. When a logon server isn't available, the utility uses the local machine or registers an error that Active Directory isn't installed.

`-u` ***`UserName`*** Specifies the name of the user account to use to log onto a remote server. The default setting relies on the user account of the currently logged on user. The user name can take several forms, as shown in the following list.

`UserName` The account name such as GeorgeS.

`Domain\UserName` The domain name combined with the username, such as `MyDomain\GeorgeS`.

`User Principal Name (UPN)` The UPN version of the username that includes the fully qualified domain, such as `GeorgeS@MyDomain.MyCompany.com`.

-p {*Password* | *} Specifies the user password. The utility prompts you for a password when you provide the asterisk (*) in place of the actual password. Using this second option is actually better from a security perspective because the prompt dialog box will replace your password with asterisks. Using the command line option displays your password in plain text.

-q Places the utility in quiet mode. The utility doesn't output any information to the command line.

{-uc | -uco | -uci} Specifies that the input or output data is in Unicode format. The following list describes each of these Unicode options.

- **-uc** Specifies a Unicode format for both input and output when using a pipe (|).
- **-uco** Specifies a Unicode format for output when using a pipe (|) or file.
- **-uci** Specifies a Unicode format for input when using a pipe (|) or file.

COMPUTER

The computer object adds a new computer to Active Directory. This object uses the following syntax:

```
dsadd computer ComputerDN [-samid SAMName] [-desc Description]
   [-locLocation] [-memberof GroupDN ...] [{-s Server | -d Domain}]
   [-u UserName] [-p {Password | *}] [-q] [{-uc | -uco | -uci}]
```

The following list describes each of the command line arguments.

-samid *SAMName* Defines the SAM account name for the computer.

-loc *Location* Specifies the physical location of the computer.

-memberof *GroupDN* ... Defines the group membership of the computer you want to add. The input argument is the distinguished name of a group. You may specify more than one group. Separate the group distinguished names with spaces.

CONTACT

The contact object adds a new contact to Active directory. A contact is someone who exists outside of the company and doesn't have access to the network. This object uses the following syntax:

```
dsadd contact ContactDN [-fn FirstName] [-mi Initial] [-ln LastName]
   [-display DisplayName] [-desc Description] [-office Office]
   [-tel PhoneNumber] [-email Email] [-hometel HomePhoneNumber]
   [-pager PagerNumber] [-mobile CellPhoneNumber] [-fax FaxNumber]
   [-iptel IPPhoneNumber] [-title Title] [-dept Department]
   [-company Company] [{-s Server | -d Domain}] [-u UserName]
   [-p {Password | *}] [-q ] [{-uc | -uco | -uci }]
```

The following list describes each of the command line arguments.

-fn *FirstName* Specifies the contact's first name.

-mi *Initial* Specifies the contact's middle initial.

-ln *LastName* Specifies the contact's last name.

-display *DisplayName* Determines the contact's display name (the name you see when you access the contact entry).

-office *Office* Defines the physical office location of the contact.

-tel *PhoneNumber* Specifies the contact's landline business telephone number.

-email *Email* Specifies the contact's email address.

-hometel *HomePhoneNumber* Specifies the contact's home telephone number. Normally, this entry is for a landline telephone, but could also contain a secondary cellular telephone number.

-pager *PagerNumber* Specifies the contact's pager telephone number and any required special codes.

-mobile *CellPhoneNumber* Specifies the contact's cellular telephone number.

-fax *FaxNumber* Specifies the contact's facsimile telephone number.

-iptel *IPPhoneNumber* Specifies the contact's Internet Protocol (IP) telephone number.

-title *Title* Specifies the contact's business title.

-dept *Department* Defines the department in which the contact works.

-company *Company* Specifies the contact's company name.

GROUP

The group object adds a new group to Active Directory. This object uses the following syntax:

```
dsadd group GroupDN [-secgrp {yes | no}] [-scope {l | g | u}]
   [-samid SAMName] [-desc Description] [-memberof Group ...]
   [-members Member...] [{-s Server | -d Domain}] [-u UserName]
   [-p {Password | *}] [-q] [{-uc | -uco | -uci}]
```

The following list describes each of the command line arguments.

-secgrp {yes | no} Determines whether the utility adds the group as a security group (yes) or as a distribution group (no). The default setting adds the group as a security group.

-scope {l | g | u} Determines the group scope. The scopes include local (l), global (g), and universal (u). Mixed mode domains don't support the universal scope. The default setting is global.

-samid *SAMName* Specifies the SAM name for the group. You must supply a unique value. The utility creates a SAM name for the group from the distinguished name when you don't supply this value.

-memberof *Group* ... Defines the group membership of the group you want to add. The input argument is the distinguished name of a group. You may specify more than one group. Separate the group distinguished names with spaces.

-members *Member* ... Defines the membership of this group. All objects that have membership in this group have the same rights as this group.

OU (ORGANIZATIONAL UNIT)

The ou object adds a new organizational unit to Active Directory. This object uses the following syntax:

```
dsadd ou OrganizationalUnitDN [-desc Description]
   [{-s Server | -d Domain}] [-u UserName] [-p {Password | *}] [-q]
   [{-uc | -uco | -uci}]
```

This object doesn't support any specialized command line arguments.

USER

The user object adds a new user to Active Directory. A user is someone who has actual access to the network and generally works for the company. This object uses the following syntax:

```
dsadd user UserDN [-samid SAMName] [-upn UPN] [-fn FirstName]
   [-mi Initial] [-ln LastName] [-display DisplayName]
   [-empid EmployeeID]
   [-pwd {Password | *}] [-desc Description] [-memberof Group ...]
   [-office Office] [-tel PhoneNumber] [-email Email]
   [-hometel HomePhoneNumber] [-pager PagerNumber]
   [-mobile CellPhoneNumber] [-fax FaxNumber] [-iptel IPPhoneNumber]
   [-webpg WebPage] [-title Title] [-dept Department]
   [-company Company] [-mgr Manager] [-hmdir HomeDirectory]
   [-hmdrv DriveLetter:] [-profile ProfilePath] [-loscr ScriptPath]
   [-mustchpwd {yes | no}] [-canchpwd {yes | no}]
   [-reversiblepwd {yes | no}] [-pwdneverexpires {yes | no}]
   [-acctexpires NumberOfDays] [-disabled {yes | no}]
   [{-s Server | -d Domain}] [-u UserName] [-p {Password | *}]
   [-q] [{-uc | -uco | -uci}]
```

The following list describes each of the command line arguments.

`-samid` ***`SAMName`*** Defines the SAM account name for the user.

`-upn` ***`UPN`*** Defines the UPN version of the username that includes the fully qualified domain such as `GeorgeS@MyDomain.MyCompany.com`.

`-fn` ***`FirstName`*** Specifies the user's first name.

`-mi` ***`Initial`*** Specifies the user's middle initial.

`-ln` ***`LastName`*** Specifies the user's last name.

`-display` ***`DisplayName`*** Determines the user's display name (the name you see when you access the contact entry).

`-empid EmployeeID` Specifies the employee identifier. This is a text field, so you can use any form of identifier you want.

`-pwd {Password | *}` Defines the user's password. Using a default password and requiring the user to reset it on first access to the network is always the most secure choice for creating a password (see the `-mustchpwd` command line switch for details). If you supply an asterisk (*), the system will prompt you for the password.

`-memberof` ***`Group ...`*** Defines the group membership of the user you want to add. The input argument is the distinguished name of a group. You may specify more than one group. Separate the group distinguished names with spaces.

`-office` ***`Office`*** Defines the physical office location of the contact.

`-tel` ***`PhoneNumber`*** Specifies the user's landline business telephone number.

`-email` ***`Email`*** Specifies the user's email address.

TIP You can use the `$username$` token to your advantage when creating scripts with this utility. This token can replace the user's name for the `-email`, `-hmdir`, `-profile`, and `-webpg` arguments. For example, you can specify the user's home directory as `-hmdir\users\$username$\home`.

-hometel *HomePhoneNumber* Specifies the user's home telephone number. Normally, this entry is for a landline telephone, but could also contain a secondary cellular telephone number.

-pager *PagerNumber* Specifies the user's pager telephone number and any required special codes.

-mobile *CellPhoneNumber* Specifies the user's cellular telephone number.

-fax *FaxNumber* Specifies the user's facsimile telephone number.

-iptel *IPPhoneNumber* Specifies the user's Internet Protocol (IP) telephone number.

-webpg *WebPage* Specifies the user's Web page URL.

-title *Title* Specifies the user's business title.

-dept *Department* Defines the department in which the contact works.

-company *Company* Specifies the user's company name.

-mgr *ManagerDN* Defines the user's manager using a distinguished name.

-hmdir *HomeDirectory* Defines the user's home directory. The home directory is where the user stores data and begins any computing session. When you supply the home directory using a UNC path, the utility requires that you also supply a drive letter for mapping this path using the -hmdrv command line switch.

-hmdrv *DriveLetter:* Defines the user's home directory drive letter. The utility maps the drive letter to the user's directory path on the server.

-profile *ProfilePath* Defines the user's profile path.

-loscr *ScriptPath* Defines the user's logon script path.

-mustchpwd {yes | no} Forces the user to change their password during the next logon when set to yes. The default setting is no, which means the user doesn't need to change their password.

-canchpwd {yes | no} Specifies whether the user can change their password. The default setting of yes allows the user to change their password. You must set this argument to yes when you use the -mustchpwd command line switch. Always force the user to change the password for a new account or after resetting the account.

-reversiblepwd {yes | no} Determines whether the system stores the password using reversible encryption. The default setting of no prevents the user from using reversible encryption. Always set this argument to no to improve system security.

-pwdneverexpires {yes | no} Determines whether the user's password expires based on a system policy. The default setting of no forces the user to change the password regularly. Always set this argument to no to improve system security.

-acctexpires *NumberOfDays* Specifies the number of days after today when the user's account expires. A value of 0 sets the account to expire at the end of today. A positive value sets the account to expire in the future. A negative value sets the account to expire in the past. You can't set the account to never expire using this argument.

-disabled {yes | no} Specifies whether the user account is disabled. The default setting of yes disables the account for use. You must specifically enable the account by setting this argument to no.

QUOTA

The quota object creates a quota specification for Active Directory. The quota specification determines the maximum number of directory objects that a given security principal can hold. This object uses the following syntax:

```
dsadd quota -part PartitionDN [-rdn RelativeDistinguishedName]
   -acct Name -qlimit Value [-desc Description]
   [{-s Server | -d Domain}] [-u UserName] [-p {Password | *}] [-q]
   [{-uc | -uco | -uci}]
```

The following list describes each of the command line arguments.

`-part` ***`PartitionDN`*** Specifies the distinguished name of the directory partition that receives the quota. If you don't supply the distinguished name on the command line, the utility will attempt to obtain the distinguished name using the standard input (StdIn) device, which can include the keyboard, a redirected file, or as piped output from another command. Always end the standard input with the Ctrl+Z character.

`-rdn` ***`RelativeDistinguishedName`*** Specifies the relative distinguished name of the quota that you want to create. If you don't specify this command line switch, the utility sets it to `Domain_AccountName` using the domain and account name of the security principal specified by the `-acct` command line switch.

`-acct` ***`Name`*** Specifies the security principal (user, group, computer, or InetOrgPerson) to whom the quota specification applies. You may use a distinguished name as input for this command line argument. The command line argument also accepts the security principal information in the form `Domain\SAMAccountName`.

`-qlimit` ***`Value`*** Specifies the number of directory objects that the security principal can own within the specified partition. Provide a value of `-1` to specify an unlimited quota.

Listing Objects Using the DSGet Utility

The DSGet utility obtains information about existing Active Directory objects. The DSGet utility supports the following common objects.

- computer
- contact
- group
- ou (organizational unit)
- server
- user
- subnet
- site
- quota
- partition

The objects all use the same basic command line. You must supply a distinguished name for the object you want to access, followed by the items you want to display, and ending with any security-related information to access a remote machine. See the "Creating New Objects Using the DSAdd Utility" section of the chapter for a description of the distinguished name and security command line switches. This utility uses the following syntax for each of the supported objects:

```
dsget computerComputerDN... [-dn] [-samid] [-sid] [-desc] [-loc]
   [-disabled] [{-s Server | -d Domain}] [-u UserName]
   [-p {Password | *}] [-c] [-q] [-l] [{-uc  | -uco  | -uci }]
   [-part PartitionDN [-qlimit] [-qused]]
dsget computerComputerDN [-memberof [-expand]]
   [{-s Server | -d Domain}] [-u UserName] [-p {Password | *}] [-c]
   [-q] [-l] [{-uc | -uco | -uci }]
dsget contactContactDN... [-dn] [-fn] [-mi] [-ln] [-display]
   [-desc] [-office] [-tel] [-email] [-hometel] [-pager] [-mobile]
   [-fax] [-iptel] [-title] [-dept] [-company]
   [{-s Server | -d Domain}] [-u UserName] [-p  {Password | *}] [-c]
   [-q] [-l] [{-uc  | -uco  | -uci }]
dsget groupGroupDN... [-dn] [-samid] [-sid] [-desc] [-secgrp]
   [-scope] [{-s Server | -d Domain}] [-u UserName]
   [-p {Password | *}] [-c] [-q] [-l] [{-uc  | -uco  | -uci }]
   [-part PartitionDN [-qlimit] [-qused]]
dsget groupGroupDN [{-memberof | -members }] [-expand]
   [{-s Server | -d Domain}] [-u UserName] [-p {Password | *}] [-c]
   [-q] [-l] [{-uc | -uco | -uci}]
dsget ouOrganizationalUnitDN... [-dn] [-desc]
   [{-s Server | -d Domain}] [-u UserName] [-p {Password | *}] [-c]
   [-q] [-l] [{-uc  | -uco  | -uci}]
dsget serverServerDN... [-dn] [-desc] [-dnsname] [-site]
   [-isgc] [{-s Server | -d Domain}] [-u UserName] [-p {Password | *}]
   [-c] [-q] [-l] [{-uc  | -uco  | -uci }]
dsget serverServerDN [{-s Server | -d Domain}] [-u UserName]
   [-p {Password | *}] [-c] [-q] [-l] [{-uc | -uco | -uci}]
   [-topobjowner Display]
dsget serverServerDN [{-s Server | -d Domain}] [-u UserName]
   [-p {Password | *}] [-c] [-q] [-l] [{-uc | -uco | -uci}]
   [-part PartitionDN]
dsget userUserDN... [-dn] [-samid] [-sid] [-upn] [-fn] [-mi] [-ln]
   [-display] [-empid] [-desc] [-office] [-tel] [-email]
   [-hometel] [-pager] [-mobile] [-fax] [-iptel] [-webpg] [-title]
   [-dept] [-company] [-mgr] [-hmdir] [-hmdrv] [-profile] [-loscr]
   [-mustchpwd] [-canchpwd] [-pwdneverexpires] [-disabled]
   [-acctexpires] [-reversiblepwd] [{-uc  | -uco  | -uci}]
   [-part PartitionDN [-qlimit] [-qused]]
dsget subnetSubnetDN... [-dn] [-desc] [-loc] [-site]
   [{-s Server | -d Domain}] [-u UserName] [-p {Password | *}] [-c]
   [-q] [-l] [{-uc | -uco  | -uci}]
dsget site SiteCN... [-dn] [-desc] [-autotopology] [-cachegroups]
   [-prefGCsite] [{-s Server | -d Domain}] [-u UserName]
   [-p {Password | *}] [-c] [-q] [-l] [{-uc  | -uco  | -uci}]
```

```
dsget quotaObjectDN... [-dn] [-acct] [-qlimit]
   [{-s Server | -d Domain}] [-u UserName] [-p {Password | *}] [-c]
   [-q] [-l] [{-uc | -uco | -uci}]
dsget partitionObjectDN... [-dn] [-qdefault] [-qtmbstnwt]
   [-topobjowner Display] [{-s Server | -d Domain}] [-u UserName]
   [-p {Password | *}] [-c] [-q] [-l] [{-uc | -uco | -uci}]
```

The following list describes each of the display arguments and unique command line switches in alphabetical order.

-acct Displays the distinguished names of accounts that have quotas assigned.

-acctexpires Displays the object's account expires status.

-autotopology Displays the object's Internet topology generation status. A value of yes means that the system automatically generates the topology for specified sites.

-c Reports any errors encountered when displaying the object, but continues to the next object in the argument list when you specify number objects. The default action is to stop displaying data when the utility encounters the first error.

-cachegroups Displays the object's universal group membership caching status. A value of yes means that logons don't check the global catalog.

-canchpwd Displays the object's that can change password status. A value of yes means the user can change the password.

-company Displays the object's company.

-dept Displays the object's department.

-desc Displays the object's description.

-disabled Displays the object's account disabled status. When the utility returns yes, the object's account is disabled.

-display Displays the object's display name.

-dn Displays the object's distinguished name.

-dnsname Displays the object's DNS hostname.

-email Displays the object's email address.

-empid Displays the object's employee identifier.

-expand Displays the object's complete group membership by recursively expanding each group. The expansion continues until the utility reaches the end of the group listing no matter how many levels the groups are nested.

-fax Displays the object's facsimile telephone number.

-fn Displays the object's first name.

-hmdir Displays the object's home directory. The home directory can include either a standard or a UNC path.

-hmdrv Displays the mapped drive associated with the object's home directory.

-hometel Displays the object's home telephone number.

-iptel Displays the object's IP telephone number.

-isgc Displays the object's global catalog status—yes when it's a global catalog and no when it isn't.

-l Displays the entries in a list format. The default setting displays the entries in a table format.

-ln Displays the object's last name.

-loc Displays the object's physical location.

-loscr Displays the object's logon script path.

-memberof Displays the object's group association. You can't use this argument when specifying multiple objects as input.

-members Displays the object's list of members.

-mgr Displays the object's manager's distinguished name.

-mi Displays the object's middle initial.

-mobile Displays the object's cellular telephone number.

-mustchpwd Displays the object's must change password status. A value of yes means the user must change the password during the next logon.

-office Displays the object's physical office location.

-pager Displays the object's pager number.

-part *PartitionDN* Connects to the specified directory partition. You must use a distinguished name to specify the directory partition.

-prefGCsite Displays the name of the preferred global catalog site used to refresh universal group membership caching for the object's domain controller.

-profile Displays the object's profile path.

-pwdneverexpires Displays the object's password never expires status. A value of yes means the password never expires.

-qdefault Displays the default quota that applies to any security principal creating an object in the directory partition. An unlimited quota displays as "-1".

-qlimit Displays any effective quota associated with the object within the specified object.

-qtmbstnwt Displays the percentage to use when reducing the tombstone object count during a quota usage calculation.

-qused Displays the amount of quota that the object has used within the specified directory partition.

-reversiblepwd Displays the object's reversible password status. A value of yes means that user can use a password with reversible encryption.

-samid Displays the object's SAM account name.

-scope Displays the object's group scope—local (l), global (g), or universal (u).

-secgrp Displays the object's security group status—yes for a security group and no for a distribution group.

-sid Displays the object's SID.

-tel Displays the object's business telephone number.

-title Displays the object's title.

-topobjowner ***[Display]*** Displays a sorted of the number objects that each security principal (users, computers, security groups, and InetOrgPersons) owns. The utility sorts the list with the largest owner first. You can specify the number of security principals to display as the argument for this command line switch. Displays all of the object owners by supplying a value of 0. The default setting displays 10 security principals.

-upn Displays the object's UPN.

Editing Existing Objects Using the DSMod Utility

The DSMod utility modifies existing objects within Active Directory. Each object requires different input to modify the object. The DSMod utility supports the following common objects.

- computer
- contact
- group
- ou (organizational unit)
- user
- quota

All of these objects require some basic input to obtain the data. For example, you can expect to provide a username. The following list provides the common inputs for each of the objects. See the "Creating New Objects Using the DSAdd Utility" section of the chapter for a description of the distinguished name and security command line switches. The arguments for modifying an object are essentially the same as the arguments for adding an object with the following exceptions. (Refer to the "Creating New Objects Using the DSAdd Utility" subsections for details on individual objects.)

-c Reports any errors encountered when modifying the object, but continues to the next object in the argument list when you specify number objects. The default action is to stop displaying data when the utility encounters the first error.

-disabled {Yes | No} Changes the object's account disabled status. Setting the object's disabled status to Yes means that the object can't log onto the network.

Moving Existing Objects Using the DSMove Utility

The DSMove utility moves or renames a single object. When moving an object, you can change the location to anywhere in the current domain. This utility uses the following syntax:

```
dsmove ObjectDN [-newname NewName] [-newparent ParentDN]
   [{-s Server | -d Domain}] [-u UserName] [-p {Password | *}] [-q ]
   [{-uc | -uco | -uci}]
```

See the "Creating New Objects Using the DSAdd Utility" section of the chapter for a description of the distinguished name and security command line switches. The following list describes each of the command line arguments.

-newname ***NewRDN*** Renames the objects using the specified relative distinguished name.

-newparent ***ParentDN*** Specifies the new parent of the object. Giving the object a new parent moves it within the object hierarchy. You must supply a distinguished name for the new parent.

Deleting Objects Using the DSRm Utility

The DSRm utility removes the specified object from Active Directory. The action is a one-way process; you can't undo it. This utility uses the following syntax:

```
dsrm ObjectDN... [-subtree  [-exclude ]] [-noprompt ]
   [{-s Server | -d Domain}] [-u UserName] [-p {Password | *}] [-c ]
   [-q ] [{-uc | -uco | -uci}]
```

See the "Creating New Objects Using the DSAdd Utility" section of the chapter for a description of the distinguished name and security command line switches. The following list describes each of the command line arguments.

-subtree [-exclude] Specifies that the utility should delete both the object and all objects within the object's subtree. Adding the `-exclude` command line switch excludes the object defined by the ObjectDN argument from deletion (essentially deleting the subtree). The default setting deletes only the object specified by the `ObjectDN` argument.

-noprompt Forces the utility to perform all deletions without prompting you. Normally, the utility prompts you to approve each deletion as a safety precaution.

Working with Users, Groups, and Computers

It's time to start working with all of the utilities you've seen so far in the chapter to create short scripts that help you get things done quickly at the command line. In many cases, you could type these scripts at the command prompt, but trying to remember the precise syntax could prove difficult. It's better to place the commands in a batch file or create an interactive script to use them. The following sections describe specific topics, but you can use these examples to create a wealth of other scripts.

Real World Scenario

KEEPING SCRIPTS SIMPLE

Many people create batch files and scripts that perform so many tasks that the code becomes too complicated to understand. The problem is feature creep. If one feature sounds good, two features must be better, and three features beyond compare. Unfortunately, despite the bad example set by many shrink-wrap application vendors, more features aren't always better. In fact, a simple single function script often works better than a script that can perform multiple tasks. Single function scripts and batch files area easier to debug and understand.

Of course, this brings up the question of remembering so many command lines that you don't really gain any benefit from all of those single function script or batch files. That's where menu systems come in handy. The "Using the *Choice* Command" section of Chapter 7 describes a very simple technique for accessing all of your batch or script files from a menu. All you need to do is create the script or batch file, and then call it from your menu. You now have all of the advantages of a multi-feature batch or script file without any of the pain.

Obtaining a User's Logon Name

Sometimes you'll receive a help desk ticket where the user expects that you'll know their logon name, despite the fact that you have several thousand users to track. In many cases, without the logon name, you can't do much for the user. Of course, you could always track down the user and ask them for the information, but there's an easier way to obtain the information for Active Directory users. The following script displays the logon name for a user based on the last name that you pass.

```
DSQUERY USER -name %1  DSGET USER -samid -display
```

In this case, the input you provide is the user's last name. The DSQuery User object sends the user information to the DSGet User object using a pipe (|). The DSGet utility, in turn, looks up the user's SAM identifier and provides it as output on the command line. (When more than one user has the same last name, you'll see a list of all of the associated logon names, but at least the list is shorter than starting from scratch.)

Obtaining a User's Full Name

Sometimes a user will provide you with their email address and a logon name and that's it. What you really want is the user's full name so that you can understand their needs better by looking up their association with the company. When this problem occurs, you can still look up the user information using Active Directory. Simply use the script shown here.

```
DSQUERY USER -samid %1  DSGET USER -samid -display
```

In this case, the input you provide is the user's logon name. The DSQuery User object sends the user information, based on a SAM identifier search, to the DSGet User object using a pipe (|). The DSGet utility outputs the user's full name. Note that there's normally more than one way to accomplish a task. If you're using an older version of Windows or a system that doesn't have Active Directory installed, you can achieve the same results using this script.

```
NET USER %1  FIND /I " name "
```

In this case, you pass the user's logon name to the Net utility. This utility outputs all of the information about the user to the Find utility using a pipe (|). The Find utility, in turn, locates just the name entries.

Discovering User Group Membership

Many support problems revolve around security. One of the most common security problems is a lack of group membership. The user attempts to perform a task that is under the purview of a specific group and the user doesn't belong to that particular group. Unfortunately, all that the user has told you is that the task is impossible to perform and the boss really needs the task completed today. Rather than play 20 questions trying to discover the user's group membership, you can use this simple script to obtain the information from Active Directory.

```
DSQUERY USER -samid %1  DSGET USER -memberof -expand
```

In this case, you pass the user's logon name to the DSQuery User object. The DSGet utility receives the output from DSQuery through a pipe (|). The DSGet User object then displays the group membership for the user and expands the information so you get all of the details.

Resetting a User's Password

One of the tasks that administrators love least, yet perform most often, is resetting a user's password. Those users who don't keep their password recorded on a sticky note next to their monitor are prone to forgetting them. After a long weekend or a holiday, the administrator's office suddenly fills with users who have no clue as to what their password is. You could use a graphical utility to reset those passwords one at a time (wasting an entire morning as a result) or you can use this simple script to reset the password based on the user's logon name.

```
DSQUERY USER -samid %1  DSMOD USER -pwd "newpassword"
```

In this case, the DSQuery User object obtains the user's information based on the logon name and passes it to the DSMod utility through a pipe (|). The DSMod User object uses the `-pwd` command line switch to change the user's password to `newpassword`. You could extend this script by passing a second argument to the batch file, but it really isn't necessary because the reader will need to change the password anyway.

NOTE Make sure you turn echo off when working with scripts that will reveal password information, even when this information is a default setting as shown here. You don't want someone peering over your shoulder to see a password that should remain private. As an alternative, you can always replace the password string with an asterisk (*). The utility will prompt you to provide a password at the appropriate time. Anything you type will appear as a series of asterisks on screen.

Displaying a List of Hostnames

Anyone working on a large network will attest to the difficulty of remembering all of the hostnames. Even if you work on the network every day, you'll run into a server that you don't work with very often and find yourself scratching your head to remember the hostname. Rather than look up the name using a graphical utility, where you could spend more than a few minutes trying to find the hostname you need, you can obtain a quick list from Active Directory using the following script.

```
FOR /F "tokens=2 delims==," %%H IN ('DSQUERY Server') DO @ECHO.%%H
```

The focus of this script is the `DSQuery Server` command, which outputs a list of all of the domain controllers. The rest of the script simply processes the output of the `DSQuery Server` command so that you see the hostnames. Notice how the script uses an at (@) sign in front of the `Echo` command so that all you see is the hostnames. It's important to include the @ sign as needed to keep the output of your scripts readable.

Getting Started with Command Line Tasks

This chapter has provided you with an overview of the tasks you can perform on Active Directory, which is the centralized storage scheme for modern Windows networks. Even if you use the Utilities described in the chapter at the command prompt, you'll find that you save considerable time performing tasks when compared to using the graphical utilities. Active Directory relies heavily on objects to store data. For example, you can create a user object that contains specific information about the users on your network. The object remains the same for each user, but each object instance will contain unique information about a particular user.

Now it's your turn to work with Active Directory. Because Active Directory is such a large and complex database, you don't want to experiment with a production system—one that you rely on to get your work done. The best thing you can do is set up a test server that you can use to work out details about your Active Directory setup and practice using the command line utilities described in this chapter. Use the test server to test your batch files and scripts as well. The thing to remember is that you won't lose your job if the test server goes down due to a poorly conceived Active Directory change. Causing the production server to lose data or even freeze is another story.

Chapter 10 describes a new scripting topic. It's one thing to create a batch file, script, or special application, but it's quite another to run it immediately. For example, you don't want to perform a maintenance action on Active Directory during peak working hours. The slowdown in network performance would be something that everyone will remember. Of course, you don't want to stay behind at work while everyone goes home. The solution is to schedule the task using Task Scheduler or the AT utility so it runs automatically at a convenient time, even if you aren't available. You can buy an expensive third party utility to perform the task, but in many cases, Task Scheduler, a utility that comes with Windows, will do the job quite well.

Chapter 10

Using Task Scheduler Effectively

- Starting and Stopping the Task Scheduler Service
- Combining the AT Utility with Batch Files
- Creating Script-Based Scheduler Activities

Using batch files or scripts represents one level of automation. You can issue a single command and expect a number of things to take place. In addition, you don't have to remember all of those arcane command line switches. However, you still have to be present at your desk to execute the command. Executing the batch file or script manually isn't such a big deal when you aren't doing anything that will interrupt anyone else, but staying the weekend so you can execute a command is undesirable to say the least. That's where the Task Scheduler comes into play. You can use the Task Scheduler to execute reliable batch files or scripts automatically. In essence, you're asking your computer to do the work for you—imagine that, the computer working for you for once.

Real World Scenario

THE TASK SCHEDULER NIGHTMARE

Some people just don't get it when it comes to Task Scheduler. A customer once had a "virus" on their machine. The only problem is that the virus didn't show up with Task List, none of the virus checkers could find it, and it didn't have any of the usual virus symptoms. The virus simply showed up at what appeared at first random intervals. After many hours of searching, I discovered that the user had added a buggy script to Task Scheduler. The buggy script was the virus of my nightmares. My client ended up paying for quite a few hours worth of consulting time to have me remove the buggy script from Task Scheduler. My actual repair time, once I located the problem, was less than 5 minutes.

You can easily misuse Task Scheduler. It's a tool like any other tool—valuable in the hands of someone who knows how to use it, dangerous for everyone else. Never use Task Scheduler to run batch files, scripts, or applications that aren't reliable. If you think there's even a small chance that the Task Scheduler entry will fail to work as anticipated, don't create it because locating the problem can require a substantial investment in time and effort. In addition, it's essential to test every Task Scheduler entry the first time while you're at the office. You don't want an errant entry to ruin the chances of a perfectly reliable batch file, script, or application running as anticipated.

This chapter describes how the Task Scheduler performs its job, shows how you can schedule tasks from the command line, and explores some productivity techniques you can use with this form of optimization. You'll also discover a few problems with using the Task Scheduler and gain an understanding of the kinds of tasks that work best with the Task Scheduler. Finally, you'll see some new utilities that make the Task Scheduler easy to use from the command line. This chapter doesn't explore the graphical utilities you can use to work with Task Scheduler.

Starting and Stopping the Task Scheduler Service

The Task Scheduler consists of multiple elements. The Task Scheduler application is actually a Windows service that you can find in the Services console in the Administrative Tools folder of the Control Panel, as shown in Figure 10.1. Because Task Scheduler is a service, it's always present in the background so it can run applications automatically for you. As a safety precaution, it's a good idea to set the service to manual and manually start it as needed. Of course, if you're running tasks every day, the automatic start option makes more sense. Notice also that the Task Scheduler logs on using the Local System account. Normally, this account provides more than sufficient rights for local activities. However, when you automatically perform tasks on remote machines, you might need to change the account to handle the increased security requirements. Always make sure you have the Task Scheduler service running when you need to execute applications automatically.

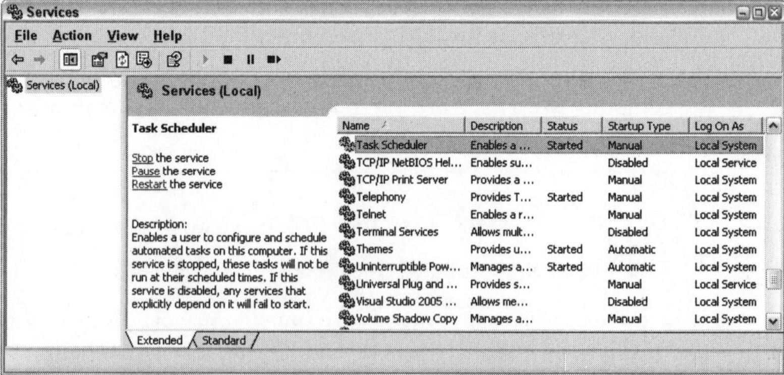

FIGURE 10.1
The Task Scheduler is a service that runs in the background as you use Windows.

The second part of Task Scheduler is a graphical utility called Scheduled Tasks that you'll find in the Start ➤ Programs ➤ Accessories ➤ Systems Tools folder. This utility displays all of the tasks you've scheduled. You can also use it to create new tasks, either directly or by using the supplied wizard. This book doesn't discuss the graphical interface, but you should know that it's available for quick tasks that you need to perform in real time.

The user interface for Task Scheduler in Vista looks considerably different from the one provided in earlier versions of Windows. However, the operation of Task Scheduler remains the same and Vista doesn't appear to provide any new features that you need to consider. When working with Task Scheduler in Vista, you need to observe the same security precautions that you do when performing the task manually. Since Vista tightens security considerably, you'll very likely have to modify the security settings to run your current Task Scheduler jobs.

WARNING Standard Vista tasks aren't visible to previous versions of Windows. To create a scheduled task in Vista that's visible to previous versions of Windows, you must use the SchTasks utility with the /V1 command line switch (see the "Managing Tasks with the SchTasks Utility" section of the chapter for details). You can also modify the Configure For field found on the General tab of any standard task you create to support other Windows versions. The Configure For field only contains Vista as an option when you create a basic task.

The third part of the Task Scheduler is a number of related utilities that are discussed in the sections that follow. These utilities make it considerably easier to schedule multiple tasks or to schedule tasks for multiple users. You can use these utilities from a remote location to ensure user machines perform required maintenance tasks automatically at a time that's convenient for the user. Because operation is automatic, you don't have to worry about users performing the task incorrectly, inconsistently, or not at all.

TIP Scripts can have payoffs other than increased personal productivity. For example, Microsoft regularly offers incentives for submitting scripts to the Community-Submitted Scripts Center at `http://www.microsoft.com/technet/scriptcenter/csc/default.mspx`. At the time of this writing, you can obtain a free e-learning course.

Managing Tasks with the SchTasks Utility

The Schedule Tasks (SchTasks) utility helps you schedule tasks at the command line. The basic command line requires that you provide a parameter (an action or command) and any arguments that the parameter requires. The list of recognized parameters includes `/Create`, `/Delete`, `/Query`, `/Change`, `/Run`, and `/End`. The following sections describe each of these parameters.

/CREATE

The `/Create` parameter helps you create new tasks. Never use this parameter to change an existing task; use the `/Change` parameter instead. This parameter uses the following syntax:

```
SCHTASKS /Create [/S system [/U username [/P password]]] [/RU username
   [/RP password]] /SC schedule [/MO modifier] [/D day] [/I idletime]
   /TN taskname /TR taskrun [/ST starttime] [/M months] [/SD startdate]
   [/ED enddate]
```

The Vista form of the SchTasks `/Create` parameter adds a few features to those found in the previous versions of Windows.

```
SCHTASKS /Create [/S system [/U username [/P password]]] [/RU username
   [/RP password]] /SC schedule [/MO modifier] [/D day] [/I idletime]
   /TN taskname /TR taskrun [/ST starttime] [/M months] [/SD startdate]
   [/ED enddate] [/RI interval] [ {/ET endtime | /DU duration} [/K]
   [/XML xmlfile] /V1]] [/IT | /NP] [/Z] [/F]
```

The following list describes each of the standard command line arguments.

/S system Specifies the remote system that you want to check. In most cases, you'll also need to supply the `/U` and the `/P` command line switches when using this switch.

/U [domain\]user Specifies the username on the remote system. This name may not match the username on the local system. You'll need to supply a domain name when working with a domain controller.

/P [*password*] Specifies the password for the given user. You can provide the command line switch without specifying the password on the command line in cleartext. The system will prompt you for the password. Using this feature can help you maintain the security of passwords used on your system.

/RU *username* Specifies the user account or user context that you want to use to run the task. Use `""`, `"NT AUTHORITY\SYSTEM"`, or `"SYSTEM"` to use the system account to run the task.

/RP *password* Specifies the password of the user account or user context you want to use to run the task. Use an asterisk (*) or a blank (nothing after the command line switch) in place of the password when you want the system to prompt you for the password. This command line switch has no effect when you use the system account to run the task.

/SC *schedule* Defines the frequency at which the system runs the task. The valid frequencies include `MINUTE`, `HOURLY`, `DAILY`, `WEEKLY`, `MONTHLY`, `ONCE`, `ONSTART`, `ONLOGON`, and `ONIDLE`.

/MO *modifier* Refines the schedule type to provide finer control over the schedule frequency. The modifier you use depends on the scheduling frequency. The following list describes each of the modifiers.

MINUTE Every 1–1,439 minutes

HOURLY Every 1–23 hours

DAILY Every 1–365 days

WEEKLY Every 1–52 weeks

ONCE No modifiers

ONSTART No modifiers

ONLOGON No modifiers

ONIDLE No modifiers

MONTHLY Every 1 to 12 months, or FIRST, SECOND, THIRD, FOURTH, LAST, or LASTDAY

/D *days* Specifies the day of the week to run the task. Acceptable values include MON, TUE, WED, THU, FRI, SAT, and SUN. When working with a monthly schedule, you can specify date numbers between 1 and 31.

/M *months* Specifies the month of the year to run a task. The default setting is the current month. Acceptable values include JAN, FEB, MAR, APR, MAY, JUN, JUL, AUG, SEP, OCT, NOV, and DEC.

/I *idletime* Specifies the amount of time to wait before running a scheduled `ONIDLE` task. Idle time is when no other application on the system is running (the system idle process is using all of the computer resources). The acceptable range of values is 1 to 999 minutes.

/TN *taskname* Specifies the name of the task. The utility requires a unique name for the purpose of identification.

/TR *taskrun* Specifies the full path and filename of the task that you want to run. Never assume that the task will run based on a `PATH` environment variable because you can't guarantee the user will have the environment variable defined. You can also specify any command line arguments that the task requires. Enclose tasks with spaces in quotes.

/ST *starttime* Specifies the time that you want the task to run. The time format is HH:MM:SS (24-hour time). Don't use a 12-hour time format that includes AM and PM. The default setting is the current time.

/SD *startdate* Specifies the first date on which to run the task. The date format is mm/dd/yyyy. Always include a 4-digit year. The default setting is the current day.

/ED *enddate* Specifies the last date that you want to run the task. The date format is mm/dd/yyyy. Always include a 4-digit year. The default is not to use an end time, so the task continues to run indefinitely.

The following list describes each of the Vista-specific command line arguments.

/RI *interval* Specifies the repetition interval of the task in minutes. You can't use this feature with schedule types of `MINUTE`, `HOURLY`, `ONSTART`, `ONLOGON`, `ONIDLE`, and `ONEVENT`. The valid range for this argument is 1 to 599,940 minutes. If you specify either the `/ET` or `/DE` command line arguments, then the default interval is 10 minutes.

/ET *endtime* Specifies the end time of the task. The time format is HH:MM:SS (24-hour time). Don't use a 12-hour time format that includes AM and PM. You can't use this feature with schedule types of `ONSTART`, `ONLOGON`, `ONIDLE`, and `ONEVENT`. It also isn't possible to use this feature with the `/DU` option.

/DU *duration* Specifies the duration of the task. The time format is HH:MM (a time interval in hours and minutes, not a specific time). You can't use this feature with schedule types of `ONSTART`, `ONLOGON`, `ONIDLE`, and `ONEVENT`. It also isn't possible to use this feature with the `/ET` option. When you specify the `/RI` argument with a `/V1` task, the default duration is 1 hour.

/K Automatically terminates the task at the end time or after the duration interval expires. You can't use this feature with schedule types of `ONSTART`, `ONLOGON`, `ONIDLE`, and `ONEVENT`. This argument is only applicable when you specify either the `/ET` or `/DU` command line arguments.

/XML *xmlfile* Creates a task based on the task XML in the specified file. Combine this command line switch with the `/RU` and `/RP` command line switches to specify a complete entry (including security). The task XML can also contain the principal, which means that you only supply the `/RU` command line switch.

/V1 Creates a task that's compatible with pre-Vista versions of Windows. If you don't use this command line switch on a Vista system, then other versions of Windows can't see the task you create. You can't use this command line switch with `/XML`.

/IT Forces the task to run interactively only. The job runs when the user is logged on, but Vista ignores it when the user is logged out.

/NP Disables password storage. The job runs noninteractively using the credentials of the specified user. The job can only access local resources. Using this command line switch improves security by not storing the password and by reducing task access to external resources.

/Z Marks the task for deletion after its final run (as specified in the schedule you provide). The job isn't actually deleted—Vista only marks it for deletion.

/F Forces task creation even if a task by that name already exists on the system. Vista doesn't display any warning messages, it simply overwrites the existing job.

/DELETE

The `/Delete` parameter deletes tasks that you no longer want to run. This parameter uses the following syntax:

```
SCHTASKS /Delete [/S system [/U username [/P password]]] /TN taskname [/F]
```

The following list describes each of the command line arguments.

/S *system* Specifies the remote system that you want to check. In most cases, you'll also need to supply the /U and the /P command line switches when using this switch.

/U [*domain*\\]*user* Specifies the username on the remote system. This name may not match the username on the local system. You'll need to supply a domain name when working with a domain controller.

/P [*password*] Specifies the password for the given user. You can provide the command line switch without specifying the password on the command line in cleartext. The system will prompt you for the password. Using this feature can help you maintain the security of passwords used on your system.

/TN *taskname* Specifies the name of the task you want to delete. You can delete all tasks using the asterisk (*) wildcard.

/F Forces the utility to delete the task and suppress any warnings when the task is currently running. Use this command line switch only when the task is frozen or unresponsive. Using this command line switch can result in data loss or other unexpected system behavior.

/QUERY

The /Query parameter requests information about any tasks you've created. This parameter uses the following syntax:

```
SCHTASKS /Query [/S system [/U username [/P password]]]
   [/FO format | /XML] [/NH] [/V] [/?] [/TN taskname]
```

The following list describes each of the command line arguments.

/S *system* Specifies the remote system that you want to check. In most cases, you'll also need to supply the /U and the /P command line switches when using this switch.

/U [*domain*\\]*user* Specifies the username on the remote system. This name may not match the username on the local system. You'll need to supply a domain name when working with a domain controller.

/P [*password*] Specifies the password for the given user. You can provide the command line switch without specifying the password on the command line in cleartext. The system will prompt you for the password. Using this feature can help you maintain the security of passwords used on your system.

/FO {TABLE | LIST | CSV} Defines the output provided by the utility. The table format is normally the easiest to view on screen. The table columns define the values for output, while each row contains one driver entry. The CSV output provides the best method for preparing the data for entry in a database. Use redirection (see the "Employing Data Redirection" section of Chapter 2 for details) to output the CSV data to a file and then import it to your database. The list format provides one data element per line. Each group of data elements defines one driver. The utility separates each driver by one blank line. Some people find the list format more readable when working in verbose mode since the table format requires multiple lines for each entry (the lines wrap).

VISTA

/XML Displays the output in XML format. This command line switch is useful when you want to learn more about creating jobs using XML files.

/NH Forces the utility to display the data without a column header. You can only use this command line switch with the table and CSV formats. Omitting the header makes it easier to incorporate the data in a report or import it into a database.

/V Displays detailed data about each of the defined tasks. The standard display shows only TaskName, Next Run Time, and Status. In addition to this basic information, the verbose display shows HostName, Last Run Time, Last Result, Creator, Schedule, Task To Run, Start In, Comment, Scheduled Task State, Scheduled Type, Start Time, Start Date, End Date, Days, Months, Run As User, Delete Task If Not Rescheduled, Stop Task If Runs X Hours and X Mins, Repeat: Every, Repeat: Until: Time, Repeat: Until: Duration, Repeat: Stop If Still Running, Idle Time, and Power Management.

/TN *taskname* Specifies the name of the task you want to query. Vista displays all of the tasks when you don't supply this parameter.

/CHANGE

The /Change parameter changes an existing task. You can't use this parameter to create a new task. However, this parameter does work well to indicate a change in task location. This parameter uses the following syntax:

```
SCHTASKS /Change [/S system [/U username [/P password]]] {[/RU
   runasuser] [/RP runaspassword] [/TR taskrun]} /TN taskname
```

The Vista form of the SchTasks /Change parameter adds a few features to those found in the previous versions of Windows.

```
SCHTASKS /Change [/S system [/U username [/P [password]]]] [/RU
   runasuser] [/RP runaspassword] [/TR taskrun] /TN taskname [/ST
   starttime] [/RI interval] [ {/ET endtime | /DU duration} [/K] ]
   [/SD startdate] [/ED enddate] [/ENABLE | /DISABLE] [/IT] [/Z] }
```

The following list describes each of the command line arguments.

/S *system* Specifies the remote system that you want to check. In most cases, you'll also need to supply the /U and the /P command line switches when using this switch.

/U [*domain*\\]*user* Specifies the username on the remote system. This name may not match the username on the local system. You'll need to supply a domain name when working with a domain controller.

/P [*password*] Specifies the password for the given user. You can provide the command line switch without specifying the password on the command line in clear text. The system will prompt you for the password. Using this feature can help you maintain the security of passwords used on your system.

/RU *username* Specifies the user account or user context that you want to use to run the task. Use "", "NT AUTHORITY\SYSTEM", or "SYSTEM" to use the system account to run the task.

/RP *password* Specifies the password of the user account or user context you want to use to run the task. Use an asterisk (*) or a blank (nothing after the command line switch) in place of the password when you want the system to prompt you for the password. This command line switch has no effect when you use the system account to run the task.

/TR *taskrun* Specifies the full path and filename of the new task that you want to run. The new task need not be a new execution; it may simply be a new version or a version of the same executable in a different location. Never assume that the task will run based on a PATH environment variable because you can't guarantee the user will have the environment variable defined. You can also specify any command line arguments that the task requires. Enclose tasks with spaces in quotes.

/TN *taskname* Specifies the name of the task to change.

VISTA

The following list describes each of the Vista-specific command line arguments.

/ST *starttime* Specifies the time that you want the task to run. The time format is HH:MM:SS (24-hour time). Don't use a 12-hour time format that includes AM and PM. The default setting is the current time.

/RI *interval* Specifies the repetition interval of the task in minutes. You can't use this feature with schedule types of MINUTE, HOURLY, ONSTART, ONLOGON, ONIDLE, and ONEVENT. The valid range for this argument is 1 to 599,940 minutes. If you specify either the /ET or /DE command line arguments, then the default interval is 10 minutes.

/ET *endtime* Specifies the end time of the task. The time format is HH:MM:SS (24-hour time). Don't use a 12-hour time format that includes AM and PM. You can't use this feature with schedule types of ONSTART, ONLOGON, ONIDLE, and ONEVENT. It also isn't possible to use this feature with the /DU option.

/DU *duration* Specifies the duration of the task. The time format is HH:MM (a time interval in hours and minutes, not a specific time). You can't use this feature with schedule types of ONSTART, ONLOGON, ONIDLE, and ONEVENT. It also isn't possible to use this feature with the /ET option. When you specify the /RI argument with a /V1 task, the default duration is 1 hour.

/K Automatically terminates the task at the end time or after the duration interval expires. You can't use this feature with schedule types of ONSTART, ONLOGON, ONIDLE, and ONEVENT. This argument is only applicable when you specify either the /ET or /DU command line arguments.

/SD *startdate* Specifies the first date on which to run the task. The date format is mm/dd/yyyy. Always include a 4-digit year. The default setting is the current day.

/ED *enddate* Specifies the last date that you want to run the task. The date format is mm/dd/yyyy. Always include a 4-digit year. The default is not to use an end time, so the task continues to run indefinitely.

/ENABLE Enables the scheduled task (so it can run).

/DISABLE Disables the schedule task (it can't run, even when scheduled).

/IT Forces the task to run interactively only. The job runs when the user is logged on, but Vista ignores it when the user is logged out.

/Z Marks the task for deletion after its final run (as specified in the schedule you provide). The job isn't actually deleted—Vista only marks it for deletion.

/RUN

The /Run parameter runs an existing task, even if the task isn't scheduled to run. Running a task using this method doesn't change the task schedule; the task will run using the schedule you set for it. You can use this feature to test your tasks to ensure they work as anticipated. Check the \Windows\SchedLgU.TXT file for the results of any task you run, especially on remote machines. This parameter uses the following syntax:

```
SCHTASKS /Run [/S system [/U username [/P password]]] /TN taskname
```

The following list describes each of the command line arguments.

/S *system* Specifies the remote system that you want to check. In most cases, you'll also need to supply the /U and the /P command line switches when using this switch.

/U [*domain*\]*user* Specifies the username on the remote system. This name may not match the username on the local system. You'll need to supply a domain name when working with a domain controller.

/P [*password*] Specifies the password for the given user. You can provide the command line switch without specifying the password on the command line in cleartext. The system will prompt you for the password. Using this feature can help you maintain the security of passwords used on your system.

/TN *taskname* Specifies the name of the task you want to run. Running a task at the command line is different from having the Task Scheduler run it for you. Using this option forces the utility to use your credentials, rather than the Task Scheduler credentials, which means that an executable that normally works could fail when used in this way.

TIP You can use the RunAs utility described in the "Impersonating a User with the RunAs Utility" section of Chapter 8 to test run a task using another person's credentials. In fact, you can use this technique to run the task using the system account. Because different people have differing rights, you need to test the task using the credentials of the person who normally runs it.

/END

The /End parameter forces a task to stop, even if the task is in the middle of processing data. Consequently, you should use this parameter with care to avoid data loss or odd system behavior. You can only use this parameter to end programs started with the Task Scheduler. Use the TaskKill utility described in the "Terminating Tasks with the TaskKill Utility" section of Chapter 5 to end other processes. This parameter uses the following syntax:

```
SCHTASKS /End [/S system [/U username [/P password]]] /TN taskname
```

The following list describes each of the command line arguments.

/S *system* Specifies the remote system that you want to check. In most cases, you'll also need to supply the /U and the /P command line switches when using this switch.

/U [*domain*\]*user* Specifies the username on the remote system. This name may not match the username on the local system. You'll need to supply a domain name when working with a domain controller.

/P [*password*] Specifies the password for the given user. You can provide the command line switch without specifying the password on the command line in cleartext. The system will prompt you for the password. Using this feature can help you maintain the security of passwords used on your system.

/TN *taskname* Specifies the name of the task you want to end.

Working with the AT Utility

The AT command line utility is an older utility that many long-time Windows users are comfortable using to create tasks. This is an alternative (albeit, less capable) to the SchTasks utility described in the "Managing Tasks with the SchTasks Utility" section of the chapter. The advantage of this utility is that it's very easy to use. In addition, because this utility has been around since Windows NT, you'll find many scripts already written to use it. Use the AT utility alone to display a list of tasks that you've created using the AT utility (the AT utility won't display any tasks created using the graphical tools). This utility uses the following syntax:

```
Remove a Task:
AT [\\Computer] [[<Id>] [/DELETE] [/YES]]
Add a Task:
AT [\\Computer] <Time> [/INTERACTIVE] [/EVERY:<Dates> | /NEXT:<Dates>] <Command>
Query the Task List:
AT
```

The following list describes each of the command line arguments.

Computer Specifies the name of a remote computer used to run the AT command.

Id Specifies the identifying number of the job. The AT command begins at 1 and increments the count as needed. Every job must have a unique identifier.

/DELETE Removes a job from the list. If you omit the Id argument, AT will remove all jobs that it created from the list. This command doesn't affect jobs that you create using the graphical utilities. AT requests confirmation before it deletes a job unless you specify the /YES switch.

/YES Prevents AT from asking whether it should delete each job in the list.

Time Determines the starting time of the job.

/INTERACTIVE Determines whether the user can interact with the job (and vice versa). The default setting runs the job in the background without any interaction.

/EVERY:*Dates* Runs the job during the specified day of the week or month. The valid values for days of the week include Monday, Tuesday, Wednesday, Thursday, Friday, Saturday, and Sunday. The month values are a number between 1 and 31. Adding more than one entry runs the job on multiple days of the week or month. If you omit the date argument, AT assumes you want to run the job monthly during the current day of the month. Vista doesn't allow you to use abbreviations for this argument.

/NEXT:*Dates* Runs the job during the next occurrence of the day of the week or month. The valid values for days of the week include Monday, Tuesday, Wednesday, Thursday, Friday, Saturday, and Sunday. The month values are a number between 1 and 31. Adding multiple dates runs the job during each of the specified dates. If you omit the date argument, AT assumes you want to run the job during the current day. Vista doesn't allow you to use abbreviations for this argument.

Command Specifies the command that you want to run. This entry must include the path of the command you want to run and any command line switches. You must enclose the command in quotes.

Combining the AT Utility with Batch Files

Before you can begin using the AT utility within a batch file, you need to know how to use it at the command line. Creating a job with AT is relatively easy. Imagine that you want to defragment your hard drive. You could create a defragmenter job that runs at 6 PM every Friday, immediately after you leave work to go home for the weekend. You can create the job using the following command line.

```
AT 6pm /Every:FRIDAY "C:\WINDOWS\SYSTEM32\DEFRAG.EXE"
```

The same job using the SchTasks utility would require a longer command line, as shown here.

```
SchTasks /Create /RU SYSTEM /SC WEEKLY /D FRI /TN "ST Defrag Hard
   Drive" /TR "C:\WINDOWS\SYSTEM32\DEFRAG.EXE" /ST 18:00:00
```

NOTE Vista doesn't let you abbreviate day or month names. Previous versions of Windows would let you use an abbreviation such as FRI for Friday. In some cases, you'll find that this change breaks macros in Vista that work fine in other Windows versions.

You don't obtain the same level of configuration features using AT that you would using the graphical or SchTasks method. Many of the special configuration features that the graphical utility supports are unavailable (they're available when you use the SchTasks utility).

NOTE Exercise care when working with AT tasks in the graphical utility. If you modify an AT task using the Scheduled Tasks window, AT won't track it any longer. The second you apply the changes AT removes the task from its list.

The Scheduled Tasks window tracks jobs created using both the graphical and the command line method. AT only tracks jobs that it creates. If you type **AT** at the command prompt and press Enter, all you'll see are the AT jobs. Figure 10.2 shows a typical example of the same jobs created using the graphical utility, SchTask, and AT. Notice that the AT job name has "At," plus the number of the job. The top screenshot shows the Windows XP version of Task Scheduler, while the bottom screenshot shows the Vista version. The entries are essentially the same in both Windows XP and Vista, but the Windows XP view is simpler, while the Vista view provides more details.

As you can see, from a Scheduled Tasks window perspective, all three jobs are the same. The only two differences are the job name and the creator name. Unless you change the default setting, the system creates all AT jobs. Any job created using the Scheduled Tasks window will appear under the user's name.

The limitations of the AT utility do bring up one additional useful feature for batch files. You can schedule a number of temporary tasks using one batch file, and remove all of those tasks from the Scheduled Tasks window using another, all without disturbing the original scheduled tasks. Because the AT utility only operates on the tasks that it creates, you can use it to create temporary tasks and simplify the method required to remove those tasks later.

Using the AT Utility Effectively

The AT utility is still useful, but many would say that it's outdated. If you're working at the command prompt, the AT utility probably is outdated; the SchTasks utility provides more functionality. However, the AT utility still provides good functionality for other purposes. One of the main reasons to use the AT utility is that there are already a wealth of scripts on the Internet for using it.

Sometimes you don't require complexity to get the job done at the command line. The AT utility tends to be simpler to use than the SchTasks utility. Sure, all you can do is query, add, and delete tasks, but sometimes that's all you really need to do. You don't want all of the details; a simple task scheduling will do just fine. Even though the AT utility might look outdated, it really does have some very useful features that make it a worthwhile utility to consider.

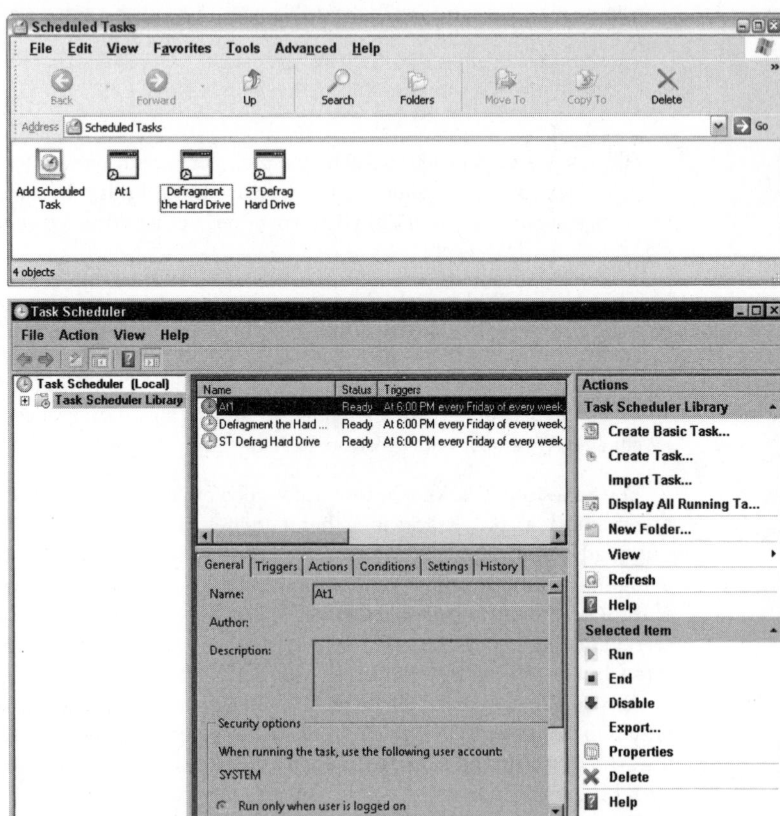

FIGURE 10.2
AT jobs appear in the Scheduled Tasks window as "at" jobs (Windows XP appears at the top and Vista appears at the bottom).

Creating Script-Based Scheduler Activities

You might wonder how you can use the Task Scheduler to improve productivity without expending a lot of energy. Some of the best Task Scheduler tasks are those that you normally perform manually or using a batch file, but don't perform consistently. For example, everyone knows that your hard drive eventually fills up with garbage if you don't remove all of those temporary files. However, many people don't get the job done because it simply isn't convenient, ever.

If you've ever tried to locate all of the temporary files on your hard drive, you know that it's a time-consuming task. In fact, I would go so far as to say that some people would rather hear fingernails screeching across a chalkboard or walk barefooted across broken glass than have to locate all of their temporary files. Fortunately, you don't have to go to such extreme measures because you can tell the computer to do all of the work for you. You can't perform this task easily using Windows Explorer because it won't find all of the files for you (many people have tried). However, the `Dir` command always tells the truth, you just need to put it to work. The batch file shown in Listing 10.1 will remove all of your temporary files. It's fully configurable and you'll find that it's quite reliable.

LISTING 10.1: Deleting Temporary Files Using a Batch File

```
@ECHO OFF

REM Verify that the file specifications file exists.
IF NOT EXIST DelFiles.TXT GOTO :NoFileError
GOTO :GetFiles

REM Display an error message that shows how to correct the problem.
:NoFileError
@ECHO This utility depends on the presence of a file named Delfiles.TXT
@ECHO that contains all of the file specifications you want to delete.
@ECHO All the file need contain is a list of entries such as *.BAK.
@ECHO Place each entry on a separate line.
GOTO :EOF

:GetFiles
REM Remove any existing list of temporary files.
REM This file is retained after the previous cleaning so you have
REM a record of the deletions.
@ECHO Removing old DeleteMe.TXT.
IF EXIST DeleteMe.TXT Del DeleteMe.TXT

REM Locate all of the temporary files on your hard drive.
@ECHO Locating temporary files to delete.
FOR /F %%F IN (DelFiles.TXT) DO Dir %%F /B /S >> DeleteMe.TXT

REM Delete the temporary files.
@ECHO Removing the temporary files.
FOR /F "delims==" %%D IN (DeleteMe.TXT) DO Del "%%D" /Q > Errors.TXT

@ECHO Deletion of Temporary Files Completed!
@ECHO ON
```

This batch file uses three basic steps. First, it ensures that you've defined a file that contains the file extension specifications to delete. Second, it uses these file specifications to locate the files you want to delete. Third, it deletes the file using the accumulated list of files. Notice that the batch file automatically erases any old file lists before it begins generating the new one.

The trickiest piece of code in this example is the second `FOR` command. Notice the `"delims=="` entry. Because the `DeleteMe.TXT` file contains filenames with spaces, you need to use this option. Otherwise, the `FOR` command will only output the filenames up to the first space and the deletion will fail. The batch file outputs any files that failed to delete to `Errors.TXT`, so you can check on them later.

Once you create and fully test this batch file, you can create a second batch file for installing it as a scheduled task on every machine on the network. Of course, you want to do all this without working with each machine individually, so it's just as well that you can tell the batch file to generate the list of machines for you. Listing 10.2 shows how to create such as batch file. Note that some of the long lines are broken in the book. All of the `FOR` commands must appear on a single line.

LISTING 10.2: Defining Tasks on Every Machine on a Network

```
@ECHO OFF

REM Obtain a list of machines from the system.
Net View > Temp.TXT

REM Remove any existing list of machines.
@ECHO Removing old Machines.TXT.
IF EXIST Machines.TXT Del Machines.TXT

REM Make the list usable by removing extraneous material.
@ECHO Generating a New Machine List
FOR /F "skip=3" %%M in (Temp.TXT) DO IF %%M NEQ The @ECHO %%M >> Machines.TXT

REM Copy the required files to each machine.
@ECHO Copying the File Specification and Deletion Batch Files
FOR /F %%M in (Machines.TXT) DO Copy DelFiles.TXT "%%M\Drive_D" /Y
FOR /F %%M in (Machines.TXT) DO Copy MyBatch.BAT "%%M\Drive_D" /Y

REM Schedule the task on each machine.
@ECHO Creating the Scheduled Task
FOR /F %%M in (Machines.TXT) DO SchTasks /Create /S %%M /RU SYSTEM
   /SC WEEKLY /D FRI /TN "Remove Temporary Files"
   /TR "D:\MyBatch.BAT" /ST 18:00:00

@ECHO ON
```

The example begins by using the Net View utility to create a list of machines. Unfortunately, the output from this utility isn't very useful for a batch file, as shown in Figure 10.3. The first three lines contain a header that you can't get rid of and the output ends with "The command completed successfully." In addition, some machines in the list contain a comment.

The first FOR command gets rid of this extraneous material using three techniques. First, it relies on the "skip=3" option to remove the top three lines from the file. The FOR command doesn't even process these lines. At this point, the FOR command does process the three lines with machine names. Because there's a space after each machine name, the result only contains the machine name and not the comment. This is one case where the natural FOR command behavior works in your favor. The FOR command passes the file output to an IF command. Remember that the first word of the last line of the file is "The." By using the code IF %%M NEQ The, you can remove the offending line. The final step copies only the good input to a new file named Machines.TXT by redirecting the output of the ECHO command.

The batch file shown in Listing 10.1 requires two files. The first is a text file containing a list of file specifications. The second is the batch file itself. The next two FOR commands copy these two files to every machine on the network. Because the file could already exist (this could be an update), you use the /Y command line switch with the Copy utility.

The final step creates the required scheduled task on every machine. Notice the use of the /S command line switch to access each machine in turn. The resulting task will run every Friday at 6 PM using the system account.

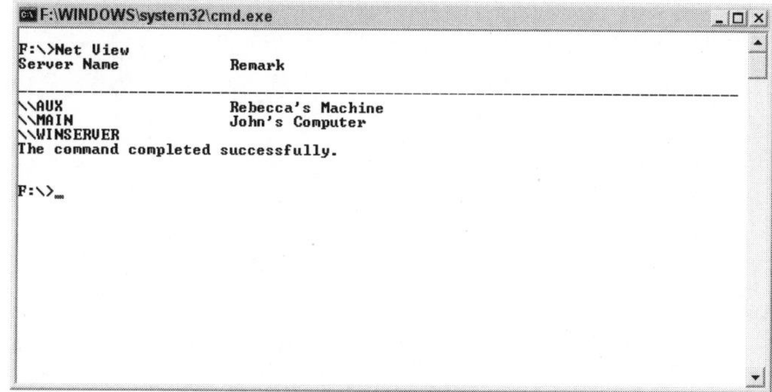
F:\WINDOWS\system32\cmd.exe
F:\>Net View
Server Name Remark
\\AUX Rebecca's Machine
\\MAIN John's Computer
\\WINSERVER
The command completed successfully.
F:\>_

FIGURE 10.3
Some utilities produce helpful output, but you can't use it for a batch file.

Getting Started with Command Line Tasks

This chapter has shown that you have to use Task Scheduler to further automate the applications, batch files, and scripts you use from the command line. Instead of being present to execute these entities, you can ask the system to do it for you. The one thing you can depend on is that the system will execute the task when you ask, using the input data you requested, unless it's unable to do so. Of course, this means that you have to make certain that the Task Scheduler entry is correct or you might get some unanticipated results.

It's time for you test this new form of automation. The best route to pursue is to experiment with a number of simple entries to see how Task Scheduler works. Try something simple and nondestructive, such as the `Dir` command. As you gain proficiency with Task Scheduler, move up to other kinds of commands—those that actually do some work you need to perform offline. When you know beyond any doubt that the entry works as anticipated, you can move on to executing the commands when you aren't sitting at your machine.

Chapter 11 is the next step in scripting, the after hours script. While this chapter provides you with a great start, Chapter 11 examines after hour scripting in greater depth and introduces you to some additional utilities that you might find helpful in automating your setup even further. It's important to remember that creating batch files and scripts, like any form of application development, is often more a process than a single event. The batch files and scripts that you have created so far in the book can always receive additional tweaks and adjustments to make them more powerful. Of course, as Chapter 11 explains, you still need to keep the concept of simplicity in mind. There isn't any need to create a complex script to accomplish a simple task.

Chapter 11

After Hours Automation Scripting

- Defining After Hours Task Candidates
- Designing and Testing the After Hours Batch File
- Designing and Testing the After Hours Script
- Creating Remote Connections with the MSTSC Utility
- Providing Fault Tolerance for an After Hours Batch or Script

You have all the scripts and batch files you need to manage your network by typing a few commands. In addition, you have automated many of these applications using the Task Scheduler. Now it's time to go that last step—choosing the applications that will run unattended when you go home at night. This particular step is the most dangerous because you aren't available any longer to do something when the batch file or script fails. You could arrive at work the next morning to find a disaster on your machine.

The most important concept you can discover in this chapter is that not every task is a good candidate for after hours scripting. The biggest problem you'll encounter with any form of automation is a lack of monitoring. Automation simply means that the task occurs in the background, while you do something else. You're still responsible for accurate and timely task completion. This chapter discusses some of the pitfalls of after hours scripts and helps you determine which applications make the best candidates.

The remainder of this chapter exposes you to the requirements for using after hours scripting effectively. For example, you'll discover some techniques for ensuring that the after hours scripts you design run well. Of course, no matter how well you design the script, you have to plan for the script to fail. The worst possible assumption that you can make is that things will always go as planned. Consequently, this chapter discusses issues such as fault tolerance.

Defining After Hours Task Candidates

You must consider a wealth of issues when you compose your list of after hours scripting candidates. For example, you wouldn't want to perform any unreliable task after hours. An application that has failed once or twice already is likely to do so again in the future. Of course, you can always look for the source of the error and provide some type of error handling as part of your batch file or script to improve the application's reliability. Make sure you test any such changes thoroughly. The point is that you have to have some assurance that the application can operate in your absence. Otherwise, you'll spend your time checking up on the application remotely, which means you may just as well be at the office.

It's also important to consider security. An application that requires administrator-level security probably isn't a good candidate. You don't want to keep an administrator account open all night, or worse yet, all weekend. If you're present when the task runs, you can make sure that any security issues are resolved as quickly as possible—before the cracker gains access to your network and has a full evening to work undisturbed. Make sure you look for hidden security flaws. For example, you might find that the application relies on impersonation to gain additional rights at some point.

Some people will run applications after hours simply because it seems like the right thing to do. However, you really do need to make sure that you gain something by running the application after hours. For example, you might need to perform a cleanup of the database when no one is using it. The exclusive access requirement is an application that you really need to run after hours. Many companies perform backups, clean up network drives, and conduct other maintenance tasks after hours to ensure that the application can work undisturbed by user activity. You'll want to avoid performing tasks that do require some level of monitoring. For example, you wouldn't want to create new users as an after hours task since it's important to monitor the setup for the right user setup details. Otherwise, you'll spend your work hours trying to figure out why a user can't start an application.

VISTA

The following sections contain utilities that you can use in an after hours environment. These aren't the only utilities you should consider. For example, the NTBackup utility described in the "Performing Backups with the NTBackup Utility" section of Chapter 2 works just fine as an after hours automation project. Vista users will want to use the newer WBAdmin utility for backups as described in the "Performing Backups with the WBAdmin Utility" section of Chapter 2.

Real World Scenario

Avoiding the Task That Can't Fail

In all of my years of working with computers (and I don't want to date myself here, but they're many), I've never found an application that can't fail. I've been surprised at some of the applications that have failed over the years. For example, who would think that something as simple as Debug could fail? This utility is working with a known good file and it doesn't do anything so special that you can't predict every failure mode in advance. Yet, there are times when this utility has failed to work as anticipated. The important thing to remember is that as applications become more complex, the number of failure modes increases and reliability decreases substantially. Any application of any size and complexity will fail.

Good after hours scripting candidates assume some level of failure and provide documented and robust methods for dealing with failure, even failures that supposedly can't occur. At one time, the programming methodology required that developers create applications that failed gracefully and avoided data loss. Today, applications can't afford to fail at all, not even gracefully, if possible. The best possible strategy relies on self-repairing applications that can completely recover from a failure and continue processing data as if nothing happened. These self-repairing applications are your best bet for after hours scripting in many cases.

Some unwary administrators make assumptions based on their knowledge of their own code that supposedly can't fail. Don't assume that simply because your batch file consists of a few lines of well-defined text that it can't fail. Batch files rely on external applications to perform their tasks. Even if you create the best batch file in the world, you can count on failure because the external application will fail. Even with completely reliable and self-repairing applications, you can count on the operating system to fail. Going a step further, you must consider hardware failures. Another step takes you to environmental failures, such as power outages and lightning. You must also consider human failure. Somewhere, somehow, your application will fail and you must plan for it.

Creating Message Queue Backups with the MQBkup Utility

Performing a system backup during work hours can be difficult because you don't know whether a particular file is in use. If it is, the backup utility usually skips it, which means you might have holes in your data store. In many cases, you'll never run into these data holes, however, so it's not fatal to perform a backup during the day. To a certain extent, databases also provide obstacles to backup during the day. If the backup routine requires exclusive database access, then you must perform the backup at night.

The Microsoft Message Queue (MSMQ) falls along the lines of a database, but in this situation, you'll find that downtime backups are essential. Unfortunately, applications are using MSMQ to send and receive server messages. Although the Message Queue Backup (MQBkup) utility attempts to perform the backup during daylight, it often fails, and you'll find that you don't receive much in the way of warning about the potential problems that restoring the backup could cause. Just consider for a moment attempting to resolve all of those partial messages in the queue or wading through the messages that the server has already handled. Consequently, the MQBkup utility is one that you should consider automating as an after hours task. (Unlike previous versions of Windows, Vista doesn't install MSMQ by default, so the MQBkup is unavailable unless you install the MSMQ software.) This utility uses the following syntax:

```
mqbkup [-b | -r] [-y] backup_path
```

The following list describes each of the command line arguments.

backup_path Specifies the location of the backup file that you want to create or restore. Make sure you include this file as part of your system backup so the data ends up on a tape, rather than simply on a system hard drive.

-b Performs a backup of MSMQ to the specified backup path.

-r Restores MSMQ from the file specified by the backup path.

-y Forces the utility to assume that you want to answer yes to all prompts. Make sure you test this feature before you use it. Of course, you must use this command line switch for an unattended backup.

Installing Applications with the MSIExec Utility

The Microsoft Installer Executive (MSIExec) utility helps you install applications on a system. The application setup package must appear in a form that MSIExec can understand which is normally a file with a Microsoft Installer (MSI) extension, although you'll see these files with an EXE extension as well. Generally, the MSI packages are robust enough that you can install them unattended after you test the application setup on a test machine. In fact, if you have many machines to setup, using this approach, coupled with automation, can save you considerable time. Unattended installations of tested application setups are an excellent choice for after hours scripting. This utility uses the following syntax:

```
msiexec /Option <Required Parameter> [Optional Parameter]
```

You can categorize the command line switches for MSIExec into several functional areas. Each area performs a specific Microsoft Installer task. The following list describes each of the command line installation options.

{/package | /i} *{Product.MSI | ProductGUID}* Installs or configures the specified application. You can specify the application as an MSI package or as a GUID. When you use the GUID form, MSIExec looks for the application information in the registry and performs a configuration, rather than an installation. This installation option relies on the credentials of the current user.

/a *Product.MSI* Performs an administrative installation. An administrative installation unpacks all of the files into a directory, normally on the network, and creates a smaller MSI file. Clients can then perform a local installation by accessing this directory on the network. Normally, you'll use this command line switch to create a centralized location from which to perform an installation for a number of machines. You'll normally specify the installation location using the `TARGETDIR` parameter.

/j{u | m} *Product.MSI [[/t TransformList | /g LanguageID]* Advertises an application on a network. Use the `/ju` command line switch to advertise to the current user. The `/jm` command line switch advertises the application to all users on the network. Use the `/jm` command line switch when you need to install a package using elevated rights (privileges). The `/t` command line switch specifies a transform list used to advertise the product. A transform is a method of customizing the MSI database to meet specific needs. It's a property that you can specify at the command line using the `TRANSFORMS` parameter. For example, `TRANSFORMS=":1033"` might select a file of advertising information in United States English based on a Locale Identifier (LCID) of 1033.You can also supply transforms as part of a Microsoft Transform (MST) file. The `/g` command line switch lets you specify a language identifier directly. The language is normally an LCID. You can find a list of common LCIDs at `http://krafft.com/scripts/deluxe-calendar/lcid_chart.htm`.

{/uninstall | /x} *{Product.MSI | ProductCode}* Uninstalls a previously installed application. You can uninstall the product based either on the original installation package or on the product's GUID.

In addition to installation options, the MSIExec utility supports a number of display options. The following list describes each of these options.

/quiet Installs the product without any user interaction. The product installs using the default arguments. However, you can override the arguments using parameters when the developer sets up the installation program correctly. For example, you can select an installation type, such as custom or typical, using the `INSTALLLEVEL` parameter. Make sure you check the product documentation for any custom parameters that the developer might create to address specific installation needs.

/passive Performs an unattended installation. The setup program won't ask the user any questions, but the user still sees a progress bar. The progress bar gives the user some idea of how far the setup has progressed and indicates continued activity. An activity indicator is essential when the user knows about the installation. Otherwise, users may overwhelm your help desk with questions about why the application setup didn't complete (even though it would have if they'd simply given it time to complete).

/q[{n | b | r | f}] Defines the user interface level. The interface level determines what the user sees during the application installation. Each of these levels has a specific meaning as described in the following list.

n Conceals the user interface (no user interface).

b Displays a basic user interface. Normally, this includes only the features required to install the application.

r Displays a reduced user interface. The package developer defines the user interface setup, which is somewhere between the basic and the full display in complexity.

f Displays the full user interface.

Once the installation has completed, you need to consider whether to restart the machine. The only time you need to restart the machine is when you need to replace a DLL or other system component that is in use. Generally, this type of update requires special programming for the setup routine and a discussion of the required programming techniques is outside the scope of this book. Here's the list of restart options.

`/norestart` Performs the installation without a restart.

`/promptrestart` Prompts the user for a restart when necessary.

`/forcerestart` Forces the system to restart after the installation is complete.

An after hours installation might not go as planned. Consequently, you'll want to log any installation events so you can review the installation process later. It's important that you review the log even when it appears the installation occurred as predicted. A small error might not stop the installation from completing, but could stop the application from working as intended. The following list defines the command line switches for logging an installation.

`/l[I] [w] [e] [a] [r] [u] [c] [m] [o] [p] [v] [x] [+] [!] [*]` ***`LogFile`*** Performs only the specified level of logging. You can combine multiple logging levels to obtain specific logging results. For example, using the `/lia` command line switch records all status messages and startup actions. The following list identifies the various logging levels that you can use.

- **i** Status messages
- **w** Nonfatal warnings
- **e** All error messages
- **a** Startup of actions
- **r** Action-specific records
- **u** User requests
- **c** Initial user interface parameters
- **m** Out-of-memory or fatal exit information
- **o** Out-of-disk-space messages
- **p** Terminal properties
- **v** Verbose output (you can only use this command line switch when you specify that you want all output by using the `\l*v` command line switch)
- **x** Extra debugging information
- **+** Append to existing log file
- **!** Flush each line to the log
- ***** Log all information, except for `v` and `x` options

`/log` ***`LogFile`*** Performs a level of logging equivalent to the `/l*` command line switch.

The MSIExec utility can do more than simply install or remove applications. You can also use it to perform an update of the application. The following command line switches tell about the update options.

`/update` ***`Update1.MSP[;Update2.MSP]`*** Performs an update based on the content of one or more Microsoft Patch (MSP) files. Separate the individual MSP entries with a semicolon (;).

NOTE Some versions of MSIExec support a `/p` command line switch file updates where you supply the update package as the input argument. This form doesn't support multiple update packages and it doesn't provide a means of removing the patch. Use the `/update` command line switch if your version of MSIExec supports it. (The utility displays an error message when you attempt to use the `/update` command line switch with a version that doesn't support it.)

/uninstall *PatchCodeGuid[;Update2.MSP]* */package* {*Product.MSI* | *ProductCode*} Removes an update based on the patch's GUID. You can remove additional, supplementary updates by supplying the MSP file.

If you've ever had an application act oddly and found that some small change in the system caused the error, you've wanted a repair option. Interestingly enough, the MSIExec option allows this action, even in cases where the product's installation interface doesn't supply the required functionality. Because it's easier to repair an application than to reinstall and configure it, you might try this option with any application that performs strangely. The following list describes the command line switch for repairing a faulty installation.

/f[p] [e] [c] [m] [s] [o] [d] [a] [u] [v] {*Product.MSI* | *ProductCode*} Repairs the product based on the original installation file or the product code. Use the original installation file for greater reliability in fixing an application. The following list describes the levels of repair that you can perform. You can combine multiple repair levels to achieve specific effects.

p Replaces a file only when the file is missing.

o Replaces a file when the setup program detects the file is missing or it finds another application has installed an older version of the file. This is the default action.

e Replaces a file when the setup program detects the file is missing or it finds another application has installed an equal or older version of the file.

d Replaces a file when the setup program detects the file is missing or it finds another application has installed a different version. This action replaces the file even when the file is newer than the one used by the application.

c Replaces a file when the setup program detects the file is missing or the file's checksum does not match the calculated value. This option often helps you locate and replace files tainted by viruses.

a Forces the setup program to reinstall all files.

u Updates all required user-specific registry entries.

m Updates all required computer-specific registry entries.

s Updates all existing shortcuts.

v Runs the setup program from a source media and caches the local package to the hard drive. This command line switch replaces the local package when it already exists.

You may have noticed more than a few references to properties in this section. Adding properties to the command line changes the way in which the MSI package unpacks. The properties that are available depend in part on the person who crafted the package, part on the version of the Microsoft Installer used to create the package, and part on your own personal requirements. The Windows Installer Property Reference at `http://helpnet.installshield.com/robo/projects/helplibdevstudio9/IHelpPropReference.htm` provides one of the most complete listings of properties you can use with Microsoft Installer. Of all these parameters, you'll use the special folder parameters, such as TARGETDIR, most often. To use a parameter at the command line, simply include the parameter name, followed by an equals sign (=), followed by the parameter value, such as `TARGETDIR="C:\Program Files\My Application"`. Always enclose parameters with spaces in quotes.

Designing and Testing the After Hours Batch File

It's important to remember the place that batch files occupy in the hierarchy of automation. A batch represents a fast and simple way of executing a series of tasks using applications, commands, and utilities. The batch file possesses basic programming structures and you can perform amazing tasks at times with those structures, but in the end, batch files are somewhat limited. Something as simple as a disk being full or a lack of rights to create a file in a specific location can cause the batch file to fail. Error trapping in such cases is difficult because you have to check for error levels from the errant application, command, or utility and not every one of them supports output error levels. The "Providing Fault Tolerance for an After Hours Batch or Script" section of the chapter discusses fault tolerance, including error handling, in detail. The following sections describe some batch file techniques you should consider using, especially when working with large systems.

Real World Scenario

REAL ADMINISTRATORS USE BATCH FILES

At one time, I thought I held the title for the number of batch files used for daily activities. That's until I ran into one network administrator who had more batch files than I'd ever seen before. He had batch files for every occasion. In fact, one of the batch files was simply there to track all of the other batch files (so he didn't reinvent the wheel at some point). The entire collection required two CDs, a considerable amount of space when you consider that many of the batch files in this book are less than 1 KB in size.

Of course, he didn't build this huge source of batch files in a day. In fact, he had been building and refining them over a period of years. This administrator customized many of the batch files to his way of working with systems and the network as a whole. In fact, that's the point of batch files. You can do things your way. Because batch files are simplicity itself, you can add, remove, and rebuild them as needed.

However, batch files are important for administrators for another reason. The examples in this book demonstrate that batch files can be quite powerful. Yet, the time required to develop a batch file is short and you don't need to become a programmer to use one. These are the two reasons that most administrators I've talked with give for using batch files instead of scripts. Although batch files can't replace scripts or full-fledged programming languages, over the years I've found that batch files serve the purpose for most administrator needs.

Adding Debug Information to Batch Files

Developers of most applications know how to add debugging statements to their code. The debugging statements aren't for general use; they simply make it easier to check the application for flaws. In addition, the debugging statements make it possible to track program flow and generally help the developer understand the application better. A batch file can also include debugging information, even though there aren't specific statements to perform the task. The following code shows one method you can use.

```
@IF NOT DEFINED DEBUG @ECHO OFF
ECHO
@ECHO ON
```

In this case, the debug trigger is an environment variable named DEBUG. You can set this environment variable to any value desired by using the Set command. Type **Set DEBUG=** and press Enter to turn debugging off. The purpose of this debugging statement is to keep echo on when you're debugging the batch file. During the debugging cycle, you want to see all of the statements, so you display them by keeping the echo on. When the batch file runs normally, the user won't have an environment variable named DEBUG, and the batch file will turn echo off so the user doesn't see all of the intervening commands. Using the ECHO command by itself displays the current echo state so you can easily test this technique for yourself.

Notice that the batch file doesn't include anything special for the @ECHO ON statement. It's bad practice to use conditional statements with commands that set the system back to a default state. In this case, you can set echo on without considering the current echo state because having echo on is the default setting.

You can extend debugging to other activities. For example, you might want to know the current value of a variable within the batch file. Because you don't have a debugging environment that you can rely on to perform such tasks, you'll need to use other methods with a batch file. Listing 11.1 shows one technique you can use to extend a batch file to output debugging information about an internal variable (note that this example also uses the DEBUG environment variable).

LISTING 11.1: Adding Simple Debugging to a Batch File

```
@ECHO OFF

REM Locate all of the temporary files on your hard drive.
@ECHO Locating temporary files to delete.
FOR /F %%F IN (DelFiles.TXT) DO CALL :GetFile %%F
GOTO :NextStep

REM This is the actual code for handling the temporary file
REM processing.
:GetFile
IF DEFINED DEBUG @ECHO Adding %1 to the list.
Dir %1 /B /S >> DeleteMe.TXT
GOTO :EOF

REM You would normally place the next step of the processing
REM task here.
:NextStep

@ECHO ON
```

This is actually a batch file within a batch file. The code begins by displaying information to the user that it's collecting a list of temporary files. At this point, the user normally waits while the batch file does its job in complete silence. However, as a developer, you really need to know what's going on within the batch file. To make this work, you need to execute multiple commands. Consequently, the batch file calls a label named `:GetFile` and passes it the %%F argument.

Now, look at the `:GetFile` label and you'll see two statements. The first displays the current %%F value when you create an environment variable named DEBUG. However, notice that it's called %1 here, not %%F. Whenever you employ a `Call` command to pass control to a label within a batch file, you create a new batch file context. As far as the `:GetFile` label is concerned, it exists in a different batch file from the original that called it. The first batch file passes %%F as an input value, so it appears as %1 to the `:GetFile` label code. The second statement in `:GetFile` is the `Dir` command that locates the files you want to delete based on the file specification.

Notice that the `:GetFile` section ends with GOTO :EOF, which should end the batch file. It does, in fact, end the `:GetFile` batch file and returns control to the FOR command that called it. Now the FOR command can process the next file extension in the list. Figure 11.1 gives you a better idea of how this batch file works with and without DEBUG defined. Notice the batch file doesn't display the file extensions the first time because DEBUG isn't defined yet.

FIGURE 11.1
Batch files can output as little or much debugging information as needed.

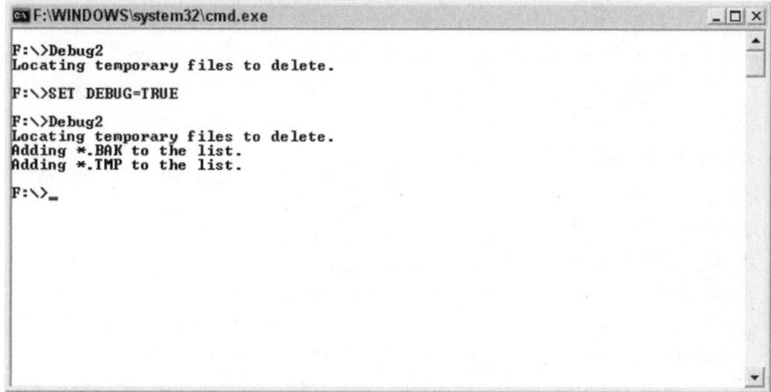

The examples in this section have only shown a single level of debugging so far. However, you can create as many levels of debugging as you want by adding some additional code. Listing 11.2 shows the example in Listing 11.1 with a second level of debugging added.

LISTING 11.2: A Batch File with Multiple Debug Levels Defined

```
IF NOT DEFINED DEBUG2 @ECHO OFF

REM Set the second level of debugging.
IF DEFINED DEBUG2 SET DEBUG=TRUE

REM Locate all of the temporary files on your hard drive.
@ECHO Locating temporary files to delete.
FOR /F %%F IN (DelFiles.TXT) DO CALL :GetFile %%F
GOTO :NextStep

REM This is the actual code for handling the temporary file
```

```
REM processing.
:GetFile
IF DEFINED DEBUG @ECHO Adding %1 to the list.
Dir %1 /B /S >> DeleteMe.TXT
Goto :EOF

REM You would normally place the next step of the processing
REM task here.
:NextStep

REM Always remember to remove additional debugging levels.
IF DEFINED DEBUG2 SET DEBUG=

@ECHO ON
```

The two levels of debugging for this example are DEBUG and DEBUG2. When you define the DEBUG2 level, the batch file automatically defines DEBUG for you and then removes the DEBUG definition when the batch file ends. As shown in the code, the DEBUG2 level displays all of the batch code as it executes. Although this display can be handy, as shown in Figure 11.2, it can also become quite messy. You don't always need it to locate a problem in your batch file. In fact, displaying the code can sometimes hide problems in plain sight.

FIGURE 11.2
Display code statements in batch files with care to avoid overwhelming yourself with too much content.

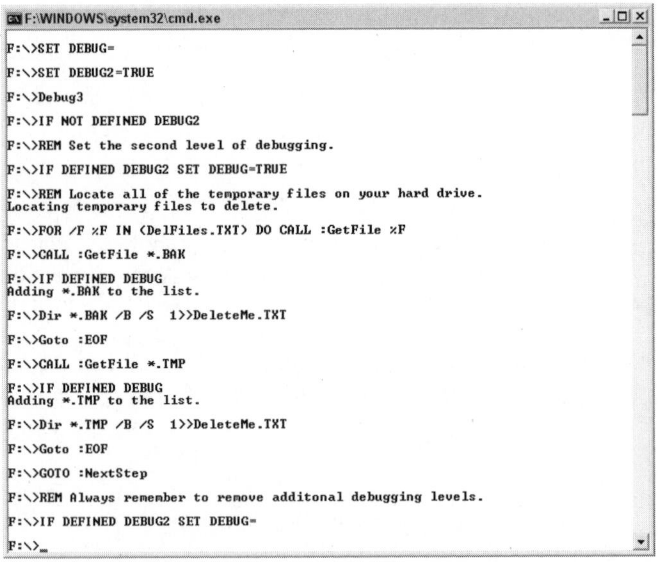

```
F:\WINDOWS\system32\cmd.exe
F:\>SET DEBUG=
F:\>SET DEBUG2=TRUE
F:\>Debug3
F:\>IF NOT DEFINED DEBUG2
F:\>REM Set the second level of debugging.
F:\>IF DEFINED DEBUG2 SET DEBUG=TRUE
F:\>REM Locate all of the temporary files on your hard drive.
Locating temporary files to delete.
F:\>FOR /F %F IN (DelFiles.TXT) DO CALL :GetFile %F
F:\>CALL :GetFile *.BAK
F:\>IF DEFINED DEBUG
Adding *.BAK to the list.
F:\>Dir *.BAK /B /S  1>>DeleteMe.TXT
F:\>Goto :EOF
F:\>CALL :GetFile *.TMP
F:\>IF DEFINED DEBUG
Adding *.TMP to the list.
F:\>Dir *.TMP /B /S  1>>DeleteMe.TXT
F:\>Goto :EOF
F:\>GOTO :NextStep
F:\>REM Always remember to remove additonal debugging levels.
F:\>IF DEFINED DEBUG2 SET DEBUG=
F:\>_
```

Many people claim that batch files don't offer any form of debugging. Admittedly, batch files don't provide the robust debugging features that full-fledged programming languages do, but batch files don't require these advanced levels of debugging either since they normally perform simple tasks. Using the techniques found in this section, you can provide at least a modicum of debugging functionality for your batch files.

Identifying Batch Files and Their Actions

If you work on a large system, you know that automation isn't just a nicety; it's a requirement if you want to stay on top of maintenance actions. However, automation brings with it all kinds of problems. One of the more critical problems is identifying which machine produced a particular data file. After all, if a machine encounters an error, you want to know which machine to fix. The same concept holds true for other kinds of data. No matter what data you collect, data without an attached context is worthless. With this in mind, you can use code as shown in Listing 11.3 to create a descriptive data file.

LISTING 11.3: Creating a Descriptive Data File Header

```
@ECHO OFF

REM Add identifying information.
@ECHO Computer: %COMPUTERNAME% > Temps.TXT
@ECHO User: %USERNAME% >> Temps.TXT

REM Add the date and time.
Date /T >> Temps.TXT
Time /T >> Temps.TXT

REM Create a header for the data.
@ECHO. >> Temps.TXT
@ECHO Temporary Files: >> Temps.TXT
@ECHO. >> Temps.TXT

REM Locate all of the temporary files on your hard drive.
@ECHO Locating temporary files to delete.
FOR /F %%F IN (DelFiles.TXT) DO Dir %%F /B /S >> Temps.TXT

@ECHO ON
```

This example uses several techniques to output descriptive data. First, it combines standard text with environmental variable expansion. Every Windows machine will include the `%COMPUTERNAME%` and `%USERNAME%` environment variables (or you can define them in the unlikely event that they don't exist). Notice the first output contains just a single > redirection symbol, so this first line always erases any existing file.

Second, the example uses the Date and Time utilities to output the date and the time. Notice the use of the /T command line switch to prevent these utilities from prompting the user for the date or time. It's a common error not to include the /T command line switch, so you should watch for the error in your own code.

Third, the example creates a header for the data. Notice the use of the special `ECHO.` command to create a blank space in the output. The addition of the period prevents echo from displaying its status. Because there isn't any other data to display, the `ECHO` command simply displays a blank line. The remainder of this example outputs a temporary file listing. Figure 11.3 shows typical output from this example.

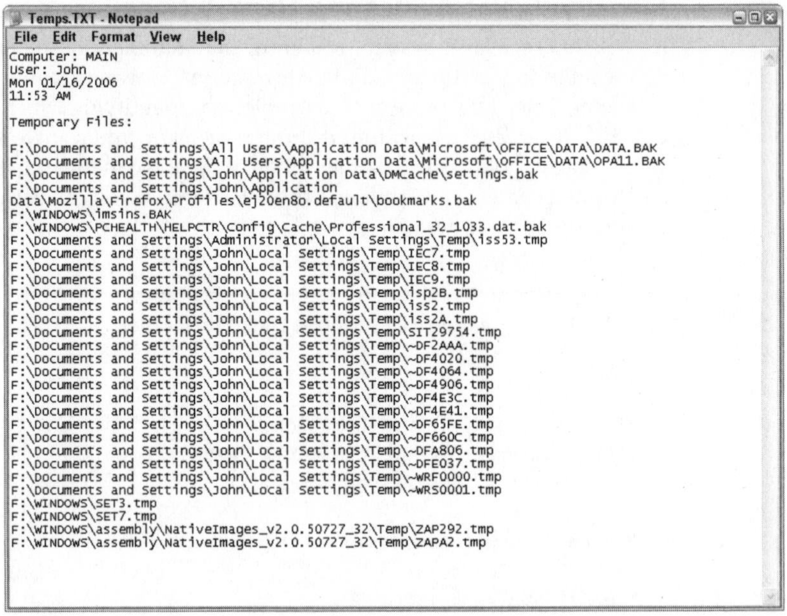

FIGURE 11.3
It's important to create identifying information for the data files you produce with a batch file.

```
Temps.TXT - Notepad
File  Edit  Format  View  Help
Computer: MAIN
User: John
Mon 01/16/2006
11:53 AM

Temporary Files:

F:\Documents and Settings\All Users\Application Data\Microsoft\OFFICE\DATA\DATA.BAK
F:\Documents and Settings\All Users\Application Data\Microsoft\OFFICE\DATA\OPA11.BAK
F:\Documents and Settings\John\Application Data\DMCache\settings.bak
F:\Documents and Settings\John\Application
Data\Mozilla\Firefox\Profiles\ej20en8o.default\bookmarks.bak
F:\WINDOWS\imsins.BAK
F:\WINDOWS\PCHEALTH\HELPCTR\Config\Cache\Professional_32_1033.dat.bak
F:\Documents and Settings\Administrator\Local Settings\Temp\iss53.tmp
F:\Documents and Settings\John\Local Settings\Temp\IEC7.tmp
F:\Documents and Settings\John\Local Settings\Temp\IEC8.tmp
F:\Documents and Settings\John\Local Settings\Temp\IEC9.tmp
F:\Documents and Settings\John\Local Settings\Temp\isp2B.tmp
F:\Documents and Settings\John\Local Settings\Temp\iss2.tmp
F:\Documents and Settings\John\Local Settings\Temp\iss2A.tmp
F:\Documents and Settings\John\Local Settings\Temp\SIT29754.tmp
F:\Documents and Settings\John\Local Settings\Temp\~DF2AAA.tmp
F:\Documents and Settings\John\Local Settings\Temp\~DF4020.tmp
F:\Documents and Settings\John\Local Settings\Temp\~DF4064.tmp
F:\Documents and Settings\John\Local Settings\Temp\~DF4906.tmp
F:\Documents and Settings\John\Local Settings\Temp\~DF4E3C.tmp
F:\Documents and Settings\John\Local Settings\Temp\~DF4E41.tmp
F:\Documents and Settings\John\Local Settings\Temp\~DF65FE.tmp
F:\Documents and Settings\John\Local Settings\Temp\~DF660C.tmp
F:\Documents and Settings\John\Local Settings\Temp\~DFA806.tmp
F:\Documents and Settings\John\Local Settings\Temp\~DFE037.tmp
F:\Documents and Settings\John\Local Settings\Temp\~WRF0000.tmp
F:\Documents and Settings\John\Local Settings\Temp\~WRS0001.tmp
F:\WINDOWS\SET3.tmp
F:\WINDOWS\SET7.tmp
F:\WINDOWS\assembly\NativeImages_v2.0.50727_32\Temp\ZAP292.tmp
F:\WINDOWS\assembly\NativeImages_v2.0.50727_32\Temp\ZAPA2.tmp
```

Adding the identifying information to the data file is fine when you don't want to maintain backups of previous data and when the data resides on the original machine. Of course, things change when you want to create a historical view of the data or store the information in a centralized location. In this second instance, you need a unique filename for every submission. Listing 11.4 shows how to add the information to the filename, rather than the data file.

LISTING 11.4: Adding Descriptive Information to a Data File

```
@ECHO OFF

REM Create a new environment variable with the identifying
REM information for this file. Start with the computer and
REM user name.
SET DataStore=%COMPUTERNAME%
SET DataStore=%DataStore%_%USERNAME%

REM Add the date.
SET DataStore=%DataStore%_%DATE:~4,2%
SET DataStore=%DataStore%_%DATE:~7,2%
SET DataStore=%DataStore%_%DATE:~10,4%

REM Add the time.
SET DataStore=%DataStore%_%TIME:~0,2%
SET DataStore=%DataStore%_%TIME:~3,2%
SET DataStore=%DataStore%_%TIME:~6,2%
```

```
REM Add the file extension.
:SetExtension
SET DataStore=%DataStore%.TXT

REM Locate all of the temporary files on your hard drive.
@ECHO Locating temporary files to delete.
@ECHO Saving files to "%DataStore%".
FOR /F %%F IN (DelFiles.TXT) DO Dir %%F /B /S >> "%DataStore%"

@ECHO ON
```

In this example, the batch files build up an environment variable named `DataStore` that contains the computer and usernames, along with the date and time. Obtaining the computer and usernames are simply a matter of using the existing `%COMPUTERNAME%` and `%USERNAME%` environment variables. However, the date and time prove more interesting.

Even though the `Set` command doesn't show them, Windows dynamically generates several environment variables each time you request them, including `%DATE%` and `%TIME%`. When working at DOS, you had to generate these environment variables yourself, which is a time-consuming and error-prone process (see the examples at `http://www.robvanderwoude.com/datetime.html` for details). Unfortunately, these environment variables contain characters that you can use for a filename including the slash (/) and colon (:). Consequently, you can't use the variables directly. The solution is to extract the numbers you need. For example, to extract the first two numbers of the time, you use `%TIME:~0,2%`, where the first number is the starting point in the string and the second number defines the number of characters to use. Strings in batch file always rely on a 0-based starting point.

TIP When extracting characters from a string, the system assumes that you want to start on the left side of the string and move to the right. You can reverse this process by using a negative number. For example, `%TIME:~-2%` would extract the last two characters in the `TIME` environmental variable.

The `%DATE%` environment variable requires a little more manipulation than `%TIME%`. In this case, the string contains the day of the week, so you must extract that information from the string as well. Consequently, the month always appears at position 4, rather than 0.

Now that the batch file has built a unique filename based on the machine name, username, date, and time, it adds a file extension of `.TXT` to it. The result appears in place of the standard filename in the `FOR` command for this example. Notice that you must enclose the filename with quotes because it could contain a space.

Using a Centralized Data Store

One problem that none of the examples in the book have addressed so far is the use of a centralized data store. Overcoming this problem with scripts is relatively easy because you have access to standard database objects. With the proper code, you can simply send the data from a client machine to a server and never have to worry about it again except for analysis purposes. However, batch files don't support database objects and the individual machine records discussed so far in the book are ill suited for import into a database. If you have a large network, it's unlikely that you'll want to view every one of those individual records.

You have options at your disposal when working with individual commands. For example, many commands and utilities support the CSV format. When working with one of these utilities, you simply specify that you don't want headers and that the system should use the CSV format.

Unfortunately, these utilities won't address special needs, such as error reports or a listing of interesting files on a machine (perhaps an unacceptable or unsupported application, temporary files, viruses, adware, or spyware). For all of these needs and many more, you must create the output in a form that lends itself to use with a database. Fortunately, creating your own CSV output (a data form commonly accepted by databases) isn't difficult. Listing 11.5 shows one way to do it with a list of temporary files.

LISTING 11.5: Creating Output for a Database

```
@ECHO OFF

REM Clean up any existing output file.
IF EXIST Output.CSV Del Output.CSV

REM Create a new environment variable to hold the static
REM data for this session.
SET DataEntry="%COMPUTERNAME%"
SET DataEntry=%DataEntry%,"%USERNAME%"
SET DataEntry=%DataEntry%,"%DATE%"
SET DataEntry=%DataEntry%,"%TIME%"

REM Locate all of the temporary files on your hard drive.
@ECHO Locating temporary files to delete.
FOR /F %%F IN (DelFiles.TXT) DO CALL :AddValue %%F
GOTO :Finished

REM Work with the individual directory entries as a set
REM and process them as part of a FOR command.
:AddValue
@ECHO Adding database values for %1.
FOR /F "delims==" %%E IN ('Dir %1 /B /S') DO @ECHO %DataEntry%,"%%E" >> Output.CSV
GOTO :EOF

:Finished
@ECHO ON
```

The idea behind CSV is that you encapsulate the individual data values in quotes and separate them with commas. This example works as most batch files that create CSV will work. You begin by creating one or more static data values that provide a snapshot of this particular session. When you combine this data with other snapshots, the static information provides the means for separating the individual data entries.

The example requires two FOR loops in this case. The first FOR command parses the file specifications located in the DelFiles.TXT file and passes them to a secondary routine.

The secondary FOR loop processes the individual file entries returned by the Dir command. Notice the two additions to the FOR command. First, you must provide the "delims==" option so that the FOR loop doesn't cut off the paths at the first space. Second, notice that this FOR loop doesn't process the data as a file; it uses the command representation instead. Remember that single quotes are for commands and double quotes are for strings. The resulting `Output.CSV` file contains a pure string representation that you could open in Notepad if desired. However, the power of this particular routine is that you can also open it as a database in a database application or even in Excel. Figure 11.4 shows typical output presented in Excel.

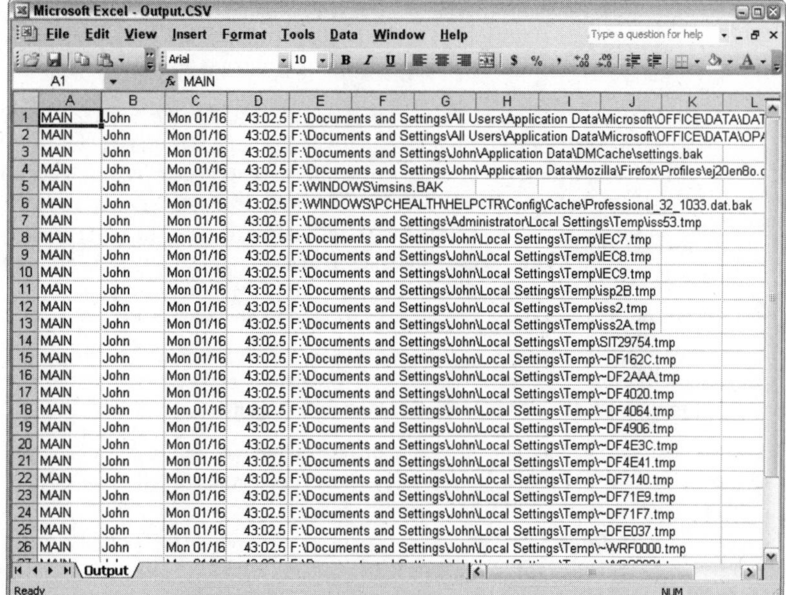

FIGURE 11.4
CSV files make it very easy to move data to a spreadsheet or database.

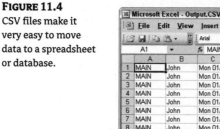

Designing and Testing the After Hours Script

Scripting languages provide far more than batch files do in the way of flow control and error handling support. In addition, you can debug your scripts with greater ease because Microsoft includes a script debugger with Windows. If you find this script debugger a tad limited (many people do), you can also use third party utilities to debug your scripts. You can learn more about the Microsoft Script Debugger at `http://msdn.microsoft.com/library/en-us/sdbug/html/sdbug_1.asp`. The following sections discuss some script techniques you can use to create robust script applications in a command line environment.

Mapping a Network Drive

You can map a network drive using a batch file, but it's more difficult and error prone than using a script. A script can provide one thing that a batch file can't in this case, great interactivity. Using a script lets you interact with the user in a way that would be difficult using a batch file. In addition, the script provides a modicum of additional error handling support that makes error handling easier. Listing 11.6 shows a typical example of how you can implement this functionality using JavaScript.

USING SCRIPTING EFFECTIVELY

Sometimes you do need to use scripting techniques to ensure you get the right results from your command line activities. The best rule of thumb to follow is that anything that requires direct application access through something other than command line switches requires a script, rather than a batch file. In addition, if you've just spent five hours trying to get a batch file to work and feel that you still haven't made any progress, then perhaps you're not using the right tool for the job.

It's this second point where many people get into endless discussions about the suitability of one technique over another. In many cases, it's part personal preference and part skill or special need. For example, at one time some people tried to use spreadsheets in place of word processors (it really was common in the 1980s). However, anyone who has used both products today knows that each tool has a particular job to perform and it's better to use the right tool for the job. The same rule applies to scripts versus batch files. You might be able to use batch files to meet most of your needs, but eventually, you'll run into a complex task that simply requires a script to perform adequately.

LISTING 11.6: Mapping a Network Drive with JavaScript

```
// Define the network object used to map the drive.
var oNetwork = new ActiveXObject("WScript.Network");

// Detect a request for command line help.
if (WScript.Arguments.length == 1)
   if (WScript.Arguments(0) == "/?")
      {
         // Display the help information
         WScript.Echo("Usage: MapNetwork <letter> <UNC target>\n");

         // Exit the script and provide an error level of 1 to
         // indicate a help request.
         WScript.Quit(1);
      }
   else
      {
         // Display an error message.
         WScript.Echo("Input argument is unknown.");
         WScript.Echo("Usage: MapNetwork <letter> <UNC target>\n");

         // Exit the script and provide an error level of 2 to
         // indicate  a data entry error.
         WScript.Quit(2);
      }

// Create variables to hold the drive letter and the UNC location.
```

```
var DriveLtr;
var UNCName;

// Detect the correct number of input arguments.
if ( WScript.Arguments.length < 2 )
{
   // Ask whether the user wants to continue.
   WScript.Echo("No input provided! Provide it interactively? [Y | N]");
   var Answer = WScript.StdIn.ReadLine();

   // If the user doesn't want to continue, dipslay help and exit.
   // Use an exit code of 2 to indicate a data entry error.
   if (Answer.toUpperCase() == "N")
   {
      WScript.Echo("Usage: MapNetwork <letter> <UNC target>\n");
      WScript.Quit(2);
   }

   // Input the drive letter.
   WScript.Echo("Type the local drive letter (X:).");
   DriveLtr = WScript.StdIn.ReadLine();

   // Input the UNC drive on the remote machine.
   WScript.Echo("Type the UNC location (\\MyServer\MyDrive).");
   UNCName = WScript.StdIn.ReadLine();
}
else
{
   // Obtain the required inputs from the command line.
   DriveLtr = WScript.Arguments(0);
   UNCName = WScript.Arguments(1);
}

// Tell the user which drive is mapped.
WScript.Echo("Mapping drive " + DriveLtr + " to " + UNCName);

// Attempt to create the connection.
try
{
   // Perform the drive mapping function.
   oNetwork.MapNetworkDrive(DriveLtr, UNCName);
}
catch(e)
{
   // Display an error when the task fails.
   WScript.Echo("Couldn't map the drive!\n" + e.description);
   WScript.Quit(3);
}
```

The example begins by creating a network object to create the connection. In this case, the code uses the new `ActiveXObject()` method. You can also use `WScript.CreateObject()` to perform the same task. The method you use depends on personal taste in most cases. This examples uses the `ActiveXObject()` method for the sake of completeness. If you want to use the other method, you would replace this line of code with `var oNetwork = WScript.CreateObject("WScript .Network");`.

The next section of code addresses the need to handle the /? command line switch. The help displayed in this example is decidedly weak. You'd provide a lot more help in a fully functional production script. The command and utility examples in this book provide you with a good idea of the kind of information you need to provide to make a script useful for everyone. Notice how the code detects the number of arguments first, and then handles the special case of the /? command line switch. Notice how the code exits with an error level of 1, so you can trap the help request in a batch file if desired.

Of course, you also need to handle the case where someone provides a single input, but it isn't the /? command line switch. The code displays a special error message along with the same help that you would normally display for the /? command line switch. Notice that in this case the script exits with an error level of 2. Using a different error level lets you trap this particular problem in a batch file.

At this point, the code begins looking at the input. The input must provide two arguments to map a network drive to a local drive letter. Consequently, when the script detects two input arguments, it places them in the appropriate variables and attempts to map the network drive. You might wonder why the script doesn't perform all kinds of odd error checking on the input arguments. The `try...catch` statement is the secret in this case. If the user provides incorrect input, the `oNetwork.MapNetworkDrive(DriveLtr, UNCName)` call fails and the `catch` part of the statement will trap the error. The script displays an error message in this case and exits again. Because this is another kind of error, the script sets the error level to 3. Notice that the script conveniently disregards any more than two inputs.

At this point, all the code needs to handle is the case where the user doesn't provide any input arguments. This is where the interactive features of scripting pay off. The script begins by asking the user whether they want to provide the input interactively. If so, the code asks some simple questions and tries to map the drive. If not, the code exits with a help message and an error level of 2. The reason the script uses an error level of 2 is that this is the same kind of error as providing a single input that isn't the /? command line switch.

Creating a CSV File

Sometimes it's important to see the same example using two different techniques. The example in this section performs the same task as the batch file example in the "Using a Centralized Data Store" section of the chapter. When you compare the code in Listing 11.7 with the code in 11.5, you'll notice that Listing 11.7 is significantly longer, even though it produces the same output. In addition, the code in Listing 11.7 is significantly more complex. However, if you perform just these two comparisons, you'll miss some of the reasons to use scripts. Mostly notably, the script version demonstrates the flexibility that this form of coding can provide. For example, you have more control over the files. The input files are read only, which means that the code can't damage them, even accidentally. Consequently, the files are safer than when you use a batch file to manipulate them. Listing 11.7 shows the script version of the CSV output example.

LISTING 11.7: Creating CSV Output Using a Script

```
// Create a File System Object to work with files.
var FSO = WScript.CreateObject("Scripting.FileSystemObject");

// Determine whether the Output2.CSV file exists and delete it.
if (FSO.FileExists("Output2.CSV"))
   FSO.DeleteFile("Output2.CSV", false);

// Create a WshShell object to obtain environment variables.
var Shell = WScript.CreateObject("WScript.Shell");

// Create variables to hold the static data.
var CompName = Shell.ExpandEnvironmentStrings("%COMPUTERNAME%");
var UserName = Shell.ExpandEnvironmentStrings("%USERNAME%");
var DateTime = new Date();

// Obtain the list of file specifications.
WScript.Echo("Locating temporary files to delete.");
var DirSpec = FSO.OpenTextFile("DelFiles.TXT", 1);

// Process each entry in the file.
while (!DirSpec.AtEndOfStream)
{
   // Get a single file specification.
   var ThisSpec = DirSpec.ReadLine();

   // Process the directory specification.
   WScript.Echo("Adding database values for " + ThisSpec);
   Shell.Run(
      "Cmd /C Dir " + ThisSpec + " /B /S > TmpDirFiles.TXT", 0, true);

   // Open the file containing the individual file entries.
   var Files = FSO.OpenTextFile("TmpDirFiles.TXT", 1);

   // Open the CSV file to accept the file entries.
   var Output = FSO.OpenTextFile("Output2.CSV", 8, true);

   // Process each of the file entries in turn.
   while (!Files.AtEndOfStream)
   {
      // Get an individual file entry.
      var File = Files.ReadLine();

      // Create the CSV file entry. Begin with the computer name and
      // the user name.
      Output.Write("\"");
      Output.Write(CompName);
      Output.Write("\",\"");
```

```
        Output.Write(UserName);
        Output.Write("\",\"");

        // Processing the date requires a little additional work. You
        // must extract the individual elements and put them together as
        // desired. Begin by converting the day number to a day string.
        var DayNum = DateTime.getDay();
        switch (DayNum)
        {
           case 0:
              Output.Write("Sun ");
              break;
           case 1:
              Output.Write("Mon ");
              break;
           case 2:
              Output.Write("Tue ");
              break;
           case 3:
              Output.Write("Wed ");
              break;
           case 4:
              Output.Write("Thu ");
              break;
           case 5:
              Output.Write("Fri ");
              break;
           case 6:
              Output.Write("Sat ");
              break;
        }

        Output.Write(DateTime.getMonth() + 1);
        Output.Write("/" + DateTime.getDate() +
                     "/" + DateTime.getFullYear());
        Output.Write("\",\"");

        // Extract the time from DateTime.
        Output.Write(DateTime.getHours() + ":" +
                     DateTime.getMinutes() + ":" +
                     DateTime.getSeconds());
        Output.Write("\",\"");

        // Finally, add the filename to the output.
        Output.Write(File);
        Output.WriteLine("\"");
    }

    // Close the working files.
```

```
        Files.Close();
        Output.Close();
    }

    // Close the file containing the file specifications.
    DirSpec.Close();
```

The code begins by removing any existing output file. JavaScript and VBScript lack file support. However, you have access to the `Scripting.FileSystemObject` object, which does provide full file system support. You can use this object to perform a multitude of tasks with files, including creating, deleting, and editing them. The `FileSystemObject` also includes functionality for working with folders.

The next step is to retrieve the username, computer name, date, and time. In many cases, you can simply use the `ExpandEnvironmentStrings()` method to obtain the information you need from the system. Notice that the example code uses the `Date` object in place of obtaining the date from the environment variables using the `Shell.ExpandEnvironmentStrings("%DATE%")` method. When working with JavaScript, you can only access the environment variables that you can see with the `Set` command. JavaScript doesn't support the extended functionality that's available at the command line. In fact, you'll find that this general rule applies to both VBScript and JavaScript; neither scripting language supports the extensions that you can access from a batch file at the command prompt. The `Date` object also provides time support, so you don't need a separate `Time` variable.

At this point, it's time to begin collecting a list of temporary files on the system. This example, like its batch file counter, relies on an external file to hold the file specifications. The code opens the file and begins processing it one line at a time. The use of a constant value of 1 for the `FSO.OpenTextFile()` method opens the file in read-only mode. The code processes the file one line at a time (one file specification at a time) using the `DirSpec.ReadLine()` method. You can read one character at a time using the `DirSpec.Read()` method instead.

This example points out a very special feature of the scripting languages. Notice the use of the `Shell.Run()` method. You can use this method to run any application. To use this feature at the command prompt, you have to begin by creating a command processor using the Cmd utility as shown. In this case, the code runs the `Dir` command with the file specification obtained from `DelFiles.TXT`. This line of code begs the question of why the code doesn't use the `FileSystemObject`. In this particular case, you can perform the task faster and without any loss of functionally by using the `Dir` command. The point is that you don't always have to use a scripting object; sometimes a command line tool works just as well or even better.

The code now has two files to work with. The first is an input file, `TmpDirFiles.TXT`, which contains the list of temporary files. The second is an output file, `Output2.CSV`, which contains the database of file entries. The `FSO.OpenTextFile()` constant of 8 opens the file in append (read/write) mode. If the file doesn't exist, the code raises an error unless you also set the third argument to `true`, which tells the method to create the file when it doesn't exist.

Now all the code needs to do is process the data and output it. The user and computer names are straightforward. Processing the date requires the most code because the code has to put the date string together. The downside of all this code is that it makes the example harder to read than the batch file. The plus side is that you can create a date string in any format required, even nonstandard formats.

As a final note on this example, make sure you close files when you finish working with them. Otherwise, the script will raise an error when you try to open the file again. In some cases, the file could remain open until you reboot the system, making it inaccessible to everyone.

Remote System Management

In many cases, you'll need to create remote connections before you can perform some types of maintenance tasks. Many of the utilities described in this book provide a method for creating a remote connection, but not necessarily a connection where you can manipulate objects as well as run utilities. In addition, some utilities don't provide a remote connection feature. Even though the Remote Desktop does open the potential for a security breach, you can generally keep security under control by ensuring you create a security connection. The following sections describe utilities you can use to perform remote system management.

Creating Remote Connections with the MSTSC Utility

The Microsoft Terminal Server Connection (MSTSC) utility provides remote connectivity using the Remote Desktop feature introduced in Windows XP. The utility relies on a Remote Desktop Connection (RDP) file to create the connection in most cases. You must have administrator privileges to use this utility. This utility uses the following syntax:

```
mstsc.exe {ConnectionFile | /v:server} [/console] [/f] [/w:width /h:height] [/
public] [/span]
mstsc.exe /edit"ConnectionFile"
mstsc.exe /migrate
```

The following list describes each of the command line arguments.

ConnectionFile Specifies the RDP file you want to use to create the connection.

/v:*server* Specifies the name of a remote computer. You can use this feature in place of an RDP file when you don't have an RDP defined.

/console Connects to the console session of the specified Windows 2000 server.

/f Starts the Remote Desktop session in full-screen mode. Using this feature overcomes issues that you might encounter displaying the remote computer's desktop in a window.

/w:*width* Specifies the width of the Remote Desktop window.

/h:*height* Specifies the height of the Remote Desktop window.

/edit Opens the specified RDP file for editing.

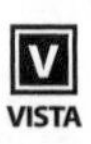

/migrate Migrates older connection files that you created with the Client Connection Manager in older versions of Windows to the new RDP file format.

/public Runs the session in public mode. When a session runs in public mode, Terminal Server doesn't save any of the private user data. For example, it won't save the user's registry settings. In addition, Terminal Server won't make use of any private user data within the session. Consequently, you might find that some application settings are missing.

/span Matches the local and remote computer screen sizes and spans multiple computer screens when required to perform the match. When working with spanned computer screens, the screens must all have the same height and you must align them vertically. Microsoft places a maximum resolution restriction of 4,096 × 2,048 pixels on this mode.

Real World Scenario

USING REMOTE DESKTOP TO BEST ADVANTAGE

Don't assume that the MSTSC utility and Remote Desktop as a whole are simple ways to create a connection. Yes, you can create a connection and even make it secure, but the Microsoft documentation for the graphical portion of this utility leaves a lot to the imagination. Fortunately, a third party has stepped in to make it easier to create useful connections with MSTSC. You can find the first of the graphical interface articles on the PETRI.co.il site at `http://www.petri.co.il/add_a_new_rdp_listening_port_to_terminal_server.htm`. The related articles section at the bottom of the Web page leads you to a wealth of additional information, including download instructions for RDP Version 5.2.

In general, this is a client-to-server connection. The only problem is that Windows 2000 Server doesn't know about Remote Desktop, so it might appear at first that MSTSC is useless. Fortunately, you can add an RDP listening port, which makes the Windows 2000 Server completely accessible. It's tips like this that the PETRI.co.il Web site excels in providing.

Performing Remote Windows Management with the WinRM Utility

VISTA

The Windows Remote Management (WinRM) utility helps you manage a remote system from the command line. This utility is Microsoft's implementation of the WS-Management protocol, which provides a secure method of connecting local and remote computers using a Web service. You can learn more about the WS-Management protocol at `http://msdn2.microsoft.com/en-us/library/aa384470.aspx`. This utility uses the following general syntax:

```
winrm OPERATION RESOURCE_URI [-SWITCH:VALUE [-SWITCH:VALUE] ...]
   [@{KEY=VALUE[;KEY=VALUE]...}]
```

The WinRM utility provides access to a number of operations (or commands) that combine with a resource Uniform Resource Identifier (URI) to perform tasks on the remote machine. The command line syntax for each of the operations is as follows:

```
winrm g[et] RESOURCE_URI [-SWITCH:VALUE [-SWITCH:VALUE] ...]
set RESOURCE_URI [-SWITCH:VALUE [-SWITCH:VALUE] ...]
   [@{KEY="VALUE"[;KEY="VALUE"]}] [-file:VALUE]
winrm c[reate] RESOURCE_URI [-SWITCH:VALUE [-SWITCH:VALUE] ...]
   [@{KEY="VALUE"[;KEY="VALUE"]}] [-file:VALUE]
winrm d[elete] RESOURCE_URI [-SWITCH:VALUE [-SWITCH:VALUE] ...]
winrm e[numerate] RESOURCE_URI [-ReturnType:Value] [-Shallow]
   [-BasePropertiesOnly] [-SWITCH:VALUE [-SWITCH:VALUE] ...]
winrm i[nvoke] ACTION RESOURCE_URI [-SWITCH:VALUE [-SWITCH:VALUE] ...]
   [@{KEY="VALUE"[;KEY="VALUE"]}] [-file:VALUE]
winrm id[entify]  [-SWITCH:VALUE [-SWITCH:VALUE] ...]
winrm quickconfig [-quiet] [-transport:VALUE]
```

The following list describes each of the command line arguments.

g[et] Obtains management information.

s[et] Modifies the management information. You can also specify this operation as `put`.

c[reate] Defines new instances of management resources.

d[elete] Removes an instance of a management resource.

e[numerate] Lists the instances of the specified management resource.

i[nvoke] Executes a method on a management resource.

id[entify] Determines whether WinRM or another compatible WS-Management implementation is running on a remote machine.

quickconfig Configures the local machine to accept WS-Management requests from other machines.

RESOURCE_URI Specifies the URI of the management resource. For example, if you want to obtain the current WS-Management configuration, you would query the `winrm/config` URI. You could access the Spooler service using the `wmicimv2/Win32_Service?Name=spooler` URI. WinRM supports a number of common URIs that you can discover by typing **winrm help uris** and pressing Enter.

-*SWITCH*:*VALUE* Specifies a switch and value pair that modifies the performance of the specified operation. The common switches appear later in this section of the chapter. Type **winrm help switches** and press Enter to obtain the complete list of switches.

@{*KEY*="*VALUE*"[;*KEY*="*VALUE*"]} Defines an argument and its associated value. The argument can control the operation of the management resource or configure the management resource in some way. For example, typing **winrm set winrm/config @{MaxEnvelopeSizekb="100"}** would change the maximum envelope size for the local copy of WinRM. The key and value pair must appear within curly braces ({}) and be preceded by an at (@) sign. You can incorporate multiple settings in one request by separating them with a semicolon (;).

-file:*VALUE* Specifies the name of a file containing key and value pairs. See the `@{KEY="VALUE"[;KEY="VALUE"]}` entry for details. The file simply makes it easier to provide the data at the command line.

-ReturnType:{Object | EPR | ObjectAndEPR} Determines the return type of the data. The `Object` return type provides a listing of the object. The `End Point Reference (EPR)` return type provides information about the resource URI and selectors for the specified instance. The `ObjectAndEPR` type returns both an object listing and the EPR data.

-Shallow Enumerates only the instances of the base class as specified by the resource URI. Otherwise, the utility returns both the base class and derived classes.

-BasePropertiesOnly Enumerates only those properties associated with the base class specified by the resource URI. The utility ignores this command line argument when you specify the `-Shallow` command line argument.

ACTION Executes the particular method (action) on the object specified by the resource URI. You specify any method arguments using key/value pairs.

-quiet Performs the configuration without prompting for confirmation. This switch is useful when you want to configure WinRM in the background.

-transport:*VALUE* Performs a quick configuration of the specified transport. The utility currently supports HTTP and HTTPS as transports. The utility defaults to using HTTP as the transport.

Most of the operations will accept a number of switches that help define how the operation performs its tasks. The following list describes the common switches.

`-timeout:`*`MS`* Defines the timeout in milliseconds for the successful completion of a command (otherwise, the system keeps retrying the command without limit). This switch limits the duration of a particular operation.

`-skipCAcheck` Specifies that the certificate issuer need not be a trusted root authority when working with a remote system using HTTPS. Use this switch when accessing a system that has a self-issued certificate, such as a server on your LAN or a machine attached to your WAN. Never use this switch when working with a system that you don't trust.

`-skipCNcheck` Specifies that the certificate common name (CN) of the server need not match the hostname of the server. Using this switch is a significant security risk, even for local servers. Generally, it's better to self-issue a certificate with all of the correct information in place.

`-dialect:`*`VALUE`* Determines the dialect of the filter expression for enumeration or fragment. For example, if you want to use a Windows Management Instrumentation (WMI) Query Language (WQL) formatted filter, then you would specify `-dialect:http://schemas.microsoft.com/wbem/wsman/1/WQL`. Likewise, if you want to use an XML Path (XPath) Language query, you would specify `-dialect:http://www.w3.org/TR/1999/REC-xpath-19991116`. The default filtering relies on WQL as described for the `-filter` command line switch.

`-filter:`*`VALUE`* Defines a filter used to limit the amount of data returned by a query. The filter looks very much like a SQL statement, but relies on the filtering dialect you choose. The default filtering dialect is WQL, where you choose objects based on WMI. For example, if you wanted to locate the BITS service on a system, you would type **`winrm enum wmicimv2/* -filter:"select * from win32_service where Name=\"BITS\" "`**. Figure 11.5 shows the results of issuing this command.

FIGURE 11.5
Filtering is an important part of using the WinRM utility because it lets you limit the output.

```
Administrator: Command Prompt

C:\Windows\system32>winrm enum wmicimv2/* -filter:"select * from win32_service w
here Name=\"BITS\" "
Win32_Service
    AcceptPause = false
    AcceptStop = true
    Caption = Background Intelligent Transfer Service
    CheckPoint = 0
    CreationClassName = Win32_Service
    Description = Transfers files in the background using idle network bandwidth
. If the service is disabled, then any applications that depend on BITS, such as
 Windows Update or MSN Explorer, will be unable to automatically download progra
ms and other information.
    DesktopInteract = false
    DisplayName = Background Intelligent Transfer Service
    ErrorControl = Normal
    ExitCode = 0
    InstallDate = null
    Name = BITS
    PathName = C:\Windows\System32\svchost.exe -k netsvcs
    ProcessId = 1028
    ServiceSpecificExitCode = 0
    ServiceType = Share Process
    Started = true
    StartMode = Auto
```

`-fragment:`*`VALUE`* Defines the section within the instance XML that you want to update or retrieve for a given operation. WinRM requires that you supply the name of the object and the fragment particulars as an object method. For example, to retrieve the description of the BITS service, you would type **`winrm get wmicimv2/Win32_Service?name=BITS -fragment:Description/text()`**.

`-options:{`*`KEY`*`="`*`VALUE`*`"[;`*`KEY`*`="`*`VALUE`*`"]}` Defines arguments used for provider-specific needs. You must consult the documentation for your provider to use this switch. If you need to provide a null value, use `$null` as the input.

-SPNPort Specifies a port number to append to the Service Principal Name (SPN) of the remote service. The utility uses the SPN for authentication purposes when using Negotiate or Kerberos authentication.

-encoding:{utf-8 | utf-16} Defines the encoding used to transmit data to and from the remote system. The default option is `utf-16`.

-f[ormat]:{xml | pretty | text} Specifies the output format of the data. The default setting is `text`, which is the human readable form shown in Figure 11.5. The `xml` setting outputs pure XML without any white space. Using the `pretty` setting outputs XML with white space to make the data more readable.

Accessing a System with the WinRS Utility

The Windows Remote Shell (WinRS) utility helps you execute commands on a remote system. This utility doesn't support interaction, which means that the command you supply has to provide all required information. The console displays the results of any command you execute. This utility uses the following syntax:

```
winrs [-r[emote]:ENDPOINT] [-un[encrypted]] [-u[sername]:USERNAME
   -p[assword]:PASSWORD] [-t[imeout]:SECONDS] [-d[irectory]:PATH]
   [-env[ironment]:STRING=VALUE] [-noe[cho]] [-nop[rofile]] COMMAND
```

The following list describes each of the command line arguments.

-r[emote]:*ENDPOINT* Specifies the endpoint (the target of the command) using either an URL or a NetBIOS name. The default setting uses LOCALHOST for all commands.

-un[encrypted] Specifies that the utility won't encrypt messages to the remote system. This feature is helpful for diagnosing problems with the setup. However, it also represents a security problem because all communication takes place as cleartext. The default setting encrypts all data using NTLM or Kerberos keys.

-u[sername]:*USERNAME* Provides the username to the remote system. If you don't supply this command line switch, the remote system will prompt you for a username and password. You must use this command line switch with the `-password` command line switch.

-p[assword]:*PASSWORD* Provides the user's password to the remote system. If you don't supply this command line switch, the remote system will prompt you for a username and password. You must use this command line switch with the `-username` command line switch.

-t[imeout]:*SECONDS* Determines the maximum time that the command will execute in seconds. This command line switch acts as a safety feature when working with a remote system that may not respond. The default setting doesn't place any limit on the time the command can execute.

-d[irectory]:*PATH* Specifies the starting location for the command. If you don't specify this command line switch, the command will begin execution in the location specified by the %USERPROFILE% environment variable.

-env[ironment]:*KEY=VALUE* Defines an environment variable to use when executing the command. You must supply the environment variables as key/value pairs. Each command line switch can only specify one environment variable, so you must use multiple instances of this command line switch to provide multiple environment variables to the remote system.

-noe[cho] Sets echo off. Using this command line switch ensures that user answers to remote prompts don't appear on the local system. The default setting leaves echo on so the user can see any input provided.

-nop[rofile] Forces the remote system to execute the command without loading the user's profile on that system. You must use this command line switch when the user issuing the command isn't a local administrator on that system. Otherwise, the command will fail even if it would normally succeed.

COMMAND Specifies any command that you want to execute on the remote system. The command must appear as it would at the local command prompt. You may use any command that the remote system can execute at the command prompt.

TIP If you find that the remote command has stalled and you need to terminate it, press Ctrl+C or Ctrl+Break. As with the local system, pressing these key combinations will terminate the command.

Providing Fault Tolerance for an After Hours Batch or Script

Chapter 10 discussed the mechanics of using Task Scheduler effectively. In most cases, you'll find that Task Scheduler is as reliable as the commands that you automate with it. In other words, Task Scheduler will start the command on time as long as no outside influence prevents it and you consider any local requirements (such as setting the computer clock correctly). However, starting the application is the least of your worries.

After hours processing means that you're letting the computer work independently. Even though the computer is following your instructions (to the letter mind you), you aren't there to monitor it. This chapter discusses a number of techniques you can use to reduce risk, but not eliminate it. Assuming that Task Scheduler starts the task on time and with all of the required information, you still have to consider failure of the application itself. When all or part of an after hours processing task fails, you have four choices:

- Let the task fail gracefully and fix it when you arrive the next morning.
- Create a batch file or script loop that automatically restarts the processing after a failure.
- Add a Task Scheduler task to check for a failure condition and attempt to execute the application again when Task Scheduler detects an error.
- Provide administrator notification so that the administrator can restart the application.

Each of these options has advantages. For example, letting the task fail gracefully means that the system will be in a known state the next morning and you can try to discover what error occurred. Unfortunately, letting the task fail gracefully is no longer an option for many enterprises where 24/7 operation is the standard and you must provide five 9's of reliability (in short, an average of 5 minutes of downtime during an average year). Including a loop in the batch file or script has the advantage of automatically restarting the task without bothering anyone. The application can attempt to succeed all night long. Unfortunately, you can still arrive at work the next morning to a nasty surprise and now you won't have that first failure to examine—the reason the application failed can remain a mystery. Having Task Scheduler check for the error is a great idea, but now you have to create a batch file or script to check for the error and act on it by starting the application. In addition, you have to schedule the task once for each attempt, which means added complexity in managing Task Scheduler. Of all the options, the one least likely to fail is alerting the administrator, but now you have to disrupt someone's evening and possibly get them out of bed to restart an application that would have run the second time using a simple batch file or script loop. In short, there aren't any perfect solutions, but you should decide on a policy for handling errors at the outset.

Make sure you also have policies in place for machines that perform after hours processing. Task Scheduler can't run if someone turns the machine off. Well-intentioned people can cause all kinds of problems for your system. Imagine what would happen if someone decided to work late on a report that requires the database and your batch file or script requires exclusive access to that database. As part of your strategy, you might want to broadcast a message across the network telling everyone about the outage. Make sure you include an automated broadcast message with Task Scheduler as well. You don't want to have to come into work just to send a message telling everyone that your automated software is about to begin its task.

Fault tolerance can consume a lot of ground. A reliable environment is one that doesn't change. For example, you might think that applying a patch to your software will make it more reliable because the vendor has fixed the problem. Like the human body, every networked system is different. Just as you can't guarantee that a new medication won't have disastrous side effects, you can't guarantee that a patch will do anything other than make your system stop working. Even though the hope is that things will go well and the application will run better than before, you don't know about side effects until you've thoroughly tested the new setup. Testing takes the guesswork out of the system, makes it stable, and therefore more reliable.

As a final consideration for making your after hours processing more robust and reliable, think about training several people to take over repairing the problem should you become unavailable. In many cases, protectionist policies by those with knowledge (making them theoretically indispensable) also serve to make the system completely unreliable. A reliable system requires redundancies in every area, including the humans who run the system. Cross-training other people to perform the tasks that you perform actually makes the system more reliable. In addition, if you really want to have some evenings at home, rather than babysit a sick system, having a backup is required. Generally, you want to consider every possible contingency before you start up that automated system the first time. Expecting it to work without help isn't going to be effective; remember that Murphy fellow who seems obliged to make our lives interesting in the worst possible way.

Real World Scenario

THINK ABOUT THE SMALL STUFF

I use checklists for everything. In fact, the book you're reading now relied on many checklists to ensure I didn't miss any details (at least not purposely). Checklists aren't perfect, but by documenting the process you use to accomplish a task, you can reduce errors and fix any procedural errors as you continue to work with the checklist. In many cases, checklists also help you avoid common, silly errors. The type of error where you wonder what you were thinking about later. Often, these errors occur when you're in a rush, such as at the end of the day when you're setting up the after hours processing for the night.

Someone once complained that the automation they'd set up didn't work. After going through all of the usual problems, I thought to ask about the computer clock. The user checked the clock and found it was set incorrectly; problem solved. However, small errors are often the cause of problems with after hours automation. Creating and using a checklist can mean the difference between sleeping well at night knowing your computer is working hard for you and coming in the next morning to a nasty surprise.

Getting Started with Command Line Tasks

This chapter has shown you how to use after hours scripting safely. As you know by now, after hours scripting is a powerful tool; one that's easy to abuse. Any time you abuse a tool, you can expect to get hurt and after hours scripting can cause considerable administrative pain. That said, after hours scripting can also save you considerable time, improve the reliability of updates, and reduce the risk of failed maintenance actions. In addition, it's the only way to run some kinds of after hour tasks simply because you need exclusive system access to perform them.

The key to this chapter is planning. First, you must get rid of the notion that just any activity runs well unattended. You should only plan to run tasks that work reliably in unattended mode. In fact, make a company policy regarding after hours scripting. Make three columns—those activities that never run unattended, those that can run unattended, and those that must run after hours (monitoring is always appreciated, so never insist that after hours tasks run unattended). Second, once you do decide on which tasks to perform after hours, plan for them to fail. Look at all of the failure modes for every task that can fail and create a plan for handling them. Even if a task supposedly can't fail, make a contingency for when it does, because it most certainly will at some point.

Chapter 12 begins a new section of the book. This chapter, and the three that follow, discuss various kinds of utilities. All three of these chapters focus on utilities that are either free or shareware (try before you buy) because most companies today are looking for a deal. They need software that works well and doesn't cost a lot. The chapters also mention some industrial strength utilities that you'll have to pay for at the outset, but may provide additional functionality you need. The focus of the utilities in Chapter 12 is enhancing your experience at the command prompt.

Part 3

Relying on Third Party Automation

In This Section:

Chapter 12

Obtaining Command Prompt Enhancers

- Using XVI32 to View Files in Depth
- Moving Data with Send To Toys
- Checking File Integrity Using FCIV
- Getting the Better XCopy with XXCopy
- Working with Shell Extensions Using ShellExView
- Examining Processes Using Process Explorer

You might have noticed by now that Microsoft has packed Windows with tools that you can use at the command prompt. In fact, until you begin working with these tools, you might feel that they answer every possible need. However, after working at the command prompt for a while, you might find yourself wishing for a few additional tools or perhaps some additional features for existing tools. For example, many people feel that the XCopy utility works fine, but they'd like it to have some additional flexibility so they could use it as a quick backup application. This chapter contains descriptions of some of the third party tools that you can use to answer these needs. These command prompt enhancers provide you with the added functionality you need to perform some advanced tasks.

Using XVI32 to View Files in Depth

You won't work at the command line for very long before you discover a need to look inside files. For example, you might need to check a file to determine whether it really is a graphic image or an executable in disguise. You need to perform this check without executing the file and viewing the image with a graphics application might not tell you want you want to know. What you really need is a program that works along the same lines as the Debug utility described in the "Examining, Modifying, and Debugging Files with the Debug Utility" section of Chapter 6, but with a better interface. The XVI32 utility lets you look inside files and it also provides a great deal of functionality in a graphical package. Figure 12.1 shows a typical view of the XVI32 utility. In this case, the application is showing the content of the `_Default.pi_` file.

Real World Scenario

WORKING WITH FILE EXTENSIONS

Windows attempts to hide file extensions and simply show you an icon to identify files. In fact, the lack of file extensions has prompted some industry leaders to warn of viruses and other problems that users encounter when they maintain the Microsoft default of hiding file extensions. Some people use this feature to make one file look like another and you could end up opening an executable instead of the text file that you thought you were opening. Nevertheless, the command line has no lack of file extensions. People who haven't worked at the command line before are suddenly shocked by the number of file extensions they see. The fact that the command prompt lacks any form of familiar icon makes things worse because you don't have any visual aid in determining the purpose or function of a particular file extension. You could inadvertently trash your system by deleting the wrong file or by running another.

The FILExt Web site at `http://filext.com/` can help you overcome the problem of figuring out what task a file performs based on its file extension. This Web site contains descriptions of thousands of file extensions. In fact, you might be surprised at the amount of information this Web site provides. For example, you can discover the Multipurpose Internet Mail Extensions (MIME) type of the file, so you know how applications such as your browser and email reader view it. You can also find identifying information for the file, such as the fact that executable files have the letters MZ as the first two characters within the file. Even if someone gives the file another name, you can use these letters as a potential means of finding the executable.

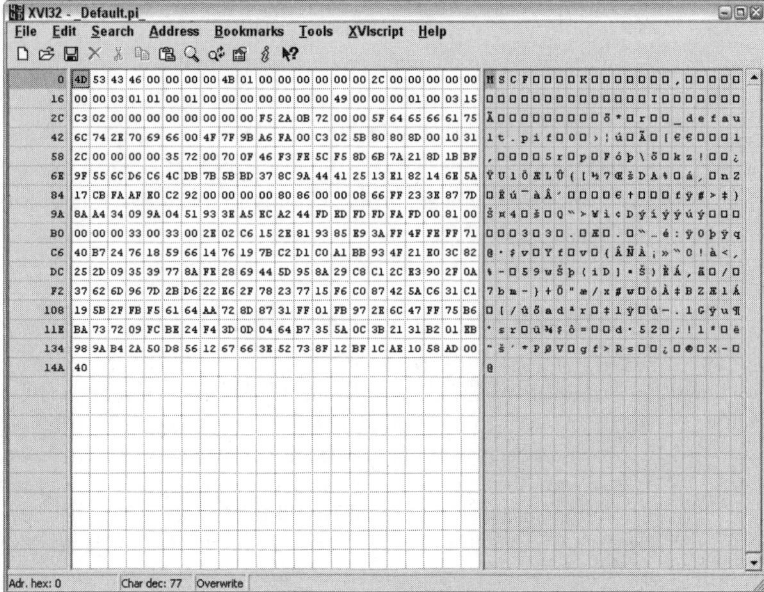

FIGURE 12.1
Use the XVI32 utility to look inside files on your machine without executing their content.

Because Microsoft compressed the file shown in Figure 12.1 as a CAB file, the file begins with the letters MSCF for Microsoft Compressed File. You can see the hexadecimal numbers in the left pane and the associated characters in the right pane. Look at the third row down and you'll see the preserved name (`_default.pif`) of this file in the right pane near the left side and continuing down to the fourth line. If you changed the filename entry, the expanded file would have a different name, whatever you typed. Of course, you have a limit of using the same amount of space as the original filename unless you want to get into some complex editing.

The same file compressed with a utility such as WinZIP begins with the letters PK. The WinZIP file would also include a catalog of filenames. The internals of most files contain information that lets you know more about how the system views the file. You can use this information to detect tampering and to see when a file has a different file extension than it really should. Some people have used applications such as this one to look for additional information inside files. For example, developers often leave interesting comments inside files that you can only see using a utility such as XVI32.

NOTE If you like XVI32, you should check the author's other freeware tools at `http://www.chmaas.handshake.de/delphi/freeware/freeware.htm`. You may find tools such as Name to Clipboard and BatMaker are exactly what you need to make your command line experience better.

The XVI32 utility is freeware, so all you need to do is download it from `http://www.chmaas.handshake.de/delphi/freeware/xvi32/xvi32.htm` and start using it. You don't have to install this program, simply unpack it into a directory on your machine. According to the utility's author, even developers at Microsoft use this utility. Even if they didn't, XVI32 has a lot to offer. You can search a file using a string or a hexadecimal number. The utility will count the number of times that a particular string or number appears in the file. You can even perform a global search and replace. The XVI32 utility comes with its own scripting language so that you can automate tasks as needed. The tools let you perform tasks such as encode or decode numbers, change the character conversion table (so the right pane meets specific conversion needs), and even calculate the Cyclic Redundancy Code (CRC) of a file so you can easily detect changes in it.

Real World Scenario

CREATING A SEND TO CONTEXT MENU ENTRY FOR ANY APPLICATION

Many administrators know the secret of using the Send To menu to their advantage. For example, one administrator told me that she uses the Send To menu for a number of tasks. In one case, she has two shortcuts to send a database used with their company's macros to both the network and a satellite office any time she updates it. The system downloads the macros to the user's PC using the login script so they always have an updated copy of the macros. This administrator goes on to say that she has several other Send To menu items that she uses to copy files to servers in both offices. In short, the Send To context menu can provide a considerable time savings.

Like many utilities, the XVI32 utility is handiest when you make it available as part of the Send To context menu that appears when you right-click a file in Windows Explorer. To make XVI32 available from this menu, locate your personal Send To folder at `\Documents and Settings\<User Name>\ SendTo`. Right-click any blank area within this folder and choose New ➤ Shortcut from this menu. Follow the steps in the Create Shortcut wizard to create a shortcut to the `XVI32.EXE` file. (Since the XVI32 utility doesn't have an installation program, you'll find the executable wherever you decompressed the archive; other applications normally appear in your `\Program Files` folder under the application or vendor name.) Adding the shortcut will add the XVI32 entry to the Send To context menu. Right-clicking any file and choosing the XVI32 entry automatically sends that file to XVI32 for display.

One of the most impressive features of XVI32 is that it doesn't choke on huge files. You can open files of significant length without worrying about data corruption or an error message. In fact, the author tells you that XVI32 can easily support a 60 MB file and offers a freeware random file generator for the purpose named `RndFileC.EXE`. Most people never need to open such a huge file, but it's nice to know that the functionality is available when you need it.

VISTA AND THIRD PARTY UTILITIES

Vista hinders use of some third party utilities. For example, when working with XVI32, you'll find that the utility can't write to its INI (initialization) file, so you'll see an error message when you close the program. In this case, you can overcome the problem by giving yourself permission to access the XVI32 folder. The settings that XVI32 is saving are global to everyone using the utility, so it's appropriate to store the INI file in the application folder. The problem is the level of security that Vista provides. Look for security issues whenever you run into a problem with a utility in Vista—a lack of permission to do something. I personally didn't run into any utilities that outright refused to work, but some of them did present some interesting issues.

Moving Data with Send To Toys

Many people are completely unaware of the functionality provided by the Send To context menu on their machine. Once people become aware of this feature, they quickly become addicted and never want to return to manually moving data to applications. In fact, with a proper setup on the Send To context menu, you can almost throw away the File ➤ Open command on many applications. The "Creating a Send To Context Menu Entry for Any Application" sidebar in this chapter tells you how to add any application to the Send To context menu. Unfortunately, this technique only works for applications. If you want to send a file to the Clipboard, for example, you're simply out of luck. The Send To Toys 2.4 utility overcomes this particular problem. You can download this utility at `http://fileforum.betanews.com/detail/Send_To_Toys/1011999707/1`. The current version performs these and other tasks as described in the following list.

- Output data to a Control Panel applet.
- Remove a file by sending it to the Recycle Bin.
- Send any shortcut or application to the Quick Launch area of the Taskbar. The Quick Launch area lets you execute your most common applications quickly. However, you could also place a batch file or script in the Quick Launch area to work at the command line more effectively.
- Send any file to the clipboard so that you can use its content directly. You can also save the data using a specific name so that you can include multiple entries on the Clipboard (you'll need to use the Clipboard Viewer to see them). In addition, you can send the output of any command to the Clipboard instead of seeing the result on screen.
- Send a file to the `\Windows\System32` folder. For a command prompt user, this feature means that you can create a file anywhere, and then move it to the system folder for execution with any of the command line utilities described in the book.
- Output the filename to the command prompt. This option lets you copy a file from its current location to the command prompt where you're working. You can additionally force the

use of `COMMAND.COM` (the old DOS command interpreter) in place of `CMD.EXE`. This feature is possibly the most helpful for people who work at the command prompt regularly because you no longer have to move things manually.

To give you an idea of how many options this utility adds to your Send To menu, look at Figure 12.2. The figure on the left shows my original Send To menu setup. Notice that it already includes a number of application entries, along with the standard Windows entries and a few entries added by third party products such as WinZIP. The menu on the right shows the updated context menu with the Send To Toys features added.

TIP The FileForum Web site has a wealth of utilities you can download to perform specific tasks. FileForm is one of the Web sites that you might have to search using Google (see the "Finding the Third Party Utilities That You Want" Real World Scenario in this chapter for details) because it offers so many great utilities. If you only want to view the utilities available for tweaking your system, check out the URL at `http://fileforum.betanews.com/browse/SystemUtilities/Tweaking`.

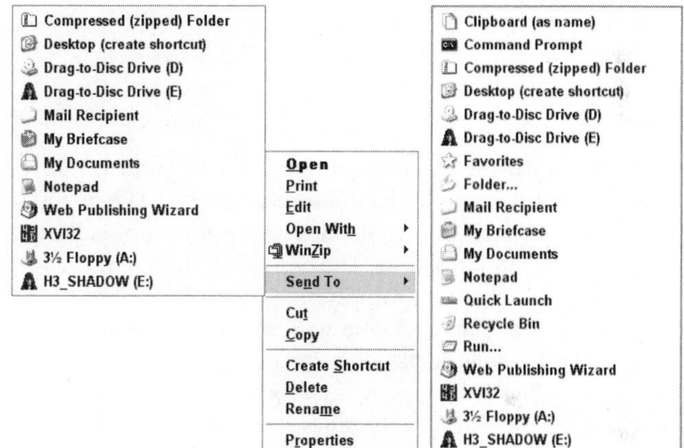

FIGURE 12.2
The main reason to use Send To Toys is to obtain new Send To context menu entries.

The feature that many people like best about this product is that you can use it to configure the Send To menu. Simply select the Send To Toys applet in the Control Panel and you'll see the Send To Toys dialog box shown in Figure 12.3. The Send To tab lets you add and remove items from the Send To menu without using the technique described in the "Creating a Send To Context Menu Entry for Any Application" sidebar. The Folders tab tells how to treat files when you move them. It defines where the file is moved and how the system reacts to the move (such as opening the folder where the file resides). The Clipboard Settings tab defines how the utility interacts with the Clipboard. For example, you can decide whether to place the entire file path on the Clipboard, or just the filename. You can also decide how to wrap filenames that contain spaces (or whether to wrap them at all). The default setting relies on quotes, but you can use any character desired.

Checking File Integrity Using FCIV

Most network administrators are deeply concerned about the damage caused by crackers, viruses, adware, spyware, and errant applications. In fact, the errant application causes considerably more damage than most administrators know or will admit to when asked. The important issue is to realize that damage does take place and have some method for detecting it. The File Checksum Integrity Verifier (FCIV) from Microsoft creates a cryptographic hash (essentially a fingerprint) for the files you specify. Use the utility as soon as you install the system or perform an update to create a set of fingerprints for every system file. When you suspect that something has changed outside your direct purview, you can run the utility again and compare the output to look for changes. You can obtain this tool from the Microsoft Knowledge Base at `http://support.microsoft.com/kb/841290/`.

FIGURE 12.3
You can also use the Send To Toys utility to configure the Send To context menu with greater ease.

Besides using this utility to track the fingerprints of your files for your own use, you can use it create a cryptographic hash for other people. When you send someone a file through email, they have no idea whether someone else has intercepted the message and changed the file. Perhaps this third party added a virus. The person receiving the file won't know who added the virus to the file, but they'll blame you. Supplying a hash value for each file as part of your upload assures the recipient that they can check and validate the attachment.

Other utilities do provide a form of file integrity. However, the majority of these utilities rely on a CRC, which is an insecure method of determining file validity because CRC doesn't always detect changes. The FCIV utility relies on the Message Digest 5 (MD5) or Secure Hashing Algorithm 1 (SHA-1) hashing methods. Using either of these two methods is very secure because every file generates a different result. Consequently, if someone as much as changes the case of a letter inside the file, you know about it. This utility uses the following syntax:

```
FCIV  -add {file | dir [-r] [-type file ...] [-exc dir ...] [-wp] [-bp basepath]}
[{-md5 | -sha1 | -both}] [-xml db]
FCIV -list [{-md5 | -sha1 | -both}] -xml db
FCIV -v {file | dir} [-bp basepath] [{-md5 | -sha1 | -both}] [-xml db]
```

The following list describes each of the command line arguments.

`-add` Adds a new entry to a database. If you don't specify the `-xml` command line switch, the utility sends the output to the display. You can redirect this output to a text file for inclusion with an email message when desired.

`-list` Displays a list of the verification entries in a database. You must supply a database name using the `-xml` command line switch.

`-v` Verifies a file or directory against the content of a verification database. The verification process returns 0 for success or 1 for failure, so you can use this utility within a batch file or script to perform complex verification checks.

{*file* | *dir*} Specifies an individual file or directory to check. When working with a directory, you can specify additional options as defined in the following list.

-r Performs recursive checks of all subdirectories. This command line switch performs the same tasks as the /s command line switch provided with many other utilities.

-type *file*... Defines the type of file you want to include in the database. For example, if you specify **-type *.exe**, the utility only adds executable files to the database. You can include this command line switch multiple times. If you included **-type *.exe -type *.txt** on the command line, the utility would include both executable and text files.

-exc *file*... Specifies a file that contains a list of directories that you don't want to include as part of the database. Place one directory specification per line in the file. Add a blank line to the end of the list.

-wp Creates a database without including the path information. Normally, the utility includes the full path of every file.

-bp *basepath* Creates a database without including the base path information. For example, if the full path to a file is C:\MyFiles\Files1\Temp.TXT and you use **-bp C:\MyFiles** as the command line switch, the output displays Files1\Temp.TXT. This option is especially useful when the source and destination directories for a verification aren't the same.

{*-md5* | *-sha1* | *-both*} Specifies the hashing algorithm used for the file or directory. The default setting relies on the MD5 hashing algorithm. You can learn more about the MD5 hashing algorithm at http://www.ietf.org/rfc/rfc1321.txt and the SHA-1 algorithm at http://www.itl.nist.gov/fipspubs/fip180-1.htm. The -both command line switch generates one hash for each standard so that you end up with two hashes per file.

-xml *db* Defines the name of a file used to store the hashes for each file in XML format.

The output from this program is a table showing the hashes for each file in your specification. For example, if you specify that you want the hash of a particular directory and that you want to use both hashing methods, you might see output similar to that shown in Figure 12.4. The MD5 hash appears first, followed by the longer SHA-1 hash. The full path to each file appears last.

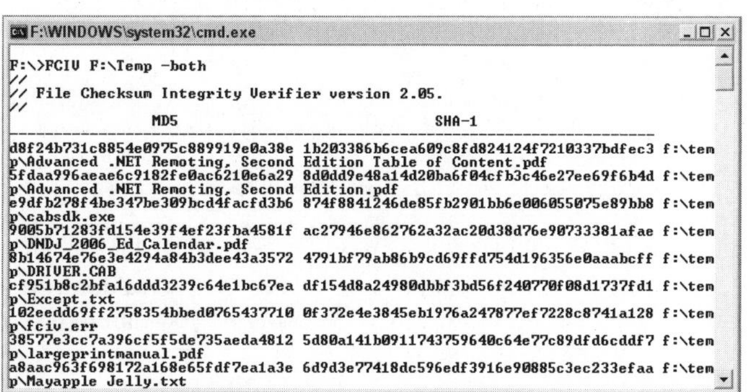

FIGURE 12.4
Even though it looks like gibberish, the hash values uniquely identify each file.

You can send the output from the utility to an XML file. The XML format is the only option that the utility offers for storing the hashes in an easily used form. It's possible to open the XML file in Internet Explorer to see how it looks. Figure 12.5 shows a typical example. Notice how each file appears as part of a <FILE_ENTRY> element. The name and hashes appear as child elements.

FINDING THE THIRD PARTY UTILITIES THAT YOU WANT

Believe me when I say that you won't ever test all of the command line–oriented third party utilities on the market. In fact, if you test even a fraction of them fully, you'll do well. Of course, this lack of testing time means that you have to find the utility you want sooner than later. Magazines often provide great reviews of shareware, but finding those reviews can be difficult. Many magazine search engines leave a lot to the imagination.

Fortunately, Google provides a great search engine. However, if you just enter search terms in Google, you're very unlikely to locate the utility you want. The selection of keywords and focusing the search is critical. Always place the most important words for your search first. For example, placing the word *shareware* first usually guarantees that you'll see the try-before-you-buy items first in Google. In addition, use special search terms as needed. I find the *site:* search term one of the most useful that Google provides. The *site: word,* followed by the site domain, such as *www.microsoft.com* (don't include the protocol in this case), performs a detailed search on Microsoft's Web site and ignores everything else. Using these techniques, you can search magazine Web sites for detailed reviews of the utilities you want.

When you perform a verification, the utility outputs a simple success message of, "All files verified successfully." However, when the verification fails, you'll see a list of entries that didn't match. You'll see a list of modified files that includes the original hash value and the new hash value. The hash values aren't actually important. What's important is that you can use them to detect changes in files.

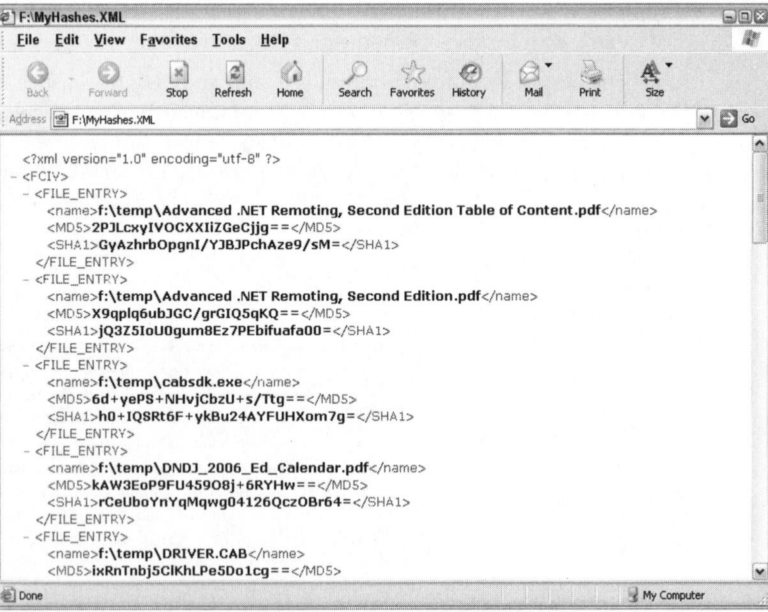

FIGURE 12.5
The FCIV offers only the XML data format to save the hashes for you.

Getting the Better XCopy with XXCopy

Magazines often provide valuable resources for the administrator who works at the command line by making you aware of certain problems. For example, the article titled, "Windows Tips: Safer Backups—The Long and Short of It," at `http://www.pcworld.com/howto/article/0,aid,41242,00.asp` makes you aware of a problem with using XCopy or XCopy32 for creating a backup of your system. The article goes on for several pages, but the short version is that these utilities sometimes don't make a perfect copy due to the way that Windows handles long filenames. Although XCopy usually works fine for moving an application from one location to another, you might not want to use it to back up all of that sensitive information on your hard drive. It's not that XCopy will damage the data, but it could damage the filenames.

In many cases, the article tells you about the problem and perhaps provides a quick fix or two, but doesn't go any further. What you end up with is a good understanding of the problem, but no real solutions. However, there are the bright spot articles that also provide a solution and this article is one of them. Along with the article, you can download the XXCopy utility from the PC World Web site at `http://www.pcworld.com/downloads/file_description/0,fid,7995,00.asp#`. If you want to work directly with the originator of the XXCopy utility, go to their Web site at `http://www.xxcopy.com/index.htm`. In fact, it's a good idea to go to the vendor Web site to obtain the most current version of this utility.

The XXCopy utility comes in a number of flavors. All of these flavors support the standard XCopy syntax described in the "Performing Bulk File Transfers with the XCopy Utility" section of Chapter 2. Consequently, any batch file or script that relies on XCopy can use XXCopy today. In addition to these standard command line switches, you have the option of using all of the XXCopy command line switches. The freeware version has 160 command line switches alone. The /? command line switch displays the most common XXCopy command line switches, but doesn't even begin to display them all. Go to the Web site at `http://www.xxcopy.com/xxcopy01.htm` to obtain a complete listing of the command line switches.

Individuals can obtain and use a freeware version of the standard XXCopy utility without paying anything. Of course, the vendor is hoping that individuals will see the value of XXCopy and want to purchase the XXCopy Pro version. Any commercial entity must purchase the XXCopy Pro version to have a valid license. You can obtain a trial version of this version at `http://www.xxcopy.com/index.htm#testdrive`.

Working with Shell Extensions Using ShellExView

Anyone who uses Windows has used a shell extension, but it's very likely that you don't know anything about it. A shell extension is a COM object that extends Windows in some way. For example, when you install WinZIP on a system, it installs several shell extensions. Clicking a ZIP file produces a new context menu that contains options for working with shell extensions. In addition, you'll see new WinZIP options for general files and even as part of the Send To menu. In most cases, these shell extensions behave properly and add to the functionality of the system.

However, every time you add something new to the operating system, especially a feature that's constantly monitoring what you do in order to display a context menu, you incur a performance penalty. When the addition provides something valuable, the performance penalty is usually worthwhile. Once you add enough items, though, you begin to see a significant performance penalty and have no idea of how to fix it. Unfortunately with shell extensions, Windows doesn't provide any means of fixing the problem and manually patching the registry is certain to cause problems. That's where ShellExView comes into play. You can use this utility to not only view the shell extensions installed on your system (you probably have no idea of how many there are), but also manage the shell extensions so you get both functionality and performance. You can download this utility at `http://www.nirsoft.net/utils/shexview.html`.

This utility is incredibly easy to use. After you download it, you can unpack it and start working immediately. Figure 12.6 shows the initial window for this utility. As you can see, this newly formatted and updated system contains 235 shell extensions (just think about how many an older system has accumulated). The utility tells you the extension name, whether it's disabled, how it modifies Windows, a description, version, product name, company, whether it appears as part of My Computer (Computer in Vista), the Desktop, or the Control Panel, filename, Class Identifier (CLSID), file and CLSID creation times, whether this is a Microsoft product, the file specifications the product affects, file attributes, and file size. In short, everything you could possibly want to know about the shell extension. Unfortunately, the window doesn't display everything in a convenient form. Double-click an entry to see everything as a single form.

FIGURE 12.6
Most Windows systems include hundreds of shell extensions, some of which you won't need.

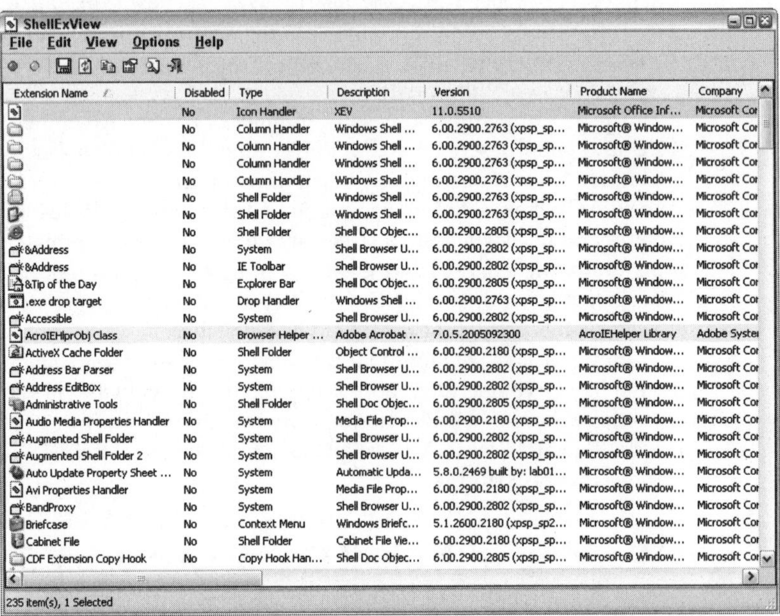

Extension Name	Disabled	Type	Description	Version	Product Name	Company
	No	Icon Handler	XEV	11.0.5510	Microsoft Office Inf...	Microsoft Cor
	No	Column Handler	Windows Shell ...	6.00.2900.2763 (xpsp_sp...	Microsoft® Window...	Microsoft Cor
	No	Column Handler	Windows Shell ...	6.00.2900.2763 (xpsp_sp...	Microsoft® Window...	Microsoft Cor
	No	Column Handler	Windows Shell ...	6.00.2900.2763 (xpsp_sp...	Microsoft® Window...	Microsoft Cor
	No	Column Handler	Windows Shell ...	6.00.2900.2763 (xpsp_sp...	Microsoft® Window...	Microsoft Cor
	No	Shell Folder	Windows Shell ...	6.00.2900.2763 (xpsp_sp...	Microsoft® Window...	Microsoft Cor
	No	Shell Folder	Windows Shell ...	6.00.2900.2763 (xpsp_sp...	Microsoft® Window...	Microsoft Cor
	No	Shell Folder	Shell Doc Objec...	6.00.2900.2805 (xpsp_sp...	Microsoft® Window...	Microsoft Cor
&Address	No	System	Shell Browser U...	6.00.2900.2802 (xpsp_sp...	Microsoft® Window...	Microsoft Cor
&Address	No	IE Toolbar	Shell Browser U...	6.00.2900.2802 (xpsp_sp...	Microsoft® Window...	Microsoft Cor
&Tip of the Day	No	Explorer Bar	Shell Doc Objec...	6.00.2900.2805 (xpsp_sp...	Microsoft® Window...	Microsoft Cor
.exe drop target	No	Drop Handler	Windows Shell ...	6.00.2900.2763 (xpsp_sp...	Microsoft® Window...	Microsoft Cor
Accessible	No	System	Shell Browser U...	6.00.2900.2802 (xpsp_sp...	Microsoft® Window...	Microsoft Cor
AcroIEHlprObj Class	No	Browser Helper ...	Adobe Acrobat ...	7.0.5.2005092300	AcroIEHelper Library	Adobe Systei
ActiveX Cache Folder	No	Shell Folder	Object Control ...	6.00.2900.2180 (xpsp_sp...	Microsoft® Window...	Microsoft Cor
Address Bar Parser	No	System	Shell Browser U...	6.00.2900.2802 (xpsp_sp...	Microsoft® Window...	Microsoft Cor
Address EditBox	No	System	Shell Browser U...	6.00.2900.2802 (xpsp_sp...	Microsoft® Window...	Microsoft Cor
Administrative Tools	No	Shell Folder	Shell Doc Objec...	6.00.2900.2805 (xpsp_sp...	Microsoft® Window...	Microsoft Cor
Audio Media Properties Handler	No	System	Media File Prop...	6.00.2900.2180 (xpsp_sp...	Microsoft® Window...	Microsoft Cor
Augmented Shell Folder	No	System	Shell Browser U...	6.00.2900.2802 (xpsp_sp...	Microsoft® Window...	Microsoft Cor
Augmented Shell Folder 2	No	System	Shell Browser U...	6.00.2900.2802 (xpsp_sp...	Microsoft® Window...	Microsoft Cor
Auto Update Property Sheet ...	No	System	Automatic Upda...	5.8.0.2469 built by: lab01...	Microsoft® Window...	Microsoft Cor
Avi Properties Handler	No	System	Media File Prop...	6.00.2900.2180 (xpsp_sp...	Microsoft® Window...	Microsoft Cor
BandProxy	No	System	Shell Browser U...	6.00.2900.2802 (xpsp_sp...	Microsoft® Window...	Microsoft Cor
Briefcase	No	Context Menu	Windows Briefc...	5.1.2600.2180 (xpsp_sp2...	Microsoft® Window...	Microsoft Cor
Cabinet File	No	Shell Folder	Cabinet File Vie...	6.00.2900.2180 (xpsp_sp...	Microsoft® Window...	Microsoft Cor
CDF Extension Copy Hook	No	Copy Hook Han...	Shell Doc Objec...	6.00.2900.2805 (xpsp_sp...	Microsoft® Window...	Microsoft Cor

Knowing as much as you do now about the various shell extensions, you can start to decide which extensions to disable. The utility helps you with this process by highlighting shell extensions that you've already disabled, from vendors other than Microsoft, or of a suspicious nature. You also have the descriptions and the purpose of the shell extensions to consider. Highlight any suspect or less than useful shell extension and click Disable Selected Items to remove it from system use. This action doesn't remove the shell extension completely, it simply makes the shell extension unusable.

If you find later that you don't want to keep the shell extension, you can get rid of it by using the RegSrv32 utility described in the "Adding and Removing Servers with the RegSvr32 Utility" section of Chapter 2. Simply locate the server file using the Filename column of the window.

WARNING Make sure any COM object you remove from the system doesn't provide services that you need. Very often, a single file includes a number of shell extensions. Unregistering one of them unregisters them all. You can register the COM object again by using the RegSvr32 utility when you make a mistake.

The interesting part about the ShellExView utility from a command line perspective is that you can also use it to find information about a system. Unfortunately, the vendor doesn't document the required command line switches as part of a `/?` command line switch for the product. However, you can find a listing of them in the vendor Web site and in this book. Here are the current ShellExView command line switches.

`/stext` ***`Filename`*** Saves the current list of shell extensions to a regular text file.

`/stab` ***`Filename`*** Saves the list of shell extensions to a tab-delimited text file that you can import into a database. Using this option makes it possible for an administrator to create a list of shell extensions for every machine on the network. Unfortunately, to obtain the listing for another machine, you need to use Terminal Server or Remote Desktop to access the machine. This utility doesn't include any remote system connectivity features.

`/stabular` ***`Filename`*** Saves the list of shell extensions into a tabular text file. You could use this option to create reports.

`/shtml` ***`Filename`*** Saves the list of shell extensions to an HTML file in tabular format. The resulting file is a nicely formatted Web page that you can view in any browser.

`/sverhtml` ***`Filename`*** Saves the list of shell extensions to an HTML file in list format. The resulting file is a nicely formatted Web page that you can view in any browser.

`/xml` ***`Filename`*** Saves the list of shell extensions into an XML file. This is actually the most versatile format. Not only can you save the resulting file into a database, you can also use XSLT to translate it into a number of other forms, such as a Web page. The use of XSLT makes it possible to create any output document you might need.

`/NoLoadSettings` Runs ShellExView using the default application settings. Normally, ShellExView saves the previous settings so it appears as it did when you last used it.

Examining Processes Using Process Explorer

Windows does provide you with process information, but it isn't always enough. Right-click the Taskbar and choose Task Manager from the context menu to see the Windows Task Manager dialog box. The Processes tab of this dialog box provides an overview of the processes on your system. Vista provides additional tabs that provide more information than previous versions of Windows. For example, you'll find a complete list of services currently running on your system on the Services tab. The TaskList utility described in the "Listing Applications and Services with the TaskList Utility" section of Chapter 5 provides even more information, but it still might not be enough. That's where Process Explorer comes into play. If you want a very detailed description of the processes running on your system, you can obtain it using Process Explorer. You can download Process Explorer from `http://www.microsoft.com/technet/sysinternals/utilities/ProcessExplorer.mspx`.

TIP An interesting bit of information about Process Explorer is that Microsoft heavily supports it. A visit to the Web page shows a list of related tools that you might want to explore, along with a list of Microsoft Knowledge Base articles that relate to Process Explorer and its use.

PERFORMING A WINDOWS MEMORY DIAGNOSTIC

Not every utility you need to run your system efficiently works at the command line. You might have a memory problem with your machine, but current Windows technology usually doesn't tell you about it. Consequently, you'll run into odd data errors and weird, unexplainable, application glitches. The events seldom repeat because memory usage changes minute by minute on a Windows machine. You don't see a pattern because the operating system constantly changes the content of memory in response to application requests. An application request could result in the operating system storing some data in the paging file and moving other data into memory from the paging file.

In most cases, the software that supposedly tests memory from within Windows does a very poor job and many administrators resorted to maintaining a DOS boot partition on disk or using boot disks to test memory using a DOS-based utility in the past. Because DOS doesn't constantly change memory, it's possible to test memory completely with a DOS utility, even though it isn't possible to do so from Windows. To overcome the problems of testing memory in Windows, Microsoft recently released a Windows Memory Diagnostic. You can download this utility from `http://oca.microsoft.com/en/windiag.asp`.

The Windows Memory Diagnostic is a low-level tool. You actually place it on a 3.5-inch floppy disk or a CD and use that media to boot your system. The reason that you have to use this approach is that you can't actually test memory inside Windows—at least not with any accuracy. People in the know have said this for years and Microsoft has finally acknowledged the fact by releasing this utility. The reason that this utility is so important is that many people do have memory problems on their system that cause all kinds of hard-to-trace problems. Because memory can fail through use, it's important to test systems regularly for memory problems. Even though this utility doesn't run at the command line, as an administrator you should have this utility (or one like it) because you never know when a memory problem will ruin your day.

Process Explorer is ready to use when you extract it from the ZIP drive. In fact, this very simple utility includes the application, help file, and license file. The main window shows a hierarchical display of the executables running on your system, as shown in Figure 12.7.

The hierarchical display shows the relationships between executables so you have a better idea of how the executable is loaded and started. Figure 12.7 shows only part of what you can expect from this utility. You'll find a wealth of options on the View menu to display yet more information. The Process menu contains options for managing processes, such as changing their priority or killing them when needed. The Find menu helps you locate a particular executable on the list.

When you double-click an entry, you see a properties dialog box like the one shown in Figure 12.8. This dialog box tells you everything the system knows about the process. In fact, when you choose the Threads tab, you'll likely see a dialog box telling you that you can obtain more information about the process by installing the Windows debug server. The point is that you can drill down into the innermost secrets of virtually any process by using Process Explorer, but those with less experience may find the amount of information overwhelming.

NOTE Many utilities in this book require administrator privileges when used in Vista. Process Explorer will ask for privilege elevation the moment you start it. You can't run this utility in any version of Windows without an administrator account.

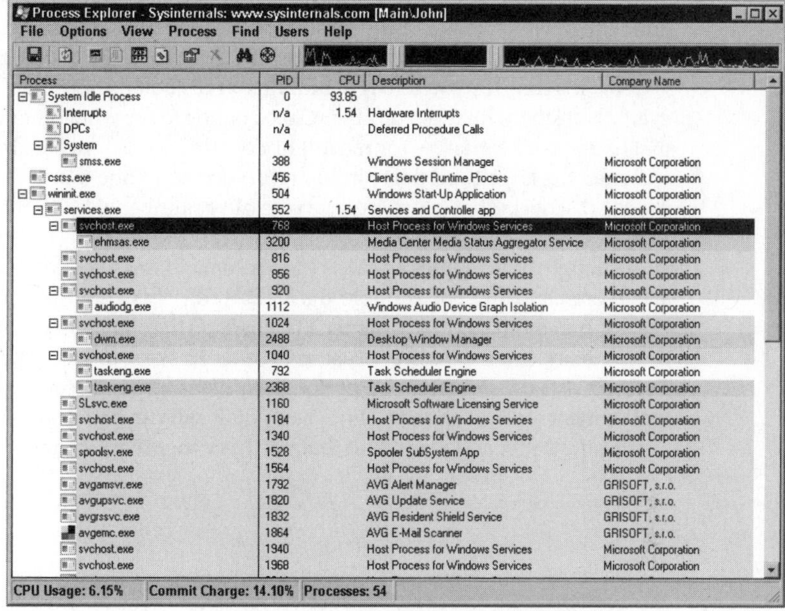

FIGURE 12.7
Process Explorer provides extremely detailed information about the processes on your system.

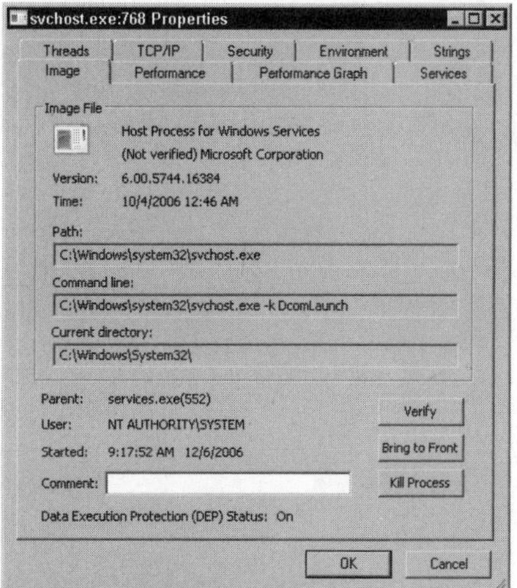

FIGURE 12.8
Use Process Explorer to learn the innermost details of the processes running on your system.

Getting Started with Command Line Tasks

This chapter has provided you with a glimpse of the many command line enhancers available on the market today. The command line has been around for well over 20 years now, so you won't find any lack of third party utilities. In fact, the trick is often more along the lines of finding just the right utility, than one that will do the job adequately. This chapter provides you with some ideas on what is available for you at the command prompt. Utilities such as XXCopy take a simple idea and make it into something far more useful. However, you might find that you need to look at files in depth quite often, which makes a utility such as XVI32 incredibly helpful. A good administrator has an entire toolbox packed with utilities such as these to address specific needs.

Now it's time for you to begin building your toolbox. Try out the utilities in this chapter. However, don't stop with these utilities. Check online to see what other utilities you can discover. A tool that happens to work fine for me might not address your needs. In fact, these differences in needs spawned the large third party industry in command line tools. Everyone has different needs; you need to discover what yours are by trying out a number of utilities and seeing which ones work best for you.

Although these utilities enhance your command line experience in some way, they don't all work at the command line. For example, the XVI32 utility has a graphical interface and you'll never actually use it at the command line. Chapter 13 focuses on the command line itself. You'll find tools that make the command line itself easier to use in Chapter 13. For example, you'll discover a method for shutting a system down faster after you perform maintenance on it. You'll also find a friendlier, graphical replacement for the command line. Yes, you'll still run batch files and use commands, but the interface itself is better and you'll find that you have more control over the entire command line interface.

Chapter 13

Increasing Productivity at the Command Line

- Obtaining Additional Information with ToggIt Command Line Helper
- Using Quick Shutdown to End a Session Fast
- Creating a Friendlier Interface with PromptPal
- Getting a More Functional Command Line with WinOne
- Automating Email Using sendEmail
- Viewing XML Files Using XML Notepad 2007

Many utilities increase your overall efficiency when working with Windows. In general, anything that affects Windows will likely affect your performance at the command line as well, even if the effect is marginal or only environmental. However, to get the most out of the command line, you really need to improve the command line itself. That's where the utilities in this chapter come into play. These utilities are unlikely to affect anything you do with Windows as a whole, but they do affect your command line efficiency.

Real World Scenario

When Not Enough Is Too Much

There's a danger that many people disregard when it comes to utilities of any sort. Too many utilities can become a liability, rather than a help. Digging through the accumulation of utilities becomes a chore and requires time that you won't normally have in an emergency. Keeping all of those utilities updated and paying for licenses when necessary adds to the problem. It all comes down to a problem of priorities—deciding which utilities you really need to get your work done and which are just so much added weight.

Of course, you want to try out new utilities and discard those that don't work as intended. In some cases, clutter is simply a matter of not getting rid of utilities that failed to meet expectations. Fortunately, you have an easy and convenient way of locating utilities that you don't really use. Simply use the `Dir` command. You can specify that you want to see only EXE files. Use the `/TA` command line switch to change the time field to the last access date. Add the `/OD` command line switch so that you can see which utilities you haven't accessed for a long time. By using this technique, you can clean up your list of utilities very quickly and keep your toolbox fit and trim.

Obtaining Additional Information with ToggIt Command Line Helper

The ToggIt Command Line Helper is a kind of a super help utility that makes it easier for you to remember command line syntax for network and hardware-related commands. The vendor originally designed the utility as a study aid for administrators obtaining their certification, but that isn't any reason you can't use it for other tasks. You can download this utility from a number of places online, but the safest location is the ToggIt Web site at `http://www.toggit.com/`. You can also obtain it from the NoNags site at `http://www.nonags.com/nonags/cl.html`. When you visit the NoNags Web site, you should also view some of the other command line utilities.

WARNING You'll run into a lot of buyer beware scenarios when working with software on the Internet. Sometimes, a piece of software that looks completely innocent can trash your system. The ToggIt Command Line Helper brought this point home to me recently. You can download this utility from a number of locations online. The URL provided in this chapter is one of the safer locations. The software itself is freeware, so no one should ask you to buy it. One of the locations that I tried to use to download this software had added a shell around the actual utility. The shell asked me to install a piece of adware in exchange for using this free utility. The deception started with the first page of the installation program where the vendor simply asked me to agree to the licensing agreement without telling me anything about that agreement. Only by opening the licensing agreement and reading it before I went forward was I spared the frustration of uninstalling some very nasty adware later. Always read the licensing agreement before you start an installation. Make sure you understand what the vendor expects from you.

The basic ToggIt Command Line Helper interface looks like a nicer form of the standard command line prompt, as shown in Figure 13.1. The interface includes a menu with predefined commands. To use a particular command, select it from the menu. In addition, you can type commands directly in the Type Command to Execute field that appears directly below the menus.

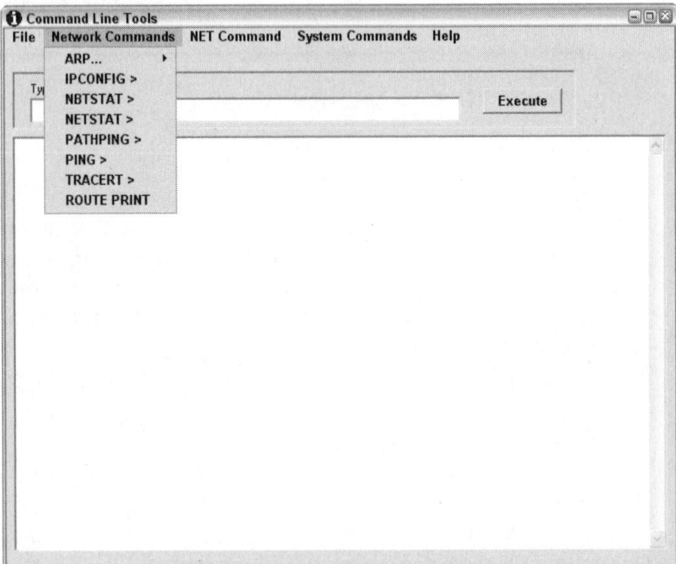

FIGURE 13.1
The ToggIt Command Line Helper provides a nicer command line interface and helpful menus.

Many of the commands that the ToggIt Command Line Helper supports execute directly. For example, when you select the `Mem /C` command from the System Commands ➤ Mem menu, the utility automatically executes the command and displays the result as shown in Figure 13.2. However, when you select the `Net Use` command from the Net Command menu, the utility displays the prompt shown in Figure 13.2. In this case, you need to provide additional information before you can execute the command. The utility prompts you for the information. Simply type the values and click Execute.

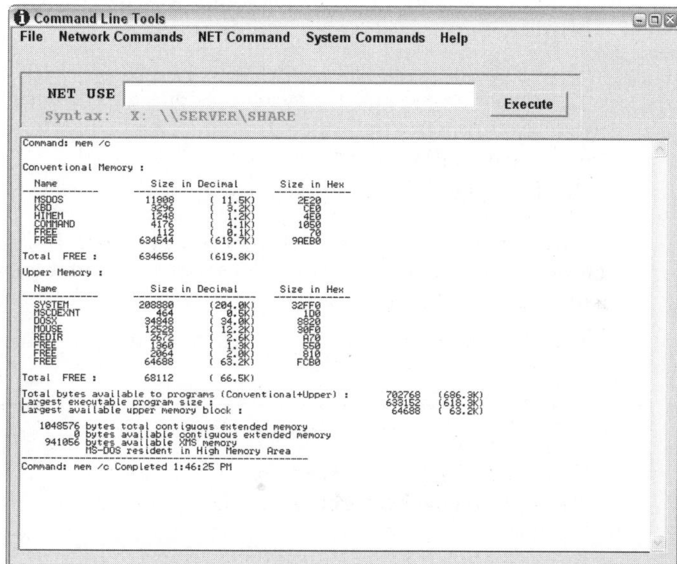

FIGURE 13.2
Sometimes you need to provide additional information before executing a command.

Although the ToggIt Command Line Helper is limited, it does provide some useful functionality for someone who needs the required commands. Theoretically, you could use this utility as a support tool. Simply have a user access the utility and read the information it provides. Because you aren't expecting the user to perform any complicated task (just select a menu entry), things will normally work as expected.

Using Quick Shutdown to End a Session Fast

The Quick Shutdown (QSD) tool helps you perform a system shutdown interactively or from the command line. You could use this tool to perform a specific kind of shutdown from a batch file or script after performing a maintenance action. In most respects, QSD is simply a more functional version of the ShutDown utility provided with Windows XP and above. To use the interactive form of this utility, simply look for the icon in the Taskbar tray. You can download this tool at `http://www.winutility.com/qsd/`. This utility uses the following syntax:

```
qsd.exe [-f] [-s] [-r] [-l] [-h] [-d] [-k] [-e:x:]
```

The following list describes each of the command line arguments.

`-f` Forces all of the running applications to exit immediately, instead of giving them time to save their data. You can use this feature when you need to shut the computer down for emergency reasons, such as a circuit meltdown. However, using this option may mean data loss. Make sure the emergency is real.

-s Shuts the computer down normally. All of your applications will have time to save data and settings. This option results in a power down of the computer. If you simply need to reboot the computer to add new drivers or DLLs, then use the `-r` command line switch instead.

-r Reboots the computer. The computer will go through an entire soft boot cycle. After the boot process completes, you can log back into the system and resume computing.

-l Logs the current user off the system. The machine doesn't reboot. You can accomplish some types of file replacement installations simply by logging off the existing user and asking them to log back into the system. This feature also lets you create batch files where you switch between users to accomplish specific tasks.

-h Places the computer in hibernation mode. The system remains on and the user remains logged into the system. The system restores the current setup when the user performs the task required to remove the system from the hibernate state, such as moving the mouse or pressing a button on the keyboard.

-d Places the computer in standby mode.

-k Locks the workstation. The user is still logged into the system, but has to supply a username and password to unlock the workstation. You would use this feature when the user goes to lunch or to a meeting.

-e:*x:* Ejects removable media from the system. You must supply the letter of the drive to eject.

Real World Scenario

NOT ALL UTILITIES RUN AS EXPECTED

The command line as it appears in most versions of Windows is the same command line that originally appeared in DOS. (Vista does place additional security restraints on the command line.) Yes, the command line today supports additional utilities, but even the old DOS utilities are available on Windows. In short, apparently nothing is new. However, appearances can be deceiving. The Windows command line doesn't rely on the older command processor, `Command.EXE`; it relies on a new command processor, `CMD.EXE`, instead. In addition, the Windows command line does provide access to a wealth of new utilities and it places limitations on how utilities work. The limitations are going to cause you grief when working with some utilities.

In order to provide a safe environment for your applications to run, the Windows command line must make some assumptions about the utilities. For example, a utility can't use certain low-level function calls because they would interrupt other applications or make the environment unusable. Unfortunately, Microsoft doesn't display a message box every time a utility violates one of these rules. The only thing that will happen is that the utility will fail—apparently for no reason at all. The only way for you to ensure that the utility works as anticipated is to view Microsoft's rules and then ensure the utility doesn't violate any of them. You can find a list of these rules at `http://support.microsoft.com/default.aspx?scid=kb;en-us;Q314106`.

Creating a Friendlier Interface with PromptPal

The PromptPal utility replaces the command line with a friendlier interface. You can download this utility from the Web site at `http://www.promptpal.com/`. This utility does require a full installation, unlike many of the utilities described so far in this chapter. In addition, the program you download from the Web site is a 30-day trial version. However, if you spend much time working at the command prompt, you'll find that your return on investment is substantial when you consider the time you'll save. Figure 13.3 shows the PromptPal interface, which looks almost nothing like the Windows command prompt you used in the past.

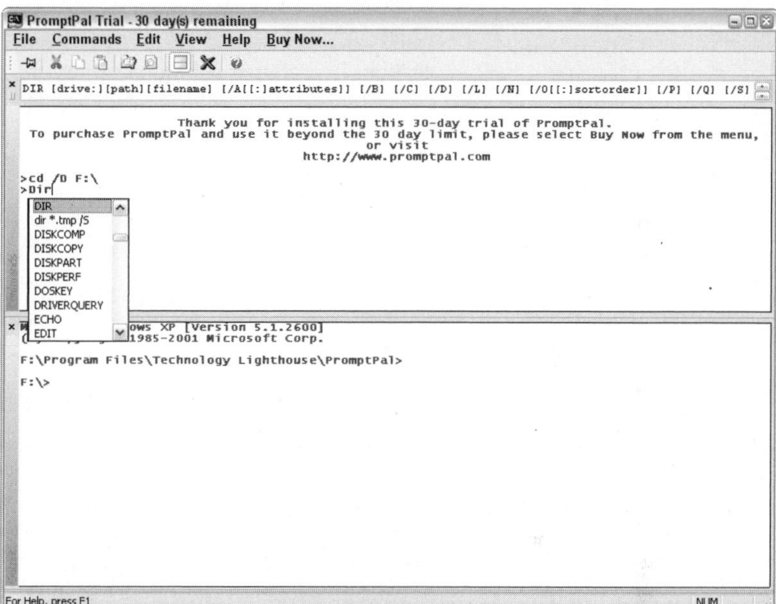

FIGURE 13.3
PromptPal supports an interface that makes working at the command prompt fun.

The utility sports a two-pane interface. The upper pane is where you type your commands; the lower pane shows the results. Using this approach means that you can always see the command you typed and the result it produced with equal ease. However, that's where the extended functionality starts. Whenever you start typing a command, PromptPal displays a list of matching commands, eliminating most typing errors. In addition, it displays the longer versions of that command that you typed in the past as shown directly below the `DIR` entry in Figure 13.3. The full command syntax appears in the bar directly below the menu as shown in the figure. Consequently, you don't have to try to remember all of those command line switches. When you type a command line switch, PromptPal displays the entire list, along with the meaning behind each command line switch, as shown in Figure 13.4 (the figure shows the explanation list, truncated for space considerations in the book).

PromptPal includes a wealth of configuration choices. You can change the appearance of the display in a number of ways. Any display change you can make with a regular command prompt is also available in PromptPal (which means you can display a green background with red letters if you want). However, the most important configuration option appears in Figure 13.5. This configuration option lets you add new commands to PromptPal, edit existing definitions, and remove commands you don't want to use from the list. Consequently, the help you receive from PromptPal is completely configurable.

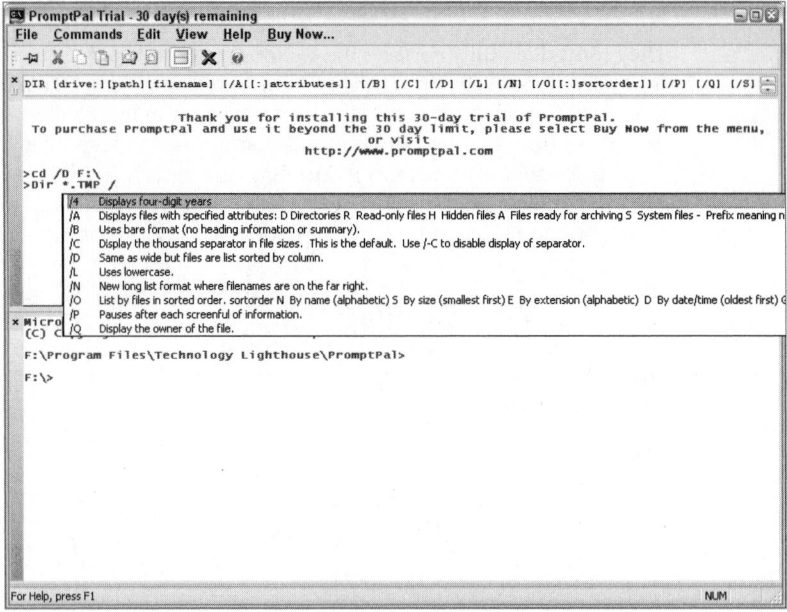

FIGURE 13.4
PromptPal helps you remember all of those command line switches and their meanings.

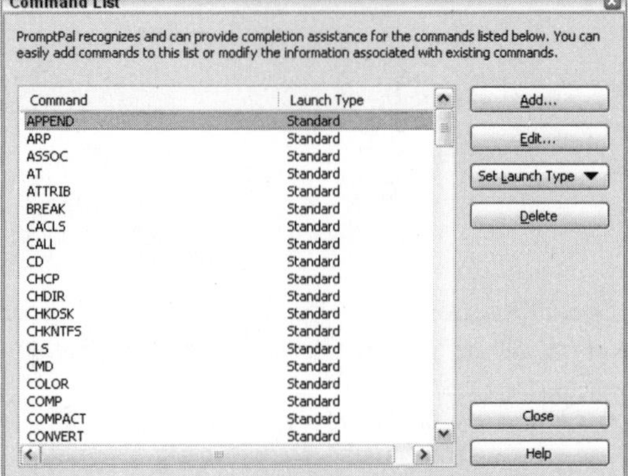

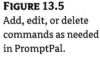

FIGURE 13.5
Add, edit, or delete commands as needed in PromptPal.

Getting a More Functional Command Line with WinOne

The WinOne utility is more along the lines of a look and feel command line prompt enhancement. What you receive is a far nicer interface than Windows provides for the command prompt, along with many options for modifying the interface. You can download this utility at `http://www.winone.com.au/`. Figure 13.6 shows how this utility appears on screen. Although you can't see it in the book, WinOne provides a significant amount of color coding that makes working with command or utility output significantly easier, especially for tabular items.

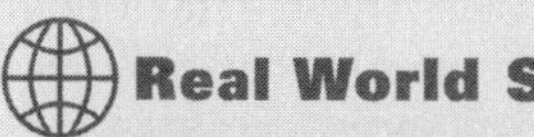

WORKING IN MIXED ENVIRONMENTS

Many administrators work in mixed environments today, so it's not surprising that they look for software that has the same functionality in as many environments as possible. PromptPal and WinOne look, more than any other utility in this chapter, like they bring the Windows command line much closer to the functionality of the Linux command line environment (CLE). Many administrators feel that the Linux CLE is much more intuitive than the Windows version, even if the commands aren't necessarily the same. If you work in both the Windows and Linux environments, you might want to use these utilities to bring the two environments closer.

Working in a mixed environment can be difficult. Although this book doesn't provide much Linux information, a few books on the market do. One of the best books for learning more about working in a mixed environment is *Windows and Linux Integration* by Jeremy Moskowitz and Thomas Boutell (Sybex, 2005).

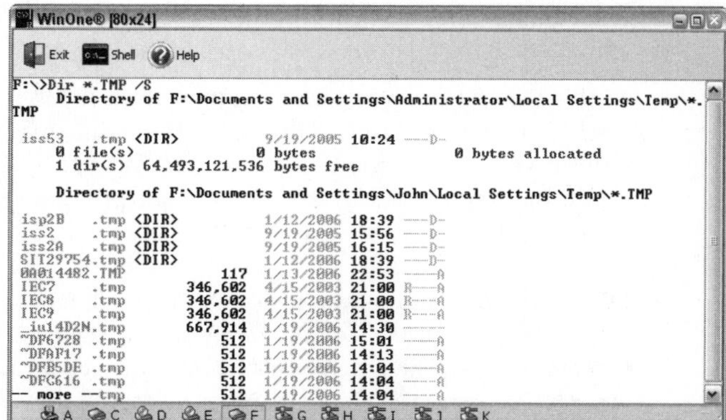

FIGURE 13.6
WinOne provides a nicer look and feel than the basic command prompt that Windows provides.

In addition, WinOne includes its own batch language that you can compile. The batch applications can include special dialog boxes, so you have an opportunity to combine the advantages of the command line with a graphical interface. The book doesn't include an example of this batch language because you can probably do better by using standard batch development techniques and a batch file compiler. Chapter 14 discusses batch and script file compilers in greater detail.

TIP Even though this chapter doesn't discuss them, you'll find a wealth of shrink-wrap products on the market to enhance the command line. Many of them started as shareware, but moved on to full commercial vendors and now provide only a product demonstration for free. You can find some of these utilities on software brokering Web sites such as BMTMicro at `http://www.bmtmicro.com/BMTCatalog/win/02system.html`. For example, the 4NT utility on this Web site is an excellent command interpreter replacement that has a long history. Many of you might have heard of it as 4DOS.

Automating Email Using sendEmail

The sendEmail program is interesting because it originally appeared on the Linux platform, not on Windows. Essentially, sendEmail is a Simple Mail Transfer Protocol (SMTP) agent, so you don't have to rely on any external application to use it. You do need an SMTP server, which the sendEmail application assumes is on Localhost unless you specify otherwise. Make sure you download the Windows version of the utility at `http://caspian.dotconf.net/menu/Software/SendEmail/`.

The really interesting feature of this product, though, is that you can use it to send an email to anyone from the command prompt, a batch file, or a script (the Web page makes it appear that you need to use Practical Extraction and Report Language or PERL, which also works of course, but isn't a requirement). Consequently, an administrator who needs to monitor a host of network machines can do so effectively simply by checking email. This utility uses the following syntax:

```
sendEmail -f ADDRESS  [-t ADDRESS [ADDRESS ...]] [-u SUBJECT] [-m
   MESSAGE] [-s SERVER[:PORT]] [-a   FILE [FILE ...]] [-cc  ADDRESS
   [ADDRESS ...]] [-bcc ADDRESS [ADDRESS ...]] [-xu USERNAME [-xp
   PASSWORD]] [-l  LOGFILE] [-v [...]] [-o NAME=VALUE]
sendEmail --help TOPIC
```

Of these arguments, you must provide the `-f` command line switch as a minimum. You must also provide at least one recipient using the `-t`, `-cc`, or `-bcc` command line switches. Finally, even though you don't absolutely have to provide it, you should include a message body using the `-m` or `-o` command line switches. You can also type the message using the standard input device (STDIN). The following list describes each of the command line arguments.

`-f` ***ADDRESS*** Defines the address of the sender. If you're using this utility to report system progress or errors, you can use the user's address and machine name for the address. For example, using an address of "John, Main<JMueller@mwt.net>" tells you that the user's name is John and that the machine name is Main. You must still provide a return address, which can be your own email address or the user's email address.

NOTE Newer Windows systems with built-in firewall support might block the sendEmail utility. Unfortunately, you'll just see an odd error message; neither the utility nor Windows will tell you what is really happening to the email. Make sure you set your firewall to allow sendEmail to transmit the message using whatever port you select. The default port for this utility is 25, but you can change the standard port using the `-s` command line switch.

`-t` ***ADDRESS [ADDRESS ...]*** Defines one or more addresses to receive the email message. These email addresses appear in the To field of the message. You can also send the email to addresses in the CC field using the `-cc` command line switch and the BCC field using the `-bcc` command line switch.

`-u` ***SUBJECT*** Defines the message subject. Make sure you place the message subject in quotes when it contains spaces. Any other argument with spaces also requires quotes.

`-m` ***MESSAGE*** Defines the message body. The message body can contain anything that you can place in a standard message, including HTML. However, at some point, this utility becomes more cumbersome than helpful for complex messages and you should consider switching to a full-fledged email application.

`-s` ***SERVER[:PORT]*** Specifies the SMTP server. Don't include a protocol with the SMTP server argument—include only the full server name such as `smtp.myserver.com`. The default server is Localhost. You may also specify a port number to use when contacting the server. The default setting is the standard SMTP port of 25.

`-a` ***FILE [FILE ...]*** Adds one or more file attachments to the email message. You can use this option to send complex test data.

-cc ***ADDRESS [ADDRESS ...]*** Defines one or more carbon copy recipients. These addresses appear in the CC field of the message.

-bcc ***ADDRESS [ADDRESS ...]*** Defines one or more blind carbon copy recipients. Even though these email addresses receive the message, they won't appear as part of either the To or CC fields. Instead, you'll normally see a default entry, such as Undisclosed-Recipient.

-xu ***USERNAME*** Specifies the username for SMTP server authentication. You may not require this input with public servers.

-xp ***PASSWORD*** Specifies the user's password for the SMTP server account. You normally must provide a username with the `-xu` command line switch to use this option.

-l ***LOGFILE*** Specifies a log file to use to record email events.

-v [...] Forces the utility to provide additional information about email events. Use this command line switch multiple times for added verbosity.

-q Forces the utility to restrict any email event output. The user won't see any messages at the command line. You can use this option to ensure a background process doesn't disturb the user.

-o ***NAME=VALUE*** Defines special email processing requirements. This book doesn't describe the email header in detail. However, the following list provides a short description of the various properties that this utility makes available.

message-file=*FILE* Specifies the message relies on a file, rather than a standard body, as the means of sending information.

message-header=*EMAIL_HEADER* Defines one or more special headings for the email message.

message-format=raw Specifies that the utility will send the email using a raw, prebuilt message.

message-charset=*CHARSET* Defines the character set used by the email message.

reply-to=*ADDRESS* Defines the address to use for replies. The default setting uses the address in the From field of the message for replies. This option provides an alternative to the default.

timeout=*SECONDS* Determines how long the utility, servers, and other elements of the mail transfer system wait for a successful email transmission.

TIP You can find a host of Web sites that describe the email message header online. If you want to understand the email process better and the tools required when working with email headers, look at the Tracking E-mail site at `http://www.expita.com/header1.html`.

--help ***TOPIC*** Obtains additional help about a particular topic. Even though you can use the /? command line switch to obtain general help, you can obtain a wealth of additional information by using this command line switch. The following list describes the additional topics.

addressing Explains the various addressing and related options.

message Explains the message body input and related options.

misc Contains all of the miscellaneous topics that don't fit under any other heading.

networking Explains all of the networking options, such as selecting a server using the `-s` command line switch.

output Explains the logging and other output options.

Real World Scenario

CONSIDERING MULTIPLATFORM REQUIREMENTS

You might not think that a book on the Windows command line would merit much thought about working on other platforms, but it does. Most administrators today don't have the luxury of just working with Windows or any other individual platform for that matter. Most companies now have multiple platforms for various tasks and the use of more than one platform isn't going to change. In fact, the problem promises to become worse, not better, as time progresses, for administrators.

The sendEmail application is a command line utility that just happens to run at the command line on multiple systems. Any time you can find a single software application that runs on multiple platforms, it's a good idea to check it out. Using the same software on multiple platforms means that you can leverage the work you perform on one platform on all of the other platforms as well. You'll reduce errors and the need for complex training in multiple packages. In some cases, you'll even be able to use the applications you create on multiple platforms because the software that your applications access is the same on every platform.

Unfortunately, software that runs on more than one platform is still the exception and not the rule. In addition, most multiplatform software runs on two platforms; software that runs equally well on three or more platforms is rare. Software that runs precisely the same on three or more platforms is even rarer, but it does exist for specific needs. If your network has an odd combination of mainframe, Linux, Windows, and Macintosh, you probably won't find a lot of software to meet your command line needs, but you should still look. When you find someone who has two of your platforms covered, try to convince them to cover the other platforms too. Multiple platform networks are here to stay—any software you can find that runs equally well on all of those platforms makes your job easier.

Viewing XML Files Using XML Notepad 2007

VISTA

Microsoft started using XML in Windows XP, but if you've noticed anything in the first six chapters of this book, Vista makes significant use of XML. In many cases, the files don't even have an XML extension. Microsoft uses a wealth of file extensions for XML files today. Any configuration file is likely to use XML. You'll also find that many log files and even some lower-level operating system data files all rely on XML. With this change in mind, you really need a good XML utility to work at the command line, but many of the free products on the market come up lacking. XML Notepad provides a decent level of XML support and you'll find that it works just fine for most, if not all, command line administration needs. You can obtain this utility at `http://www.microsoft.com/downloads/details.aspx?familyid=72D6AA49-787D-4118-BA5F-4F30FE913628`.

NOTE Microsoft has produced a number of versions of XML Notepad. Old versions of XML Notepad won't install in Vista. You must download and install XML Notepad 2007 from the Web site provided in this section in order to obtain a working copy of XML Notepad. Even XML Notepad 2006 fails to install in Vista.

After you install XML Notepad, the setup program automatically opens an HTML page containing information about XML Notepad. You'll typically find this file at `C:\Program Files\XML Notepad 2007\Readme.htm`. One of the links opens a sample XML folder. In this folder you'll find the `Basket.XML` file that appears in Figure 13.7. Right-click the file in Windows Explorer and choose Edit with XML Notepad to open the file.

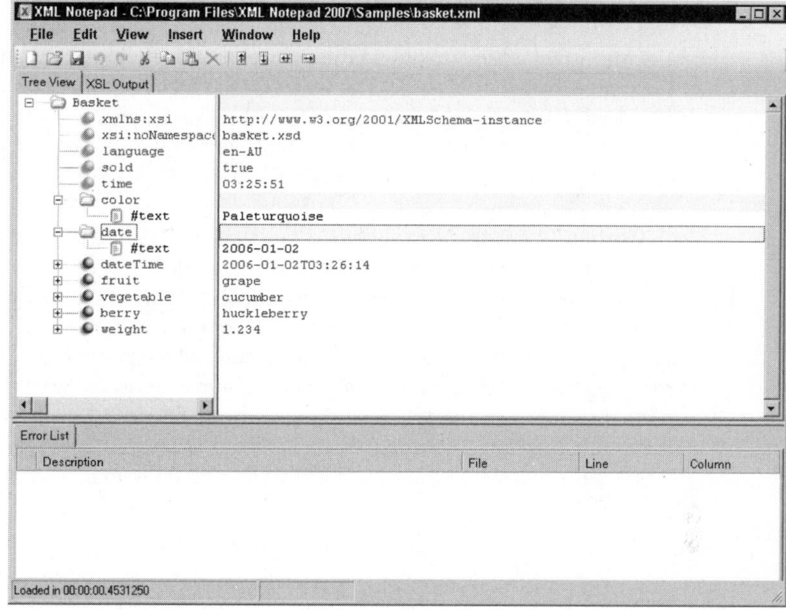

FIGURE 13.7
XML Notepad provides a safe editing environment for your XML files.

The XML Notepad display color codes entries by type and includes special icons to identify various types. For example, value entries appear with a special icon to differentiate them from elements.

You add a new entry by selecting it from the Insert menu. As an alternative, you can add new entries by right-clicking an existing entry and choosing the entry type from the context menu. In both cases, the new entry appears as a child of the currently selected entry in the left pane. You type a value for the new entry in the right pane. When you make a mistake in creating an entry, such as not adhering to a restriction in an XSD file, XML Notepad provides an entry in the bottom pane. Double-clicking the error entry takes you to that position in the file.

If your file has an XSLT processing instruction, you can view the output by clicking the XSL Output tab. The `RSS.XML` file provides a sample of this XML Notepad feature. You can change XSL files by clicking the ellipses button (...) and choosing another XSL file in the Open dialog box. Click Transform to display the transformed XML file.

One of the more interesting features of XML Notepad is the ability to compare two XML files. Begin by loading the primary XML file into XML Notepad. Choose View ➤ Compare XML Files to display an Open dialog box. Select the secondary XML file and click Open. You'll see an XmlDiff window open that has a complete comparison of the two files. This feature is helpful when performing configuration tasks where you want one machine to have some, but not all, of the settings of another machine or you need to check XML files for damage.

Getting Started with Command Line Tasks

This chapter has addressed efficiency at the command line. It considers the matter of making you more efficient at the command line when you have manual tasks to perform. The utilities in this chapter all affect the command prompt in some way. For example, when you use PromptPal, what you actually create is a better interface for working at the command line. Anything you can do to make the environment easier from your perspective is a plus that you shouldn't avoid.

The utilities in this chapter are just a small sampling of what is available online. In some cases, these utilities won't meet any of your needs and you'll wonder why I included them in the book. The important issue is to obtain the utilities that do meet your particular needs, which are going to be very personal in this case. The way you work at the command line determines which utilities you need. Of course, you have many other ways to become more efficient at the command line. Don't forget to use automation and after hours tasking as required. Sometimes, it's more a matter of balancing all of the efficiency methods, rather than focusing on a single way to work faster and with greater ease.

Chapter 14 moves into a slightly different area of command line work. The batch files and scripts you created are a source of inefficiency, especially when they perform complex tasks. The problem is that the system must interpret the files every time you use them. Interpreting is a process where the system converts the words that you understand into something the system understands. It's often a time-consuming process, at least from the computer's perspective. Chapter 14 discusses how to use compilers to perform the interpretation once and convert the result into an executable file. You won't notice much of a change when working with small batch files or scripts, but the change can be significant with large or complex applications. In addition, using this technique translates words that everyone can read into executable format that no one can read conveniently (if at all).

Chapter 14

Editing and Compiling Batch Files and Scripts

- Editing All File Types with WinVi
- Obtaining a Better Notepad with Notepad+
- Creating Executable Batch Files with Batch File Compiler 5.2
- Develop and Compile Batch Files with Quick Batch File Compiler
- Understanding JavaScript and VBScript Compilers
- Understanding the JSC Compiler Supplied with .NET

Any full automation effort at the command line will likely require batch files and scripts. You can use any technique that you want to write the batch file or script. For example, you can use the simple command **`Copy CON: C:MyBatch.BAT`** and press Enter to start an editing session right there at the command prompt. If the batch file is small and simple enough, this environment may be all that you need. However, most people use an editor of some kind. In fact, Notepad is one of the more popular options. Of course, you can find more powerful editors and this chapter examines a few of those choices. The point is that you should use the editor that feels comfortable to you and achieves any task that you want to complete. You don't need the IDE of a full-fledged programming language to complete most tasks at the command line.

Nothing says that you must do anything more than write the lines of instructions to create a perfectly usable solution. In fact, for many years, this is all that people did. They wrote their batch files and used them as is. However, you can obtain some additional efficiencies by compiling your batch file or script. In some cases, you might see slightly faster executing speeds. Compiling your batch file or script also hides the content from prying eyes, so your coding secrets remain safe. In addition, compiling the batch file or script makes it difficult to edit; you don't have to worry about someone else modifying the content of the file. Editing is a major concern in the corporate environment where an administrator might have hundreds of machines to manage and an equal number of curious users.

Editing All File Types with WinVi

When working at the command line, you often require a versatile editor that does more than simply edit text. Unfortunately, most low-cost editors on the market either edit text or edit binary information, but not both. Normally, to obtain an editor that does both, you have to buy a full-fledged programming language such as Visual Studio. Obviously, buying Visual Studio to write batch files

LOCATING SCRIPTING EXAMPLES

Many people will look at the scripting examples provided as part of a product and then not get any further because the examples are limited or don't meet their needs. However, you don't have to learn every aspect of scripting before you can become productive with it. You can find many scripting Web sites online. Many of them have coding samples you can use. Others provide tools, tips, or techniques you can use when working with scripts.

One of the most interesting of these Web sites is Rob van der Woude's Scripting Pages at `http://www.robvanderwoude.com/index.html`. This particular Web site not only provides a wealth of scripts in various languages (most of which haven't appeared in this book), but explanations provided are unusually clear and easy to understand. Because of the diversity of these scripts, you can often find what you need and use it without writing a single line of code yourself. In other cases, you can make simple changes to adapt the script to meet your specific needs.

is significant overkill. If you find you need both text and binary editing capabilities in a single editor, WinVi might provide everything you need. As shown in Figure 14.1, this editor features a full binary editing mode. It edits text equally well. You can download this product at `http://www.winvi.de/en/`.

The WinVi editor has a few interesting features that make it exceptionally useful to administrators. One of the more interesting features is that it supports multiple character sets. You can choose between the ANSI, DOS, or EBCDIC character sets. The third character set comes in handy for examining older mainframe data.

FIGURE 14.1 You can use WinVi to edit text files and binary files with equal ease.

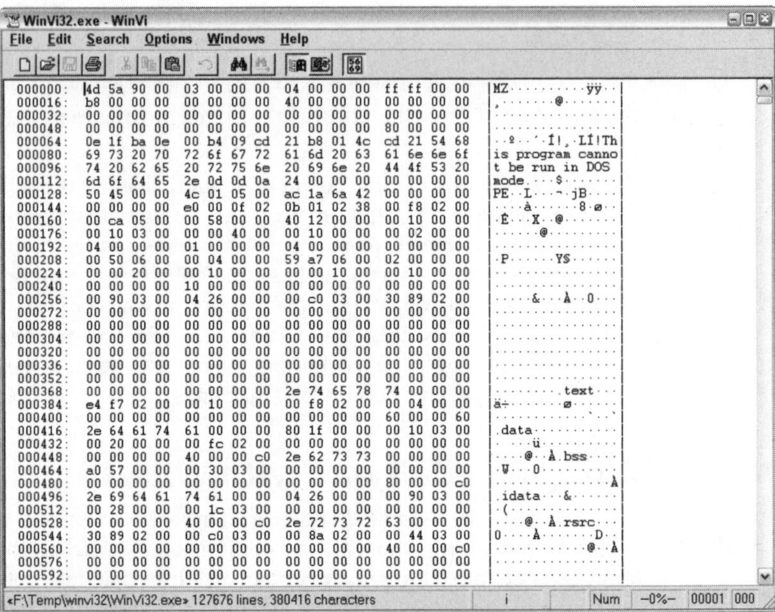

Unlike many low-cost editors on the market, WinVi also supports multiple language options. You can choose between English, French, German, or Spanish as your language. The automatic selection feature chooses a language based on the current system setup. Consequently, if you use multiple languages, you can change language setups and start a new copy of WinVi. The editor will automatically change languages for you as long as it supports the language you're using.

Printing might not seem like such an important issue, but developers often print out their code listings. The printing features of WinVi match those of Notepad in many respects. However, it includes a two-column printout feature that can save a significant number of pages. You can also have the editor add line numbers to the printout so you can discuss the code with someone else over the telephone or email with greater ease.

If you want support for automation for your editor, WinVi includes keyboard macro support. You can create short macros of tasks that you want performed and assign them to a key combination. Whenever you use that key combination, the editor automatically performs the preprogrammed series of steps. Overall, you'll find this feature is less capable than a full-fledged editor such as Microsoft Word, but definitely better than most low-cost editors provide.

The editor also supports a number of programmer features. You can set it to support automatic indenting and define the number of characters for each indent. In addition, you can select the end of line sequence. WinVi supports the standard carriage return/line feed combination for Windows, the line feed only character used by Unix, or the carriage return only character used by the Macintosh. Best of all, you can save all of your settings as a profile. The editor supports multiple profiles so you can switch between them as needed for your editing needs. All of these settings appear in one location—the Settings dialog box shown in Figure 14.2.

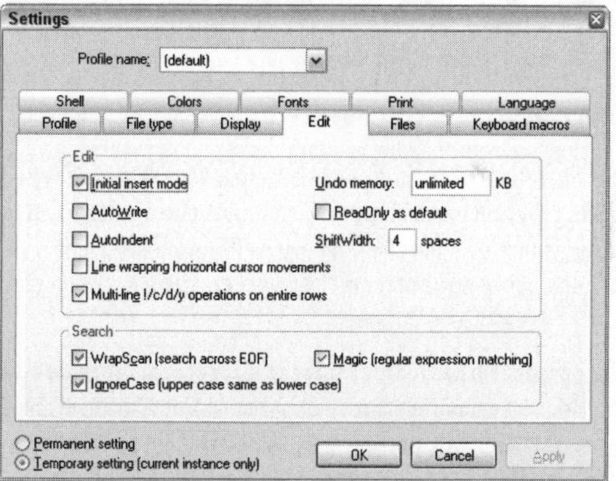

FIGURE 14.2
Use the WinVi Settings dialog box to access all of the features of this highly configurable editor.

Obtaining a Better Notepad with Notepad+

Many people use Notepad for all of their development needs. After all, you really don't need anything fancy when working on a batch file or a simple script. Of course, it would be nice if Notepad had some additional features. For example, you can only open one file at a time in Notepad. Notepad+ looks strikingly similar to Notepad at first. It even has the same name. The vendor envisions this freeware utility as a replacement for Notepad and gives it the same name for that reason. However, one look at this utility as shown in Figure 14.3 tells you that it's different from Notepad. Notice that the figure shows two documents opened and the editor supports more. You can download Notepad+ at `http://www.mypeecee.org/rogsoft/`.

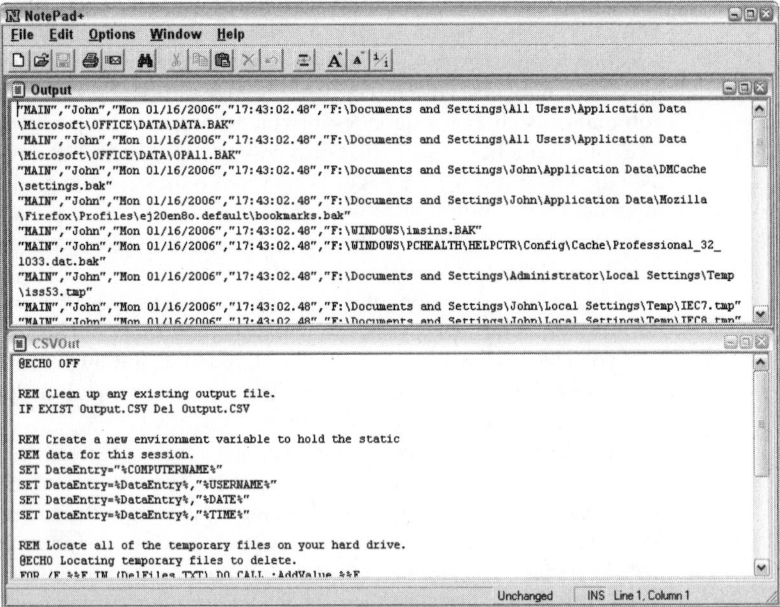

FIGURE 14.3
Notepad+ looks very much like the Windows Notepad, but with important differences.

Real World Scenario

EXPLORING THE ALTERNATIVES TO APPLICATION DEFICIENCIES

Most applications have deficiencies. The deficiency is something that you perceive the application is lacking. When enough people feel that the application has a deficiency, the vendor normally does something about it. However, many deficiencies reflect a personal requirement that the vendor will never address. Consequently, either you continue to use the application or you obtain another application that addresses the concern.

The applications in this chapter address various deficiencies in Windows applications. However, you should also consider the alternatives. For example, Notepad only opens one file at a time, but you can open multiple copies of Notepad. Sure, it's a little inconvenient moving between copies of Notepad to compare files, but it works. Whether this alternative addresses the deficiency of not opening multiple files depends on your particular tastes and needs. The important issue is to consider alternatives before you obtain a third party alternative that might have other deficiencies that you must address.

Make sure that when you do look at the third party application alternatives, that you review enough products to ensure the new selection meets all of your needs. For example, you might find that EditPlus (`http://www.softwarerate.com/EditPlus-Version-2-download-9666.htm`) meets your needs more effectively than Notepad+ does. Only you can decide when an application meets enough of your needs and provides enough functionality that any required workarounds are minor.

Notepad+ includes a number of interesting features. If you ever ran into the file size barrier when using older versions of Windows, you don't have to worry about this issue with Notepad+. In fact, I was able to open very large files quickly and without any problems.

Besides opening rather large files, Notepad+ supports one feature that many administrators find saves considerable time. You can click a single button to send the content of the file that you're editing to someone else. This makes it very easy to communicate with other administrators without ever leaving the editing environment.

Notepad+ includes a number of interesting configuration options, some of which appear in the Preference dialog box shown in Figure 14.4. The Dialogs tab lets you set the filters used for the Open and Save dialog boxes—an unusual feature that you probably won't see in many other utilities. Having this feature means that you can set up Notepad+ to edit text files of any kind. You can choose the filter for that file directly from the Open or Save dialog boxes as needed. This support is very important when you need a flexible editing environment.

FIGURE 14.4
Configure Notepad+ to open and save any file type using these options.

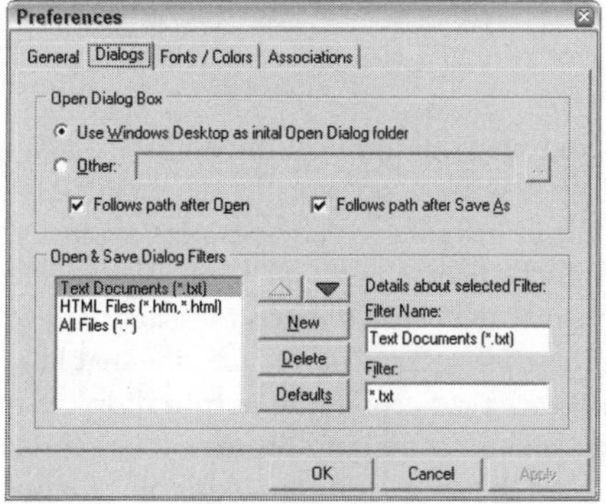

You can also associate Notepad+ with any file using the features on the Association tab of the Preferences dialog box. This feature means that you can double-click the file in Windows Explorer and have Notepad+ open it for you automatically. Notepad+ includes a number of other helpful configuration options, such as the ability to use proportional fonts that should make your editing experience nicer. Generally, this is a very helpful update for a utility that most people have used at one time or another to create or edit batch or script files.

Creating Executable Batch Files with Batch File Compiler 5.2

The main reason to use the Batch File Compiler is to create an executable from your batch file—a task this utility performs very well. However, this utility does a lot more. The Batch File Compiler is a shareware product that works with pure batch files, but it can also augment batch files so that they do more. For example, you can perform math within your batch file when you compile it using this utility. You can download the Batch File Compiler at `http://www.topshareware.com/Batch-File-Compiler-download-45.htm`.

The feature I like best about this product is that it's very simple. Figure 14.5 shows the interface for this product. The main window lets you access and edit your batch files. Select an option from the Extended Commands menu when you want to add more functionality to your batch file. You can find a complete list of these features in the `bfcped.HTM` file provided as part of the application.

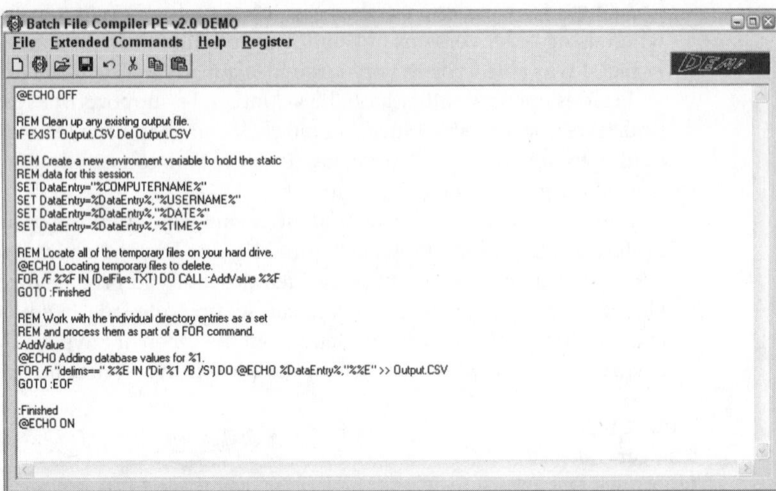

FIGURE 14.5
Batch File Compiler supports a simple interface that makes it easy to create batch file executables.

To compile your application, edit the batch file code and then click Compile. The utility opens a dialog box where you type the name of the executable you want to create. After you provide the name, the utility asks which operating system you're using to execute the batch file (the choices are essentially DOS or Windows). Once you select an operating system, the utility completes the compilation and displays a success message. A few odd things happened when I used the resulting application. First, it seemed to assume that I would use some of the extended features to place the cursor on screen. Second, the output didn't use the colors I selected for the command prompt—it used the default command prompt colors instead. Otherwise, the batch file worked precisely as it should. When using the demonstration version of the product, you also have to live with the developer's commercial messages.

Develop and Compile Batch Files with Quick Batch File Compiler

The Quick Batch File Compiler has all the look and feel of a development platform. This isn't the kind of utility that you use for a quick application—it's an environment you can use to perform in-depth coding with your batch files. Everything about this product feels solid. For example, when you load your batch file for editing, you'll immediately notice that the editor uses color coding to make the code more readable. In addition, I found that the help file was an easy read and put together in a way that made accessing the various topics fast. You can download this utility at `http://www.abyssmedia.com/quickbfc/index.shtml`.

The best way to use the Quick Batch File Compiler is with the IDE shown in Figure 14.6. However, you can also use it in batch mode by supplying an input filename and an output (executable) filename. The IDE has an upper window where you edit the code and a lower window where you can see the results of any tasks you perform. For example, the utility uses this window when it compiles the application for you.

Unlike most utilities, this one includes a number of customizations that you need to produce a professional looking executable. The Custom Resources tab shown in Figure 14.7 shows the customizations you can perform. You can include a file description, company name, version, and an icon. Everything works as it should. Displaying the executable's Properties dialog box shows the results of these entries.

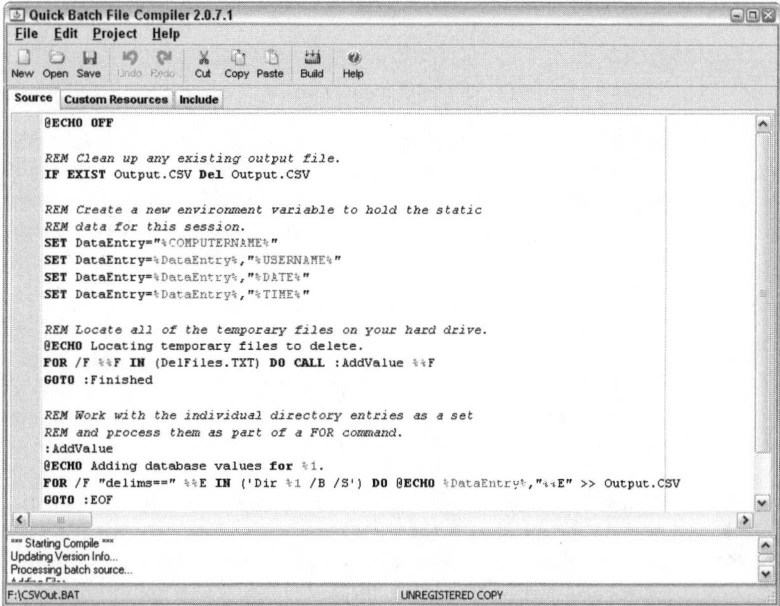

FIGURE 14.6
Color coding and great help features make Quick Batch File Compiler easy to use.

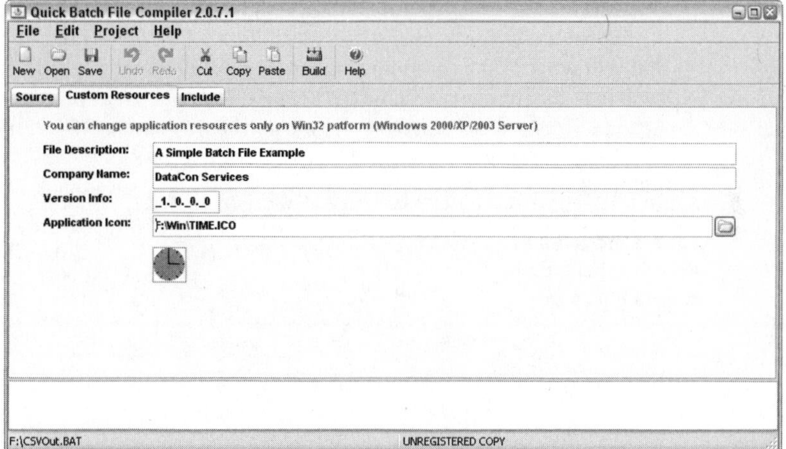

FIGURE 14.7
The Custom Resources tab helps you customize your application as needed.

Understanding JavaScript and VBScript Compilers

Generally, you aren't going to find a JavaScript or a VBScript compiler that works at the command line. The problem is that you need to have the support of the Windows Scripting Host (WSH) at the command line and WSH only provides an interpreted environment. Consequently, what you'll find is a vast array of JavaScript and VBScript editors, some of which are extremely complex and provide just about anything you could ask for, except WSH support. For example, the C-Point Antechinus JavaScript Editor (`http://www.c-point.com/javascript_editor.php`) shown in

LOOK FOR APPLICATION ADVANTAGES

Sometimes, the feature you need is the one that is hidden in the documentation or not immediately obvious when you start working with the product. For example, Quick Batch File Compiler includes a number of helpful features that can help you produce better command line applications. For example, you can perform some advanced tasks with this utility, such as including external files with the executable. This feature lets you combine several batch files into one executable, so you don't have multiple files floating around.

The program also comes with a decompiler you can use to recover your code should you lose it. Simply right-click the executable and choose Decompile with QuickBCF from the context menu. You can protect your code from others by adding a password using the fields on the Decompilation tab of the Options dialog box that you access with the Project ➢ Options command.

Figure 14.8 provides all of the functionality that you would expect from a full-fledged programming language at a fraction of the cost. Unfortunately, while this editor will provide everything you need, including IntelliSense support, to build a Web application, it won't help you create a JavaScript application that relies on WSH. Yes, it will help you write the code, but you can't compile it.

An important issue to remember is that any time you see HTML Application (HTA), what you're really talking about is a Web application of some sort. Yes, you can create stand-alone HTA versions for the local machine with the right editor, but an HTA can't rely on the functionality that WSH provides, which means that you'll lose a lot of functionality. The best place to look for tools that will work at the command line is on the Microsoft site at `http://www.microsoft.com/technet/scriptcenter/createit.mspx`. Another great place to look is the Asp4Hs: Add-On's: ActiveScripts / WSH Scripts Web site at `http://www.wilk4.com/asp4hs/list5.htm`.

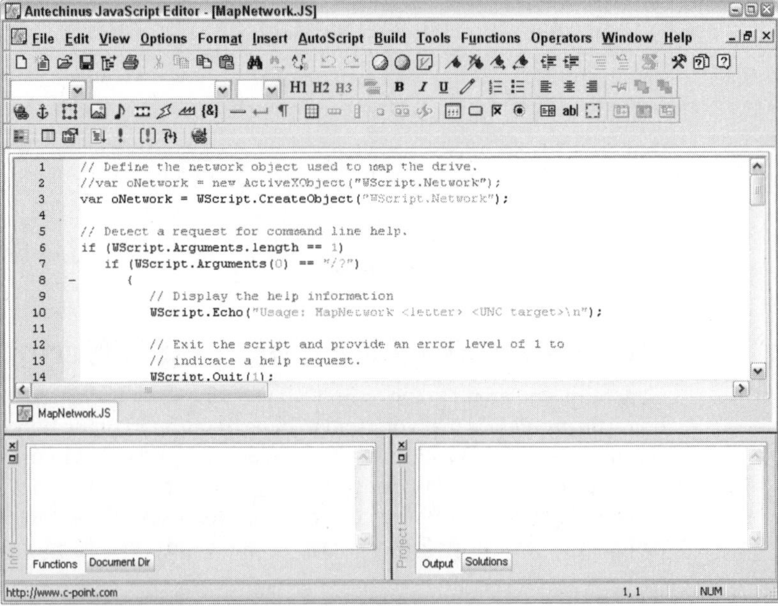

FIGURE 14.8
Most JavaScript editors and compilers focus their attention on Web pages.

Fortunately, you can find editors that make your task significantly easier. For example, the AdminScriptEditor described at `http://www.adminscripteditor.com/editor/` provides you with a number of features that make working with WSH easier. For example, you can use it to create scripts that use Windows Management Instrumentation (WMI). This Windows feature provides access to various Windows management functions that you can control from your script. This particular product isn't shareware and it doesn't come with a fully functional demonstration program. The 45-day trial version does give you a good idea of how the product works though.

CONSIDERING THE WSH ALTERNATIVES

Microsoft created WSH many years ago. It's amazing that this interpreted environment still meets so many needs and will continue to meet them well into the future. However, you still need to consider what WSH offers as part of your application-building task. At some point, you might need to consider giving up the convenience that WSH provides and using an entirely different environment. You can find a wealth of third party utilities such as OnScript (`http://www.onscript.com/en/home.asp`) and ExeScript (`http://www.hide-folder.com/overview/hf_7.html`) online. In addition, you might want to try Microsoft's new JavaScript Compiler (JSC) described in the "Understanding the JSC Compiler Supplied with .NET" section of this chapter. The important consideration is finding the right tool for your particular needs.

Understanding the JSC Compiler Supplied with .NET

Even though this chapter doesn't discuss the .NET Framework (see Chapter 15 for the introductory material on the .NET Framework), this is the most appropriate chapter to introduce one useful .NET Framework feature. Because the .NET Framework is finding its way to more computer systems and many script developers are looking for more in the way of powerful scripting languages, you might want to look at JScript.NET. It's a form of JavaScript with a definite .NET Framework slant.

You can create a JScript.NET script using any standard text editor such as Notepad and compile it with the JSC compiler to an executable form. However, you also need to be aware that JScript.NET isn't just a simple upgrade of JScript, the Microsoft form of JavaScript. For example, you don't execute JScript.NET using the Microsoft Scripting Engine. Consequently, objects such as WScript that you may have used in the past aren't available. Only pure JavaScript features are available, along with any .NET Framework features that you might want to use. You can find a number of JScript.NET programming topics at `http://msdn.microsoft.com/library/en-us/jscript7/html/jsoriJScript.asp`.

Using the JSC Compiler

Despite the differences with other forms of JavaScript you might use at the Windows command line, JScript.NET provides a significant gain in programming functionality. It helps you create advanced scripting applications, but also requires you to know more about the language environment to perform any given task. The important consideration is not to confuse JScript.NET, a compiled version of JavaScript that uses the .NET Framework, with standard JavaScript. The JSC utility uses the following syntax:

```
jsc [options] <SourceFiles> [[options] <SourceFiles>...]
```

The JSC compiler groups the command line options by purpose, including output files, input files, resources, code generation, miscellaneous, and advanced. The following list describes each of the output file command line arguments.

NOTE The version of the JSC compiler that comes with Vista works precisely the same way as it does for other versions of Windows. However, don't look for JSC in the .NET Framework 3.0 folder. Instead, look for it in the `\Windows\Microsoft.NET\Framework\v2.0.50727` folder.

`/out:`*`file`* Determines the name of the output file. The default is to use the name of the source file as the name of the output file and to add the required extension such as EXE or DLL.

`/t[arget]:exe` Creates a console application, one that executes at the command line. A console application can still use message boxes and other graphical elements, but it starts execution at the command line. Most console applications have the same appearance as the command line utilities that have appeared throughout the book.

`/t[arget]:winexe` Creates a Windows application. This application will begin running in a windowed environment. This option produces about the same result as running a JavaScript application using WScript instead of CScript.

`/t[arget]:library` Creates a library. A library is a method of storing code for use in multiple applications. The result is a DLL file.

`/platform:{x86 | Itanium | x64, anycpu}` Determines the platform on which the application will run. The default setting of `anycpu` means that you can run the application on any system. The only time you would specify the other options is when you really do need the functionality these other platforms provide—a discussion that's well outside the scope of this book.

You use input files to determine the output from the compiler. Of course, you need source files that contain the steps you want to perform. However, you can provide other kinds of input, such as library files. The following list describes the input file command line options.

`SourceFiles` Specifies the source code files, the files that you write, to use to create the output application or library.

`/autoref{+ | -}` References any assemblies that you define using an import statement within your source code. The compiler automatically uses the most current version of the assemblies. You can turn this feature off by using the `/autoref-` command line switch. In this case, you must manually reference the required assemblies using the `/reference` command line switch.

`/lib:`*`path`* Specifies additional directories that the compiler should use to search for references.

`/r[eference]:`*`FileList`* References one or more files for inclusion in the resulting application. A reference file provides code resources for the application. For example, if you reference the `System.Windows.Forms.DLL` file, you can create message boxes within your application.

Resources are a different kind of input file. A resource can include anything you use to create the user interface such as strings, icons, and bitmaps. The following list describes the resources you can use with your application.

`/win32res:`*`file`* Specifies a Win32 resource file. A resource file has a RES file extension and you usually create it as part of an application development effort. However, you can also create RES files using any of a number of shareware and freeware editors. See the list at thefreecountry.com (`http://www.thefreecountry.com/programming/resourceeditors.shtml`) for additional details.

/res[ource]:*filename*[*, name*[*, {public | private}*]] Embeds a single resource into the application. The resource is part of the application and you can access it directly without any concern that the resource might not be available. You can give the resource a unique name to make it easier to access. You can also set the visibility of the resource (which determines whether anything outside the application can use it).

/linkres[ource]:*filename*[*, name*[*, {public | private}*]] Links a single resource to the application. The resource remains a separate entity, which means that you must check to ensure it's available when needed. However, this option makes it easier to update the resource later. You don't have to recompile the application to make a resource change; simply add the new resource.

In some cases, you want to change the way the compiler generates the code to ensure the application runs as quickly as possible or to ensure you obtain the best error information possible. The following list describes all of the command line switches, even though you might find that some of the command line switches aren't that useful.

/debug{+ | -} Adds debugging information to the application. However, this option is unusable unless you have a debugger to use. Given that there aren't any third party debuggers for JScript.NET applications (if you hear of one, let me know at `JMueller@mwt.net`), you'd need a full version of Visual Studio to use this option, which would negate many of the benefits of working at the command line.

/fast{+ | -} Disables some language features to enhance code generation. The resulting application is smaller and executes faster. However, the code doesn't perform all of its usual checks, which means that some errors could go undetected until they cause an application crash.

/warnaserror{+ | -} Forces the compiler to treat warnings as errors. The compiler produces an executable when it encounters a warning, but doesn't when it encounters an error. This feature is a safety switch of sorts and ensures that the application you receive has no errors or warnings associated with it.

/w[arn]:*level* Sets the warning level from 0 to 4. A higher warning level produces applications that are more precise by tracking more potential problems during compilation. However, setting the warning level too high can also make the debugging process very difficult and frustrating. The best policy is to begin with the warning level at 0, fix the warnings at that level, and progress through the levels until you reach 4.

The compiler provides a number of miscellaneous options that you might find helpful. The following list describes the miscellaneous options.

@*filename* Uses a response file to provide input to the compiler. The compiler reads the content of the response file first and then adds (or changes) any command line switches that you provide.

/d[efine]:*symbols* Defines conditional compilation. Conditional compilation is a technique where you add code based on a specific requirement. For example, you might include conditional code with debugging messages as you debug your application, and then leave that code out for the final version of the application.

/nologo Compiles the application without displaying the compiler's copyright banner.

/print{+ | -} Adds or removes the print function, which provides basic command line output.

The JSC compiler also provides a number of advanced options. You won't need these objects for basic command line development. However, the options can come in handy when you begin sending the application to others. The following list describes the advanced options.

/codepage:*id* Specifies which code page to use for open source files.

/lcid:*id* Specifies the Locale Identifier (LCID) to use for messages and the default code page.

/nostdlib{+ | -} Adds or removes the standard library, MSCorLib.DLL, from the application. Also sets the /autoref- command line switch. You must have the standard library available for the application to run.

/utf8output{+ | -} Outputs the applications using UTF-8 character encoding.

/versionsafe{+ | -} Creates a version-safe application that can use multiple versions of the .NET Framework by specifying default members not marked as override or hide. This option could result in applications that have less functionality, including less support for newer security features.

Creating a Simple Example

As previously mentioned, there isn't anything secret about JScript.NET. It provides a full implementation of the JScript language that you've used at the command prompt. However, the objects you use with JScript.NET differ from those that you normally use with JavaScript at the command line. Here's a simple example that tells you the JScript version number, which I named Version.JS.

```
var Version;

// Create a string with the JScript version information.
Version = ScriptEngine() + " Version ";
Version += ScriptEngineMajorVersion() + ".";
Version += ScriptEngineMinorVersion() + ".";
Version += ScriptEngineBuildVersion();

// Display the output.
print(Version);
```

You can compile this example by typing **JSC Version.JS** at the command line and pressing Enter. After a few seconds, the compiler will create Version.EXE for you. You can execute the resulting executable to see the version information. Figure 14.9 shows typical results.

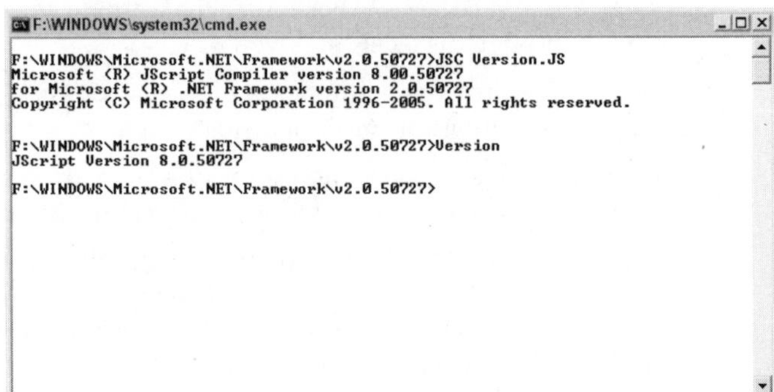

F:\WINDOWS\system32\cmd.exe
F:\WINDOWS\Microsoft.NET\Framework\v2.0.50727>JSC Version.JS
Microsoft (R) JScript Compiler version 8.00.50727
for Microsoft (R) .NET Framework version 2.0.50727
Copyright (C) Microsoft Corporation 1996-2005. All rights reserved.
F:\WINDOWS\Microsoft.NET\Framework\v2.0.50727>Version
JScript Version 8.0.50727
F:\WINDOWS\Microsoft.NET\Framework\v2.0.50727>

FIGURE 14.9
JSC produces an executable application that you can use like any other application.

Working with the .NET Framework

Anything you can do with any other language using the .NET Framework, you can do with JScript. Microsoft doesn't place any limitations on you. The biggest problem in using the .NET Framework is learning about all of the required objects. You can find a .NET Framework reference online at http://msdn.microsoft.com/library/en-us/netstart/html/cpframeworkref_start.asp. In addition, you need to know about the import statement, which lets you use .NET Framework objects in your code. Here's a fully functional .NET Framework example that I named NET.JS.

```
import System;
import System.Windows.Forms;

System.Windows.Forms.MessageBox.Show("Hello World");
```

After you type this example, type **JSC NET.JS** and press Enter at the command line. The compiler creates NET.EXE for you. In addition, it adds all of the required libraries to use the .NET Framework for you. At this point, you can test the example by typing **NET** at the command prompt and pressing Enter. You'll see a simple dialog box with Hello World as the message.

NOTE You'll find that Vista comes with several versions of the .NET Framework. The version used for this section appears in the \Windows\Microsoft.NET\Framework\v2.0.50727 folder. The .NET Framework entries in the \Windows\Microsoft.NET\Framework\v1.0.3705 and \Windows\Microsoft.NET\Framework\v1.1.4322 folders are there for compatibility purposes only. The contents of the \Windows\Microsoft.NET\Framework\v3.0 folder are for new Vista features, such as the Windows Communication Foundation, Windows Workflow Foundation, and Windows Presentation Foundation (WPF). WPF is the part of Vista that provides features such as Aero Glass.

Getting Started with Command Line Tasks

This chapter has discussed a number of products you can use to edit or compile your batch or script files. The important issue to remember about editors is that most of them have a feature that makes them special. Whether the feature is actually useful to you determines whether the editor is a good choice for your particular needs. For example, the binary file editing features of WinVi are only useful if you perform editing on binary files. Otherwise, you might want the added functionality provided by an editor such as Notepad+. The important issue is that there aren't any right choices—only the choice that works best for you. Remember that compiling your batch file or script is optional. These programs work just fine at the command prompt even if you don't compile them. The three essential reasons for compiling your batch file or script are hiding the content from others, keeping others from changing the content, and getting a small performance gain.

One of the problems with looking for new utilities is the need to focus on what you need, rather than what looks interesting. The interesting features might make you aware of other possibilities, but more often than not, they only serve to distract you from the task at hand (not that this is always bad, even administrators need play time). The best way to begin looking for a new utility is to define the goal of that utility before you do anything else. Write down the tasks the utility must perform and then search for the utility that performs those tasks. Of course, sometimes you'll find several utilities that perform the required tasks and you'll need to test them out. The important thing is to find an editor and compiler that do the kinds of things that you need to perform at the command line.

Chapter 15 begins a new section of the book. This section looks at a new addition to the Windows environments: the .NET Framework. The .NET Framework is an application environment along the same lines as Java. In fact, people often view the .NET Framework and Java as competitors. Because newer versions of Windows ship with the .NET Framework and some applications are installing the .NET Framework on systems, you need to know a little about the command line utilities that the .NET Framework supports. Chapter 15 introduces the .NET Framework and provides you with a few insights about it.

Part 4

Working with the .NET Framework Utilities

In This Section:

Chapter 15

Understanding the .NET Framework Versions

- Locating the .NET Framework on Your System
- Understanding the Concept of Side-by-Side Versions
- Viewing the Assembly Folder
- Discovering the Essential .NET Framework Assemblies

The .NET Framework is Microsoft's answer to Java, or maybe it isn't. It really depends with whom you talk as to whether the .NET Framework is the best thing since sliced bread or Microsoft's latest attempt to control the world. No matter how you view the .NET Framework or what you've heard about it, it's here to stay. Earlier versions of Windows require that you install the .NET Framework; future versions will have the .NET Framework installed. Even if you're using an earlier version of Windows, it's a good bet that you have the .NET Framework installed. Not only does Microsoft regularly update the .NET Framework through Windows Update, the .NET Framework now appears as part of many application distributions as well.

This book isn't going to make you a .NET Framework guru. In fact, we won't spend much time discussing the .NET Framework as an entity. The focus of this book is the .NET Framework at the command line. For example, would you know what to do if all of the ASP.NET applications on your server suddenly stopped working? A simple command line utility can fix the problem, in many cases, and you'll learn about it in Chapter 17. The focus of this chapter is the .NET Framework itself. You'll discover what the .NET Framework is, where you can find it, and what it means to you from a command line perspective.

Your goal in reading this chapter is to become familiar with the .NET Framework, which seems to be a bit of a mystery to anyone who doesn't write applications for a living (and it's a mystery to many who do). You'll discover a little about what Microsoft is attempting to accomplish and what you can do to make sure your copy of the .NET Framework continues to work as anticipated. In addition, you'll see how the .NET Framework will eventually make your life easier.

NOTE All of the .NET Framework tools require administrator privileges to run—even if you only want to see the help screen using the /? command line switch. In most cases, getting the correct privilege won't be a problem. However, in Vista, you must open a command prompt using the Run as Administrator option on the context menu or you'll see the message "Error: You must run as an administrator to run this tool." Whenever you see this message, open a new command prompt that has the administrator privileges. An administrator command prompt uses Administrator: Command Prompt as the title.

Locating the .NET Framework on Your System

The .NET Framework is Microsoft's technology for running applications based on the same tokenized technique that other modern development environments, such as Java, use. Compiling the program into tokens that rely on the Microsoft Intermediate Language (MSIL) means that the application can theoretically run on multiple platforms. Although Java makes good on this promise, so far the .NET Framework hasn't. Given that the .NET Framework represents an entirely different method of working with applications, Microsoft decided to place it in a different location on your hard drive. You'll normally find it in the `\WINDOWS\Microsoft.NET\Framework` folder of your system.

NOTE Because applications produced with the .NET Framework differ from those produced with standard application development technology, developers have had to create terminology to describe both application types. A .NET application relies on the Common Language Runtime (CLR) to execute based on the .NET Framework libraries. On the other hand, a native executable (application) relies on the Windows libraries located in the `\Windows\System32` directory to execute. All versions of Windows can run native executables, but older versions of Windows require that you install the .NET Framework to run .NET applications.

Any system that has the .NET Framework installed will have the `\WINDOWS\Microsoft.NET\Framework` folder. If you don't see this folder and want to have .NET Framework support on your machine, you can download the full version of the .NET Framework by going to Windows Update. You can also find a wealth of .NET Framework downloads at the Microsoft .NET Developer Center at `http://msdn2.microsoft.com/en-us/netframework/aa731542.aspx`. Here's a list of a few of the more important .NET Framework URLs.

.NET Framework 3.0 `http://www.microsoft.com/downloads/details.aspx?FamilyId=10CC340B-F857-4A14-83F5-25634C3BF043&displaylang=en`

NOTE You'll find that Vista comes with several versions of the .NET Framework. The version that most applications use appears in the `\Windows\Microsoft.NET\Framework\v2.0.50727` folder. The .NET Framework entries in the `\Windows\Microsoft.NET\Framework\v1.0.3705` and `\Windows\Microsoft.NET\Framework\v1.1.4322` folders are there for compatibility purposes only. The contents of the `\Windows\Microsoft.NET\Framework\v3.0` folder are for new Vista features, such as the Windows Communication Foundation, Windows Workflow Foundation, and Windows Presentation Foundation (WPF). WPF is the part of Vista that provides features such as Aero Glass. Because the .NET Framework 3.0 is so specialized, this chapter won't discuss it in any detail.

Microsoft Windows Software Development Kit for Windows Vista and .NET Framework 3.0 Runtime Components `http://www.microsoft.com/downloads/details.aspx?familyid=C2B1E300-F358-4523-B479-F53D234CDCCF&displaylang=en`

.NET Framework 2.0 `http://www.microsoft.com/downloads/details.aspx?FamilyID=b44a0000-acf8-4fa1-affb-40e78d788b00&DisplayLang=en`

.NET Framework 2.0 Software Development Kit (SDK) x86 Version: `http://www.microsoft.com/downloads/details.aspx?displaylang=en&FamilyID=FE6F2099-B7B4-4F47-A244-C96D69C35DEC`

.NET Framework 2.0 Software Development Kit (SDK) x64 Version: `http://www.microsoft.com/downloads/details.aspx?familyid=1AEF6FCE-6E06-4B66-AFE4-9AAD3C835D3D&displaylang=en`

.NET Framework 1.1 `http://msdn2.microsoft.com/en-us/netframework/aa569264.aspx`

.NET Framework 1.1 Service Pack 1 `http://www.microsoft.com/downloads/details.aspx?familyid=a8f5654f-088e-40b2-bbdb-a83353618b38&displaylang=en`

.NET Framework 1.1 SDK `http://www.microsoft.com/downloads/details.aspx?familyid=9b3a2ca6-3647-4070-9f41-a333c6b9181d&displaylang=en`

.NET Framework 1.0 `http://www.microsoft.com/downloads/details.aspx?familyid=d7158dee-a83f-4e21-b05a-009d06457787&displaylang=en`

.NET Framework 1.0 Service Pack 3 `http://www.microsoft.com/downloads/details.aspx?familyid=6978d761-4a92-4106-a9bc-83e78d4abc5b&displaylang=en`

You might ask yourself why all of these versions are important. A .NET application works better when it has access to the version of the .NET Framework used to write it. The "Understanding the Concept of Side-by-Side Versions" section of the chapter tells how you can maintain several versions of the .NET Framework on your system and know that you'll never run into the compatibility problems you encounter when working with Windows applications.

Real World Scenario

THE .NET FRAMEWORK VERSIONS IN REALITY

The .NET Framework is, indeed, in its third version. Many machines will have all three versions installed on them. However, the reality of the .NET Framework is that the public received the first version with a lot less enthusiasm than Microsoft would like. The reason is important in that many administrators are concerned about the amount of space that the .NET Framework consumes on the hard drive. The 1.0 version consumes upwards of 75 MB for a typical installation, while the 1.1 version consumes 81 MB and the 2.0 version consumes 165 MB.

If hard drive space is a concern, you can safely eliminate the 1.0 version because very few applications use it. In fact, unless you have a custom-built .NET application that relies on the .NET Framework 1.0, you'll probably never run into this version. Unfortunately, eliminating just one version might not free sufficient space. The next step is to remove either the 1.1 or 2.0 .NET Framework versions. When you already have an investment in .NET technology and don't have any pending new applications, keep the 1.1 version installed. Otherwise, keeping the 2.0 version is your best choice.

Once you have a version or two of the .NET Framework installed, you'll find some additional folders under the `\WINDOWS\Microsoft.NET\Framework` folder. Each of these folders represents a different version of the .NET Framework and contains similar utilities. For example, the `\WINDOWS\Microsoft.NET\Framework\v1.1.4322` folder contains the 1.1 version of the .NET Framework and the `\WINDOWS\Microsoft.NET\Framework\v2.0.50727` folder contains the 2.0 version of the .NET Framework. The last number in the folder, 4322 or 50727, can change depending on updates that Microsoft provides.

WARNING The utilities in a particular .NET Framework version folder are for that version and support that version. For example, if you want to add support for an ASP.NET application that relies on the .NET Framework 1.1 to IIS, you must use the utilities in the `\WINDOWS\Microsoft.NET\Framework\v1.1.4322` folder, not those found in any other folder.

To access the utilities for a specific version of the .NET Framework from anywhere on your system, you must add the folder for that version to your path statement. Avoid adding more than one version to the path because you'll find that Windows will stop with the first path it finds anyway and the first path might not contain the utilities you want to use. In fact, this is a good time to use a batch file to add the path when you open the command prompt. The following batch file named `Framework.BAT` sets up .NET Framework support for you.

```
@ECHO OFF

REM Add .NET Framework support as needed.
@ECHO Add .NET Framework Support
@ECHO.
@ECHO 1) Version 1.1
@ECHO 2) Version 2.0
@ECHO 3) Don't Add Support
@ECHO.
CHOICE /C:123 Select a .NET Support Option

REM Act on the selection.
IF ERRORLEVEL 3 GOTO :EOF
IF ERRORLEVEL 2 GOTO :Add20
IF ERRORLEVEL 1 GOTO :Add11

REM Add the .NET Framework 2.0
:Add20
SET PATH=%PATH%;%WINDIR%\Microsoft.NET\Framework\v2.0.50727
GOTO :EOF

:Add11
SET PATH=%PATH%;%WINDIR%\Microsoft.NET\Framework\v1.1.4322

@ECHO ON
```

As you can see, this menu system relies on the `Choice` command to request input from the user. You could easily add this to the Command Prompt shortcut that appears in the Start ➤ Programs ➤ Accessories folder. Simply change the Target field to read **`%SystemRoot%\system32\cmd.exe /KF:\Framework`**. Every time you open a command prompt using this shortcut, the system will ask which version of the .NET Framework you want to use to execute commands.

Of course, if you always use the same version of the .NET Framework, it pays to skip the selection process and add the path directly. In this case, right-click My Computer and choose Properties from the context menu. Select the Advanced tab of the System Properties dialog box and click Environment Variables. You'll see the Environment Variables dialog box shown in Figure 15.1. Select the Path entry in the System Variables listing and click Edit. Add the .NET Framework path to the list and click OK three times to close all of the dialog boxes.

TIP This book won't tell you precisely how the .NET Framework works. It does provide you with useful information for managing the .NET Framework and its applications. You can get a good overview of the .NET Framework on the MSDN Web site at `http://msdn2.microsoft.com/en-us/netframework/aa497336.aspx`. The overview includes block diagrams, reasons you might want to use the .NET Framework, and a list of resources. The MSDN Web site at `http://msdn2.microsoft.com/en-us/netframework/default.aspx` contains a handy list of resources that help you understand the .NET Framework and discover what you need to use it. Get your .NET Framework questions answered on the .NET Development General newsgroup at `http://forums.microsoft.com/msdn/showforum.aspx?forumid=39&siteid=1`.

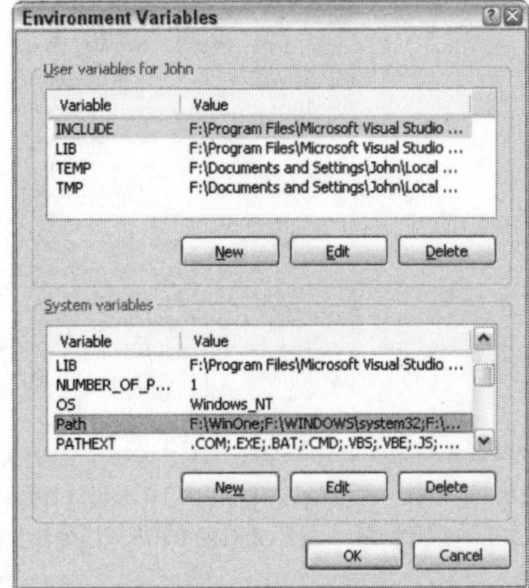

FIGURE 15.1
Add the .NET Framework path permanently when you only work with one version.

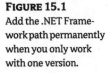

Understanding the Concept of Side-by-Side Versions

In the past, a Windows application would tell Windows that it required a certain DLL and Windows would respond by loading it. Unfortunately, Windows would load whatever version of the DLL appeared in the `\Windows\System32` directory. The version of the DLL that the developer used to create the application might differ from the version that appeared on the hard drive. If the developer had to overcome a problem with the previous DLL by writing code that used its peculiar functionality, the application might break if Microsoft fixed that behavior in the new DLL. In short, applications of the past normally required a certain version of the DLL, but didn't have any means to request it from Windows.

Applications created with the .NET Framework are different from those created for Windows. However, you won't see the difference when you view the two applications using a hexadecimal editor such as the Debug utility described in the "Examining, Modifying, and Debugging Files with the Debug Utility" section of Chapter 6 or the XVI32 utility described in the "Using XVI32 to View Files in Depth" section of Chapter 12. Figure 15.2 shows two utilities. The one on the top is a .NET application, while the one on the bottom is a native executable. Notice that both application files start with the letters MZ and they both have the same error message about not running as DOS applications. Both applications look the same to a hexadecimal editor.

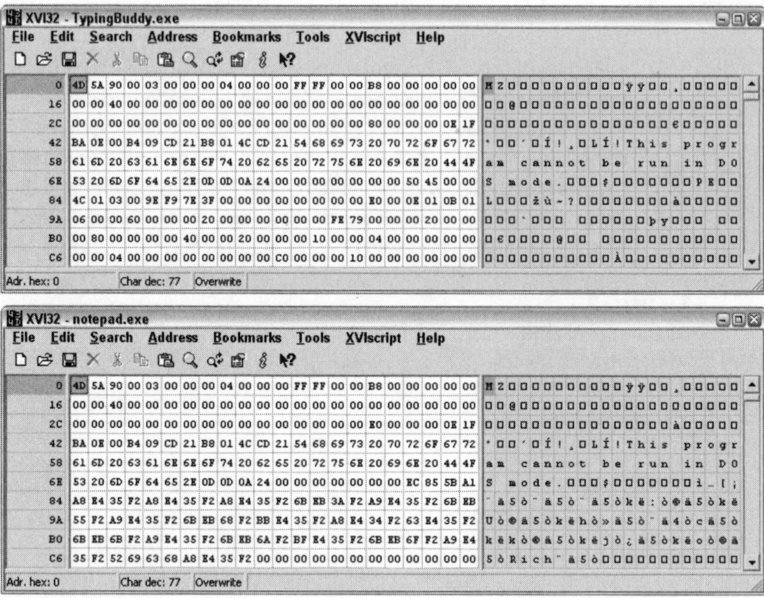

FIGURE 15.2
Hexadecimal editors can't tell the difference between .NET applications and native executables.

However, a .NET application differs significantly from a native executable. You can disassemble a .NET application using a special utility named Intermediate Language Disassembler (ILDASM). You get this utility as part of the SDK mentioned in the "Locating the .NET Framework on Your System" section of this chapter. The SDK provides full documentation for this tool. In addition, articles such as the one on C# Corner at `http://www.c-sharpcorner.com/vsnet/IldasmTool.asp` abound on the Internet. Most of the information you see when using this utility will appeal only to developers. It's interesting to look at though and you can't harm the program by viewing it. However, as shown in Figure 15.3, every .NET application includes a manifest that's of interest to administrators.

FIGURE 15.3
Use the ILDASM utility to view the contents of .NET applications.

Double-click the Manifest entry and you'll see what appears at first as incomprehensible gibberish as shown in Figure 15.4. The manifest tells you about the application—what it needs to work. This manifest begins by telling you that the application requires the Microsoft Core Library (MSCorLib) assembly, which is a requirement for every .NET application because it contains the core .NET Framework functionality. The developer of this application, me, used Visual Basic to write it and you can tell because it requires the Microsoft VisualBasic library. The next entry is important because it tells you the version number of the .NET Framework used for the main calls for this application. Look at the System entry and you'll see two subentries. The first tells you the token number (special key) for the assembly. The second tells you the assembly version number, which is 1:0:5000:0 in this case. A System assembly number of 1:0:5000:0 relates to the .NET Framework 1.1. Consequently, this application works best using that version of the .NET Framework, even though it will attempt to use all other versions unless the developer adds special checks to ensure that the application only runs under the original .NET Framework version. Don't worry too much about how assemblies work just yet; the "Viewing the Assembly Folder" section of the chapter describes them in detail.

FIGURE 15.4
View the manifest to determine what a .NET application requires to run.

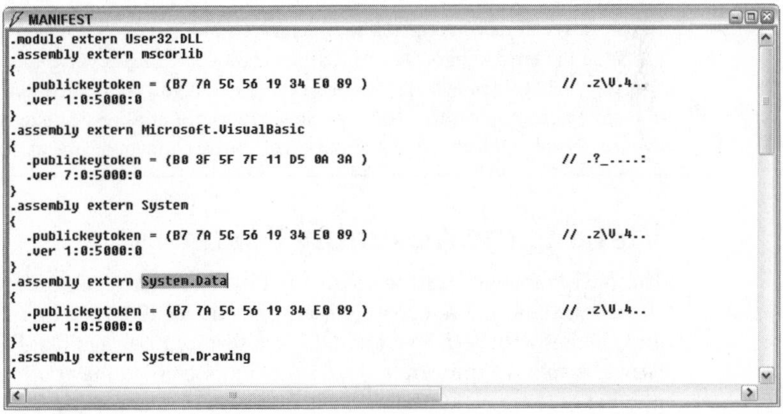

```
MANIFEST
.module extern User32.DLL
.assembly extern mscorlib
{
  .publickeytoken = (B7 7A 5C 56 19 34 E0 89 )                         // .z\V.4..
  .ver 1:0:5000:0
}
.assembly extern Microsoft.VisualBasic
{
  .publickeytoken = (B0 3F 5F 7F 11 D5 0A 3A )                         // .?_....:
  .ver 7:0:5000:0
}
.assembly extern System
{
  .publickeytoken = (B7 7A 5C 56 19 34 E0 89 )                         // .z\V.4..
  .ver 1:0:5000:0
}
.assembly extern System.Data
{
  .publickeytoken = (B7 7A 5C 56 19 34 E0 89 )                         // .z\V.4..
  .ver 1:0:5000:0
}
.assembly extern System.Drawing
{
```

The important idea to grasp in this section is that you finally have the resources required to understand why an application isn't working properly. When you have a Windows application that suddenly stops running correctly, you usually have to guess as to the cause and you can't verify the required DLL version numbers unless you request the information from the vendor. In short, native executables are very hard to troubleshoot. The demonstration in this chapter shows that you can take any .NET application apart with relative ease, diagnose precisely what it needs to run correctly, and fix it without spending hours doing it. When you run across a .NET application that doesn't run correctly and eliminate the resource files as the cause of the problems, you're left with a few small things to check before you call the vendor and ask for help with a bug that you're pretty certain is a bug.

Side-by-side version support also means that you don't have to worry about a host of native executable issues such as DLL hell (see the "Understanding DLL Hell" Real World Scenario for details). When you find that an application fails to run because you have the wrong version of the .NET Framework installed, you can simply download the version you need and install it. No longer do you have concerns about breaking another application when you perform the required installation. Although the .NET Framework is far from perfect, it's a step in the right direction and knowing how to interpret .NET applications makes your job considerably easier.

Real World Scenario

UNDERSTANDING DLL HELL

If you work in the computer industry for very long, you'll hear the term *DLL hell*. My hope is that the term will eventually become as antiquated as phrases such as 23 Skidoo (you can read about 23 Skidoo at `http://www.phrases.org.uk/meanings/393450.html` and one of its implementations at `http://www.explorehistoricalif.com/twenty-three%20skidoo.html`). DLL hell is a term that describes a condition where you have two applications, both of which require the same DLL. Unfortunately, one application requires one version of the DLL and the other application requires a different version of that same DLL. Now you face the prospect of supporting just one application since the `\Windows\System32` directory can only have one version of the DLL in place. If both of these applications are critical to your business, the choice becomes difficult indeed. This problem is so significant that you can find hundreds of thousands of hits for it on Google. The quintessential article on the topic though is titled, "The End of DLL Hell." You can find it on the MSDN Web site at `http://msdn2.microsoft.com/en-us/library/ms811694.aspx`.

Despite any claims you read to the contrary, no one's actually solved DLL hell. It's very likely that you'll continue to battle it for quite some time to come. As long as you have two applications on your system that rely on native code DLLs, there's a chance that you'll run into DLL hell. However, the introduction of technologies such as the .NET Framework, where side-by-side execution keeps DLL hell at bay, may eventually solve the problem and make the entire concept of DLL as old as horse-drawn carriages.

Viewing the Assembly Folder

The .NET Framework introduces a number of new terms. One of the more important terms to know about is assembly. An assembly is any executable file. As with native executables, assemblies can include files with both EXE and DLL extensions. Look again at Figure 15.3 and you'll see why the term *assembly* is appropriate. The compiler assembled the application shown in the figure from a number of components that include forms, classes, and other features. The concept of an assembly isn't that new, but because of the way that the .NET Framework interacts with assemblies, developers needed a new name.

Assemblies are either private or public. Private assemblies are essentially inaccessible unless they appear in the same directory as the application that requires them or the application creates a specific reference to them. Developers use private assemblies in situations where other applications won't require code or resources that the assembly contains. All public assemblies appear in the Global Assembly Cache (GAC). No matter where the public assembly physically appears on the hard drive, an application can find it by looking in the GAC.

Although it's just fine that applications can locate a public assembly, you often need to find them as well. The `\WINDOWS\assembly` folder contains a special view of the GAC you can use to manage the public assemblies. Figure 15.5 shows a typical view of the `\WINDOWS\assembly` folder.

The display shown in Figure 15.5 contains several essential pieces of information that you need to know about to manage the assembly correctly. The first piece of information isn't actually available. Every file in this list is a DLL. Consequently, the Accessibility entry is actually `Accessibility.DLL`. Notice that the listing contains two Accessibility entries. Normally, a folder can't contain two files with the same name. It's essential to remember that the `\WINDOWS\assembly` folder isn't a standard folder; it's a view into the GAC. The GAC can contain two files with the same name as long as the files differ by some criteria, such as version number.

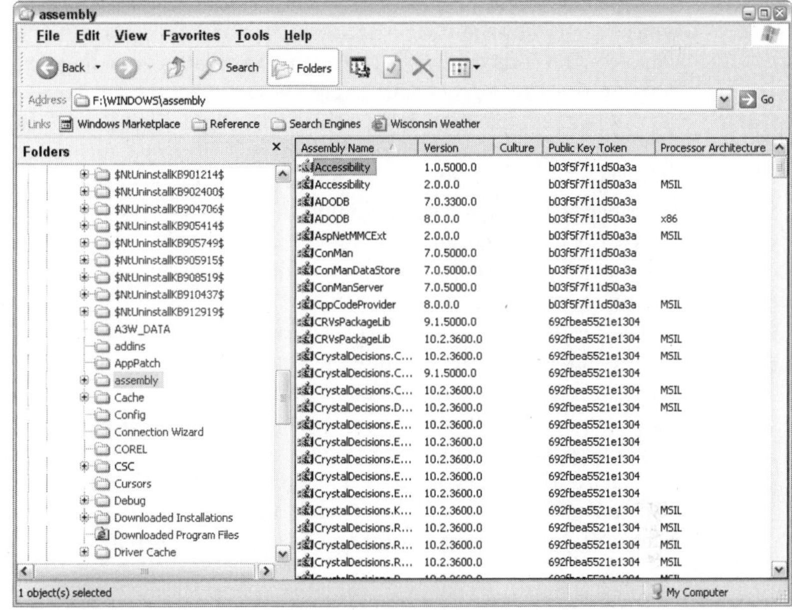

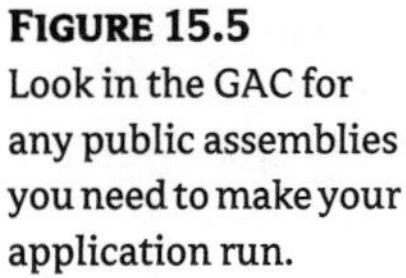
FIGURE 15.5
Look in the GAC for any public assemblies you need to make your application run.

NOTE Not every assembly in the GAC is associated with the .NET Framework. For example, if you install SQL Server 2005 on your system, you'll see a number of SQL Server–related assemblies in the list. In addition, any third party that produces a .NET application or resource can add an assembly to the GAC. Consequently, you should only assume that files that actually appear in the `\WINDOWS\Microsoft.NET\Framework` folder are part of the .NET Framework.

The assembly version number is next in the list. The assembly version number need not match the .NET Framework version. In fact, for the .NET Framework 1.1, the numbers definitely don't match. If the assembly is for a specific language other than English, the next column contains a cultural code. Normally, it's a two-letter designation, such as fr for French.

The public key token comes next. This is the most important piece of information for an administrator looking for modified files. Unlike a Windows DLL, a developer must sign a .NET assembly before adding it to the GAC. Most references call the process of signing an assembly giving it a strong name. The point is that this digital certificate is your guarantee of knowing who signed a public assembly. The token value for an assembly is unique. If someone makes any change to the assembly at all, the token is no longer valid and the GAC won't accept the assembly. Should someone make a change using devious means, the CLR still won't run the assembly because the values inside the assembly won't match the token value any longer. In short, no one can modify a .NET assembly file without leaving a fingerprint behind and making it very easy for you to detect the change.

TIP If you ever doubt the validity of a .NET assembly, you can always verify the token with the vendor. The token doesn't give away any information about your machine; every machine that has a particular version of an assembly installed has the same token. Consequently, it's very easy to check token numbers with the vendor to ensure you have an unmodified assembly installed on your system.

The final column shows the target processor for an assembly. Most assemblies target the MSIL, which means they should run on any platform that supports the .NET Framework. A few assemblies could contain code that won't run on just any platform, so they provide a platform-specific target. If you don't see any target at all, you can assume that the developer targeted the assembly at MSIL.

You can perform two tasks in this view. Right-click any assembly and you'll see the Uninstall and Properties options on the context menu. Selecting Uninstall will remove the assembly from the GAC. However, the assembly is still available on the system. You can use the GACUtil utility described in the "Placing Assemblies in the Global Assembly Cache with GACUtil" section of Chapter 16 to reinstall an assembly that is removed accidentally. In fact, this information is essential when you have curious users who might damage their systems by cleaning up assemblies they don't think they need any longer.

The Properties option displays a Properties dialog box like the one shown in Figure 15.6. The General tab provides essentially the same information as you saw in Figure 15.5. The Version tab is where you find additional assembly information. Notice that the File Version field doesn't match the assembly version. In this case, the number you see is the .NET Framework version number. The File Version helps you match an assembly to the .NET Framework version that supports it (assuming that the assembly is actually part of the .NET Framework). You can always verify that an assembly is part of the .NET Framework by looking at the Product Name field. This field contains Microsoft .NET Framework for any assembly that is part of the .NET Framework.

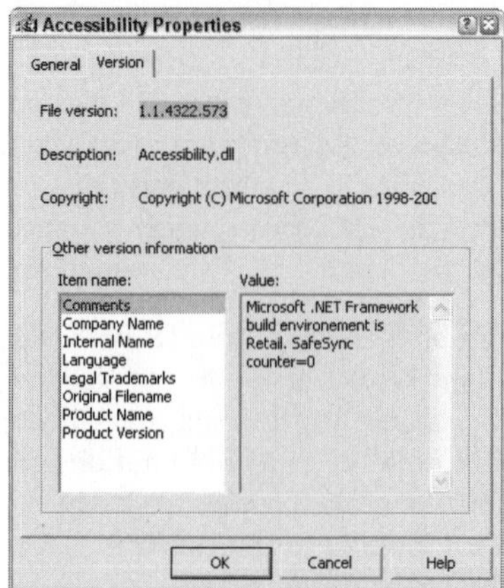

FIGURE 15.6
The Properties dialog box provides you with additional information about an assembly.

Always look at the Comments field for an assembly if you think that you have the wrong support installed. A production system, one that you aren't using for development, should always have a retail version of the assembly installed. The Comments field tells you which kind of assembly you have installed when working with .NET Framework assemblies.

Discovering the Essential .NET Framework Assemblies

You have just about every piece of information you need now to work with the .NET Framework and manage it in a way that improves overall system security and reliability. Of course, Chapters 16 and 17 discuss the essential utilities you need, but you do have an understanding of the .NET Framework itself. However, it's important to know a little more about discovering assemblies on your system. So far, you know that the .NET Framework assemblies physically appear in the `\WINDOWS\Microsoft.NET\Framework` folder and that all public assemblies appear in the GAC.

This is enough information to work with simple applications, but not enough to work with anything complex.

The first kind of supplemental assembly that you'll need to know about is the local reference. A local reference generally doesn't appear in the GAC because the developer assumes that no other application will require the assembly. The local reference always physically appears in the same folder as the application. It must also appear in the application's manifest. Figure 15.7 shows a manifest with a local reference named `MyMath`. Notice that all of the other assemblies in this figure have a `.publickeytoken` entry, but that `MyMath` doesn't. Any assembly that is missing the `.publickeytoken` entry is a local reference. Without a public key token, you can't register the assembly in the GAC. Consequently, if you don't see this assembly in the directory with the application, then you know the user has deleted it and you need another copy. Local references of this type normally come from the application vendor so they should appear on the product media.

FIGURE 15.7
Learn to spot local references in your applications so you know if something is missing.

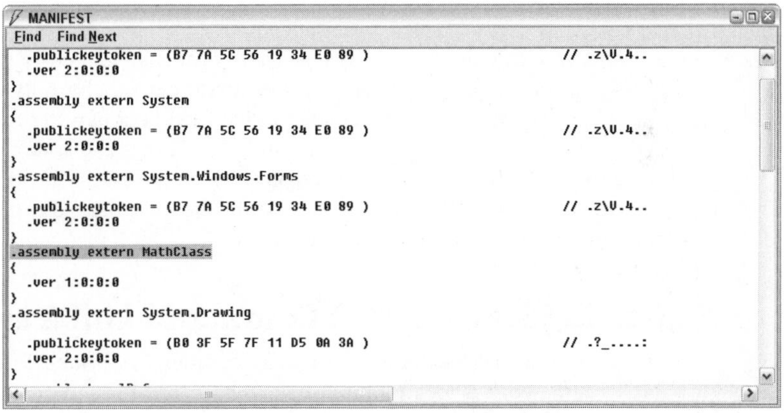

```
MANIFEST
Find   Find Next
  .publickeytoken = (B7 7A 5C 56 19 34 E0 89 )                         // .z\V.4..
  .ver 2:0:0:0
}
.assembly extern System
{
  .publickeytoken = (B7 7A 5C 56 19 34 E0 89 )                         // .z\V.4..
  .ver 2:0:0:0
}
.assembly extern System.Windows.Forms
{
  .publickeytoken = (B7 7A 5C 56 19 34 E0 89 )                         // .z\V.4..
  .ver 2:0:0:0
}
.assembly extern MathClass
{
  .ver 1:0:0:0
}
.assembly extern System.Drawing
{
  .publickeytoken = (B0 3F 5F 7F 11 D5 0A 3A )                         // .?_....:
  .ver 2:0:0:0
}
```

The second kind of supplemental assembly is the third party product. The third party product can appear in the GAC, which means that you should see it in the `\WINDOWS\assembly` folder or as a local reference, which means that you should see it in the application folder. These are the only two possibilities. Consequently, troubleshooting should be very short. However, knowing where to find the third party assembly when you need to reinstall it can take longer. Hopefully, it appears on the application media, but if it doesn't the vendor documentation should say something about the third party product.

The third kind of supplemental assembly is the external service. Not every .NET assembly contains code that the application accesses directly. For example, an assembly could require the use of a Windows service. In fact, it's possible to write the code for the Windows service using the .NET Framework, but the application won't know because Windows strictly controls service access. However, the assembly will contain breadcrumbs to tell you about this requirement. When an assembly requires use of a Windows service, it contains a reference to the System.ServiceProcess assembly in the manifest. If the assembly uses other kinds of external services (such as a Web service), then you'll find the appropriate assembly reference in the manifest.

Unfortunately, the service assembly reference doesn't tell you much about the required service. Hopefully, the vendor documentation will tell you about this requirement, but often it doesn't. Fortunately, when tech support also fails to tell you which service that the application requires, you can usually rely on ILDASM to help you. Notice the highlighted entry in Figure 15.8. This entry is the service that requires the System.ServiceProcess assembly.

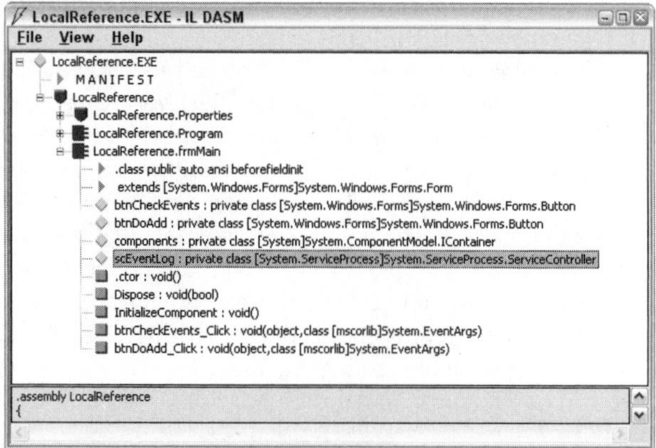

FIGURE 15.8
Fortunately, .NET applications can't hide requirements the way native executables do.

The key in this case is the `[System.ServiceProcess]` entry that you see immediately after `.field private` class. The name of the entry, `scEventLog`, tells you the application requires the Event Log service. Even if the developer isn't kind enough to provide you with this kind of information, you can usually poke around in the `InitializeComponent()` method to see how the developer initialized the `scEventLog` object. In short, unless the developer takes extreme measures, you can always find out what a .NET application requires to run properly with a little research—no more secrets, no more hidden obstacles.

Getting Started with Command Line Tasks

This chapter has considered a few .NET Framework issues. First, you discovered where the .NET Framework is located on your machine and how to determine which version you have installed. This information is very important because Microsoft continues to update the .NET Framework. Second, you discovered how you can have multiple copies of the .NET Framework installed on your machine at one time so that older applications can continue to use the version of the .NET Framework that they prefer. Third, you've discovered some of the internal workings of the .NET Framework; not enough to amaze developers, but enough that you can work with the .NET Framework comfortably.

Now it's time to explore a bit so that you become familiar with the .NET Framework directories on your system. Make sure you update your machine to the latest version of the .NET Framework as well. This is one case where updating doesn't mean breaking every application on your system. Remember that the .NET Framework allows side-by-side execution, so you have multiple versions on your machine at the same time.

Chapter 16 continues exploration of the .NET Framework. This chapter tells you about the command line utilities that affect all .NET applications. For example, you'll learn about the .NET Framework alternative to the RegSvr32 utility, the RegAsm utility. Knowing about these utilities can spare you the frustration of trying to learn about a new Microsoft technology without knowing about any of the utilities to manage it.

Chapter 16

Configuring the .NET Framework

- Understanding .NET Framework Configuration
- Understanding the Use of CONFIG Files
- Setting Policies Using the CASPol Utility
- Placing Assemblies in the Global Assembly Cache with GACUtil
- Installing Assemblies with the InstallUtil Utility
- Registering Assemblies with the RegAsm Utility
- Registering Services with the RegSvcs Utility
- Using the .NET Framework 3.0 Utilities

The .NET Framework provides a wealth of configuration options. Some of these options control how the application runs, but you'll also find configuration options that control how the .NET Framework controls security or whether an assembly appears in the Global Assembly Cache. You can also control how the system works with the assembly code and define who can use a particular assembly and how they can use it. In short, you have completely flexible control over assemblies when working with the .NET Framework—more control than you can possibly imagine having when working with a native executable application.

This chapter discusses the utilities that you use to work with the .NET Framework in general. These utilities affect all assemblies, no matter how you use them. For example, if you have a DLL that you need to register in the GAC, you use the Global Assembly Cache Utility (GACUtil) to do it. You'll also find that the .NET Framework supports special utilities you use when working with a particular product such as SQL Server or a service such as IIS. These utilities appear in Chapter 17.

Understanding .NET Framework Configuration

The .NET Framework and Common Language Runtime (CLR) (pronounced clear) can do a lot to make administration easier. In addition, because of the extreme flexibility of configuring .NET applications, you can also receive a significant gain in application reliability and security. However, to obtain all of these pluses over native executables, you must also deal with additional complexity. An administrator must understand how the .NET Framework works with both users and applications, instead of simply managing users. In fact, the new way of accomplishing tasks is the one thing that most administrators find difficult to understand about the .NET Framework.

With the difficulty in grasping a new way of accomplishing tasks in mind, this chapter begins by looking at a graphical utility, instead of looking immediately at the command line. The .NET Framework Configuration console that appears in the Administrative Tools folder of the Control Panel shows how the .NET Framework manages objects, both users and code, more effectively than trying to describe them as part of a command line utility. Yes, you'll learn all about the command line utilities later in the chapter, but this section is important because it shows graphically what the command line tools do at the command line.

NOTE Every version of the .NET Framework has a similar .NET Framework Configuration console. Make sure you use the correct version of the .NET Framework Configuration console for the version of the .NET Framework you want to use for your application. This chapter views the latest version of the .NET Configuration console for the .NET Framework 2.0. Older versions of the .NET Framework console provide equivalent features, so you can use this information with any version of the .NET Framework Configuration console you choose to use. Older versions may differ in screen presentation and offer a few less features than this version.

The .NET Framework Configuration console has a lot to offer the administrator. It's a tool that you should spend time learning, even if you aren't using it for configuration needs because it helps you understand the command line better. The following sections describe the portions of the .NET Framework Configuration console that you'll normally use to administer .NET applications on any machine.

Working with the Global Assembly Cache

Managing the Global Assembly Cache (GAC) is an important task because the GAC determines which assemblies are available for public use. The .NET Framework Configuration console lets you view registered assemblies and add new ones using a graphical interface, as shown in Figure 16.1.

This console works approximately the same as viewing the information in the `\WINDOWS\assembly` folder as described in the "Viewing the Assembly Folder" section of Chapter 15. However, unlike using the `\Windows\assembly` folder, you can also add new assemblies to the list by right-clicking the Assembly Cache folder and choosing Add from the context menu. To delete an assembly from the GAC, select it and click Delete (the icon on the toolbar with a red X).

Understanding .NET Security

Many of the .NET Framework configuration features have something to do with security. Anyone familiar with Windows security understands that everything focuses on the user and that the user always has the same rights no matter where the user accesses the system. The problem with this approach is that modern viruses, adware, spyware, and crackers don't just attack the user; they also attack the code. Because Windows doesn't secure the code, these nefarious elements can trick the code into doing things that it wouldn't normally do and create holes in security as a result. For example, the code might request access to a file when it normally doesn't do anything with files. The code could also make a remote request, despite the fact that it doesn't provide remote capabilities.

When working with .NET security, you must consider three elements. First, you need to consider the user's role. The role considers the user's activity and you can define activity based on a computing need. The role can also change as the user's computing requirements change. Second, you must consider the zone from which a request originates. A local request is far less likely to have security implications than one that comes from the Internet. By changing security to meet the requirements of a particular zone, you can ensure that Internet requests never access a file on the system even though local requests from the same party can. Third, it's important to secure the code. An application that doesn't normally handle files should never have the right to do anything with a file. Even if the application has a security hole and a cracker exploits that hole, if CLR determines that the code can't access a file the cracker wants, the cracker hasn't gained anything. The following sections discuss these three elements in detail.

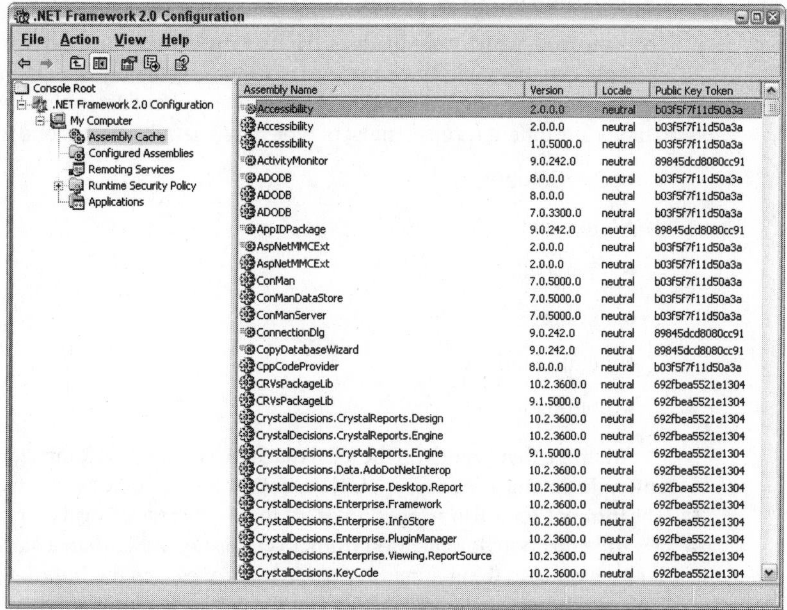

FIGURE 16.1
Add the .NET Framework Configuration console to your list of security aids.

CONSIDERING USER ROLES

The user role is the closest to the standard Windows security, even though a role isn't precisely the same as Windows security. A user's role depends partly on the user's membership in groups. In addition, a developer can create custom roles and add the user to them. The method you use to set a user's role depends on the application. For general roles, you use the group membership features of Windows. A developer might also choose to use COM+ to provide application services. You access COM+ roles through the Component Services console. The MSDN article at `http://msdn.microsoft.com/archive/en-us/dnarexnt00/html/ewn1100.asp` describes this process in detail. In some cases, the developer might define roles using the application's CONFIG files (see the "Understanding the Use of CONFIG Files" section of the chapter for details) or rely on a SQL Server database. The point is that the user's role determines what a user may nominally access on a system.

An application controls the role access in a number of ways. From an administrative perspective, the two most important methods are through accounts and zone recognition. The user's account has a lot to do with the user's role. If you ensure the user must use a different account to log on from a remote location, you can control the user's role and therefore access to system resources. Likewise, a developer can add zone control to the application. Even if a user is in a particular role, the application can restrict access based on the zone.

NOTE The .NET Framework supports policies at three scope levels: enterprise, machine, and user. The scope defines how much of the network a policy affects. For example, you might decide that it's a bad idea for any application to access the registry from the Internet zone. Consequently, you could restrict that right at the enterprise level. A user who calls in from home might have a machine policy that restricts access to certain client files. Another user who just joined the company might have a user policy that restricts access to sensitive company information. It's important to remember the scope of a policy when you create it to avoid making a sweeping change that breaks applications.

CONSIDERING REQUEST ZONES

The zone from which code loads or the user makes a request determines a basic level of security. For example, code contained on your local machine is generally safer than code downloaded from the Internet. Knowing the original location of code can help you determine its trustworthiness. By default, CLR defines five different zones (most of which look familiar to anyone who uses Internet Explorer).

- MyComputer
- Intranet
- Trusted
- Internet
- Untrusted
- NoZone

Anything that resides on the local machine is in the MyComputer zone. The Intranet zone includes any code downloaded using a UNC location such as `\\ServerName\Drive\Folder\Filename.TXT`. The Intranet zone also applies for anything you access using a mapped drive. CLR also uses the Intranet zone for code downloaded from a WINS site, rather than a standard IP site, such as a local Web server. Anything outside of these two zones is in the Internet zone. Initially, the Trusted and Untrusted zones are empty. However, the network administrator can place sites that are normally in the Internet zone into either the Trusted zone (to raise its confidence level) or the Untrusted zone (to lower its confidence level). The NoZone zone is a temporary indicator for items that CLR has yet to test. You should never see this zone in use.

CONSIDERING CODE ACCESS

The word *evidence* brings up the vision of a court with judge and jury for many people. The image is quite appropriate for the .NET Framework because any code that wants to execute must present its case before CLR and deliver evidence to validate any requests. CLR makes a decision about the code based on the evidence and decides how the evidence fits within the current policies (laws) of the runtime as set by the administrator. Theoretically, controlling security with evidence as CLR does allow applications built on the .NET Framework to transcend limitations of the underlying operating system. Largely, this view is true. However, remember that CLR is running on top of the underlying operating system and is therefore subject to its limitations. Here's the typical evidence-based sequence of events.

1. The assembly demands access to data, resources, or other protected elements.
2. CLR requests evidence of the assembly's origins and security documents (such as a digital signature).
3. After receiving the evidence from the assembly, CLR runs the evidences through a security policy.
4. The security policy outputs a permission based on the evidence and the network administrator settings.
5. The code gains some level of access to the protected element if the evidence supports such access; otherwise, CLR denies the request.

Note that the assembly must demand access before any part of the security process occurs. The Win32 API normally verifies and assigns security at the front end of the process—when the program first runs based exclusively on the rights of the user and not on the rights of the code. (A program can request additional rights later or perform other security tasks.) CLR performs verifications as needed based on a combination of the user's and the code's rights to enhance system performance. For example, a user in the local administrator role might have the right to access a file, but if the code doesn't have this right as well, CLR will deny access to the file. Likewise, a user in the Web user role might not have access to a file, even if the code has access to the file, and CLR will deny access based on the user's lack of rights.

The .NET Framework bases the concept of code trust on a number of code features. CLR divides code into verifiable and non-verifiable types. Verifiable code is safe and adheres to all of the policies defined by the .NET Framework. When CLR encounters verifiable code, it allows access to system resources automatically based on the evidence the code and user provide. Non-verifiable code isn't safe because it might access memory directly or perform other unsafe operations. Older code, such as that found in most Windows DLLs and COM objects, is always non-verifiable because it doesn't rely on the methodology that CLR uses to verify both code and user access. In this case, you must often tell CLR to allow resource access—effectively overriding the default actions because CLR doesn't know whether it can trust the code. In short, the code is safe because the system doesn't perform any unexpected action without your approval.

CLR defines two kinds of evidence: assembly and host. A developer can create any number of custom evidence types to support specific application needs, but you'll find that this is the exception, rather than the rule. For example, your company might decide as a business rule that only users who are in the manager role can access a particular part of a loan application that grants the loan. A developer could implement that rule as custom evidence that the user must satisfy. Custom evidence resides within the assembly as assembly evidence. CLR also ships with seven common evidence categories that cover most needs. These seven categories provide host evidence because Microsoft implemented them as part of the host (CLR).

- Application Directory
- Hash
- Publisher
- Site
- Strong Name
- URL
- Zone

The Application Directory, Site, URL, and Zone categories show where the code originates. For example, if a local application makes a request of a DLL on the server, the server code originates in the Intranet zone and you can treat it differently than if the local application makes the same request from the DLL on the local machine. The Publisher and Strong Name categories tell who wrote the code. You might decide to trust code from one publisher, but not another. Finally, the Hash category defines a special number that identifies the assembly as a unique entity—it shows whether someone has tampered with the content of the assembly. The application code checks the hash and denies the right to execute when it detects tampering.

Working with Code Groups

Code groups define the execution rights of assemblies on the local machine. The .NET Framework only comes with one code group by default, the All_Code group. The Enterprise, Machine, and User policies all support this code group and you'll generally use it for all local programs. However, you can modify how the code groups work and even add new code groups as the need arises. Any new code group you add will appear below the All_Code group in the hierarchy.

When you first select the Runtime Security Policy\<Scope>\Code Groups\All_Code entry in the left pane of the .NET Framework Configuration console, you'll see a help screen. This screen contains options for adding new code groups or configuring the existing code group, as shown in Figure 16.2. (This figure also shows the location of the All_Code entry in the hierarchy.)

FIGURE 16.2
Add or edit code groups using this help screen.

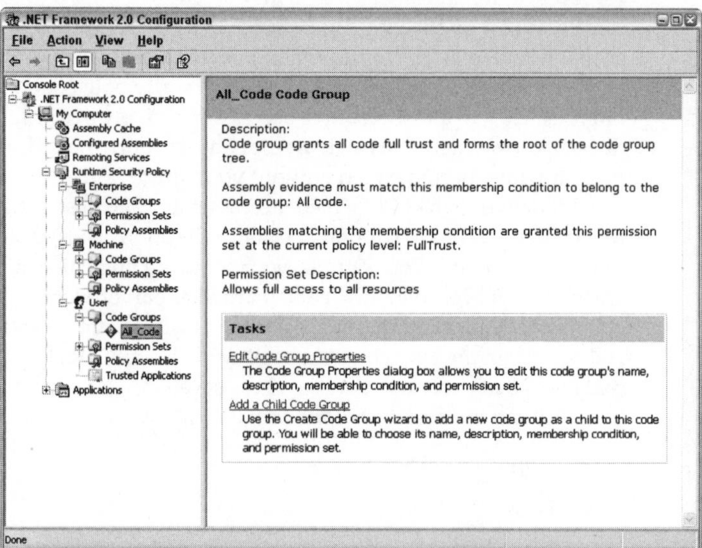

You can use one of three ways to create a new code group. Click the Add a Child Code Group link (you can also right-click an existing code group and choose New from the context menu) and you'll see a Create Code Group dialog box. This dialog box contains an option to create the code group manually (the first method). You can import an XML file that contains the code you want to use (the second method). Finally, you can right-click an existing code group and choose Duplicate from the context menu (the third method). This technique creates a code group with the same characteristics as the parent.

When you choose to create a code group manually, you pass through several dialog boxes. Each dialog box asks a question about the new code group including the condition type (such as ApplicationDirectory, Zone, or Hash) and the permission set (such as Full Trust, Execution, or Internet).

Editing a code group means changing features such as the condition type and the permission set. When you click Edit Code Group Properties on the help screen, you see a Properties dialog box similar to the one shown in Figure 16.3.

Notice that you can use this dialog box to determine how the code group will work with the policy levels. The first check box lets you set the code group to use permissions associated with the permission set for the code group exclusively. The second tells CLR not to evaluate policy levels below the existing policy level. In other words, this check box creates an exclusive code group.

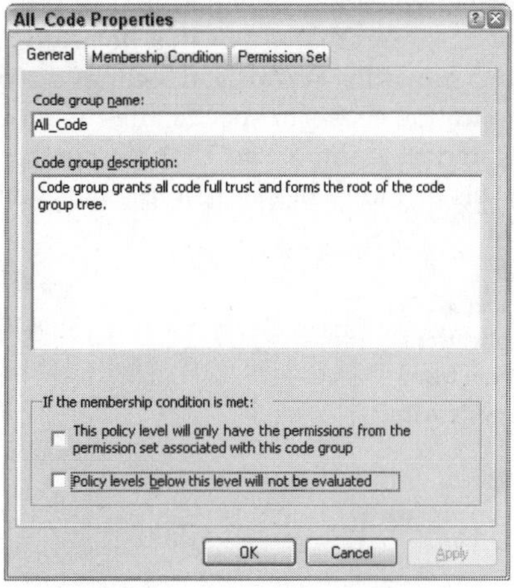

FIGURE 16.3
Use this dialog box to change the characteristics of a code group.

Creating and Defining Permission Sets

The .NET Framework comes with a standard set of permissions. You can create additional permission sets as required to meet specific programming needs. In addition, you can modify the definitions for existing permissions. However, modifying a current permission isn't a good idea because that action will change the default meaning of the permission and could cause other applications to fail. (CLR prevents you from changing .NET Framework–specific permission sets.)

You have the same options for creating a new permission set as described in the "Working with Code Groups" section. When you create a new permission manually, you'll see the Create Permission Set dialog box. The first screen asks for a name and description for the permission set. The second screen asks you to define the permission for the permission set, as shown in Figure 16.4.

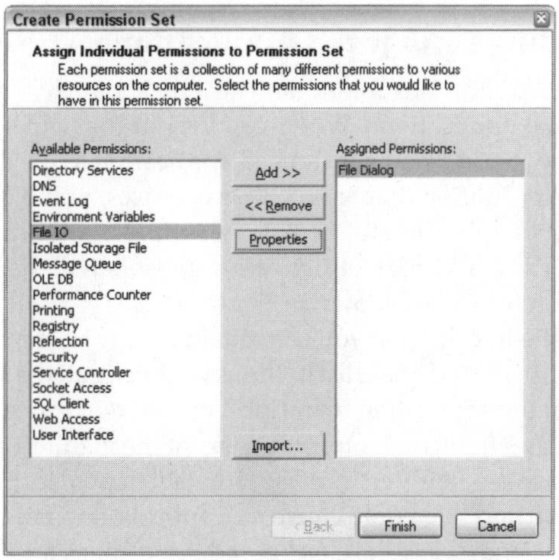

FIGURE 16.4
Define the permissions for your new permission set carefully to avoid security breaches.

Whenever you add a new permission, the .NET Framework Configuration console displays a Permission Settings dialog box that helps you configure that particular permission. For example, Figure 16.5 shows the Permission Settings dialog box for the File IO permission. Notice that you can limit application access to specific files when desired. The dialog boxes vary by permission. You can click Import to import an XML file containing the permissions you want to use. Custom permission sets include a help screen that lets you view, change, and rename the permission set.

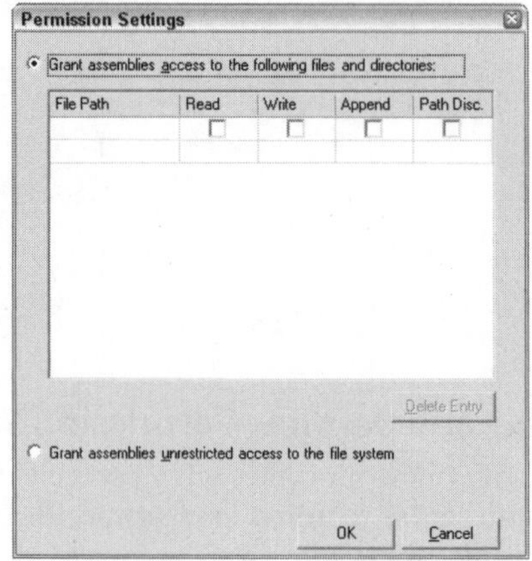

FIGURE 16.5
Create very specific rights for applications to prevent them from harming the system in any way.

Defining Policy Assemblies

Policy assemblies contain the code used by CLR to evaluate the evidence presented by an object to obtain a permission. The default .NET Framework configuration is all you need unless you design a special policy that requires additional code. As an administrator, you only need to configure this folder when an application you purchase comes with the required assembly. Make sure you follow the vendor instructions for installing and using the assembly.

Adding Configured Applications

The Applications folder isn't strictly a security setting, but entries in this folder can affect individual applications. When you look at the help screen for the Applications folder, you see an entry to add a new configured application to the list. Click this entry and you'll see the Configure an Application dialog box. In most cases, you'll click Other to add the new application. Adding a new application to the list is a simple matter of locating the executable on the hard drive. The .NET Framework Configuration console will display the application, along with three configuration folders as shown in Figure 16.6.

The information you can obtain here is interesting. First, select Assembly Dependencies and you'll see a complete list of the assemblies that the application needs to run. This information comes from the application manifest. You can't do much with this information, other than verify that it matches the actual information from the manifest as described in the "Understanding the Concept of Side-by-Side Versions" section of Chapter 15. Sometimes you'll find that the versions don't match and that could cause an application to fail.

Second, select the Configured Assemblies folder. You use this folder to change the system configuration for a particular application. For example, you might find that the application has decided to use the 2.0.0.0 version of the Accessibility assembly when it really requires the 1.0.5000.0 version.

You can change this behavior by configuring the assembly. Right-click Configured Assemblies and choose Add from the context menu. You'll see the Configure an Assembly dialog box. Select an assembly to configure. The easiest method is to select Choose an Assembly from the List of Assemblies this Application Uses and click Choose Assembly. Locate the assembly you want to change, and click Select. Click Finish and you'll see the Properties dialog box for that assembly.

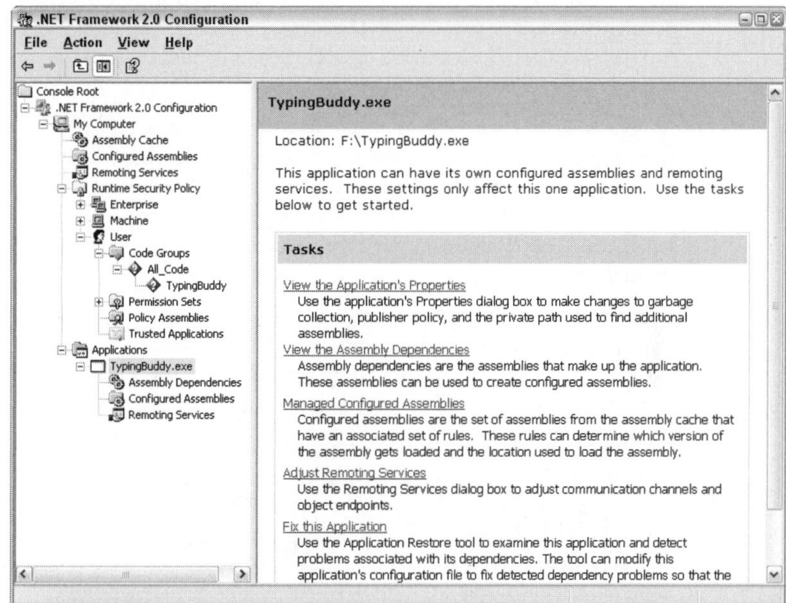

FIGURE 16.6
The .NET Framework Configuration console helps you perform a range of application configuration tasks.

You can change two features for an assembly. The first is the binding policy. The binding policy determines which version of the assembly the application uses for execution. Type the version number that the assembly is using now in the Requested Version field and type the version you want the assembly to use in the New Version field. The second feature is the code base for the assembly. Changing the code base lets the application request the assembly from another location when it isn't installed on the local machine. You shouldn't need to use this feature in most cases. Follow the vendor documentation when you do encounter an application that requires an assembly in a remote location.

Understanding the Use of CONFIG Files

Perhaps the most powerful feature for .NET applications is the use of configuration files. Configuration files always have a CONFIG file extension and rely on an XML format to define application settings. Some administrators are already aware that ASP.NET applications rely on configuration files for basic settings. However, configuration files appear in many other locations and you can use them for more than just setting ASP.NET application requirements. Desktop applications can also rely on configuration files. When working with a desktop application, the configuration file has the executable filename, plus the CONFIG extension. For example, when your application has `MyApp.EXE` as its name, the configuration file has `MyApp.EXE.CONFIG` as its name. In general, an application configuration file always appears in the same directory as the application.

UNDERSTANDING HOW .NET ROLE-BASED SECURITY DIFFERS

For many developers, the main issue in shifting gears from Win32 to .NET is how each system manages security. Under .NET an object doesn't have any rights until it provides evidence that CLR feeds through a policy to produce a permission. The idea is that CLR grants all rights. An object seeks permission to perform a task. If you can keep this basic concept in mind, then all the complexities discussed in this book become easier to understand.

Anyone who's spent time working with the security features provided by the Win32 API knows that these measures concentrate on individuals and groups. (Don't assume that any user is necessarily a person—it could be another application, remote computer, or other device.) If you give an individual user access to a system resource, they always have access to that resource no matter how they access the resource. They have access to the resource from the desktop or from the Internet. This kind of security doesn't consider the environment.

Groups only add to the problem because you can inadvertently give a user access to resources through a group membership that the user shouldn't have. Perhaps a manager hasn't trained the user on how to make entries in the accounting system yet. However, because the user belongs to the accounting department, they have access to the accounting system and can make entries in it.

The Win32 API technique also has other problems. Remember that this system has two kinds of lists. The first grants access to a resource, while the second denies access to a resource. It's possible that a single resource could have entries that both grant and deny access. When this situation occurs, a user who should have access to a resource may not be able to access it because the entry granting access to the resource appears earlier in the list than the entry denying access to the resource. The reverse situation can also occur, which means there's a hidden security hole in your system.

The following sections further refine the differences between role-based, code access, and user identity security. The coding examples show how to overcome some of the limitations of Win32 API security using the new features in the .NET environment. The big thing to remember, however, is that CLR still depends on the Win32 API, so you need to exercise care in saying that these measures are perfect. Until the underlying operating system is secure, you'll always have to look at these security features as useful, but not complete.

The application configuration file affects everyone who uses the application. The application developer can also create personal configuration files. These configuration files appear in the `\Documents and Settings\`*`User Name`*`\`*Application Data*`\`*`Application Name`* folder using a file with the CONFIG extension. The filename need not match the application filename. A personal configuration file always takes precedence over an application configuration file. The system applies the application settings first and then modifies them as needed with the personal settings.

This chapter can't provide a complete discussion of every possible configuration file setting. However, you can find all of the settings documented on the MSDN site at `http://msdn2.microsoft.com/en-us/library/ms228147.aspx`. However, it's helpful to look at a quick example. Let's say that you need to modify an application to use the appropriate assembly and you want to do it in a way that doesn't require individual machine configuration.

To use a specific assembly version, you must tell CLR about the requirement. Begin by creating a configuration file for your application that has a name such as `MyApp.EXE.CONFIG`. Use any text editor such as Notepad to perform this task. You can specify a file version in a couple of ways. If you're looking to use a particular version of the runtime, all you need to do is say you want to use that version with an entry in the configuration file such as this one.

```
<?xml version="1.0" encoding="utf-8" ?>
<configuration>
   <startup>
      <requiredRuntime version="v1.0.3705"
                       safemode="true"/>
   </startup>
</configuration>
```

This entry tells CLR that your application relies on the .NET Framework 1.0. If the host machine doesn't have this version, then CLR displays an installation error message that effectively says that the host machine needs the 1.0 version. The application won't start. Of course, not every .NET application will use the .NET Framework 1.0. If you want to specify a different version, simply set the value to something other than v1.0.3705. For example, the current 1.1 version would use a value of v1.1.4322 and the current 2.0 version would use a value of v2.0.50727.

Sometimes you need to control something other than the runtime. In this case, you can use a configuration file entry similar to this one:

```
<?xml version="1.0" encoding="utf-8" ?>
<configuration>
   <runtime>
      <assemblyBinding
         xmlns="urn:schemas-microsoft-com:asm.v1">
         <dependentAssembly>
            <assemblyIdentity
               name="MyAssembly"
               publicKeyToken="b77a5c561934e089"
               culture="neutral" />
            <bindingRedirect oldVersion="1.1.0.0"
                             newVersion="1.0.0.0"/>
         </dependentAssembly>
      </assemblyBinding>
   </runtime>
</configuration>
```

In this case, you would force the application to use an older version of MyAssembly. The `<bindingRedirect>` element shows the preferred version of the assembly. The important thing to remember is that anything you can set using the .NET Framework Configuration console, you can also set using a configuration file.

Setting Policies Using the CASPol Utility

The Code Access Security Policy (CASPol) utility helps you set the code access security for an application. This utility is the command line version of the .NET Configuration utility described in the "Understanding .NET Framework Configuration" section of the chapter. You can perform all of the same tasks at the machine, user, and enterprise levels. This utility uses the following syntax:

```
caspol -en[terprise] <args> ...
caspol -m[achine] <args> ...
```

```
caspol -u[ser] <args> ...
caspol -cu[stomuser] <path> <args> ...
caspol -a[ll] <args> ...
caspol -ca <path> <args> ... or caspol -customall <path> <args> ...
```

The following list describes each of the request levels for a command.

-en[terprise] Performs a task that affects the system at the enterprise level.

-m[achine] Performs a task that affects the system at the machine level.

-u[ser] Performs a task that affects the system at the user level.

-cu[stomuser] ***path*** Performs a task that affects a user other than the one currently executing CASPol. You must specify a path to the user's settings file to perform this task.

-a[ll] Performs a task that affects the enterprise, machine, and user levels. The user level change affects the current user. If you want to change another user, you must use the `-customuser` or `-customall` command line switch.

-ca ***path*** or **-customall** ***path*** Performs a task that affects the enterprise, machine, and user levels of a custom security configuration file. You must specify a path to the custom security configuration file to perform this task.

Once you define the level you want to work with, you can specify a particular action that you want to perform. The default level is machine for most commands. To obtain information at a different level, precede the action with a level command line switch. For example, typing **CASPol -enterprise -list** at the command line displays all of the security settings for the current user at the enterprise level. The following list describes each of these actions.

-l[ist] Lists all of the security settings.

-lg or **-listgroups** Lists the code groups.

-lp or **-listpset** Lists the permission sets.

-lf or **-listfulltrust** Lists the full trust assemblies.

-ld or **-listdescription** Lists the code group names and descriptions.

-cft or **-checkfulltrust** Checks the full trust list. The utility displays a list of any discrepancies it finds in the full trust list.

-ap { ***named_xml_file*** **|** ***xml_file name*** **}** or **-addpset {** ***named_xml_file*** **|** ***xml_file name*** **}** Adds a named permission set to the policy file. The permission set must appear as an XML file. When the permission set is a named permission set, all you need to provide is the name of the file. Otherwise, you must provide both the name of the file and a name for the permission set. You can find the XML file specification at `http://msdn.microsoft.com/library/en-us/cpguide/html/cpconnewpermissionsets.asp`. Another good place to look for examples is the `Security.CONFIG` file in the `\Documents and Settings\`*User Name**Application Data**Microsoft**CLR Security Config**.NET Framework Version*\\ folder on your hard drive.

-cp ***xml_file pset_name*** or **-chgpset** ***xml_file pset_name*** Modifies the named permission set. The permission set must appear as an XML file. You must specify the name of the permission set you want to change. See the `-addpset` command line switch discussion for details on creating a permission set.

-rp ***pset_name*** or **-rempset** ***pset_name*** Removes the specified permission set.

-af ***assembly_name*** or **-addfulltrust** ***assembly_name*** Adds the specified full trust assembly. The assembly must have a strong name (the vendor must sign the assembly). Generally, you'll use this command line switch with assemblies that implement a custom security feature. You must add any referenced assemblies to the full trust list before you add the specified assembly.

-rf ***assembly_name*** or **-remfulltrust** ***assembly_name*** Removes the specified full trust assembly.

-rg {***label*** | ***name***} or **-remgroup** {***label*** | ***name***} Removes the code group with the specified label or name. The CASPol utility automatically removes any child groups.

-cg {***label*** | ***name***} {***mship*** | ***pset_name*** | ***flag***}+ or **-chggroup** {***label*** | ***name***} {***mship*** | ***pset_name*** | ***flag***}+ Changes the code group with the specified label or name. You may modify the membership, permission set, or flags. See the discussion of the membership and flag values later in this section. The permission set is a string indicating an existing permission set.

-ag {***parent_label*** | ***parent_name***} ***mship*** ***pset_name*** [***flag***] or **-addgroup** {***parent_label*** | ***parent_name***} ***mship*** ***pset_name*** [***flag***] Adds a new code group to the specified parent. You may specify the parent name or label. You must specify the membership and permission set. Setting the flags argument is optional. See the discussion of the membership and flag values later in this section. The permission set is a string indicating an existing permission set.

-rsg ***assembly_name*** or **-resolvegroup** ***assembly_name*** Lists the code group associated with the specified assembly.

-rsp ***assembly_name*** or **-resolveperm** ***assembly_name*** Lists the permissions associated with the specified assembly.

-s[ecurity] { on | off } Enables or disables .NET Framework security. The default setting is enabled.

-e[xecution] { on | off } Enables or disables the right to run checking that CLR performs when starting an application. The default setting is enabled.

-pp { on | off } or -polchgprompt { on | off } Enables or disables the policy change prompt that appears every time you change a policy. The default setting is enabled.

-q[uiet] Disables the policy change prompt for the current command.

-r[ecover] Recovers the most recently saved version of the enterprise, machine, or user level. This feature is a type of undo.

-rs or **-reset** Resets the enterprise, machine, or user level to its default state. This feature removes any changes you've made since installing the .NET Framework.

-rsld or **-resetlockdown** Resets a level to its default lockdown state.

-f[orce] Forces CASPol to perform a save without performing a self-destruct check. The utility normally verifies that a policy change won't prevent it from running. Using this feature could disable CASPol functionality.

-b[uildcache] Builds the security policy cache file.

Some of the command line switches that you use with the CASPol utility require that you specify a membership. The membership command line switches appear in the following list.

-allcode Specifies the All Code membership.

-appdir Specifies the Application Directory membership.

-custom *xml_file* Specifies a custom membership. You must define the details within an XML file. See the discussion on the MSDN Web site at `http://msdn.microsoft.com/library/en-us/cpguide/html/cpconimportingcodegroupfromxmlfile.asp` for details on this technique.

-hash *hashAlg* {*-hex* *hashValue* | *-file* *assembly_name*} Specifies a Hash membership. You must provide the name of the algorithm used to create the hash. In addition, this membership requires the actual hash value as a hexadecimal number or the name of the assembly file that contains the hash.

-pub {-cert *cert_file_name* | *-file* *signed_file_name* | *-hex* *hex_string*} Specifies a Software Publisher membership. You must provide a certificate filename, a signed filename, or a hexadecimal string to identify the publisher identity. In all cases, the input is based on a digital signature.

-gac Specifies a GAC membership.

-site *website* Specifies a Site membership. Normally, you must provide the site domain such as `www.mysite.com`.

-strong {-file *assemblyfile_name* | *-hex* *public_key*} {*name* | *-noname*} {*version* | *-noversion*} Specifies a Strong Name membership. You must specify three pieces of information. First, you must identify the assembly using an assembly name or a public key token. Second, you must specify the assembly name or tell the utility that you don't want to provide a name using the `-noname` command line switch. Third, you must provide a version number or indicate that you don't want to provide a version number using the `-noversion` command line switch.

-url *url* Specifies a URL membership. When specifying a URL on the Internet, you must provide the protocol as part of the URL. For example, you could use `http://www.mysite.com/`. When specifying a UNC URI, you must include the information using the standard UNC format such as `\\myserver\myshare`.

-zone *zone_name* Specifies a Zone membership. The zone values can include any member of the following list.

MyComputer

Intranet

Trusted

Internet

Untrusted

Some of the command line switches that you use with the CASPol utility require that you specify a flag value. The flag value command line switches appear in the following list.

-exclusive {on|off} Sets the policy statement Exclusive flag.

-levelfinal {on|off} Sets the policy statement LevelFinal flag.

-n[ame] *name* Sets the code group name to the specified value.

-d[escription] *desc* Sets the code group description to the specified value.

Placing Assemblies in the Global Assembly Cache with GACUtil

You use GACUtil to register an assembly in the GAC or remove it from the GAC from the command line. An assembly that you want to register must meet specific criteria, the most important of which is that it must have a strong name. A strong name indicates that someone has signed the utility using a digital certificate. In short, someone is taking responsibility for the code in a way that's difficult to counterfeit. You can create a digital certificate to use to sign assemblies using the Strong Name (SN) utility, but generally the vendor selling the product will perform this task for you. This utility uses the following syntax:

```
Gacutil /i <assembly_path> [/r [{assemblyName | assemblyPath}]] [/f]
   [/nologo] [/silent]
Gacutil /il <assembly_path_list_file> [/r [{assemblyName |
   assemblyPath}]] [/f] [/nologo] [/silent]
Gacutil /u <assembly_display_name> [/r [{assemblyName | assemblyPath}]]
Gacutil /uf <assembly_name> [/nologo] [/silent]
Gacutil /ul <assembly_display_name_list_file> [/r [{assemblyName |
   assemblyPath}]] [/nologo] [/silent]
Gacutil /l [<assembly_name>] [/nologo] [/silent]
Gacutil /lr [<assembly_name>] [/nologo] [/silent]
Gacutil /cdl [/nologo] [/silent]
Gacutil /ldl [/nologo] [/silent]
```

The following list describes each of the command line arguments.

`/i` *`assembly_path`* Installs the specified assembly to the GAC. You must provide the assembly name and path.

`/il` *`assembly_path_list_file`* Installs the list of files provided in a separate file. You must provide a text file that has one assembly listed per line.

`/u` *`assembly_display_name`* Removes the specified assembly from the GAC. You must use the display name of the assembly as it appears in the `\Windows\assembly` folder. Don't use the filename and path. If you provide a partial assembly name, the utility will remove all assemblies that match the partial name.

`/uf` *`assembly_name`* Forces the system to remove an assembly from the GAC by removing all traced references to the assembly. The only exception is when the Windows Installer has a reference to the assembly. Using this option can cause applications to stop responding.

`/ul` *`assembly_display_name_list_file`* Removes the list of assemblies provided in a separate file. You must provide a text file that has one assembly listed per line.

`/l` *`[assembly_name]`* Lists the contents of the GAC. Use the optional assembly name input to reduce the list size. Specifying a partial assembly name lists all assemblies that match the specified criteria.

`/lr` *`[assembly_name]`* Lists the contents of the GAC including all traced references to the assemblies. Use the optional assembly name input to reduce the list size. Specifying a partial assembly name lists all assemblies that match the specified criteria.

`/cdl` Deletes the contents of the download cache.

`/ldl` Lists the contents of the download cache.

`/r` *`[assemblyName | assemblyPath]`* Specifies a traced reference to an assembly that you want to install or uninstall. The traced reference includes a schema type, an identifier, and a description. You must use the same options to uninstall an assembly as you use to install it. This feature helps overcome problems where uninstalling an application doesn't necessarily remove it from the GAC or vice versa. For example, you might install an assembly using the FILEPATH schema type with **/r FILEPATH c:\MyProject\MyApp.EXE "My Application"** as the arguments. The following list describes the schema types.

UNINSTALL_KEY Specifies that the installer adds the application to the Add/Remove Programs applet in the Control Panel. The application entry appears in the `HKLM\Software\Microsoft\Windows\CurrentVersion` registry key. You only supply the application's registry key as an identifier when using this option; don't provide the full registry path.

FILEPATH Specifies that the installer doesn't add the application to the Add/Remove Programs applet in the Control Panel. You must specify the full file path an identifier when using this option.

OPAQUE Specifies that the assembly doesn't require a registry key or file path for installation. Use this value to specify custom information for the identifier.

/f Forces the utility to install the assembly in the GAC even when there's another assembly with the same name, version, and token information.

/nologo Suppresses the display of the GACUtil banner. This option is helpful when creating batch files when you don't want to disturb the user.

/silent Suppresses all utility output. This option is helpful when creating batch files when you don't want to disturb the user.

Installing Assemblies with the InstallUtil Utility

The InstallUtil performs an installation of .NET applications based on the installer code within each assembly. You may specify more than one assembly and each assembly can have its own set of options. This section only lists common options; a developer can create unique assembly options that you must discover from the vendor documentation. The installation takes place in a transactional manner; if one assembly fails to install, they all fail and InstallUtil backs up the installation. This utility uses the following syntax:

```
InstallUtil [{/u | /uninstall}] [/AssemblyName] /LogFile=[filename]
   /LogToConsole={true | false} /ShowCallStack assembly [[options
   [...]] assembly] [...]]
```

The following list describes each of the command line arguments.

{/u | /uninstall} Uninstalls the specified assemblies. If you don't use this command line switch, the utility assumes that you want to install the assemblies.

/AssemblyName Specifies that the utility should interpret the assembly argument as an assembly name from the GAC that includes the Name, Locale, PublicKeyToken, and Version information. The default setting interprets the assembly argument as a filename and path to the assembly on disk.

/LogFile=[*filename*] Specifies the name of a file to use to write installation progress information. If you specify this command line switch without a filename, then the utility doesn't write a log for the assembly installation. The default setting creates a log with the name of the assembly with an InstallLog extension added.

/LogToConsole={true | false} Displays the installation progress to the console when set to true and suppresses the information when set to false. The default setting is true.

/ShowCallStack Sends the call stack to the log file when an exception occurs. The call stack can help a developer locate the source of an installation error.

Registering Assemblies with the RegAsm Utility

When working with native executables, you use the RegSvr32 utility to register the executable as a component in the registry. The registration process makes the executable accessible from other applications. By reviewing the registry entries, a calling application can locate the component on disk and use the code that it provides. A .NET application doesn't always require access to the registry to locate a component. When working with a .NET component, the application can locate the required files and know how to use the component without relying on the registry. However, native executables that require access to the .NET component still require registry entries. The RegAsm utility performs the same task as RegSvr32 for .NET components. This utility uses the following syntax:

```
RegAsm AssemblyName [/unregister] [/tlb[:FileName]]
   [/regfile[:FileName]] [/codebase] [/registered] [/asmpath:Directory]
   [/nologo] [/silent] [/verbose]
```

The following list describes each of the command line arguments.

AssemblyName Specifies the name of the assembly that you want to register. You must include the full assembly filename as a minimum.

/unregister Removes the registry entries for the .NET component.

/tlb[:*FileName*] Creates a type library for the .NET component. Normally, you won't need a type library unless you're writing an application. However, you might find that you need the type library, in some cases, such as when you register the component with COM+ for use in COM+ applications. Type libraries always have a TLB file extension.

/regfile[:*FileName*] Generates a REG file that contains the .NET component registry entries instead of placing the entries in the registry. This option is useful when you need to register the .NET component on multiple machines using a batch file. You can't use this command line switch with the /unregister or /tlb command line switches.

/codebase Sets the code base for the component in the registry.

/registered Specifies that the utility should only reference type libraries that you've already registered.

/asmpath:*Directory* Specifies the path that the utility should use when looking for .NET components to register.

/nologo Suppresses the display of the RegAsm banner. This option is helpful when creating batch files when you don't want to disturb the user.

/silent Suppresses all utility output. This option is helpful when creating batch files when you don't want to disturb the user.

/verbose Displays additional information during the registration process. The amount of additional information depends on the .NET component.

Registering Services with the RegSvcs Utility

You use the RegSvcs utility to create a COM+ application. As part of creating the COM+ application, this utility registers the assembly in the registry, creates the COM+ application, and configures any services found within the assembly. Make sure you follow any vendor recommendations when installing a COM+ application. Always configure the COM+ application after you install it to provide proper security and meet other application requirements. This utility uses the following syntax:

```
regsvcs.exe AssemblyName [/fc] [/c] [/exapp] [/tlb:<tlbfile>]
   [/appname:<name>] [/parname:<name>] [/extlb] [/reconfig]
   [/noreconfig ] [/u] [/nologo] [/quiet ] [/componly] [/appdir:<path>]
```

The following list describes each of the command line arguments.

AssemblyName Specifies the name of the assembly that you want to register. You must include the full assembly filename as a minimum.

/fc Finds or creates the target application.

/c Creates the target application. Displays an error if the application already exists.

/exapp Specifies that there's an existing application.

/tlb:*tlbfile* Specifies the filename of the exported type library for the assembly.

/appname:*name* Specifies the name of the target application.

/parname:*name* Specifies the name or identifier for the target partition.

/extlb Forces the utility to rely on an existing type library.

/reconfig Reconfigures an existing target application.

/noreconfig Specifies that the utility shouldn't reconfigure an existing target application.

/u Uninstalls the target application.

/nologo Suppresses the display of the RegSvcs banner. This option is helpful when creating batch files when you don't want to disturb the user.

/quiet Suppresses the display of both the RegSvcs banner and the success message. This option is helpful when creating batch files when you don't want to disturb the user.

/componly Configures only the component. The utility doesn't configure any required methods or interfaces.

/appdir:*path* Sets the application's root directory to the specified path.

Using the .NET Framework 3.0 Utilities

The .NET Framework 3.0 ships with Vista. Even though you can download it and install it with other versions of Windows, the main purpose of this .NET Framework version is to provide special feature support for Vista. For example, the Windows Presentation Foundation (WPF) provides support for the Aero Glass interface found in Vista. Most of the .NET Framework 3.0 DLLs affect developers, not administrators. A developer will use these DLLs to create an application for Vista. The only utilities you need to consider appear in the Windows Communication Foundation folder. The following sections describe these utilities.

Configuring COM+ Applications with the ComSvcConfig Utility

The ComSvcConfig utility helps you define the Service Model integration with COM+ applications. The result of using this utility is to expose a COM+ application interfaces as Web services. Anyone with access to the Web service can then use the application through a standard interface from a remote location. Vista doesn't configure any COM+ applications as a default because exposing a COM+ application interface as a Web service carries security penalties. This chapter won't define how Web services work or help you understand how COM+ interfaces appear as Web services. This utility uses the following syntax:

```
ComSvcConfig.exe mode [Options]
```

The ComSvcConfig utility provides three modes of operation as described in the following list.

/i[nstall] Adds Service Model integration to the application's component interfaces. This mode makes the interfaces available as a Web service. Before you use this mode, make sure you test the COM+ application completely. Any failure on the part of the COM+ application will result in a failed installation.

/u[ninstall] Removes Service Model integration from the application's component interfaces. The Web service becomes unavailable on successful completion of this mode.

/l[ist] Displays a list of the COM+ applications and interfaces that you have configured for Service Model integration.

The following list describes each of the command line arguments.

/a[pplication]:{*ApplicationID* | *ApplicationName*} Specifies the Globally Unique Identifier (GUID) or name of the COM+ application that you want to configure.

/c[ontract]:*ClassID* | *ProgID* | *, *InterfaceID* | *InterfaceName* | * [.* | {*Method1* [, *Method2* ...]}] Specifies the interfaces and methods that you want to configure as part of the Web service. The default is to use all interfaces and methods as part of the Web service, but you might find that you want to keep some of them hidden from public view. This command line switch accepts the asterisk (*) as a wildcard. Consequently, if you wanted to use all classes, you'd use an * instead of the class identifier. You follow the class identifier or program identifier with a comma and the interface identifier or interface name. You may optionally provide specific method names by following the interface name or interface identifier with a period and the method name. Separate multiple methods with a comma. For example, `/contract:MyApp,ITest.TestMethod` would create a contract for the `TestMethod()` found in the `ITest` interface of the `MyApp` application.

/allowreferences Specifies that the system should permit object reference parameters.

/h[osting]:{complus | was} Defines the hosting process for the Service Model services. You may choose between using the standard COM+ hosting or the Web Process Activation Service (WAS). Using WAS lets the system automatically activate the COM+ application as required, which means the system uses resources more efficiently, but that you also lose a certain level of control over the application process. When using WAS, the application executes as part of an Internet Information Server (IIS) process for library COM+ applications or as a `DLLHost.exe` process for server COM+ applications. You can learn more about WAS hosting at `http://msdn2.microsoft.com/en-us/library/ms734677.aspx`.

/w[ebSite]:*WebsiteName* Specifies the Web site to use for Web hosting.

/webDirectory:*WebDirectoryName* Specifies the virtual directory to use for Web hosting. You may also specify this command line switch as `/D`.

/mex Includes an additional WS-MetadataExchange endpoint. The WS-MetadataExchange standard provides the means for a client to obtain policy, schema, and Web Services Description Language (WSDL) information about a Web service. You may also specify this command line switch as `/x`.

TIP As Web services mature, you'll find more and more standards with the WS (Web Service) moniker. One of the best places to find a list of these standards is on MSDN at `http://msdn.microsoft.com/webservices/webservices/understanding/specs/default.aspx`. Click the associated link, such as Metadata Specifications, and you'll be able to download a specification that explains the standard.

/id Displays the application, component, and interface information as identifiers (GUIDs), rather than as human readable names. Sometimes you require the identifiers to perform other management tasks. You may also specify this command line switch as `/k`.

/n[ologo] Prevents the utility from displaying the logo.

/v[erbose] Displays additional information in the output, which includes all warnings.

Installing and Configuring Windows Communication Foundation Using the ServiceModelReg Utility

The ServicesModelReg utility manages installation and uninstallation of the Windows Communication Foundation on a machine. It's important to note that uninstallation doesn't actually remove any files—it simply makes the Windows Communication Foundation unavailable for use by the operating system and applications that rely on it. The main use for this utility is to repair a Windows Communication Foundation installation that has stopped working properly. This utility uses the following syntax:

```
ServiceModelReg.exe [-i[r | ru] | -u | -ua | -r | -s:<path> |
   -sn:<path> | -k:<path> | -kn:<path> | -lv | -lk | -vi] [-y] [-x]
   [-q | -v] [-nologo] [-?]
```

The following list describes each of the command line arguments.

-i Installs the version of the Windows Communication Foundation referenced by `ServiceModelReg.exe`. The installation process updates script maps at the IIS metabase root, in addition to all of the script maps below the roots. The installation process updates all script maps to the current version.

-ir Installs the version of the Windows Communication Foundation referenced by `ServiceModelReg.exe`. However, the installation process performs a registration only—the installation process doesn't update the script maps in IIS.

-iru Installs the version of the Windows Communication Foundation referenced by `ServiceModelReg.exe`. The installation performs an optional update of the IIS script maps. The update only occurs if the system doesn't currently have any applications that use Windows Communication Foundation.

-u Uninstalls the version of the Windows Communication Foundation referenced by `ServiceModelReg.exe`. The uninstall process remaps any IIS script maps to the highest remaining version of Windows Communication Foundation on the machine. If this is the last version installed on the machine, then the uninstall process removes the script maps.

-ua Uninstalls all versions of the Windows Communication Foundation found on the machine.

-r Reinstalls the current version of the Windows Communication Foundation. The installation process updates script maps at the IIS metabase root, in addition to all of the script maps below the roots. The installation process updates all script maps to the current version.

`-x` Includes the Windows Communication Foundation custom action script as part of the installation process.

`-s:`***`path`*** Installs the script maps for the version of Windows Communication Foundation referenced by `ServiceModelReg.exe` to the specified path. The script maps are installed recursively according to their original layout.

`-sn:`***`path`*** Installs the script maps for the version of Windows Communication Foundation referenced by `ServiceModelReg.exe` to the specified path. The script maps are installed in the specified path without regard to their original layout.

`-k:`***`path`*** Removes the script maps for all versions of Windows Communication Foundation from the specified path. The script maps are removed recursively.

`-kn:`***`path`*** Removes the script maps for all versions of Windows Communication Foundation from the specified path.

`-lv` Lists all versions of Windows Communication Foundation installed on the machine. The listing includes status information and installation path.

`-lk` Lists the paths of all IIS metabase keys for Windows Communication Foundation scripts-maps. The information includes the version. This feature only lists the top level script maps—keys that inherit from a parent key don't appear in the list.

`-vi` Verifies the installation of target components and generates a report. The components can include the following states:

- Unknown
- Not Installed
- Installed Default
- Installed Custom

`-y` Uninstalls or reinstalls components without asking for confirmation. This option works well for scripts and batch files that execute in the background.

`-q` Performs the specified task in quiet mode, which produces little or no output.

`-v` Performs the specific task in verbose mode, which provides additional information including warnings.

`/nologo` Prevents the utility from displaying the logo.

Interacting with WS-AtomicTransaction Using the WSATConfig Utility

The WS-AtomicTransaction Configuration (WSATConfig) utility helps your system support the WS-AtomicTransaction standard used for Web services. You can find out more about this standard at `http://www.service-architecture.com/web-services/articles/web_services_atomictransaction_ws-atomictransaction.html` and `http://www-128.ibm.com/developerworks/library/specification/ws-tx/`. From an administration perspective, the basic idea behind WS-AtomicTransaction is to ensure that any data activity either completes when it's successful or rolls back to a known good state when it fails. You use WSATConfig to define how the system works with the Web service to support WS-AtomicTransaction. This utility uses the following syntax:

```
WSATConfig [-network:{enable | disable}] [-port:<portNum>]
   [-endpointCert:{machine | <thumb> | "Issuer\SubjectName"}]
```

```
   [-accounts:<account>[, <account> ...]]
   [-accountsCerts:{<thumb>| "Issuer\SubjectName"} [,<thumb>|
   "Issuer\SubjectName" ...]] [-virtualServer:<virtualServer>]
   [-timeout:<sec>] [-maxTimeout:<sec>] [-traceLevel:{Off | Error | Critical |
Warning | Information | Verbose | All}]
   [-traceActivity:{enable|disable}] [-traceProp:{enable|disable}]
   [-tracePII:{enable|disable}] [-show] [-restart]
```

The following list describes each of the command line arguments.

-network:{enable | disable} Enables or disables the WS-AtomicTransaction network support.

-port:*portNum* Sets the HyperText Transport Protocol Secure (HTTPS) port for WS-AtomicTransaction communication.

-endpointCert:{machine | *thumb* | "*Issuer\SubjectName*"} Specifies the endpoint certificate to use. You may use the machine certificate, a thumbprint, or an issuer and subject name pair. When working with an issuer and subject name pair, you may specify the *SubjectName* value as {EMPTY}.

-accounts:*account*[, *account* ...] Provides a comma-separated list of accounts that can participate in WS-AtomicTransaction transactions.

-accountsCerts:{*thumb* | "*Issuer\SubjectName*"} [,*thumb* | "*Issuer\SubjectName*" ...] Provides a comma-separated list of thumbprints or issuer and subject name pairs that can participate in WS-AtomicTransaction transactions. When working with an issuer and subject name pair, you may specify the *SubjectName* value as {EMPTY}.

-virtualServer:*virtualServer* Specifies the Distributed Transaction Coordinator (DTC) resource cluster name.

-timeout:*sec* Specifies the default outgoing message timeout in seconds.

-maxTimeout:*sec* Specifies the maximum incoming message timeout in seconds.

-traceLevel:{Off | Error | Critical | Warning | Information | Verbose | All} Sets the trace level for logging or displaying WS-AtomicTransaction activity.

-traceActivity:{enable|disable} Enables or disables the tracing of WS-AtomicTransaction activity events.

-traceProp:{enable|disable} Enables or disables the tracing of propagation events.

-tracePII:{enable|disable} Enables or disables the tracing of Personally Identifiable Information (PII).

-show Shows the current WS-AtomicTransaction protocol settings.

-restart Restarts the Microsoft Distributed Transaction Controller (MSDTC) to make any changes active immediately, rather than wait for a reboot of the system or other MSDTC restart event. The default action is to wait until the next MSDTC restart to reduce the effect of any changes on ongoing transactions and other applications.

Getting Started with Command Line Tasks

This chapter has introduced you to the general utilities provided by the .NET Framework. You can use the techniques in this chapter to manage both users and code in any .NET application. It's important to remember that the configuration of an application resides partly with the application developer. The features that the developer includes in an application can make administration significantly easier. However, the .NET Framework also gives the administrator far more flexibility in working with application than the native executables of the past.

One of the features that distinguish the .NET Framework is your ability to set security at a very fine level. It's important to remember that .NET applications rely on roles; the user and the code both fulfill roles within the application environment. The ability to set user security exists with native executables too, but not with the level of flexibility that the .NET Framework provides. However, remember that you also have the ability to determine what the code can do, which can be your buffer against coding errors and other problems that exist with native executables today. As part of discovering more about the .NET Framework configuration flexibility, make sure you spend time working with the .NET Configuration console for whatever version of the .NET Framework you use. In addition, begin working now to set up roles using the command line tools such as CASPol.

Chapter 17 continues with the task of reviewing the .NET Framework utilities. These utilities work with services and help you create a useful Web environment for your applications. In general, the utilities in Chapter 17 work in some way with ASP.NET, so they're much more targeted than the utilities described in this chapter. When you complete Chapter 17, you'll know all about the various management utilities that the .NET Framework provides. The .NET Framework does provide other utilities that aren't described in this book, but they're all oriented toward developer needs, such as compiling Visual Basic applications.

Chapter 17

Configuring ASP.NET

- Locating ASP.NET Errors
- Creating Web Applications with the ASPNet_Compiler Utility
- Providing Multiple Browser Support with the ASPNet_RegBrowsers Utility
- Adding ASP.NET Support to IIS with the ASPNet_RegIIS Utility
- Adding ASP.NET Support to SQL Server with the ASPNet_RegSQL Utility
- Understanding the ASPNet_State Service

More administrators have problems with ASP.NET than any other portion of the .NET Framework. Part of the problem is that they don't realize that the .NET Framework is involved. IIS tends to hide the information and so does the .NET Framework. In fact, you can't even implement .NET Framework support to get an ASP.NET application going outside of the command line. Consequently, if you're having a problem with complete failure of your ASP.NET Application, this is the place to look. This chapter discusses the special utilities you need to keep your ASP.NET applications going.

In addition to ASP.NET itself, you also need to consider how your applications will access a database. When working with SQL Server, you can integrate database support with ASP.NET to make it easier to obtain database support. The .NET Framework includes a special utility for registering SQL Server support. In addition to SQL Sever registration, you'll find utilities for monitoring ASP.NET and even compiling ASP.NET applications. This final task is important when you want to remove all of the source files from the server and rely only on the executable so that you keep your business secrets safe from prying eyes.

Locating ASP.NET Errors

Some people don't know that the .NET Framework lurks in their Web server, but ASP.NET relies on the .NET Framework to perform its work. Without the .NET Framework, there isn't any ASP.NET. Unfortunately, administrators run into a number of common problems—most of which you either repair with a command line utility or are caused by using a command line utility. The following sections don't provide a comprehensive list of ASP.NET errors, but they do discuss the most common errors and provide information on how to fix them.

Of course, one of the first problems to check is whether ASP.NET is even installed on your system. You can perform this task by opening the Internet Information Services console found in the Administrative Tools folder of the Control Panel. Right-click the Default Web Site entry and choose Properties from the context menu. When you see the Default Web Site Properties dialog box, look for the ASP.NET tab. If you don't see the ASP.NET tab, then install ASP.NET support using the ASPNet_RegIIS utility described in the "Adding ASP.NET Support to IIS with the ASPNet_RegIIS Utility" section of the chapter.

WHEN IT JUST STOPS WORKING

Administrators are used to hearing users say that something just stopped working. In most cases, the administrator locates a problem that shows the user didn't understand what to do and caused their own woe. However, in rare cases the administrator really does find something that just stopped working and has to fix it. Many cases of ASP.NET errors fall into this category. For no obvious reason at all, ASP.NET just stops working.

Like every computer problem, there's always a reason that it stops working, but ASP.NET hasn't been around long enough for administrators to recognize these sources of problems instantly. For example, a developer might deploy a new version of an application to the server. The deployment process can cause problems. The application might stop working because the deployment process failed to create the required application or it relies on a newer version of the .NET Framework.

Installing a new version of the .NET Framework can cause problems. Sometimes the installation routine doesn't properly register the file associations. In some cases, you'll find there's a conflict between the expectations of the application and the settings on the server. It's important to know that updating the .NET Framework can cause problems that are hard to diagnose when you don't know where to look.

As with every computer problem, always begin the ASP.NET diagnostic process by asking what has changed. Something must have changed to cause the problem. Even if the problem's hardware related, something's changed. Make sure you check with developers to ensure that the application hasn't changed in any way. Look for problems with the file associations and ensure you have the correct version of the .NET Framework installed. Always work methodically because there really is a reason that something stopped working, even when it appears that it simply stopped for no reason at all.

Fixing Application Registration Errors

Application registration errors can happen for a number of reasons—too many reasons to list here. However, the symptoms and the fix are always the same. An ASP.NET application isn't just a folder on your server. IIS must see the ASP.NET application as an application or it won't work at all. Consequently, if you suddenly find that one or two of your ASP.NET applications aren't working, even though other applications are, then you might want to check for a registration problem. Figure 17.1 shows an application on a server.

Notice the special icon that both IISHelp and Test1 use. This icon tells you that IIS recognizes the folder as an application. If you don't see this icon for one of your ASP.NET applications, then you can easily fix it. Right-click the application folder and choose Properties from the context menu. Select the Virtual Directory or Directory tab and you'll see a dialog box similar to the one in Figure 17.2. Look at the Application Name field. If IIS has grayed this field out and you see a Create button, rather than the Remove button shown in Figure 17.2, click Create. IIS will register the directory as an application and your ASP.NET application should begin working again.

Fixing File Association Problems

One of the most common problems that you'll experience with IIS is that it forgets how to process the ASP.NET and associated pages. Your first clue that something is wrong is that IIS suddenly starts displaying error messages whenever someone requests an ASP.NET page. Of course, a good many other problems can occur to cause this problem, but don't rule out IIS as a source of the problem. You can verify IIS as a source of problems by looking in two areas.

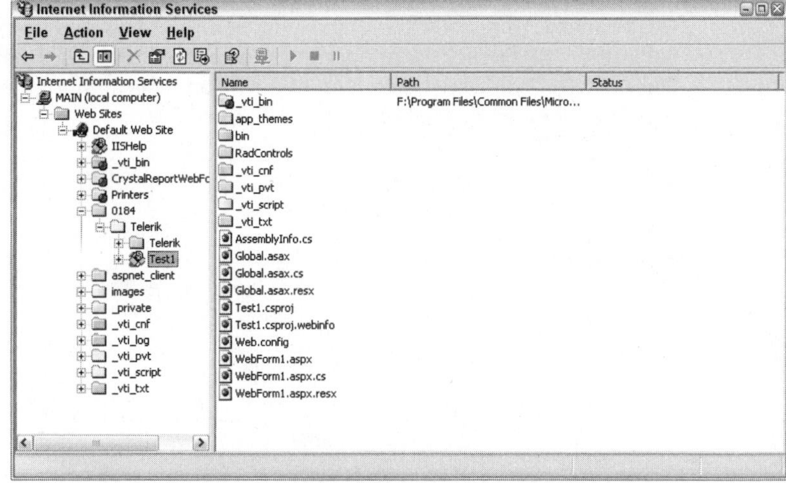

FIGURE 17.1
Make sure you have the application registered on the server so that IIS recognizes it as an application.

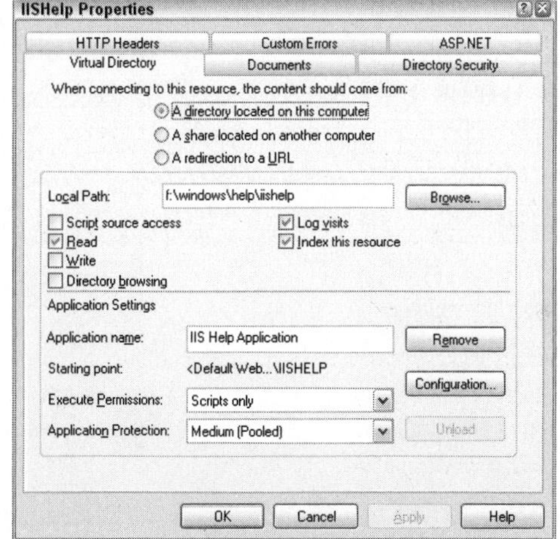

FIGURE 17.2
Fix an application registration problem by re-creating it when necessary.

The first source of problems occurs when the ASP.NET services don't startup correctly. You can verify this source of problems by opening the Services console found in the Administrative Tools folder of the Control Panel. Check the ASP.NET Admin Service and ASP.NET State Service entries shown in Figure 17.3. If these entries show Stopped status, even though the service is set for automatic startup, the problem is usually one where a registration problem has occurred and the service can't locate the resources it needs. Remember that you can also perform this check using the TaskList utility described in the "Listing Applications and Services with the TaskList Utility" section of Chapter 5. Using the command line means that you can easily check a server from your workstation, rather than walk over to the server to use the graphical utility.

Another problem that occurs is that IIS actually loses the file extension support it requires. If IIS doesn't know what to do with a particular file extension, it usually displays an error message or does something unexpected (such as displaying your source code when available on screen).

You can verify a file extension problem by opening the Internet Information Services console located in the Administrative Tools folder of the Control Panel. Open the Web site that hosts your application. Right-click the application and choose Properties from the context menu. Select the Directory tab. You'll see the Properties dialog box. Click Configuration and you'll see the Application Configuration dialog box shown in Figure 17.4.

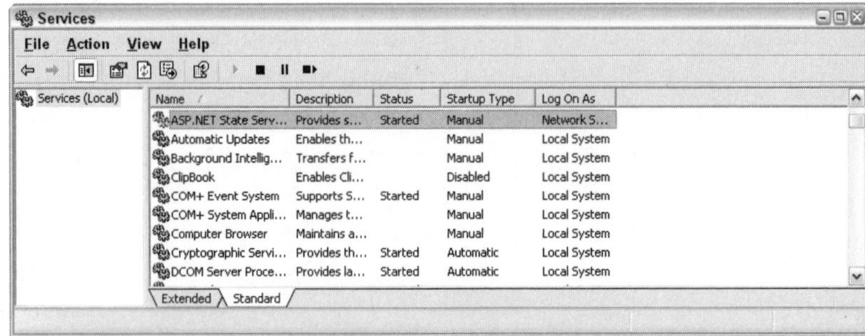

FIGURE 17.3
Determine whether the ASP.NET services can access the resources they need.

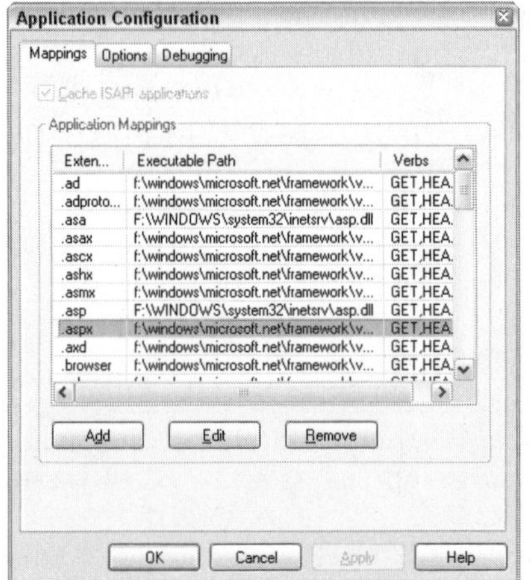

FIGURE 17.4
Set the default page so the user automatically sees the first page of your Web application.

Notice that the Application Configuration dialog box contains entries for every file extension that this copy of IIS supports. The extensions appear in the first column of the Application Mappings table and, in this case, ASPX is one of them. The second column contains the path and name of the DLL that supports the file extension, while the third column shows which verbs (actions) the DLL can handle. An error in any of the three columns usually indicates a problem with the IIS setup.

Make sure that the DLL path points to the correct version of the .NET Framework for your application. A common cause of problems is that the server has a DLL registered, but it's for the wrong version of the .NET Framework and the application relies on updated ASP.NET features. If you're working with the .NET Framework 2.0, then the DLL should point to the `\Windows\Microsoft.NET\Framework\v2.0.50727\aspnet_isapi.dll` file. You can fix this particular problem using the ASPNet_RegIIS utility described in the "Adding ASP.NET Support to IIS with the ASPNet_RegIIS Utility" section of the chapter.

NOTE Always locate the ASPNet_RegIIS utility for the version of ASP.NET that you want to use with your Web application. Each version of the .NET Framework will have a separate folder in the `\WINDOWS\Microsoft.NET\Framework` folder. Select the folder that contains the version you want to use. (The actual folder might vary between Windows versions; for example, the .NET Framework appears in the `\WINNT\Microsoft.NET\Framework` folder when working with Windows 2000 and the `\Windows\Microsoft.NET\Framework64` folder when working with the 64-bit version of Windows XP.)

Fixing Configuration Problems

IIS can experience a number of configuration problems with ASP.NET. It's important to describe the configuration problems. Even though you'll use the ASPNet_RegIIS utility to fix some problems, using this utility is akin to taking a sledgehammer to your configuration information. The ASPNet_RegIIS utility resets everything. Sometimes, what you really need is a screwdriver. One of the features that this book doesn't discuss, but you need to know about, is the ASP.NET configuration tab for an application and for the Web server as a whole. Figure 17.5 shows the Web server configuration on the left and the application configuration on the right.

For the purposes of this chapter, the important issue is the selection of the version of ASP.NET. You must select the proper version in the ASP.NET Version field. A problem that many administrators encounter at this point is that they don't see the version they need. This problem indicates that you didn't register the ASP.NET versions correctly using the ASPNet_RegIIS utility. You can verify the installed versions using the `-lv` command line switch. Make sure you use the `-r` command line switch when necessary to obtain the correct version support on your system.

Configuration problems can take other routes. Click Edit Configuration. The General tab, shown in Figure 17.6, should contain a SQL Server entry when you rely on SQL Server to provide database support for your application. If you're missing this entry, then you probably need to run the ASPNet_RegSQL utility described in the "Adding ASP.NET Support to SQL Server with the ASPNet_RegSQL Utility" section of the chapter. Even if you see the entry shown, make sure the connection is correct. You may find that running the ASPNet_RegSQL utility will clear up connectivity problems as well, but check with the developer for specifics on how the connection string should appear.

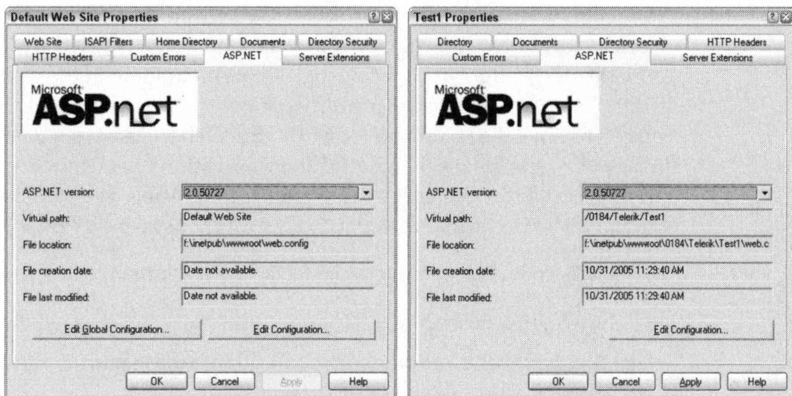

FIGURE 17.5
Verify that the Web server and individual application settings are correct.

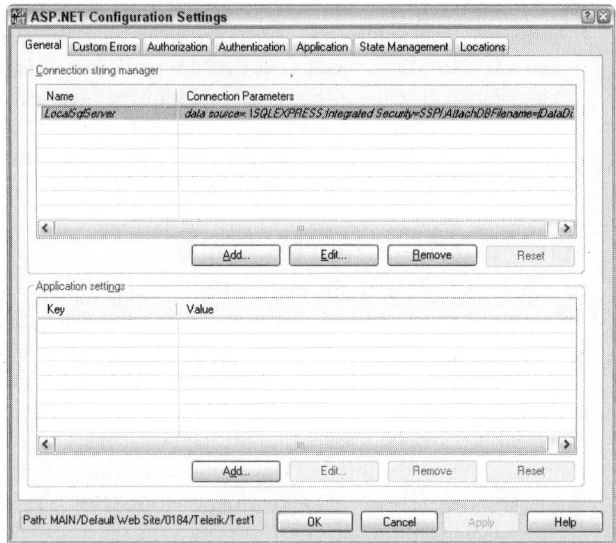

FIGURE 17.6
Make sure you have the proper SQL Server support installed.

Gone are the days when you could write an application that supports Internet Explorer and call it done. Users rely on a wealth of browsers today. To its credit, ASP.NET supports a number of browser types, not just Internet Explorer, but you may find that you still need additional browser support. When an application runs into browser support problems and you know that the developer has added the correct support, make sure you use the ASPNet_RegBrowsers utility described in the "Providing Multiple Browser Support with the ASPNet_RegBrowsers Utility" section of the chapter to add the required support. As with file associations and many other ASP.NET features, IIS tends to forget the browser settings should certain events occur, such as a .NET Framework update.

Creating Web Applications with the ASPNet_Compiler Utility

Production Web sites often keep source code from view because they don't want prying eyes to obtain any business information. However, if you've worked with Web sites for very long, you know that they often do have source code in plain view in the form of Web pages and associated scripts. The ASPNet_Compiler utility compiles the application for you and creates an executable. You can remove the rest of the code from the Web site and rely on the executable to serve up pages. Because executables are essentially binary, they don't have much in the way of human readable text and you can obtain a certain level of code hiding using an executable. In addition, using an executable can boost performance slightly. This utility uses the following syntax:

```
ASPNet_Compiler [-m MetabasePath | -v VirtualPath [-p PhysicalDir]] [TargetDir]
```

The following list describes each of the command line arguments.

`-m` ***`MetabasePath`*** Provides the full IIS metabase path to the application. You can't use this switch with either the `-v` or `-p` switches.

NOTE The metabase is essentially a database of information about IIS. Think of it as a kind of IIS registry. Microsoft moved the IIS settings out of the registry and into the metabase to allow developers to make changes to IIS without rebooting the system. Because the metabase is separate from the registry, you can also move the IIS settings to another machine with few problems. You can learn more about the metabase at `http://www.microsoft.com/technet/prodtechnol/windows2000serv/technologies/iis/tips/metabase.mspx`. Another good article to read is the one on the WindowsNetworking.com site at `http://www.windowsnetworking.com/kbase/WindowsTips/WindowsNT/AdminTips/IIS/IISMetabaseRegistry.html`.

`-v` ***`VirtualPath`*** Provides the virtual path to the application you want to compile. The virtual path is the location of the application, as the user would see it. For example, if the user accesses the application using `http://myapp`, you would provide `/myapp` as the virtual path. You can't use this switch with the `-m` switch.

NOTE If you omit both the `-m` and `-v` switches, the ASPNet_Compiler utility assumes that you want to compile the default application as listed in the IIS metabase.

`-p` ***`PhysicalDir`*** Provides the physical location of the application on the hard drive. If you omit this switch, the ASPNet_Compiler utility uses the IIS metabase to locate the application. You must use this switch with the `-v` switch.

`-nologo` Runs the ASPNet_Compiler utility without displaying a logo. You can use this switch with automated processing techniques.

`TargetDir` Defines the physical path of the compiled application. If you don't provide this argument, the ASPNet_Compiler utility compiles the application in place (within the same physical location as the application source code).

Providing Multiple Browser Support with the ASPNet_RegBrowsers Utility

ASP.NET provides improved control over Web page display by using custom browser setups. Each browser setup defines a specific browser based on the browser name and version (among other things). Instead of waiting for Microsoft to add support for a particular browser, you can add this functionality yourself using a specially formatted file with a `BROWSER` extension. You can find the list of browsers that ASP.NET supports in the `\WINDOWS\Microsoft.NET\Framework\`*`.NET Version`*`\CONFIG\`*`Browsers`* folder. These custom browser setups make it easy to add and remove support as needed by your system. In addition, you can fix a browser setup with relative ease when it fails to work as intended.

NOTE The old method of detecting a browser relies on `BrowserCap.DLL`. This DLL detects the user agent entry provided by the client machine using a simple wildcard match. It then looks in the `BrowserCap.INI` file to locate information about that browser. This particular method doesn't work well because it assumes too much about the user agent entry and you can't update the `BrowserCap.DLL` file to support new browsers.

Even though you don't need to know the details, it's good to know where ASP.NET stores this information. Hidden deep within the `Machine.CONFIG` file found in the `\WINDOWS\Microsoft.NET\Framework\`*`.NET Version`*`\`*CONFIG* folder is a special section called `<browserCaps>`. This section contains a series of XML entries that define the configurations for various browsers. The ASPNet_RegBrowsers utility takes the information found in the BROWSER file and adds it to the `Machine.CONFIG` file so that users with that browser can access your Web site. To use the ASPNet_RegBrowsers utility, place the BROWSER file in the `\WINDOWS\Microsoft.NET\Framework\.NET Version`\CONFIG\ *Browsers* folder and perform an installation. This utility uses the following syntax:

```
aspnet_regbrowsers [{-i | -u}]
```

The following list describes each of the command line arguments.

`-i` Creates and installs the runtime browser capabilities assembly. This assembly contains the list of all of the `BROWSER` files.

`-u` Uninstalls the browser capabilities assembly from the GAC. IIS doesn't stop supporting a browser when you uninstall the browser capabilities assembly. It uses the old runtime browser capabilities (those found in the `BrowserCap.DLL` file) instead.

Adding ASP.NET Support to IIS with the ASPNet_RegIIS Utility

The ASPNet_RegIIS utility registers a particular version of ASP.NET on your system. This utility only works with one version of ASP.NET. You must use the utility for the particular version of the .NET Framework that you need to register. IIS can support multiple versions of ASP.NET. You can select the version you need. See the "Locating ASP.NET Errors" section of the chapter for usage ideas for this utility. This utility uses the following syntax:

```
.NET Framework 1.1
    aspnet_regiis.exe [-i] [-ir] [-enable] [-s <path>] [-sn <path>]
    [-r] [-u] [-ua] [-k <path>] [-kn <path>] [-lv] [-lk] [-c] [-e]
    [-ea]
.NET Framework 2.0
    ASPNet_RegIIS [-i] [-ir] [-iru] [-enable] [-disable] [-s <path>]
    [-sn <path>] [-r] [-u] [-ua] [-k <path>] [-kn <path>] [-lv] [-lk]
    [-c] [-e] [-ea] [-ga <user>] [pe <section>] [pd <section>]
    [-pef <section> <web-app-physical-dir>]
    [-pdf <section> <web-app-physical-dir>] [-pc <container>]
    [-pz <container>] [-pi <container> <file>] [-px <container> <file>]
    [-pa <container> <account>] [-pr <container> <account>]
```

The following list describes each of the command line arguments.

`-i` Installs this version of ASP.NET on IIS. Using this option updates all of the script maps, updates the file extensions, registers any DLLs, and generally makes the same changes that a new Visual Studio .NET installation would make. This option also updates any existing features to the version of ASP.NET that you're installing. Use this option when you want to ensure the ASP.NET installation completely refreshes and fixes any major errors in the system.

`-ir` Performs all of the tasks required to register ASP.NET on IIS. This option doesn't perform any updates. Consequently, this option completes much faster than the `-i` option, but isn't as complete.

`-iru` Installs this version of ASP.NET on IIS. This switch is the same as the `-i` option, but it verifies that no existing applications are using ASP.NET first. When the utility detects existing applications, it performs the installation and registration, but maintains any existing script maps so the existing applications don't break.

NOTE Script mapping is the process of matching an application to a particular version of the .NET Framework for execution. ASP.NET supports the concept of maintaining multiple versions of the .NET Framework on a machine so that you can use the version that the application relies on, rather than the latest version installed. This approach makes it less likely that your application will break because of an upgrade to ASP.NET. During an update, you must decide whether to maintain the current mapping—support for the current version of the .NET Framework—or update to the latest version of the .NET Framework. All of the options that discuss the script map (some sources use scriptmap) are referring to this process of maintaining the correct version of ASP.NET for each application. The ASP.NET Web site at `http://www.asp.net/faq/SideBySide.aspx` has an article that details the process for using more than one version of ASP.NET on a system.

`-enable` Enables ASP.NET in the IIS security console (IIS 6.0 or later) when used with the `-i`, `-ir`, or `-r` command line switches. You don't need to use this switch with older versions of IIS (including Windows XP or Vista, which is version 5.1 or above in most cases).

`-disable` Disables ASP.NET in the IIS security console (IIS 6.0 or later) when used with the `-i`, `-ir`, or `-r` command line switches. You don't need to use this switch with older versions of IIS (including Windows XP, which is version 5.1 in most cases).

`-s` ***`Path`*** Installs the script maps for this version of ASP.NET at the specified path, rather than use the default path. This instruction follows the script map path recursively to install all subdirectories as well. Generally, you don't want to use this option unless you have a custom IIS setup.

`-sn` ***`Path`*** Installs the script maps for this version of ASP.NET at the specified path, rather than use the default path. This instruction doesn't use recursive installation, so you only obtain the script map at the top level. Generally, you don't want to use this option unless you have a custom IIS setup.

`-r` Installs this version of ASP.NET and updates all of the script maps starting at the IIS metabase root for all of the script maps below the root. (See the note about the IIS metabase in the "Creating Web Applications with the ASPNet_Compiler Utility" section of the chapter.) This switch updates all of the script maps regardless of the original version.

`-u` Uninstalls this version of ASP.NET. This switch automatically updates existing script maps to the highest version of ASP.NET still installed on the machine. If this is the last version of ASP.NET on the machine, then the application removes the existing script maps and your ASP.NET applications will no longer run.

`-ua` Uninstalls all versions of ASP.NET on the machine. This switch also removes all script maps—your ASP.NET applications will no longer run.

`-k` ***`Path`*** Removes all script maps to any version of ASP.NET from the specified path. This switch removes the script maps recursively, so it removes all of the script maps for an entire application. Any subapplications will also stop working.

`-kn` ***`Path`*** Removes all script maps to any version of ASP.NET from the specified path. This switch doesn't remove the script maps recursively, so other applications in a path are unaffected. Only the application specified by the path variable is affected by the change.

`-lv` Lists all versions of ASP.NET installed on the machine. The output information includes the version status and installation path.

`-lk` Lists the paths of the IIS metabase keys where the ASP.NET script map is defined, along with the ASP.NET version. Keys that inherit the ASP.NET script map from a parent don't appear in the listing.

-c Installs the client-side scripts for this version of ASP.NET to the `\aspnet_client` subdirectory of each IIS site directory.

-e Removes the client-side scripts for this version of ASP.NET from the `\aspnet_client` subdirectory of each IIS site directory.

-ea Removes the client-side scripts for all versions of ASP.NET from the `\aspnet_client` subdirectory of each IIS site directory.

-ga *user* Grants the specified user or group access to the IIS metabase and other directories that ASP.NET uses.

-config{- | +} Enables or disables remote access to configuration information. Enabling this support is a good option for team development on a private network, but an open invitation to cracker activity on a public system. Always disable this feature for public Web sites.

NOTE **Performing a fresh installation of ASP.NET can require several minutes to complete. Don't disturb the system during this process—go get a cup of coffee instead. Be patient—the process won't complete for several minutes even on a fast system.**

The .NET Framework 2.0 added a number of encryption command line switches. You use encryption to increase the security of your Web site by keeping more information out of sight. The following list describes these encryption options.

-pe *section* Encrypts the specified section. You can augment this command line switch with a number of optional command line switches. The following list describes each of these options.

> **-prov *provider*** Defines the provider used to encrypt the data.
>
> **-app *virtual-path*** Specifies the virtual path to use as a starting point for the encryption. The path must begin with a forward slash (/). Use a single forward slash to designate the root of the Web site. The utility encrypts the root `Web.CONFIG` file when you don't provide the `-app` command line switch.
>
> **-site *site-name-or-ID*** Specifies the site name or identifier of the virtual path specified with the `-app` command line switch. The utilities use the default Web site when you don't specify the `-app` command line switch.
>
> **-location *sub-path*** Specifies the location of the subpath.
>
> **-pkm** Encrypts or decrypts the `Machine.CONFIG` file (the global settings), rather than the `Web.CONFIG` file.

-pd *section* Decrypts the specified section. You can augment this command line switch with a number of optional command line switches. See the `-pe` command line switch for a list of options.

-pef *section web-app-physical-dir* Encrypts the specified configuration section in the specified Web application directory. You may optionally include a provider using the `-prov` command line switch. See the `-pe` command line switch for a list of options.

-pdf *section web-app-physical-dir* Decrypts the specified configuration section in the specified Web application directory.

-pc *container* Creates an Rivest, Shamir, and Adleman (RSA) key pair in the specified container. You can augment this command line switch with a number of optional command line switches. The following list describes each of these options.

> **-size *key-size*** Defines the key size for the key pair. Larger key sizes result in better security, but also incur a greater performance hit. The default size is 1,024 bits.

-pku Creates a user container for an individual instead of a machine container that everyone can use.

-exp Creates private keys that you can export and use on another system.

-csp *provider* Specifies the Cryptographic Service Provider (CSP) to use.

-pz *container* Deletes the specified container. You can delete a user container by adding the -pku command line switch.

-pi *container file* Imports an RSA key pair from the specified XML file into the specified container. You can augment this command line switch with a number of optional command line switches. The following list describes each of these options.

-pku Creates a user container for an individual instead of a machine container that everyone can use.

-exp Creates private keys that you can export and use on another system.

-csp *provider* Specifies the CSP to use.

-px *container file* Exports an RSA key pair from the specified container to the specified file. The file is in XML format. You can augment this command line switch with a number of optional command line switches. The following list describes each of these options.

-pku Creates a user container for an individual instead of a machine container that everyone can use.

-pri Creates a file that includes the private keys. You can only use this option if you created the private keys using the -exp command line switch. See the -pc and -pi command line switches for details.

-csp *provider* Specifies the CSP to use.

-pa *container account* Adds access for the specified account to the specified container. You can augment this command line switch with a number of optional command line switches. The following list describes each of these options.

-pku Creates a user container for an individual instead of a machine container that everyone can use.

-csp *provider* Specifies the CSP to use.

-full Creates the account with full access rights. The default setting creates an account with read access rights.

-pr container account Removes access for the specified account from the specified container. You can augment this command line switch with a number of optional command line switches. The following list describes each of these options.

-pku Creates a user container for an individual instead of a machine container that everyone can use.

-csp *provider* Specifies the CSP to use.

Adding ASP.NET Support to SQL Server with the ASPNet_RegSQL Utility

As with ASP.NET, sometimes you'll lose the SQL Server connection for your Web applications. The ASPNet_RegSQL utility helps you fix any connectivity problems without reinstalling SQL Server and ASP.NET. This utility operates separately from the ASPNet_RegIIS utility, so you might have to use both to restore application functionality completely when you rely on a database to implement certain features.

Unlike the ASPNet_RegIIS utility, the ASPNet_RegSQL utility comes with two interfaces. The first operates at the command line, while the second uses a wizard to accomplish its work. Because the ASPNet_RegSQL utility is more complex than the ASPNet_RegIIS utility, you'll want to use the wizard version of the utility whenever possible. However, the command line version works best within batch files and scripts, which is the best option for automation of common tasks. The following sections describe both interfaces.

Using the Command Line

You'll use the command line interface for the ASPNet_RegSQL utility when you work with scripts or when you don't feel the wizard provides sufficient access to a particular feature. Generally, the command line version is harder to use and error prone. This utility uses the following syntax:

```
ASPNet_RegSQL [-W] [-S <Server> [-U <Username> [-P <Password>]]] [-E]
   [-C <ConnectionString>] [-sqlexportonly <Filename>] [-A [{all | m |
   r | p | s | c | w}]] [-R [{all | m | r | p | s | c | w}]] [-d
   <Database>] [-Q] [-d <Database>] [-ed] [-dd] [-et] [-et] [-t
   <Table>] [-lt] [-ssadd] [-ssremove] [-sstype [{t | p | c}]]
```

The following list describes each of the command line arguments.

WARNING The command line switches are case sensitive. If you use the wrong case, the utility will fail, in most cases, and might perform unanticipated and unwanted actions in other cases. You must use the dash (-) rather than a slash (/) when typing a command line switch. Failure to use the dash always results in an error.

-W Places the utility in wizard mode. This is the best mode to use for reconfiguring the SQL Server connection. See the "Working with the ASPNet_RegSQL Utility Wizard" section for details.

-S *Server* Specifies the name of the server when creating a connection.

-U *Username* Defines the name of the user when creating a connection.

-P *Password* Defines the user password when creating a connection.

-E Sets the utility to authenticate the user with Windows credentials, rather than a username and password when creating a connection.

-C *ConnectionString* Contains the arguments required to create the connection. The connection string takes the place of the username, password, and server name command line switches. Don't include a database name as part of the connection string.

-sqlexportonly *Filename* Sets the utility to generate a SQL script file for adding and removing the desired SQL Server features. The utility doesn't actually perform any changes when you specify this switch. You can use this switch with the `-A`, `-R`, `-ssadd`, and `-ssremove` switches.

Once you create a connection to SQL Server, you can perform various application service tasks. Here's a list of application service command line switches.

-A [{all | m | r | p | s | c | w}] Use this switch with any of the optional keywords to add a feature to the SQL Server connection. You can use multiple switches together by specifying them as separate switches (-A m -A r) or by combining them into one switch (-A mr). The features include:

all All features

m Membership

r Role manager

p Profiles

s Site counters

c Personalization

w SQL Web event provider

-R [{all | m | r | p | s | c | w}] Use this switch with any of the optional keywords to remove a feature from the SQL Server connection. You can use multiple switches together by specifying them as separate switches (-R m -R r) or by combining them into one switch (-R mr). The features include:

all All features, including all common tables and stored procedures

m Membership

r Role manager

p Profiles

s Site counters

c Personalization

w SQL Web event provider

-d *Database* Contains the name of the database to use with application services. ASP.NET uses a default name of aspnetdb when you don't supply this value.

-Q Sets the utility to perform all tasks quietly. You don't see confirmation or error messages. This is the mode to use with scripts and other forms of automation.

Besides application services tasks, you can also use the ASPNet_RegSQL utility to modify the cache dependency options. Here's a list of the command line switches you use to perform this task.

-d *Database* Contains the name of the database to use for the cache dependency options. ASP.NET uses a default name of aspnetdb when you don't supply this value.

-ed Enables the database for SQL cache dependency.

-dd Disables the database for SQL cache dependency.

-et Enables a particular table for SQL cache dependency. You must specify the -t command line switch to use this switch.

-dt Disables a particular table for SQL cache dependency. You must specify the -t command line switch to use this switch.

-t *Table* Contains the name of the table to enable or disable for SQL cache dependency. You must also supply the -et or -dt command line switch.

-lt Lists all of the tables enabled for SQL cache dependency.

The final set of command line switches let you use the ASPNet_RegSQL utility to modify the session state options. Here's a list of the command line switches you use to perform this task.

`-d Database` Contains the name of the database to use for the session state when the `-sstype` command line switch type is set to `c` (custom).

`-ssadd` Adds support for the SQL Server mode session state.

`-ssremove` Removes support for the SQL Server mode session state.

`-sstype [{t | p | c}]` Defines the type of session state that SQL Server supports. These options include:

> **`t`** Defines a temporary session state. ASP.NET uses the `tempdb` database to store information. Stored procedures for managing the session appear in the ASPState database. ASP.NET doesn't persist any information when you start SQL Server. This is the default setting.
>
> **`p`** Defines a persisted session state. ASP.NET uses the ASPState database to store both state information and the stored procedures for managing the session. The information stays in place even after you restart SQL Server.
>
> **`c`** Defines a custom session state. ASP.NET stores both the state data and the stored procedures used to manage the session state in the custom database that you supply. You must combine this option with the `-d` command line switch.

Working with the ASPNet_RegSQL Utility Wizard

The command line version of the ASPNet_RegSQL utility works great for scripts, but you have a better option when making manual changes. Use the `-W` command line switch to place the ASPNet_RegSQL utility into wizard mode. When you use this switch, you'll see the ASP.NET SQL Server Setup Wizard appear. The following steps take you through the process of using this wizard.

1. Click Next to get past the Welcome dialog box. You'll see a Select a Setup Option dialog box. When you select the Remote Application Services Information from an Existing Database, the wizard takes you through a three-step process that removes SQL Server support from the system and then exits. The steps that follow assume that you're using the Configure SQL Server for Application Services option.
2. Select Configure SQL Server for Application Services and click Next. You'll see the Select Server and Database dialog box shown in Figure 17.7. This dialog box lets you choose the server and database that you want to work with, along with supplying your credentials for access to the server.
3. Choose the server and database you want to work with. Choose an authentication option. Click Next and you'll see a confirmation dialog box.
4. Click Next. The application will work for a few minutes as it configures the database. Eventually you'll see a completion dialog box.
5. Confirm that the configuration succeeded without error. Click Finish.

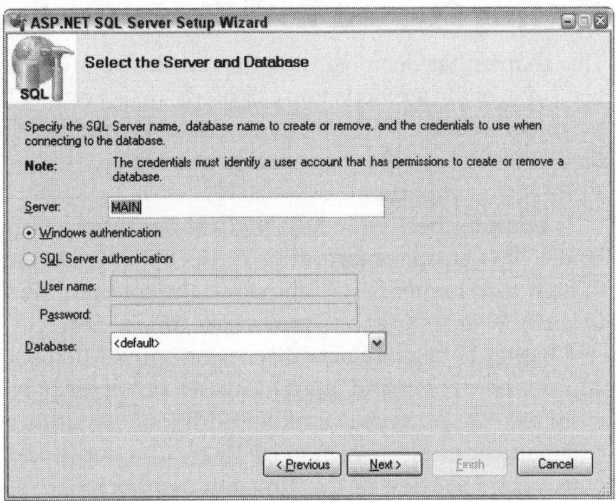

FIGURE 17.7
Choose the server and database that you want to configure.

Understanding the ASPNet_State Service

The ASPNet_State service is important for ASP.NET applications because it provides a centralized means of storing state information for every ASP.NET application on the system. State information is the user data that an application requires to track requests. IIS uses a single ASPNet_State service to handle all state requests, no matter which version of ASP.NET an application uses. Generally, IIS uses the latest version of the ASPNet_State service to ensure that all ASP.NET applications work as anticipated.

It may not seem like the ASPNet_State service should require any more attention than any other service. You can use all of the same utilities described in other areas of the book to start, stop, pause, and continue this server. (See the SC utility in the "Controlling Services with the SC Utility" section of Chapter 6 as an example of a utility that controls services.) As with all services, this one has to run to provide any functionality. Consequently, if your ASP.NET applications run, but don't maintain state information (settings, configuration information, or variable data), then you know there's a problem with the ASPNet_State service. A lack of status support is a real problem if you're running a shopping cart or other state intensive application.

The ASPNet_State service does differ in one important respect. This is a .NET application, so you must register it differently from other services. In addition, you need to make sure that the system is actually using the current version. You can verify the version by viewing the ASP.NET State Service Properties dialog box accessible from the Services console found in the Administrative Tools folder of the Control Panel. The General tab contains the location of the executable in the Path to Executable field. The path should point to the latest version of the .NET Framework on your system.

You have several options for fixing this service if it didn't install correctly. First, you can use the ASPNet_RegIIS utility described earlier to reinstall the support completely. Use this option when you feel there are other configuration issues to consider. Second, you can use the InstallUtil utility described in the "Installing Assemblies with the InstallUtil Utility" section of Chapter 16 to perform the installation. Use this second option when you see the wrong version of the ASPNet_State service installed or when the service doesn't work as anticipated. Make sure you set the service to start automatically after you install it (see the Knowledge Base article at `http://support.microsoft.com/default.aspx?scid=kb;en-us;839800` for additional information).

Getting Started with Command Line Tasks

This chapter has demonstrated the utilities you need to work with ASP.NET and also has shown you some of the methods you can use to detect errors. It's important to remember that many of the major configuration errors you face when working with ASP.NET have no graphical utility solution; you must use the command prompt to fix them so knowing the correct utility to use to repair a problem is important.

It's time to check your ASP.NET configuration (assuming you have one). Many ASP.NET installations have small configuration errors that prevent applications from working well or at all. Even though this chapter hasn't discussed the configuration settings themselves, you should take time to verify your settings and make sure they're correct.

Chapter 18 begins a new discussion about Microsoft Vista. This latest version of Windows will add yet more command line features and Chapter 18 previews them for you. As Microsoft becomes more security conscious, look for additional security features in the operating system and more command line utilities to manage them. Chapter 18 has more than a few surprises and provides you with a good preview of the direction that Microsoft is headed with the command line in Vista.

Part 5

Windows Vista Special Features Preview

In This Section:

Chapter 18

Using Windows PowerShell

- An Overview of Windows PowerShell
- Why Use the Windows PowerShell?
- Downloading and Installing Windows PowerShell
- Understanding the Windows PowerShell Difference
- Using the Windows PowerShell Commands

Vista was supposed to come with a new command line shell called Windows PowerShell. This new command line shell provides direct access to the .NET Framework, improved security, and helps you perform tasks at the command line that you could never perform in the past. However, Microsoft decided to drop Windows PowerShell from Vista (they didn't provide a reason, but the probable reason is that Windows PowerShell for Vista was still in testing when Microsoft released Vista to manufacturing). You can obtain Windows PowerShell as a separate download for Vista, the next version of Windows Server (Longhorn), Windows Server 2003, and Windows XP. This chapter provides an overview of Windows PowerShell: why you should use it and where you can get it.

NOTE Microsoft hasn't released a version of Windows PowerShell that's compatible with the Vista RTM version at the time of this writing. Consequently, Chapters 18 and 19 rely on the version of Windows PowerShell for Windows XP SP2. If you're using Vista, you may notice slight differences between it and the version of Windows PowerShell that ships for Windows XP SP2. In fact, there may be slight differences with Windows Server 2003 and Windows Server Longhorn as well. In all cases, the basic principles and usage instructions do remain the same across all platforms.

An Overview of Windows PowerShell

Although Microsoft hasn't made a statement on the matter, many industry experts view Windows PowerShell as a highly extensible equivalent to many UNIX shells on the market. Under UNIX, many graphical utilities simply provide a convenient way to use the well-defined command line utilities. Working at the command line is the main event and the graphical environment serves to make working with the command line utilities easier for those who need it. If this is the direction that Microsoft is taking, you may eventually see all of the old, poorly documented and virus-prone utilities disappear from Windows, replaced by Windows PowerShell equivalents. Of course, this won't happen in Vista or perhaps even the next version of Windows, but because of the security problems with current utilities, Microsoft may feel forced to move in this direction.

Of course, the basic issue that many administrators are concerned about is what Windows PowerShell provides that the old command line doesn't provide. The "Why Use the Windows PowerShell?" section of the chapter discusses why you would want to use it in detail. However, here are some issues to consider:

- The Windows PowerShell provides a greater level of reliability than the command line.
- Using the Windows PowerShell improves security because you need the required credentials to execute commands.
- Windows PowerShell helps the administrator obtain the full resources of the .NET Framework without becoming a programmer.
- In many cases, the commands are easier to remember and use because they use human readable terms (the older commands are also available, for the most part, should you decide to use them).
- Scripting is considerably more powerful in Windows PowerShell, albeit not always as easy as working at the old command prompt.
- Instead of using plain text for data, Windows PowerShell uses .NET objects, which means you can obtain consistent output of complex data.

These basic reasons for using Windows PowerShell also tell you what Microsoft is trying to accomplish. If you take a hard look at Vista, many of the low-level operating system features still don't rely on the .NET Framework, but many of the higher-level features do. For example, you can no longer talk about IIS without also talking about the .NET Framework. The .NET Framework also makes an appearance in security, graphics, and communications. Consequently, it isn't any surprise that the Windows PowerShell also has a very heavy connection to the .NET Framework. In general, you're going to find that Microsoft moves more and more in the direction of using the .NET Framework for the majority of operating system features. This change in focus means that you really do need a .NET Framework connection at the command prompt to get useful work done today and that the connection will only get stronger as time passes.

Why Use the Windows PowerShell?

The fact that the .NET Framework hasn't taken over yet may leave some people considering not using Windows PowerShell today. It's true; you can work with Windows XP, Windows 2003, and Vista at the command line without ever looking at Windows PowerShell. In fact, you'll very likely be able to work with Windows Server Longhorn with nary a glimpse at Windows PowerShell too. Microsoft doesn't throw out old technology very quickly. However, they do throw it out. If the Vista entries in this book tell you anything, they demonstrate that Microsoft is doing some serious housecleaning at the command prompt and you need to keep on top of it. However, there are many other personal reasons to use Windows PowerShell as described here:

- It provides better automation features so you can do more with less effort.
- You can create scripts more quickly in many cases.
- Scripts created with Windows PowerShell tend to execute faster for a given task than performing the task at the old command line.
- Using Windows PowerShell reduces potential mistakes.

- You get more information from Windows PowerShell than you do from the command line utilities of the past.
- It's easier to obtain usable help in Windows PowerShell than it is at the command prompt (which sometimes doesn't provide any help at all).

Of course, this begs the question of whether you should just throw away that old command prompt. Unfortunately, you can't do that either. Many individuals and most companies have a significant base of existing batch files and scripts that they aren't going to be willing to throw away. Unfortunately, this established base might not run very well under Windows PowerShell for the very reasons that you want to use it—improved security and reliability. Consequently, during this transitional phase, you'll probably have to use both the command line and Windows PowerShell for maximum productivity. To make the transition smoother, you may want to begin moving those old batch files and scripts to Windows PowerShell as time permits.

Downloading and Installing Windows PowerShell

Before you can use Windows PowerShell, you need a copy of it. The version of Windows PowerShell you obtain depends on the version of Windows you use. You can find all of the latest Windows PowerShell downloads at `http://www.microsoft.com/technet/scriptcenter/topics/msh/download.mspx`. The important issue is to download the version of Windows PowerShell you actually need. For example, when working with Windows XP Service Pack 2 (SP2), you have a choice of x86 (32-bit) and x64 (64-bit) versions. In addition to a platform choice, you can also choose between language versions.

After you download the installation file, double-click it. You'll see the usual licensing agreement. After you accept the licensing terms, following the remaining prompts to perform the installation. The process should require just a few minutes to complete. When the installation is complete, you'll see a new Windows PowerShell 1.0 entry on your Start ➤ Programs menu. The features include several pieces of documentation and the Windows PowerShell entry that opens a Windows PowerShell prompt.

NOTE When working in Vista, you'll need to right-click the Windows PowerShell entry and choose Run as Administrator from the context menu. Otherwise, most of the commands you execute using Windows PowerShell will fail.

Understanding the Windows PowerShell Difference

Working at the Windows PowerShell command line shell is intrinsically different from working at the `CMD.EXE` command line. One of the first things you'll notice is that using the /? command line switch doesn't work for many commands and utilities. For example, if you want to find out about the `Dir` command, you must type **`Help Dir`** and press Enter. The command line help is also significantly different. Some people will feel that they're reading a programming manual, rather than a help listing. Figure 18.1 shows a typical example. You'll see immediately Windows PowerShell doesn't provide the same command line help you used in the past.

NOTE Windows PowerShell uses a relatively large font and a 120-character screen size by default. The figures in this chapter use a somewhat smaller font and an 80-character screen size to ensure you can see the text within the book.

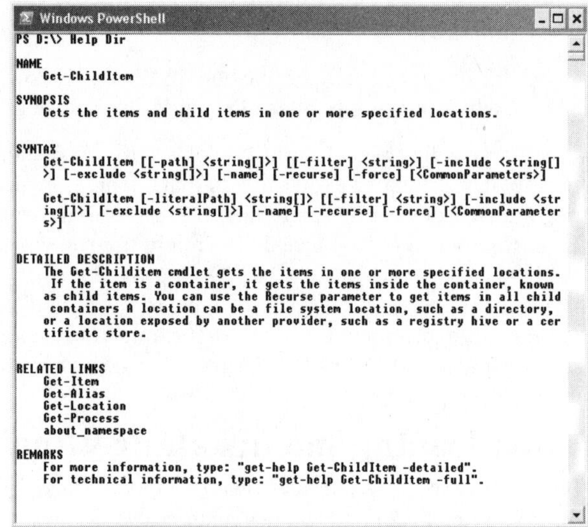

FIGURE 18.1
Windows PowerShell provides a different sort of help than you used in the past.

Most commands and many utilities don't work the same when using Windows PowerShell. For example, say you want to locate all of the temporary files on your system and place the results in the `Temp.TXT` file. Using the old method, you would type **`Dir *.TMP /S >> Temp.TXT`** and press Enter. This technique doesn't work under Windows PowerShell. Instead, you type **`get-childitem -Include *.TMP -Recurse >> Temp.TXT`** and press Enter. The results are similar; the syntax is completely different. You can substitute `Dir` for `get-childitem`, but that's about the limit of the similarities. The `Dir` command does work differently under Windows PowerShell. The output appears in Figure 18.2. Notice the use of the `get-childitem` command. You could substitute `Dir *.TXT` and obtain the same results.

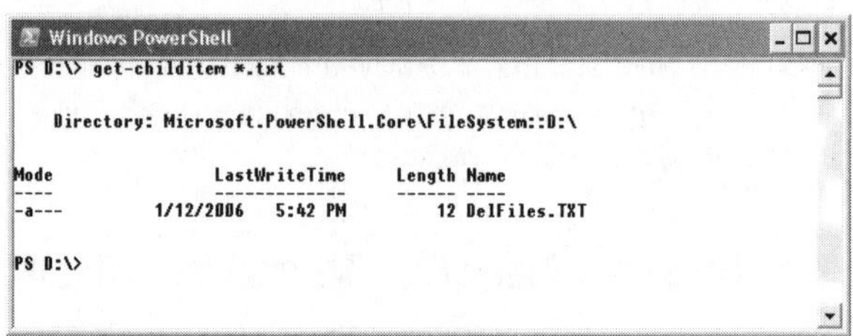

FIGURE 18.2
The output of the directory command, no matter which syntax you use, differs in Windows PowerShell.

Windows PowerShell uses a wealth of new names for old commands. For example, the `CD` command from days past is now the `set-location` command. You can see a list of the Windows PowerShell commands by typing **`Help *`** and pressing Enter. Figure 18.3 shows part of the list. This list might look a little daunting at first. However, it represents a major change in the way that the command shell works with commands from ancient UNIX to a more modern object-oriented methodology. The bottom line is that Windows PowerShell provides a vast wealth of commands, many of which don't appear in the old command prompt, but which require you to learn a new way of working with those commands.

Real World Scenario

EXPECTING THE VISTA SECURITY DIFFERENCE

Microsoft has made the claim that Vista is more secure than any previous version of Windows. In fact, if you use all of the Vista features and don't disable the features Microsoft includes for system protection, you'll find that the entire environment is more secure. The changes are going to be welcome in a world filled with all kinds of nefarious individuals, adware, viruses, and spyware. The plus side is that you might not have to worry as often about users shooting themselves and everyone around them in the foot with the latest attachment in an email that somehow gets through your filtering process. The negative side is that some of those old scripts and batch files might not work as anticipated, when they work at all.

One of Microsoft's goals for Windows PowerShell, the command line interface for Vista, is to keep batch files and scripts working as they always have. However, this goal is the direct opposite of good security, in some cases, because many of those old batch files and scripts performed tasks in an insecure manner. For example, deleting all of the temporary files on a drive might seem like an innocuous task and it is. However, what happens when a cracker changes that script, just for fun, and now it deletes all of the executable files on the hard drive? The script is no longer benevolent and requires some level of control. The old command line would simply delete the executable files and you'd have a mess on your hands.

Working with Windows PowerShell, you'll see a message about the pending deletion. If you're like many advanced users, the warning is going to be incredibly annoying and you might simply disregard it. Windows PowerShell will attempt to protect you from shooting yourself in the foot, but you can override the features it provides. After all, there's a point at which you can't protect people from themselves. Consequently, you need to expect the Vista security to be different and react appropriately to it. When you see a message from the operating system, don't get annoyed; make sure you really want to do the task that the operating system is warning you about.

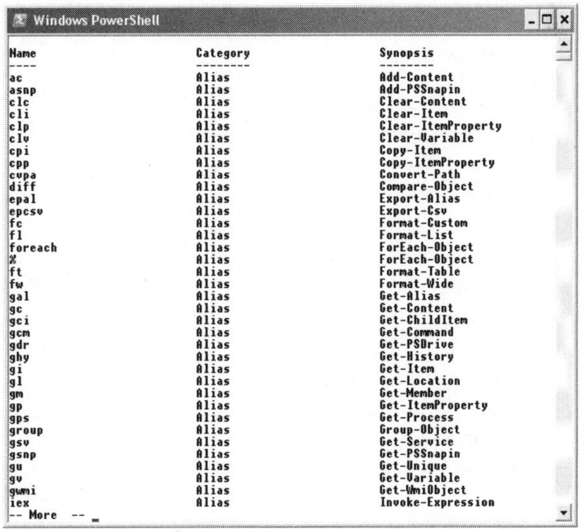

FIGURE 18.3
Before you begin using Windows PowerShell in earnest, you'll want to review the command list.

```
Windows PowerShell

Name                Category            Synopsis
----                --------            --------
ac                  Alias               Add-Content
asnp                Alias               Add-PSSnapin
clc                 Alias               Clear-Content
cli                 Alias               Clear-Item
clp                 Alias               Clear-ItemProperty
clv                 Alias               Clear-Variable
cpi                 Alias               Copy-Item
cpp                 Alias               Copy-ItemProperty
cvpa                Alias               Convert-Path
diff                Alias               Compare-Object
epal                Alias               Export-Alias
epcsv               Alias               Export-Csv
fc                  Alias               Format-Custom
fl                  Alias               Format-List
foreach             Alias               ForEach-Object
%                   Alias               ForEach-Object
ft                  Alias               Format-Table
fw                  Alias               Format-Wide
gal                 Alias               Get-Alias
gc                  Alias               Get-Content
gci                 Alias               Get-ChildItem
gcm                 Alias               Get-Command
gdr                 Alias               Get-PSDrive
ghy                 Alias               Get-History
gi                  Alias               Get-Item
gl                  Alias               Get-Location
gm                  Alias               Get-Member
gp                  Alias               Get-ItemProperty
gps                 Alias               Get-Process
group               Alias               Group-Object
gsv                 Alias               Get-Service
gsnp                Alias               Get-PSSnapin
gu                  Alias               Get-Unique
gv                  Alias               Get-Variable
gwmi                Alias               Get-WmiObject
iex                 Alias               Invoke-Expression
-- More  --
```

NOTE A number of people are starting to compare the Windows PowerShell interface to the interface provided with Linux. You can find an interesting article on the topic at `http://arstechnica.com/guides/other/msh.ars`. Most people who've used both Windows PowerShell and Linux agree that Microsoft has taken a significant step in the right direction by making the command line easier to use overall and more object oriented. The result is that you have a more consistent interface to work with, even if it's significantly different from what you used in the past.

Using the New Windows PowerShell Commands

Using Windows PowerShell is a different experience from working with the command line in a number of ways, not the least of which is how Windows PowerShell provides functionality. Instead of individual utilities, Microsoft is placing a strong emphasis on Cmdlets and scripts, which let you access the power of the .NET Framework in a secure manner. The Windows PowerShell interface is significantly different as described in the "Understanding the Windows PowerShell Difference" section of the chapter. Table 18.1 shows a list of the new commands available as part of Windows PowerShell as of the time of writing.

NOTE You'll see Windows PowerShell abbreviated as PS in more than a few locations. When you see PS, think PowerShell.

TABLE 18.1: New Commands Available in Windows PowerShell

COMMAND	DESCRIPTION
`add-content`	Adds the content of one or more objects to another object. For example, you could use this command to add the content of one or more files to a master file.
`add-history`	Adds an entry to the session history even though you haven't actually executed the command.
`add-member`	Adds the user-defined custom member to an existing object.
`add-pssnapin`	Adds the requested Windows PowerShell snap-in to the current console. A snap-in is a set of features for manipulating a particular application or system resource such as a snap-in for Microsoft Exchange.
`clear-content`	Removes the content from a file or other object. The file or other object remains intact; it simply doesn't have any information stored in it.
`clear-item`	Sets an item to contain a specific value that represents a clear condition.
`clear-itemproperty`	Removes the value from an object property. The system sets the property to a blank value, rather than a null (nothing) value.
`clear-variable`	Removes the value from a variable. The variable still exists; it simply doesn't contain any information.
`compare-object`	Performs a comparison of two objects.

TABLE 18.1: New Commands Available in Windows PowerShell *(CONTINUED)*

COMMAND	DESCRIPTION
`convertfrom-securestring`	Converts a secure string into an encrypted standard string. The most common reason to perform this conversion is to save the standard string to a file for later use. Use the `convertto-securestring` Cmdlet to convert the string from a standard string to a secure string. You can learn more about the `SecureString` class at `http://msdn2.microsoft.com/en-us/library/system.security.securestring.aspx`.
`convert-path`	Converts the path to the specified object from a Windows PowerShell path to a provider path. Normally, this means creating a full path specification, including the drive letter.
`convertto-html`	Converts the input information into an HTML table. For example, you could use this command to convert a directory listing into an HTML format.
`convertto-securestring`	Converts an encrypted standard string into a secure string. You can also use this Cmdlet to convert plain text strings into secure strings.
`copy-item`	Copies the contents of one item to another item.
`copy-itemproperty`	Copies the contents of one object property to another object property.
`export-alias`	Exports a command alias that you've created for the current session to a file. For example, the alias of the `Dir` command is `get-childitem`.
`export-clixml`	Creates an XML representation of one or more Windows PowerShell objects.
`export-console`	Exports the changes made to the current console so that you can import them later to another console. Any changes you save overwrite the content of any existing console file.
`export-csv`	Exports the requested data to a CSV format.
`foreach-object`	Performs a `foreach` looping function. This command normally appears in a script.
`format-custom`	Displays output data using a custom format. You specify the output format as part of a formatter file that describes the format.
`format-list`	Displays the output data in a list format where each data element appears on a separate line.
`format-table`	Displays the output data in a tabular format where each element appears in a separate column.
`format-wide`	Displays objects as a list of the properties that contain the object's data.
`get-acl`	Obtains an Access Control List for the specified object.

TABLE 18.1: New Commands Available in Windows PowerShell *(CONTINUED)*

COMMAND	DESCRIPTION
`get-alias`	Obtains the alias for the specified command.
`get-authenticodesignature`	Obtains the signature object (the digital signature) associated with a file.
`get-childitem`	Displays a list of the children for a particular object. This command is normally associated as the alias for the `Dir` command and used to display a directory. However, you can use it for any object.
`get-command`	Obtains information about a specified command. The information is different from help in that you receive a short synopsis of the command and its command line switches.
`get-content`	Displays the content for an object. When used for a file, this command displays the file contents in a manner similar to the `Type` command.
`get-credential`	Obtains a credential object based on a particular password.
`get-culture`	Obtains the culture information for the current command line session.
`get-date`	Displays the current date and time.
`get-drive`	Obtains the specified drive object. Unlike `CMD.EXE`, you don't provide the colon after the drive letter. The current utility version doesn't support UNC drive specifications.
`get-eventlog`	Obtains the specified event log.
`get-executionpolicy`	Obtains the current execution policy for Windows PowerShell. The default setting is Restricted. Potential values include Restricted, AllSigned, RemoteSigned, and Unrestricted. The execution policy determines the requirements for running code on a system, with Restricted providing the most protection and Unrestricted providing the least.
`get-help`	Obtains help information about a specific command. You can also use this command to obtain a list of matching commands by using wildcard characters.
`get-history`	Displays the command line history for the session. You can also use this command to select a command from the list to execute.
`get-host`	Displays information about the current host, including the session identifier and basic cultural information.
`get-item`	Displays information about the specified item.
`get-itemproperty`	Obtains the content of an object property.

TABLE 18.1: New Commands Available in Windows PowerShell *(CONTINUED)*

COMMAND	DESCRIPTION
`get-location`	Displays the current hard drive location on the system.
`get-member`	Displays specifics about the supplied object including properties, methods, type information, and property sets.
`get-pfxcertificate`	Obtains the Personal Information Exchange (PFX) certificate information. You can learn more about the PFX certificate at `http://msdn2.microsoft.com/en-us/library/bb172338.aspx`.
`get-process`	Displays a list of the processes running on the machine.
`get-psdrive`	Returns information about the Windows PowerShell drives. The default output information includes the drive name, provider, and root directory.
`get-psprovider`	Obtains information about the specified provider.
`get-pssnapin`	Displays a list of the existing Windows PowerShell snap-ins loaded within the current session. The information includes the name, version, and description.
`get-service`	Displays a list of all of the services installed on a machine along with the service status.
`get-tracesource`	Lists the properties for a given trace source. You can learn more about the `TraceSource` class used for creating a trace source at `http://msdn2.microsoft.com/en-us/library/system.diagnostics.tracesource.aspx`.
`get-uiculture`	Displays the culture information used for the user interface.
`get-unique`	Displays a list of unique items in a collection. This command lets you remove repeated entries from the list. You normally use this command as part of a script.
`get-variable`	Displays the content of one or more variables. You can use this command while diagnosing errors in scripts or as a means of saving state information for later use.
`get-wmiobject`	Obtains the Windows Management Instrumentation (WMI) object for the machine. You can use this object to perform a broad range of tasks, such as obtaining information about the network. This command provides a superset of the information you can obtain and manipulate using the WMIC utility described in Chapter 6.
`group-object`	Groups objects that contain the same value for a given property. You can use this command to compare objects.

TABLE 18.1: New Commands Available in Windows PowerShell *(CONTINUED)*

COMMAND	DESCRIPTION
`import-alias`	Imports an alias from a file. This feature lets you use aliases that you've stored for later use.
`import-clixml`	Imports an XML representation of one or more Windows PowerShell objects.
`import-csv`	Obtains objects from a CSV listing and transmits them to another command or utility through a pipeline. You'll normally use this feature to perform object analysis or process a number of objects that include the same properties, such as a directory listing.
`invoke-expression`	Executes the specified expression, normally a Cmdlet. This is one of the default command line actions, so you won't use this command at the command line in most cases. However, you can use it within a script to execute a supplementary command.
`invoke-history`	Executes a previously executed command based on its position in the history list.
`invoke-item`	Invokes an executable or opens a file. Essentially, this command performs the default actions associated with a file.
`join-path`	Creates a single path element from several path elements.
`measure-command`	Tracks the running time for scripts and Cmdlets. You can use this command to measure system performance while performing a task. However, a more common use is to track the time that a task is running and when to terminate it if it takes too long. Many people will associate the functionality of this command with the watchdog timer used to reset hardware. Generally, you'll use this feature in a script to keep the script from freezing the system.
`measure-object`	Measures the specified element of an object or object property. For example, you could count the number of directory entries using this command. You always use the output of another command as input to this command through a pipe.
`move-item`	Moves an item from one location to another. For example, you can use this command to move a file from one location to another.
`move-itemproperty`	Moves a property from one object to another.
`new-alias`	Creates a new alias for an existing Cmdlet. The Cmdlet must exist or this command will fail.
`new-item`	Creates a new item in the specified namespace.
`new-itemproperty`	Sets a new property for an item at a specific location. For example, you could use this feature to set a Cmdlet property value.

Table 18.1: New Commands Available in Windows PowerShell *(continued)*

Command	Description
`new-object`	Creates a new .NET Framework object. You can create any object within the .NET framework. Even though you could use this command at the command line, you'll normally use it within a script to create objects necessary to manipulate data, show status information, or perform other tasks.
`new-psdrive`	Mounts a new drive on the system. This command provides a superset of the functionality provided by the Mount utility described in the "Mounting a Volume with the MountVol Utility" section of Chapter 6.
`new-service`	Installs a new service on the system.
`new-timespan`	Defines a time span using a `TimeSpan` object. Normally, you'll use this feature within a script to track the time span required to perform a task or to create other time-related statistics. You can learn more about the `TimeSpan` object at `http://msdn.microsoft.com/library/en-us/cpref/html/frlrfsystemtimespanclasstopic.asp`.
`new-variable`	Creates a new variable that you can use either at the command line or within a script. Variables act as storage containers for data that you want to retain in memory.
`out-default`	Specifies the default controller of output data.
`out-file`	Specifies the output device to use for file information. This file receives the output of the specified command, script, or pipeline.
`out-host`	Sends the pipelined output of a series of commands to the console.
`out-null`	Sends the output to the null device. Essentially, this places the output in the bit bucket. This command takes the place of the NUL: device used in older versions of the command line.
`out-printer`	Sends the output to the printer. If you don't specify a printer, the system uses the default printer.
`out-string`	Sends the pipelined output of a series of commands to a string variable.
`pop-location`	Removes a path from the top of the stack. This command provides a superset of the functionality provided by the PopD command described in the "Storing and Retrieving Directories with the *PushD* and *PopD* Commands" section of Chapter 2.
`push-location`	Adds a directory path to the stack. This command provides a superset of the functionality provided by the `PushD` command described in the "Storing and Retrieving Directories with the *PushD* and *PopD* Commands" section of Chapter 2.

TABLE 18.1: New Commands Available in Windows PowerShell *(CONTINUED)*

COMMAND	DESCRIPTION
`read-host`	Reads a line of input from the host console. Normally, you'll use this command within a script to query the user for input.
`remove-item`	Requests that a provider remove the specified item. Generally, this command works with directories and files. It provides a superset of the features found in the RD, `RmDir`, `Del`, and `Erase` commands. You can learn more about the RD command in the "Removing a Directory with the *RD* and *RmDir* Commands" section of Chapter 2. The `Del` and `Erase` command information appears in the "Removing Files with the *Del* and *Erase* Commands" section of Chapter 2.
`remove-itemproperty`	Removes the specified property value from an object.
`remove-psdrive`	Dismounts a drive currently attached to the system. See the `new-drive` command for details.
`remove-pssnapin`	Removes the specified Windows PowerShell snap-in from the current session.
`remove-variable`	Removes a variable from the current session. This action deletes the variable.
`rename-item`	Requests that a provider rename the specified item. Generally, this command works with directories and files. It provides a superset of the functionality of the `Ren` and `Rename` commands. You can learn more about these commands in the "Renaming a File with the *Ren* and *Rename* Commands" section of Chapter 2.
`rename-itemproperty`	Renames the specified property in the requested location.
`resolve-path`	Resolves the wildcards in a path so that you can see the actual path information. You can also use this feature within a batch file to provide actual path information to utilities that require it.
`restart-service`	Restarts the specified Windows service after you stop it. Don't use this command with paused services.
`resume-service`	Resumes the specified Windows service after you pause it. Don't use this command with stopped services.
`select-object`	Selects an object based on the arguments you provide to a Cmdlet.
`select-string`	Searches through strings or files for data with a specific pattern. This command provides a superset of the functionality provided by the FindStr utility described in the "Locating Information in Files with the Find and FindStr Utilities" section of Chapter 4.

TABLE 18.1: New Commands Available in Windows PowerShell *(CONTINUED)*

COMMAND	DESCRIPTION
`set-acl`	Modifies the contents of an ACL. Use this command to change user, group, or machine security.
`set-alias`	Modifies an existing alias. Use the `new-alias` command to create a new alias for an existing command.
`set-authenticodesignature`	Modifies the Authenticode signature of an object such as a file.
`set-content`	Changes the content of the specified object at the requested location. For example, you could use this command to output a data to a file.
`set-date`	Changes the system time and date.
`set-executionpolicy`	Changes the current execution policy for Windows PowerShell. The default setting is Restricted. Potential values include Restricted, AllSigned, RemoteSigned, and Unrestricted. The execution policy determines the requirements for running code on a system, with Restricted providing the most protection and Unrestricted providing the least.
`set-item`	Requests that a provider set the value of an item using the specified pathname. For example, you can use this command to set the value of a variable.
`set-itemproperty`	Sets an object property to the specified value.
`set-location`	Sets the working directory to the specified location. The working directory is where Windows looks for data files and places output when you don't specify a particular location as part of the output argument.
`set-psdebug`	Places the command line in a debug state. You use this feature to debug your scripts. Unlike previous versions of the command line, Windows PowerShell includes built-in debugging support to go with the built-in scripting support.
`set-service`	Sets the properties of a service. For example, you can use this command to set a service to start automatically. You can also use it to change the description or the logon account. This command lets you modify any editable service property. Note that some services offer more editable features than others do based on the design features included by the developer.
`set-tracesource`	Sets or removes the specified trace listeners and options from the requested trace source. See the `get-tracesource` command for additional information.
`set-variable`	Changes the value of a variable.

TABLE 18.1: New Commands Available in Windows PowerShell *(CONTINUED)*

COMMAND	DESCRIPTION
`sort-object`	Sorts the data provided. For example, you could use the command to sort a directory listing by the length of the file. However, this command works with any sortable object, such as files.
`split-path`	Separates one or more paths into a qualifier, parent path, or leaf item and places the result in a string. You'll normally use this feature from within a script to ensure you can locate specific places on the hard drive, determine the current hard drive location, process or access files, or perform other path-related tasks.
`start-service`	Starts a stopped service. Don't use this command with a service that's paused.
`start-sleep`	Places the console, script, Cmdlet, or other executable code into a sleep state for the specified amount of time. You can use this feature within a script to stop script execution while you wait for the system to perform a task. For example, you might use this feature when waiting for a download to complete from the Internet.
`start-transcript`	Creates a log of the console session. You can use this feature to keep track of tasks performed at the command line or diagnose the sequence of events used by a script to complete a task. The log file contains a complete record of the session from the time you use the `start-transcript` command until you issue the `stop-transcript` command or end the current session.
`stop-process`	Stops the specified process. The process terminates, which means that you could lose data. This command provides a superset of the functionality provided by the TaskKill utility discussed in the "Terminating Tasks with the TaskKill Utility" section of Chapter 5.
`stop-service`	Stops the specified service. You must use the `start-service` command to restart the service.
`stop-transcript`	Ends the logging of console input. See the `start-transaction` command for additional information.
`suspend-service`	Pauses the specified service. The service is still in memory and retains any property values. You must use the `resume-service` command to restart a paused service.
`tee-object`	Sends input object to two places. In short, this command creates a copy of the specified input object so you can use it for multiple commands.

TABLE 18.1: New Commands Available in Windows PowerShell *(CONTINUED)*

COMMAND	DESCRIPTION
`test-path`	Provides a method for testing a path. The command returns true when the path exists. Although you could use this command at the command line, you'll generally use it in a script to ensure a path exists before you attempt to perform tasks that involve the path.
`trace-command`	Enables you to track trace sources for the duration of the command. This is a debugging feature. See the `set-tracesource` and `get-tracesource` commands for additional information.
`update-formatdata`	Updates and appends format data files. These files let you format data using custom parameters. See the `format-custom` command for additional information.
`update-typedata`	Updates the `Types.PS1XML` file with additional type information for objects.
`where-object`	Filters the data from a pipeline so the recipient receives only the data required to execute a command or manipulate data.
`write-debug`	Sends debugging information to the console display. You use this command to debug scripts and Cmdlets by viewing information about specific objects and variables.
`write-error`	Sends error information to the console display. You use this feature to perform debugging and when you need to know the error status of both scripts and Cmdlets. Errors are coding mistakes that cause the script or Cmdlet to stop working, seriously degrade performance, damage data in some manner, or cause other serious damage.
`write-host`	Displays a list of the objects supported by the current host.
`write-object`	Sends an object to the pipeline. This command lets you use objects with a series of Cmdlets.
`write-progress`	Sends a progress indicator to the console display. Using this command lets you track script or Cmdlet progress and ensure that the script or Cmdlet hasn't stopped. This feature is also useful for scripts and Cmdlets to let the user know that the command is working during an interactive session.
`write-verbose`	Displays maximum information about any command.
`write-warning`	Sends warning information to the console display. You use this feature to perform debugging and when you need to know the warning status of both scripts and Cmdlets. Warnings are coding mistakes that cause the script of Cmdlet to perform in a manner other than intended by the developer. A warning usually indicates a problem that isn't serious, but that you still need to know about in order to take any required repair action.

WHY USE A DIFFERENT SET OF COMMANDS?

Many network administrators will wonder why Microsoft has chosen to introduce a new set of commands. After all, they already understand the commands that CMD.EXE uses and generally find them usable. However, the problem isn't one of usage. Most people can use the existing commands without too much trouble. The problem is one of remembering which command to use in a particular situation. After reviewing the current commands and utilities in this book, you must admit that it's quite a menagerie of disparate features.

The purpose in creating a new command set is to reduce the requirement to remember the commands at all. The combination of an action, followed by an object or task, makes it likely that you'll enter the right word for a search. Because the system uses a centralized help scheme and you can perform wildcard searches for commands, it's very likely that you'll find the command you want in seconds, rather than hours. The point is that you don't have to remember any commands, even though you'll likely remember those you use most often.

The new command set will also reduce training costs for new administrators and make it less likely that a new administrator will make a catastrophic error. The old system requires years to learn because there isn't any cohesiveness to the choice of command syntax. For example, even though most commands respond to the /? command line switch, some don't. In addition, the use of the /? command line switch presupposes that you know which command to use. The lack of centralization causes significant problems for new administrators and even administrators who have been working at the computer for many years.

Getting Started with Command Line Tasks

This chapter has helped you understand the new utilities that Microsoft is providing as part of Windows PowerShell. The essential reasons to use Windows PowerShell include higher reliability, better security, shorter learning curve, faster execution, and ease of use. Unfortunately, Windows PowerShell can't meet every need today. You'll still need to keep a copy of the old command line around for a while until the transition is complete. Just when the old command line will fall out of favor is anyone's guess. Just consider how long DOS was around after Windows appeared on the scene and you'll realize that old software lingers seemingly forever.

Windows PowerShell is a very good product. Yes, it's in its infancy today, but Microsoft has already done a lot of things right with Windows PowerShell. Of course, the only way that you'll know for yourself is to work with Windows PowerShell, which means getting a copy, installing it, and working with the Cmdlets it provides. After you spend enough time with Windows PowerShell, you can begin building your own Cmdlets and start tossing those old batch and script files aside.

Chapter 19 is the final chapter of the book. This chapter tells you more about the new and exciting command interpreter, Windows PowerShell. You'll find that Windows PowerShell is an entirely new command line experience that comes with its own scripting language. Working with Windows PowerShell promises to enhance the command line experience and make it easier than ever before for anyone to create useful and well-designed command line utilities. Hopefully, you'll find the command line experience with Windows PowerShell as exciting as many other people have. Chapter 19 is your introduction to this wonderful new computing experience.

Chapter 19

Working with Windows PowerShell

- Using the PS Command Interpreter
- Creating a Shell Extension with the Make-Shell Utility
- Creating a Windows PowerShell Script
- Creating a Windows PowerShell Cmdlet and Shell

Even though Windows PowerShell doesn't appear as part of Vista, you can download it for a number of platforms, including Windows XP, Vista, Windows Server 2003, and Windows Server Longhorn as described in Chapter 18. Many people will turn to Windows PowerShell because it offers a distinct set of new features that should make working at the command prompt significantly easier. In fact, Windows PowerShell provides the following features that the remaining sections of the chapter discuss in as much detail as is possible.

Simplified Navigation Windows PowerShell provides easier access to operating system elements including disk drives, startup files, and the registry. Easier access should translate into fewer problems working at the command line. You may even find that you don't need some of the very simple older scripts you used in the past to overcome difficulties in navigating your hard drive.

Command Extensibility This feature lets you write scripts faster and customize existing commands. In addition, you can use this feature to create your own command line tools.

Object Manipulation Previous versions of the command line never talked about objects because objects don't exist except as part of specific command line environments. Windows PowerShell provides access to a number of objects that the administrator can manipulate directly to access other tools or databases.

Direct System Data Access Accessing system data using older command line technologies is error prone because you have to save the data in text files and then parse it to obtain the information you need. Windows PowerShell makes it possible to access most system data directly so that you don't have to perform any error-prone manipulation.

Improved Output and Formatting Capabilities You can now define how you want data to appear when you output it, which means the information is often ready for reports and other needs. Older command line technologies output pure text and the format of that output is often limited to what Microsoft thought you needed at the time.

NOTE Microsoft hasn't released a version of Windows PowerShell that's compatible with the Vista RTM version at the time of this writing. Consequently, Chapters 18 and 19 rely on the version of Windows PowerShell for Windows XP SP2. If you're using Vista, you may notice slight differences between it and the version of Windows PowerShell that ships for Windows XP SP2. In fact, there may be slight differences with Windows Server 2003 and Windows Server Longhorn as well. In all cases, the basic principles and usage instructions do remain the same across all platforms.

Real World Scenario

A NOTE ABOUT COMPATIBILITY

I'll admit it: I'm just as excited as everyone else about working with Windows PowerShell. The excitement of something new is always hard to resist. Because Windows PowerShell has so much potential, there are many practical reasons to use it as well. In short, Windows PowerShell is the kind of product addition that attracts attention. However, it's important to step back for a moment and consider the potential side effects of using Windows PowerShell too. One of the most important effects to remember is that Windows PowerShell is new; it's not necessarily compatible with older versions of Windows (except those specifically mentioned). Anything new that you create with Windows PowerShell may only work with Windows PowerShell, which means older systems, such as Windows 2000, can't use it.

Microsoft has some very distinct goals for Windows PowerShell. These goals define what Windows PowerShell will do for you and determine how you can use Windows PowerShell effectively. Even though Microsoft plans to provide as much backward compatibility as possible, they always provide new features as well. One of the unwritten goals for every Microsoft product is to make it difficult for you to continue to use the older version of the product; in essence, they create an environment of forced update. Any new technique you discover in this chapter, even the very appealing ones, will cost you some level of compatibility with older systems. The question you need to ask is how much incompatibility you can afford.

Using the PS Command Interpreter

Windows PowerShell, like `CMD.EXE`, is essentially a command interpreter—a special kind of utility. In this case, you're using the `POWERSHELL.EXE` file. The first indication you have that Windows PowerShell is different is what appears when you execute the PS utility the first time. As shown in Figure 19.1, Windows PowerShell is extremely security conscious and asks whether you actually want to run it the first time. The message you see is just one indication of how serious Microsoft has become about security in Vista. In fact, you'd better get used to seeing this message because Windows PowerShell will constantly remind you about the security implications of certain actions.

NOTE Most of the error messages described in this chapter only appear when you use Windows PowerShell with Vista or Windows Server Longhorn. The errors don't appear when you work with Windows XP or Windows Server 2003 because these operating systems don't provide the high level of security that Vista and Windows Server Longhorn provide.

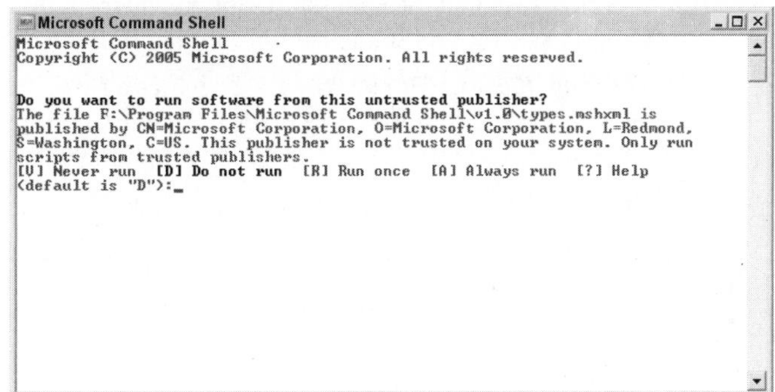

FIGURE 19.1
The security message you see when you run PS the first time tells you that Windows PowerShell is different.

As with `Command.COM` and `CMD.EXE`, `POWERSHELL.EXE` has a number of useful command line switches. You use these command line switches to change the way that Windows PowerShell works and the environment it provides to the user. This utility uses the following syntax:

```
PowerShell.exe [-PSConsoleFile cf | Version version] [-Help] [-NoLogo]
   [-NoExit] [-NoProfile] [-NonInteractive]
   [-OutputFormat {Text | XML}] [-InputFormat {Text | XML}]
   [-Command { - | <script-block> [-args <arg-array>]
   | <string> [<CommandParameters>] }]
```

The following list describes each of the command line arguments.

`-PSConsoleFile` ***`cf`*** Loads the specified PS console file during startup.

`-Version` ***`version`*** Starts a particular version of PS. This feature goes along with general side-by-side execution for the .NET Framework. You can read about the side-by-side version support in the "Understanding the Concept of Side-by-Side Versions" section of Chapter 15.

`-NoLogo` Forces the command line interpreter to start without displaying the copyright banner.

`-NoExit` Forces the command line interpreter to continue running after it completes running all startup commands.

`-NoProfile` Initializes the command line environment without executing a user initialization script. Normally, you want to run the initialization script to obtain specific command line functionality.

`-OutputFormat {Text | XML}` Specifies how the shell formats output data. The current shell values can include TEXT for text string output and XML for serialized XML format. The text format is most useful for entering commands manually. The XML format works well with scripts, especially when you intend to send the data to a database.

`-InputFormat {Text | XML}` Specifies the format of the input data. The current shell values can include TEXT for text string output and XML for serialized XML format.

`-Noninteractive` Performs one or more tasks without presenting an interactive prompt to the user. This feature lets you execute commands or Cmdlets in the background without disturbing the user.

`-Command` Executes the remainder of the command line arguments as though you typed them at the command line. The command line interpreter exits when it completes the commands, unless you provide the `-NoExit` command line switch. You can use the following formats for a command.

- Specifies that the command input come from the standard input device. In other words, you'll type the commands at the command line.

string [CommandParameters] Specifies a single command as a string. If you specify a dash (-) as the command, PS reads the command text from the standard input. PS passes all text after the command string to the command as part of its input arguments.

script-block [-args arg-array] Specifies one or more commands as a script block. You can only use the option if you are currently running the PS shell. Enclose the script box within curly brackets ({}). The parent shell automatically serializes any data to the child shell using a pipeline. Always send arguments to the child shell using the `-args` command line switch as an array.

Creating a Shell Extension with the Make-Shell Utility

You can create extended command shells for the Windows PowerShell environment. The Make-Shell utility (also know as the make-kit) helps you create these extensions. You use this utility to add the Cmdlets you create to the shell so that you can execute them directly from the command line as you would any other command. The Make-Shell utility always creates an executable file as output. This utility uses the following syntax:

```
make-shell -out n.exe -namespace ns [ -lib
   libdirectory1[,libdirectory2,..] ] [ -reference
   ca1.dll[,ca2.dll,...] ] [ -formatdata
   fd1.format.mshxml[,fd2.format.mshxml,...] ] [ -typedata
   td1.type.mshxml[,td2.type.mshxml,...] ] [ -source c1.cs [,c2.cs,...]
   ] [ -authorizationmanager authorizationManagerType ] [ -win32icon
   i.ico ] [ -initscript p.PS ] [ -builtinscript s1.PS[,s2.PS,...] ]
   [ -resource resourcefile.txt ] [ -cscflags cscFlags ] [-verbose] [ -
   ? | -help ]
```

The following list describes each of the command line arguments.

NOTE The Make-Shell utility used to appear as part of the Windows PowerShell installation program. However, Microsoft moved this utility to the Windows SDK because most users will create snap-ins for Windows PowerShell, rather than create their own shell. To obtain the Make-Shell utility, you must download the Windows SDK at `http://www.microsoft.com/downloads/details.aspx?FamilyId=C2B1E300-F358-4523-B479-F53D234CDCCF`. The Windows SDK includes shell examples using C#, all of the required reference assemblies, `Make-shell.EXE`, the required templates (`Format.PS1XML` and `Types.PS1XML`), and the documentation (getting started guide, programmer's guide, conceptual help, and managed reference).

-out *n.exe* Specifies the name of the shell that you want to produce. You must specify the path as part of this argument. The Make-Shell utility automatically appends `.EXE` to the filename if you don't specify it. You must provide this command line switch or the Make-Shell utility will fail.

-namespace *ns* Specifies the namespace to use for the `RunspaceConfiguration` table and the `main()` function that the Make-Shell utility generates and compiles for you. The `main()` function is the entry point for the executable. You must provide this command line switch or the Make-Shell utility will fail.

-lib *libdirectory1[,libdirectory2,..]* Specifies the directories to search for .NET assemblies that your Cmdlet requires to run. You don't need to specify this command line switch for assemblies that appear in the GAC or in the current directory. You may need to use this command line switch for any Windows PowerShell assemblies that you reference. Always include this argument for assemblies that you access with the `-reference` command line switch unless the assemblies appear in the GAC. You must also provide directory entries for any assemblies that a main assembly references that don't appear in the GAC.

-reference *ca1.dll[,ca2.dll,...]* Specifies the assemblies that you want to include in the shell. Don't include system or .NET Framework assemblies in this list; the Make-Shell utility finds these assemblies automatically. Reserve this command line switch for special assemblies that the Cmdlet requires to run, that contain the Cmdlet, and that contain resources used by the Cmdlet. If you don't include this command line shell, the resulting executable contains only the intrinsic Cmdlets (those produced by the Windows PowerShell team). You may specify the references using a full path. Otherwise, use the `-lib` command line switch to provide the path information as needed.

-formatdata *fd1.format.mshxml[,fd2.format.mshxml,...]* Provides a comma-separated list of format data to include as part of the shell. If you don't include this command line switch, then the resulting shell contains only the intrinsic format data (those produced by the Windows PowerShell team). The current shell provides formatting for text and serialized XML.

-typedata *td1.type.mshxml[,td2.type.mshxml,...]* Provides a comma-separated list of type data to include as part of the shell. If you don't include this command line switch, then the resulting shell contains only the intrinsic format data (those produced by the Windows PowerShell team).

-source *c1.cs [,c2.cs,...]* Specifies the names of the source files to use to create the shell additions. The source code must appear as C# code. The code can provide any functionality that you want to include at the command line. In addition to the code required to provide the new shell functionality, the code may include an Authorization Manager implementation that overrides the default Authorization Manager. You can also supply the Authorization Manager information (when you want to override the Authorization Manager) using the `-authorizationmanager` command line switch. The code can also include a number of assembly informational declarations including the overrides in the following list.

- AssemblyCompanyAttribute
- AssemblyCopyrightAttribute
- AssemblyFileVersionAttribute
- AssemblyInformationalVersionAttribute
- AssemblyProductAttribute
- AssemblyTrademarkAttribute

-authorizationmanager *authorizationManagerType* Defines the type in a source code (C#) file or a compiled assembly that the new shell should use as an Authorization Manager. The new shell will use the default Authorization Manager when you don't specify this command line switch or include an Authorization Manager as part of the shell source code. When you do specify a new type, you must include the full type name, including any required namespaces.

-win32icon ***i.ico*** Specifies the name of the file containing the icon you want to use for the new shell. (The icon file can contain multiple icons, one for each major resolution, if desired.) The new shell will use the C# compiler icon (if any) when you don't specify this command line switch.

-initscript ***p.PS*** Specifies the startup profile for the new shell. The Make-Shell utility doesn't verify this file in any way. Consequently, a faulty profile can prevent the new shell from running. A user can always override the default shell that you provide using the `-NoProfile` command line switch for the PS utility. Therefore, you shouldn't assume that the profile you provide is absolute, even when the profile works as anticipated.

-builtinscript ***s1.PS[,s2.PS,...]*** Defines a list of built-in scripts for the shell. The new shell discovers these scripts before it discovers scripts in the path. The scripts you provide as part of this command line switch are absolute; the user can't change them. The Make-Shell utility doesn't validate the scripts in any way. Consequently, even though an errant script won't keep the new shell from running, it will cause problems when the user attempts to run the script.

-resource ***resourcefile.txt*** Specifies a text file containing the resources that the shell uses. You must name the first resource ShellHelp. This resource contains the help text that the user sees when using the `-help` command line argument. The ShellHelp resource doesn't affect the output of the `Help` command used to display help for a particular shell command. The second resource is ShellBanner. This resource contains the text and copyright information that appears when the user invokes the shell in interactive mode. The new shell uses a generic help and banner when you don't provide these overrides.

-cscflags *cscFlags* Determines which flags the C# compiler (`CSC.EXE` located in the .NET Framework directory) receives as part of compiling the new shell. The Make-Shell passes these command line switches to the compiler unchanged. Always surround this command line switch with quotes. Otherwise, the Make-Shell utility may not pass all of the C# compiler command line switches and the compilation process will fail.

-verbose Displays detailed information during the shell creation process. The Make-Shell utility created the detailed information, so the output won't include any details of the C# compilation. If you want to see details of the C# compilation as well, you need to include additional command line switches for the C# compiler.

Creating a Windows PowerShell Script

Windows PowerShell supports both scripts and Cmdlets. A script is a series of commands contained in a text file that PS interprets. It's possible to execute scripts from the command line or make them part of the shell using the Make-Shell utility. A Cmdlet is a compiled executable in DLL format. As with the script, you begin with a text file containing commands that the C# Compiler (CSC) turns into an executable. To use a Cmdlet, you must make it part of the shell. The "Creating a Windows PowerShell Cmdlet and Shell" section of the chapter describes this process in detail.

Most administrators will want to start working with Windows PowerShell scripts before they move on to working with Cmdlets. The following sections describe how to create a basic script and run it at the command line. If you want to add the script to the shell, add them using the `-initscript` or `-builtinscript` command line switches of the Make-Script utility. The scripts then become part of the shell and you can use them whenever you want.

Real World Scenario

WORKING WITH SCRIPTS AND SHELLS

Scripts and shells represent two different levels of working with Windows PowerShell. When you create a script, you don't need to compile it. The system interprets the script and you work with it interactively at the command line. Unless you build a script into the shell, you can change it in an ad hoc manner until you get it right. Scripts are simple text that Windows PowerShell executes for you. They replace the batch files and JavaScript scripts that you've used in the past. Unlike these older alternatives, however, Windows PowerShell scripts are quite functional and powerful. You have the full functionality of the .NET Framework readily available.

A shell, on the other hand, is executable code. A shell contains a number of intrinsic (built-in) commands supplied by the Windows PowerShell development team. It also includes any number of extrinsic commands that you create as Cmdlets. You add a Cmdlet to Windows PowerShell by building a new shell to house it. Only after you create the new shell can you test the Cmdlet. Windows PowerShell doesn't know anything about the Cmdlet until you perform both a compilation and a shell creation process.

Unlike the command line of old, scripts and shells aren't necessarily mutually exclusive. You can build a script, test it for a while, add functionality as needed, and eventually turn it into a Cmdlet if you want. In other words, there's now a distinct process from quite simple and ad hoc to complex and part of the shell. Unlike the old static `CMD.EXE`, `POWERSHELL.EXE` is fully extensible so you can create the environment you want, rather than live with the environment that Microsoft thinks you need. Consequently, scripts and shells require a different viewpoint in Windows PowerShell because what you build today can easily become part of the environment tomorrow.

NOTE This chapter isn't going to provide a description of the Windows PowerShell scripting language or its programming elements, but will show you how to use them to create a script. The authoritative resource for the Windows PowerShell scripting language is the current documentation available from Microsoft at `http://www.microsoft.com/downloads/details.aspx?FamilyId=B4720B00-9A66-430F-BD56-EC48BFCA154F`. In fact, you may want to review the entire list of Microsoft resources for Windows PowerShell at `http://www.microsoft.com/technet/scriptcenter/hubs/msh.mspx`.

Creating a Simple Script

As with most scripts, a Windows PowerShell script is simply a series of executable statements that the system interprets to perform tasks. However, a Windows PowerShell script is built on a combination of the C# language, special objects that the Windows PowerShell developers create for you, the .NET Framework, and any special Cmdlets that you create. You can find a great overview of the language on the ars technica Web site at `http://arstechnica.com/guides/other/msh.ars`. If you want the short version, check out the basic list of elements Arul Kumaravel's WebLog at `http://blogs.msdn.com/arulk/archive/2005/02/24/379732.aspx`.

Script files are text files with a PS1 file extension. However, if you try to edit a file with a PS1 extension, the system will display an error message like the one shown in Figure 19.2. You must rename the file to have a TXT or other editable file extension and perform any required changes. Just in case you're thinking about creating scripts with a TXT extension, that won't work either. The file must have a PS1 extension to execute it as a script. If you give the file some other extension and load it, Windows PowerShell won't execute it. These security features prevent you from accidentally executing a partially created script. In addition, the security feature reduces the risk of someone modifying your script later.

FIGURE 19.2 You can't edit Windows PowerShell scripts directly, you must edit them as text files and then change the extension.

A Windows PowerShell script can include a wealth of features. As with any command line script, you can include any command that the command interpreter supports, as well as calls to utilities. In addition, Windows PowerShell scripts support all of the same statements that full-fledged programming languages do, including both conditional and looping statements. Unlike JavaScript, Windows PowerShell scripts also include the concept of data type.

TIP Windows PowerShell scripting has taken off. You can find sample scripts on many Web sites. However, some samples are better than others are. The first place you should look for sample scripts is on the Microsoft site at `http://www.microsoft.com/technet/scriptcenter/scripts/msh/default.mspx`. You'll also want to check out the community scripts at `http://www.reskit.net/monad/samplescripts.htm`.

It's often educational to view different ways of performing the same task using different languages. Listing 11.6 shows how to map a network drive using JavaScript. The example relies on the `MapNetworkDrive()` method of the `WScript.Network` object to perform the task. The only problem is that you can't access WScript from Windows PowerShell, so you need to take a different approach. Listing 19.1 shows the Windows PowerShell version of the JavaScript example in Listing 11.6.

LISTING 19.1: Mapping a Network Drive with Windows PowerShell

```
#Input arguments Local Drive and Network UNC location.
Param ($DriveLtr = "", $UNCName = "")

# Detect the correct number of input arguments.
if (($DriveLtr -eq "") -or ($UNCName -eq ""))
{
   # Detect a request for command line help.
   if ($DriveLtr -eq "/?")
   {
      # Display the help information
      [system.console]::Out.WriteLine(
         "Usage: MapNetwork <letter> <UNC target>")

      # Exit the script and provide an error level of 1 to
      # indicate a help request.
      return(1)
   }
```

```
      else
      {
         # Ask whether the user wants to continue.
         [system.console]::Out.WriteLine(
            "No input provided! Provide it interactively? [Y | N]")
         $Answer = [system.console]::In.ReadLine()

         # If the user doesn't want to continue, dipslay help and exit.
         # Use an exit code of 2 to indicate a data entry error.
         if ($Answer -eq "N")
         {
            [system.console]::Out.WriteLine(
               "Usage: MapNetwork <letter> <UNC target>")
            return(2)
         }

         # Input the drive letter.
            [system.console]::Out.WriteLine(
               "Type the local drive letter (X:).");
            $DriveLtr = [system.console]::In.ReadLine();

         # Input the UNC drive on the remote machine.
            [system.console]::Out.WriteLine(
               "Type the UNC location (\\MyServer\MyDrive).");
            $UNCName = [system.console]::In.ReadLine();
      }
   }

   # Define the network object used to map the drive.
   $oNetwork = new-object -COM WScript.Network

   # Attempt to create the connection.
   Trap [Exception]
   {
      # Display an error when the task fails.
      [system.console]::Out.WriteLine("Couldn't map the drive!")
      [system.console]::Out.WriteLine($_.Exception.Message)
      return 3
   }

   # Perform the drive mapping function.
   $oNetwork.MapNetworkDrive($DriveLtr, $UNCName);
```

Comparing the JavaScript version in Chapter 11 with the example in this chapter tells you quite a bit about Windows PowerShell. First, the script is slightly shorter and you need to perform the checks a little differently than you do with JavaScript. Notice the way that this example creates the input arguments. Instead of accessing an argument list, this example simply places the values directly in the variables, which ends up saving time because you don't have to check the argument list several times before you can even create the variables.

The example uses the pound sign (#) for comments. In addition, you might notice the odd method of performing logical operations with `-eq` (for equals) and `-or` (for or). You'll find a complete list of these logical operators in the Getting Started document provided as part of the Windows PowerShell documentation. All variables in a Windows PowerShell script must begin with the dollar sign ($), as shown in the example.

For anyone who has worked with the .NET Framework, the `[system.console]::Out.WriteLine()` method call will look familiar and that's precisely what it is. The example makes a call to the `console` class of the `system` namespace. The console class contains an `Out` property that's actually a container for the standard output stream. The `stream` object includes the `WriteLine()` method that the example uses to output text. You can use any .NET Framework feature in precisely the same way, which means that Windows PowerShell has a very large list of language features from which to choose.

One feature that differs from standard .NET application coding is the lack of a `try...catch` structure. When working with Windows PowerShell, you use a `Trap` instead. The `Trap` relies on the .NET Framework exception classes. Once you set a trap, it remains in effect until it either goes out of scope or you set another trap. To access the data that the exception provides, you use the `$_.Exception` property, followed by the exception property that you want to access. The example simply displays the `Message` property so that the user knows what happened during an attempted drive mapping.

Windows PowerShell can use `COM` objects, just like your JavaScript scripts do. In this example, the script creates the `WScript.Network` object like the example in Listing 11.6. To perform this task in Windows PowerShell, you must use the `new-object` Cmdlet and call it with the `-COM` command line switch. The result is the `$oNetwork` object that calls the `MapNetworkDrive()` method using the same syntax as the JavaScript counterpart. The `Trap` statement that appears before the `MapNetworkDrive()` method call provides error trapping in this case.

TIP Now that you have a taste for Windows PowerShell scripting, you might want to obtain some additional tutorial type resources. You can find a series of articles about Windows PowerShell script on Computerworld. The four part scripting series begins at `http://www.computerworld.com/softwaretopics/os/windows/story/0,10801,107669,00.html`. The second part is at `http://www.computerworld.com/softwaretopics/software/story/0,10801,107673,00.html`. You'll find the third part at `http://www.computerworld.com/softwaretopics/os/windows/story/0,10801,107681,00.html`. The fourth part is at `http://www.computerworld.com/softwaretopics/os/windows/story/0,10801,107683,00.html`.

Running the Script

You're ready to try a script. However, running a script with Windows PowerShell is nothing like running a script under the old command line. You can't simply type the script name and let the process take over. The first step is to load the script into memory. To perform this task, type **`get-content MapNetwork.PS1`** and press Enter. When working with another script, you type the name of that script. Now that you have the script loaded into memory, you can execute it. Type **`./MapNetwork`** and press Enter. At this point, you're probably seeing the error message shown in Figure 19.3. The default Windows PowerShell setting doesn't allow you to execute any scripts at all.

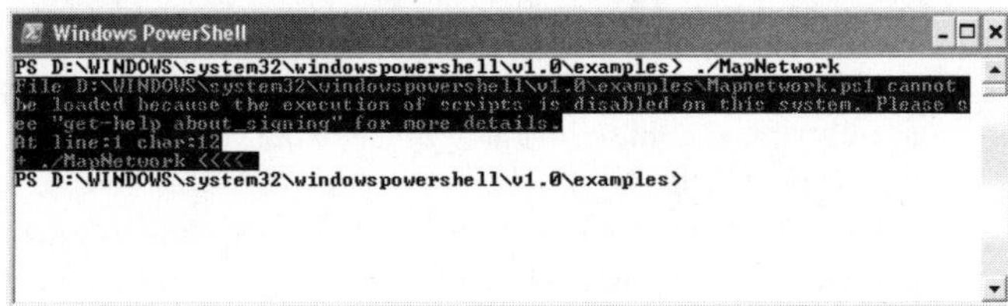

FIGURE 19.3
Windows PowerShell scripts won't run without the proper permission.

You have to make a decision now. The issue is what level of script to allow on your system. Before you disable the protection that Windows PowerShell provides, consider using the security to your advantage and set the system to execute only signed scripts. To set the system to use only signed scripts, type **`Set-ExecutionPolicy Unrestricted`** and press Enter (see the "Defining a Company Policy for Scripts" sidebar for a description of the various policies you can use for scripts).

Now that you have the permission problem solved with Windows PowerShell, try running the script again. This time the script will tell you that it requires input. You can add the required input and map a drive. The script also accepts the input arguments from the command line. Try entering incorrect arguments and you'll find that the exception handling works fine, too.

 **Real World Scenario**

DEFINING A COMPANY POLICY FOR SCRIPTS

You might think that the default Windows PowerShell setup of not running any scripts is terrible. However, consider how many users have downloaded scripts from the Internet and run them without having any idea of what the script could do or even that they were downloading a script. It's important to consider how scripts running amok on user machines create infections that waste everyone's time and energy, not to mention damaging both systems and data. In fact, you might have been involved in cleaning up such a problem at some time in the past. Consequently, you need to weigh this factor against the few minutes required to sign your script so the system knows that it's safe to execute. Most companies today have a zero-tolerance policy regarding executable content because it's become too expensive to continually clean infected machines.

Generally speaking, you should maintain the default Restricted policy of not running any scripts for all of the users on the network. If users don't run scripts, you don't need to worry about them loading something that will destroy their machine even accidentally.

When you must allow the user to run scripts, set the policy to AllSigned. At the AllSigned level, the user can't run a script unless someone you trust signs it. You could set the policy so that only scripts signed by someone at your company run on the user machine. Using only signed scripts on user machines ensures that you know who created the script and understand the potential pitfalls of using the script.

Administrators and developers will likely want to share code from time to time. You should still ensure that someone has signed the code. Consequently, setting the policy to RemoteSigned could make sense for those who have more knowledge about Windows and need to execute code that someone else created. In most cases, you want to use this level with care because anyone can send you a signed script and your system will execute it, even if the individual used fake credentials.

The final level of is Unrestricted. Using the Unrestricted level is returning to previous versions of Windows where you don't have any protection. Windows PowerShell will allow you to shoot yourself in the foot, but why do it? Always keep your system safe by using signed code.

Creating a Windows PowerShell Cmdlet and Shell

Windows PowerShell uses an object-oriented strategy for running code. Part of that strategy is the use of scripts—the method you'll use to answer the vast majority of your applications. However, sometimes a script won't answer the requirement. You might want to create an application that performs complex tasks and can therefore benefit from compilation, rather than waiting for the command line to interpret it at runtime. The second type of Windows PowerShell application is a Cmdlet. Unlike scripts, you always create a Cmdlet as compiled code and it always appears as part of the shell. Consequently, a Cmdlet represents a significant investment in additional coding time.

TIP **Many administrators want a quick overview of the PS scripting language and want to know how it compares to the existing Windows Scripting Host (WSH) technology. You can find a great overview on the topic at `http://arstechnica.com/guides/other/msh.ars/2`. One of the features that most administrators will find interesting is that all Cmdlets inherit the same base class, which means that they all use the same methods, parse the arguments in the same way, and output data using the same PS framework. Consequently, Cmdlets offers a significant level of consistency over other scripting technologies.**

Creating the Cmdlet Code

It's important to note that the Windows PowerShell scripting language is similar, but not precisely the same as the C# code that you'll use to create a Cmdlet. In fact, you can create the Cmdlet using Visual Studio 2005 (you can't use earlier versions of the IDE) should you wish to do so. However, a Cmdlet isn't supposed to be a full application, in most cases, and it's never a stand-alone executable, so you can also write the code for it using a simple editor such as Notepad (the editor used for the example in this chapter). Listing 19.2 shows an example of the code for a Cmdlet. The example uses a filename of `Reverse-String.CS` for this code.

LISTING 19.2: Creating a Cmdlet for the Microsoft Command Shell

```
// Define the .NET Framework namespaces that the Cmdlet will use.
using System;
using System.Text;
using System.Management.Automation;

// Define a Cmdlet class to hold the code for the new Cmdlet.
// This class will let the user reverse a string on screen.
[Cmdlet("reverse", "string")]
public class ReverseStringCommand : Cmdlet
{
   // Create a private variable to hold the string the user passes.
   private string _initString;

   // Create a property to request the string from the user.
   [Parameter(Mandatory=true, Position=0)]
   public string InitString
   {
      get
      {
```

```
            return _initString;
         }
         set
         {
            if (value.Length == 0)
               _initString = "Empty";
            else
               _initString = value;
         }
      }

      // Perform the string reversal and return a value.
      protected override void ProcessRecord()
      {
         // Create a variable to hold the reversed results.
         StringBuilder Output = new StringBuilder();

         // Create a Char array to hold the characters.
         Char[] Characters = _initString.ToCharArray();

         // Reverse the String.
         for (Int32 Count = Characters.Length - 1; Count >= 0; Count--)
            Output.Append(Characters[Count]);

         // Output the result.
         WriteObject(Output.ToString());
      }
   }
```

The code begins by defining the namespaces that the code uses. You don't have to add these references, but doing so makes your code considerably easier to read. It's possible to write a Cmdlet using just two namespaces, `System` and `System.Management.Automation`. The first provides basic .NET Framework functionality, while the second provides access to the special features you need for creating a Cmdlet. The example includes the `System.Text` namespace to provide access to the text manipulation features of the .NET Framework.

TIP Visual Studio 2005 users will find the DLLs for the namespaces referenced in this example in the `\WINDOWS\system32\windowspowershell\v1.0` folder and in the folders you used to install the Windows SDK. Simply add a reference to these DLLs as needed to build Cmdlets directly in the Visual Studio 2005 IDE. The installation process automatically installs the DLLs in the GAC as well.

Every Cmdlet must include the `[Cmdlet]` attribute written as `[Cmdlet("reverse", "string")]`. In this case, the attribute includes just the Cmdlet name, `reverse-string`. When you type this value at the command line using the new shell, you'll execute the `reverse-string` Cmdlet. The name of the class comes next. You can use any name you want, but using something close to the name of the Cmdlet usually works best. You must inherit the `Cmdlet` class as part of creating a Cmdlet, as shown in the example.

You don't have to include custom parameters with your Cmdlet, but most Cmdlets will require one or more parameters. This Cmdlet includes one parameter named `InitString`. As shown in the code, it's good coding practice to define a parameter that relies on a local private variable. The code places the public input from the user into the private variable after testing it for any problems. In this case, the `InitString` parameter (actually a C# property) places the value in the private variable `_initString` only after checking to verify the input is meaningful. If the input isn't meaningful, then the `set` method automatically creates a default value. To make this property visible at the command line, you must include the `[Parameter]` attribute. The arguments shown are optional. These arguments tell the command line that it must display this parameter first (`Position=0`) and that the user must provide a value (`Mandatory=true`).

Every Cmdlet has three opportunities to work with the data the user provides at the command prompt. The `BeginProcessing()` method lets you modify the data before the system sees it. It's also possible to perform any required startup tasks in this method, such as creating objects you need. Normally, you won't perform any data manipulation in this method. The `ProcessRecord()` method is where you perform the main processing tasks. The `EndProcess()` method is where you perform any shutdown tasks for the Cmdlet, such as releasing objects you no longer need. In all three cases, you must override the existing methods provided by the `Cmdlet` class, as shown in the listing, to accomplish tasks in your Cmdlet.

The actual code for this example converts the input data the user provides into a character array. This technique allows the code to access the characters in the input string one at a time. The `for` loop starts at the end of the character array and adds one character at a time to the `StringBuilder` object, `Output`. The result is that the loop reverses the string elements from their original order.

It's important to remember that a Cmdlet isn't freestanding code. You don't have access to the console, for example, so you need to rely on the `WriteObject()` method to output data to the screen. In this case, the example converts Output to a string and sends the value to the display.

Compiling the Cmdlet Executable

Before you can do anything with the Cmdlet, you must create an executable. You can perform this task as part of the Make-Shell utility, but it's actually easier to perform the compilation as a separate step. Start this section at the Windows PowerShell command line. The first task you need to perform is to create an alias for the C# compiler. This compiler appears in the .NET Framework folder on your machine. Creating an alias makes the compiler accessible by typing a simple command, CSC, as the command line. Here's the command for creating the alias on my system; you'll need to change the directory for `CSC.EXE` to match your system. Remember to use the .NET Framework 2.0 version of the CSC command; the older versions won't work.

```
set-alias csc F:\WINDOWS\Microsoft.NET\Framework\v2.0.50727\csc.exe
```

The next step is to create a variable to reference the required library for this example. This example only uses one of the libraries. Complex examples could use multiple libraries and you can include them all in one variable. Here's the command for creating a reference variable (type the entire command as a single entity; don't press Enter as you type it).

```
$ref = "F:\Program Files\Microsoft Command
   Shell\v1.0\System.Management.Automation.Dll"
```

At this point, you can compile the executable using the C# compiler. You need to tell the compiler what kind of output you want to create, a library (DLL), the name of the input file, the name of the output file, and any libraries that the Cmdlet needs, as shown here.

```
csc /target:library /out:reverse-string.dll reverse-string.cs /reference:$ref
```

The compiler will display a logo as a minimum. If the file contains errors or you miss a library reference, you'll also see error messages. In general, you can now create a new shell with the resulting library.

Using the Make-Shell Utility to Create the Shell

It's time to create the new shell. You use the Make-Shell utility to perform this task. The following command line will create the new shell for this example.

```
make-shell -out NewShell -ns DataCon.Demos -reference reverse-string.dll
```

This command line represents a minimal implementation. You must specify the output filename, the namespace for the shell, and the list of any DLLs you want to add as Cmdlets. The output is an executable named `NewShell.EXE`.

Before you can use the new shell, you must provide a registry entry for it. You can perform this task at the command line, but it's easier to use the Registry Editor to perform the task in this case. Select Start ➤ Run. You'll see the Run dialog box. Type **`RegEdit`** and click OK. You need to add a new key to the `HKEY_LOCAL_MACHINE\SOFTWARE\Microsoft\PS\1\ShellIds` key. In fact, you have to add a new key every time you create a new shell. For the purposes of this example, create a key named `DataCon.Demos.newshell`. This key contains two values, both of which are strings. The first value, `ExecutionPolicy`, contains one of the values described in the "Defining a Company Policy for Scripts" sidebar. The second value, `Path`, contains the path to the new shell you just created. It's best if you place the new shell and any associated DLLs in the `\Program Files\ Microsoft Command Shell\v1.0` folder if possible. The `Path` value on my system points to the `F:\Program Files\Microsoft Command Shell\v1.0\NewShell.EXE` folder.

Now that you have the registry values in place, you can start the new shell. You can choose one of two techniques. The first is to double-click the executable for the new shell you created. The second method is to type the name of the shell at an existing command line prompt. The system will create a new shell and you can begin using it immediately. In either case, you should be able to execute the `reverse-string` Cmdlet as you would any other Cmdlet on the system, as shown in Figure 19.4. (This screenshot shows the results of all of the other steps used to create the new shell as well.)

FIGURE 19.4
The new command line shell contains the reverse-string Cmdlet that you can access like any other Cmdlet.

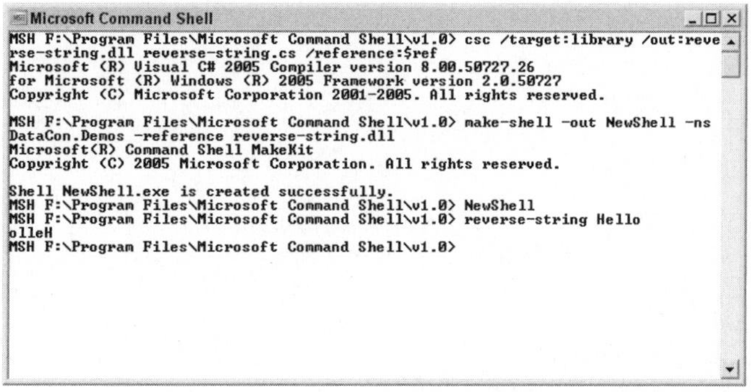

```
Microsoft Command Shell
MSH F:\Program Files\Microsoft Command Shell\v1.0> csc /target:library /out:reve
rse-string.dll reverse-string.cs /reference:$ref
Microsoft (R) Visual C# 2005 Compiler version 8.00.50727.26
for Microsoft (R) Windows (R) 2005 Framework version 2.0.50727
Copyright (C) Microsoft Corporation 2001-2005. All rights reserved.

MSH F:\Program Files\Microsoft Command Shell\v1.0> make-shell -out NewShell -ns
DataCon.Demos -reference reverse-string.dll
Microsoft(R) Command Shell MakeKit
Copyright (C) 2005 Microsoft Corporation. All rights reserved.

Shell NewShell.exe is created successfully.
MSH F:\Program Files\Microsoft Command Shell\v1.0> NewShell
MSH F:\Program Files\Microsoft Command Shell\v1.0> reverse-string Hello
olleH
MSH F:\Program Files\Microsoft Command Shell\v1.0>
```

Getting Started with Command Line Tasks

This chapter has provided you with an overview of Windows PowerShell and provided basic information on what you can expect from this command shell. The update is long overdue. Windows has used the same command interpreter from the days of DOS and many people find using this older command interpreter difficult, to say the least. Of course, using Windows PowerShell alone won't make you an instant success at the command line. As with anything, you need to invest time into the new command interpreter to get anything from it.

Now that you have some idea of how Windows PowerShell works, try it out. You can download the current version of Windows PowerShell and try it on your existing Windows XP or Windows 2003 system. Better yet, try Windows PowerShell out with Vista to see all of the new graphical features it provides. The important thing to remember as you test out this new toy is how it fits within your existing infrastructure. Look for compatibility problems as well as the new bonuses that Windows PowerShell can provide to your productivity.

Congratulations! You've reached the last chapter of the book. However, your journey should include the appendix and glossary as well. The appendix provides 52 helpful tips you can use to work at the command line better and faster. Try reading one at the start of every week and you'll find that you have a wealth of new ideas by the end of the year. You'll also want to use the glossary as needed to find the meaning of terms as they apply to this book. Make sure you contact me at `JMueller@mwt.net` if you have any questions about this book. I'd also love to hear about your experiences working at the command line. Also, look on my Web site at `http://www.mwt.net/~jmueller/` for updates and additional information.

Appendix A

52 Indispensable Command Line Tricks and Techniques

This appendix contains 52 helpful hints that you can use to work at the command line more efficiently and successfully. There's one tip for each week of the year. As you continue working at the command line, build batch files and scripts, and discover new commands and utilities that Microsoft has hidden there, you'll discover just how much of a resource the command line can be. Now that I've shared my tips with you, I'd love to hear about any tips you might have. Write me at `JMueller@mwt.net` to share them with me.

1. Always test new scripts and batch files using a test machine. Verify that the script or batch file works as anticipated before you test it on production machines. Even after you test scripts and batch files, make sure you provide additional monitoring while the script or batch file is new to allow potential bugs to surface.
2. Consider learning to use batch files for automation before you move on to scripts. Many automation tasks don't require scripts to succeed. Batch files are a very simple and easily understood way to add automation to the command line.
3. Third party utilities are a tempting way to make the command line more accessible. However, it's usually a better idea to determine whether Windows provides a command or utility to accomplish the task first. Even if the Windows command or utility won't accomplish the task in the manner in which you want to accomplish it, the exercise of working with the command or utility will help you select third party products with a greater potential for success.
4. Use the PushD and PopD utilities to save and restore directories as needed while working at the command line. These two utilities can save you considerable typing time. Use these utilities to create batch files that move between directories as needed to perform work. In many cases, you'll find that this feature makes it considerably easier to perform complex tasks with less typing because you don't have to type the full path to every file.
5. Environment variables come in three forms. The first is system variables that affect all computer users. The second is user variables that affect a single user permanently. You can find the first and second forms listed in the Environment Variables dialog box accessible by clicking Environment Variables on the Advanced tab of the System Properties dialog box. The third environment variable form is the temporary variables you create at the command line using the `Set` command.
6. Always use the most current version of a utility when possible. For example, even though many people are familiar with the older WinMSD utility, the MSInfo32 utility replaces it in Windows XP and above. Generally, you'll find that the newer utilities provide added functionality and reliability.

7. There aren't any absolutes when working at the command line. Sometimes you must break the rules in order to devise a reliable and secure method of automating a task. For example, even though the SchTasks utility is newer and more functional than the AT utility, you'll find that the AT utility often works better in batch files because of its simplicity. In this case, even though the SchTasks utility is more functional, the AT utility can produce a better batch file as long as you don't need the features the SchTasks utility provides.
8. Use after hours scripting carefully. Restrict after hours scripting to those tasks that actually require it. For example, an application, command, or utility that requires exclusive access to a database is a good candidate for after hours scripting. Don't use after hours scripting for any application, command, or utility that is unreliable or presents security risks.
9. Remember that a command is an internal feature of the command processor or another executable environment, such as the FTP application. A utility is an external, freestanding application. Even though commands and utilities are both executable code, commands depend on the resources of their enabling environment.
10. Even though a utility exists, that doesn't mean you should use it. For example, Microsoft disables the Messenger service by default in newer versions of Windows because crackers can use it to gain access to your system. However, the Msg utility requires access to the Messenger service. Unless you want to create a security hole in your system, you'll refrain from using the Msg utility except where the network has no outside access.
11. Remember, this book documents a number of command and utility features that don't appear as part of the command or utility help, the local Windows help, or even the Windows Resource Kit. Some of these additions come from third party Web sites (the sites appear in the book whenever possible). Some come from reader input for past books. Still other information comes from my personal experimentation. If you find a feature that doesn't work or you locate a feature that I should know about, contact me at `JMueller@mwt.net`.
12. More people use JavaScript than use VBScript. You can use both scripting languages (and many others) at the command line. However, if you're learning a new scripting language and want to obtain the maximum benefits from your efforts, JavaScript is by far the more popular of the two scripting languages. Not only can you use it with ease for work at the command line, you'll also find it in use on many Web sites. JavaScript is also standardized across multiple platforms, which means it's conceivable that an application you create can run equally well on a Macintosh or a Linux system as it does on your Windows system. Of course, you must use standards-based programming techniques to obtain this level of platform support.
13. Always document your batch files using the `REM` command. The batch file you document might require modifications later and you don't want to spend hours relearning how the batch file works. Make things easier for yourself; use lots of comments to document your batch files.
14. The RunDll32 utility is possibly the most powerful single utility on your system because you can use it to access code within any DLL that provides a list of public calls. For example, you can use the RunDll32 utility to shut down the system or display a message box on screen. The number of tasks you can perform is only limited by the number of DLLs installed on the system.
15. Look in the `\WINDOWS\Microsoft.NET\Framework` directory for .NET Framework commands. The commands you require for a particular version of the .NET Framework appear

in the version numbered directories within this main directory. Always verify that you're using the most current version of the .NET Framework to perform tasks unless an application specifically states that it requires an older version of the .NET Framework.

16. One of Microsoft's focuses with Vista is improved security. Consequently, many commands and utilities that work fine with older versions of Windows appear with reduced functionality in Vista. You may also find yourself using the RunAs utility more often to support command line development. Of course, Vista includes many new commands and utilities as well.

17. Use the ASP.NET command line utilities found in the `\WINDOWS\Microsoft.NET\Framework\v2.0.40607` folder of your hard drive to your advantage. For example, the ASPNET_RegBrowsers utility lets you register the capabilities of the browsers you expect Web site users to use. The browser definitions appear in the `\WINDOWS\Microsoft.NET\Framework\v2.0.40607\CONFIG\Browsers` folder. Use the ASPNET_RegIIS utility to register or unregister a particular version of ASP.NET on a system. Likewise, you use the ASPNET_RegSQL utility to register a particular version of ASP.NET with SQL Server.

18. Microsoft continuously updates the commands and utilities for Windows. Make sure you perform regular system updates to ensure you have access to the latest command and utilities. When you do obtain an updated piece of software, spend time learning its new features. The time you spend will pay off in greater productivity later.

19. Always configure the command window to meet your viewing needs. In addition, you can change settings, such as color, to add aesthetic appeal to the command line. Always remember that the system saves your settings based on title, so a command window with a different title can have different settings.

20. The `SET` command is a powerful feature that many people don't use effectively. A `SET` command can store any data you require at the command prompt. For example, you can easily use it to store numeric information as well as paths to files and user information. Generally, you'll use the `SET` command to store short information sequences.

21. Use temporary files to store large amounts of cumbersome data. You can also use a temporary file as a kind of database. Parse through the temporary file using the `FOR /F` command format. For example, with the proper code, you can use a directory listing as a means for locating and deleting temporary files on your machine.

22. Windows PowerShell is a new scripting platform that Vista supports. You may see this scripting platform ported to older versions of Windows as well. The main Windows PowerShell executable is the PowerShell utility. Use this utility to execute your Windows PowerShell scripts much as you currently use CScript to execute scripts at the command line and WScript to execute scripts using a graphical environment.

23. It's important to remember that .NET applications require special utilities to make them useful to the system in many cases. For example, instead of using RegSvr32 to register a new object on the system, you use RegAsm instead. In addition, you need to make the application DLLs visible to the system with GACUtil. Running a .NET service means registering it with the RegSvcs utility.

24. Always assume that every application, batch file, script, command, and utility on your system is going to fail. Try to list every possible failure mode, even when you think that such a failure mode is unlikely. Provide for the detection, recovery, and workaround for each failure mode so that the software continues to run, rather than failing gracefully.

25. The Microsoft Knowledge Base at `http://support.microsoft.com/default.aspx?scid=fh;EN-US;KBHOWTO` is the greatest help for the command line user. Often, Microsoft document changes and new software appear here long before you see them anywhere else. In fact, you can find material here that you won't find anywhere else.

26. The only good time to compile your script file is after you've tested it thoroughly. In most cases, you can use third party utilities to obtain a native executable file. However, the JSC compiler supplied with the .NET Framework also does a great job as long as you abide by the JScript requirements and can use a .NET application in place of a native application.

27. The DS utilities, such as DSQuery, provide you with extensive access to Active Directory. Even though these utilities don't appear as part of a standard Windows installation, you can install them from a server that supports them. Using the various DS utilities, you can add, delete, query, edit, and get Active Directory objects.

28. Redirection is an important part of working at the command line at any time. You can redirect both input and output using the redirection symbols. For example, instead of displaying a directory listing at the command prompt, you can send it to a file instead. By placing the output in a file, you can perform sequential processing of the individual file entries.

29. The `XCopy` command is the most versatile method of copying bulk data from one location to another. If you need to copy just a few files in the same directory, use the `Copy` command for greater efficiently (it executes more quickly than `XCopy` does). Avoid using older commands such as `DiskCopy` because Microsoft designed them in an era when floppies were the main form of data transfer from one machine to another.

30. Rely on the TypePerf utility to track performance characteristics at the command line. Use PerfMon when you need to perform long-term performance tracking or require use of the graphical performance monitoring interface that Windows supplies.

31. Use automation with great care. Always test the applications, batch files, and scripts you intend to automate before you let them run unmonitored. Never automate unreliable applications, batch files, or scripts.

32. Remember to use the `AutoExec.NT` and `Config.NT` files to modify the application execution environment. You can perform any task in `AutoExec.NT` that you would with a standard batch file.

33. Many .NET applications don't use the registry to store settings anymore. You can find the application specific settings in a CONFIG file. For example, if the name of the application is `MyApp.EXE`, then the application configuration settings appear in the `MyApp.EXE.CONFIG` file. User specific settings generally appear in the `\Documents and Settings\`*`UserName`*`\`*Application Data*`\`*`ApplicationName`* directory (where *`UserName`* is the name of the user and *`ApplicationName`* is the name of the application). As with the application settings, the user-specific settings appear in a CONFIG file, but the name of this file isn't set in stone and you may find it under any name, including the user's name.

34. Keep in mind that you have multiple methods for performing remote access tasks at the command line. Many people immediately think about using Terminal Server for remote tasks, but many utilities provide direct machine access through command line arguments. Use the direct access method when you only require the services of a single utility. Remember that newer versions of Windows also include Remote Desktop, but that you must make registry changes to systems in some cases to use this technique. You can also rely on older

technologies to perform remote tasks, such as TelNet. In short, don't limit yourself to one technique for remote access; use the technique that works best for a particular scenario.

35. Killing tasks using utilities such as TaskKill might seem like a good idea when the system isn't responding as anticipated. However, a seemingly frozen application may simply be performing a task in the background, so it's important to wait before you kill the task. Always assume that killing a task will result in data loss of some kind. In addition, killing the task might not revive the system; you could still end up having to reboot the system to restore its responsiveness.

36. Assume that someone is going to break into your system and cause significant damage to it, because someone almost certainly will. Treat security as a barrier that keeps honest people honest. A determined cracker will always find a way in, so your only defense is to rely on monitoring and constant maintenance to detect the intrusions when they occur.

37. One of the essential issues to remember about working with scripts is that they can use any registered object on the machine. In addition to the special WScript object, a script can access any other object on the system, such as the media player. All you need to remember is the `CreateObject()` method used to create new objects based on existing system classes.

38. The .NET Framework currently comes in 1.0, 1.1, and 2.0 versions, so you could have up to three versions installed on your system. (The newest 3.0 version augments the capabilities of the .NET Framework 2.0 and you'll automatically install it with Vista.) The 1.0 version of the .NET Framework wasn't very popular. Unless you have an application that specifically calls for it, remove the 1.0 version from your machine to reduce complexity.

39. Use wildcard characters to create file specifications when you need to process more than one file with a single command. Some commands and utilities don't support wildcard characters at all. However, most utilities support at least the asterisk (*) wildcard and many support the single character question mark (?) wildcard character as well. Some utilities support exotic string specification techniques and you should employ these wildcard character combinations whenever possible.

40. Most commands and utilities support the /? command line switch when you need help. However, some don't support this standard. When you find a utility that doesn't support the /? command line switch, try the `/help` command line switch instead. You can also try the `Help` command to obtain information about the command or utility.

41. Remember that using pipes to connect Active Directory utilities together is one of the most powerful techniques for working with Active Directory. Using a pipe makes it possible to perform tasks with Active Directory without knowing the names of the object in advance. In addition, you can perform tasks on object sets, such as a group of users.

42. Microsoft is working hard to ensure that you can use Windows PowerShell with all their new products. For example, you'll find Windows PowerShell support already provided as part of Exchange. Of course, to get the Windows PowerShell support, you'll need to update these applications and services. Windows PowerShell Cmdlets won't work with older versions of applications because the application isn't Windows PowerShell aware.

43. Always consider the security issues of using any application, command, or utility. Never automate an application, command, or utility that presents a potential security problem. For example, applications, commands, or utilities that require administrative privileges often present a significant security risk that you won't want to leave open for crackers to exploit.

44. Never assume that users will perform any particular task. For example, even if you send a message across the network to close all open files on your system before you perform a maintenance task, you still need to verify that users have followed through by using the OpenFiles utility. The OpenFiles utility tells you about any open files on your system, giving you peace of mind when you perform the maintenance task.

45. Always run applications using the lowest number of rights that you can. Logging in with administrator rights for every task is an open invitation to cracker invasion. If you need to run a task that requires temporary extended rights, then use the RunAs utility to perform the task. The RunAs utility lets you execute just one command using Administrator rights, rather than using Administrator rights all of the time.

46. Remember that your system might have more than one version of the .NET Framework installed. Microsoft has created the .NET Framework with side-by-side installation in mind. A side-by-side installation overcomes some of the problems that users experienced in the past when one application required an earlier version of a DLL to run than another application.

47. Scripting languages are more powerful than batch files because they include better flow control. In addition, you can possibly compile a script for better execution speed. However, with power comes complexity. Creating a script is an order of magnitude more complex than working with batch files.

48. Don't assume a limitation in a Windows graphical utility necessarily translates to the command line. For example, most people realize that Windows Explorer does a very poor job of finding content on your system. In fact, it does such a poor job that many people have resorted to third party products to locate information on their systems. However, a combination of the `Dir` command and the FindStr utility can help you locate any information on your system for free and often faster than these third party utilities can perform the task. Of course, you need to know how to use these command line utilities to take advantage of this command line feature that works far better than its Windows counterpart does.

49. The system creates a number of environment variables for you. For example, you'll find that the `OS` environment variable tells you whether you're using Windows as an operating system (preventing people from using batch files intended for the Windows environment on a DOS system). You can always list the environment variables on your system using the `SET` command. Simply type **SET** and press Enter to see the list.

50. Create custom versions of `AutoExec.NT` and `Config.NT` for applications that require them. The custom versions can use different settings to ensure that the application runs as anticipated. You specify these custom files using the Windows PIF Settings dialog box that you access by clicking Advanced on the Program tab of the application's Property dialog box.

51. Use the error level output of commands and utilities to detect errors in batch files. An `IF ERRORLEVEL` command can detect the error. A simple `GoTo` command can redirect the flow of the batch file to an error-handling section, and then redirect program flow for another attempt at the failed command or utility. Using this looping approach helps you create a certain level of error handling and fault tolerance even in batch files. Make sure you record all error information possible in an output file.

52. The command line is like the submerged part of an iceberg. Few people see it, many people don't know about it, yet it exists and it comprises the greater part of the Windows operating system. Every time you think that a graphical utility will replace the command line, look again because someone will find a way to automate it with a batch file or script.

Appendix B

A Summary of New and Modified Commands in Vista

TABLE B.1: Vista significantly changes the command line by adding new commands and modifying others. These changes, coupled with the new security features and the requirement to constantly give yourself permission to perform tasks, might make the job of moving to the new operating system difficult. This appendix eases the transition a little by telling you which commands and utilities are new and which are changed. You can use this handy reference to locate the required usage information in the book.

COMMAND OR UTILITY NAME	CHAPTER	NEW, MODIFIED, OR NOT SUPPORTED
ARP	5	Modified
ASR_Fmt	6	Not supported
ASR_LDM	6	Not supported
ASR_PFU	6	Not supported
AT	10	Modified
ATMAdm	5	Not supported
Attrib	4	Modified
AuditPol	5	New
AuditUsr	5	Not supported
BCDEdit	5	New
BlastCln	5	Not supported
BootCfg	5	Not supported
CACL	4	Not supported
Change	8	New

TABLE B.1: Vista significantly changes the command line by adding new commands and modifying others. These changes, coupled with the new security features and the requirement to constantly give yourself permission to perform tasks, might make the job of moving to the new operating system difficult. This appendix eases the transition a little by telling you which commands and utilities are new and which are changed. You can use this handy reference to locate the required usage information in the book. *(CONTINUED)*

COMMAND OR UTILITY NAME	CHAPTER	NEW, MODIFIED, OR NOT SUPPORTED
ChgLogon	8	New
ChgPort	8	New
ChgUsr	8	New
ChkDsk	4	Modified
Choice	7	Modified
Cipher	4	Modified
Clip	7	New
CMD	7	Modified
CmdKey	7	New
ComSvcConfig	16	New
ConvLog	5	Not supported
Copy	2	Modified
CrpConv	4	Not supported
CScript	8	Modified
Defrag	6	Modified
DelTree	2	Not supported
Dir	4	Modified
DiskRAID	6	New
DispDiag	5	New
ESEnTUtl	2	Modified
EventTriggers	3	Not supported
ForceDOS	6	Not supported

TABLE B.1: Vista significantly changes the command line by adding new commands and modifying others. These changes, coupled with the new security features and the requirement to constantly give yourself permission to perform tasks, might make the job of moving to the new operating system difficult. This appendix eases the transition a little by telling you which commands and utilities are new and which are changed. You can use this handy reference to locate the required usage information in the book. *(CONTINUED)*

COMMAND OR UTILITY NAME	CHAPTER	NEW, MODIFIED, OR NOT SUPPORTED
ForFiles	7	New
Format	7	Modified
FSUtil	3	Modified
FTP	5	Modified
ICACL	4	New
IISReset	5	Not supported
IPConfig	5	Modified
IPSec6	5	Not supported
IPV6	5	Not supported
IPXRoute	5	Not supported
LPQ	2	Not supported
LPR	2	Not supported
MountVol	6	Modified
Msg	5	Not supported
MSTSC	11	Modified
Net	5	Modified
NetCfg	5	New
NetDiag	5	Not supported (downloadable)
NetSH	8	Modified
NetStat	5	Modified
NTBackup	2	Not supported
NTSD	6	Not supported

TABLE B.1: Vista significantly changes the command line by adding new commands and modifying others. These changes, coupled with the new security features and the requirement to constantly give yourself permission to perform tasks, might make the job of moving to the new operating system difficult. This appendix eases the transition a little by telling you which commands and utilities are new and which are changed. You can use this handy reference to locate the required usage information in the book. *(CONTINUED)*

COMMAND OR UTILITY NAME	CHAPTER	NEW, MODIFIED, OR NOT SUPPORTED
NW16	7	Not supported
OCSetup	5	New
OSUninst	6	Not supported
PathPing	5	Modified
PING	5	Modified
PING6	5	Not supported
PkgMgr	5	New
PnPUnattend	3	New
PnPUtil	3	New
PowerCfg	4	Modified
ProxyCfg	5	Not supported
Query	4	New
QUser	5	New
RCP	5	Not supported
RegTLib	6	Not supported
RExec	5	Not supported
RoboCopy	2	New
Route	5	Modified
RPCPing	5	New
RSH	5	Not supported
SchTasks	10	Modified
SDBInst	6	Modified

TABLE B.1: Vista significantly changes the command line by adding new commands and modifying others. These changes, coupled with the new security features and the requirement to constantly give yourself permission to perform tasks, might make the job of moving to the new operating system difficult. This appendix eases the transition a little by telling you which commands and utilities are new and which are changed. You can use this handy reference to locate the required usage information in the book. *(CONTINUED)*

COMMAND OR UTILITY NAME	CHAPTER	NEW, MODIFIED, OR NOT SUPPORTED
ServiceModelReg	16	New
SetX	3	New
SFC	5	Modified
ShutDown	6	Modified
SRDiag	6	Not supported
SxSTrace	6	New
SysOCMgr	5	Not supported
TakeOwn	2	New
TFTP	5	Not supported (downloadable)
TimeOut	7	New
TraceRpt	5	Modified
TraceRt	5	Modified
TraceRt6	5	Not supported
TSShutDn	4	Not supported
Verifier	5	Modified
VSSAdmin	3	Modified
VWIPXSPX	7	Not supported
W32Tm	4	Modified
WaitFor	7	New
WBAdmin	2	New
WEvtUtil	3	New
Where	4	New

TABLE B.1: Vista significantly changes the command line by adding new commands and modifying others. These changes, coupled with the new security features and the requirement to constantly give yourself permission to perform tasks, might make the job of moving to the new operating system difficult. This appendix eases the transition a little by telling you which commands and utilities are new and which are changed. You can use this handy reference to locate the required usage information in the book. *(CONTINUED)*

Command or Utility Name	Chapter	New, Modified, or Not Supported
WhoAmI	5	New
WinRM	11	New
WinRS	11	New
WinSAT	3	New
WSATConfig	16	New
WScript	8	Modified
XCopy	2	Modified

Glossary

This book includes a glossary so that you can find terms and acronyms easily. It has several important features you need to know about. First, every nonstandard acronym in the entire book appears here. I have left out common acronyms. (The glossary does exclude common acronyms such as units of measure and most file extensions because these terms are easy to find in other sources and most people know what they mean.) This way, there isn't any doubt that you'll always find everything you need to use the book properly.

Second, these definitions are specific to the book. In other words, when you look through this glossary, you're seeing the words defined in the context in which they're used in this the book. This might or might not always coincide with current industry usage since the computer industry changes the meaning of words so often.

Finally, I've used a conversational tone for the definitions in most cases. This means that the definitions might sacrifice a bit of puritanical accuracy for the sake of better understanding. The purpose of this glossary is to define the terms in such a way that there's less room for misunderstanding the intent of the book as a whole.

WHAT TO DO IF YOU DON'T FIND IT HERE

While this glossary is a relatively complete view of the words and acronyms in the book, you'll run into situations when you need to know more. No matter how closely I look at terms throughout the book, there's always a chance I'll miss the one acronym or term that you really need to know. In addition to the technical information found in the book, I've directed your attention to numerous online sources of information throughout the book and few of the terms the Web site owners use will appear here unless I also chose to use them in the book. Fortunately, many sites on the Internet provide partial or complete glossaries to fill in the gaps:

Acronym Finder `http://www.acronymfinder.com/`

Free Online Dictionary Of Computing (FOLDOC) `http://nightflight.com/foldoc/`

Microsoft Encarta `http://encarta.msn.com/`

Microsoft .NET Glossary `http://www.microsoft.com/net/basics/glossary/glossary_a_z.asp`

Microsoft Security Glossary `http://msdn2.microsoft.com/en-us/library/ms950397.aspx`

More Microsoft Glossaries `http://www.winlexic.com/more_microsoft_glossaries.htm`

TechEncyclopedia `http://www.techweb.com/encyclopedia/defineterm.jhtml?term=COM`

Webopedia `http://webopedia.internet.com/`

yourDictionary.com `http://www.yourdictionary.com/`

Some entries in this list are quite specialized. For example, the Microsoft Security Glossary discusses the Microsoft view of security terms. You can find other Microsoft Glossaries listed at `http://www.microsoft.com/resources/glossary/default.mspx`. If you still don't find what you need, try the Microsoft Search page at `http://search.microsoft.com/`, type the word **`glossary`**, add a specific area such as network, and click Go.

A

Access Control Entry (ACE)

Defines the object rights for a single user or group. Every ACE has a header that defines the type, size, and flags for the ACE. Next comes an access mask that defines the rights a user or group has to the object. Finally, there's an entry for the user's or group's Security Identifier (SID).

Access Control List (ACL)

Part of the Windows-based operating system security Application Programming Interface (API) used to determine both access and monitoring properties for an object. The ACL originally appeared in Windows NT. Each ACL contains one or more Access Control Entries (ACEs) that define the security properties for an individual or group. There are two major ACL groups: Security Access Control List (SACL) and Discretionary Access Control List (DACL). The SACL controls Windows auditing feature. The DACL controls access to the object.

ACE

See Access Control Entry

ACL

See Access Control List

Active Directory (AD)

A method of storing machine, server, and user configuration within Windows versions, starting with Windows 2000. Active Directory supports full data replication so that every domain controller has a copy of the data. This is essentially a special purpose database that contains information formatted according to a specific schema. Active Directory is designed to make Windows more reliable and secure, while reducing the work required by both the developer and administrator for application support and distribution. The user benefits as well since Active Directory fully supports roving users and maintains a full record of user information, which reduces the effects of local workstation downtime.

AD

See Active Directory

Address Resolution Protocol (ARP)

A method of computing the specific address of any entity on any Transmission Control Protocol/Internet Protocol (TCP/IP) network. The network driver sends out a broadcast message asking which piece of hardware is associated with a particular IP address. If a piece of hardware responds with a combination of its IP address and hardware identification number, then the network driver makes the association. This technique is normally used with devices such as Small Computer System Interface (SCSI) host adapters, where using the SCSI ID is much easier than using the 48-bit Ethernet hardware address.

ARP

See Address Resolution Protocol

ASR

See Automated System Recovery

Asynchronous Transfer Mode (ATM)

A data transfer method that relies on packets (cells) of a fixed size. The cell size used with ATM is smaller than used with older technologies, which enhances network efficiency by reducing the number of padding characters required to create complete cells. An ATM network typically transfers data at 25 to 622 Mbps. Most ATM services use one of four types of transmission. The Constant Bit Rate (CBR) service uses a constant stream that's equivalent to working with a leased line. The Variable Bit Rate (VBR) service varies the stream as needed to accommodate bursts in activity. This is a good option for voice and videoconferencing. The Available Bit Rate (ABR) service guarantees a minimum constant bandwidth, but allows bursts when the network is otherwise unused. The Unspecified Bit Rate (UBR) service is a low cost alternative that doesn't guarantee a specific bandwidth. This is a good option for file transfers and other tasks that can tolerate delays.

ATM

See Asynchronous Transfer Mode

Attribute

An attribute expresses some feature peculiar to an object. When referring to a database, each field has an attribute that expresses what type of information it contains, the length of the field, the field name, and the number of decimals. When referring to a display, the attribute expresses pixel color, intensity, and position. In programming, an attribute can also specify some type of object functionality, such as the method used to implement security.

Automated System Recovery (ASR)

A Windows technology that stores enough system information to recover from a number of system failures, such as an application installation that doesn't succeed well. ASR attempts to cover every contingency and does very well in recovering from many errors, but doesn't recover from every potential system error.

C

CAB

See Cabinet File

Cabinet File (CAB)

1. A compressed-format file similar to ZIP files used to transfer code and data from one location to another. For example, many Web sites use the CAB file to download applications to a user system using a browser as the intermediary. Use the Compress utility to create the file and the Expand utility to decompress the file. 2. A single file created to hold a number of compressed files. A related set of cabinet files can appear within a folder. During application installation, the compressed files in a cabinet are decompressed and copied to an appropriate directory for the user.

CACL

Change Access Control List

CI

See Container Inherit

Clear to Send (CTS)

A serial port signaling line that indicates the Data Communications Equipment (DCE), such as a modem, can receive data from the Data Terminal Equipment (DTE), such as a computer.

CLR

See Common Language Runtime

Comma Separated Value (CSV)

A type of text database file where the data fields are separated from one another using commas. Each carriage return/line feed combination (new line) creates a new record. Many applications can retrieve CSV files and convert them to other database representations.

Command Line

The input area allocated for entering instructions executed by the command processor. The operating system provides a standard prompt where you begin typing the instruction. In most cases, the prompt remains unavailable until the instruction completes.

Common Language Runtime (CLR)

The engine used to interpret managed applications within the .NET Framework. All Visual Studio .NET languages that produce managed applications can use the same runtime engine. The major advantages of this approach include extensibility (you can add other languages) and reduced code size (you don't need a separate runtime for each language).

Container Inherit (CI)

Signifies that this particular user inherited the Access Control Entry (ACE) from a parent directory.

Cracker

A hacker (computer expert) who uses their skills for misdeeds on computer systems where they have little or no authorized access. A cracker normally possesses specialty software that allows easier access to the target network. In most cases, crackers require extensive amounts of time to break the security for a system before they can enter it. Some sources call a cracker a black hat hacker.

CRC

See Cyclic Redundancy Code

Cryptographic Service Provider (CSP)

A specialty company that deals in certifying the identity of companies, developers, or individuals on the Internet. This identification check allows the company to issue an electronic certificate, which can then be used to conduct transactions securely. Several levels of certification are normally provided within a specific group. For example, there are three levels of individual certification. The lowest merely verifies the individual's identity through an Internet email address; the highest requires the individual to provide written proof along with a notarized statement. When you access a certified site or try to download a certified document such as a component, the browser displays the electronic certificate on screen, allowing you to make a security determination based on fact.

CSP

See Cryptographic Service Provider

CSV

See Comma Separated Value

CTS

See Clear to Send

Cyclic Redundancy Code (CRC)

A technique used to ensure the reliability of information stored on any media, transported across network cabling, or sent from one place to another using other techniques. It uses a cyclic calculation to create a numeric check number. The computer performs the same calculation when it retrieves the data and compares it to the CRC. If the two match, there's no data error. Otherwise, the sender must transmit the data again or the recipient must reconstruct it. If neither the sender nor the recipient can reconstruct the data, the system registers an error and informs the user of the data loss.

D

DACL

See Discretionary Access Control List

Data Set Ready (DSR)

A serial port signaling line that indicates that the Data Communications Equipment (DCE), such as a modem, is turned on.

Data Stream

One of several methods to send or access information that resides either in local or remote storage. A data stream consists of a series of bits taken from any location within a data storage unit (such as a file). The information can flow continuously (as in an Internet transfer for music) or in blocks (as occurs when reading data from a file on the local hard drive). The reading and writing sequence need not use blocks of any given size and the transfer often works with individual bits rather than characters or words.

Data Terminal Ready (DTR)

A serial port signaling line that indicates that the Data Terminal Equipment (DTE), such as a computer, is turned on.

DDF

See Diamond Directive File

Defragmenting

1. The process of organizing files on a storage media so that the file system can access each sector of the file sequentially. Defragmenting the file improves overall system performance by reducing the head movement of the hard drive. 2. The process of organizing and cleaning the Windows registry. The defragmentation application reorders the entries for faster access and locates entries that the system no longer requires. In most cases, the application removes the extraneous entries with user permission to enhance registry performance. In addition, the registry exists in multiple physical locations on the hard drive, which become physically fragmented. However, since Windows locks the registry files, standard defragmentation doesn't reorganize these files, so this process normally includes physical disk file organization as well.

DHCP

See Dynamic Host Configuration Protocol

Diamond Directive File (DDF)

Similar to an INF (information) or BAT (batch) file, the DDF provides instructions to a CAB (cabinet) creation utility such as DIANTZ for compressing one or more files into a single storage file. CAB files are normally used to distribute data locally, using a CD or other similar type of media, or remotely, through an Internet or other server connection. The DDF can also list files needed for a complete installation, but stored in other locations. Normally, these missing files already appear on the user's computer, so downloading them again would waste time. The DDF makes it possible to download them only as needed.

Directory

A logical unit of storage for most forms of media. Directories provide a means of separating files into different locations based on type or use. Using directories makes it easier to locate data and use applications.

Directory Information Tree (DIT)

All or part of the Active Directory database. A Directory Service Agent (DSA) can contain all or part of the Active Directory database. Each DSA has its own DIT. All of the DSA database pieces, when combined, form all of the data for Active Directory for a particular domain, but an individual DSA may contain only part of the database. In Active Directory, the top of the Active Directory database information tree is an object of the `DomainDNS` class that contains the Domain Controller object.

Discretionary Access Control List (DACL)

A Windows security component. The DACL controls access to an object. You can assign both groups and individual users to a specific object.

Disk Quota

A limit placed on the amount of hard drive space that a user can rely on to hold data. Many administrators use disk quotas to keep hard disk resource usage under control. In a shared environment, disk quotas ensure that each user receives a fair share of the available disk space.

Distributed Link Tracking (DLT)

A service that monitors all of the links on the system. The type of link can include file, shortcut, and Object Linking and Embedding (OLE), among others. The main purpose of the service is to detect and fix broken links so they don't damage the system or its data. For example, when a user changes the name of a linked file, the system updates the links so they point to the correct file again.

DIT

See Directory Information Tree

DLL

See Dynamic Link Library

DLT

See Distributed Link Tracking

DNS

See Domain Name System

Domain Name System (DNS)

An Internet technology that allows a user to refer to a host computer by name rather than using its unique IP address.

DOS Protected-Mode Interface (DPMI)

A method of accessing extended memory from a DOS application using the eXtended Memory Manager (XMM) that Microsoft introduced for Windows 3.0. The main feature of DPMI is that it provides a means of protecting the extended memory using a method that Windows understands.

DPMI

See DOS Protected-Mode Interface

DSR

See Data Set Ready

DTR

See Data Terminal Ready

Dynamic Host Configuration Protocol (DHCP)

A method for automatically determining the IP address on a TCP/IP connection. A server provides this address to the client as part of the setup communications. Using DHCP means that a server can use fewer addresses to communicate with clients and that clients don't need to provide a hard-coded address to the server. You must configure your server to provide these services.

Dynamic Link Library (DLL)

A specific form of application code loaded into memory by request. It's not a stand-alone executable like an EXE file. A DLL does contain one or more discrete routines that an application may use to provide specific features. For example, a DLL could provide a common set of file dialogs used to access information on the hard drive. More than one application can use the functions provided by a DLL, reducing overall memory requirements when more than one application is running. DLLs have a number of purposes. For example, they can contain device-specific code in the form of a device driver. Some types of COM objects also rely on DLLs.

E

ECMA

See European Computer Manufacturer's Association

EFI

See Extensible Firmware Interface

EFS

See Encrypting File System

EMM

See Expanded Memory Manager

EMS

See Expanded Memory Specification

Encapsulated PostScript (EPS)

A graphics file format used by the PostScript language. PostScript is a page description language that uses text to define the elements of a drawing. Like all vector graphic formats, PostScript allows infinite scaling and provides better resolution characteristics than bitmapped graphics. Use of PostScript requires an interpreter on every machine where the language is used.

Encrypting File System (EFS)

A component of the Windows NT File System (NTFS) that performs encryption and decryption of files in a transparent manner. The user that originally encrypted the file can access it seamlessly, but any other user is denied access. The user must mark the file as encrypted to use this feature.

End Of File (EOF)

The physical or logical end of a file. In text files, the end of file is the control character 26 or ^Z. In database files, the end of file marker is a logical element that depends on the database in use. Other file types have similar end of file markers.

End of Line (EOL)

The character or characters that define the end of a line of text within any data source on a computer system. The PC relies on the line feed (character 10) and carriage return (character 13) control character combination. A UNIX system uses only the carriage return character, while a Macintosh uses the line feed character.

Environment Variable

An operating system-supported means of storing temporary data in memory. The data appears as name value pairs and the operating system can access the variable by name or as a value (in expanded form). The expanded form of an environment variable appears within percent signs (%) such as %PATH%. The user can set, view, and clear environment variables at the command line using the `Set` command. The environment variable settings also appear on the Environment Variables dialog box that the user can access through the Environment Variables button on the Advanced tab of the System Properties dialog box.

EOF

See End of File

EOL

See End of Line

EPS

See Encapsulated PostScript

European Computer Manufacturer's Association (ECMA)

A standards committee originally founded in 1961. ECMA is dedicated to standardizing information and communication systems. For example, they created the ECMAScript standard used for many Web page designs today. You can also find ECMA standards for product safety, security, networks, and storage media.

Expanded Memory Manager (EMM)

A device driver such as `EMM386.EXE` that provides expanded memory services on an 80386 and above equipped machine (which definitely includes all modern machines). An application accesses expanded memory using a page frame or other memory-mapping techniques from within the conventional or upper memory area (0 to 1,024 KB). The EMM usually emulates expanded memory using extended memory managed by an eXtended Memory Manager (XMM) such as `HIMEM.SYS`, which provides access to the eXtended Memory Specification (XMS) memory. An application must change the processor's mode to protected mode to use XMS.

Expanded Memory Specification (EMS)

A method (specification) for older DOS and console applications to access memory outside of the 640 KB conventional memory area. This specification defines one method of extending the amount of memory that a processor can address from the conventional memory area. It uses an area outside of system memory to store information. An Expanded Memory Manager (EMM) provides a window view into this larger data area. The old 3.2 EMS specification requires a 64 KB window in the Upper Memory Block (UMB). The newer 4.0 specification can create this window anywhere in conventional or UMB memory.

eXtended Memory Specification (XMS)

A device driver that emulates expanded memory by using extended memory (the memory above the 1 MB limit imposed by DOS). The original version of this specification (developed by Quarterdeck) appeared in 1986. It allowed an 80286 or above processor to access up to 64 KB of extended memory from within the conventional memory area by enabling the A20 address line. This specification makes it possible to multitask from within DOS by freeing more application memory. In 1990, Microsoft revised its `HIMEM.SYS` driver with the release of Windows 3.0. The scope of XMS memory increased to multitask Windows applications. Versions of Windows starting with Windows NT don't require `HIMEM.SYS` to provide access to extended memory, but the DOS applications run by these versions of Windows do, so newer versions of Windows makes a version of `HIMEM.SYS` available for these applications.

Extensible Firmware Interface (EFI)

A standard method of providing boot information to the operating system that replaces the Basic Input/Output System (BIOS). The information that EFI provides includes platform specifics such as hardware configuration, boot setup, and runtime service calls. The operating system and its loader receive all of this information prior to starting the boot cycle.

eXtensible Markup Language (XML)

1. A method used to store information in an organized manner. The storage technique relies on hierarchical organization and uses special statements called tags to separate each storage element. Each tag defines a data attribute and can contain properties that further define each data element. 2. A standardized Web page design language used to incorporate data structuring within standard HTML documents. For example, you could use XML to display database information using something other than forms or tables. It's actually a lightweight version of Standard Generalized Markup Language (SGML) and is supported by the SGML community. XML also supports tag extensions that allow various parts of a Web-based application to exchange information. For example, once a user makes a choice within a catalog, that information could be added to an order entry form with a minimum of effort on the part of the developer. Since XML is easy to extend, some developers look at it as more of a base specification for other languages, rather than a complete language.

eXtensible Stylesheet Language (XSL)

A technology that separates the method of presentation from the actual content of either an eXtensible Markup Language (XML) or HyperText Markup Language (HTML) page. The XSL document contains all of the required formatting information so that the content remains in pure form. This is the second style language submitted to the World Wide Web Consortium (W3C) for consideration. The first specification was for Cascading Style Sheets (CSS). XSL documents use an XML-like format. This term is also listed as eXtensible Style Language by some sources.

eXtensible Stylesheet Language Transformation (XSLT)

The language used within the eXtensible Style Language (XSL) to transform the content provided in an eXtensible Markup Language (XML) file into a form for display on screen or printing. An XSL processor combines XML content with the formatting instructions provided by XSLT and outputs a new document or document fragment. XSLT is a World Wide Web Consortium (W3C) standard.

F

FAT

See File Allocation Table

Fault Tolerance

The ability of an object (application, device, or other entity) to recover from an error. For example, the fault tolerance provided by a transaction server allows a network to recover from potential data loss induced by a system or use failure. Another example of fault tolerance is the ability of a Redundant Array of Inexpensive Disks (RAID) system to recover from a hard drive failure.

FFT

File Allocation Table (FAT) File Times

File Allocation Table (FAT)

The method of formatting media used by DOS and other operating systems. This technique is one of the oldest formatting methods available. There have been several different versions of FAT based on the number of bits used to store disk locations. The original form was 12 bits, which was quickly followed by the 16-bit version used by many computers today. A 32-bit version of FAT, also called FAT32, was introduced with the OEM Service Release 2 (OSR2) version of Windows 98. The 32-bit version of FAT stores data more efficiently on the large hard drives available on today's computers. FAT also appears on many other media, such as the memory cards used for cameras.

File Replication Service (FRS)

A service used to copy file system policies and logon scripts for Windows. In addition, this service can copy content as needed between servers with the assistance of the Distributed File System (DFS).

Firewall

Hardware or software (or a combination of both) used to prevent unauthorized access to a private network. The firewall can use any of a number of techniques to detect unauthorized packets and deny access to them. Some firewalls not only check incoming packets, but outgoing packets as well. There are many types of firewalls including packet filter, application gateway, proxy server, and circuit-level gateway. For maximum protection, the proxy server normally works best in a hardware configuration.

Fully Qualified Domain Name (FQDN)

The combination of a host and domain name, including the top-level domain name. For example, `www.microsoft.com` is a Fully Qualitifed Domain Name (FQDN). In this case, www is the host, microsoft is the second-level domain, and com is the top-level domain.

FQDN

See Fully Qualified Domain Name

FRS

See File Replication Service

G

GAC

See Global Assembly Cache

Global Assembly Cache (GAC)

A central repository used by the .NET Framework for storing public-managed components. The GAC contains only components with strong names, ensuring the integrity of the cache. In addition, the GAC can hold multiple versions of the same component, which ensures that applications can access the version of a component that they need, rather than the single version accessible to all applications.

Globally Unique Identifier (GUID)

A 128-bit number originally used to identify a Component Object Model (COM) object within the Windows registry. Microsoft now uses the GUID wherever a system requires a unique identifier. When working in COM, the system uses the GUID to find the object definition and allow applications to create instances of that object. However, the system can use the GUID for other purposes as well. GUIDs can include any kind of object, even nonvisual elements. In addition, some types of complex objects are actually aggregates of simple objects. For example, an object that implements a property page will normally have a minimum of two GUIDs: one for the property page and another for the object itself.

GUID

See Globally Unique Identifier

H

Hacker

An individual who works with computers at a low level (hardware or software), especially in the area of security. A hacker normally possesses specialty software or other tools that allows easier access to the target hardware or software application or network. The media defines two types of hackers, which includes those that break into systems for ethical purposes and those that do it to damage the system in some way. The proper term for the second group is *crackers* (see Cracker for details). Some people have started to call the first group "ethical hackers" or "white hat hackers" to prevent confusion. Ethical hackers normally work for security firms that specialize in finding holes in a company's security. However, hackers work in a wide range of computer arenas. For example, a person who writes low-level code (like that found in a device driver) after reverse engineering an existing driver is technically a hacker. The main emphasis of a hacker is to work for the benefit of others in the computer industry.

Hard Link

A connection between two files. The new file is a pointer to the existing file. In essence, the system creates another directory entry to a single file. The file continues to exist until the system removes all of the directory entries pointing to it. Any change an object makes to the content of the new file also appears within the existing file, and vice versa.

Hierarchical Storage Manager (HSM)

Manages the user's data storage hierarchy. A hierarchy might consist of several hard drives, a compact disk (CD), digital video disk (DVD), and tape drive.

High Memory Area (HMA)

The first 64 KB area of memory beyond the 1 MB boundary that the processor can access in real mode on an 80286 or above processor. The system accesses this memory area by activating the A20 memory line.

HMA

See High Memory Area

HSM

See Hierarchical Storage Manager

HTTP

See Hypertext Transfer Protocol

HTTPS

See Hypertext Transfer Protocol Secure Sockets

Hypertext Transfer Protocol (HTTP)

One of several common data transfer protocols for the Internet. HTTP normally transfers textual data of some type. For example, the HyperText Markup Language (HTML) relies on HTTP to transfer the Web pages it defines from the server to the client. The eXtensible Markup Language and Simple Object Access Protocol (SOAP) also commonly rely on HTTP to transfer data between client and server. It's important to note that HTTP is separate from the data it transfers. For example, it's possible for SOAP to use the Simple Mail Transfer Protocol (SMTP) to perform data transfers between client and server.

Hypertext Transfer Protocol Secure Sockets (HTTPS)

A secure form of HyperText Transport Protocol (HTTP) that relies on the Secure Sockets Layer (SSL) encryption technology to transfer data.

I

ICACL

Improved Change Access Control List

IDE

See Integrated Development Environment

IGMP

See Internet Group Multicast Protocol

IIS

See Internet Information Server

Integrated Development Environment (IDE)

The development environment used to write application code. An IDE provides all of the tools needed to write an application using one or more specialized editors. The IDE normally includes support for development language help, access to any tools required to support the language, a compiler, and a debugger. Some IDEs include support for advanced features such as automatic completion of language statements and balloon help showing the syntax for functions and other language elements. Many IDEs also use color or highlighting to emphasize specific language elements or constructs.

Inter-Packet Gap (IPG)

The distance, measured in milliseconds, between packets on a TCP/IP network.

Internet Group Multicast Protocol (IGMP)

Controls the remote systems that receive a packet based on the RFC1112 specification. IGMP keeps neighboring multicast routers informed of the host group memberships present on a particular local network. To support IGMP, every level 2 host must join the all-hosts group (address 224.0.0.1) on each network interface at initialization time and must remain a member for as long as the host is active.

Internet Information Server (IIS)

Microsoft's Web server that runs under the Windows operating system. IIS includes all of the standard Web server features including File Transfer Protocol (FTP) and HyperText Transfer Protocol (HTTP), along with both mail and news services in older versions of the product. The latest version of IIS concentrates on developer requirements and doesn't provide mail and news services. This newer version of IIS relies on a modular approach that depends on the .NET Framework, rather than the monolithic architecture used in older versions of IIS.

Internet Packet Exchange (IPX)

A peer-to-peer communication protocol based on the Internet Protocol (IP) portion of the TCP/IP pair. IPX is a security datagram protocol used for connectionless communication. It offers superior functionality to IP, but never became popular because it's a proprietary Novell technology.

IPG

See Inter-Packet Gap

IPX

See Internet Packet Exchange

L

LCID

See Locale Identifier

LDAP

See Lightweight Directory Access Protocol

Lightweight Directory Access Protocol (LDAP)

A set of protocols used to access directories and is based on a simplified version of the X.500 standard. Unlike X.500, LDAP provides support for TCP/IP, a requirement for Internet communication. LDAP makes it possible for a client to request directory information like email addresses and public keys from any server. In addition, since LDAP is an open protocol, applications need not worry about the type of server used to host the directory.

Line Printer Daemon (LPD)

A special application that provides printing services.

Line Printer Queue (LPQ)

A special application that provides spooling services for print jobs sent from a client to a print service. The application normally places the print job on a local hard drive until the printer can output it.

Line Printer Remote (LPR)

The client-side software used to make requests of a remote print server using TCP/IP as the protocol. The LPR protocol normally appears as part of a UNIX setup, but also appears on operating systems such as Windows.

Locale Identifier (LCID)

A number that uniquely identifies a country, language, or other nationalistic information. An application, online resource, or data manager uses the LCID to provide specific information, services, or resources in a form that the user can understand. For example, many applications support more than one language and the application would use the LCID to change the prompts to match the user's language.

LPD

See Line Printer Daemon

LPQ

See Line Printer Queue

LPR

See Line Printer Remote

M

MAC

See Media Access Control

Master File Table (MFT)

A file that contains information about all of the directories and files on the associated hard drive. The current MFT implementation uses the first sixteen 1,024-byte records in the file to tell the operating system about itself. Afterward, each record contains information about a file or directory. The records tell the operating system how to retrieve the files or interact with the directory. For example, the records contain file permissions, the name and size of the file, the date and time the operating system created it, and the date and time any operating system object modified it.

Master File Table Zone (MFT Zone)

The physical location of the Master File Table (MFT) on a hard drive.

MDAC

See Microsoft Data Access Components

Media Access Control (MAC)

The unique address assigned to every Network Interface Card (NIC) that identifies each node on a network. The MAC layer is at the data link control (DLC) layer of the OSI reference model for networks. It directly interacts with the network media, which means that each type of network will have a different MAC that identifies the nodes on that network. The MAC layer also referred to the DLC layer on some networks.

Memory Fragmentation

A type of memory bottleneck that occurs when an operating system is left running for an extended time. The allocation and deallocation of memory by applications can leave pockets of memory too small to handle typical application requests, even though there's more than enough memory to handle the request. The result of memory fragmentation is a loss of performance due to increased disk thrashing as the operating system moves data from physical memory to the hard drive and back again.

MFT

See Master File Table

MFT Zone

See Master File Table Zone

Microsoft Data Access Components (MDAC)

A set of components designed to make data access easier. MDAC is actually a software development kit (SDK) that includes components, sample code, headers, libraries, and other elements that allow the developer to use newer Microsoft technologies such as Object Linking and Embedding-Database (OLE-DB).

Microsoft Database Engine (MSDE)

This term also appears as Microsoft Desktop Engine and Microsoft Data Engine in various references. MSDE is a miniature form of SQL Server that enables developers to create test database applications. Microsoft designed this engine for use by one person, usually the developer, although, you can potentially use it for up to five people. The developer accesses

MSDE through a programming language Integrated Development Environment (IDE) or using command line utilities. In some cases, MSDE also provides access to a remote copy of SQL Server. Some third party products, such as MSDE Query, provide a Graphical User Interface (GUI) for MSDE.

Microsoft Installer (MSI)

1. A technique for installing applications within Windows that allows later removal even if the system configuration has changed. This technique also provides support for additional vendor information, partial installations, multiple configurations, and installation recovery. 2. A file format containing instructions for installing Windows applications. The file is actually a database that contains specialized instructions and data in a specific format that's read by the Microsoft installer application.

Microsoft Intermediate Language (MSIL)

The tokenized output of all .NET language compilers. The Common Language Runtime (CLR) reads the MSIL output and converts it to platform-specific code, which the platform then executes.

Microsoft Message Queuing Services (MSMQ)

A technology that enables a developer to create applications that rely on asynchronous data transfer. The data passed between client and server is recorded in a message and stored in a local or remote queue until the recipient can process it. A local listener alerts the affected application component to the presence of the message in the queue. A player interprets the content of the message for the application component so that the application component can react to it. The asynchronous application support provided by MSMQ has a number of useful applications including disconnected application support and load balancing.

MIME

See Multipurpose Internet Mail Extensions

Modifier

An addition that changes the way that a command, utility, interface, programming instruction, or other computer technology works. When used with a command or a utility, a modifier changes the way a command line switch works, the way the application processes data, the way the user perceives or interacts with the data, or the way the application outputs information. When used with a programming instruction, a modifier can change the internal workings of the instruction or provide amplifying information to the instruction. Modifiers typically augment the computer technology in some way, rather than define the precise workings of the technology.

MSDE

See Microsoft Database Engine

MSI

See Microsoft Installer

MSIL

See Microsoft Intermediate Language

MSMQ

See Microsoft Message Queuing Services

Multipurpose Internet Mail Extensions (MIME)

The standard method for defining the content of Internet messages. This standard allows computers to exchange objects, character sets, and multimedia using email without regard to the computer's underlying operating system. MIME is defined in the Internet Engineering Task Force (IETF) Request for Comment (RFC) 1521 standard.

N

NCSA

National Center for Supercomputing Applications

Network Time Protocol (NTP)

A technique for synchronizing computer time with a time source. NTP is a standardized technology based on RFC1305.

NTFS

See Windows New Technology File System

NTLM

See Windows NT LAN Manager Security

NTP

See Network Time Protocol

O

Object Inherit (OI)

Signifies that the Access Control Entry (ACE) reflects a right inherited by the file and not a user.

ODBC

See Open Database Connectivity

OEM

See Original Equipment Manufacturer

OI

See Object Inherit

Open Database Connectivity (ODBC)

One of several methods for exchanging data between Database Management Systems (DBMSs). In most cases, this involves three steps: installing an appropriate driver, adding a source to the Data Sources (ODBC) applet in the Control Panel, and using specialized statements, such as Structured Query Language (SQL), to access the database. The precise functionality and configuration requirements of ODBC depend on the ODBC driver used to create the connection.

Open System Interconnection Reference Model (OSI)

A theoretical seven layer protocol model of network connectivity commonly used to teach how network protocols interact. Data is passed from one layer to the next until the sender physically transmits it to another machine. The reverse process takes place when the data arrives at the receiving machine, unwrapping layer after layer of protocol information, until the data appears in its original form. The OSI reference model was originally supposed to unite all network models, but proprietary formats prevented full acceptance by vendors and the OSI reference model became a teaching tool instead. (The X.400 and X.500 standards are directly based on the OSI reference model.) The seven OSI reference model layers include application, presentation, session, transport, network, data link, and physical.

Original Equipment Manufacturer (OEM)

Used to identify manufacturers that produce some type of PC hardware. In this case, hardware can include anything from individual chips to entire systems. For example, a vendor that designs and builds display adapters is considered an OEM. An OEM is normally responsible for writing device drivers and other software required to use the hardware it sells.

OSI

See Open System Interconnection Reference Model

P

Path Maximum Transmission Unit (PMTU)

A standardized method that two Transmission Control Protocol (TCP) peers can use to discover the size of the Internet Protocol (IP) Maximum Transmission Unit (MTU). This feature helps the peers maximize performance by using the largest packet size to transmit data between them.

PBK

See Phonebook File

PDC

See Primary Domain Controller

Phonebook File (PBK)

A file containing the telephone numbers and other information for user contacts stored in various applications including Microsoft Office and Outlook Express.

PID

See Process Identifier

PIF

See Program Information file

PIM

See Protocol Independent Multicast

Pipe

A method of transferring data from one process to another. When used with a command line utility, the user types the pipe symbol (|) to represent the connection between two commands or utilities. Pipes usually provide a streamed data transfer, but can also perform block transfers depending on the capabilities of the processes.

PMTU

See Path Maximum Transmission Unit

Primary Domain Controller (PDC)

The Windows server responsible for tracking changes made to the domain accounts and storing them in the directory database (usually Active Directory with newer versions of Windows). In addition, the PDC provides user authentication and other services. A domain has one PDC. Windows 2000 and above doesn't have an actual PDC. Instead, newer Windows servers use Active Directory as the authentication database. All Domain Controllers (DCs) are equal with regard to functionality. However, many utilities and applications that work with a PDC also work with the Windows 2000 setup.

Process Identifier (PID)

A numeric value associated with a process running on a specific machine. Every process has a unique PID, making it possible to locate a specific process, even if multiple copies of a single application are running on the machine. The PID is used by a wide variety of monitoring applications. It's also used to access an application or as a means of identification when terminating an errant application.

Program Information file (PIF)

A means of storing application configuration settings as a separate file. Windows automatically looks at the configuration settings when you execute the corresponding application and makes any required environment changes. The PIF usually includes various memory settings along with the application's command path and working directory.

Protocol Independent Multicast (PIM)

Defines the type of routing the server uses.

R

RAS

See Remote Access Server

RCP

Remote Copy Protocol

Ready to Send (RTS)

A serial port signaling line that indicates the Data Terminal Equipment (DTE), such as a computer, is ready to send data to the Data Communications Equipment (DCE), such as a modem.

Relative Identifier (RID)

An Active Directory term that denotes the unique part of a Security Identifier (SID) for an object. The RID ensures that each SID is truly unique, even when other objects have the same name or other attributes. A RID is always a number that's drawn from a pool of numbers. No two SIDs have the same number.

Remote Access Server (RAS)

An optional Windows service that allows an outside entity (such as a user) to create a connection into the server from a remote location. Generally, the outside entity uses this service to access server resources such as files or applications. An outside entity can access this service in a variety of ways, including as a callback mechanism.

Remote Installation Services (RIS)

A Windows 2000 and higher feature that allows administrators to install a copy of Windows on a remote client system without physically visiting the client machine. This feature is part of the Remote Operating System Installation feature in Windows 2000. Microsoft has added extended forms of this feature to all versions of Windows since Windows 2000.

Remote Procedure Call (RPC)

One of several techniques for accessing a procedure or a method (some code) within another application. RPC is designed to look for the application first on the local workstation and then across the network at the applications stored on other workstations.

Resource Reservation Protocol (RSVP)

A set of network rules that allows an object (usually an application or a service) to request the resources it needs to run from the server in advance, which ensures that the network administrator can manage resource usage and that the operating system can plan ahead for application requirements. This is an especially important feature for resource hungry applications like multimedia or Voice Over IP (VOIP).

Resultant Set of Policy (RSoP)

Defines the rights of a particular object based on all of the security entries for that object in an Access Control List (ACL) attached to an operating system resource. For example, a user inherits rights from groups and the parent directory, and has personal rights to a file. Whether the user gains access to the file depends on the result of comparing all of those sources of rights.

RID

See Relative Identifier

RIS

See Remote Installation Services

Rivest Shamir Adleman algorithm (RSA)

An authentication technology named after its creators that relies on a private-public key pair to create a set of credentials. The credentials are then used as a means of identification for logging into various network resources. Using this methodology allows for secure data transmission as well as user-oriented features like one password logon to the network.

RPC

See Remote Procedure Call

RSA

See Rivest Shamir Adleman algorithm

RSHD

Remote Shell Daemon

RSoP

See Resultant Set of Policy

RSVP

See Resource Reservation Protocol

RTS

See Ready to Send

S

SACL

See Security Access Control List

SAM

See Security Access Manager

Script

A type of simple interpreted application, productivity enhancer, or automated data manipulator developed using a macro or simplified programming language. Most operating systems support at least one scripting language. You'll also find scripting capability in many higher-end applications such as Web browsers and word processors. Scripts are normally used to write small utility type applications rather than large-scale applications that require the use of a compiled language. In addition, many script languages are limited in their access of the full set of operating system features.

SCM

See Service Control Manager

Secure Hashing Algorithm 1 (SHA-1)

The mathematical basis for encrypting and decrypting data used with the Digital Signature Standard (DSS) introduced by the National Institute of Standards and Technology (NIST). DSS also relies on Digital Signature Algorithm (DSA) to provide the digital signature functionality.

Security Access Control List (SACL)

One of several specialized Access Control Lists (ACL) used to maintain object integrity. This list controls Windows' auditing features. Every time a user or group accesses an object and the auditing feature for that object is turned on, Windows makes an entry in the audit log.

Security Access Manager (SAM)

A service that manages a database containing information about an object (such as a user) and its security settings. Some sources also call this service the Security Accounts Manager. In either case, the security database normally appears within a special hive of the registry. Windows secures this hive using the Registry Editor to make it difficult to access. The SAM can also use alternative input sources such as Active Directory.

Security Identifier (SID)

The part of an access token that identifies the object throughout the network; it's the same as having an account number at a bank or other organization. The identifier is unique. The access token that the SID identifies tells what groups the object belongs to and what privileges the object has.

Sequential Packet Exchange (SPX)

The part of the IPX/SPX protocol pair that guarantees delivery of a message sent from one node to another. Think of SPX as the postal clerk that delivers a certified letter from one place to another. In network terms, each page of the letter is called a packet. SPX delivers the letter one page at a time to the intended party.

Service Control Manager (SCM)

The part of Windows that controls the various services loaded to provide background support. The SCM starts, stops, pauses, and continues services, as well as providing service status information. The SCM is also part of the load-balancing technology used by Windows servers. When a client makes a DCOM call to the load-balancing router, it's the SCM that actually receives the request. The SCM looks up the component in the load-balancing router table, then makes a DCOM call to one of the servers in the application cluster to fulfill the request. The server in the application cluster creates an instance of the request object, then passes the proxy for it directly to the client. At this point, the server and the client are in direct communication; the router is no longer needed.

SHA-1

See Secure Hashing Algorithm 1

Shell Extension

A special application that gives some type of added value to the operating system interface. Many shell extensions provide added functionality by working with a specific file type or provide increased user access by offering additional commands. In most cases, the application must register itself with the registry before the operating system will recognize it.

SID

See Security Identifier

Simple Mail Transfer Protocol (SMTP)

One of the most commonly used protocols to transfer text (commonly mail) messages between clients and servers. This is a stream-based protocol designed to allow query, retrieval, posting, and distribution of mail messages. Normally this protocol is used in conjunction with other mail retrieval protocols such as point of presence (POP). However, not all uses of SMTP involve email data transfer. Some Simple Object Access Protocol (SOAP) applications have also relied on SMTP to transfer application data.

Simple Network Management Protocol (SNMP)

A network protocol (originally designed for the Internet) used to manage devices from different vendors. The protocol originally appeared in the 1980s and relies on Protocol Data Unit (PDU) messages to transmit requests. SNMP-compliant devices, known as agents, respond to these requests by sending information from Management Information Bases (MIBs) to the requestor.

Smart Card

A type of user identification used in place of passwords. The smart card contains an encrypted chip that provides the user identification information; most smart cards are about the size and shape of a credit card. The use of a smart card makes it much harder for a third party to break into a computer system using stolen identification. However, a lost or stolen smart card still provides user access. The most secure method of user identification is biometrics.

SMTP

See Simple Mail Transfer Protocol

SNMP

See Simple Network Management Protocol

Sparse File

A file that allocates a lot of space on a hard drive, but actually uses very little of that space. For example, a data cache might allocate 1 MB of hard drive space, but only use a few KB of that space to hold data. The system allocates the space because it could require it to keep applications running, but the system doesn't need all of the space all of the time. A sparse file is a type of reservation system where the system reserves hard drive space for a future need.

SPX

See Sequential Packet Exchange

SQL

See Structured Query Language

Structured Query Language (SQL)

Most Database Management Systems (DBMSs) use this language to exchange information; many also use it as their native language. SQL provides a method for manipulating data controlled by the DBMS. It defines which table or tables to use, determines what information to get from the table, and resolves how to sort the information. A typical request will include the name of the database, table, and columns needed for display or editing purposes. SQL can filter a request and limit the number of rows using special features. Developers also use SQL to manipulate database information by adding, deleting, modifying, or searching records. The IBM research center designed SQL between 1974 and 1975. Oracle introduced the first product to use SQL in 1979. SQL originally appeared on mainframe and minicomputers. Today it's a favorite language for most PC DBMS as well. There are many versions of SQL.

Symbolic Link

A pointer to a physical file or folder somewhere else on the drive, another local drive, or even a network drive. The symbolic link makes it unnecessary to track where a file or folder exists. Instead, you focus on the data itself. A directory entry marked as a symbolic link has no real content—just the pointer to the actual file or folder.

T

Tab Separated Value (TSV)

A type of text database file where the data fields are separated from one another using tabs. Each carriage return/line feed combination (new line) creates a new record. Many applications can retrieve TSV files and convert them to other database representations.

TAPI

See Telephony Application Programming Interface

TCP/IP

See Transmission Control Protocol/Internet Protocol

TDR

See Time Domain Reflectometer

Telephony Application Programming Interface (TAPI)

A set of DLLs and other system resources used by applications to interact with various types of communication equipment. Developers can use TAPI to create communication applications or applications that use communications to provide services such as help. The TAPI service provides functionality for dial-up services such as modems and faxes. Windows also uses it for networking services such as Internet connectivity no matter what form the connectivity takes (dial-up, broadband, digital subscriber line, and so on).

Time Domain Reflectometer (TDR)

A special device that detects and analyzes cabling problems by sending a signal through the cable and measuring the return signal. Unlike a resistance check, a TDR can measure partial breaks, stress fractures, and other conditions that a technician can't see using visual inspection.

Time-to-Live (TTL)

An Internet Protocol (IP) packet entry that controls the lifetime of the packet. The router forwards the datagram when the TTL in the IP header is greater than the TTL threshold for the interface. This value limits the distances that packets can travel.

Token

The representation of data, an object, database element, programming syntax, or other information using a code word, phrase, number, or object. For example, in programming, a token could represent a statement, punctuation mark, argument, or other syntactical element. Users often receive tokens describing their rights as part of the security features of an operating system. Networks also use tokens to control data flow and perform other tasks.

Transmission Control Protocol/Internet Protocol (TCP/IP)

A standard communication line protocol (set of rules) developed by the United States Department of Defense. The protocol defines how two devices talk to each other. TCP defines a communication methodology where it guarantees packet delivery and also ensures the packets appear at the recipient in the same order they were sent. IP defines the packet characteristics.

TSV

See Tab Separated Value

TTL

See Time-to-Live

U

UAC

See User Account Control

UDP

See User Datagram Protocol

UMB

See Upper Memory Block

UNC

See Universal Naming Convention

Unicode Character

A double byte (16-bit) character used to represent more than the character set used by the English language. Unicode character sets are standardized by international convention. Advanced operating systems such as Windows and Linux normally rely on Unicode for enhanced language support and consistent data handling. Older versions of Windows, such as Windows 98, rely on the American Standard Code for Information Interchange (ASCII), an 8-bit code that works well only for English. Unicode is the standard character set used by newer versions of Windows, although all versions of Windows can still use ASCII characters when needed for compatibility purposes.

Uniform Resource Identifier (URI)

A generic term for all names and addresses that reference objects on the Internet. A URL is a specific type of URI. See Uniform Resource Locator (URL).

Uniform Resource Locator (URL)

A text representation of a specific location on the Internet. URLs normally include the protocol (http:// for example), the target location (World Wide Web or www), the domain or server name (mycompany), and a domain type (com for commercial). (Many URLs don't include the www portion of the address anymore.) It can also include a hierarchical location within that Web site. The URL usually specifies a particular file on the Web server, although there are some situations when a Web server will use a default filename. For example, asking the browser to find `http://www.mycompany.com`, would probably display the `DEFAULT.HTM` or `INDEX.HTM` file at that location. The actual default filename depends on the Web server used. In some cases, the default filename is configurable and could be any of a number of files. For example, Internet Information Server (IIS) offers this feature, so the developer can use anything from an HTM, to an ASP, to an XML file as the default.

Universal Naming Convention (UNC)

A method for identifying network resources without specifying a local resource such as a drive letter. In most cases, a user will employ this convention with drives and printers, but the user can also apply it to other types of resources. A UNC normally includes a server name followed by a device name in place of a locale identifier. For example, a user might refer to a disk drive on a remote machine as "`\\AUX\DRIVE_C.`" The advantage of using UNC is that the resource name won't change, even if the user's local device mappings do.

Universally Unique Identifier (UUID)

Another name for a Globally Unique Identifier (GUID). The two terms are interchangeable. The UUID is part of the Distributed Computing Environment (DCE) standardized by the Open Software Foundation (OSF), while Microsoft created the GUID acronym.

Update Sequence Number (USN)

Provides a persistent log of all of the changes made to the files on the system. As users add, delete, and modify files and directories, the Windows NT File System (NTFS) makes an entry in the USN. Each volume has a separate USN. The main use of the USN for administrators is to check the changes made to one or more files. Using the USN is more efficient than relying on time stamps and the administrator receives more information as well.

Upper Memory Block (UMB)

The area of memory between 640 KB and the 1 MB boundary. IBM originally set aside this area of memory for device ROMs and special device memory areas. Various memory managers, including the one supplied with Windows, let you load applications and device drivers in this area to free more memory in the lower 640 KB area.

URI

See Uniform Resource Identifier

URL

See Uniform Resource Locator

User Account Control (UAC)

A Windows security feature that increases security by reducing the chance that an application can perform any act on the user's behalf, without the user's knowledge. This feature first appeared as part of Windows Vista. The operating system displays a dialog box asking permission to perform the required task. When the user answers yes, the system performs a privilege elevation that allows the task to progress.

User Datagram Protocol (UDP)

Provides the means for applications to exchange individual packets of information over an IP network. UDP uses a combination of protocol ports and IP addresses to get a message from one point of the network to another. More than one client can use the same protocol port as long as all clients using the port have a unique IP address. There are two types of protocol ports: well-known and dynamically bound. The well-known port assignments use the ports numbered between 1 and 255. When using dynamically bound port assignments, the requesting applications queries the service first to see which port it can use. Unlike TCP/IP, UDP/IP provides very few error recovery services, making it a fast way to deliver broadcast messages and performing other tasks where reliability isn't a concern.

USN

See Update Sequence Number

UUID

See Universally Unique Identifier

V

Valid Data Length (VDL)

The length of the valid data within a file, rather than the actual file length as indicated by an End of File (EOF) marker.

VDL

See Valid Data Length

VDS

See Virtual Disk Service

Virtual Disk Service (VDS)

Device drivers that provide specialized disk support on Windows. This service is normally associated with a Redundant Array of Inexpensive Disks (RAID) setup.

Virtual Terminal Windows NT (VTNT)

An emulation of the Telnet Terminal Type Option standard specified in RFC884. The VTNT emulation supports a remote Telnet console session by transmitting display coordinates and character attributes using structures defined in the Microsoft Console Application Programming Interface (API).

Volume Shadow Service (VSS)

A service that tracks changes to individual files on the system. The system can use the shadowed information to restore the previous state of the file.

VSS

See Volume Shadow Service

VTNT

See Virtual Terminal Windows NT

W

WAS

See Web Process Activation Service

WBEM

See Web-Based Enterprise Management

Web-Based Enterprise Management (WBEM)

A technique for managing computers and other devices using Web-based tools, rather than traditional desktop applications originally introduced by Microsoft.

Web Process Activation Service (WAS)

Lets the operating system automatically activate COM+ applications as required, which means the system uses resources more efficiently, but that you also lose a certain level of control over the application process. When using WAS, the application executes as part of an Internet Information Server (IIS) process for library COM+ applications or as a `DLLHost.exe` process for server COM+ applications.

Wildcard Character

A special character used to represent one or more letters, numbers, punctuation characters, or other special characters. For example, the `Dir` (directory) command can use the asterisk (*) to represent any number of characters and the question mark (?) to represent a single character. Applications also use wildcard characters. For example, word processors often use wildcard characters to help you search for strings. Programming languages implement a complex wildcard character scenario called regular expressions used to match patterns in strings such as a telephone number.

Windows Management Interface (WMI)

A Windows service and interface that helps an administrator or developer remotely monitor, control, and configure workstations or servers. This particular technology falls into the agent category and is very common on many network operating systems. An agent (special files executing on the client machine) allows the server to gain access to client machine resources and configuration information. Obviously, only machines that have the agent installed are accessible to the requestor.

Windows New Technology File System (NTFS)

The method of formatting a hard disk drive used by Windows NT/2000/XP/2003 and Vista. While it provides significant speed advantages over other formatting techniques, only these newer versions of the Windows operating system and applications designed to work with that operating system can access a drive formatted using this technique. Windows 2000 uses NTFS5, a version of this file system designed to provide additional features, like enhanced security. Each newer version of Windows from Windows XP to Vista provides an updated version of NTFS as well that includes additional features. An older version of Windows usually can't read a newer version of NTFS than Microsoft designed it to use.

Windows NT LAN Manager Security (NTLM)

A security scheme based on a challenge/response scenario. The server challenges the client, which must then provide an appropriate username and password. If the user name and associated password are found in the server's security list for the service that the client has requested, then access to the service is granted. This security scheme is relatively easy to break and has been replaced by more reliable security schemes like Kerberos in later versions of Windows.

Windows Presentation Foundation (WPF)

Provides special graphics feature support for newer Windows operating systems such as Vista. For example, the WPF provides support for the Aero Glass interface found in Vista.

Windows Side-by-Side Execution (WinSxS)

A technology for maintaining multiple versions of DLLs on a system so that each application can use the version of the DLL it requires.

WinSxS

See Windows Side-by-Side Execution

WMI

See Windows Management Interface

WPF

See Windows Presentation Foundation

X

XML

See eXtensible Markup Language

XML Schema Definition (XSD)

The portion of the eXtensible Markup Language (XML) specification that defines data types and other data elements. Most browsers and other applications use XSD to verify the XML document. XSD is also related to a Web site containing such information by use of XML parsers. A designer can create a custom XSD for use with a particular application.

XMS

See eXtended Memory Specification

XSD

See XML Schema Definition

XSL

See eXtensible Stylesheet Language

XSLT

See eXtensible Stylesheet Language Transformation

Index

B

C

E

F

I

J

K

L

O

P

S

U

V

W

X

Z